PROJECT MK-ULTRA AND MIND CONTROL TECHNOLOGY

Edited by

Axel Balthazar

Other Books in the *Mind Control* Series:

• Mind Control, World Control
• Mind Control and UFOs: Casebook on Alternative 3
• Liquid Conspiracy: JFK, LSD, the CIA, Area 51 & UFOs
• Mind Control, Oswald & JFK
• Mass Control: Engineering Human Consciousness
• Saucers of the Illuminati
• HAARP: The Ultimate Weapon of the Conspiracy

See more astounding mind control books at:
www.adventuresunlimitedpress.com

PROJECT MK-ULTRA AND MIND CONTROL TECHNOLOGY

Edited by

Axel Balthazar

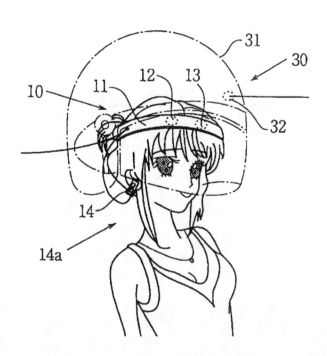

Project MK-Ultra and Mind Control Technology
Edited by Axel Balthazar

Published by:
Adventures Unlimited Press
One Adventure Place, Box 74
Kempton, Illinois 60946 USA
auphq@frontiernet.net

www.adventuresunlimitedpress.com

PROJECT MK-ULTRA AND MIND CONTROL TECHNOLOGY

Edited by

Axel Balthazar

DISCLAIMER

This book is presented for informational purposes only. Inclusion of reports and patents does not imply harmful intentions by the authors or inventors. This compilation seeks to demonstrate the existence of this technology and the government papers related to the subject of mind control. The implications are open to interpretation.

The editor and publisher of this compilation are in no way endorsed by the authors, inventors, or agencies herein. The authors, inventors, publisher, and editor are not liable for anything done with this information.

The content herein is in the public domain or is otherwise protected under the fair use doctrine for the purpose of comment or criticism.

SPECIAL THANKS

Special thanks to the writers and researchers who have laid the groundwork in this field. They include: Jim Keith, Jerry E. Smith, Kenn Thomas, John D. Marks, Colin A. Ross, Neil Sanders, Ted Gunderson, Walter Bowart, Alex Constantine, John Hall, Mark Phillips, Cathy O'Brien, and truth seekers around the world. Special thanks to my family, friends, and publisher for their continued support.

axelbalthazar@protonmail.com

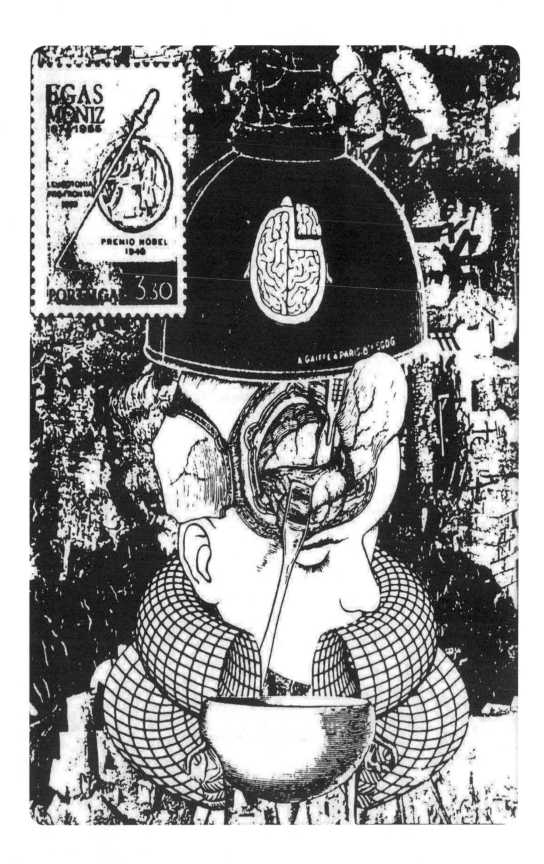

Table of Contents

Chapter 1
Overview Documents

1977 memo for the Secretary of Defense RE: Experimentation Programs
1963 memo for the Director of Central Intelligence RE: Report of Inspection
of MK-Ultra

MEMORANDUM FOR THE SECRETARY OF DEFENSE

SUBJECT: Experimentation Programs Conducted by the
          Department of Defense That Had CIA Sponsor-
          ship or Participation and That Involved the
          Administration to Human Subjects of Drugs
          Intended for Mind-control or Behavior-
          modification Purposes

     On August 8, 1977 you requested that the Office of
General Counsel coordinate a search of Department of Defense
records to determine the extent of Department of Defense
participation in three projects identified by the Director
of Central Intelligence on August 3, 1977 as including the
administration of drugs to human subjects for mind-control
or behavior-modification purposes. In addition, you
requested that the search attempt to identify any other
project conducted or participated in by the Department of
Defense in which there was any Central Intelligence Agency
involvement and which included the administration of drugs
to human subjects for mind-control or behavior-modification
purposes. That search was conducted during the period
August 15, 1977 through September 15, 1977 and covered the
records of the Military Departments from 1950 to the
present.

     The results of the search indicate that there were three
such programs in which the Army participated over the period
1969 to 1973; five such programs in which the Navy participated over the period 1947 to 1973; and no such programs in
which the Air Force participated. In four of these eight
programs the Department of Defense participation was limited
to channeling funds to outside contractors in order that the
sponsorship of the Central Intelligence Agency be covered.
In two of the remaining four programs there was no testing
on human subjects. Four of the programs were terminated in
the 1950's or early 1960's and the remainder were terminated
in 1973.

It appears from the documents that the three codeword projects of the Central Intelligence Agency identified by the Director in his testimony as basically Department of Defense projects were, in fact, planned, directed and controlled by the Central Intelligence Agency. Each of these projects and the participation of the military services is described below.

I. Codeword Projects Identified by the Central Intelligence Agency

In testimony on August 3, 1977, before a joint session of the Senate Select Committee on Intelligence and the Senate Subcommittee on Health and Scientific Research, the Director of Central Intelligence reported that the Central Intelligence Agency had located a number of boxes of documents, consisting largely of financial records, relating to experiments using human subjects in which drugs were tested for mind-control and behavior-modification purposes. The Director testified that it appeared that three of the projects described by these documents -- projects designated MKSEARCH, MKOFTEN and MKCHICKWIT -- were Department of Defense programs with which the Central Intelligence Agency had had some contact. The Director also described three other projects -- designated MKULTRA, MKDELTA and MKNAOMI -- which were primarily Central Intelligence Agency projects but which might have had some Department of Defense involvement.

It appears from the available documents that these projects cover subject matters as follows:

MKDELTA: This was apparently the first project established by CIA in October, 1952, for the use of biochemicals in clandestine operations. It may never have been implemented operationally.

MKULTRA: This was a successor project to MKDELTA established in April, 1953, and terminating some time in the late 1960's, probably after 1966. This program considered various means of controlling human behavior. Drugs were only one aspect of this activity.

MKNAOMI: This project began in the 1950's and was terminated, at least with respect to biological projects, in 1969. This may have been a successor

project to MKDELTA. Its purpose was to
stockpile severely incapacitating and
lethal materials, and to develop gadgetry
for the dissemination of these materials.

MKSEARCH: This was apparently a successor
project to MKULTRA, which began in 1965
and was terminated in 1973. The objective
of the project was to develop a capability
to manipulate human behavior in a predictable manner through the use of drugs.

MKCHICKWIT or CHICKWIT: This was apparently
a part of the MKSEARCH program. Its
objective was to identify new drug
developments in Europe and Asia and to
obtain information and samples.

MKOFTEN or OFTEN: This was also apparently
a part of the MKSEARCH project. Its
objective was to test the behavioral and
toxicological effects of certain drugs
on animals and humans.

Beginning on August 4, 1977, Army and Navy investigators
undertook a search of the boxes of Central Intelligence
Agency records identified by the CIA code words OFTEN and
CHICKWIT in order to locate documents relevant to possible
Department of Defense involvement in these projects. On
September 7, 1977, the Agency permitted DoD representatives
to search additional boxes containing MKULTRA records. Both
sets of materials consisted of approvals of advances of funds,
vouchers and accounting records relating to these projects.

II. Army Programs

It appears from the available documents that the Army was
involved in one aspect of the Central Intelligence Agency
project designated as MKCHICKWIT and two aspects of a counter-
part project designated as MKOFTEN. The document search is
described in section A below, and each of the Army programs
is described in section B below.

A. Records searched

The search of Army records was coordinated by the Director
of the Staff. The search included the files of the Edgewood

Arsenal Research Laboratories, the Dugway Proving Grounds,
the Department of Defense Investigative Service (with respect
to the Special Operations Division at Fort Detrick), the
Department of the Army Inspector General, the Army activity
in the U.S. Biological Warfare Program, and the Army
Intelligence Agency.

B. Programs identified

(1) Identification of new drugs with behavioral
effects

This project began in 1967 and was terminated in 1973.
It was carried out primarily by a contractor in California.
The project was apparently funded jointly by the Army,
through Edgewood Arsenal Research Laboratories, and the
Central Intelligence Agency. The funds contributed by the
Agency were used by Edgewood for payments to a private
contractor. This project was a part of the project
designated as MKCHICKWIT.

This project was involved solely with the collection
of information. No testing on human subjects was conducted.
The Central Intelligence Agency apparently provided $12,084
in 1967 and $5,000 in 1969 for this project. The extent of
the Army's financial contribution to this project is unknown.

(2) Data bases on evaluation of pharmacological
products

This project apparently began in 1968 and was completed
by 1971. It was carried out by the Edgewood Arsenal Research
Laboratories. The Central Intelligence Agency transferred
funds to the Army for this purpose in 1968, 1970 and 1971.
This project was a part of the project designated as MKOFTEN.

Edgewood created data bases for computer use with respect
to information on pharmacological products. These included
human clinical data obtained from volunteer subjects in other
Edgewood projects, not connected with the Central Intelligence
Agency. (b)(3):50 USC §403(g) Section 6

15

This project involved only the transfer of information to computer usable form. No testing on human subjects was conducted. The amount of funding is not known.

(3) Determination of clinical effects of a glycolate class chemical

This project began in 1971 and was terminated in 1973. It was carried out by the Edgewood Arsenal Research Laboratories and was funded by the Central Intelligence Agency. This project was a part of the project designated as MKOFTEN.

It appears from the available documents that Edgewood had been testing a number of incapacitating agents in its own programs without Central Intelligence Agency participation. Edgewood identified a compound designated as EA#3167 as particularly effective and tested it on animals. Edgewood also engaged in clinical testing on human volunteers at the Holmesburg State Prison in Philadelphia, Pennsylvania, using prisoners as test subjects and at the Edgewood laboratories using military personnel as test subjects. It appears that all of the test subjects were volunteers and that stringent medical safeguards and followup procedures were used.

In 1971, the Central Intelligence Agency reviewed prior Edgewood work and identified EA#3167 as relevant to the MKOFTEN program. The Agency set up a joint effort with Edgewood to pursue further testing of this compound. In 1971, the Agency transferred to Edgewood $37,000 for this purpose. Most of the testing under CIA sponsorship was with animals. The primary effort was to determine whether EA#3167 could be used effectively if applied to the skin through some type of adhesive tape. There was only one experiment that involved human subjects. In June, 1973, two military volunteers were apparently tested using EA#3167. The documents do not give any details with respect to these tests.

---

*/ The Navy contributed a similar data base to the MKOFTEN project but it appears from the available documents that the work to create the data base was undertaken as an independent Navy project not designed for any CIA use, and that there was no transfer of CIA funds to the Navy for this purpose.

C. Documents released

The Army has identified nine documents related to the programs described in Section B. A list identifying those documents is set out in Appendix A.

III. Navy Programs

It appears from the available documents that the Navy was not involved in any aspect of the Central Intelligence Agency projects designated MKSEARCH and MKCHICKWIT. It appears that the Navy did act as a financial intermediary through which the Central Intelligence Agency dealt with an outside contractor that conducted one research effort that was a part of the MKOFTEN project. It also appears that the Navy conducted, directly or through contractors, five programs in which there was Central Intelligence Agency sponsorship or participation and which included the administration of drugs to human subjects for mind-control or behavior-modification purposes. The records that were searched are described in section A below. Each of the projects discovered is described in section B below.

A. Records Searched

The Special Assistant to the Secretary of the Navy coordinated the search of Navy records. The search covered archival material with respect to the activities of the Office of Naval Intelligence, Bureau of Medicine and Surgery, and the Office of Naval Research.

B. Programs identified

(1) Synthesis of analogs of certain central nervous system stimulants

This project began in 1971 and was terminated in January, 1973. It was performed by a contractor located in Massachusetts The involvement of the Navy was only as a conduit for funds between the contractor and the Central Intelligence Agency. Some of the funding documents identify this project as a part of project OFTEN.

In December, 1970, the contractor contacted the Central Intelligence Agency project officer directly and suggested research work on two types of drugs: analogs of DOPA and dopamine and analogs of picrotoxin. After the work was undertaken, the contractor added a third aspect, the study of analogs of the hallucinogen ibogaine. In March, 1972, the contractor suggested enlarging the scope of the work to include narcotic antagonists or blocking agents. One document indicates that "The overall objective of these studies is to synthesize new classes of pharmocologically active drugs affecting the central nervous system so as to evaluate their modification of man's behavior." (Doc. No. CIA-1.) The purpose of creating analogs, rather than using the parent compounds, was to find drugs "which will be more specific in action as well as more reliable." (Doc. No. CIA-2.)

The Central Intelligence Agency may have transmitted as much as $117,938 for this project to the Office of Naval Research during the period February 26, 1971 through June 23, 1972. The Central Intelligence Agency authorization document stated: "This project is funded through the Office of Naval Research. This arrangement protects the Agency's association with this area of research and provides the contractor with credible sponsorship. The work will be unclassified, but Agency association will be confidential." (Doc. No. CIA-1, 3.)

There is no indication in the documents available to the Navy that human testing was performed by the researchers. One of the documents reports: "The relative merits of the synthetic compounds will be determined in mice, and information as to the underlying biochemical basis for the observed pharmacological activities will be deduced from the comparative effects of the various compounds." (Doc. No. CIA-8.)

One of the researcher's progress reports indicates an intention to publish the results of the first phase of this work, on analogs of DOPA and dopamine, at a professional meeting in the fall of 1972 but there is no indication that publication was accomplished. (Doc. No. N-2.)

(2)   Identification of nonaddictive substitute for codeine

This project began in 1954 and was continued at least until 1964. It was performed at the facilities of another government agency located in Kentucky. The involvement of the Navy was only as a conduit for funds between the Central Intelligence Agency and a researcher who was associated with a federal government agency. One of the funding documents identifies this as part of project MKPILOT.

According to the information available to the Navy, the purpose of the project was to find a nonaddictive substitute for codeine. The work was done at the Addictive Research Center, U.S. Public Health Service Hospital, in Lexington, Kentucky. It is unclear from the information available to the Navy whether the researcher was an independent scientist using government facilities or a government employee.

It appears that the researcher tested some 800 compounds on addicted patients. There is no indication in the documents as to the number of persons involved or the compounds tested. Three compounds were retained and all are now common drugs: darvon which is used as a pain killer; dextromethorphan which is used in cough syrup; and lomotil which is used as an antidiarrhea drug.

The Central Intelligence Agency transferred at least $282,215 to the Office of Naval Research for this program with instructions to make the funds available to the researcher at the U.S. Public Health Service Hospital. The project costs appear to have been between $34,000 and $45,000 per year. These documents specify that "the interest of CIA in this project is classified Secret and is not to be revealed ... ." (e.g., Doc. No. N-18.)

(3) Identification of effects of blast concussion

This project began in October, 1954 and was terminated, at least with respect to the Navy, in December, 1955. It was performed by a contractor located in California. The involvement of the Navy was primarily as a conduit of funds from the Central Intelligence Agency to the contractor. A small amount of Navy funds may also have been used for this contract. In December, 1955 this project was terminated as far as the Navy involvement was concerned and it thereafter apparently became subproject 54 of the MKULTRA project.

While the Navy was involved with this project it did not include any drug testing and apparently did not include any testing on humans. The contractor was investigating a new theory of the dynamics of brain concussion. Fluid-filled flasks were used to measure the effect of blast impacts from a 2 1/2 lb. charge of dynamite 10 feet away. The results of this work were published in 1957 in a 17-page report entitled "On the Impact Thresholds of Brain Concussion." (Doc. N-19.)

The Central Intelligence Agency transferred $20,000 to the Office of Naval Research for use on this project. The Office of Naval Research may have contributed as much as $5,000 of its own funds to this project.

In December, 1955, the contractor submitted a proposal for a continuation of the research for 1956. In that proposal the contractor pointed out that brain concussion "is always followed by amnesia for the actual moment of the accident" and suggested that "if a technique were devised to induce brain concussion without giving either advance warning or causing external physical trauma, the person upon recovery would be unable to recall what had happened to him. Under these conditions the same technique of producing the concussion could be re-used many times without disclosure of its nature." (Doc. No. CIA-4.) In discussing the techniques envisioned, the contractor described non-drug means for inducing concussion, but went on to describe a technique for providing immunity to concussion that "involves the introductioi of a small quantity of gas, approximately 1 cc, into the spinal cord." (Doc. No. CIA-4.)

When this project proposal was received, CIA decided to convert it to the MKULTRA project rather than using the Navy as a conduit for funds. A memorandum dated January 10, 1956 explained:

> The first year's work on this program was financed through the Navy for several reasons ... .
>
> When [the contractor] was cleared and informed of our true interests in this research, the whole scope of the project changed, and it became apparent that developments might be expected in the second year which would make it impossible to operate the program securely under the previous cover. Specifically, human experiments of a type not easily justifiable on medical-therapeutic grounds would be involved. ...
>
> For the reasons given above and because this project in a general way will begin to become involved in the subjects of interrogation and some aspects of brain-washing,

TSS/CD has decided that it should be funded
through project MKULTRA rather than by less
secure methods.

(Doc. No. CIA-5.) The project thereafter became subproject
54 of the MKULTRA project and there is no indication of further
involvement by the Navy.

(4) Administration of LSD to human subjects

This project began in 1952 and was apparently completed
by 1956. It was performed by a researcher located in New York.
Navy is listed as a sponsor in only one CIA document prepared
at a later date, and not otherwise corroborated. If Navy was
involved, it was solely as a conduit for funds between the
Central Intelligence Agency and the researcher. This project
has been identified as subprojects 7, 27 and 40 of the
MKULTRA project.

(5) Development and administration of speech-
inducing drugs

This project apparently began in 1947 and ended in 1953.
It was performed primarily by a contractor located in New
York and, in one aspect, by the Navy at a location in Europe.
The involvement of the Central Intelligence Agency was appar-
ently only as an interested observer. The project was funded
by the Navy through the Naval Medical Research Institute.
The Central Intelligence Agency records of this project are
apparently in the BLUEBIRD and ARTICHOKE project files.

The Navy arranged in 1950 to obtain marijuana and heroin
from the FBI for use in experiments and entered a contract
with a researcher in New York to develop drugs and instrumentation for use in interrogation of prisoners of war, defectors
and similar persons. The security cover for the project was
a study of motion sickness. The study began with six of the
researcher's staff as knowing volunteers. The project was
expanded to cover barbituates and benzedrine. Other substances were evaluated.

In August, 1952 the Office of Naval Intelligence informed
the Central Intelligence Agency that it had developed drugs
that might have the desired characteristics and was about to
test them on human subjects who would be unaware of the test.
The drugs were administered to about eight subjects, each of
whom was a Soviet defector, and each test was done in Europe

in September, 1952. The tests were apparently not satisfactory because the drugs used had such a bitter taste that it was
not possible to keep the human subjects from knowing about
the test.

By September, 1952 it was apparent that this project was
not producing useful results and the Navy began to consider
ending it. By 1953 most work had apparently been phased out.

C. Documents released

The Navy has identified 42 documents which are related
to the programs described in section B. A list identifying
those documents is set out in Appendix B.

IV. Air Force Programs

It appears from the available documents that the Air
Force was not involved in any aspect of the Central Intelligence Agency projects designated MKSEARCH, MKOFTEN and
MKCHICKWIT. It also appears that the Air Force was not
involved in any program in which there was Central Intelligence
Agency sponsorship or participation and which included the
administration of drugs to human subjects for mind-control
or behavior-modification purposes.

A. Records searched

The search was conducted by the Office of the Assistant
Secretary of the Air Force for Research, Development and
Logistics. The Air Staff offices in which records were
searched are: The Surgeon General, the Deputy Chief of Staff
for Research and Development, the Air Force Office of Special
Investigations, and the Air Force Intelligence Service.

B. Programs identified

There were no records or information found relating to
projects designated MKSEARCH, MKOFTEN or MKCHICKWIT or
corresponding to the description of the subject matter of
those projects available through Central Intelligence Agency
files.

There were no documents or information found indicating any CIA involvement in any experimentation program conducted by the Air Force that included administration of drugs to human subjects.

C. Documents released

None.

VI. Current Programs

There are no programs currently maintained by any Department of Defense component or contractor involving drug testing on human subjects in which the Central Intelligence Agency is in any way involved.

All current Department of Defense programs involving the use of investigational drugs on humans, including its contractor programs, have been approved by the Food and Drug Administration.

26 July 1963

MEMORANDUM FOR: Director of Central Intelligence

SUBJECT   : Report of Inspection of MKULTRA

     1. In connection with our survey of Technical Services Division, DD/P, it was deemed advisable to prepare the report of the MKULTRA program in one copy only, in view of its unusual sensitivity.

     2. This report is forwarded herewith.

     3. The MKULTRA activity is concerned with the research and development of chemical, biological, and radiological materials capable of employment in clandestine operations to control human behavior. The end products of such research are subject to very strict controls including a requirement for the personal approval of the Deputy Director/Plans for any operational use made of these end products.

     4. The cryptonym MKULTRA encompasses the R&D phase and a second cryptonym MKDELTA denotes the DD/P system for control of the operational employment of such materials. The provisions of the MKULTRA authority also cover [   ] The administration and control of this latter activity were found to be generally satisfactory and are discussed in greater detail in the main body of the report on TSD.

     5. MKULTRA was authorized by the then Director of Central Intelligence, Mr. Allen W. Dulles, in 1953. The TSD was assigned responsibility thereby to employ a portion of its R&D budget, eventually set at 20%, for research in behavioral materials and [   ] under purely internal and compartmented controls, (further details are provided in paragraph 3 of the attached report). Normal procedures for project approval, funding, and accounting were waived. However, special arrangements for audit of expenditures have been evolved in subsequent years.

6. The scope of MKULTRA is comprehensive and ranges from the search for and procurement of botanical and chemical substances, through programs for their analysis in scientific laboratories, to progressive testing for effect on animals and human beings. The testing on individuals begins under laboratory conditions employing every safeguard and progresses gradually to more and more realistic operational simulations. The program requires and obtains the services of a number of highly specialized authorities in many fields of the natural sciences.

7. The concepts involved in manipulating human behavior are found by many people both within and outside the Agency to be distasteful and unethical. There is considerable evidence that opposition intelligence services are active and highly proficient in this field. The experience of TSD to date indicates that both the research and the employment of the materials are expensive and often unpredictable in results. Nevertheless, there have been major accomplishments both in research and operational employment.

8. The principal conclusions of the inspection are that the structure and operational controls over this activity need strengthening; improvements are needed in the administration of the research projects; and some of the testing of substances under simulated operational conditions was judged to involve excessive risk to the Agency.

9. Attached for the signature of the Deputy Director of Central Intelligence is a memorandum transmitting the report to the Deputy Director/Plans requesting a summary of action taken or comments on the recommendations contained therein.

J. S. Earman
Inspector General

Attachments - as stated

REPORT OF INSPECTION OF MKULTRA/TSD

I. Introduction

1. Technical Services Division (TSD), (then Technical Support Staff), received authorization from the then Director of Central Intelligence, Mr. Allen W. Dulles, on 3 April 1953 to develop and maintain continuing operational capabilities in the fields of a) [_____] and b) chemical and biological materials capable of producing human behavioral and physiological changes, (see Tab A). The cryptonym MKULTRA was assigned to encompass TSD's research, development and equipment activities in these two fields. The cryptonym MKDELTA had already been assigned by DD/P Notice No. 220-1 on 20 October 1952 (since revised - see Tab B) as the indicator covering DD/P policy and procedure for the use of biochemicals in clandestine operations.

2. The MKULTRA charter provides only a brief presentation of the rationale of the authorized activities. The sensitive aspects of the program as it has evolved over the ensuing ten years are the following:

a. Research in the manipulation of human behavior is considered by many authorities in medicine and related fields to be professionally unethical, therefore the reputations

of professional participants in the MKULTRA program are

on occasion in jeopardy.

    b. Some MKULTRA activities raise questions of

legality implicit in the original charter.

    c. A final phase of the testing of MKULTRA products

places the rights and interests of U. S. citizens in jeopardy.

    d. Public disclosure of some aspects of MKULTRA

activity could induce serious adverse reaction in U. S.

public opinion, as well as stimulate offensive and defensive

action in this field on the part of foreign intelligence services.

3. In recognition of the sensitivity of MKULTRA, TSD was

authorized exclusive control of the administration, records, and

financial accountings of the program. Simple statements of certification

were all that were required of TSD to obtain advances of funds from

Finance Division. The DCI's memorandum also exempted MKULTRA

from audit, but this provision was modified to permit limited audit

before the end of the first year. Funding of MKULTRA was eventually

stabilized at 20 percent of TSD's annual research and development budget.

It has fallen in the neighborhood of [   ] per year over the ten-year

history of the program, of which about 30 percent has been allocated to support of the _____ | cf. Tab C for MKULTRA _____

funding record FY 60-63._____

    4. The inspection of TSD activities in the field of _____ |

| while chartered under MKULTRA is discussed for reasons

noted below in the section of the Inspector General's Survey dealing

with the _____ | of TSD, cf. dis-

cussions beginning with paragraphs _____ |

The security considerations applying to _____ | were found to

be significantly different from those governing manipulation of human

behavior. a) Many ____ | external projects in support of the _____ |

| are being funded and managed securely outside the

MKULTRA mechanism. b) Chief, Support, TSD, believes that it may

also be possible in the future to fund _____ | MKULTRA projects by

secure methods more compatible with DD/S responsibilities. c) The

very nature of the _____ | requires that a high

percentage of its staff contribute and be witting of each operation.

security practices are tight and the Inspector General's survey recom-

mends further refinements in security procedures. _____

    5. The inspection of MKULTRA projects in biochemical controls

of human behavior raised questions in the following area of policy and

management which are dealt with in the balance of this report:

a. Scope of the MKULTRA charter:

(1) Over the ten-year life of the program many additional avenues to the control of human behavior have been designated by the TSD management as appropriate to investigation under the MKULTRA charter, including radiation, electro-shock, various fields of psychology, psychiatry, sociology, and anthropology, graphology, harrassment substanc s, and paramilitary devices and materials.

(2) Various projects do not appear to have been sufficiently sensitive to warrant waiver of normal Agency procedures for authorization and control.

(3) Other secure channels for establishment and funding of Agency-sterile activities have been evolved over the past ten years by Deputy Director/Support (DD/S) and in some cases could reasonably be employed by TSD in lieu of MKULTRA procedures.

In view of these developments there is substantial agreement among all parties concerned that redefinition of the scope of MKULTRA is now appropriate.

b. MKULTRA management policies:

(1) The original charter documents specified that TSD maintain exacting control of MKULTRA activities.

In so doing, however, TSD has pursued a philosophy of minimum documentation in keeping with the high sensitivity of some of the projects. Some files were found to present a reasonably complete record, including most sensitive matters, while others with parallel objectives contained little or no data at all. The lack of consistent records precluded use of routine inspection procedures and raised a variety of questions concerning management and fiscal controls.

(2) Lack of records essential to inspection of MKULTRA moved to the forefront among issues as the present survey proceeded. Under normal circumstances the inspectors would have examined an inventory of dis-crediting, disabling, and lethal substances perfected or procured from whatever sources. The records on representative items would have been reviewed according to such standard criteria as:

(a) How were the substance and its properties identified?

(b) What researcher was selected to perform the research, and why?

(c) When was the work begun, where, involving what costs, at what rate of progress, based on what tests?

(d) What are the present capabilities and limitations of the substance for clandesinte operations?

(e) What further research is being conducted on this and related substances and how does this reflect existing TSD capabilities, operational requirements and budget factors?

(3) MKULTRA records afforded no such approach to inspection. There are just two individuals in TSD who have full substantive knowledge of the program and most of that knowledge is unrecorded. Both are highly skilled, highly motivated, professionally competent individuals. Part of their competence lies in their command of intelligence tradecraft. In protecting the sensitive nature of the American intelligence capability to manipulate human behavior, they apply "need to know" doctrine to their professional associates and to their clerical assistants to a maximum degree. Confidence in their competence and discretion has been a vital feature of the management of MKULTRA.

c. Advanced testing of MKULTRA materials:

It is the firm doctrine in TSD that testing of materials under accepted scientific procedures fails to disclose the full pattern of reactions and attributions that may occur

31

in operational situations. TSD initiated a program for covert testing of materials on unwitting U. S. citizens in 1955. The present report reviews the rationale and risks attending this activity and recommends termination of such testing in the United States, cf. paragraphs 10-18 below.

II. Modus Operandi

6. The research and development of materials capable of producing behavioral or physiological change in humans is now performed within a highly elaborated and stabilized MKULTRA structure. The search for new materials; e. g., psilocybin from Mexican mushrooms, or a fungi occurring in agricultural crops, is conducted through standing arrangements with specialists in universities, pharmaceutical houses, hospitals, state and federal institutions, and private research organizations who are authorities in the given field of investigation in their own right. Annual grants of funds are made under ostensible research foundation auspices to the specialists located in the public or quasi-public institutions. This approach conceals from the institution the interest of CIA and permits the recipient to proceed with his investigation, publish his findings (excluding intelligence implications), and account for his expenditures in a manner normal to his institution. A number of the grants have included funds for the construction and equipping of research

facilities and for the employment of research assistants.]Key individuals

must qualify for top secret clearance and are made witting of Agency

sponsorship. [As a rule each specialist is managed unilaterally and is

not witting of Agency support of parallel MKULTRA research in his

field. The system in effect "buys a piece" of the specialist in order to

enlist his aid in pursuing the intelligence implications of his research.]

His services typically include systematic search of the scientific

literature, procurement of materials, their propagation, and the appli-

cation of test dosages to animals and under some circumstances to

volunteer human subjects. No quarrel is found with the rationale of

this program to the extent that it fits the original MKULTRA charter.

However, for inspection purposes, there were lacking records, year

by year, of the progress of each project and the recorded judgments

of the project monitors on operational benefits vis-a-vis costs.

7. [The funding of sensitive MKULTRA projects by sterile grants

in aid as noted in the preceding paragraph disclosed one of the principal

controversial aspects of this program.] The original charter of MKULTRA

assumed that the sensitivity of activities would be sufficient to justify

both a) special protection for the researcher; and b) compartmentation

of MKULTRA knowledge within the Agency. On this basis the inherent

safeguards of DD/S procedures were waived, the DD/S was not consulted

in the design of the MKULTRA management system, and established Agency audit procedures were waived. In the subsequent administration of the program, however, TSD has found it feasible to contract for some of the research on MKULTRA objectives in accordance with prescribed DD/S procedures. The DD/S, in turn, has evolved various secure systems for the funding of sensitive activities. It appears feasible and appropriate, therefore, to propose that the DD/S be consulted during the re-chartering of MKULTRA in the design of an administrative system that does justice to his responsibilities as well as to the management and security requirements of TSD. The Inspector General accordingly has recommended at the end of this report that the DD/S be consulted in the re-design of the system; that the Chief, Support, TSD, be assigned responsibility for the day-to-day support of MKULTRA and that the latter constitute a bridge to the DD/S for monitoring the future evolution of the system.

8. The next phase of the MKULTRA program involves physicians, toxicologists, and other specialists in mental, narcotics, and general hospitals and in prisons, who are provided the products and findings of the basic research projects and proceed with intensive testing on human subjects. These specialists are also recipients for testing purposes of the flow of new products from pharmaceutical laboratories. Materials and procedures with intelligence potential may be identified through this

relationship. The testing programs are conducted under accepted
scientific procedures including the use of control populations, the
employment of placebos, and the detailed observation, measurement,
recording, analysis, and publication of findings. Where health permits,
test subjects are voluntary participants in the program.

9. A current development in the testing of new products is the
tightening of controls over dosages and procedures by the U. S. Food
and Drug Administration. Since MKULTRA files contained no documentation on this subject, it was not possible to appraise the significance of this development for MKULTRA objectives. However,
interviews with the TSD officers concerned indicated that the new rules
are affecting procedures and causing controversy in research hospitals
and pharmaceutical houses. The TSD officers have close relationships
with key individuals in many of the leading U. S. pharmaceutical houses
and count on their continued close cooperation in obtaining materials
and services deemed vital to U. S. intelligence.

10. The final phase of testing of MKULTRA materials involves
their application to unwitting subjects in normal life settings. It was
noted earlier that the capabilities of MKULTRA substances to produce
disabling or discrediting effects or to increase the effectiveness of
interrogation of hostile subjects cannot be established solely through
testing on volunteer populations. Reaction and attribution patterns are

clearly affected when the testing is conducted in an atmosphere of confidence under skilled medical supervision.

11. TSD, therefore, entered into an informal arrangement with certain cleared and witting individuals in the Bureau of Narcotics in 1955 which provided for the release of MKULTRA materials for such testing as those individuals deemed desirable and feasible. The initial arrangement obtained the services of a senior representative of the Bureau and one of his assistants on the West Coast. A parallel arrangement was established on the East Coast in 1961. The Director of the Bureau has been briefed on the activity, but the Deputy Chief, TSD, who has guided MKULTRA from its inception, is of the opinion that the former would disclaim all knowledge and responsibility in the event of compromise. The MKULTRA program director has, in fact, provided close supervision of the testing program from the beginning and makes periodic visits to the sites. The sum of $10,000 has been provided annually to each of the two projects to cover cost of cultivation of targets and of maintenance of a safehouse in each area for the observation of effects of substances on selected test individuals.

12. The particular advantage of these arrangements with the Bureau of Narcotics officials has been that test subjects could be sought and cultivated within the setting of narcotics control. Some subjects

have been informers or members of suspect criminal elements from whom the Bureau has obtained results of operational value through the tests. On the other hand, the effectiveness of the substances on individuals at all social levels, high and low, native American and foreign, is of great significance and testing has been performed on a variety of individuals within these categories.

13. A significant limitation on the effectiveness of such testing is the infeasibility of performing scientific observation of results. The Bureau agents are not qualified scientific observers. Their subjects are seldom accessible beyond the first hours of the test. The testing may be useful in perfecting delivery techniques, and in identifying surface characteristics of onset, reaction, attribution, and side-effect. In a number of instances, however, the test subject has become ill for hours or days, including hospitalization in at least one case, and the agent could only follow-up by guarded inquiry after the test subject's return to normal life. Possible sickness and attendant economic loss are inherent contingent effects of the testing.

14. The MKULTRA program officer stated that the objectives of covert testing concern the field of toxicology rather than medicine; further, that the program is not intended to harm test individuals, and that the medical consultation and assistance is obtained when appropriate through separate MKULTRA arrangements. The risk of compromise of

the program through correct diagnosis of an illness by an unwitting medical specialist is regularly considered and is stated to be a governing factor in the decision to conduct the given test. The Bureau officials also maintain close working relations with local police authorities which could be utilized to protect the activity in critical situations.

15. There have been several discussions in the public press in recent months on the use of certain MKULTRA-type drugs to influence human behavior. Broadly speaking, these have argued that research knowledge of possible adverse effects of such substances on human beings is inadequate, that some applications have done serious harm, and that professional researchers in medicine and psychiatry are split on the ethics of performing such research. Increasing public attention to this subject is to be expected.

16. The final step in the research and development sequence is the delivery of MKULTRA materials into the MKDELTA control system governing their employment in clandestine operations. The subject is discussed further in the next section; however, it is appropriate here to note that the employment of MKDELTA materials remains an art rather than a scientific procedure. A significant number of variables in the target individual, including age, sex, weight, general health, social status, and personality structure, may account for widely varying and unpredictable reactions to a given drug in a given dosage.

/

17. The final stage of covert testing of materials on unwitting subjects is clearly the most sensitive aspect of MKULTRA. No effective cover story appears to be available. TSD officials state that responsibility for covert testing is transferred to the Bureau of Narcotics. Yet they also predict that the Chief of the Bureau would disclaim any knowledge of the activity. Present practice is to maintain no records of the planning and approval of test programs. The principal responsibility for the propriety of such testing rests with the MKULTRA program director and the Deputy Chief of TSD. The handling of test subjects in the last analysis rests with the Narcotics agent working alone. Suppression of knowledge of critical results from the top TSD and CIA management is an inherent risk in these operations.

18. Final phase testing of MKULTRA substances or devices on unwitting subjects is recognized to be an activity of genuine importance in the development of some but not all MKULTRA products. Termination of such testing would have some, but an essentially indeterminate, effect on the development of operational capability in this field. Of more critical significance, however, is the risk of serious damage to the Agency in the event of compromise of the true nature of this activity. As now performed under Bureau of Narcotics auspices, non-Agency personnel are necessarily fully witting of the true nature and significance of their assignments, and of the sponsorship of CIA. Compromise of

this information intentionally or unwittingly by these individuals at some
time in the future is a hazard that cannot be ruled out. A test subject
may on some occasion in the future correctly attribute the cause of his
reaction and secure independent professional medical assistance in
identifying the exact nature of the substance employed, and by whom.
An extreme reaction to a test substance could lead to a Bureau request
for cooperation from local authorities in suppressing information of the
situation. This would in turn broaden the circle of individuals who
possessed at least circumstantial evidence of the nature of the activity.
Weighing possible benefits of such testing against the risks of compromise
and of resulting damage to CIA has led the Inspector General to recommend
termination of this phase of the MKULTRA program. Existing checks
and balances on the working level management of such testing do not
afford the senior command of CIA adequate protection against the high
risks involved.

19. [It does not follow that termination of covert testing of MKULTRA
materials on unwitting U. S. citizens will bring the program to a halt.
Some testing on foreign nationals has been occurring under the present
arrangements. Various U. S. deep cover agents overseas would appear
to be more favorably situated than the U. S. narcotics agents to perform
realistic testing.] Finally, the operational use of the substances clearly
serves the testing function in view of the lack of predictability of human
reactions.

III. Current estimate of the MKULTRA/MKDELTA capability

20. The present Deputy Chief of TSD, Dr. Sidney Gottlieb, in his then capacity of scientific advisor to the Deputy Director/Plans (DD/P), released a study (hereafter referred to as the Gottlieb report) on 21 April 1960, covering his six-month investigation of "Scientific and Technical Problems in Covert Action Operations". Appendix B of the report was entitled, "The Applicability of Special Chemicals and Biologicals to Clandestine Operations". The inspectors found this Appendix to be a carefully prepared and very useful treatment of the subject. The remaining paragraphs draw on the Gottlieb report, take account of developments since that date, and discuss management and funding aspects of MKULTRA.

21. The author opened his discussion with the question of what the operational returns had been from an eight-year program involving an investment of approximately   // He observed that the Clandestine Services had encouraged TSD on various occasions to develop and maintain the operational capability in special drugs and chemicals, but that TSD had received little or no guidance in directing the work and that the Clandestine Services had up to that time shown little inclination to use the end products operationally. He indicated that there had been approximately 100 operations over the eight years

41

employing harrassment materials (not controlled under the MKDELTA regulation) and only nine operations employing disabling drugs, (NB: two-thirds of these involved the use of drugs in interrogations). No use of lethal substances was reported.

22. The factors accounting for the low rate of use of this capability were considered to be the following:

    a. the technical shortcomings of the drugs
    b. the problem of testing in realistic pilot operations
    c. limitations on the dissemination of pertinent
       information to operations officers
    d. organizational and administrative restrictions on
       operations
    e. negative attitudes toward the use of MKDELTA materials
    f. problems in the training of case officers in this field
    g. the risk of stimulating increased use of MKDELTA
       materials by opposition intelligence services

23. Technical shortcomings of the drugs:

As of 1960 no effective knockout pill, truth serum, aphrodisiac, or recruitment pill was known to exist. MKDELTA was described as inherently a high-risk, low-yield field of operations. Three years later the situation remains substantially unchanged, with the exception that real progress has been made in the use of drugs in support of interrogation. Ironically, however, the progress here has occurred in the development of a total psychological theory of interrogation, in which the use of drugs has been relegated to a support role.

24. The problem of testing in realistic pilot operations:

This subject has been discussed above, beginning with

paragraph 10. It should also be noted that testing on operational

targets overseas is considered by some operations officers to

be quite impracticable. Unilateral operations are imperative

which substantially complicates the delivery problem. The

possibilities of unexpected or critical reactions in test subjects

and of ensuing compromise of the activity make most senior

command personnel unwilling to take the risks involved.

25. Limitations on the dissemination of pertinent information to

case officers; organizational and administrative restrictions on

operations:

The present-day situation concerning both of these problem

areas is improved over 1960. TSD now regularly briefs a variety of senior officers on its MKDELTA capability. Approval of

the use of MKDELTA materials is now accomplished within

the chain of command of the DD/P. The DD/P may consult,

for example, with the Chief, Medical Staff, concerning

medical risks involved in MKDELTA operations, but the

latter surely would not expect to exercise final authority for

the disapproval of operations.

26. TSD has found that TDY visits of MKULTRA officers to the

field in support of specific operations increases the awareness of the

MKDELTA capability and stimulates proposals for additional projects.

Of equal significance, however, has been the TSD decision in 1961 to

station in the   officer who is

informed on MKDELTA matters. A second officer is scheduled to

move PCS to   during the summer of 1963 to support   and

adjacent stations. While the principal responsibility of these officers

lies in the field   the arrangement in the

has proved useful in the MKDELTA field--notably in interrogation--as

well. It now appears that increased reliance can be placed on this

approach to promoting responsible use of the MKDELTA capabilities.

27. Negative attitudes toward the use of MKDELTA materials;

problems in the training of case officers in this field:

The 1960 [Gottlieb] report observed that some case officers

have basic moral objections to the concept of MKDELTA and

therefore refuse to use the materials. Some senior officers were reported to believe that the proper employment of the capability required more sophistication than most case officers possessed and that there would be a tendency toward over-reliance on and misuse of drugs in lieu of perfecting classic espionage techniques. Finally, it was suggested that MKDELTA controls were so restrictive as to have generated a general defeatism among case officers concerning the chances of getting approval for use of materials in routine rather than extreme situations. These matters will be reviewed in future field inspections of DD/P area divisions. In the meanwhile, the stationing of qualified TSD consultants in the field and increasing operational experience will tend to develop over time a category of case officers who have acquired direct appreciation of the potential and limitations of the MKDELTA capability.

28. The risk of stimulating increased use of MKDELTA materials by opposition intelligence services:

The Gottlieb report stated that opposition intelligence services are active in the MKDELTA field and recommended that the CI Staff of the DD/P conduct a systematic study of the evidence. This recommendation has not been implemented. It is a subject of increasing significance as new materials and techniques become available.

It is recommended that:

Deputy Director/Plans instruct Chief, CI Staff, to perform a study of the evidence of use of MKDELTA materials by opposition intelligence services and recommend appropriate measures for training DD/P case officers to recognize and counter hostile activity in this area.

29. In summary, present evidence concerning the operational value of the MKDELTA capability would appear to confirm the principal judgments of the 1960 Gottlieb report. There is an extremely low rate of operational use of the controlled materials. On the other hand, significant progress has been achieved in the development of an interrogation theory employing chemical substances, and in providing competent guidance to the field in MKDELTA matters through TSD officers working overseas.

IV. Management of MKULTRA

30. TSD has initiated 144 projects relating to the control of human behavior; i.e., during the ten years of operation of the MKULTRA program. Twenty-five (25) of these projects remain in existence at the present time, while a number of others are in various stages of termination.

31. Active projects may be grouped under the following arbitrary

headings. Many projects involve activity in two or more of the areas

listed.

    a. basic research in materials and processes
    b. procurement of research materials
    c. testing of substances on animals and human beings
    d. development of delivery techniques
    e. projects in offensive/defensive BW, CW, and radiation
    f. miscellaneous projects; e.g. (1) petroleum sabotage,
       (2) defoliants, (3) devices for remote measurement of
       physiological processes

32. The current management of TSD has initiated a policy of

directing the activities of MKULTRA and of the Behavioral Activities

Branch towards operations and away from long-range research. Prior

to this change in policy which occurred in 1962, MKULTRA sponsored

a large number of projects in the fields of applied psychology, sociology,

anthropology, and graphology. The present management is unlikely to

return to these fields of research under the MKULTRA charter. The

inspectors concluded that many of these projects were of insufficient

sensitivity to justify waiver of normal Agency control procedures. It

is recommended at the end of this report that projects falling outside the

authorized scope of MKULTRA henceforth require the prior written

approval of the DD/P to qualify for MKULTRA processing.

33. The TSD chain of command for administration of the MKULTRA

program comprises the following:

    a. Chief, TSD providing overall management
    b. Deputy Chief, TSD, (a trained scientist) providing
       top substantive guidance for the MKULTRA program
    c. Assistant Chief, TSD, for Research and Development,
       contributing management but not substantive guidance

d. Chief Scientist (reporting to c., above), (a trained scientist), contributing substantive guidance in some areas and responsible for the technical administrative processes of MKULTRA. He is supported by a GS-12 budget officer.

e. program manager for MKULTRA, also serves as Chief of Biology Branch, (a trained scientist)

f. project monitors located in various branches of TSD and specialized in the subject fields of the specific projects for which they are assigned responsibility

To date this chain of command has relied primarily on oral communication in the management of MKULTRA. Files are notably incomplete, poorly organized, and lacking in evaluative statements that might give perspective to management policies over time. A substantial portion of the MKULTRA record appears to rest in the memories of the principal officers and is therefore almost certain to be lost with their departures. The senior officers in the MKULTRA chain of command who are not substantively qualified need better records to measure the validity of projects through time and to identify key areas in which to require detailed periodic briefings from working specialists.

34. It will be noted that the Chief of Support, TSD, does not participate in the MKULTRA administration. The predecessor of the present Chief of Support served in TSD throughout the life of the program until 1962 without ever being associated with its management. In his stead, the Chief Scientist and a GS-12 budget officer have provided administrative support. The Chief Scientist has set policy on the funding of MKULTRA

projects in all respects including salaries, overhead rates, fees, material, equipment, facilities, travel, and the like. The support officer was only added in 1962 under pressure of critical audit findings. This use of the Chief Scientist in a field where Chief of Support possesses superior qualifications and facilities constitutes a misuse of talent. The proposed new charter for MKULTRA should take account of this anomaly and also provide that Chief of Support advise in the future on decisions to fund projects under the MKULTRA authority and thereby to waive the application of DD/S procedures.

It is recommended that:

Deputy Director/Plans draft and submit for the approval of the Director of Central Intelligence a revision and re-confirmation of the authority granted him in 1953 (Tab A) to operate the MKULTRA program, incorporating the following provisions:

a. Deputy Director/Plans assign Chief, Technical Services Division, to operate MKULTRA as a program for research and development of chemical, biological, and radioactive materials, and of techniques for the employment of electro-shock, capable of producing human behavioral or physiological change. Subsequent changes in scope of MKULTRA shall require the written approval of the Deputy Director/Plans.

b.   Deputy Director/Plans arrange with Deputy Director/
Research for the coordination of research relating
to MKULTRA objectives to control duplication of
effort and to provide for exchange of information of
new capabilities.

c.   Chief, Technical Services Division, consistent with
established policy, may negotiate for research in
MKULTRA materials and techniques to be conducted
by Deputy Director/Research and by other component
offices of CIA. He shall consult regularly with the
appropriate officers of such components to control
duplication of effort.

d.   Chief, Technical Services Division shall approve the
addition of MKULTRA developed materials to the
list of operationally available MKDELTA substances.
and keep the Deputy Director/Plans advised of such
additions. (cf. Clandestine Services Instruction :
No. 220-10, MKDELTA MATERIALS, dated 22 July
1960--Tab B--which governs the employment of
behavioral control materials in clandestine operations.)

e.   Deputy Director/Plans, jointly with the Deputy Director/
Support, establish policy for the administration of
support functions under MKULTRA. Such policy shall
seek to limit to the maximum the waiver of established
Agency support procedures for activities of unusual
sensitivity.

f.   Chief, Technical Services Division shall maintain
exacting internal controls and records of all substantive
and support matters within each MKULTRA project.
Records shall include:

(1) A plan of the research and development to be
performed.

(2) An administrative annex setting forth security,
budget and accounting arrangements agreed to
by the parties to the project. Chief of Support,
TSD, shall then certify to the DD/S for each
such project that this annex is in accord with
the agreed DDS/DDP policy. Pursuant to this

responsibility, Chief of Support, TSD,
shall have right of unlimited access to
the substantive and administrative records
of MKULTRA.

(3) An annual written review by the project
monitor setting forth in reasonable detail
the nature of the work performed, the
prospects for results of eventual operational significance, and a recommendation
for continuance or termination of the project.

g. Testing of MKULTRA materials and devices shall only
be performed in accredited research institutions under
accepted scientific procedures.

h. Chief, Technical Services Division, shall brief the
Deputy Director/Plans at least semi-annually on
MKULTRA activities. The Deputy Director/Plans
after each briefing shall promptly notify the Deputy
Director of Central Intelligence that he has personally
conducted a semi-annual review of the program.

i. The MKULTRA program be audited in accordance
with the provisions of HR 31-1, including auditor access
to substantive as well as administrative records.

Allen Welsh Dulles, first director of the CIA, started Project MK-Ultra on April 13, 1953.

Chapter 2
Drugs

1955 memo regarding desirable drugs to be found or created. Document retrieved via the 1977 Senate hearing on MK-Ultra.
1954 CIA Scientific Intelligence Memo "Potential New Agent for Unconventional Warfare - LSD"
1953 memo RE: LSD
1954 memo RE: Experiments with LSD-25 on "at least 12 human subjects of not too high mentality."
News headlines RE: CIA drug testing

Project MK-Ultra and Mind Control Technology

[document begins]

DRAFT
[deletion]
5 May 1955

A portion of the Research and Development Program of TSS/Chemical Division is devoted to the discovery of the following materials and methods:

1. Substances which will promote illogical thinking and impulsiveness to the point where the recipient would be discredited in public.

2. Substances which increase the efficiency of mentation and perception.

3. Materials which will prevent or counteract the intoxicating effect of alcohol.

4. Materials which will promote the intoxicating effect of alcohol.

5. Materials which will produce the signs and symptoms of recognized diseases in a reversible way so that they may be used for malingering, etc.

6. Materials which will render the induction of hypnosis easier or otherwise enhance its usefulness.

7. Substances which will enhance the ability of individuals to withstand privation, torture and coercion during interrogation and so-called "brain-washing".

8. Materials and physical methods which will produce amnesia for events preceding and during their use.

9. Physical methods of producing shock and confusion over extended periods of time and capable of surreptitious use.

10. Substances which produce physical disablement such as paralysis of the legs, acute anemia, etc.

11. Substances which will produce "pure" euphoria with no subsequent let-down.

12. Substances which alter personality structure in such a way that the tendency of the recipient to become dependent upon another person is enhanced.

13. A material which will cause mental confusion of such a type that the individual under its influence will find it difficult to maintain a fabrication under questioning.

14. Substances which will lower the ambition and general working efficiency of men when administered in undetectable amounts.

15. Substances which promote weakness or distortion of the eyesight or hearing faculties, preferably without permanent effects.

16. A knockout pill which can surreptitiously be administered in drinks, food, cigarettes, as an aerosol, etc., which will be safe to use, provide a maximum of amnesia, and be suitable for use by agent types on an ad hoc basis.

17. A material which can be surreptitiously administered by the above routes and which in very small amounts will make it impossible for a man to perform any physical activity whatsoever.

The development of materials of this type follows the standard practice of such ethical drug houses as [deletion] It is a relatively routine procedure to develop a drug to the point of human testing. Ordinarily, the drug houses depend upon the services of private physicians for the final clinical testing. The physicians are willing to assume the responsibility of such tests in order to advance the science of medicine. It is difficult and sometimes impossible for TSS/CD to offer such an inducement with respect to its products. In practice, it has been possible to use outside cleared contractors for the preliminary phases of this work. However, that part which involves human testing at effective dose levels presents security problems which cannot be handled by the ordinary contractor.

The proposed facility [deletion] offers a unique opportunity for the secure handling of such clinical testing in addition to the many advantages outlined in the project proposal. The security problems mentioned above are eliminated by the fact that the responsibility for the testing will rest completely upon the physician and the hospital. [one line deleted] will allow TSS/CD personnel to supervise the work very closely to make sure that all tests are conducted according to the recognized practices and embody adequate safeguards.

[document ends]

SCIENTIFIC INTELLIGENCE MEMORANDUM

POTENTIAL NEW AGENT FOR UNCONVENTIONAL WARFARE

Lysergic Acid Diethylamide (LSD)
(N, N-Diethyllysergamide)

CIA/SI 101-54
5 August 1954

CENTRAL INTELLIGENCE AGENCY

OFFICE OF SCIENTIFIC INTELLIGENCE

POTENTIAL NEW AGENT FOR UNCONVENTIONAL WARFARE

Lysergic Acid Diethylamide (LSD)
(N, N-Diethyllysergamide)

Lysergic acid diethylamide (LSD) (N, N-diethyllysergamide), a drug derived from ergot, is of great strategic significance as a potential agent in unconventional warfare and in interrogations.* In effective doses, LSD is not lethal, nor does it have color, odor or taste. Since the effect of this drug is temporary in contrast to the fatal nerve agents, there are important strategic advantages for its use in certain operations. Possessing both a wide margin of safety and the requisite physiological properties, it is capable of rendering whole groups of people, including military forces, indifferent to their surroundings and situations, interfering with planning and judgment, and even creating apprehension, uncontrollable confusion and terror.

Of all substances now known to affect the mind, such as mescaline, harmine and others, LSD is by far the most potent. Very minute quantities (upwards of 30 millionths of a gram) create serious mental confusion and sensual disturbances, or render the mind temporarily susceptible to many types of influences. Administration of the drug produces in an individual such mental characteristics of schizophrenia as visual or auditory hallucinations and physiological reactions of dizziness, nausea, dilation of the pupils, and lachrymation. These reactions, however, are not necessarily obvious and only a trained observer, after giving psychological tests, may definitely ascertain that a psychogenic drug has been administered. Data, although still very limited, are available which indicate its usefulness - for eliciting true and accurate statements from subjects under its influence during interrogation. It also revives memories of past experiences. In at least one case there was complete amnesia of events during the effective period.

To date, no antidote nor specific counteragent is available. The effect of LSD may, however, be shortened in duration by the use of chlorpromazine, barbiturates, or the intravenous injection of glucose. Very limited methods of detection and identification are known, such as fluorescence, staining and spectrophotometry. Although the mechanism of action of this drug in the human body is not fully understood, it is nevertheless known to interfere with the carbohydrate metabolism and to affect the central nervous system, certain of the brain hormones, and other body functions.

---

*OSI is now completing a detailed study of LSD that will deal with the composition of the drug, its psychogenic properties, its development, experimental use, and distribution. This study entitled "Strategic Medical Significance of Lysergic Acid Diethylamide (LSD)" will be made available to those with a paramount interest in the subject.

interrogation lasts for a long period the dosage by inhalation can be repeated as often as necessary, but not more frequently than every half to three quarters of an hour by inhalation or every two and a half to three hours by ingstion. It must be pointed out that the dosage suggested is the average. It is our observation that if the individual is slight, tired, or has not been on a proper diet they will have more reaction than a well-fed American.

The maximum effect is obtained in 20 to 30 minutes by inhalation and in two hours if given by mouth. Effect by inhalation continue for two hours and by mouth for from 5 to 8 hours. The behavior of each individual under the effect of this drug varies definitely with the personality of the subject. That is: a timid individual may become paralyzed with fear, while hyper-active individuals may have active halucinations. These are, of course, toxic reactions and not to be expected with the dosage suggested.

SIGNS AND SYMPTOMS FOLLOWING ADMINISTRATION

1. Sense of well-being.

2. Increase in confidence.

3. Feeling of amiability and rapport with the interrogator.

4. Driving necessity to discuss psychologically charged topics. Whatever the individual is trying to withhold will be forced to the top of his subconscious mind and the necessity to discuss this topic is one of the most valuable aspects of the material. (This last sentence is not based on scientific fact

but on observation using the material)

5. Loquacious

6. Marked _____*motor activity*_____ and increased rate volume
of speech.

The following signs and symptoms are considered as undesirable
and as minor toxic effects. As with the proceeding list
they follow in order of occurrence.

1. Thickening and slurring of speech.

2. Loss of control of muscle movements.

3. Asthenia.

4. Difficulty in remembering events only a few
seconds past.

5. Sweating and a feeling of warmth. (It is advisable
to keep the room warm so that you can complain
at the same time of being warm)

6. "Free floating", anxiety or fear.

7. Vertigo and lightheadedness.
nausea
8. Nausia, belching and other gastro-intestinal
symptoms, which may include vomiting.

The following toxic results have occurred only with much
higher dosages but include marked hyper-activity and physical
and auditory halucinations.

The substance has maximum usefulness when there is a
friendly rapport between the interrogator and the subject.
It is suggested that procedure be carried out as far as
possible in a relaxed and informal social setting. If the
subject should begin to show hostility, this is a toxic symptom
and it would be unusual if anything was gained from the

ew because subject usually withdraws at this point.
Most people under the effect have a desire to boast, proclaim
their ability both in the past and of what they can do in the
future. The most should be made of this. The interrogator
should encourage any discussions along this line. It is
obviously necessary for the interrogator to have a good background of the subject's past and possible future in order to
direct the thought in the sphere in which the interrogator
is most interested. The great value of the substance is
that the subject is not aware at any time during the actual
proceeding that he under the influence of a drug. However,
due to the toxic effects which may occur it is well to have
some suitable cover story such as a stove in the room which
gave out obnoxious fumes which the interrogator could complain
about, or food or xxhx alcohol which the interrogator could
also complain caused him to have peculiar symptoms. In the
ideal case this will not be necessary for within an hour after
inhalation there should be no ill effects and within 2 hours
and ½ after ingestion the subject should be able to conduct
himself in a normal fashion. It is felt s visable that the
substance might be given in another room and after the interrogation some additional procedure be undertaken to keep the
subject under observation.

60

Memorandum • UNITED STATES GOVERNMENT

Files   DATE: 3 February 1953

Lysergic Acid (LSD)

1. Lysergic Acid is a synthetic chemical having similar molecular
structures of various ergot derivatives. As is well-known, ergot is a
rust which affects rye during its growth. Also well-known is the fact
that ergot has certain properties which produce mental derangement,
mental and physical disorders, and in certain forms can produce death.
Ergot, however, has very valuable medicinal value, particularly in
connection with treatment of women before and after childbirth and in
curing certain types of migraine headaches.

2. Lysergic Acid (LSD) has, up until recently, been produced by
the SANDOZ Chemical organization whose main headquarters are at Basel,
Switzerland. The synthetic ergot (LSD) was developed by a Dr. Hoffman,
who is the chief researcher for Sandoz. One of Dr. Hoffman's many outstanding assistants, and apparently a protege of Dr. Hoffman's, is
Dr. Rudolph Bircher also a Swiss National.

3. For many years, it has been well-known that various doctors,
psychiatrists, scientists in various countries in Europe have been
experimenting with ergot or Lysergic Acid. This has been, as far as
is known, almost always purchased from the Sandoz organization which
sells chemicals to the world. This experimentation generally is of
a psychiatric nature but there have been certain indications that some
countries, and possibly the Soviet Union, have considered the use of
Lysergic Acid for either chemical warfare, psychological warfare, or
military purposes.

4. Since the unusual properties of ergot and more importantly
Lysergic Acid have been known to ARTICHOKE for some time, the development of this chemical has been of intense interest.

5. In connection with this, the writer learned long ago that
███████████████ of ████████ (one of the outstanding researchers
in the field of narcotic, hypnotic and soporific chemicals and drugs)
was doing research work in Lysergic Acid and was reportedly advocating
its study and use. Subsequently, ████████████ made several trips to
Europe and during these trips to Europe he visited numerous individuals
and discussed Lysergic Acid with them and spent a considerable amount
of time with officials of the Sandoz Company including ████████████
████████████, and others. ████████████████ upon his return from Europe in
1952, made a report in connection with this and again stressed the interest in and importance of Lysergic Acid.

6. Over a month ago, this office received a dispatch through the Contact Division which indicated that ████████████████ (mentioned above) was then visiting the United States, apparently for the purpose of visiting Sandoz's New York representatives and having general discussions concerning Sandoz's productions (particularly Lysergic Acid). The information forwarded to this office indicated in a not too specific manner that ████████'s trip had some military significance but this has never been checked out. This dispatch indicated that ████████ was in contact with ████████ and that ████████ would apparently spend some time either at the home of ████████ or in ████████'s company and ████████ desired some authorization to proceed in an attempt to "pump" ████████ for information concerning Lysergic Acid and other pertinent related information. Since it was indicated after consultation between ████████ of OTS, ████████ of Security, and the writer that ████████ could possibly C secure more information from ████████ than anyone else, a very general authorization was given to him to attempt to obtain from ████████ such information that he thought pertinent. The results of this have not yet been made available to this office. It should be noted for the record that ████████ is not in as far as is known a 𝒮 consultant to this Agency but is a Consultant to the ████████ ℬ of the ████████ and holds an ████ contract for many thousands of ℬ dollars for research purposes. The writer is not certain whether or 𝑒 not this Agency in any way is indirectly financing ████████ but it has been established that ████████ of OTS is well aware of ████████ work and apparently through ████████ channels is more or less ℬ able to control the activity of ████████. C

7. On 29 January 1953, ████████ and the writer had a 𝐴 long discussion with ████████ of OTS and much of this material was covered in this conference. What ████████ usefulness to this Agency ⟨ will be has not yet been ascertained, but apparently ████████ feels that ████████ in some ways a problem.

8. For matter of record, apparently chemists of the ████████ /. ████████ working for OTS have in the past few weeks succeeded in breaking the secret formula held by Sandoz for the manufacture of Lysergic Acid and have manufactured for this Agency a large quantity of Lysergic Acid which is available for our experimentation. This work is a closely guarded OTS secret and should not be mentioned generally.

Chief, Medicine Division, SI

Acting Chief, Biochemistry and Pharmacology, M/SI

Experiments with LSD-25

1. According to ████████████████████████ experiments with LSD-25 have been carried on in ████████ In order to test the doses required, at least 12 human subjects of not too high mentality were selected. They were told only that a new drug was being tested and promised that nothing serious or dangerous would happen to them. They were given doses of from 50 to 150 , some on alternate and others on every fourth day. During the intoxication they realized that something was happening, but were never told exactly what. All of the testing was done under the supervision of a trained psychiatrist.

2. A dose of 150 was finally selected to be used on a test subject in the interest of intelligence. The subject is believed to have been an ████████████████████. He was told the nature of the test and then given the LSD-25 in water by a psychiatrist who was the only person to witness the test. Although no direct questions were asked, the psychiatrist led the general conversations into appropriate channels and the subject disclosed certain information which he had been previously warned against revealing. At the conclusion of the experiment, the subject stated that to the best of his knowledge he had disclosed nothing. When confronted by the statements he had made, he was amazed.

3. The dosage varies greatly from person to person, but it seems that the higher the mentality, the higher the dose, and conversely.

4. The source of LSD-25 was Sandoz, Ltd., of Switzerland. Further, Sandoz has supplied several laboratories with ample LSD-25 to conduct research, including the ████████████████████ In addition, anyone in the world who wants samples of this material may obtain them providing, of course, they are legitimately engaged in research pertaining to the subject. This presumably applies to East Germany and any other Bloc countries, as well as to the USSR.

5. ████████████ feels that the USSR could produce this material at any time, if it has not already done so, and if it is not obtaining adequate samples directly from Sandoz.

6. It appears as though the activity of LSD-25 decreased rather markedly around the fourth day after it is put into solution. One explanation for this fact, advanced by ▓▓▓▓▓▓▓▓, is that the few bacteria in water are either metabolizing the LSD-25 or their by-products are destroying it or otherwise inactivating it. The magnitude of the decrease in activity in four days is roughly forty per cent or thereabouts.

7. This is the only experiment of its kind known by ▓▓▓▓▓ to have been conducted in the interest of intelligence in ▓▓▓▓▓ *H·L* He had no knowledge of any future tests with LSD-25. It must be kept in mind that, other than planning the experimental design and reviewing the results, he took no active part in the experiment. Finally, inasmuch as LSD-25 is a relatively new drug, the dosages of which are still regarded as undetermined for eliciting specific responses, ▓▓▓▓▓▓feels that many more experiments should be conducted before more definitive ansers can possibly be elicited.

A ▓▓▓▓▓▓▓▓▓▓

▓▓▓▓▓ 21 Jul 54

COPY: 13 Aug 54

CIA says 54 institutions got '50's, '60's drug-tests data

By ALBERT SEHLSTEDT, JR.

The Central Intelligence Agency said yesterday that approximately 54 institutions have requested and received hitherto secret documents linking them to the agency's experimental drug program in the 1950's and 1960's.

In all, about 80 institutions had been unwittingly involved in the secret project, called MK-ULTRA, dealing in part with so-called mind-bending tests and other experiments.

The Central Intelligence Agency began the process of notifying each institution in mid-August.

The University of Maryland and the Johns Hopkins University were two of the 80 institutions that were involved. However, neither university's work seemed to be directly associated with drug tests.

MK-ULTRA, conducted between 1953 and 1954, was an umbrella project with a number of objectives. It was aimed, among other things, at enabling the CIA to perfect interrogation techniques; detecting the use of similar techniques by a potential enemy, and helping the agency to induce amnesia in its own as well as enemy agents.

A spokesman for the intelligence agency said yesterday that 15 of the 80 institutions had not responded at all to the agency's August notification of involvement with MK-ULTRA. In addition, there were 8 organizations the agency was unable to locate because they no longer exist.

Three other institutions declined to accept the agency documents linking them to MK-ULTRA. The papers for two more institutions are still being processed, the spokesman said.

One organization declined to accept the agency documents but requested the agency to respond to several questions by mail.

The agency has refused to disclose the name of any university or other organization that was involved in the project. The decision to reveal the CIA link was left to each institution, which included prisons, mental hospitals and research laboratories, as well as universities.

Asked what response the CIA received from the contacted institutions, the agency spokesman said they were "generally appreciative of us being forthcoming."

Only a few expressed any deep con-

cern, primarily because of the length of time that had elapsed between the period of the tests and the time of the notification, he said.

The notification process began after Adm. Stansfield Turner, director of the CIA, presented two Senate panels with a classified list of the institutions that had been involved with MK-ULTRA.

Admiral Turner told the Senate Intelligence committee and the health subcommittee that no similar programs were now being conducted by the CIA, adding that if he ever discovered any "heads would roll."

A number of the CIA documents given the various institutions were fragmentary and it was difficult to establish the precise nature of the work that had been conducted under the title of MK-ULTRA.

The University of Maryland's involvement with the project was traced to a 1956 Medical School study which may have been aimed at arresting the spread of cancer cells.

The Hopkins project apparently dealt with a study of "allergic substances," a spokesman for the university said.

Harvard outlines its CIA work

By Al Larkin Jr
Globe Staff

Harvard University said yesterday that it conducted two research projects for the CIA's controversial MK-ULTRA human behavior project but denied involvement in the program's testing of LSD and other drugs on humans.

A spokesman for the university, outlining the extent of the university's participation for the first time, said a full statement detailing the specific research projects was being prepared.

The announcement came shortly after Stanford University in California released a lengthy statement outlining its involvement in seven CIA-funded projects after a report was issued by the Massachusetts Institute of Technology on its CIA research.

The universities' disclosures followed several weeks of reluctance to discuss the research until after the universities were apprised of their involvement by the CIA.

But the new openness also appears to point up the inadequacy of records kept by both the CIA and the individual research institutions on how, where, and for how long the projects operated.

For example, MIT's admission of involvement in only one MK-ULTRA project—a contention supported by CIA officials in Virginia yesterday— directly contradicts information The Globe has obtained involving at least two, and perhaps other, MK-ULTRA projects.

Dr. Edgar Schein, an MIT professor, said two weeks ago that he knowingly accepted CIA money for research into brainwashing techniques that later resulted in the publi-

MIT's admission of involvement in only one MK-ULTRA project—a contention supported by CIA officials in Virginia yesterday—directly contradicts information. The Globe has obtained involving at least two, and perhaps other, MK-ULTRA projects.

cation of a book entitled "Coercive Persuasion."

A spokesman for MIT said yesterday that the CIA had not notified the school of Schein's research. The university previously had disclosed only a project involving a study of Soviet scientists as possible defectors.

Other researchers at the university also have reported knowledge of "a number of CIA projects" during the 1950s and early 1960s, but said they did not know if the re-

search was done as part of the MK-ULTRA project.

CIA Director Stansfield Turner has repeatedly emphasized that the agency lacks detailed records on the research project because most of those documents were destroyed in 1973. Only financial documents pertaining to certain projects remain.

Stanford revealed yesterday that between 1953 and 1961 the CIA covertly spent more than $385,000 on faculty research designed "to identify materials and methods useful in altering human behavior."

A Stanford spokesman said yesterday there "was mention of human experimentation" in the documents supplied by the CIA but that the university was unable to determine if that research had been carried out.

One of the projects apparently involved a "practicing psychiatrist" on the Stanford faculty who served as a consultant to the controversial George H. White, a CIA operative who established a "safe house" in San Francisco and used prostitutes to administer LSD to unsuspecting citizens.

Other projects at Stanford included research on alcoholic intoxication, analysis of sedatives (including a species of ticks) used in developing a knockout drug, development work on a miniaturized lie detector and a literature search on blood-type groupings.

The Boston Globe 27 Sept. 1977

CIA Says It Has New Details Of Its Drug Tests on Humans

By Robert G. Kaiser
Washington Post Staff Writer

The White House revealed yesterday that the Central Intelligence Agency has uncovered new details of its own experiments with exotic drugs from 1953 to 1964.

In what appeared to be a pre-emptive announcement to the press, the White House released a letter from CIA Director Stansfield Turner to Sen. Daniel K. Inouye (D-Hawaii), chairman of the Senate intelligence committee, briefly describing the new evidence found in CIA files.

The White House did not release any detailed information on the new discoveries, however, and what it did release added very little to the documented history of CIA drug experimentation—including the administration of drugs like LSD to unwitting human guinea pigs—revealed by Sen. Frank Church's (D-Idaho) investigation of the agency.

The Senate Intelligence Committee plans to hold public hearings on the new information next week, probably on Wednesday or Friday, and the skimpy outline of facts released yesterday could blossom into substantial new revelations.

The newly discovered documents reported by Turner are financial records of MK-ULTRA, a supersecret CIA research and development program involving exotic drugs and their possible uses for intelligence or military purposes.

The CIA files describing MK-ULTRA were destroyed in 1973 at the suggestion of then-Director Richard Helms, according to testimony before the Church committee.

But a continuing search through CIA files has discovered records on disbursements made for MK-ULTRA, according to Turner's letter to Inouye.

Turner's letter enumerated these activities for which money was apparently disbursed:

• Testing of drugs on American citizens without their knowledge, in cases beyond those already revealed.

• Research on the surreptitious administration of drugs.

• Research on a knockout or "K" drug, including tests on "advanced cancer patients."

• Experiments using drug addicts or alcoholics.

• A possibly illegal payment to a "private institution."

All of these except the "K" drug were discussed in the Church committee's final report in April 1976. The committee found that MK-ULTRA gave LSD to unwitting subjects (one of whom, Dr. Frank Olson, died as a result), used private institutions clandestinely to conduct research, and used prisoners and patients as subjects.

The committee found that the CIA went to great lengths to conceal the MK-ULTRA project because of its sensitivity.

In his letter Turner said that the newly found financial records don't present "a complete picture" but "provide more detail than was previously available."

Turner said he wanted to testify about this material to the intelligence committee "in keeping with the President's commitment to disclose any errors of the intelligence community which are uncovered."

Jody Powell, Carter's press secretary, said the material was released quickly to head off any charge that the administration was trying to hide new information.

Powell said the resignation this week of E. Henry Knoche, deputy director of central intelligence, had nothing to do with the newly discovered MK-ULTRA financial records.

On another CIA matter, Powell denied that Carter has offered the deputy's job to Prof. Lyman B. Kirkpatrick of Brown University, a former executive director of the CIA. The New York Times reported Thursday that he had been offered the job. Asked if Kirkpatrick would be offered it later, Powell replied, "Not that I know of, no."

The Washington Post 16 July 1977

'Canadian Suit Ties CIA to LSD, Brainwashing Studies

By KENNETH FREED, *Times Staff Writer*

TORONTO—Between 1953 and 1963, nine people entered a Montreal psychiatric clinic seeking treatment for a variety of illnesses ranging from depression to alcoholism to arthritis. However, instead of being helped, the six men and three women charge, they became test subjects for American intelligence agents exploring ways to control the human mind.

Their claim is that without their knowledge or consent, they were fed doses of drugs, including mind-altering LSD, and subjected to radical brainwashing experiments, involving long periods of forced sleep and other unorthodox procedures, proposed and financed by the Central Intelligence Agency.

In a long-running lawsuit, the nine Canadians allege that their stay at the Allan Memorial Clinic and their treatment by its director, the late Dr. Ewen Cameron, left them with permanent mental damage and has affected their ability to lead normal lives.

Each is asking for $175,000 (in U.S. dollars) in damages and an apology from the U.S. government. Although the suit was filed in a federal district court in Washington, D.C., five years ago, the case still has not come to trial and lawyers for the nine people say they are frustrated by the government's tactics.

Joseph Rauh, a well-known civil liberties attorney who represents the nine, said in a telephone interview from his Washington office that the government has prevented key witnesses, particularly former CIA agents, from giving depositions and has forced him to file time-consuming pretrial motions sometimes taking two years to resolve.

"The CIA strategy," he said, "is to stonewall until I'm not able to continue with the case. At my ripe old age of almost 75 there is only a limited time I can practice, and they are stalling for all it's worth."

The CIA says it does not discuss cases in litigation and the State Department and the U.S. Embassy in Ottawa add only that Secretary of State George P. Shultz's legal adviser is studying the matter.

Rauh and some Canadian government officials who do not want to be identified are nearly as critical of the Canadian government's attitude as they are of the CIA, charging that External Affairs Minister Joe Clark has not acted firmly in the matter for fear of upsetting Shultz and other Reagan Administration officials.

Canadian Asks Shultz

A spokesman for Clark said the minister has brought up the case with Shultz on two occasions since mid-May but has received no reply other than that the matter is being reviewed by the State Department's attorney.

Calling this an overly cautious approach, Rauh said, "The Canadian government is weaker than water for four shifts of relatives. I am flabbergasted at the lack of response. . . . Clark can't even get a 'no' from Shultz.

Rauh and some Canadians want Clark to threaten to take the case to the World Court at The Hague. They say that the CIA and the U.S. government breached Canadian sovereignty.

"This could be settled in five minutes if Clark said he was going to The Hague," the American lawyer went on, but "Shultz treats him like a gnat on his forehead; he just brushes him away."

A Canadian external affairs official added, "It is clear that Clark doesn't want to upset the Americans right now and it is government policy to downplay any differences that crop up" between the two countries.

Although the American government has refused to settle or apologize and is fighting the case in the court, the CIA—both in 1977 and in court papers filed in 1980—acknowledged its involvement with Cameron's work after charges were made public.

American author John Marks first disclosed the CIA role after noting in a 1975 report of the Rockefeller Commission a brief mention of the agency's interest in exploring mind control through the use of drugs and other techniques.

He asked for all pertinent documents under the Freedom of Information Act, received 16,000 pages of material and found references to Cameron's work at the Allan clinic and the fact that he had received funds from a CIA front organization.

Marks presented his findings in a 1977 book called "In Search of the Manchurian Candidate." In it, he referred to several articles that Cameron had written for various American and Canadian medical journals.

In a deposition, former CIA Director Stansfield Turner told Rauh that the experiments had taken place and that "the (CIA) unit conducting the experiment simply had such autonomy that not many outsiders could look in and ask what was going on."

Also, sources close to the case have said that two former CIA operations officers based in Canada in the late 1970s acknowledged the agency's involvement and even secretly apologized to the Canadian government.

The same sources said the two men, Stacy Hulse and John Kenneth Knaus, agreed to give a deposition to Rauh confirming the CIA role and their apology but that they were prevented from doing so by the CIA's invoking of regulations limiting public testimony by even retired employees.

Rauh has filed a motion to compel the CIA to permit their testimony, but the judge has delayed a ruling.

In addition, there are more than 2,000 pages of documentation in the public archives in Ottawa concerning Cameron's experiments, including several documents that deal with letters between high Canadian health officials and Cabinet members concerning the work at the Allan Memorial Clinic, which is associated with Montreal's prestigious McGill University.

These papers point to radical uses of drugs, including LSD, and the injection of large doses of insulin to induce comas, sometimes for 16 hours. Cameron, whose work was highly regarded by his professional peers, according to contemporary news accounts, also used

Continued

Chapter 3
Hypnosis (H)

Mori doc ID# 17447 - MK-Ultra Subproject 49. Note the interest in "flicker light" on page 73, which some have speculated would later be used in the flicker rate of television and computer monitors.
Mori doc ID# 17448
Mori doc ID# 140393 - One of the most disturbing MK-Ultra documents to come to light. The writer details how an unknown hypnotist used hypnotism for "inducing young girls to have sexual intercourse with him." The document goes on to suggest that hypnotism could be used to pass along state secrets.

23 May 1955

MEMORANDUM FOR THE RECORD

SUBJECT: Project MKULTRA, Subproject 49

1.   Subproject 49 of Project MKULTRA is being instituted as a means by which ███████████ work on hypnosis will be continued at the ████████████████ for the period 1 June 1955 to 31 May 1956.

2.   Two financial proposals are attached.   They entail $8,150.00 to ████████ and $10,450.00 to the ████████████████ To this is added $744.00 which represents a 4% service charge to the ████████████████   The ████████████████ will function as cut-out and cover for this grant.   The cover title of the project is ████████████████████████████ and is presumably being supported by a research grant from the ████████████████

3.   The total cost of the project will therefore not exceed $19,344.00.

4.   ████████ is cleared through TOP SECRET.

████████████████████████

SIDNEY GOTTLIEB
Chief, TSS/Chemical Division

APPROVED FOR OBLIGATION
OF FUNDS:

████████████████   A

Research Director

Date: ████████████

70

PROPOSAL FOR RESEARCH IN HYPNOSIS AT THE ███████████████ *B*
(June 1, 1956 to May 31, 1957)

Introduction:

Since the initiation of this project in September 1952, various
phases of hypnotic research have been completed. Two papers have
been published: ███████████████████████████████████ and
████████████████████████████████ *C*

Unpublished work consists of: ████████████
██
██
████████████████████████████████

At the present time, work is being conducted on: ████████████ *C*
████████████████████ (copy attached hereto). As
an ancillary activity, work is currently being conducted on measuring
the difference in psychogalvanic responses under questioning between
the waking and hypnotic states.

In an attempt to revitalize and reorient research activities in
the field of hypnosis, the following proposal of experimental investigation is submitted to the ████ for consideration for fiscal year 1957.
The following experimental design is an outgrowth of present and past
efforts conducted to date. *B*

Criteria for Determining "Genuineness" of Hypnosis:

At the present time, there are no good criteria for determining
the "genuineness" of hypnosis. It is felt that there are strong
possibilities that valid criteria can be established through physiological
and/or biochemical patterns of measurement.

By utilizing hypnotically induced states of anxiety and/or stress
as emotional stimuli, "true" responses will be reflected in the bio-
chemical and/or physiological changes within the human organism. Unless
the hypnotically induced stimuli is "genuine" or effective, there would
be no demonstrable response, either biochemically or physiologically.

It is felt that by establishing "normal" waking patterns and comparing them with patterns of those "under hypnosis", a dependable and
reliable criteria for determining the state and "genuineness" of hypnosis
will be formulated.

A. Biochemical Measurements:

    1. Hippuric acid tolerance test (measure of detoxication by the liver to estimate the ability of the organism to mobilize glycine)..

    2. Plasma amino acid level (check on possible alteration of glycine level which might merely be part of a total amino-acid change; secondary index of an altered adreno-cortical function).

    3. Blood reduced glutathione level (to further determine whether the glycine utilized for the synthesis of hyppuric acid was derived from preformed glycine, the change in level of a glycine-donating substance such as glutathione is concurrently measured).

    4. Blood eosinophil level (stress response index).

B. Physiological Measurements:

    1. Simultaneous recordings of physiological responses by means of a multi-channel recorder; to incorporate heart pulsations, respiratory rate and amplitude, psychogalvanic skin response, and cortico-electro activity.

Variations in the Techniques of Induction:

    In order to determine the extent and effectiveness of various other factors, such as non-verbal, visual and auditory, in the induction of hypnosis, the following experiments are proposed:

    1. Auditory techniques (verbal stimulation):

    In an attempt to separate the mechanical aspects of the induction technique, i.e. tone, rhythm, quality of the voice from the substantive aspects, i.e., content, association patterns; different induction "patters" or "talks" will be attempted and compared with standard "sleep talk".

    (a) Ordinary "sleep" talk.
    (b) Nonsense syllables or words.
    (c) Double talk.
    (d) Changes in cadence and tone .
    (e) Standard method presented in a foreign language (e.g., Spanish).

2. Non-verbal and/or visual techniques:

    (a) Monotoncus audio stimulation:

        (1) Soft music
        (2) Sub-liminal voice
        (3) Combination of both

    (b) Visual Stimulation:

        (1) Flicker-light
        (2) Colored lights in varying patterns
        (3) Combination of both

It is felt that a technique of induction can be devised from the results of the above experiments that will enable an operator to by-pass a subject's resistance to hypnosis and/or induce hypnosis in an unwitting subject.

Other Fields of Investigation:

Time permitting, within the framework of this investigation, other pertinent areas of interest will be pursued, namely, the following:

1. Auto-hypnosis

2. Effectiveness of hypnotists as determined by personality patterns, prestige and sex of the operator.

3. Duration and durability of hypnotic block.

Proposals for Research in Hypnosis at the ████████████
for the year, June 1, 1956 to May 31, 1957.

Introduction

Since this ~~project~~ was started in September of 1952, work

has been done on various projects which were outlined by the

fund representative and myself. Some of these have been ████

██

████████████████████████████ (These two have

been published), ████████████████████████████

██

██

████████████ and various pilot studies concerning subconscious

retention of material and ability to deliver same without the

subject's knowing consciously that he had even had this material;

i.e., an unwitting message carrier. At the present time work is

being conducted on my dissertation topic ████████████████

████████████████████, a copy of which is attached. We

are also completing the work on the study on the difference in

psychogalvanic responses under questioning between the waking

and hypnotic states. Some of this work will not be completed

by June 1, but will be well on its way.

As an outgrowth of this, and some work that has been done by

others, the following experimental work in the field of hypnosis

should be carried out.

Topics for Experimental Investigation

Criteria of Hypnosis

1. Since at the present time we have no absolute criteria of whether a person is hypnotized or is faking, and since there seems to be a strong possibility of being able to find such a criterion in the field of induced physiological changes, there should be an investigation or experiment in the area of induced bio-chemical changes, ~~in physiological~~; i.e.;

(1) An experiment on whether or not hypnotic produced anxiety may produce bio-chemical blood change—in blood sugar or hormone balance which would differ from that produced by simply imagining the anxiety situation.

(2) An experiment should be set up using multi-channel recordings of psychogalvanic skin response, heart and lung action, and brain waves. This should be inspected for pattern changes in comparing the hypnotic and waking states in an individual to see whether or not there is a pattern change. Other experimenters have tried these measurements separately; and while they have found some variations, they have found nothing that can be used as an absolute criterion. However, if these variations, in combination, would form a pattern we might be able to develop a criterion of hypnosis in this way.

Induction Methods

In order to investigate the possibilities of hypnotic
induction of non-willing subjects or subjects who have only
a knowledge of some other language than that of the hypnotist
experimental work should be done in the following fields

1. An experiment should be set up so as to try to hypnotise
   the subjects when:

   a. the hypnotist uses nothing but nonsense words or syllables
      but holds the same general tone and cadence.

   b. Since there may be a phonetic similarity of language
      of long sounds, such as sleep, an experiment should be
      set up using the direct hypnotic commands only in a
      foreign language (Since both my assistant and myself
      speak Spanish this could be done with subjects who have
      no knowledge of Spanish).

2. An investigation should be made into non-verbal induction
   techniques, such as long duration of monotonous audio or
   visual stimulation. A variation of this in which I am
   interested and in which I have done some work, a few pilot
   studies, is to use soft restful music in which my voice
   was also recorded at a sub-liminal level. With some subjects
   in the past this has been very effective. However, the
   degree of effectiveness for an experimental group has not
   been tried.

Other Fields for Investigation

Other work which needs to be done and which we could well do here includes the following topics:

1. Can a subject keep up his efficiency under hypnosis when he is subjected to a very strong audio stress?

2. Can auto-hypnosis be taught so as to be as effective as hetero-hypnosis in the canceling out of pain or other stress conditions; i.e., if this can be done a person could create his own world and be happy in it even though he were actually confined in a very small place which was extremely filthy.

3. To my knowledge little has been done to determine the effectiveness of male-versus-female hypnotists. An experiment should be set up to test whether or not there are personality patterns which are more amenable to hypnosis by hypnotists of one sex or the other.

There are a great many areas which need investigation in the field of hypnosis. However, some of these (especially those connected with the use of drugs) could not be handled in the University stiuation. Still others will probably arise after we have answered some of the questions outlined in the above experiments. It is true that we could not handle all the above outlined experiments this year even though we enlarge our staff by putting on one more assistant. Consequently, an order of precedence will have to be worked out between your representative and myself; and there is a possibility that there will be unfinished

work again at the end of next year which will need some time
to complete. However, the above experiments all have to do
with things that are pertinent to the ████████ and which I
am interested in doing research.

Budget and Personnel

I have attached a budget for the coming year. This includes
the salaries for ████████ (who will take the place of ████████
who will complete her Ph. D. work this summer and will put her
whole time on the project. She has been trained in both counseling
and guidance, and psycho-therapy, with a strong background in
psycho-metric techniques. We are at the place now where more
subjects are available and we can enlarge the work so as to
carry on more research during this year, so I have included
the salary for a new full time assistant which I will have to
select and train this summer in order to be ready for the
experimental work next year. I will select for this a person
who is as well qualified for the place as I can find. If the
bio-chemical experiment is approved, I have arranged with the
chemistry department to get a graduate student to work on
this experiment for two quarters. The cost for this would be
$1000, or $500 a quarter; and this would be classed as a half-
time assistant. ████████ has been with us now for over a
year and has charge of test administration, scoring, and
statistical work. We have had no trouble getting experimental
subjects at $1.00 per hour. However, we do have trouble in
78

keeping track of subjects in a university setting since their
program changes and they are not always available.

In putting on another assistant next year and going into
some additional experimental work, we will have to get some
new equipment (title of which will remain with the fund) and
set up another office; consequently, I have had to increase
the items 2, 3, 4, and 5 in the University budget.

Summary

In this application for research funds we have offered
(1) a list of topics of needed research which could be conducted at the ▮▮▮▮▮▮▮▮▮▮ . (2) a list of personnel *B*
needed to conduct this research, (3) a budget of salaries,
supplies and equipment to finance the year's work, (4) a
statement that these topics will be given an order of preference
to be worked out between your representative and myself, and
(5) an acknowledgement that this research may not be completed
by May 31, 1957, or that new topics may be opened up which
should be followed up by other research.

Signed, _____

▮▮▮▮▮▮▮▮▮▮ *C*

MEMORANDUM FOR THE RECORD *(H)*

SUBJECT: Visit to Project ████

(C) *(H)*

1. On this day the writer spent the day observing experiments with Mr. ████ on project ████ and in planning next year's work on the project (Mr. ████ has already submitted his proposal to the ███████████████). *(C)*

2. The general picture of the present status of the project is one of a carefully planned series of five major experiments. Most of the year has been spent in screening and standardizing a large group of subjects (approximately 100) and the months between now and September 1 should yield much data, so that these five experiments should be completed by September 1. The five experiments are: (N stands for the total number of subjects involved in the experiment.)

Experiment 1 - N-18 Hypnotically induced anxieties to be completed by September 1.

Experiment 2 - N-24 Hypnotically increasing ability to learn and recall complex written matter, to be completed by September 1.

Experiment 3 - N-30 Polygraph response under Hypnosis, to be completed by June 15.

Experiment 4 - N-24 Hypnotically increasing ability to observe and recall a complex arrangement of physical objects.

Experiment 5 - N-100 Relationship of personality to susceptibility to hypnosis.

3. The work for next year (September 1, 1953 to June 1, 1954) will concentrate on:

Experiment 6 - The morse code problem, with the emphasis on relatively lower I.Q. subjects than found on University volunteers.

26 March - A demonstration was given for selected representatives of Senior Staffs and Area Divisions.
Limb catalepsy, reproduction of written material
and visualization and verbal description were
demonstrated.

Discussion:

At all times when subjects were being hypnotized a CD representative (Dr. Gottlieb or Major ██████) was present. His presence
served a double purpose of reassurance to the subject and observation of technique for possible later exploitation.

It should be emphasized that from the hypnotist's point of
view the entire operation was carried out under the most difficult
conditions. He had no previous contact with subjects, hence, no
initial rapport existed. He had no background knowledge of subjects from which to develop leads indicating depth of trance. It
is an established fact that trance depth develops most satisfactorily if time (a few days) is allowed between interviews. Here
subjects took part in four developmental interviews within a period of 48 hours thus allowing very little assimulatory time.

Despite the difficulties under which he worked, Mr. ████ was
able to demonstrate medium trance phenomena quite satisfactorily.

With respect to techniques used by Mr. ████ in suggestibility
testing and hypnosis, the methods are essentially as follows: A
constant speed black on white spiral color wheel was used for
visual fixation along with verbal suggestion in initial testing.
With these subjects demonstrating susceptibility, suggestions were
made that future trance induction would be accomplished on verbal
command to sleep. In later interviews verbal suggestions and commands were given with a background of metronome beats.

Results:

As indicated previously, three subjects were chosen for further development. Results with each subject will be treated separately. Subject A ████ attained a medium trance state. In the
short time for development, however, he was unable to reach a som-
nambulistic state as characterized by amnesia. In the preliminary
demonstration subject A demonstrated arm catalepsy and hypnotic recall of written material. In the final demonstration Subject A demonstrated arm paralysis and induced pain as a form of physical and
psychological control.

81

Subject B ███ attained medium trance state and in both demonstrations produced under hypnosis a quite accurate copy of written material previously observed. Unfortunately both A and B proved to have excellent memories. They were able to recall the material quite accurately without hypnosis so that little, if any, improvement could be noticed.

Subject C ███ attained medium trance state with a particular flair for visualization and verbalization. In the preliminary demonstration "C" reproduced the layout of the room observed noting additional features and correcting erroneous relationships evident in a previous conscious recounting. Interrogation indicated that further information as to detail could be obtained. In the final demonstration subject C was regressed to the time in 1948 when he visited ███████ and asked to describe the scene. Verification as to accuracy of the description came from an observer who had recently visited the area. It is interesting to note that the description was in terms of the 1948 appearance and did not allude to extensive fire destruction which occurred later.

Written productions of subjects are attached in their original state.

Comments:

Whereas the experiment was only partially successful in the light of failure to achieve amnesiac states and the lack of marked improvement in hypnotic recall, the interest aroused among observers of the demonstration attests to the success of one of the main objectives—stimulation of thinking in the operational fields.

Chemical Division, TSS

MEMORANDUM FOR THE RECORD

SUBJECT: Project MKULTRA, Subproject 84

1. The purpose of this Subproject is the partial support of the activities of Dr. ▓▓▓▓▓▓▓ of ▓▓▓▓▓▓▓▓▓▓ in his work on the induction of high motivation in individuals by means of the development of specific interpersonal relationships. The attached proposal indicates the general areas of coverage and the techniques that will be exploited. Dr. ▓▓▓▓ project will require two years to complete and will cost a total of $34,000.00 for that period. He has requested that ▓▓▓▓▓▓▓▓▓▓▓▓▓▓▓▓▓▓ tender a grant of $25,000.00 to supplement funds which are available to him from other sources.

2. The Board of Directors of ▓▓▓▓▓▓▓ has considered this proposal and recommends that it be accepted on its merits and upon the demonstrated capability of its chief investigator.

3. Agency interest in work along the lines which will be pursued by Dr. ▓▓▓ centers around three salient points. First of all, even though the study is oriented in a very extensive and little understood field, i.e. individual motivation, the work itself will be divided into segments of a practical and realistic size, both from the standpoint of the research itself and that of later practical application of the results in Agency-type situations. Secondly, the development of techniques for altering or generating high motivation in individuals is the logical extension of the program of development of techniques for individual assessment now being carried out by the Agency. The ability to assess an agent adequately will only become a powerful operational tool when it is accompanied by the ability to use such knowledge in conjunction with techniques for the production of high motivation toward Agency goals. Finally, in carrying out this work, it appears that Dr. ▓▓▓ will probably establish in fair measure the limits of usefulness of hypnosis, since it is one of the motivating techniques which will be investigated. It would serve a useful purpose to the Agency to have this information developed on a sound scientific basis.

4. The cost of this project for a period of two years beginning 1 May 1958 will not exceet $25,000.00. Charges should be made against Allotment 8-2502-10-001.

MEMORANDUM FOR: THE RECORD

SUBJECT : Continuation of MKULTRA, Subproject 84

1. The purpose of Subproject 84 is to support in part the research program of Dr. ███████████████ of ███████████████ to study the induction of high motivation in individuals by means of the development of specific interpersonal relationships. Expansion of this project along lines of major Agency interest requires a grant of $30,000.00 to supplement funds which are available from ███████████████ ████ and ███████████████████████████████. It is expected that no future funds will be provided for this research although, considering the scope of this study, time extensions may be granted.

2. Three major areas of interest encompass the scope of this research program:

    a. Basic research on the nature of special states of consciousness which to date has focused upon particular aspects of the trance state.

    b. Methodological studies which have dealt with the solution of problems which are a prerequisite to progress in basic research.

    c. Methodological studies dealing with instrumentation problems which have major importance for some current research interests.

Considerable progress has been made to date in each of these areas. A statement of progress is appended.

3. An additional reason for supporting this project is to provide a sound scientific setting for the operational use of a physician ●

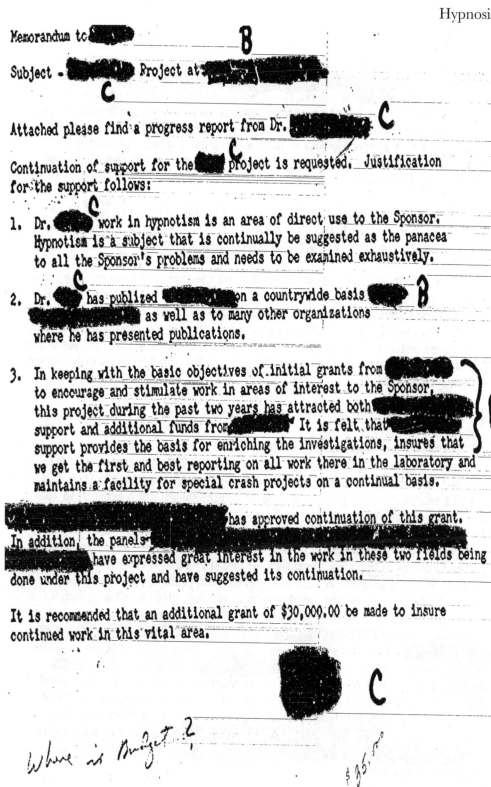

Memorandum to █████

Subject - █████ Project at ███████████

Attached please find a progress report from Dr. ███████████

Continuation of support for the ██ project is requested. Justification for the support follows:

1. Dr. ████ work in hypnotism is an area of direct use to the Sponsor. Hypnotism is a subject that is continually be suggested as the panacea to all the Sponsor's problems and needs to be examined exhaustively.

2. Dr. ████ has publized ███████████ on a countrywide basis ████ █████████████ as well as to many other organizations where he has presented publications.

3. In keeping with the basic objectives of initial grants from ████████ to encourage and stimulate work in areas of interest to the Sponsor, this project during the past two years has attracted both ████████ support and additional funds from █████████ It is felt that █████████ support provides the basis for enriching the investigations, insures that we get the first and best reporting on all work there in the laboratory and maintains a facility for special crash projects on a continual basis.

████████████████████████████ has approved continuation of this grant. In addition, the panels ███████████████ have expressed great interest in the work in these two fields being done under this project and have suggested its continuation.

It is recommended that an additional grant of $30,000.00 be made to insure continued work in this vital area.

Where is Budget ?

$35

In this report I would like to first express my appreciation to the Directors and Officers of ████████████████████████████████████ for the assistance which ████████████ has given to our work. Not only have we had considerable financial support but of equal importance have been the very fruitful suggestions by several of the scientists associated with ████████████ as well as the continuing active supporting role which the group has played. Without both the financial and psychological support much of the research would never have been successfully undertaken.

This report will describe briefly the activities supported by ████████ funds in whole or in part since May 1, 1958. Some of the papers which have evolved from the research supported by ████████████ are appended to this report.

The research which has been undertaken may be thought of as covering three separate but interdependent areas. 1. Basic research on the nature of special states of consciousness which to date has focused upon particular aspects of the trance state. 2. Methodological studies which have dealt with the solution of problems which are a prerequisite to progress in basic research. 3. Methodological studies dealing with instrumentation problems which have major importance for some current research interests.

1. Studies dealing with the Nature of the Hypnotic State.

The theoretical framework in which our studies of hypnosis have been conducted has been to view the hypnotic state as having two well demonstrated components; 1.) an increased motivation to comply with the suggestions of the hypnotist, and 2.) the tendency on the part of the subject to play the role of a hypnotized subject. A third more basic but less understood aspect is, what we have termed, "the essence of hypnosis". While the source of the increased motivation and an understanding of the desire to role-play are basic issues, we have concentrated on the "essence of hypnosis" in the belief that it is this, rather than the other factors, which is uniquely related to a variety of psychological experiences, such as mystical experiences, sensory deprivation effects, placebo effects, and, of course, hypnosis. A paper conceptualizing one particular aspect of this problem is appended, ██, ████████████. This project has been fortunate to have had Dr. ████ associated with it from the onset. First as a ████████████████ and currently as a ████ ████ follow. In a previous study the concept of trance logic was discussed. A study of hallucinations in hypnosis compared the performance given by faking subjects with that of deeply hypnotized individuals. A paper discussing this research was read ████████████████████████████████ and will soon appear in ██████████████████████████████████████ A preliminary draft in ditto form is appended.

The differences between deeply hypnotized subjects and simulators seemed to present a way of asking questions as to what the hypnotic state adds above and beyond high motivation and role-playing. This line of investigation is currently being followed and pilot work is being done using films of both simulators and real subjects, thus making possible judgement at various uniform points by observers who all see the same thing. It is hoped that this will help to reveal that which distinguishes real and simulating subjects and thus shed light on the nature of the process itself.

A major investigation was undertaken on the suppression of pain by hypnosis. This study is currently being re-written into a major publication. Three major findings emerged from this study: 1.) for just about all practical purposes there were no differences in physiological reactivity to pain among any of our experimental conditions, 2.) in general, only tiny physiological responses to pain occurred even in the waking control condition, and 3.) our subjects showed far less signs of stress in this experimental situation than in other experiments at using roughly comparable amounts of electric shock. The study strongly suggests that hypnotic analgesia reduces the overreaction to pain under conditions of apprehension and stress but has no effect on the physiological response to painful stimulus under conditions of minimal anxiety. Having established this point, the need for another experimental study becomes apparent to investigate the effect of hypnotic analgesia in conditions where anxiety is maximized. We would anticipate that under these conditions marked differences would emerge. A very interesting point, however, will be to determine whether or not similar differences may emerge even in the simulating subjects. In other words, whether hypnosis as a process or state protects the individual experiencing intense anxiety or whether the hypnotic situation, regardless of the subjective experience, serves this function.

A pilot study was undertaken has been affiliated with this project for some time. The response of hypnotized and simulating subjects to requests to express fear, depression, happiness, and anger was studied. Pilot studies have suggested that simulators are able to control their emotions to a far greater degree than assumed heretofor and that this control is no less than an individual in hypnosis. This study does not deal with an artificially induced situation but merely with the effect of direct suggestions and a rigorous study of this phenomenon is now being conducted.

For the past one and one-half years a study has been conducted of the trance phenomena occurring in the Pentecostal churches with the view toward understanding their relationship to other states of consciousness. A considerable amount of observational data is now available and is in the process of being analyzed. As a part of this study, the personal experiences which one might expect of good hypnotic subjects and Pentecostal church members who are trance reactors and non-trance reactors are being investigated. This study has been facilitated by the availability of Mr. ███████████████████████████████

███████████████ Mr. ████ is ideally suited to act as research assistance in this project. This study will not be completed until sometime this summer.

2. Methodology.

In the area of methodology, a paper has been contributed to the symposium ████████████████. This deals primarily with ████████████████ ████████████████████████. This paper will appear in a book edited by ██████████████ in the near future. A pilot study has been conducted with ████████████ students dealing with demand characteristics in sensory depri-vation type situations which demonstrated the utility of a process ████████ called the pre-experimental interview. A preliminary draft is appended.

3. Instrumentation.

A new electrode has been developed for the more adequate measurement of potential GSR. This promises to be more useful for psycho-physiological work than the classical resistance GSR. A description of the electrode is be-ing readied for publication and a careful evaluation of the electrode in compari-son with three other electrodes currently used has been performed. A copy of the study, which is being submitted for publication, is appended.

One further study which has been of considerable interest to us has been the investigation of the subjective pain experience associated with electric shock. A preliminary attempt has been made to scale this along the lines of Wolff, Hardy, and Goodell's efforts. In conjunction with this, a new kind of shock electrode is being developed which may control spacing of contact points better than previously possible.

Largely through the initial help which was given by ██████████ it has been possible to obtain substantial support from ████████████████████ ████ and, in the form of a contract, from ████████████████████ ███████████████████████. Current studies now in progress are a continuation of the investigation of real and fake differences in part in collaboration with other investigators in other laboratories. Another major effort being undertaken is the study of hypnotizability and its relationship to responsivity in sensory deprivation under mescaline, etc. Also, we are studying the occurrence of trance-like behavior in the normal experience of subjects. Part of this major research undertaking will be the replication of a previous report which claimed to predict hypnotizability using parts of the TAT, Rosenzweig's Picture Frustra-tion Test, and the Zeigarnik effect, the sway test, the heat illusion test, and personality instruments. Questionnaires developed by our group are also used and we hope that these will aid not only in the prediction of hypnotizability but permit specific predictions to be made about the type of response obtained from each subject. A preliminary report on one questionnaire is in press.

Another investigation which is currently being undertaken along these lines is the evaluation of the newly reported audio-analgesia and the relationship which this technique has to hypnotic pain suppression. Informal working relationships have been established with ████████████████████ and Dr. ███████████████████████████████ It is hoped to evaluate good and bad reactions to this technique of analgesia in regard to subjects trance-like experiences and hypnotizability.

Finally, the controversial question of anti-social behavior in hypnosis will be re-evaluated experimentally. It is hoped to be able to shed considerable light on the limitations of hypnosis as a technique of controlling behavior in this manner. A paper has been written, in part under the auspices of ██████████ dealing with the potential uses of hypnosis in interrogation and is to be published ██

C

TO : ████Morse Allen████   *A*   Date: 9 July 1951

FROM : ████████████████████

SUBJECT: ████████████████   *H-B/6*

On 23 June 1951, ████████████████████████ was contacted by telephone by ████████████████ a lie detector operator, of █ regarding a course of instruction in hypnotism. At that time ████ stated that instruction could begin anytime that the student presented himself

On 2 July 1951 approximately 1:00 p.m. the instruction began with ████████ relating to the student some of his sexual experiences. ████████ stated that he had constantly used hypnotism as a means of inducing young girls to engage in sexual intercourse with him. ████████████ a performer in ████████ orchestra was forced to engage in sexual intercourse with ████ while under the influence of hypnotism. ████████ stated that he first put her into a hypnotic trance and then suggested to her that he was her husband and that she desired sexual intercourse with him. ████████ further stated that many times while going home ██████████████ he would use hypnotic suggestion to have a girl turn around and talk to him and suggest sexual intercourse to him and that as a result of these suggestions induced by him he spent approximately five nights a week away from home engaging in sexual intercourse.

████████ claimed that during the Second World War he had worked for (characterized by ████████ as such a top secret intelligence organization that he was not permitted to give the words that the initials represented). His work for ████████ consisted in hypnotizing subjects and causing them to memorize detailed material while under the influence of hypnotism. After the subject was awakened he would go to some other place and there be re-hypnotized and repeat verbatim the material he had memorized while previously under the influence of hypnotism. ████████ stated that while mentally transporting this information the subject could not be made to reveal any of the material as due to post hypnotic suggestion he had completely forgotten it until he was re-hypnotized.

████████ stated that ████████████████████ and a former student of ████████ was considerably advanced in thought projection by hypnotism. ████████ could cause a subject in hypnotic trance to read from a closed book a considerable distance away. ████ stated that about one out of twenty subjects have sufficient clairvoyance to be able to do thought projection.

On the last day of the period of training ████████ introduced the student to a man who was waiting for an appointment with ████████ The student was introduced as an expert hypnotist who wished to try an experiment on the man. The student at that time hypnotized the man and suggested that he would feel no pain. The student then suggested that he would be deaf for two minutes after he awoke. When the man awoke he could hear nothing, and to test for fakery the

Chapter 4
Subconscious Isolation (SI)

Mori ID# 144823 - This document, titled "Subconscious Isolation," disproves the notion suggested by some researches that S.I. (an abbreviation used throughout MK-Ultra documentation) stands for "sleep induction." The true meaning is defined on page one: A method of exerting immediate or prolonged influence on the subconscious mind.

Mori ID# 190527 - SI and H Experimentation 25 Sept. 1951

SUBCONSCIOUS ISOLATION

1. Introduction

    a. Present scope of National Defense

        (1) Recognized defense problems

            (a) Atomic bomb

            (b) Submarine

            (c) Biological warfare

            (d) Espionage agents

            (e) Etc.

        (2) Unrecognized defense problems

            (a) Subconscious isolation

                1. Method of exerting immediate or prolonged influence on the subconscious mind.

    b. Purpose of presentation of this information.

        (1) Present fundamental principles involved.

        (2) Possible applications by an unfriendly country.

        (3) Present use by other countries.

        (4) Common techniques in use.

        (5) Suggested future action

            (a) Learn how to recognize

            (b) Learn how to combat

            (c) Security implications

                (a) Reason for security

                    1. Cause user to refine techniques

                    2. Stimulate interest among non-users

                    3. Material not safe for public consumption

                    4. Ridicule from mis-informed groups.

2. Fundamental principles involved

    a. Psychological concept of the mind

        (1) Conscious mind

            (a) Its power

                1. Control of certain bodily movements

                2. Conscious thought process

            (b) Its limitations

                1. Lack of control of certain organic actions

                2. Comparatively weak memory

        (2) Subconscious mind

            (a) Control of physiological functions

            (b) Powerful memory

    b. Uncontrollable manifestation of the subconscious mind

        (1) Talking in sleep

        (2) Dreaming

        (3) Spontaneous reaction

            (a) Lack of memory concerning emergency actions

    c. Desirable for one to contact subconscious memory

3. Possible uses of "SI" by an unfriendly country

    a. Interrogation

        (1) Extraction of classified information

            (a) Many more details retained subconsciously

        (2) Psychological regression for past details and memory restoration

    b. Subconscious assignment

        (1) Espionage guidance

        (2) Sabotage guidance

(3) Informant guidance

c. Other uses

    (1) Instilling of false information

    (2) Eradication of information

    (3) Surveillance

d. Practical example

    (1) Well trained U. S. Employee

        (a) Working in sensitive area

    (2) Application of SI by unfriendly element

        (a) Interrogation

            1. Regression

        (b) Subconscious assignment

            1. Cue

            2. Espionage guidance

            3. Eradication of information

            4. Instilling of false information

            5. Policy direction after recall

4. Present Use by Other Countries

a. Extent unknown

    (1) Specific examples

        (a) Moscow trials

        (b) Mindszenty trial

        (c) Vogeler trial

        (d) Various newspaper and magazine articles

5. Common techniques in use - brief

   a. Fixed attention

      (1) Psychologist

      (2) Psychiatrist

      (3) Conversation

      (4) Relaxation

   b. Emotional Stimulation

      (1) Stage

      (2) Emergency

   c. Drugs

      (1) Doctor

      (2) Dentist

      (3) Surreptitious administering

   d. Sleep Conversion

      (1) Sleep learning

      (2) Ordinary sleep

   e. Shock treatment

      (1) Insulin

      (2) Electric

6. Present work in this field

   a. Research

      (1) Theory

      (2) Active experimentation

7. Future action

   a. Combative measures

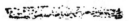

     (1) "Combative Measure" Research Program

        (a) Written material

        (b) Experienced technicians in allied field

        (c) Intelligence reports

        (d) Experimental work

     (2) "Combative Measure" Instruction Program

        (a) To whom taught

            1. Key personnel in sensitive positions

        (b) Material

            1. Fundamental principles of subconscious isolation

            2. Possible applications by unfriendly elements

            3. Common techniques in use

            4. How to recognize

            5. How to combat

     (3) "Combative Measure" Investigation Facility

        (a) Investigate all suspected use of subconscious isolation

B. Conclusion.

To: Files

Subject: SI and H Experimentation (25 September 1951)

On 25 September 1951, ██████████ and the writer conducted SI and H experimentation with ██████████ and ██████████ ████ as subjects.

In view of the successful experimentation of Tuesday, 18 September 1951 with ██████████ and ██████████ it was decided to continue experiments along more or less related lines during this session. However, prior to actually beginning the more complex experiments, several simple post H were worked with both of the girls participating. In this connection, it is interesting to note that whereas ██████████ was capable on each test tried of producing the desired post H effect, ██████████ was unable to do so. No explanation was offered for this, but it should be noted for the record that ██████████ and the writer did not make continuous and serious efforts to produce the desired effect for these simple post H tests.

The first major experiment of the evening was set up as follows without previous explanation to either ██████████ or ██████████ child. Both subjects were placed in a very deep trance state and while in this state, the following instructions were given:

(A) ██████████ was instructed that when she awakened, she was to procede to ██████████ room. She was told that while there, she would receive a telephone call from an individual whom she would know only as "Joe". This individual would engage her in a normal telephone conversation. During this conversation, this individual would give her a code word and upon mentioning the code word, ██████████ would go into a deep SI trance state but would be "normal" in appearance with her eyes open. ██████████ was then told that upon the conclusion of the telephone conversation, she would procede to the ladies room where she would meet a girl who was unknown to her. She was told that she would strike up a conversation with this girl and during the conversation she would mention the code word "New York" to this other girl who, in turn, would give her a device and further instructions which were to be carried out by ██████████ She was told that after she carried out the instructions, she was to return to the Operations Room, sit on the sofa and go immediately into a deep sleep state.

(B) ██████████ was instructed that upon awakening, she would procede to ██████████ room where she would wait at the desk for a telephone call. Upon receiving the call, a person known as "Jim" would engage her in normal conversation. During the course of the conversation, this individual would mention a code word to ██████████ When she heard this code word

97

she would pass into an SI trance state, but would not close her
eyes and remain perfectly normal and continue the telephone conversation. She was told that thereafter upon conclusion of the
telephone conversation, she would then carry out the following
instructions:

███████████ being in a complete SI state at this
time, was then told to open her eyes and was shown an electric
timing device. She was informed that this timing device
was an incendiary bomb and was then instructed how to attach
and set the device. After ███████████ had indicated that
she had learned how to set and attach the device, she was
told to return to a sleep state and further instructed
that upon concluding the aforementioned conversation, she
would take the timing device which was in a briefcase and
procede to the ladies room. In the ladies room, she would
be met by a girl whom she had never seen who would identify
herself by the code word "New York". After identifying
herself, ███████████ is then to show this individual
how to attach and set the timing device and further instructions would be given the individual by ███████████
that the timing device was to be carried in the briefcase
to ███████ room, placed in the nearest empty electric-
light plug and concealed in the bottom, left-hand drawer
of ███████ desk, with the device set for 82 seconds and
turned on. ███████████ was further instructed to tell
this other girl that as soon as the device had been set
and turned on, she was to take the briefcase, leave ███
███ room, go to the operations room and go to the sofa
and enter a deep sleep state. ███████████ was further
instructed that after completion of instructing the other
girl and the transferring to the other girl of the incendiary bomb, she was to return at once to the operations
room, sit on the sofa, and go into a deep sleep state.

For a matter of record, immediately after the operation was begun it was noted that a member of the charforce was cleaning the floor
in the ladies room and subsequently, both ███████████
and ███████████ had to be placed at once again in a trance state and
instructions changed from the ladies room to Room 3.

It should be noted that even with the change of locale in the
transfer point, the experiment was carried off perfectly without any
difficulty or hesitation on the part of either of the girls. Each
girl acted out her part perfectly, the device was planted and set
as directed and both girls returned to the operations room, sat on
the sofa and entered a deep sleep state. Throughout, their meove-
ments were easy and natural and the member of the charforce and the
guard were, to all intents and purposes, completely unaware of what
was taking place although they could clearly observe the movements
of ███████████ and ███████████

Before the girls were awakened, they were given instructions

████████ was unable to recall any of the incident, except going to the desk in ████████ room before the experiment was completely under way. However ████████ had partial recall of some of the incidents that transpired.

The entire experiment from original instructions to conclusion consumed twenty-seven minutes and it should be noted for the record that at the conclusion of the experiment, ████████ did not completely respond to instructions to awaken and, hence, was returned to a sleep state and reawakened. Both subjects were, of course, "cleared" of all post H words, etc. in the experiment before awakening.

This long and rather complex experiment was regarded by ████████ and the writer as being successful, although ████████ partial recall of some of the incidents was not according to instructions, but it should be remembered that ████████ memory in such matters has continually been remarkable and she has remembered from week to week, numbers which she had memorized considerable time before.

The second major experiment of the evening concerned the proposition of whether or not individuals of normal and proper training, background, and teaching would commit an act which they would not, under normal circumstances, do. This experiment was carried on as follows:

Both subjects were placed in a deep SI state and were instructed that they were to procede, when awakened, to the laboratory and sit at the desk and wait for a telephone call. Each girl would be called in turn and would be given a code word. Upon completion of the telephone call, the girls were told that they would procede to the operations room where they would find a man lying on the sofa who had passed out from drinking or was drugged and was possibly asleep. It was further explained to them that this man had been picked up in a local bar and brought here to this room. They were instructed that they were to enter the room as quietly as possible, approach the individual, making certain they did not awaken him, and examine his clothing and determine if he carried a wallet. They were told that if the individual carried a wallet, they were to remove the wallet from this person and immediately and quietly leave the room. They were told further that they were to deliver the wallet to ████████ or ████████ who would be waiting in the darkroom and after that, they were told that they would return to the desk, put their heads down, and go into a deep sleep. In each case, after the girls were called on the phone and given the designated code word, they went to the operations room and removed a wallet first from ████████ and then ████████ who acted as bodies in the instant case. Both girls were under observation at all times in the act of removal and both moved very cautiously in a very deft manner and removed the item as instructed.

This experiment is regarded by ████████ and the writer as being successful, although as in all these experiments, it must be borne in mind that a possibility exists that the subjects realize that the experiments are nothing more than this and are not in fact actual operations, although by instructing and by wording, every effort has been made to convince the subjects when they are in the SI state that these are actual operations. The word experiment or test is never used under any circumstances when the operations are being carried out.

For a matter of record and of interest is the fact that at the conclusion of this experiment, which ran about twenty-two minutes, ████████ refused to awakened as instructed and it was necessary to return her to a trance state and again awaken her before she became fully awake. Furthermore, for a matter of record, it should be noted that again in this case, ████████ had a complete amnesia for the activity whereas ████████ although instructed to have complete amnesia, had a partial recall of events.

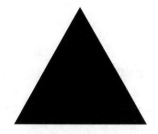

Chapter 5
Extrasensory Perception (ESP)

Mori doc ID# 17395 - A memo RE: Subproject 136 and extrasensory perception

23 August 1961

MEMORANDUM FOR: THE RECORD

SUBJECT   : Project MKULTRA, Subproject 136

1. The purpose of this subproject is to support the research of ██ an "Experimental Analysis of Extrasensory Perception." A proposal describing his research activities is attached.

2. ███████████████ esearch effort is moving beyond the question of whether the phenomenon, extrasensory perception (ESP), exists. He is attempting to approach the twin questions of what are the functional relation- ships between other personality factors and ESP skills, and what are the factors that must be considered in using ESP as a method of communication. Any positive results along these lines would have obvious utility for the Agency. It is not expected that answers would emerge from ███████████ initial efforts. He is one of the few individuals sophisticated in ESP research who has been willing, however, to orient his efforts along these fundamental lines.

3. This project will be funded through the ████████████████████ security and cover purposes, and the accounting for funds expended shall conform to the established practices of that organization. The title to any equipment purchased shall remain with th████████████████ lieu of higher overhead costs.   *B C*

4. The total cost of this research for a period of one year is estimated not to exceed $8,579.00. Charges should be made against Allotment 2125-1390-3902.

5. ████████████ is not witting of any relationship between the ████████████████████ Since he has made separate contact with the Director's office and may in time become aware of the ██████ relationship, a request for covert security approval has been initiated.

████████████

Chief
TSD/Research Branch

Approved for Obligation of Funds:

██████████████

Research Director

A
B
C

_____
Date

Distribution: Original Only
Attachment : Proposal

103

When St. Denis was decapitated, he is supposed to have picked up his head and walked off with it. This led his custodian to comment, "Dans des cas pareils, ce n'est que le premier pas qui coûte."* Unfortunately, this maxim does not seem to apply to research in parapsychology. If extrasensory perception (ESP) exists, it is of fundamental importance, and fundamental problems are never easy to solve. But a large body of evidence has been adduced in favor of the existence of ESP, and while this evidence has left most scientists unconvinced, there is general agreement that further research is justified. In a survey of 349 fellows of the American Psychological Association, only 17% said that ESP was an "established fact" or a "likely possibility", but 90% considered its investigation a "legitimate scientific undertaking". (J. Parapsychol., Vol.16, 1952, pp. 284-95)

I. Objectives

It is difficult to state the long range objectives of a research program in parapsychology. The present investigators are by no means certain that ESP exists or that it is possible to experiment with it. They do feel that the parapsychologists have made a strong case and are willing to devote research time to further study of this subject.

There are three overlapping areas which require special exploration and where it is hoped that substantial progress can be made. These are: the design of 'repeatable' experiments; the determination of functional relationships between a variety of psychological variables and ESP test scores; and mapping limits for the utilization of the phenomenon, with special reference to the channel capacity, the kinds of messages which can be transmitted and spatio-temporal constraints.

The present research team have concluded that these objectives would be best served by initiating three closely connected experimental studies. The first consists in conducting group experiments, in which each individual is treated as possessing a modicum of ESP and test scores are predicted on the basis of ratings on a number of psychological and physiological scales. The second is to develop a method to relate patterns of subjective probability

---

* In such cases, only the first step requires any effort.

reflected in response sequences to test scores and to
psychological and behavioural factors. The third is an
exploration of the postulated ESP abilities of a few
specially gifted subjects, who will be intensively studied
under flexible conditions.

A large number of group experiments have been
carried out by previous investigators. They have apparently
succeeded in discriminating between levels of scoring for
persons characterised by different ratings on a number of
psi-variables. These include IQ, extroversion, effects of
certain drugs, Rorschach protocols, self-confidence, belief
in ESP, subject-experimenter relations &c. But in each
case only one variable was studied at a time, even though
it should have been clear that other variables than the
one selected for analysis were also influencing the results.

If a phenomenon is caused by a number of factors,
or if at a given stage of investigation it must be treated
as if it were, it would be permissible to allow one factor
to vary at a time, the other factors being held constant,
or to consider the combined effect of a number of relevant
factors. If one varied one factor at a time and ignored all
the others, he would be ill informed about the use of
experimental design. This is unfortunately the situation
which obtains in parapsychology.

Experiments in which ESP emerges as a function of
the interrelations of a number of psi-variables should yield
results which meet any reasonable criterion of repeatability.
Comparatively crude one-variable studies, such as those of
Anderson and White at Duke University where ESP depends on
the inter-personal attitudes of school-children subjects
and their teacher, experimenters have apparently been
successful about 50% of the time, even though the variables
have been dichotomous and significance has been estimated
with relatively crude tests (a student either likes or does
not like his teacher and vice versa; a student either scores
above the expected mean or scores below it).

The study of response sequences is based upon the
assumption, defensible in the light of recent psychological
research, that guessing patterns represent subjects'
evaluation of the uncertainty situation in the experiment.
There will be certain gross departures from randomness for
all subjects, but there will also be idiosyncratic departures.
These are related to general behavioural differences, because
what a person considers to be probable determines to an
important extent what he will do. It is predicted that

105

when subjects are divided into response types, these types
will tend to score at different levels in ESP tests. Of
course it is not assumed that adopting a particular pattern
can in any way effect scores (except in experiments where
the model involved in comparing guess and target sequences
is the matching distribution rather than the binomial
distribution, in which case the variance may be increased,
though the expectation is not effected). It is assumed
that the guessing pattern and the ESP score are both
related to a third factor.

The work with individual subjects who give
promise of extraordinary abilities will introduce a number
of experimental techniques which have been ignored or
barely hinted at in the past. A variety of models of the
manner in which information is transferred will be tested
by simple variation of the tasks imposed on the subject.
Preliminary learning studies, in which feedback of results
and other kinds of reinforcement are utilised, will be
introduced at the same time. If a subject is found who can
score reliably, an attempt will be made to increase the
quantity of transmitted information without increasing
the average probability of success, by making use of
straightforward techniques borrowed from the mathematical
theory of communication.

In working with individual subjects, special
attention will be given to disassociative states, which
tend to accompany spontaneous ESP experiences. Such states
can be induced and controlled to some extent with hypnosis
and drugs. Some of this work will make use of qualitative
stimuli, such as drawings and ideas with special
associations.

II. Methods

Group Experiments

Numerous mathematical models and experimental
designs enable the simultaneous assessment of two or more
independent predictors. Chief among these are multiple
regression analysis and factorial experimental designs,
which are closely related logically and mathematically.
The essential idea of the regression model is that each
individual's scores on the n independent variables and
the ESP criterion may be located at a point in an n + 1
dimensional space. The relation between the criterion
and the predictors is given by a multiple regression
equation which takes the form:

$$\tilde{Y} = A + \beta_{y1.23...N} X_1 + \beta_{y2.134...n} X_2 + \cdots + \beta_{yn.123...r}$$

where A is an intercept and the coefficients of the X's are partial regression coefficients and indicate the weighting allotted to each predictor.

The regression equation and each of the independen predictors may be tested for significance. If the null hypothesis is rejected, the accuracy of prediction is of interest. This is best considered in the language of estimation statistics, where one may speak of confidence intervals. That is, for a subject characterised by a certain pattern of scores on the independent variables, one may predict with .95 confidence that the subject's ESP score will fall somewhere between A and B percent success. The clearest meaning of 'repeatability' is expressed in statements of this kind, whereby the results of a series of experiments, not the probabilities attached to them, may be compared to see if they fit the same pattern. The width of the predicted interval and the confidence coefficient of course vary inversely and the definition of 'repeatability' depends on assigning an a priori ESP-probability.

The variables to be considered can be classed in several ways. They will be intrinsic psychological and physiological factors and experimentally manipulable factors. Intrinsic factors may be temporary and characteristic of the experimental situation, such as annoyance, or general personality characteristics, such as intelligence. Experimentally manipulable factors include induced attitudes, such as motivation produced by positive reinforcement, and purely formal factors, such as the number of ESP trials yielding the most accurate predictions. The selection of variables will depend on a detailed analysis of the results of past research, incidental observations in experiments with single subjects, apparent common factors in 'spontaneous' ESP, and intelligent guessing. In the selection of variables, special attention will be paid to technical problems in scaling and to the reliability and validity of existing scales. In some cases ad hoc procedures, such as the Q sort, will be used.

Response Patterns. Human beings are notoriously inefficient randomisers, so would not be inappropriate to treat response patterns as having two components, ESP and guessing habits. Guessing habits represent subjects' subjective evaluation of the sequential uncertainty situation in the experiment and depend on such factors as ability to judge probabilities and imitate randomness, compulsions with respect to symmetry &c. Such habits will necessarily interfere with exercise of ESP, because every time a choice is made habit and psi-information are in

/competition

107

competition unless they should agree fortuitously. It might be, for example, that the well known decline effect phenomena are due to the gradual build up of habits and their dominance over ESP.

It is, however, not only desirable to correct for the destructive effects of guessing habits. It may be that such habits could be used to predict ESP test scores. When one decides to cross the street, his decision about when to cross depends on his estimate of the chance that he will be run over. Behaviour is largely determined by concepts of probability, and systematic bias in assessments of uncertainty situations are known to be related to personality types. It is quite possible that some of these types, whether or not they are similar to the ones derived by psychometric techniques or ordinary common sense, may be related to ESP ability. It might in fact be possible to derive an ESP-typology from the non-ESP component of the ESP guessing pattern.

The techniques which will be used to analyse response sequences are too complicated to enter into here, but will include the informational estimation of redundancy, as used in the study of languages and the construction of pseudo-languages, autocorrelation, and ad hoc methods to reduce and classify the number of possible patterns. The actual analysis will be carried out by an electronic computer. It should be made clear that the quantity of ESP in the results of even the best subjects is too small to interfere with the elucidation of guessing habits. The data used in this study will be obtained from group ESP experiments which have yielded significant results, high scoring subjects (including control series and records taken after they 'lost' their ability), from special groups such as psychotics, children and mediums, and from psychological and educational tests in which answers are of the multiple choice type. The ESP data have been promised by ████████████████████████████████

Individual Subjects. The amount of information transmitted on the average per trial in ESP experiments is: $\log_2 5 + (r/25)\log_2(r/25) + 4[(25-r)/100]\log_2[(25-r)/100]$ in binits, where r is the number of correct guesses. (This appears to be the correct model, since there is evidence that subjects produce the same deviation from chance when aiming below it as when they aim above, in spite of the fact that $p \neq 1/2$). Good subjects will tend to have somewhere between .2 and .6 bits of information generally

/available

available to them. This is one of the reasons why ESP
experiments are so difficult. But it may still be possible
to learn a good deal about the phenomenon, even if learning
studies should fail. For it is possible to vary the
experimental paradigm to discriminate between various
models for the operation of the phenomenon, such as:
ESP occurs sporadically but gives perfect information;
ESP always occurs and multiplies chances of success by
a constant factor; ESP tells the subject one of the
things the target is not; ESP, when it occurs, answers
a question of the form— is the target an X?. In addition
to psi-models, it will also be necessary to introduce
models which provide more sensitive estimates of ESP. For
example, target material will be introduced whereby guesses
instead of being of the 'all or nothing' type can be more or
less right. Again, a number of different p values will be
introduced and intermixed to imitate real life situations.

Learning studies will be instituted in which the
subject will be rewarded or punished for his overall
performance and reinforced in various ways – by being
told whether he was right, by being told what the target
was, with electric shock etc. In addition, an attempt
will be made to increase the transmitted information in
cases where the average probability of success remained
constant. Thus if N_{ia} = the number of trials in which
the ith distinguishable target is guessed to be the ath,
t_i = the frequency of a as a target, g_a = the frequency
of guesses of A, and N = the number of trials, $(N_{ia})N/g_a(t_i)$,
which states the ratio of the frequency with which i is
guessed A to the expected frequency if there were no guessing
preference, may be used to determine which guess was the
best estimate of the target, and the resultant estimate,
which will depend on the number of trials and the quantity
of information available to the subject, will approach
certainty asymptotically.

But the main consideration will be the attitude
and general disposition of the subject. Wherever possible,
every attempt will be made to tailor the tasks required to
his preferences and his estimate of good working conditions.
In one case the experimental procedure will be designed to
achieve favorable motivation by such devices as instructing
him that he is participating in a study of subception. In
other cases drugs and psychological tricks will be used to
modify his attitudes. The experimenters will be particularly
interested in disassociative states, from the abaissement de
niveau mental to multiple personality in so-called mediums,
and an attempt will be made to induce a number of states of
this kind, using hypnosis. Hypnosis is seen not as a

/variable

109

variable in itself but as a technique for creating various
subjective states through suggestion. In these studies and
some others use may be made of qualitative target material,
which may be evaluated with the use of elaborate matching
methods, which have their origin in Euler's solution of
the 'Rencontre' problem.

We are very fortunate in having the co-operation
who ~~~~~~~~ returned ~~~~~~ several years in
~~~~~~. The experimen~~~~ Dr. S.G. Soal did with
~~~~~ discussed in the book Modern Experiments in
Telepathy, are probably the best controlled and most
convincing evidence yet offered for ESP. Exploratory
experiments with ~~~~~~~~ are already in progress.

III. Time Required.

Support is being requested for a twelve month
period. This will allow studies to be carried out in each
of the three areas discussed above. If at the end of that
period no results favoring the ESP hypothesis have been
found, the project will be dropped. If the hypothesis is
supported, the project will be revalued and its objectives
will be modified. Then a further request for support may
be made to the ~~~~~~~~~~~~~~~~~~~~~~~~~~   *B*

IV. Estimated Budget.

Item	Amount Requested
Apparatus for recording data	$300
Microfilm camera and projector	250
Computer time* and programming	300
Office Equipment	150
Office expenses (postage, 'phone, duplicating)	300
Repairs to premises at ~~~~~~~~~ *H*	560
Manual computing and checking data	300
Inducements for subjects	500
Experimental assistants	200
~~ (full time)	3,600
Travel	1,000
	7,460
+ 15% indirect costs	1,119
	$8,579

████████ will be available without charge, but a small contribution is expected.

The ████████████████████████████████████ will provide and construct experimental apparatus without charge.

The ████████████████████ will provide desk calculators, furniture, and a limited amount of secretarial and clerical assistance without charge.

The ████████████████████████████████ has allocated premises a████████████ to this █████████ without charge. These consist of the basement of the ████████ ████████ about 570 square feet in area and comprising two rooms and three large closets.

Experimental workers other than ████████████ will contribute most of their time without charge.

V. Qualifications and Tax Exemption.

The ESP research project is to be a research study officially approved by the ████████████████████ ████████████████████████ and will be conducted ████ parapsychological laboratory attached to the ████████████████████████████████████

There will be an informal advisory committee who will review the progress of the work, offer suggestions about its conduct and consult on technical proglems. The members of this committee are:

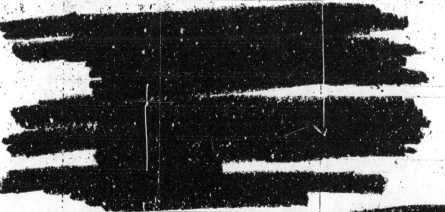

The chief investigator will be ████████████████ ████████ for the degree D.Phil. working under the ████████████████████ was born in ████████████ and attended the ████████████████████████

The following persons have agreed to assist █████ █h experiments:

██
██,

█████████████████ who is ultimately responsible for the conduct of this research, is joint editor of the ██████████ and the author of three books and numerous technical papers on statistics and biometrics. ██████

As the project will be carried out ████████████ ████████████ and the ██████████████ is willing to receive and disseminate the funds, any funds granted us should be considered tax exempt by the U.S. Government.

VI. Related Work at Other Universities.

There are or have been research centers for parapsychology at Duke University, Cambridge University, City College of New York, Harvard University, Stanford University, The University of Chicago, The University of Utrecht (which has a chair of Parapsychology), London University, Pittsburgh University &c.

A general survey of the methods and findings of parapsychology may be found in Rhine and Pratt (14), an exhaustive analysis of the research up to 1940 in Rhine et all (13), and a general review of the subject in Soal and Bateman (16).

/Research

Research into psi-variables has been summarised by Mangan, 1959 (9). A recent review of the experiments initiated by Anderson and White is Van de Castle (19). A detailed account of a major research project in this is Schmeidler & McConnell (15). Work relevant to the study of response sequences has been done by Pratt and by Soal (10, 11, 12). General factors presumed related to ESP and studies of individual subjects are discussed in (13), (14) and (16), where references are given.

The idea of using multivariate designs in group experiments appears to be original. Some of the ideas about studying response █████████████ go back to conversations with ██ The ████ history ████████████ by them seem █████ have been a Ph.D. thesis.

████████████████████████████ ████ of the ideas involved in the individual studies have been discussed at one time or another in the past, but little has been done about them. ████████ has done mathematical work on the experimental discrimination of psi-models (18); the method of differential scoring is due to ██████████████████████ █████████████████████ has discussed the method for ████████████ ████████ mentioned (17). In general, much useful information and man██████ for research have come out of conversations with ███████████████████

References:

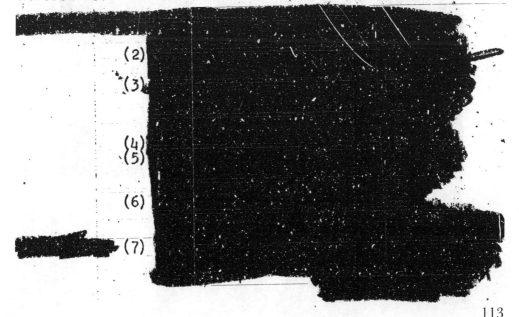

(2)

(3)

(4)
(5)

(6)

(7)

CIA Director Richard Helms ordered all MK-Ultra files destroyed in 1973. Only a small percentage survived.

Chapter 6
Victims

The first two documents are letters regarding CIA use of human subjects. The third document is from 1963 and states: individuals to be subjected to testing must be unwitting.

The next document shows the CIA's interest in creating a mind controlled assassin. The writer asks, "Can an individual of [deleted] descent be made to perform an act of attempted assassination involuntarily under the influence of ARTICHOKE?"

4 OCT 1977

Dear

        Receipt is acknowledged of your letter, dated
14 September 1977, to the Director of Central Intelligence in which you cited the Freedom of Information
Act and requested information regarding certain tests
you believe may have been performed on you.

        The recently discovered files of Project MKULTRA
do contain evidence that research involving human testing
was conducted in the fields of behavior control using
techniques involving hypnosis, drugs, etc. Our records
indicate such testing on unwitting subjects ceased in
1964. Unfortunately, neither Project MKULTRA files nor
any other files thus far located contain the names of
persons who may have been used as test subjects.

        Admiral Turner has assured the Congress that the
CIA will attempt to identify those persons who were the
subjects of unwitting testing conducted under Project
MKULTRA. To this end, the institutions where Project
MKULTRA testing took place have been notified of their
involvement with the project. Admiral Turner has offered
these institutions his full cooperation in helping them
identify the persons who were test subjects. Please be
assured I will inform you immediately if any institution
notifies the CIA that is has identified you as having been
a Project MKULTRA test subject.

FEB 10 1953

PERSONAL

Dr. Sidney Gottlieb
Chief, Chemical Division
Technical Services Staff

Dear Dr. Gottlieb:

I have personally reviewed the files from your office concerning the use of a drug on an unwitting group of individuals. In recommending the unwitting application of the drug to your superior, you apparently did not give sufficient emphasis to the necessity for medical collaboration and for proper consideration of the rights of the individual to whom it was being administered. This is to inform you that it is my opinion that you exercised poor judgment in this case.

Sincerely,

Allen W. Dulles
Director

O/IG/LBKirkpatrick:rm 29 Jan 54
Rewritten by DDCI/CPCabell:rm 1 Feb 54
Rewritten by DDCI/CPCabell:rm 6 Feb 54

17 December 1963

EYES ONLY

MEMORANDUM FOR: Deputy Director of Central Intelligence

SUBJECT: Testing of Psychochemicals and Related Materials

1. At the conclusion of a meeting in your office on 29 November dealing with the problem of testing of psychochemicals and related materials, you asked that I submit a short paper to you on this subject. In discussing this matter, I would appreciate it if you would consider two aspects of the problem:

    a. For over a decade the Clandestine Services has had the mission of maintaining a capability for influencing human behavior; and

    b. Testing arrangements in furtherance of this mission should be as operationally realistic and yet as controllable as possible.

2. Most of our difficulty stems from the fact that, in our opinion, the individuals to be subjected to testing must be unwitting. This, unfortunately, is the only realistic method of maintaining the capability, considering the intended operational use of materials to influence human behavior. In the circumstances of potential operational use of this technique, it is virtually certain that the target will be unwitting. Any testing program which does not attempt to approximate this real situation will be "pro forma" at best and result in a false sense of accomplishment and readiness.

3. If one grants the validity of the mission of maintaining this unusual capability and the necessity for unwitting testing, there is only then the question of how best to do it. Obviously, the testing should be conducted in such a manner as to permit the opportunity to observe the results of the administration on the target. It also goes without saying that whatever testing arrangement we adopt must afford maximum safeguards for the protection of the Agency's role in this activity, as well as minimizing the possibility of physical or emotional damage to the individual tested.

4. In considering possible alternatives to our present arrangement with the Bureau of Narcotics, we have considered the following:

a. Arrangements with one of several police department located in the principal cities of the United States. Co tacts between the Agency and police departments in ███████ ██████████████████████, for example, could be e plotted.

b. Similar arrangements with prisons or prison hospi through contacts in the Department of Justice could be i vestigated.

c. Various foreign intelligence and/or security org zations having a current and continuing interrogation pro ████████████████████████ could be queried with this obje in mind.

5. I believe that none of the alternatives cited in the p paragraph satisfies the requirements for an acceptable testing Potential arrangements with local police departments necessita enlargement of the knowledgeable group to include individuals in local politics with its attendant unacceptable security pro Past experience with the Bureau of Prisons in the Department c Justice has established their unwillingness to participate in programs involving unwitting testing. We have attempted sever times in the past ten years to establish a testing program in seas setting, using indigenous subjects. In every case the ne of making an inordinate number of foreign nationals witting of role in this very sensitive activity has made the program unde on security grounds.

6. Our present arrangements with the Bureau of Narcotics to me. to be the most practical and secure method available to implement this program. While it is true that there is an ele of risk in the present arrangement, it still affords us more s than any other method we can conceive.

7. In sum, if we are to continue to maintain a capabilit influencing human behavior, we are virtually obliged to test o witting humans. The best method for conducting these tests se is our relationship with the Bureau of Narcotics — an arrange which has stood up through eight years of close collaboration. tinued attention to observation and control of the results of testing, as feasible, would be exercised.

8. While I share your uneasiness and distaste for any pr which tends to intrude on an individual's private and legal pr

tives, I believe it is necessary that the Agency maintain a centra
role in this activity, keep current on enemy capabilities in the
manipulation of human behavior, and maintain an offensive capabili
I, therefore, recommend your approval for continuation of this tes
ing program with the Bureau of Narcotics.

Richard Helms
Deputy Director for Plans

Distribution:
    Original - DDCI
        1 cc - C/TSD
        1 cc - DD/P

120

A R T I C H O K E

1. The ARTICHOKE Team visited ████████ during period 8 January to 15 January 1954. The purpose of the visit was to give an evaluation of a hypothetical problem, namely: Can an individual of ****** descent be made to perform an act of attempted assassination involuntarily under the influence of ARTICHOKE?

2. <u>PROBLEM</u>:

    a. The essential elements of the problem are as follows:

        (1) As a "trigger mechanism" for a bigger project, it was proposed that an individual of ****** descent, approximately 35 years old, well educated, proficient in English and well established socially and politically in the ****** Government be induced under ARTICHOKE to perform an act, involuntarily, of attempted assassination against a prominent ***** politician or if necessary, against an American official. The SUBJECT was formerly in ████████ but has since terminated and is now employed with the *** Government. According to all available information, the SUBJECT would offer no further cooperation with ████████ Access to the SUBJECT would be extremely limited, probably limited to a single social meeting. Because the SUBJECT is a heavy drinker, it was proposed that the individual could be surreptitiously drugged through the medium of an alcoholic cocktail at a social party, ARTICHOKE applied and the SUBJECT induced to perform the act of attempted assassination at some later date. All the above was to be accomplished at one involuntary uncontrolled social meeting. After the act of attempted assassination was performed, it was assumed that the SUBJECT would be taken into custody by the *** Government and thereby "disposed of." Other than personal reassurances by ████████ means of security involving the

project, techniques, personnel and disposal of the SUBJECT were not indicated. Whether the proposed act of attempted assassination was carried out or not by the SUBJECT was of no great significance in relation to the overall project.

3. CONCLUSIONS:

a. In answer to the hypothetical question, can an individual of ****** descent be made to perform an act of attempted assassination, involuntarily, under ARTICHOKE, according to the above conditions, the answer in this case was probably "No" because of the limitations imposed operationally as follows:

(1) The SUBJECT would be an involuntary and unwitting SUBJECT.

(2) We would have none, or, at most, very limited physical control and custody of the SUBJECT.

(3) Access to the SUBJECT is strictly limited to a social engagement among a mixed group of both cleared and uncleared personnel.

4. The final answer was that in view of the fact that successful completion of this proposed act of attempted assassination was insignificant to the overall project; to wit, whether it was even carried out or not, that under "crash conditions" and appropriate authority from Headquarters, the ARTICHOKE Team would undertake the problem in spite of the operational limitations.

ADDENDUM:

Two main problems presented itself in relation to answering the above hypothetical question.

a. Security: Insufficient consideration was given to the fact that any leakage of ARTICHOKE through performance of the proposed problem would jeopardize the entire future application and proposed activity of the ARTICHOKE Team in the area.

b. It was the unanimous opinion of all ARTICHOKE members that unless the ARTICHOKE Team had more detailed access to the operational plan it would be extremely difficult, if not impossible, to carry out the assigned mission.

Montreal Hospital Pays Woman Who Sued Over C.I.A.

By HENRY GINIGER
Special to The New York Times

OTTAWA, May 15 — A Montreal hospital has settled out of court to end a suit begun by the wife of a member of the House of Commons from Winnipeg, who alleged that she had been unknowingly subjected to psychiatric experiments sponsored by the United States Central Intelligence Agency.

David Orlikow, the Member of Parliament, said in a telephone interview yesterday that his wife, Velma, became aware of the role of the C.I.A. in July 1977.

when she read an article in The New York Times about a secret 25-year, $25 million research program in mind control. This was 13 years after she had ended treatment for acute depression at the Allan Memorial Institute, the psychiatric wing of the Royal Victoria Hospital, which was one of the institutions that participated in the experiments.

Soon after reading the article, Mrs. Orlikow began proceedings in a Montreal court, but the case did not come to trial until this month. Mrs. Orlikow, who said she was still suffering ill effects from the treatment and had sued for some $190,000, agreed to accept about $41,000 plus court costs.

Mr. Orlikow said a suit against the C.I.A. in Washington by his wife and five other Canadians was pending.

Deterrent Effect Stressed

A statement by Mrs. Orlikow's lawyer said, "We believe that the testimony heard will deter not only the Allan Memorial Institute but all hospitals from experimental therapy being undertaken without first advising the patient of the nature of the experimentation and even then only after obtaining express permission."

Mrs. Orlikow, who began treatment in Montreal in 1956, testified that she was "outraged and heartbroken" when she learned that she had been part of the experimental program.

"I find the whole thing despicable," she said in court. "It runs against everything I believed in. I felt outraged that an organization from another country had done this."

She said that she had been regularly forced to take LSD and a dozen other drugs and that "sometimes I thought I would die."

A psychiatrist testifying for Mrs. Orlikow, whose code name in C.I.A. documents was "Miriam," said Mrs. Orlikow had been subjected to "psychological torture" and had suffered irreparable damage.

Documents introduced at the trial alleged that Dr. Douglas Ewen Cameron, who directed the experiments, had accepted subsidies between 1949 and 1964 from a C.I.A. front group called the Society to Investigate Human Ecology.

The documents were part of an affidavit from John D. Marks, a freelance journalist who first obtained information on the C.I.A. program under the United States Freedom of Information Act. Dr. Cameron, an American citizen and a well-known psychiatrist, resigned from the hospital institute in 1964 and died three years later, reportedly from a heart attack while mountain climbing in the Adirondacks.

MP's wife 'tortured' €

Court told of tests with LSD

By JENNIFER ROBINSON
of The Gazette

A Winnipeg psychiatrist said yesterday the wife of federal New Democratic Party MP David Orlikow was subjected to "psychological torture" at Montreal's Allan Memorial Institute, alleged to be the site of secret brainwashing experiments on unwitting patients for the U.S. Central Intelligence Agency (CIA).

Dr. Gordon Lamberd of Winnipeg testified yesterday in Quebec Superior Court that Velma Orlikow, 64, suffered irreparable damage from the brainwashing experiments conducted on her between 1956 and 1964.

Orlikow is suing the Royal Victoria Hospital for about $80,000 for damages allegedly resulting from treatment received from Dr. Douglas Ewen Cameron, former director of the institute, the psychiatric wing of the hospital. Cameron was killed in a mountaineering accident in 1967.

Cameron's experiments were allegedly known as Subproject 68 — the largest behavior control project in the brainwashing research program, called MK Ultra, operated by the CIA.

Orlikow alleges she was used as a guinea pig for unethical experiments that left her with permanent brain damage.

During four hours of emotional, highly descriptive testimony yesterday, Orlikow said she was forced regularly to take lysergic acid diethylamide (LSD) and at least a dozen other controversial drugs.

"Once I thought I was a squirrel running around in a cage unable to escape," she said.

"Sometimes I thought I would die."

She told Judge Marcel Belleville she was drugged daily and expected to write down all her thoughts as she listened to tapes played over and over for up to five hours a day. The tapes were recordings of con-

Velma Orlikow leaves court with her MP husband David

versations she had with Cameron.

"I really tried hard," she said. But after several months of listening to the same tapes she could only write "lost, lost, lost" over and over again.

She said Cameron did not want her to go back to her husband and daughter who lived in Winnipeg at the time. She said he told her to take an apartment in Montreal when she was released from the hospital.

The suit alleges that Cameron received subsidies from a CIA front group, the Society to Investigate Human Ecology, to carry out his experiments.

Orlikow said she was never told what the medical staff was doing

to her. She said she was forced several times to dress skimpily and be filmed by Cameron's assistant, who would call out instructions to her like "sit down" or "stand up."

Orlikow's lawyer, Phil Cutler, said that CIA documents used the code name Miriam to refer to Orlikow in the brainwashing experiments, which were part of a $25-million mind control program to find ways of breaking down enemy agents and manipulating behavior.

Orlikow and several other patients suspected to have been treated by Cameron are also each suing the CIA for $1 million in damages. That case is before U.S. courts.

Hearings here continue today.

Montreal Gazette 5 May 1981

25 Years Of Nightmares

Victims of CIA-Funded Mind Experiments Seek Damages From the Agency

By David Remnick
Washington Post Staff Writer

Harvey Weinstein, a quiet, bearded man who practices psychiatry at Stanford University, says there are days when he is "ashamed" of his profession, nights when he cannot stop thinking about the Canadian psychiatrist who "ruined my father's life . . . Left him with nothing. It's a nightmare that never ends."

With funding from the CIA, the late Dr. D. Ewen Cameron did a series of mind-control experiments on 53 people, including Harvey Weinstein's father, Louis, a prosperous Montreal businessman. All had come to the Allan Memorial Institute of McGill University in Montreal between 1957 and 1961 for treatment of various psychological ailments.

The experiments, Weinstein says, left his father "a human guinea pig, a poor pathetic man with no memory, no life. He lost his business, he lost everything." Weinstein is one of nine plaintiffs in a lawsuit, seeking damages from the CIA.

To erase or "de-pattern" personality traits, Cameron gave his subjects megadoses of LSD, subjected them to drug-induced "sleep therapy" for up to 65 consecutive days and applied electroshock therapy at 75 times the usual intensity. To shape new behavior, Cameron forced them to listen to repeated recorded messages for 16-hour intervals, a technique known as "psychic driving." Cameron and the CIA were interested in brainwashing and the ability to redirect thought and action. The patients did not consent to the treatment and were never told they were being used for research.

"When you're 13 years old and you see your father—an independent, kind, smart person—become a different man before your eyes, it's impossible to accommodate that," Weinstein says. "I remember one of his first visits home from the hospital. He didn't talk much, and when he did talk it made no sense. When he wasn't sleeping he was drowsy. He asked us things about his parents, even though they'd been dead for years. His memory was gone. At night once, when I was in bed, I saw him come into my room and urinate on the floor. He didn't know where he was.

"My father has ended up feeling guilty that he had done something to deserve this punishment. He is convinced the CIA listens to his telephone. He's ashamed, embarrassed. My mother died without seeing the end of this. It will be a tragedy if my father dies without

restoring some sense of dignity to his life."

Today Louis Weinstein lives alone in Montreal, cared for by his two grown daughters.

No one knows the whereabouts of all the subjects, some of whom may be dead. But Louis Weinstein and eight others, including Velma Orlikow, the wife of a New Democratic Party member of the Canadian parliament, claim they have been injured irreparably by the experiments. "I'd say Velma operates at about 20 percent of capacity," David Orlikow says. "It's horrific."

The CIA's involvement in mind control experiments has been coming to light for years. The suit filed by the group against the U.S. government has been pending here in U.S. District Court since December 1980 before Judge John Garrett Penn. The plaintiffs originally asked for $1 million each in damages but have cut that to $175,000. The government has offered to pay $25,000. The group's attorney, Joseph Rauh Jr., calls the settlement offer "demeaning" and contends that the CIA has managed to delay the proceedings by "stonewalling."

The CIA's counsel, Lee Strickland, declined to comment on the case. Agency spokeswoman Kathy Pherson said, "We don't comment on cases under litigation. It's inappropriate to try cases in the press."

In Cameron's defense, Brian Robertson, the present director of the Allan Institute, and James Farquhar, a psychiatrist there, wrote in the Montreal Gazette that "we have not been able to uncover a single shred of evidence that Dr. Cameron knew of the CIA connection with his research funding." They said Cameron's work "must be placed in its historical context" and that "in Cameron's day [researchers] were not expected to inform their patients of the nature of their research in the way that they are today."

The CIA has asked Judge Penn to block Rauh from taking depositions from two key agency figures—Stacey Hulse and John Knaus, who have been publicly identified as former CIA station chiefs in Ottawa. They are both retired.

Cameron, who died of a heart attack while mountain climbing in 1967, had been one of the most prominent psychiatrists in North America. A former president of both the Canadian and American psychiatric associations, he was selected to diagnose Nazi

The Victims of MKULTRA

The Post is quite right in urging that victims of CIA-supported brain-washing experiments "must be found and cared for" ["The Victims of MKULTRA," editorial, April 18].

Long before my wife and eight other Canadian victims of MKULTRA sued the U.S. government, then CIA Director Stansfield Turner publicly promised two U.S. Senate committees that the CIA would begin "the process of attempting to identify the individuals and determining what is our proper responsibility to them." Had the CIA honored these commitments, the Canadian victims of MKULTRA would have not been forced to sue for reparations, and the hundreds of other victims would have long since learned of their unwitting involvement in CIA experiments so they too could seek medical and financial assistance.

As for the suit by the Canadian MKULTRA victims, the CIA has done everything in its power to stall in the hope that attrition will wear down my wife and the eight other Canadians who were subjected to CIA-supported brainwashing experiments with LSD and other damaging techniques.

Until compensation is secured, we will continue our court fight, confident that justice ultimately will prevail

DAVID ORLIKOW
Member of Parliament
Winnipeg North

The Washington Post 25 Apr. 1985

Chapter 7
Glossary

January 1, 1956 index cards labeled Drug Cards Index. CIA Mori ID# 189903. Reformatted.

Project MK-Ultra and Mind Control Technology

ALCOHOL	See Ethyl Alcohol
	Sedative Deprivations
ALTERATIONS	See Deprivations
AMANITA	See Fungus Toxins
Muscaria	
Pantherina	
Phalloides	
AMMONIUM	See Tetraethylammonium

ACETYLCHOLIN & CHOLINESTERASE

The constantly changing balances between these substances at innumerable points in the body, relate to the transmission of all nerve impulses. "Cholinergic" and "Adrenergic" drugs throw the balance in one direction, or the other. "Ganglion-block" drugs have special relationships. See Nerve Gases also.

Because of their overall importance in neurology and psychiatry, any psychiatric project needs to keep track of the literature on Acetylcholin & Cholinesterase.

AMNESIA

One of the questions most commonly asked of A is, "Can you guarantee amnesia?" This, of course, is a very logical question and its answer--if it could be given in the affirmative would be of extreme importance in many types of operations as well as in A use. At present, however, we do not know of any technique, chemical, treatment, etc. which will guarantee complete amnesia. A is very interested in this problem but to date our research and experimentation is disappointing.

In hypnosis, certain of our good subjects have, with some degree of consistency, had amnesias but the same subjects in other tests have had recall even after the strongest suggestions were made for amnesia. It appears that under hypnosis, even if a complete amnesia cannot be obtained a blurred or fuzzy memory can be, induced and a partial amnesia is often obtained. Some subjects seem to experience memory blank when placed in deep hypnotic states without efforts being made to produce an amnesia--but this too is not consistent.

Certain chemicals seem effective. Scopolamine, for instance, comes closer than the barbiturates although we have apparently produced good amnesias with amytal and pentothal. Some new chemicals may be valuable along these lines (LSD). However, our professional consultants emphatically support the A view that short of cutting a subject's throat, a true ~~confession~~ cannot be guaranteed.

It should be recalled also that most drugs leave a tell tale "hangover" with the subject and while he may be very vague as to what has occurred, he nevertheless will realize that something "unusual" has happened to him. Such chemicals as LSD, mescaline etc. having weird and bizarre effects in heavy dosages clearly indicate something has been done to the individual. Particularly sensitive to drugging, of course, would be good intelligence agents since drug effects are known by all the nations of the world and we believe are very well known by the Soviets.

The A group has considered shock--both electro and chemically-induced as an amnesia-producing technique but even in this results are spotty and medical authorities are certainly not in agreement. This, coupled with the dangers involved, the clumsy apparatus necessary and the medical problems present more or less rule out shock for our use.

The A group would recommend this for research.

Amnesia for words mentioned in the hypnotic state was suggested to a

somnambule. Despite subject's inability to recognize or recall these

words in the posthypnotic period, they could be determined from records

of physiological changes which were made (polygraph) during the tests

of recognition.

Bitterman & Marcuse
(Cornell)

AMPHETAMINS

· See Narco-Analysis, and Narcotizing Drug Combinations.
Of the several in use, the best for Narco-Analysis, either alone or for partially
arousing the S. from a drug-induced sleep, are the two: Methedrin or Pervitin, and
Dexedrin. Methedrin may be slightly more powerful. Either can be given orally or
intravenously. If I.V., then it may be wise to try a small dose first before using
an average dose. Some persons are sensitive enough to be convulsed on an average
intravenous dose; anyone's convulsive threshold will be lowered. There are reports
of an acute psychosis being caused by an intravenous overdose of Methedrin.

The convulsive threshold may be lowered enough to produce convulsion on exposure to
Flicker, but the behavior of amphetamines is more erratic in this connection than is
that of intravenous Azczol, or Metrazol.

One unsettled question here is: could enough Benzedrin (another amphetamin, more
volatile) be inhaled to produce a certain Flicker-convulsion, without producing too
much other effect, chiefly too high a blood-pressure? The answer seems to be "No".

Further study of these Amphetamins is recommended.

Pervitin is said to have a marked objective sobering effect on alcoholic intoxication.

AMYGDALOID NUCLEUS

At present this brain-center can be specifically stimulated by a current passed
through wires inserted through the brain by operation.
                              to this project:
Such a procedure is obviously useless; but ultrasonics or other means of radiant
energy may yet be improved or modified so that a "cross-fire" (as with X-rays)
                            on
arrangement could be focussed a selected small region in the brain without affecting
                          ^
the surrounding areas.
The Amygdaloid nucleus is interesting because it has been stimulated in humans (as
in first paragraph above); producing fear or anger. Monkeys' amygdaloids have been
removed; producing tameness.

Temporary inhibition of this region (possibly also of others), should tame humans.

ANALGESIC DRUGS
}
C
_____   recently stated
that a new era in medicine was about to begin. He was referring to new drugs such as
DOLITRONE which are capable of obliterating pain without removing consciousness. Whether
or not these new drugs may be of value to ARTICHOKE remains to be seen but theoretically
at least they are of interest to us both offensively and defensively.

    Many questions arise in considering these drugs:

        1) Is there a dissociation between feeling and thinking?
        2) Is there a tendency toward euphoria?
        3) Is amnesia developed (some indication here)?
        4) Could it serve as a defense against torture?
        5) Would these drugs have any form of potentiating effect?
        6) Could they be used as a confusion agent? After--or combined with
              other chemicals.

H Note: DOLITRONE was obtained as a result of a trip by   in October
A   1954 and turned over to _   for research. (Dolitrone came from
 B C
  G
    See DOLITRONE
ANESTHETIC GASES

                                    ·

Patients going under and coming out of surgical anesthesia are notorious for revealing
material otherwise concealed.

ETHER is too easily inflammable and explosive, for one objection. There are also other Ethers than the common one, that are faster — but likewise inflammable. This drug I would forget.

NITROUS OXID or "laughing gas" may cause uncontrollable laughing, or else weeping, for a good part of an hour after recovery of consciousness. Not enough usefulness to us. This too can be forgotten.

CHLOROFORM is worth remembering. A good deal of literature-searching might be required, but a cleared contact told us of an American Civil War case of an agent being questioned under Chloroform with remarkable success. It may be that other drugs could advantageously/added to Chloroform, while keeping its dose small because it can be fairly toxic to the liver.

ANIMAL TOXINS

1. Paralyzing toxins in the flesh of certain fishes, and shellfish (mussels especially), produce numerous well known neurological effects. Psychological effects, if any, have not been emphasized. The literature deserves more study than this reporter has given it.

2. Toxins in the sting of most insects, seem of little or no interest. Again, the literature on black widow and other spiders, scorpions, etc., has not been closely searched.

3. Snake venoms (as cobra & rattlesnake) are most interesting, and have been used by injection:

    (a) to reduce chronic pain; and

    (b) to relieve symptoms of epilepsy.

    These uses are not well or generally accepted medically; but they do suggest that further study of the literature may well bring out something of value.

ANTI-HISTAMINICS

Anti-histaminic drugs such as Anahist, Benadryl and Pyribenzamine have two possibly useful properties.

1. They cause emotional instability in children; less so in adults, therefore some experimentation would be required to select the most generally disturbing one. Probably there is too little to be gained in this direction exclusively, but the other (doubtless related) property is more promising:

2. They sensitize a Subject to alcohol. People become intoxicated sooner and nearer semiconsciousness with less alcohol. (A patient of mine fell asleep and fell down while climbing a stairway; it is notorious that persons under both drugs' influence may fall asleep suddenly if attempting to drive).

This condition seems well worth further study.

Antimetabolites
_____
(see also Deprivations, p. 2)

Many of these substances are known, each one of which is specifically antagonistic to the action of a certain enzyme, hormone, etc.

E.g., the antimetabolite "desoxypyridoxin" counteracts the vitamin pyridoxin (B_6) and so sensitizes the subject to convulsion; thereupon a means intended to produce a convulsion will do so on shorter exposure and/or in smaller dose. If pyridoxin is counteracted rapidly and completely enough, a convulsion may be produced.

An antimetabolite to glutamin (glutamic acid, an amino-acid essential to human health) would likewise sensitize to convulsion; or produce one, if glutamin were counteracted rapidly and completely enough.

A diet naturally low in B_6 could be fed, and drugged with the above antimetabolites.

It is also possible that edibles could be grown, under radioactivity, to contain less B_6 than normally.

Research in experimentation along these lines is not worth the project's effort; but the literature merits an occasional survey.

130

ASPIRIN

Recently a report has appeared that ascribes some Cortisone-effect to Aspirin. Aspirin is such a commonly used drug, and this property (if true) so promptly suggests that combinations of Aspirin with other drugs that we use may possibly distort their effects: a sharp eye should be directed at whatever further reports appear in this connection.

ATMOSPHERIC PRESSURE

Low.

Low oxygen (12% to 11%, i.e., about half-normal) for respiration has desirable effects (#4): exhilaration, talkativeness, & over-confidence; but with poor memory and comprehension, also headache and nausea, and pugnacity.

A severe oxygen deprivation -- 6% O_2 + 94% N_2 -- produces unconsciousness gradually.

High.

Pure (100%) oxygen breathed can produce unconsciousness promptly, but this procedure is dangerous.

Measurable alteration in either direction, of the O_2 for respiration, would require an oxygen-chamber type of installation. This seems not worthwhile.

Also, a means to protect the Operator from the same symptoms as the subject's, is not available.

ATROPIN

See Narcotizing Drug Combinations.

Atropin is a belladonna derivative, used sometimes in place of, or in addition to, Scopolamin in a Scopolamin + Morphin technique ("twilight sleep").

Atropin is also an antidote, but not a good one, to the "nerve gases."

AZOZAL   See METRAZOL
                        FLICKER

BACTERIAL TOXINS

Few if any bacterial toxins seem to lend themselves to the project's aims. Botulinum toxin may have possibilities. This reporter has read too little, to say more than that its literature deserves a survey.

BARBITURATES   See Ethyl Alcohol
                        Sedative-Deprivations
                        Unwitting Subject
                        Narco Analysis

BLOOD ELECTROLYTES   See Electrolytes

BLOOD POTASSIUM   See Potassium
BRAIN CENTERS   See Amygdaloid Nucleus
                        Frontal Lobe
                        Iontophoresis
                        LSD-25
                        Lobotomy
                        Radiant Energy
                        Ultrasonics

BRAIN-WASHING

Isolation as a means applied over an extended time, within a program of Brain-Washing, produces a Mental State of apathy and purposelessness (a #14). Whether isolation produces suggestibility (#6) when combined with other brainwashing techniques, is uncertain; a special form (see Isolation) does sometimes produce suggestibility.

Other elements of brainwashing may produce some confusion (#8); and a tendency too readily to fall asleep (#10). See next page.

Overall, brainwashing has the medium- or long-term objective of weakening or eradicating a Subject's philosophy of life and his drive to pursue it, along with his allegiance and the motivation to maintain it.

A Mental State of degradation (#14) may then improve the product of interrogation, by removing the Subject's motivation to conceal. However, in a short-term preparation for interrogation, degradation could do more harm than good.

First steps in brainwashing are deprivations:

Project MK-Ultra and Mind Control Technology

DEPRIVATIONS OF:		PRODUCE:
Sleep;	discomfort & frequent awakening	tendency to confusion (# d) & chronic drowsiness (#10)
Warmth;	exposure to distressing cold	
Food — quantity	chronic hunger & mild starvation	tendency to drowsiness (#10)
Food components	deficient proteins, vitamins, minerals, &c	ill defined "sub-clinical" Mental States
	(Deprivations of Vitamins C,B₁,B₂, are usually not enough to produce	scurvy, beri-beri, pellagra)

If DEGRADATION is included, add

DEPRIVATION OF:		
Dignity;	dirt, discomfort, humiliation, threats, abuse & beatings	tendency to violence & defeatism, with no outlet for hostility; hence only defeatism remains (a #14)

BRAIN-WASHING
See also: Vitamins
            Electrolytes
            Anti-metabolites
            Deprivations

BUFOTENIN

This substance has been synthesized, and is the equivalent of the narcotic principle of Cohoba Snuff, used in the Antilles somewhat like Peyote in North America.

Study of this drug is recommended.

BULBOCAPNIN

This drug is best known for its property of producing a cataleptic state, like catatonic schizophrenia in some respects, but only temporary. This state is abolished by cocain, or an amphetamin; rapidly, if either of these antidotes is injected; even more rapidly if a mixture of 40% CO_2 + 60% O_2 is inhaled.

A smaller dose of bulbocapnin produces Under-Anxiety (col. #1), a state of tranquillity which may include some degree of suggestibility.

Use of this drug in interrogation is well worth further study, both alone and in combination.

CARBON DIOXID

Most of the current medical literature on CO_2 in treatment of psychiatric conditions, describes methods that give 30% CO_2 + 70% O_2 , or 40 & 60 respectively, through a facemask. Unconsciousness comes rather quickly, but there is much anxiety (without amnesia after awakening) involved, as well as apparatus and an anesthetist's skill.
There seems to be no future for this method, in Interrogation.
Small concentrations are much more promising. While an oxygen-chamber type of room would be desirable, it might not be necessary. The driver of an ordinary station-wagon fell asleep gradually on driving a few blocks, after storing 100 lb. dry ice in the car, which had been standing in the sun. Under laboratory conditions, as low a concentration as 6% CO_2 causes headache and confusion; how long it would take to produce unconsciousness, is uncertain. Eventually, as the S. breathes he increases the CO_2 concentration, which complicates the problem. Also eventually, he ceases to breathe, and it will take artificial respiration for recovery. The safety margin at various ranges of concentration, must be determined.
This reporter guesses that he has not sufficiently searched the literature, and that already enough has been worked out to give CO_2 a place in our program. If a room were only relatively tight, the amount of dry ice to be sublimed to provide a given concentration of CO_2 in a given cubic yardage, should be readily calculable; the Subject's breathing might maintain or increase the concentration gradually. He might well become unconscious without being alarmed. More difficult would be the problem of how to keep the Operator alert at the same time: no answer to this, at the moment.

132

CA (Calcium)	See Electrolytes
	Prophylaxis against Revealing
CAFFEIN	See Ethyl Alcohol
CALCIUM	See Ca (above)
CANNABIS	See Unwitting Subject
CARDIAZOL	See Metrazol

CAROTID SINUS PRESSURE

Sudden strong pressure on certain small areas on either side of the neck under the lower jaw, will alter the bloodsupply to parts of the brain and may cause fainting; in a few subjects, it may cause a convulsion.

In highly susceptible subjects, a constant (not sudden) milder pressure from too tight a collar, can produce similar results.

While it is true that this carotid-sinus-reflex can be sharpened, or dulled, by one or another drug, research on this topic has not seemed to promise enough return.

Our purpose does not contemplate judo-techniques among its ordinary means.

CENTERS, BRAIN	See Brain Centers
Changes in Temperature	See Heat
	Cold
Chemical Lobotomy	See Chloropromazine
	Cocain
	Lobotomy

CHLORAL

Chloral, as knockout drops or Mickey Finn, has a better reputation for clandestine than for the medical production of sleep. In medicine it was deemed riskier for the heart than any barbiturate; but at this year's (1954) Amer. Psychiatric Assn. convention it had a renewed vogue. Two commercial firms, Squibb and Fellows, were there advertising preparations of Chloral for sleep-producing.

In a Subject already alcoholized it is doubtless more potent and quicker-acting than when given alone.

See: Unwitting Subject (page 1)
     Narcotic Drug Combinations (item 2)
     Sedative Deprivations (para. 1)

CHLOROFORM   See Anesthetic Gases

CHLORPROMAZINE

This drug by mouth or intramuscular injection, produces under-anxiety (col. #1), through a ganglion-blocking property. Especially it tames a violent subject; makes aggressive psychopaths less aggressive, and active paranoids less deluded.

Unlike Rauwolfia, Chlorpromazine is somewhat toxic; 2 to 3% of subjects develop a liver complication. It produces a mild non-permanent lobotomy-like effect. Subject is dulled, sometimes drowsy but not confused. Bloodpressure drops (sometimes too far for comfort) and pulse rises; this effect may alarm a neurotic subject. More details in Section 14 of my report on Amer. Psychiat. convention of 1954.

No revealing-tendency seems to have been reported. Cardiovascular effects would make polygraphy difficult to interpret.

Further study of this drug is recommended for its anxiety-reducing and possibly other properties (as further study of other ganglion-blocking drugs seems worth a mild recommendation): its deconditioning property is most interesting.

See Conditioning (foot of page).

CHOLINESTERASE	See Nerve Gases
	Acetylcholin and Cholinesterase
CO$_2$	See Carbon Dioxide

COCAIN

Cocain's general effects have been somewhat neglected. By injection this means will produce elation, talkativeness and etc. (#4 of Mental States). Larger doses may cause fearfulness and alarming hallucinations.

It also counteracts the catatonia produced by bulbocapnin, and the catatonia of catatonic schizophrenia.

It seems worth further study.

COCAIN DERIVATIVES

Procaine injected into the brain's frontal lobes, through trephine holes in the skull, produced free and spontaneous speech within two days in mute schizophrenics. Too surgical for our use.

However (see card on Iotophoresis) it is possible that such a drug could be gotten into the general circulation of a subject without surgery, hypodermic or feeding.

Possibility seems remote, and worth little if any further study.

COHOBA SNUFF   See Bufotenin

See Deprivations (p.3).

There are procedures for making a human hibernate like a bear, and with relative safety. Since that objective seems outside this project, I have neglected it.

COLORED LIGHT   See Colors

COLORS

1. Colors notoriously influence the emotions.
2. Some impression of a Subject's personality can be gained by his choices of, and reactions to, various colors.

This reporter has neglected colors, perhaps wrongly. They may belong in this project.

3. The colored goggles used to avoid flicker-sickness in technicians and operators, are intended merely to reduce light-intensity.

COMBINATIONS   See Aspi:
                         Ethyl Alcohol
                         Interrupted Sound
                         Mescalin
                         Narcotizing Drug Combinations
CONDITIONING   (& Deconditioning)

Roughly stated, this training teaches the Subject to respond to a signal or symbol, in the same manner as he would respond to the stimulus for/which the symbol stands. Classically, Pavlov's dog's mouth waters when he hears the bell that goes with food — without the food. When food has been omitted often enough, the dog no longer responds to the signal; he is "deconditioned".

Jones learns to respond to stimuli intended for a Smith, as though he were that Smith. He has been "conditioned" to Smith, "deconditioned" to Jones.

Such trainings are integrated on all levels, conscious and subconscious. Hypnosis can assist in establishing the desired conditioned responses.

A C. R. (condit. resp.) is meant to stick. It can be interfered with, or abolished, by new training in another direction, or back to the earlier state.

Deconditioning can probably be expedited by hypnotizing procedures. Also, a C.R. can be interfered with or abolished by violent physical shocks (e.g., electric shocks to the brain; although this reporter has not found a specific electric-shock procedure that would assuredly decondition any particular kind or number of C.R.'s).

Still problematic is the use of drugs for deconditioning. Chlorpromazine (which see) ought theoretically to have some such value, and some deconditioning effect has been produced in laboratory animals. However, hospitalized patients taking daily doses of this drug seem to have been deconditioned only selectively, against certain psychotic behavior. It may be that this property is exactly what we are looking for; perhaps it could decondition an enemy agent out of his simulated personality and back to his real one.

Deconditioning possibilities demand more study, in this order: Hypn., Chlorpr., Elec.Shocks.

CONFUSION

Ethyl alcohol, barbiturates, barbiturate + amphetamin, scopolamin + morphin, and other combinations; marijuana, mescaline, LSD25: all can produce some form or degree of confusion, but are not ordinarily given for that purpose alone.

(See the individual cards for these specific chemical Means).

Confusion is better controlled during the period of recovery from, than during the period of sinking into, unconsciousness. A tendency to reveal, as well as to be confused, would be expected especially under barbiturate + amphetamin, or scopol.+morph. Confusion is usual during recovery from an epileptiform convulsion. Its duration may be short or long, and it may be complicated by violent excitement. An especially revealing-tendency is not expected, but does appear in some Subjects. (See Convulsion; Flicker; Electric Shock.)

Some confusion has been reported from electromagnetic and high frequency fields. Radar also may have confusing effects. No one of these three seems to have been used for the purpose; but a vast deal of literature is still unsearched, and deserves searching.

CONVULSIONS (Epileptic-type Fits)

The A group has for a long time considered the possible uses of artificially induced convulsions for several interesting reasons:

    a. The convulsion or fit itself, if capable of being induced at will, would be a very strong physical and psychological harrassment to any given subject particularly if used after threat, or to convince a subject of his "serious" illness.

    b. The post-convulsion period is one of confusion, disorientation, weakness and often a semi-comatose condition. During this state, it is possible that a subject is more suggestible than normal and that conceivably hypnosis could be achieved in an otherwise unwilling subject. This latter is theoretical only and requires research--medical literature is unavailable in this connection.)

    c. Quite often amnesia occurs for events just prior to the convulsion, during the convulsion and during the post seizure state. It is possible that hypnosis or hypnotic activity induced during the post-seizure state might be lost in amnesia. This would be very valuable.

In studying this problem, it is noted that convulsion can be produced in many ways-- chemically, electronically (shock) or through flicker or interrupted sound (particularly after sensitization by certain chemicals such as Isoniacid). (Note-(unfavorable comments under Isoniazid) which of these techniques that could be used in a surreptitious manner or simply produced is at present unknown but the A group feels that this field deserves more study. A

CONVULSION

        Sensitizing to Convulsion, Flicker, Interrupted Sound,
See also: Antimetabolites, Convulsive Threshold Lowered, Convul. Thres. Raised, Deprivations, Sedative Deprivations, Electric Shocks, Vitamin B₆, individual convulsant drugs as Metrazol, Amphetamins, ec.

CONVULSION-SENSITIZING   See Sensitizing to Convulsion
                              Convulsive Threshold Lowered

Convulsive Threshold Lowered

                             (this lowering is a mild degree of)
A number of means will lower the convulsive threshold/(a 9, sensitizing to convulsion).

In practical use is a drug (Metrazol or equivalent) given intravenously. Flicker, applied after this injection, is said to convulse any Subject.

                                (applied over a period of days, lower
Question: can a biochemical or dietary means (the convulsive threshold far enough to
                                (assure that Flicker will then convulse?
More study seems worth while.

See: Metrazol.
    Cortisone.
    Sensitizing to Convulsion.
    Deprivations.
    Potassium.
    Electrolytes.
    Glutamic Acid or Glutamin.

CONVULSIVE THRESHOLD RAISED

A few reasonably normal persons will be markedly disturbed, or even convulsed, by Flicker, without having been sensitized beforehand.

Question: can a sure means be applied beforehand, to prevent a mild or serious effect of Flicker--so protecting an Operator exposed with his Subject?

Project MK-Ultra and Mind Control Technology

More study seems worthwhile.

See: Chlorpromazine
      Barbiturates

COPRINUS ATRAMENTARIUS   See Fungus Toxins

CORTISONE & A C T H

Cortisone may sensitize to convulsion, or convulse, persons who take it over a considerable period of time; it is given by physicians for a number of chronic illnesses — chiefly chronic arthritis, and chronic asthma — so that if a Subject has been taking it, his convulsive threshold may be appreciably lower than normal.

ACTH (adrenocorticotropic hormone) stimulates the body's production of Cortisone, along with some other effects. The Cortisone-effect, as above, might interest us.

Neither of these would be used actually to sensitize or to convulse, for our purposes. They would be too slow, and would involve a number of complications very undesirable).

CURRENT, galvanic	See Iontophoresis
Current, high frequency	See Iontophoresis High Frequency and Radar Fields
Current, induced	See Electric Shocks Electromagnetic Field
Current, Alternating	See Electromagnetic Field Electric Shocks
DECONDITIONING	See Conditioning
DEPRIVATION-CONVULSIONS	See Deprivations
	Sedative-Deprivations
DEPRIVATIONS	

(1

See Brainwashing.   See also SEDATIVE DEPRIVATIONS; &, DEPRIVATION OF FOOD, QUANTITATIVE.

Deprivations of dietary components, and Alterations of physical environments, can also be applied over a period of time (without other brainwashing stresses) weaken a Subject non-specifically (#14), i.e., to make him more easily fatigued and to lower his resistance generally.

Specifically desirable mental states should be sought, in addition to a non-specific (#14) weakening of the Subject which would lower his resistance and make him more easily fatigued.

Mentioned under Brainwashing, is the drowsiness-tendency (#10) produced by a mild degree of starvation.

Under Sensitizing to Convulsion (page 2) is a list of biochemical and dietary means that may so act, viz.

DEPRIVATIONS   (2

Questions:

Dietary Means that probably Sensitize to Convulsion (not listed in order of probable effectiveness, which is unknown)	MENTAL STATES produced (other than generally lowered resistance, raised fatiguability, & the Sensitizing -to-Convulsion)	Is it practical to alter the proportions of blood-electrolytes? by feeding as a part of the regular meals:
Bio-Chemical Low.tot.bl.electrolytes) Lowered blood-magnesium) Raised blood-potassium)	other effects unknown	a) certain salts? b) certain ion-exchange resins? c) vegetables of ordinary spe- cies, but grown in especi-
Vitamins Niacin (B2)deficiency Pyridoxin (B2) " Riboflavin (B2) "	(if severe deficiency, irritability & confusion) other effects unknown " " " "	ally altered soils? d) "mutant" vegetables, i.e., new species selected from freaks grown under influence of radio-activity?
Amino-Acids Glutamin deficiency	other effects uncertain	
Antimetabolites (producing deficiency of a specific Vit. or Am.Ac)	effects, as above	Or to alter the vitamin-content of edible plants, by (c) or (d) above?

DEPRIVATIONS		(3
Dietary (continued)	MENTAL STATES produced	Further study of the lit- erature seems desirable.

DEPRIVATIONS	MENTAL STATES produced
(Certain vegetables show a niacin-deficiency effect; suspected, that they have like effect, though mild, on central nervous system)	
Parsnips) Buckwheat)	unknown, whether any

DEPRIVATIONS IN, or ALTERATIONS OF, the PHYSICAL ENVIRONMENT	
Reduced CO_2, in blood, as from deep breathing	(sensitizes to convulsion (& betters hypnotizability
Reduced O_2, in air	(if mild: worsens judgment & (concentration; tends toward (elation & over-confidence (#4)
Reduced relative humidity (if to 30% or lower)	(irritability certainly; lower- (ed convulsive thresh. probably
Reduced body-warmth (no heating, little clothing)	(frustration, & aggravated in- (tensity of dependancy-needs

DEPRIVATION OF FOOD, QUANTITATIVE

See Brainwashing (page 2)
    Deprivations ("   2)

A 12-hour fast makes subjects more liable to Flicker-Sickness (which see).

Quantitative food deprivations of different durations doubtless have numerous other effects in great variety — like making males more fertile, possibly through a ductless-gland mechanism (pituitary gland?).

The literature ought periodically to be searched to pick up dietary (quantitative & qualitative) influences that can add to, or subtract from, the effects of drugs & other means.

DEXEDRIN   See Amphetamins
                              Unwitting Subject

DIET   See Deprivation of Food, Quantitative
                              Deprivations
                              Antimetabolites

DIZZINESS   See Barbiturate (see also other drugs)
                              Equilibrium
                              Flicker Sickness
                              Middle Ear Disorder
                              Motion Sickness
                              Vibration

DISPOSAL PROBLEMS (Disposal of Subjects)   See AMNESIA
                                                  LOBOTOMY
DOLITRONE

1. Dolitrone is a new drug. Injected intravenously, it renders a subject insensible to pain but conscious, unparalyzed, and able to follow directions.
There is no report yet of any mental state useful to interrogation. Whether some such drug could be or has been developed for oral use by an agent, as prophylaxis against third-degree methods, is unknown.

2. It is known that very rare individuals seem to be naturally insensitive to pain--not simply hardened or conditioned.
Research on the pharmacology of (1), and the pathology of (2), seems worth following.

137

Project MK-Ultra and Mind Control Technology

Dormison

This practically tasteless drug, given by mouth in dosage of 0.25 to 2.5 gm., will produce a few hours' sleep fairly rapidly. However, since the stated range of doses is so broad, it is obvious that a relatively small dose will produce sedation and not sleep in some Subjects. In intentionally small doses it reduces anxiety (col. #1).

Therefore to assure sleep, a large dose is required. This is safe (but may make S. sleep longer than intended, if it is a large dose for him), since 2.5 gm. is believed non-toxic; 5.0 gm. may be toxic.

Dormison has this advantage over barbiturates, that is does not cause a hangover as the latter sometimes do. It should not be given with barbiturates: effect is excessive.

Nothing found in the references read, to suggest that Dormison should not be given at the same time as alcohol; nor is it stated whether such a combination has other effects.

No revealing-tendency reported. To reduce anxiety, or to produce sleep — according to dose — seem to be its only uses.

See Unwitting Subject.

ELECTRIC SHOCKS

An electric shock of high amperage (say 500 to 800 milliamperes), 60-cycle A.C., for a fraction of a second through the frontal area of a Subject's brain, can give him a sudden epileptiform convulsion. This is more violent than an ordinary epileptic fit; also, breathing ceases and may not resume spontaneously. Machines are available to deliver different types, strengths, and durations of current for psychiatric uses.

Two to four operators shock one patient, in a fairly involved procedure that includes precautions against a fatal stray current through the heart, fractures of the spine, dislocation of the jaw, burns, &c. Artificial respiration is routinely given. Fracture complications are not rare, even with a well-trained team. A previous injection of curare or an equivalent will practically eliminate the danger of broken bones, but introduces other dangers and adds another step to the procedure. If we desire an epileptiform convulsion, it ought to be less violent and complicated than that. A number of modifications are already in psychiatric use.

Modified procedures with different types of current have succeeded in avoiding most of the above complications, but the current is so painful that the Subject must be first anesthetized.

Possible advantages of electric, instead of other, means of producing convulsion with unconsciousness, are suddenness and amnesia. A high amperage electric shock to the head acts somewhat like concussion from a blow; after recovery from unconsciousness, there is a loss of memory for the convulsion and also for a period of a few seconds' or minutes' time just preceding the convulsion. If the Op. had had to give an intra-venous anesthetic first, its administration will be remembered; giving a shock next, is pointless.

ELECTRIC SHOCKS   (2

If the amnesia-for the-event, which the strong electric shock produces, would invariably extend backward in time far enough to keep Subject from recalling that a pair of electrodes had been clapped on his head, then we would have a highly desirable amnesia.

Since one cannot be sure of this, Electric Shocks though electrodes applied to the head, may as well be dropped.

See Electro-Narcosis. *See also, Conditioning.*

There is another vague possibility. Could a coil be arranged in chair or wall, so that switching it on would induce a current in Subject's head? Perhaps; but the inducing current would have to be uncommonly heavy, while the induced current would stray all over and as likely kill the S. as convulse him. Electrical experts disapprove.

See Electromagnetic Field.

ELECTROLYTES

Possibilities of so disturbing the electrolyte balances in the blood as to produce a variety of recoverable weaknesses, confusions & convulsions, was intriguing when this project was joined by this reporter. Considerable reading persuades him that useful ones would be hard to attain, and many would as likely be non-recoverable.

Low total electrolytes, low Potassium, low Magnesium, may all lower the convulsive threshold and so dispose to convulsion; but too many complications are involved, besides the problem of how certainly to reshuffle the electrolytes to a desired imbalance.

138

Ion-exchange resins were given up, and no other practicable procedures were found.
See: Ion Exchange.
      Potassium.

ELECTROMAGNETIC FIELD

An alternating current in a Solenoid coil suspended around a subject's head, has been reported to distryb, confuse and cause a sensation of lights flashing at the rate of alternation.

> Q 1. Could such effect be obtained by A.C. of practicable strength, if the coil were concealed beyond the room's walls?

> Q 2. If the alternations were at the rates at which flashing lights may convulse a sensitized subject (see FLICKER), would these sensations-of-light be strong enough to give the same effect as actual lights?

These questions seem worth investigation--at a low priority.

ELECTRO-NARCOSIS

So-called "Electro-Narcosis" is not so good as it sounds. A barbiturate must first be given to reach a level of anesthesia deep enough so that the Subject will not react to the painfulness of the unidirectional current to be used (10 milliamperes or more, for at least 4 minutes).

Sodium pentothal, from 50 to 600 mgm., is slowly injected intravenously, with precautions against giving too little or too much.

Its good results for interrogation should be obtained by injecting the sodium pentothal and omitting the electro-narcosis.

ENERGY, Radiant	See Radiant Energy
ENVIRONMENT	See Deprivations
EPILEPSY	See Convulsion
EPILEPTIFORM CONVULSION	

	Caffein moderately counter-acts its depressive signs	Pervitin (an amphetamin) has marked objective sobering effect
D Levulose		
o or Fructose		
t slows it		
..		
S		

mild or severe dizziness.

The Internal Ear's labyrinth controls equilibrium, which is typically disordered in Meniere's Disease (see POTASSIUM).

This re-orter has given up the notion of tinkering with the blood-potassium, but still believes that Flicker Sickness is worth a laboratory experiment.

Severe Motion Sickness is highly distressing; but for it to reach a revealing-tendency level, it would amount practically to a third-degree procedure. See the card on vibration for its production.

| ETHANOL | See Ethyl Alcohol |
| ETHERS | See Anesthetic Gases |

ETHYL ALCOHOL

Intoxication

Adrenalin or an Amphetamin increases sensitivity to it	Nicotin aggravates its subjective symptoms	Morphin worsens it by increasing its depressive signs	It (alcoholic intoxication) deepens & longthens the sleep produced by barbiturate

Other Combinations

Alcohol + antihistaminic drugs may cause sudden unconsciousness.

Coprinus atramentarius (a mushroom) may be edible alone, poisonous if preceded or
followed by alcohol.

Project MK-Ultra and Mind Control Technology

EXCHANGE   See Ion-Exchange

EXTRAVERT PERSONALITY   See Subject's Personality

FEAR (Terror, Anxiety, Worry, Etc.)

All intelligence servides and police organizations use fear or its related psychological reactions as a weapon. This is particularly true in communist areas or in dictator states. Its value as a weapon is enormous. Since we do not support third degree-type activities and even psychological harassment of the more severe variety would not be condoned, this very powerful weapon cannot be fully exploited by us. To offset this, we feel that research should be carried out to find how fear can be induced by chemistry or electronically without harm to the individual. This is an unexplored.field and wide open for exploitation. Commercially used psycho-chemicals or medicinal chemicals that would create terror, dread, anxiety, etc. would be thrown away in this country. For instance, Metrozal which has been very useful in shock therapy, is no longer popular because, for one thing it produces a feeling of overwhelming terror and doom prior to the convulsion.

But terror, anxiety, worry would be valuable for many purposes from our point of view. We have some information (not in detail and not confirmed) that the Soviets and their satellites have used drugs which work along these lines. Therefore, this should be studied both from our use offensively and defensively and to find antidotes or counteracting agents.

FLICKER

Flickering light will produce an epileptiform convulsion in about 5% of so-called "normal" persons; these probably have, inherited or acquired, a low convulsive threshold.

Flicker will — if the right rate is used (see below) — convulse any Subject who has at the time been sufficiently sensitized by other means.

Of many possible sensitizers, Metrazol or Azozol is generally used.

Metrazol by mouth in a heavy dose (say between 700 : 1000 mgm.) will give most Subjects dizziness and nausea along with sensitization. Theoretically, the nausea might be avoided by a previous oral dose of Chlorpromazine for its anti-nausea effect; however, this drug-combination I have not seen in the literature, and — until tried and found safe — it must be considered dangerous, since both Metrazol and Chlorpromazine would affect the heart. Metrazol in a smaller dose, given rapidly by intravenous injection, will sensitize most Subjects enough for flicker to convulse them. Azozol is surer, can sensitize all Subjects.

Light of an intensity of from 100 to 200 foot-candles is interrupted by an electronically operated pendulum-type shutter, giving rates of from 2 to 30 flashes per second, from a lighted circle about 30 inches in diameter; the S. could, however, be surrounded by lucite-type walls so that he could not look away from the light (closing the eyes would not avoid the flicker-effect). (A 13 to 18 flash-rate is most effective for most people, especially a rate of 16; 9 is more effective for a few.)

The Op. should be protected by ground-glass goggles, else he may prove to be one of those "normals" who is either convulsed, or nauseated and distressed, by the Flicker alone.

See FLICKER-SICKNESS.

"FLICKER SICKNESS"

Is noted under Flicker, an appropriate flash-rate convulses few non-sensitized, or insufficiently sensitized, Subjects. Yet it may produce some dizziness, nausea, and particularly an Emotional Instability (column #3) of more or less severity. Persons already neurotic or unstable are the more liable to flicker-sickness of this sort. The effect is cumulative; exposure for several hours daily, for days or weeks or longer, stands a chance of producing flicker sickness in anyone, stable or not, who works with the apparatus.

When it occurs on one exposure, it may develop before, not instead of, a convulsion; this happening could mean that the Subject had been insufficiently sensitized beforehand.

The emotionalism of flicker-sickness might be sought for its own usefulness, in place of a convulsion. In that case, previous sensitizing would be omitted to avoid convulsion. On this point, the reporter recommends an experiment which could be set up with little trouble in almost any room, using any normal personnel as subjects, viz.:

Without too much instrumentation, it should be possible to set an ordinary two-bladed fan to give 16 flashes per second, the most disturbing rate for most people (other rates between 13 : 18 might be tried), when placed in front of a strong enough light. The Subject would face this, the Op. face away and wear heavily colored or smoked goggles. (In a restaurant this reporter timed such a fan at about 6 or 8 flashes per second; too slow, but still it spoiled his appetite).

FOOD DEPRIVATION, QUANTITATIVE   See Deprivation of Food, Quantitative

FREQUENCY   See Flicker

                                       High Frequency

FUNGUS TOXINS

Narcotic mushrooms have long been known — some, used by primitive peoples.

Amanita, Russula, Coprinus, are examples of the commoner genera recognized as toxic in one way or another. A Coprinus that is customarily eaten without toxic effects, is reported to be toxic if Subject has taken alcohol at about the same time.

Most fungi have been insufficiently studied, even by mycologists, to allow our determining whether or how they could serve the project. *See also Piule.*

This vast field seems well worth more exploration.

GAS CHAMBERS, AIRTIGHT ROOMS, ETC.

      The possibility of using gas chambers or airtight rooms as a means for surreptitiously rendering a subject unconscious or to cause him to breathe some type of gas which would make the subject either more suggestible or pliable has been long considered. We have felt that this could possibly be done at a specially designed permanent-type installation but the chances of doing it in the normal safe house in the field or in open field conditions appears quite remote. Numerous problems obviously appear such as the preparation of the area, protection of the operator to prevent his being affected by the fumes and inherent dangers such as lethal dose, etc.

      The possibility of using an automobile with the windows closed has been explored but presents certain technical problems most of which are the same as outlined above.

      Deprivation of oxygen, which could be brought about in specially-built rooms, is commented on under Oxygen.

GLUTAMIC ACID   or   GLUTAMIN

See Deprivations (page 2).

A low Glutamic-acid (or Glutamin, a derivative or antecedent form) content in the brain sensitizes to convulsion, of which it may be a competent-producing-cause.

Right now the relationships between Glutamin and epilepsy are being intensively studied by the Public Health at Bethesda. More will be learned of Glutamin metabolism, and the findings stand a good chance of being important to our project.

GRAND MAL   See Convulsion

GANGLION-blocking DRUGS   See Acetylcholin and Cholinesterase

                                         Chlorpromazine

                                         Tetraethylammonium

GASES   See Anesthetic Gases

                                         Carbon Dioxid

                                         Nerve Gases

                                         Oxygen

HEAT

Artificial fever can be produced by certain high-frequency-electrical, and other forms of apparatus used in physical medicine. These means have been neglected in this report; irascibility might be produced, but with little else for a usable mental state, and too expensively.

A persistently hot climate makes for fatiguability and irritability, and seems to increase the body's requirements of Vitamins B_1 and B_2-complex. To some extent it also increases sensitivity to alcohol. Undoubtedly it affects the action of other drugs in one way or another. This reporter has omitted to survey the relevant literature.

HIGH FREQUENCY AND RADAR FIELDS

HIGH FREQUENCY   (see also Iontophoresis, item 2)

Persons working at the level of a highpowered sending antenna have been reported to become dizzy and confused.

      Q.   Could a high-frequency machine of medical type be modified to confuse a Subject in another room (such machines, of old styles no longer permitted, did emit short radio waves)?

RADAR

This radiation confuses flying birds at considerable distances.

      Q.   Can it confuse (and not heat or otherwise injure) a subject, at low power?

141

Project MK-Ultra and Mind Control Technology

Both these means deserve some research--the radar more so than the high frequency--but at a low priority, since confusion is too small a gain to warrant much expense.

HISTAMIN

Shock, similar to Insulin-shock, can be produced by histamin injections. Anxiety may be caused, or aggravated.

Histamin alone seems not useful enough for our purposes. It may have a place if combined with other drugs: to determine which ones, would call for more study than it has been given. Since a barbiturate and an amphetamin in alternation do provide a type of confusion that includes some anxiety and revealing-tendency, an alternation of histamin with anti-histaminics sounds promising.

Further study in this direction would take experimentation too, which could be dangerous. See also Anti-Histaminics.

HUMIDITY	See Relative Humidity
HYOSCINE	See Narcotizing Drug Combinations
(same as Scopolamin)	
HYOSCYAMIN	
HYDERGIN	

This relatively new chemical is derived from ergot (alkaloid). Its patent is held by Sandoz. The action of HYDERGIN is sedative in a general sense and probably would be used against hypertension, anxiety, etc. However, movies show that it very definitely disturbs the unusual motor activity of the Sandoz "waltzing mice" while not affecting sensory perception. It has a very low toxic quality and the lethal danger apparently is also low.

HYPNOSIS

Too extensive a topic for brief synopsis, it will be shortened here to two phases.

1. Hypnotizing an unwilling/subject is apparently unusual but not unheard of. Much depends on subject's susceptibility (not easily assessed beforehand), and operator's skill--especially his ability to shift from one to another method, meeting unexpected obstacles. (See also, UNWITTING SUBJECT).

One principle is certain: the operator says nothing about "sleep." He may be able to promote a subject's suggestibility, by telling him that certain visual phenomena wil occur under given experimental circumstances: e.g., optical illusions, after-images, color-contrasts. The operator must be very familiar with these; and the subject very unfamiliar; the trick is, to claim that the phenomena are suggested to the subject when actually they would occur naturally.

There are means of making any subject more easily hypnotized, before or during the process itself.

   a) A state of mild narcosis, produced by any barbiturate.

   b) A reclining, or at least semi-reclining and comfortable posture.

   c) Deep breathing (a lowered O_2 content of the air would automatically promote this; or it might be suggested, for some cover reason; a metronome helps to hold a rate and also assists by a hypnotizing influence).

HYPOSPRAYS, GASES, AEROSOLS

As early as 1951, experimentation was carried out using the then standard Hypospray instrument as a possible weapon in the ARTICHOKE work. At that time, we felt that this technique had considerable merit. At least it presented the possibility that chemicals could be induced into the human body without noticeable rupture of the skin or wounding and to a large extent painlessly. We requested the Medical Division to explore this further and the medics ultimately gave us a report of a negative nature.

The main difficulty with the Hypospray was that it could not penetrate through clothing and that unless it were carefully applied, it could create bruises or wounds and possibly other complications. Further there did not appear at this time a suitable agent for our purposes as yet developed (intra-muscular injection type).

Our last information was that Squibb was considering the development of super-powerful Hyposprays which, instead of being fired by a spring mechanism as in the common Hypospray, would be fired by a compressed gas which would be much more powerful. We do not have any details on this at the present time.

Similar to the Hypospray, we have long thought that some technique could be devised whereby a gas, aerosol or possibly a dust could be discharged at short range

142

into the face of a person and produce a coma or other desired effect rapidly and quietly. We have experimented with tear-gas pencils and they are effective in closed areas at from six to ten feet. We feel that a gasgun could be designed, shaped like a pencil to discharge gas that might have a coma-producing effect on a given subject. We have not yet been able to find any suitable device and we have as yet no knowledge of a gas, aerosol or dust that fits this use.

INDUCED CURRENT   See Electric Shocks
                                  Electromagnetic Field

INSULIN

By injection, Insulin has several uses outside the treatment of diabetes.

1. It reduces the blood-sugar; a far-enough-reduced blood-sugar lowers the convulsive threshold. Large doses of insulin can eventually lower it enough to produce unconsciousness, finally a convulsion. This procedure is dangerous, and offers no advantage over other means of convulsing when convulsion is desired.

2. In smaller repeated doses over a period of time, Insulin:
   a. Renders anxious neurotics somewhat less so.
   b. Assists in some methods of treatment of drug addiction.
   c. Expedites recovery from chronic illnesses marked by emaciation, or starvation.

3. The effects of Insulin (by injection) + alcohol (by mouth) are uncertain.

Except possibly for Item (3) above, Insulin has little or nothing to offer this project.

INTERNAL EAR DISORDERS   See Equilibrium

INTERRUPTED LIGHT   See Flicker
INTERRUPTED LIGHT +
    INTERRUPTED SOUND   See Interrupted Sound

INTERRUPTED SOUND

Like Interrupted Light, Interrupted Sound also can produce convulsion in a sufficiently sensitized Subject. One loud sound alone, may produce it.

1. To attain this effect of Interrupted Sound in 100% of Subjects, a heavier dose (perhaps too strong) of sensitizing means would be required. That is, a reasonable dose would yield convulsion always after Inter. Light, not quite always after Inter. Sound: while the literature is not so sure as to Sound, as it is for Light, it gives this impression.

2. The Op., as well as other persons in the vicinity, could be less well protected against Sd
Hence Inter. Sound may as well be omitted from consideration as a practicable means.

    INTERRUPTED SOUND + INTERRUPTED LIGHT
    A combination of interruptions of both Sound & Light, might be more effective than either means alone. Either a smaller sensitization, or a shorter exposure, might do.
However, the literature I have read on this point . . .

INTERRUPTED SOUND + INTERRUPTED LIGHT   See Interrupted Sounds (foot of page
INTOXICATION   See Ethyl Alcohol
INTROVERT PERSONALITY   See Subject's Personality

ION EXCHANGE

Ion-exchange resins (used commercially to soften water) have been suggested for use in electrolyte disturbances; that is, when the blood-sodium and blood-potassium balance is disordered as in Méniere's Disease (severe attacks of dizziness, sometimes with convulsion).

However, it appeared that resins for such a purpose as upsetting electrolyte balances, would be too bulky, unappetizing and probably nauseating.

The ion-exchange-resin notion was dropped.

See POTASSIUM, & ELECTROLYTES.

IONS   See Ion-Exchange
               also Iontophoresis

IONTOPHORESIS (or IONIC GALVANISM)

A galvanic current can introduce the ions of soluble substances into body tissues.

1. If electrodes are applied to one hand for polygraph determination of the psychogalvanic current — iontophoresis electrodes might be applied to another limb. THIS IS PURE SPECULATION on my part; did not find it alluded to; it may have been explored and discarded. Such a circuit might inevitably interfere with the others.

2. Bombarding an area of the brain with ions by iontophoresis, or with molecules by a high frequency current, appears to be prevented by the skull's impermeability.

The cocain ion of a dissolved cocain salt, will penetrate the skin from the positive pole. Ordinarily it will not pass deeply enough to enter the blood-stream and so produce a generalized effect. Cocain would also give a strong and undesirable local effect.

Only very powerful drugs could be so administered, since so little (if any) could be expected to enter the circulation; and the S. would be no more unwitting than if very small doses had been given disguised by mouth. However, if gotten into the circulation at all, a smaller dose (than that by mouth) would be effective, and much more rapidly. It might prove possible so to use an Antimetabolite, or a drug to disturb the cholin-cholinesterase balance: either one aimed at confusing, or sensitizing to convulsion. More study, and vast experimentation, would be necessary; probably without success.

ISONIAZID

Isoniazid can be given orally, or by injection, to sensitize a subject to convulsion; specifically, enough so that Flicker (which see) will convulse. (See also Unwitting Subject)

However, the range of effective dosage is great (from 22 to 35 mgm. per kilogram of body weight); even at top dosage, an occasional subject will not convulse under flickering light. Also, these large sensitizing doses are nauseating, and definitely toxic.
It is recommended that this drug be given no further consideration in the project.

K   See Potassium
                  Electrolytes

LABYRINTH DISORDERS   See Equilibrium

Laughing Gas   See Anesthetic Gases

Light, Colored   See Colors

Light, Flickering   See Flicker
    Interrupted

Lobectomy   See Lobotomy

LOBOTOMY and Related Operations   See AMNESIA

The problem of disposal of subjects is constantly present in intelligence operations. Even with fully cooperative subjects the matter is simple but where disposal involves totally unwilling subjects or subjects who cannot be trusted, the problem is complex, expensive and very difficult. Since disposal does not mean shooting a subject by our standards we are faced with at least three serious issues:

    1) Placing the subject somewhere (confinement, re-settlement).
    2) Insuring his adherence to our views and/or
    3) Preventing his giving away our secrets.

If by some means we could create a perfect and thoroughly controlled amnesia, the matter would be simplified but amnesia is not certain and cannot be guaranteed. Because of this a number of individuals who are fully cognizant of the disposal problem, suggested that LOBOTOMY or one of the related operations might be the answer or at least a partial solution. It was argued that in general a lobotomy would create a person "who no longer cared," who had lost initiative and drive, whose allegiance to ideal or motivating factors no longer existed and who would probably have, if not complete amnesia at least a fuzzy or spotty memory for recent and past events. It was also agreed that certain lobotomy types of operations were simple, quickly performed and not too dangerous.

The A group examined the idea of LOBOTOMY for our purposes and are totally agreed that this technique has no place in our operations for the following reasons:

    1) It is inhumane.

    2) It is against all concepts of "fairplay" and the American way of life and it could never be officially sanctioned or supported.

    3) Its use, if discovered, would be a terrible propaganda weapon against us -- it would wreck our nation's prestige--it would tend to destroy the effectiveness of the Agency.

    4) It is extremely dangerous
        a) Surgical risk is great
        b) Brain damage is extensive
        c) It could, if faulty, produce a "vegetable."

    5) It requires hospitalization, surgical ability, proper anesthesia.

    6) It is doubted if any American surgeon could be found to perform the operation for the above purposes.

7) It leaves a telltale scar.

8) It would invite horrible reprisals.

(See also following comments on LOBOTOMY by

LOBOTOMY

Lobotomy of a Subject would produce several days of a gradually recovering confusion (#8). Against its use are: (a) the ordinary surgical risks; (b) the leaving
of a scar; (c) the permanent brain-injury.

The simplest type--"transorbital lobotomy" or the "ice-pick operation"--involves
little (a) or (b), but appreciable (c).

permanently   ("14), and to reduce anxiety (# 1).
Lobotomy operations tend/to "tame" a violent Subject/ In psychiatric practice, he
is usually a violent psychopathic-personality; or an insane or near-insane person
with a compulsion toward homicide or suicide.

A continuing check of the literature is desirable, as to three substitutes for
lobotomy:

i) A so-called "chemical lobotomy," viz., a taming but of temporary
    duration. See Rauwolfia, and Chlorpromazine.

    If one or more small regions in brain or brain-stem can be
    identified, whose stimulation would produce a temporary taming,
    then:

ii) A non-toxic drug may be found, by radioactive-tracer techniques,
    that will be attracted to such an area, and so produce a taming
    that can last for some time. See Amygdaloid Nucleus; also,
    Temporal Lobe.

iii) Ultrasonics, or some other radiating energy, may be developed
     to give a physical stimulus to such an area without injury. At
     present, Ultrasonics can produce a surgical-type (permanent)
     lobotomy; but the skull must be opened to apply it. See
     Ultrasonics.

LOWERING, CONVULSIVE THRESHOLD   See Convulsive Threshold Lowered

LSD25

Of this ergot-derivative or synthetic equivalent, 40 to 60 gamma or an even smaller
single dose, is effective by mouth and practically tasteless. The effects resemble,
also differ from, those seen in some temporal lobe (of brain) disorders; and those
caused by Mescalin, Marijuana, Bufotenin, bulbocapnin, and amphetamins — these in an
approximate descending order of similarities.

For the purposes of interrogation, one of LSD25's most important features is its tiny
dose. (See Unwitting Subject). It produces very marked emotional instability, of
which both the excitements and the depressions may prove more hindrance than help.
There is little, or much/confusion, but no amnesia after recovery.

Suggestibility increases little if at all. Some Subjects have spontaneously undergone
regression to childhood or youth, somewhat like that which is suggestible under hypnosis.
There are many distortions of time, place, and person, in all Subjects. Hallucinations
may be pleasing, or terrifying/but not especially helpful to an Operator. During the
several hours or day that the effects remain prominent, there may or may not be periods
marked by a strong revealing-tendency.

An LSD25 Subject tends to behave like a hebephrenic schizophrenic ; a Mescalin S., and
a Bulbocapnin S. to a greater or less extent (according to the bulbocapnin dose),
behaves like a catatonic schizophrenic.

LSD25 lowers the convulsive threshold; may occasionally convulse, as with larger doses.

At the moment, no known antidote is available; Serotonin may prove to be one.

Further study of LSD25 is strongly recommended.

MAGNESIUM	See Electrolytes
MAREZINE	See Chlorpromazine
MARIJUANA	See Unwitting Subject
MEANS, Choice of	See Subject's Personality
Meniere's Disease	See Potassium
Mephenesin	See Myanesin

MESCALIN

Mescalin, or Peyote, derived from a cactus, produces an artificial catatonic schizophrenia. (See LSD25; and Bulbocapnin). It can be given by mouth.

Compared with LSD25 effects, Mescalin causes more pronounced hallucinations,

more worsened critical judgment,
less pronounced euphoria (elation),
more intense experience of split personality,
common (instead of rare) persecutory and/or
grandiose delusions.

Color sensations are brilliant, but colors change and are misplaced, and may give other sensations, e.g., a color may give the sensation of something tasted, or heard. As with LSD25, space, time, and the body-scheme, are distorted.

Mescalin-symptoms have been terminated with Sodium Succinate by mouth.

Given by itself, Mescalin seems to offer Interrogation less assistance than does LSD25. However, its literature should not be neglected.

Of greater interest is the possibility of combining Mescalin with some potato-plant-family drug. Mescalin + stramonium, it is reported, has caused criminals to confess. This lead is well worth following.

METHEDRIN   See Amphetamins
                   Unwitting Subject

METHYLPENTYNOL   See Oblivon

METRAZOL
See Unwitting Subject.

Metrazol by mouth in a heavy dose (say between 700 x 1000 mgm.) will give most Subject dizziness and nausea along with sensitization. Theoretically, the nausea might be avoided by a previous oral dose of Chlorpromazine for its anti-nausea effect; however, this drug combination I have not seen in the literature, and — until tried and found safe — it must be considered dangerous, since both Metrazol and Chlorpromazine would affect the heart. Metrazol in a smaller dose, given rapidly by intravenous injection, will sensitize most Subjects enough for flicker to convulse them. Azozol is surer, can sensitize all Subjects

A larger dose of Metrazol intravenously will convulse many Subjects forthwith, without the added means of Flicker. However, a second injection may be required (if flicker is not to be added), and even this may not convulse. These non-convulsing large doses do cause a terrifying anxiety and put considerable strain on the heart. If anxiety is the mental state desired; or else, convulsion: it would seem wiser to use a means that will definitely produce the one, and a different means to produce the other.

MIDDLE EAR DISORDERS

When the Eustachian tube (connected with the middle ear) of one or both sides, is blocked — say by a mild inflammation — some psychological effect is expected. For a few days at least, until he becomes used to it or its intensity tends to lessen, the Subject is rendered irritable, sometimes dizzy.

This finding is probably useless to the project.

Motion Picture Screen   21 November 1955

Screen Hypnosis
Dr. Med Hans Sutermeister

A reduction of alpha amplitudes is a symptom of general reduction in cortical activity.

Psychologically the general lowering of consciousness during the picture facilitates the phenomenon of identification and suggestion as in hypnosis.

Cohen-Séat, Gastaut, Bert: Modification de l'EEG pendant la projection cinematographique, Revue de Filmologie, V, 16, 3, Paris 1954

Cohen-Séat, Faure:Retentissement du "fait filmique" sur les rhythmes bioelectriques du cerveau. Rev de Filmol. V, 16, 7, Paris, 1954

Gastaut: Effects psychologiques, somatiques et electro-encephalographiques du stimulus lumineux intermittent rhythmique. Rev. de Filmol. II, 7/8, 215, Paris, 1951

Heuyer, Cohen-Séat, Lebovici: Note sur l'electroencephalographic pendant la projection cinematographique chez des adolescents inadaptes. Rev. de Filmol, V, 16, 51, Paris, 1954.

Kluge, Friedel: Ueber die Einwirkung einformiger akustischer Reize auf den Funktionszustand des Hirns. Zeitschrift fuer Psychother und mediz. Psychol.

1953, 5, 212, Stullgort, 1953

Pflanz, Einfluss rhythmischer Sinnenreize auf den Organismus. Deutscher medizinische Wochenschrift, 1953, 23/24, 579

Sutermeister: Film and Mental Health. Ges. N. Wohlf. Orell-Fussli, Zurich 1950, 2, 249. Film und Psychogiene, Praxis, 1955, 15, 328.

British Journal of Medical Hypnotism, Vol. 7, No. 1, Autumn 1955

MORPHINE	See Ethyl Alcohol
MOTION SICKNESS	See Equilibrium
MUSHROOMS	See Fungus Toxins

Myanesin

Myanesin (Mephenesin, Tolserol, & other synonyms) by mouth, reduces anxiety mildly. To produce only this effect, its usefulness seems limited.

Possibly it could be used in connection with some other means, advantageously. The literature might be further searched; more fruitful, perhaps, than searching further for a similar usefulness of Obliven, or Tetraethylammonium.

Na	See Electrolytes

NARCO-ANALYSIS
See Narcotizing Drug Combinations, & Twilight Sleep.

(here distinguished as Narco-Analysis)

No conclusion has been reached here, on whether a barbiturate + an amphetamin/is generally superior to a belladonna derivative (or relative) + an opiate. I am inclined to favor the former; possibly because of some psychiatric experience with it, and none with the scopolamin/morphin team.

Evidence favors one conclusion, that barbiturate + amphetamin is superior to a barbiturate alone. In some circumstances, an amphetamin alone would be much more expeditious, since the Operator starts with the Subject as is, without having to put him first to sleep. Another comment; since the amphetamins Dexedrin and Methedrin are strong antagonists to any barbiturate, one must not give his amphetamin in so strong a dose as wholly to destroy the barbiturate effect. He might as well have omitted the sleep-producing drug altogether — unless sleep was brought into the picture for some other reason. Dexedrin or Methedrin can equally well be used to lift a S. moderately out of an alcoholic narcosis. See Amphetamins.

NARCOSIS	See Oxygen
	Narcotizing Drug Combinations
NARCOTICS	See Narcotizing Drug Combinations

NARCOTIZING DRUG COMBINATIONS
Our best-known chemical means can conveniently, if rather arbitrarily, be classed as:
(1) "Twilight Sleep", and (2) "Narco-Analysis", which see. See also individual special psychiatric drugs like LSD25, Mescalin, Marijuana, Bulbocapnin, Cocain, &c., which are arbitrarily left outside these two classes. See also Anesthetic Gases, similarly handled.

(1) A "potato-family" drug + an analgesic drug.
Traditionally, scopolamin + morphin.
Numerous combinations of belladonna or its other derivatives (atropin, hyoscyamin, &c), or relatives (stramonium; syntropan); + other opiates (heroin, &c), are used.

Since new combinations, and new applications of old ones, are frequently described, a constant check of the considerable literature should be maintained on narcotic drugs — the above, and others as they appear.

See "Twilight Sleep".

(2) A hypnotic (sleep-producing, not hypnotizing) drug + a stimulant (which could produce an epileptiform convulsion, if given in a dose much larger than used in this connection). For the mental states produced, see Narcoanalysis.
Traditionally, a barbiturate + an amphetamin.
In psychiatric medicine, the barbiturate may oftener be used alone; for our purposes, adding the amphetamin amplifies the take without over-complicating the procedure.

By injection: Sodium Amytal (or Pentothal, faster-acting but less safe). Or by mouth: Seconal or other barbiturate, or the related Chloral (slightly less safe). Methedrin or Dexedrin, to arouse (partially) the then sleeping Subject.

NATURAL POISONS	See Plant, Fungus
	Bacterial Toxins
	Animal

Project MK-Ultra and Mind Control Technology

NERVE GASES

The toxicity of Parathione, "DFP", "TEPP", &c., derives chiefly from their destruction of Cholinesterase, and so allowing Acetylcholin to accumulate and halt certain essential processes in the body economy.

So far as this reporter has searched, he has not yet found a use for Nerve Gases in Interrogation. Search in other directions should be more productive.

NICOTIN	See Ethyl Alcohol
(i.e.,Tobacco, not Nicotinic Acid)	
Nicotinic Acid	See Deprivations (p.2, Niacin)
NITROGEN	See Atmospheric Pressure
NITROGEN NARCOSIS	See Oxygen
NITROUS OXID	See Anesthetic Gases
NOVOCAINE	See Iontophoresis
NUCLEUS	See Amygdaloid Nucleus

Oblivon

Either Oblivon (Methylpentynol), or Tetraethylammonium chlorid, in small dosage by mouth, will reduce anxiety. Effect is relatively mild.

Since anxiety-reduction alone seems to have limited usefulness, further search of the literature in this connection seems unwarranted at the moment.

ODORS

Odors give emotional responses; but this reporter has not hit upon one that could be usefully adapted to our purposes.

Among third-degree methods, terror has been produced by exposing the Subject, Operator being masked, to a harmless odor (e.g., geranium) simulating the smell of a lethal gas.

OPIATE	see Ethyl Alcohol
	Sedative-Deprivations
	Twilight Sleep
	Narcotizing Drug Combinations

OXYGEN

See Deprivations (foot of page 3)

Oxygen comprises about 21% of the air at sea-level. A reduction of the concentration to about half-normal (12.5 to 11.5 %), early affects the memory — before it is as low as 12.5%. With less O_2 than that, judgment & concentration are worsened, while elation & over-talkativeness, irritability and a lack of self-criticism, appear. When the O_2 is around 11.5% or below, emotional outbursts are added. This progression of symptoms goes on to some degree with the passage of time, even if the O_2 falls little below 12.5%. As with Carbon Dioxid (which see), it is a question of how tight a room, and how close a measurement of gas, would be needed. Oxygen might well take more fine detail in its use, than would CO_2, but it would produce a wider range of desirable mental states. Again the Q, how to protect the Op. from the same states: this I do not know either.

Nitrogen Narcosis.

Six % O_2 + 94% N_2 causes confusion, then unconsciousness. This finding accounts for the "Nitrogen Narcosis" of "skin-divers" (who wear a tank, not a suit); they use up too much of their O_2 before they are aware of its lack.

It sounds as though there was too narrow a safety-margin here, for our use. I am too un-informed to have an opinion as to this.

PAIN	See Dolitrone
PANAEOLUS	See Piule
	Fungus Toxins
PENTYLENETETRAZOL	See Metrazol
PERSONALITY OF SUBJECT	See Subject's Personality
PERVITIN	See Amphetamins
PEYOTE	See Mescalin
PETITE MAL	See Unconsciousness
PHYSICAL ENVIRONMENT	See Deprivations
PIULE	
(not Peyote)	

If correctly read, Piule is a Datura (a potato-family or belladonna-group, member), and its toxic principle is almost or quite the same as that of the fungus Panaeolus.

Whether superior or inferior to other belladonna relatives, for interrogation purposes, is unknown to me. Species of Panaeolus are very common, and their toxins might well repay investigation.

PLANT TOXINS

Narcotic properties have been ascribed to hundreds, perhaps thousands, of plants, vines, shrubs & trees. A small 1933 volume mentions nearly a hundred growing in the Pacific Coast region alone.

Other sources describe many plants in use by primitive peoples for narcotic purposes. A few have been noted individually in this card file. Most were not followed through. The field as a whole deserves far more attention than this reporter has given it. It is also probable that much of the literature, while describing everything else about a plant, will have little to say of its toxicology. Much experimentation is needed.

POISINS, NATURAL   See Fungus
                              Bacterial   Toxins
                              Animal
                              Plant

POTASSIUM.

See also Potassium Chlorate.

                               with a low   (low blood-potassium)

Low blood-potassium is associated/convulsive threshold; and it/is characteristic of Menière's Disease with its severe attacks of dizziness and sometimes convulsions. But " " cannot be simulated by merely reducing the blood-potassium; besides, such a reduction would be very hard to control, and not easy to measure, and could progress to a fatality.

If a low blood-potassium should prove useful in any other way, it can be readily obtained — with the reservations already noted — by administering Desoxycorticosterone.

Like Potassium Chlorate (which see), the blood-potassium seems worth no more attention.

POTASSIUM CHLORATE

It has been claimed that this chemical, added to smoking tobacco, gave a narcotic-like effect. Not having tried to track this down, I do not know the mechanism or the effects, and whether referable to the K or the ClO_3 ions.

However, since Chlorate is fairly toxic, it seemed unprofitable to study it farther.

"POTATO-FAMILY" Drugs   See Narcotizing Drug Combinations

 PRESSURE   See Atmospheric Pressure
                                Carotid Sinus Pressure

 PROCAINE   See Iontophoresis
                                Cocain

PROPHYLAXIS AGAINST REVEALING

Studies of how to encourage a revealing-tendency, engender notions of how to discourage.

1. Any enduring boost of a friendly agent's resistance to interrogation, would be valuable. Long-lasting antidotes to drugging may be available — this reporter has not found them. Required would be substances that the body could store (immobilize) in liver, muscle, bone , &c., and use (mobilize) on demand.

(a) NEBULOUS & (Calcium can be stored in bone; whether it could (& would) have usefulness
    SPECULATIVE (beyond a possible mild prophylaxis against anxiety, is unknown to me
               (Vitamin C, if it could be rendered storable by some combination, might tend
               (to postpone fatigue (alone, it is notoriously non-storable).
               (Serotonin, intensively studied recently by physiologists, may be promising.

(b) Post-hypnotic Suggestion, or some further development of Conditioning & Deconditioning, are the approaches that look most productive at this time.

2. The captured unfriendly agent may have been well prepared by some such means. How well prepared, would be hard to say. Some drugs' influence could be detected by electro-encephalography; offhand, this sounds profitless, as too little seems known about it.

Of the above, experiment with 1(b) rates a/good priority; the rest, a low one — or no study at all, except of Serotonin.

    PYRIDOXIN   See Vitamin B6
                            Deprivations

    QUANTITATIVE FOOD DEPRIVATIONS   See Deprivation of Food, Quantitative
    QUATERNARY AMMONIUM   See Tetraethylammonium
    RADAR   See High Frequency

RADIANT ENERGY,
 Unidentified.

Various electric currents, ultrasonics, &c., are noted elsewhere in this file. It is
also possible that some newer form of radiant energy, some atomic particles, could be
aimed at sleep centers in the brain , or at brain centers that inhibit the waking state.
Sudden sleeping might be produced in this way, with an unwitting subject if the apparatus
were worked from another room.
This reporter admits that he has not found a hypothetical "sleep ray" in the literature.
He believes it either is, or will is, there. It would be so valuable that more
searching is highly recommended. Certainly there are sleep-centers in the brain.

RAISING CONVULSIVE THRESHOLD   See Convulsive Threshold Raised
RAUDIXIN   See Rauwolfia

RAUWOLFIA

Raudixin (Squibb) and Serpasil (CIBA) are available and give approximately equivalent effects (but the dosages are different).

The drug "tames" the subject, producing essentially an under-anxiety (col. #1),
along with some reduction of bloodpressure; notably, without drowsiness.

Given three times daily, it becomes effective gradually after several days.

One intravenous injection of Serpasil will produce tranquillity, with very
little or no drowsiness, after 30 or 40 minutes and lasting several hours.

Subject under strong Rauwolfia influence is so unemotional and unresponsive to
anxiety-provoking stimuli, that he would be expected to show nothing diagnostic
on the polygraph.

It is likely that a dosage can be arrived at, to reduce anxiety enough and not
too much for P.G. (ambulatory patients under daily oral doses of Rauwolfia carry
 on their business normally and do react appropriately--though less vigorously--
to anxiety-producing stimuli).

Experimentation with this drug is strongly recommended. It is so non-toxic that
anyone should be willing to play guineapig.

 Rauwolfia + amphetamin has been tried; should be compared with barbiturate + amphetamin.
Rauwolfia followed by enough alcohol to mildly intoxicate, may produce the symptom of "per-
severation" — S. says the same thing over & over again. This would be disadvantageous.

Rauwolfia alone, lately reported to cause bizarre dreams: might be an advantageous property.

Recall   21 November 1955

      Normal recall is more effective than hypnotic recall in the case of
nonsense material, but hypnotic recall is greater than 50% more effective
than normal recall in the case of poetry, and over eighty percent more
effective in the case of motion picture screens.

      Light trances (may be) more favorable for hypermnesia than deeper hypnosis,
at least for recent material.

      Items learned under anxiety producing conditions are normally less well
recalled than those learned without anxiety. But this difference is eliminated
under hypnosis.

      All the above refers to hypnotic recall of material learned in the normal,
nonhypnotic state.

                                           Hypnodynamic
                                           Psychology
                                           by Milton V. Kline
                                           The Julian Press, 1955

RELATIVE HUMIDITY
   I. Low
      (a) It is probable that a low relative humidity of the atmosphere (30% or
           below), tends to lower the convulsive threshold of persons in it.
           That is, means producing a convulsion will do so on shorter exposure,
           or in small doses.
      (b) A low relative humidity tends to provoke irascibility.
           (a) might be advantageous, (b) disadvantageous.
Since an artificially controlled humidity would require an oxygen-chamber type
of installation, it seems not worthwhile.
However, the effects of a naturally occurring very low (say 10%) relative humidity--
on both subjects and operator--should be kept in mind. It is possible that an
operator could be protected from becoming irascible, by a taming drug (Rauwolfia).

II. High

When degradation is included in brain-washing, excessive dampness is commonly included in the dirty environment. Wetness add to discomfort and probably reduces resistance to respiratory illness.

RESINS   See Ion-Exchange
RUBBER ROOM   See Vibration
RUSSULA EMETICA   See Fungus Toxins
RESERPINE   See Rauwolfia
SALICYLATES   See Aspirin
SCENTS   See Odors
SCOPOLAMIN   See Twilight Sleep
                       Narcotizing Drug Combinations
SECONAL   See Narcoanalysis
                       Unwitting Subject

SEDATIVE DEPRIVATIONS

When a Subject is addicted to the long-term use of a sedative (probably of any type), e.g., Alcohol, Chloral, Barbiturate, Opiate, and is suddenly and wholly deprived of his drug, then within several hours or a day he will have an epileptiform convulsion — perhaps a series of convulsions.

This fact might be put to use, with a known alcoholic Subject, if the Operator were prepared to take advantage of the convulsion whenever it occurred. Whether a post-convulsion confusion so procured would last longer, show more revealing tendency, or be more rarely complicated by a disturbing excitement, than is an epileptiform convulsion produced by more direct and immediate means, is uncertain.

SENSITIZING TO CONVULSION (i.e., a considerable Lowering of the Convulsive Threshold) (1

A sure and powerful means of sensitizing-to-convulsion (#9) is an intravenous injection of Metrazol or equivalent.

There are also various less potent means.

Question: could several such be combined advantageously?
           would their effects be additive, and so more potent?
           would certain ones tend to neutralize others, and so defeat the
              purpose of combination?

Further study seems worthwhile.

Next page gives table of various Means which produce sensitivity to convulsion (#9).

Theoretically, a large enough dose of most such means would go on to produce convulsion (#12).

Practically: some can be so used;
              others cannot be, since a convulsion-producing dose is too large,
                 i.e., toxic in other respects.

See itemized Means for details.

Some such means produce a possibly-useful confusion (# 6), preceding or replacing #12.

SENSITIZING TO CONVULSION

Literature States, OR Suggests, that reasonable doses of these Means are sensitizing:

(2

(rather fast)				(rather slow)	
States	Suggests	This list is not exhaustive; more study is necessary.	States	Suggests	
Lowered bloodsugar				Lowered total blood-electrolytes	
Insulin				Lowered blood-magnesium	
				Raised blood-potassium	
Scopolamin					
Hashish				Cortisone	
Mescalin			Sudden deprivation of an accustomed *strong* sedative, as opiate, alcohol, barbiturate	Sudden deprivation of certain vitamins or amino-acids	
LSD-25					
Amphetamins				Certain antimetabolites	
Metrazol				Mild deprivation of O_2	
Isoniazid					
Loss of CO_2					
Electronarcosis					

Project MK-Ultra and Mind Control Technology

SEROTONIN

Serotonin is a hormone derived from body tissues, lately publicized as a "sanity hormone". LS025 (which see) acts somewhat like an antimetabolite toward Serotonin; therefore the latter, possibly in some combination not yet discovered, may be useful in developing an antidote to LS025.
Further study of this substance' properties is strongly recommended.

SERPASIL	See Rauwolfia
SHOCKS, ELECTRIC	See Electric Shocks
	Conditioning
SINUS PRESSURE, Carotid	See Carotid Sinus Pressure
SLEEP	See Anesthetic Gases
	Electric Shocks
	Electro-narcosis
	Hypnosis
	Narco-analysis
	Radiant Energy
	Twilight Sleep
SMELL	See Odors
SODIUMA	See Electrolytes
SOUND, INTERRUPTED	See Interrupted Sound
STARVATION	See Brainwashing
	Deprivation of Food, Quantitative
	Drprivations

Sleep-atropine

We have found in our own research that if we inject atropine followed within thirty minutes by prostigmine and then finally acetylcholine, we produce in normals an increase in sleep both subjectively and objectively as measured with the electroencephalogram. - page 11

> Atropine 3 mgm 1-M
> 30 mins. later give
> Prostigmine SO_4 2 mgm 1-M
> 15 mins. later give
> Acetylcholine 200 mgm 1-V

Atropine was given to block the muscarine activity of acetylcholine while leaving its nicotinic activity untouched, and to protect the subject against acetylcholine induced cardiac arrhythmias. Atropine also inhibits acetylcholine esterase and thus elevates parasympathetic activity. Prostigmine markedly inhibits esterase. Acetylcholine was given to produce a sudden boost in parasympathetic activity.... after the injection of the acetylcholine there was a sudden production of sleep and fatigue in two of three normal subjects followed by sleep....the induction of high parasympathetic nicotinic activity by means of atropine, prostigmine and acetylcholine appears to decrease the level of consciousness...The change in the level of consciousness in normals was manifested by an increase in fatigue, in a desire to sleep, and a decrease in insight. - page 46

> 85% of normals show an increase in systolic pressure after atropine
> 81% of acute schizos show a decrease in   "   "   "
> 63% of chronic schizos " "   "   "   "   "   "

Schizophrenia Research in Saskatchewan
Project 607-5-135 (Three-Year Report)
Project 607-7-12 and 607-5-135 (1954 Annual Report)

SOUND (General Comments)

It appears to be well established that harmonious sound (music) in certain industrial areas has markedly increased productive rates. Sound experts have told us that sound in the form of music or otherwise could also increase accidents, lower output and quite probably disrupt work almost completely or bring about a strike. Mood music or background music is a commercial reality at present. Very intense sound or highly distracting sounds promote anxiety, nervous tension, instability and if carried to extremes can cause physical damage. Whether or not sound can be used in the A techniques is unknown but the effects of sounds (within or above or below the human range) might be a worthwhile subject for advanced study although cost would probably be high.

We believe that monotonous sounds have somewhat of a hypnotic effect. We have reports of psychiatrists using slowly timed metronomes to assist in hypnotic induction. The effects of drums or tom-toms may be along these lines. One specialist in accoustics believes that sleep could be induced by sound.

There is some information available that high-pitched sounds, generated continuously in a confined area tend to lower the resistance to suggestion or possibly have a seda-

152

tive quality. This information is not confirmed by acceptable authority. It could, however, be fairly easily tested.

STRAMONIUM.

Mixture of alkaloids, chiefly Scopolamin (which see) and Atropin.

See also: Narcotizing Drug Combinations

SUBJECT'S PERSONALITY   (:

The out-dated typing of persons as Introvert & Extrovert, while oversimplified, is useful.

Roughly, the Introvert is the lean thinker, self-absorbed & self-critical, interested in fine detail. The Extrovert is the better-fed doer, the outgoing friendly fellow with high self-confidence and low opinion of fine detail. The Average man has some introvert traits, some extravert, and some indistinguishable.

More exact — and more complicated — is a three-way instead of a two-way scheme. Again roughly, it describes cerebral, visceral, and muscular types: several such classifications.

For our purposes, the INTROVERT-EXTRAVERT classification will do.

Introvert Types	Extravert Types
tend to be:	
1. Better able to pursue two ideas or purposes at one time.	1. More one-track-minded.
2. Less easily diagnosed as to emotional feelings — emotions are more mixed, & less openly expressed.	2. More consistent in emotions — i.e., mo whole-heartedly nonchalant, fearful, angry, &c, at any one time.
3. More compulsive — i.e., more determined in a narrow course of action, and less able to shift promptly & consistently to a different and more expedient course.	3. More responsive to the Operator's mood.
4. Probably more responsive to some drugs — a moot point. Certainly not true for all drugs.	4. More easily hypnotized.
5. More interested in tobacco.	5. More interested in food.

SUBJECT'S PERSONALITY   (2

There is plenty of literature that would be applicable in suiting Means to Personality — the Subject's, and also the Op.'s. This reporter has not studied it closely enough to add further suggestions to the page preceding.

Experienced Operators learn by practice what Means are the more effective for a given S. Their rough appraisal will be more useful than the elaborations of a formal assessment. Corrections of the moment, to vary a Means or go on to another one, may be required. Generally, heavier and older Subjects take higher doses of drugs for effectiveness. Chronic alcoholics require heavier doses of sleep-producing drugs to attain sleep. To a S. already under the influence of alcohol, other drugs' addition must regulated accordingly (those that then become more powerful or dangerous, are referred to else- where in these cards).

Further study of the suiting of Means to S's Personality, is recommended.

    "   "   " combinations of other drugs with alcohol, "   "   more strongly.

Personality is referred to also under Adrenalin (which see)

SURGICAL LOBOTOMY   See Lobotomy

Tetraethylammonium

Either Oblivon (Methylpentynol), or Tetraethylammonium chlorid, in small dosage, by mouth, will reduce anxiety. Effect is relatively mild.

Since anxiety-reduction alone seems to have limited usefulness, further search of the literature in this connection seems unwarranted at the moment.

TETRAHYDROCANNABINOL   See Unwitting Subject

THORAZINE   See Chlorpromazine

THRESHOLD   See Convulsive Threshold Lowered
                         Convulsive Threshold Raised

TOBACCO
        (which see)

1. Nicotin is not a Means (to produce a Mental State), although it may produce one that is undesirable, viz.: it heightens the subjective sensations of alcoholic intoxication, making a Subject feel more drunk than he is. We would prefer him to feel less drunk.

2. Tobacco is noted here as a vehicle for other Means:

    a) for LSD25. (See Unwitting Subject)

    b) for Potassium Chlorate (which see).

TRACER TECHNIQUES

The use of certain types of liquids and solids which can be traced in their passage through the human body is well known. We have been advised that either at the Massachusetts General Hospital or in one of the Harvard units that there was a very advanced unit being developed for the tracing of radio-active material throughout the human body and particularly in the brain. It is also believed that advanced work along these lines has been done at Mayo and Johns Hopkins. Some of the large drug and chemical manufacturing companies are also working in this field.

We have received information from competent people that almost any element can be made "active" in some way or another and its passage throughout the body and to the brain can be observed.

Our information concerning the equipment to conduct tracer tests is to the effect that the equipment is bulky and quite. expensive.

Along these lines, several of our most important consults have constantly urged exploration of the tracer techniques as a method of advancing ARTICHOKE studies.

TWILIGHT SLEEP

See Narcotizing Drug Combinations, & Narco-Analysis.

No conclusion has been reached here, on whether a barbiturate + an ur hetamin is generally superior to a belladonna derivative or relative + an opiate. I am inclined to favor the former; possibly because of some psychiatric experience with it, and none with the scopolamin/erehin team.

Besides the latter, stramonium with morphin; or, either stramonium or scopolamin with heroin: the less familiar combinations like these should of course be first sought out in the literature. Piule (which see) might be tried.

Most important would be, to leave out the opiate — provided the authorities say nothing against this plan. Using the opiate and omitting the belladonna, would certainly be far less useful than the other way around; this I would recommend against.

Omitting the opiate and using the scopolamin, has another variant recommended in the literature: instead of scopolamin alone, one authority (one whose report I can take at par) used scopochloralose with most satisfactory results of interrogation.

ULTRASONICS

Two windows, each an inch in diameter, must be cut through the top of the skull. An applicator cup that transmits the ultrasonic beam, is placed on the membrance that covers the brain. The beam of high intensity ultra-sound waves (far beyond the range of hearing), is aimed and concentrated through lenses: direct, 5 min.; then sweeping, 7 min. A lobotomy (which see) effect is obtained, resembling a localized concussion of the frontal lobes.

Though improbable, it is possible that a temporal approach (instead of the present vertical approach) will eventually be devised without the cutting of a hole in the skull. Now, and then too, some of the lobotomy-effect is temporary, some permanent. Modifications in techniques that use Ultrasonic energy should be followed for our purposes. It may be that not only frontal lobes, but temporal lobes, amygdaloid nuclei, sleep-centers, etc., can eventually be usefully stimulated without being destroyed, by Ultrasonics.

UNWITTING SUBJECTS

The problem of how to effect control of a subject by the use of hypnosis or chemicals or a combination thereof, without the subject being aware that he is being approached (actuated), is one of the most interesting and complex problems studied by the ARTICHOKE group. This approach could (can) be made through any of the following techniques:

    a) The subject who is brought under H control by the use of the indirect techniques (relax-rest or possibly monotonous sounds, etc.).
    b) The subject who falls under H control by accident.
    c) Use of "medical cover" for:
        1) Narco-interrogation and control;
        2) Narco-hypnotic interrogation and control.
    d) Use of surreptitious agents
        1) Concealable chemicals
        2) Odorless gases or aerosols

    3) Dusts
    4) Possible deprivation of oxygen or food
  e) By-products of medical treatment
    1) Shock therapy
    2) Medical pre-conditioning with chemicals, etc.
    3) Medical treatment for illness or accident
    4) Psycho-analysis or psycho-therapy

Certain comments can be made in connection with the above categories:

a) The A group has experimentally placed a great number of individuals under hypnosis by the indirect technique but it is doubted if this would apply to hardcore-agent types done on individual basis although it is possible that it might be done disguised as some type of group activity or entertainment.

b) In the A experimentation, we have noted a number of people who have been placed in hypnotic trances by accident. Again it is doubted if this could be done directly against a hardcore or intelligent type. It might be done through some type of group activity or entertainment. For the record, it should be noted that this has not yet been attempted against personnel of interest to us from an operations point of view.

c) At the present time, the use of a carefully laid on medical cover to obtain either a narco-interrogation or narco-hypnotic interrogation appears to be the best weapon presently available. It is not necessary to go into detail as to how this is done but experience indicates it is our best technique.

d) Always linked to the problem of the unwitting subject is the technique of giving a chemical in any form to the subject without his knowledge. Many gadgets and ideas have been considered. Micropellets, substances that can be concealed in common liquids, odorless gases, electric currents, magnetic currents, dusts, aerosols, etc., but each one of these presents a difficult problem. At present, the closest approach appears to be a potent, tasteless, odorless chemical such as LSD but at the present time the value of these chemicals in interrogation or control work is very, very uncertain.

It seems pertinent to comment that the ARTICHOKE group feels that by depriving subjects of food over a considerable period of time, the will to resist can gradually be worn down. This appears to be part of the Communist brainwashing technique which we have been able to observe from our examination of the P.O.W.'s in Korea. The A group feels that food deprivation and possibly oxygen deprivation if carried on over a long period of time might be valuable in these techniques, but this would call for extensive research and in the case of oxygen deprivation specially built interrogation chambers which would possibly rule out this approach.

e) The A group feels that possibly chemical or hypnotic control could be induced as a by-product of certain parts of medical treatment such as elecctro-shock or by placing of an individual under medical prescription over a considerable period of time. Certainly an ideal approach could be made to any subject if that subject had offered himself for or was taking psychoanalysis. This is a very strong reason for prohibiting Agency personnel overseas from being treated in any way except by fully authorized physicians, psychiatrists or company doctors.

Closely coupled with the above is the related problem: if a subject can successfully and unwittingly be approached and rendered either unconscious or hypno- or narco-controlled, how can his memory be made blank for events leading up to the coma or trance and for what transpired while under control and/or possibly extending throughout the "hangover" period after he awakens. Ideally, control of the subject obtained without his knowledge or consent and followed by a total amnesia is the goal but at the present time this appears impossible. Much research and experimentation is necessary to achieve these ends and as stated above, for the present at least a smooth, carefully designed medical cover appears the best approach. (See also Amnesia)

Finally some words should be noted in regard to the use of chemicals (or hypnosis in some ways for that matter) which complicate the problem of the unwitting subject--and in a large sense recommend the use of medical cover.

a) Certain chemicals such as LSD, mescaline, cannabis, opium produce bizarre, weird and startling effects. A person experiencing these effects would recognize this and undoubtedly suspect something unusual had occurred to him.

b) Most chemicals, in effective dosages, carry some type of hangover. This can take the form of confusion, nausea, illness, sweating, headache, tremors, or combinations of these, etc. Again, a subject would suspect the reason.

c) Human beings do not respond in identical ways to identical dosages of chemicals. A dose that may have no noticeable effect on one subject might produce a convulsion or even death in another. The best results are always obtained in using chemicals by competent medical personnel using special knowledge of chemical reactions. A subject in a coma is useless for interrogation or control and an underdose may blow an operation.

d) Under the Heading AMNESIA, we commented on attempts to produce amnesias on hypnotic subjects. For the record, it should also be noted that quite often a hangover effect is felt from deep hypnosis. The ARTICHOKE group has seen subjects emerging from hypnosis effected in the following ways:

    1) Illness--including nausea, headache, sweating.
    2) Psychological reactions--fear, hysteria, confusion, disorientation.
    3) Extreme fatigue, tendencies to return to sleep states, feeling of weakness.

Hence, even if a good amnesia is developed, a subject could certainly suspect he had been subjected to something unusual.

UNWITTING SUBJECT: If Operator could surely produce prompt sleep, without a hypodermic. (1

Enough CO_2 in the room could produce sleep rapidly, but	' S. would later recall ' having fallen asleep.	Unknown how surely to keep Op. awake. Also, a fixed installation required? Possibly, any room would do.
Enough Dormison (about tasteless in food or drink), Chloral (disguisable by alcohol), or Seconal (possibly disguisable, not tasteless), produces sleep,	but S. would later recall the circumstances	
If S. had earlier been hypnotized deeply enough by the same Op., and given post-hypnotic suggestion to fall asleep instantly on a simple signal (like Op. snapping fingers), for some time thereafter he would do so.	Rarely can a S. be hypnotized unwittingly; and if so, probably not deep enough. Also, such suggestion's duration is unknown.	Hypnotic sleep is not genuine sleep. All happenings in it can be recalled thereafter — more or less of it by the S. consciously, and the rest by another Op.'s hypnosis or analysis.

If Operator could surely produce epileptic fit, without a hypodermic.

If S. sensitized enough by appropriate drug by mouth, flickering light convulses. See Flicker.	Metrazol or Isoniazid orally is toxic or nauseating in such doses, & not tasteless. Combination with other drugs must be sought; also, possible safe & effective aerosols or gaseous sensitizers.	Op. can probably be protected by other drugs.

(See also: ELECTRIC SHOCKS.)
            RADIANT ENERGY.)

UNWITTING SUBJECT

Methedrin or Dexedrin (probably disguisable by most drinks)	)			
Methedrin ≠ barbiturate (may be disguisable)	)		Under questioning, S. tends to reveal	
Other possible combinations by mouth	)			
LSD25 in drink (very small dose, tasteless)	)			
Ordinary cigarette with filter tip, whose edge has been wiped with LSD25	Extremely unsure dosage. CQ: how to apply a small enough dose to the tip, & how much will be licked & so absorbed by the S.	)		Effects peculiar to LSD25
Ordinary unfiltered cigarette to which .02 gm. Tetrahydrocannabinol acetate has been added;	stronger drugging may be exposed by "woozy" sensation.	Strong coumarin flavor (as Camels) required to mask marijuana taste	Under questioning, S. tends to reveal	

(See also card on IONTOPHORESIS)

VERTIGO   See Barbiturate (also other drugs)
                        Equilibrium
                        Flicker Sickness
                        Middle Ear Disorder
                        Motion Sickness
                        Vibration

VIBRATION

1. A rubber room that vibrated in several directions was reported used by Russians to produce overanxiety and emotional instability (columns numbered 2 and 3 of Mental States). Even the bouncing tendency of a soft rubber floor will produce some sense of insecurity; a famous piece of rubber pavement yars ago in Edinburgh was said to alarm and confuse pedestrians.

For our purpose a quaking room is too much of a torture chamber; however, if some third-degree approach is contemplated at a permanent installation, this one is interesting.

2. Less formidable would be some possible modification of the "Anatometer", exhibited this year at the American Psychiatric convention (illustrated and described in Section 26 of my report thereon). As manufactured, it is a padded table on which subject lies; it slides back and forth longitudinally, and is intended to make him calm, perhaps drowsy. Naturally it does not vibrate; but if vibration were added, and tipping and sliding were in the directions most conducive to motionsickness, an apparatus of this sort could be devastating to a subject's mental as well as physical equilibrium.

Again, too third-degree for any but exceptional use.

3. Another form of vibration is in relatively low-frequency sound waves, below the range of hearing. Frequencies below 2000 cycles per second cause a strong sense of vibration throughout the head; half an hour's exposure, at 145 to 150 decibels,

VITAMINS

Effects on Intoxication, of Other Drugs (Before, With or After) Alcohol
ALCOHOL plus Vitamins A, B_1, B_2, and B_2-complex, and C: effects uncertain
Vitamin B6 (Pyridoxin)--see Deprivations
Vitamin C (Pyridoxin)--see Prophylaxis against Revealing

WASHING   See Brain Washing

Frank Church led the Church Committee, which first brought the MK-Ultra program to public attention in 1975.

Chapter 8
Artificial Telepathy

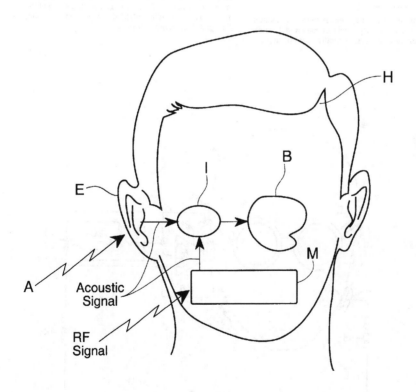

United States Patent

[11] **3,629,521**

[72] Inventors **Henry K. Puharich**
Ossining;
Joseph L. Lawrence, New York, both of
N.Y.
[21] Appl. No. **1,334**
[22] Filed **Jan. 8, 1970**
[45] Patented **Dec. 21, 1971**
[73] Assignee **Intelectron Corporation**
New York, N.Y.
Continuation-in-part of application Ser. No.
682,152, Nov. 13, 1967, now Patent No.
3,497,637, and a continuation-in-part of
446,267, Apr. 6, 1965, now abandoned.
This application Jan. 8, 1970, Ser. No.
1,334

[54] **HEARING SYSTEMS**
11 Claims, 3 Drawing Figs.

[52] U.S. Cl. .... 179/107 R
[51] Int. Cl. **H04r 25/00**
[50] Field of Search .... 179/107 R,
107 BC, 107 E, 107 H, 107 S; 128/1.5

Primary Examiner—Kathleen H. Claffy
Assistant Examiner—Thomas L. Kundert
Attorney—Mandeville and Schweitzer

ABSTRACT: The present invention relates to the stimulation of the sensation of hearing in persons of impaired hearing abilities or in certain cases in persons totally deaf utilizing RF energy. More particularly, the present invention relates to a method and apparatus for imparting synchronous AF or "acoustic" signals and so-called "transdermal" or RF signals. Hearing and improved speech discrimination, in accordance with one aspect of the present invention, is stimulated by the application of an AF acoustical signal to the "ear system" conventional biomechanism of hearing, which is delivered to the brain through the "normal" channels of hearing and a separate transdermal RF electrical signal which is applied to the "facial nerve system" and is detectable as a sensation of hearing. Vastly improved and enhanced hearing may be achieved by imparting an AF acoustic signal to the ear system by means of "conventional" transducers, such as electroacoustic speakers of "in the ear" hearing aids; piezoelectric or mechanical transducers of conventional "bone conduction"-type hearing aids; and so-called "intraoral bone conduction transducers" of the type employed in the hearing system disclosed in Puharich and Lawrence U.S. Pat. No. 2,995,633 and No. 3,170,993 and No. 3,156,787, and by simultaneously applying a transdermal signal, which signal is an RF carrier signal amplitude modulated with AF information across the head of the subject, the head acting as capacitance in LC series resonance of the RF carrier frequency. Importantly, the applied balanced transdermal signal is in the form of a substantially pure sine wave, and it is applied to the head through one bare and one insulated electrode. The applied transdermal signal is applied to the periaural and stylomastoid regions of the head and, accordingly, the apparatus of the invention may be readily adapted for use in the temples of "eyeglass" hearing aid devices.

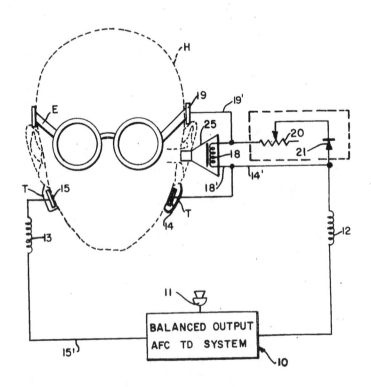

United States Patent

Flanagan

[15] **3,647,970**

[45] **Mar. 7, 1972**

[54] **METHOD AND SYSTEM FOR SIMPLIFYING SPEECH WAVEFORMS**

[72] Inventor: **Gillis P. Flanagan**

[22] Filed: **Aug. 29, 1968**

[21] Appl. No.: **756,124**

[52] U.S. Cl. ....179/1.5, 179/1.5 M, 179/1.5 E,
325/32, 328/31
[51] Int. Cl. H04k 1/00
[58] Field of Search ....179/1.5 MS, 1.5 E, 15.55, 1 AS;
340/15.5 FC; 328/31; 307/237

[56] **References Cited**

UNITED STATES PATENTS

2,479,338   8/1949   Gabrilovitch 179/1.5
2,953,644   9/1960   Miller 179/15.55
2,979,611   4/1961   Halina 179/15.55

Primary Examiner—Rodney D. Bennett, Jr.
Assistant Examiner—H. A. Birmiel
Attorney—Richards, Harris & Hubbard

[57] **ABSTRACT**

A speech waveform is converted to a constant amplitude square wave in which the transitions between the amplitude extremes are spaced so as to carry the speech information. The system includes a pair of tuned amplifier circuits which act as high-pass filters having a 6 decibel per octave slope from 0 to 15,000 cycles followed by two stages, each comprised of an amplifier and clipper circuit, for converting the filtered waveform to a square wave. A radio transmitter and receiver having a plurality of separate channels within a conventional single side band transmitter bandwidth and a system for transmitting secure speech information are also disclosed.

19 Claims, 4 Drawing Figures

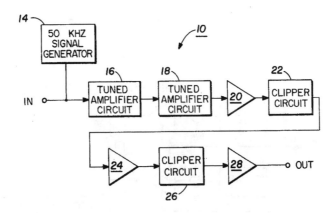

United States Patent [19]

Stocklin

[11] **Patent Number:** **4,858,612**

[45] **Date of Patent:** **Aug. 22, 1989**

[54] **HEARING DEVICE**

[76] Inventor: **Philip L. Stocklin**

[21] Appl. No.: **562,742**

[22] Filed: **Dec. 19, 1983**

[51] Int. Cl.⁴ A61N 1/36
[52] U.S. Cl. .... **128/422**; 178/419 S
[58] Field of Search .... 128/419 R, 419 S, 422,
128/653, 771, 732, 741, 746, 791, 804; 340/407

[56] **References Cited**

U.S. PATENT DOCUMENTS

3,490,458	1/1970	Allison	128/421
3,751,605	8/1973	Michelson	128/1 R
3,951,134	4/1976	Malech	128/131
4,428,377	1/1984	Zollner et al.	128/419 R

FOREIGN PATENT DOCUMENTS

893311	2/1972	Canada	128/422
2811120	9/1978	Fed. Rep. of Germany	128/419 R
591196	1/1978	U.S.S.R.	128/419 R

OTHER PUBLICATIONS

Gerkin, G., "Electroencephalography & Clinical Neurophysiology", vol. 135, No. 6, Dec. 1973, pp. 652–653.
Frye et al., "Science", vol. 181, Jul. 27, 1973, pp. 356–358.
Bise, William, "Low Power Radio–Frequency and Microwave Effects on Human Electroencephalogram and Behavior", Physiol. Chem. & Physics 10 (1978).

Primary Examiner—William E. Kamm
Attorney, Agent, or Firm—Wegner & Bretschneider

[57] **ABSTRACT**

A method and apparatus for simulation of hearing in mammals by introduction of a plurality of microwaves into the region of the auditory cortex is shown and described. A microphone is used to transform sound signals into electrical signals which are in turn analyzed and processed to provide controls for generating a plurality of microwave signals at different frequencies. The multifrequency microwaves are then applied to the brain in the region of the auditory cortex. By this method sounds are perceived by the mammal which are representative of the original sound received by the microphone.

29 Claims, 7 Drawing Sheets

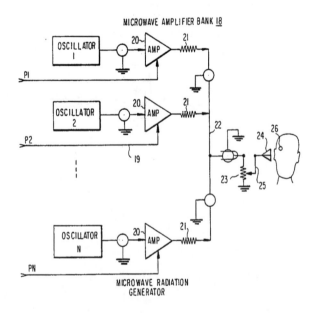

MICROWAVE AMPLIFIER BANK 18

MICROWAVE RADIATION
GENERATOR

4,858,612

1

HEARING DEVICE

BACKGROUND OF THE INVENTION

1. Field of the Invention

This invention relates to devices for aiding of hearing in mammals. The invention is based upon the perception of sounds which is experienced in the brain when the brain is subjected to certain microwave radiation signals.

2. Description of the Prior Art

In prior art hearing devices for human beings, it is well known to amplify sounds to be heard and to apply the amplified sound signal to the ear of the person wearing the hearing aid. Hearing devices of this type are however limited to hearing disfunctions where there is no damage to the auditory nerve or to the auditory cortex. In the prior art, if there is damage to the auditory cortex or the auditory nerve, it cannot be corrected by the use of a hearing aid.

During World War II, individuals in the radiation path of certain radar installations observed clicks and buzzing sounds in response to the microwave radiation. It was through this early observation that it became known to the art that microwaves could cause a direct perception of sound within a human brain. These buzzing or clicking sounds however were not meaningful, and were not perception of sounds which could otherwise be heard by the receiver. This type of microwave radiation was not representative of any intelligible sound to be perceived. In such radar installations, there was never a sound which was generated which resulted in subsequent generation of microwave signals representative of that sound.

Since the early perception of buzzing and clicking, further research has been conducted into the microwave reaction of the brain. In an article entitled "Possible Microwave Mechanisms of the Mammalian Nervous System" by Philip L. Stocklin and Brain F. Stocklin, published in the TIT Journal of Life Sciences, Tower International Technomedical Institute, Inc. P.O. Box 4594, Philadelphia, Pa. (1979) there is disclosed a hypothesis that the mammalian brain generates and uses electro magnetic waves in the lower microwave frequency region as an integral part of the functioning of the central and peripheral nervous systems. This analysis is based primarily upon the potential energy of a protein integral in the neural membrane.

In an article by W. Bise entitled "Low Power Radio-Frequency and Microwave Effects On Human Electroencephalogram and Behavior", Physiol. Chemistry Phys. 10, 387 (1978), it is reported that there are significant effects upon the alert human EEG during radiation by low intensity CW microwave electromagnetic energy. Bise observed significant repeatable EEG effects for a subject during radiation at specific microwave frequencies.

SUMMARY OF THE INVENTION

Results of theoretical analysis of the physics of brain tissue and the brain/skull cavity, combined with experimentally-determined electromagnetic properties of mammalian brain tissue, indicate the physical necessity for the existence of electromagnetic standing waves, called modes in the living mammalian brain. The mode characteristics may be determined by two geometric properties of the brain; these are the cephalic index of the brain (its shape in prolate spheroidal coordinates)

2

and the semifocal distance of the brain (a measure of its size). It was concluded that estimation of brain cephalic index and semifocal distance using external skull measurements on subjects permits estimation of the subject's characteristic mode frequencies, which in turn will permit a mode by mode treatment of the data to simulate hearing.

This invention provides for sound perception by individuals who have impaired hearing resulting from ear damage, auditory nerve damage, and damage to the auditory cortex. This invention provides for simulation of microwave radiation which is normally produced by the auditory cortex. The simulated brain waves are introduced into the region of the auditory cortex and provide for perceived sounds on the part of the subject.

BRIEF DESCRIPTION OF THE DRAWINGS

FIG. 1 shows the acoustic filter bank and mode control matrix portions of the hearing device of this invention.

FIG. 2 shows the microwave generation and antenna portion of the hearing device of this invention.

FIG. 3 shows a typical voltage divider network which may be used to provide mode partition.

FIG. 4 shows another voltage divider device which may be used to provide mode partition.

FIG. 5 shows a voltage divider to be used as a mode partition wherein each of the resistors is variable in order to provide adjustment of the voltage outputs.

FIG. 6 shows a modified hearing device which includes adjustable mode partitioning, and which is used to provide initial calibration of the hearing device.

FIG. 7 shows a group of variable oscillators and variable gain controls which are used to determine hearing characteristics of a particular subject.

FIG. 8 shows a top view of a human skull showing the lateral dimension.

FIG. 9 shows the relationship of the prolate spherical coordinate system to the cartesian system.

FIG. 10 shows a side view of a skull showing the medial plane of the head, section A—A.

FIG. 11 shows a plot of the transverse electric field amplitude versus primary mode number M.

FIG. 12 shows a left side view of the brain and auditory cortex.

FIG. 13 shows the total modal field versus angle for source location.

DETAILED DESCRIPTION OF THE PREFERRED EMBODIMENT

This invention is based upon observations of the physical mechanism the mammalian brain uses to perceive acoustic vibrations. This observation is based in part upon neuro anatomical and other experimental evidence which relates to microwave brain stimulation and the perception of sounds.

It is has been observed that monochromatic acoustic stimuli (acoustic tones, or single tones) of different frequencies uniquely stimulate different regions of the cochlea. It has also been observed that there is a corresponding one to one relationship between the frequency of a monochromatic acoustic stimulus and the region of the auditory cortex neurally stimulated by the cochlear nerve under the physiologically normal conditions (tonotopicity).

It is has been observed that for an acoustic tone of a frequency which is at the lower end of the entire acous-

United States Patent [19]

Brunkan

[11] **Patent Number:** **4,877,027**

[45] **Date of Patent:** **Oct. 31, 1989**

[54] **HEARING SYSTEM**

[76] Inventor: **Wayne B. Brunkan**

[21] Appl. No.: **202,679**

[22] Filed: **Jun. 6, 1988**

[51] Int. Cl.⁴ **A61N 5/00**
[52] U.S. Cl. **128/420.5**
[58] Field of Search .... 128/420.5, 804, 419 R, 128/421, 422, 746; 381/68

[56] **References Cited**

U.S. PATENT DOCUMENTS

3,629,521	12/1971	Puharich et al.	128/402.5
3,766,331	10/1973	Zink	128/420.5

OTHER PUBLICATIONS

Cain et al, "Mammalian Auditory Responses . . . ", IEEE Trans Biomed Eng, pp. 288–293, 1978.
Frey et al, "Human Perception . . . Energy" Science, 181,356–358, 1973.

Jaski, "Radio Waves & Life", Radio–Electronics, pp. 45–45, Sep. 1960.
Microwave Auditory Effects and Applications, Lin, 1978, pp. 176–177.

Primary Examiner—Lee S. Cohen
Attorney, Agent, or Firm—Harry W. Brelsford

[57] **ABSTRACT**

Sound is induced in the head of a person by radiating the head with microwaves in the range of 100 megahertz to 10,000 megahertz that are modulated with a particular waveform. The waveform consists of frequency modulated bursts. Each burst is made up of ten to twenty uniformly spaced pulses grouped tightly together. The burst width is between 500 nanoseconds and 100 microseconds. The pulse width is in the range of 10 nanoseconds to 1 microsecond. The bursts are frequency modulated by the audio input to create the sensation of hearing in the person whose head is irradiated.

8 Claims, 1 Drawing Sheet

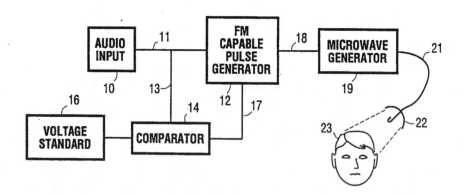

4,877,027

1

HEARING SYSTEM

This invention relates to a hearing system for human beings in which high frequency electromagnetic energy 5 is projected through the air to the head of a human being and the electromagnetic energy is modulated to create signals that can be discerned by the human being regardless of the hearing ability of the person.

THE PRIOR ART

Various types of apparatus and modes of application have been proposed and tried to inject intelligible sounds into the heads of human beings. Some of these have been devised to simulate speech and other sounds 15 in deaf persons and other systems have been used to inject intelligible signals in persons of good hearing, but bypassing the normal human hearing organs.

U.S. Pat. No. 3,629,521 issued Dec. 21, 1971 describes 20 the use of a pair of electrodes applied to a person's head to inject speech into the head of a deaf person. An oscillator creates a carrier in the range of 18 to 36 KHz that is amplitude modulated by a microphone.

Science magazine volume 181, page 356 describes a 25 hearing system utilizing a radio frequency carrier of 1.245 GHz delivered through the air by means of a waveguide and horn antenna. The carrier was pulsed at the rate of 50 pulses per second. The human test subject reported a buzzing sound and the intensity varied with 30 the peak power.

Similar methods of creating "clicks" inside the human head are reported in I.E.E.E. Transactions of Biomedical Engineering, volume BME 25, No. 3, May 1978. 35

The transmission of intelligible speech by audio modulated Microwave is described in the book Microwave Auditory Effects and Applications by James C. Lin 1978 publisher Charles C. Thomas.

BRIEF SUMMARY OF THE INVENTION 40

I have discovered that a pulsed signal on a radio frequency carrier of about 1,000 megahertz (1000 MHz) is effective in creating intelligible signals inside the head of a person if this electromagnetic (EM) energy is pro- 45 jected through the air to the head of the person. Intelligible signals are applied to the carrier by microphone or other audio source and I cause the bursts to be frequency modulated. The bursts are composed of a group 50 of pulses. The pulses are carefully selected for peak strength and pulse width. Various objects, advantages and features of the invention will be apparent in the specification and claims.

BRIEF DESCRIPTION OF THE DRAWINGS 55

In the drawings forming an integral part of this specification:

FIG. 1 is a block diagram of the system of the invention.

FIG. 2 is a diagram of an audio wave which is the 60 input to be perceived by the recipient.

FIG. 3 is a diagram on the same time coordinate as FIG. 2 showing bursts that are frequency modulated by the wave form of FIG. 2.

FIG. 4 shows, on an enlarged time coordinate, that 65 each vertical line depicted in FIG. 3 is a burst of pulses. (A burst is a group of pulses).

2

FIG. 5 shows, on a further enlarged time coordinate, a single continues pulse, Depicted as 'a vertical line in FIG. 4.

DETAILED DESCRIPTION OF THE INVENTION

Inasmuch as microwaves can damage human tissue, any projected energy must be carefully regulated to stay within safe limits. The guideline for 1,000 MHz, set by the American Standards Institute, is 3.3 mw/cm2 (3.3 milliwatts per square centimeter). The apparatus described herein must be regulated to stay within this upper limit.

Referring to FIG. 1 a microphone 10 or other generator of audio frequencies, delivers its output by wire 11 to an FM capable pulse generator 12 and by branch wire 13 to a comparator 14. The comparator 14 also receives a signal from a voltage standard 16. When the peak voltage of the audio generator 10 falls below the standard 16 the comparator delivers a signal by wire 17 to the FM capable pulse generator 12 to shut down the pulse generator 12. This avoids spurious signals being generated. The output of the FM pulse generator 12 is delivered by wire 18 to a microwave generator 19 which delivers its output to the head of a human being 23. In this fashion the person 23 is radiated with microwaves that are in short bursts.

The microwave generator 19 operates at a steady frequency presently preferred at 1,000 megahertz (1,000 million). I presently prefer to pulse the microwave energy at pulse widths of 10 nanoseconds to 1 microsecond. For any one setting of the FM capable generator 12, this width is fixed. The pulses are arranged in bursts. The timing between bursts is controlled by the height of the audio envelope above the voltage standard line. In addition the bursts are spaced from one another at a non-uniform rate of 1 to 100 KHz. This non-uniform spacing of bursts is created in the FM capable generator 12.

Referring to FIG. 2 there is illustrated an audio wave 27 generated by the audio input 10 wherein the horizontal axis is time and the vertical axis is voltage. For illustrative purposes the wave 27 is shown as having a voltage peak 28 on the left part of FIG. 2 and a voltage peak 29 of the right side of FIG. 2. The voltage standard 16 of FIG. 1 generates a dc voltage designated at 31 in FIG. 2. This standard voltage is preferably at about 50% of the peak voltage 28. The comparator 14 of FIG. 1 actuates the FM capable generator 12 only when the positive envelope of the audio wave 27 exceeds the voltage standard. The negative portions of the audio wave are not utilized.

Referring now to FIG. 3 there is illustrated two groups of bursts of microwave energy that are delivered by the antenna 22 of FIG. 1 to the head of the person 23. FIG. 3 has a horizontal time axis identical to the time axis of FIG. 2 and has a vertical axis that in this case represents the power of the microwaves from generator 19. At the left part of FIG. 3 are a plurality of microwave bursts 32 that occur on the time axis from the point of intersection of the standard voltage 31 with the positive part of the audio wave 27, designated as the time point 33 to time point 34 on FIG. 2. It will be noted in FIG. 3 that the bursts 32 are non-uniform in spacing and that they are closer together at the time of maximum audio voltage 28 and are more spread out toward the time points 33 and 34. This is the frequency modulation effected by the FM pulse generator 12.

(12) **United States Patent**
O'Loughlin et al.

(10) **Patent No.:** **US 6,587,729 B2**
(45) **Date of Patent:** **Jul. 1, 2003**

(54) **APPARATUS FOR AUDIBLY COMMUNICATING SPEECH USING THE RADIO FREQUENCY HEARING EFFECT**

(75) Inventors: **James P. O'Loughlin**, Placitas, NM (US); **Diana L. Loree**, Albuquerque, NM (US)

(73) Assignee: **The United States of America as represented by the Secretary of the Air Force**, Washington, DC (US)

(*) Notice: Subject to any disclaimer, the term of this patent is extended or adjusted under 35 U.S.C. 154(b) by 0 days.

(21) Appl. No.: **10/131,626**

(22) Filed: **Apr. 24, 2002**

(65) **Prior Publication Data**

US 2002/0123775 A1 Sep. 5, 2002

Related U.S. Application Data

(62) Division of application No. 08/766,687, filed on Dec. 13, 1996, now Pat. No. 6,470,214.

(51) Int. Cl.^{7} H03C 1/54
(52) U.S. Cl. 607/55; 128/897; 332/167; 381/151; 600/586

(58) Field of Search 332/167; 381/151; 607/56, 55; 340/384.1; 600/559, 23, 586; 128/897, 898

(56) **References Cited**

U.S. PATENT DOCUMENTS

3,563,246	A	*	2/1971	Puharich et al.	607/55
3,629,521	A	*	12/1971	Puharich et al.	607/56
4,835,791	A	*	5/1989	Daoud	375/301
5,450,044	A	*	9/1995	Hulick	332/103

* cited by examiner

Primary Examiner—Kennedy Schaetzle
(74) *Attorney, Agent, or Firm*—James M. Skorich

(57) **ABSTRACT**

A modulation process with a fully suppressed carrier and input preprocessor filtering to produce an encoded output; for amplitude modulation (AM) and audio speech preprocessor filtering, intelligible subjective sound is produced when the encoded signal is demodulated using the RF Hearing Effect. Suitable forms of carrier suppressed modulation include single sideband (SSB) and carrier suppressed amplitude modulation (CSAM), with both sidebands present.

11 Claims, 3 Drawing Sheets

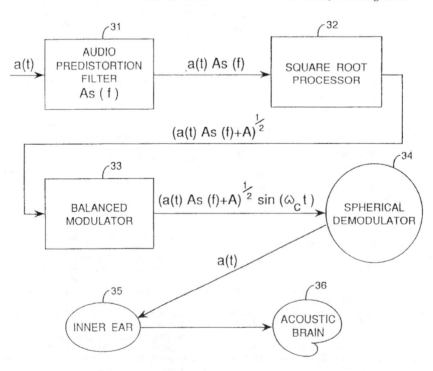

1

APPARATUS FOR AUDIBLY COMMUNICATING SPEECH USING THE RADIO FREQUENCY HEARING EFFECT

This application is a division of U.S. patent application Ser. No. 08/766,687 filed on Dec. 13, 1996, now U.S. Pat. No. 6,470,214, and claims the benefit of the foregoing filing date.

The invention described herein may be manufactured and used by or for the Government for governmental purposes without the payment of any royalty thereon.

BACKGROUND OF THE INVENTION

This invention relates to the modulating of signals on carriers, which are transmitted and the signals intelligibly recovered, and more particularly, to the modulation of speech on a carrier and the intelligible recover of the speech by means of the Radio Frequency Hearing Effect.

The Radio Frequency ("RF") Hearing Effect was first noticed during World War II as a subjective "click" produced by a pulsed radar signal when the transmitted power is above a "threshold" level. Below the threshold level, the click cannot be heard.

The discovery of the Radio Frequency Hearing Effect suggested that a pulsed RF carrier could be encoded with an amplitude modulated ("AM") envelope. In one approach to pulsed carrier modulation, it was assumed that the "click" of the pulsed carrier was similar to a data sample and could be used to synthesize both simple and complex tones such as speech. Although pulsed carrier modulation can induce a subjective sensation for simple tones, it severely distorts the complex waveforms of speech, as has been confirmed experimentally.

The presence of this kind of distortion has prevented the click process for the encoding of intelligible speech. An example is provided by AM sampled data modulation

Upon demodulation the perceived speech signal has some of the envelope characteristics of an audio signal. Consequently a message can be recognized as speech when a listener is pre-advised that speech has been sent. However, if the listener does not know the content of the message, the audio signal is unintelligible.

The attempt to use the click process to encode speech has been based on the assumption that if simple tones can be encoded, speech can be encoded as well, but this is not so. A simple tone can contain several distortions and still be perceived as a tone whereas the same degree of distortion applied to speech renders it unintelligible.

SUMMARY OF THE INVENTION

In accomplishing the foregoing and related object the invention uses a modulation process with a fully suppressed carrier and pre-processor filtering of the input to produce an encoded output. Where amplitude modulation (AM) is employed and the pre-processor filtering is of audio speech input, intelligible subjective sound is produced when the encoded signal is demodulated by means of the RF Hearing Effect. Suitable forms of carrier suppressed modulation include single sideband (SSB) and carrier suppressed amplitude modulation (CSAM), with both sidebands present.

The invention further provides for analysis of the RE hearing phenomena based on an RF to acoustic transducer model. Analysis of the model suggests a new modulation process which permits the RF Hearing Effect to be used following the transmission of encoded speech.

2

In accordance with one aspect of the invention the pre-processing of an input speech signal takes place with a filter that de-emphasizes the high frequency content of the input speech signal. The de-emphasis can provide a signal reduction of about 40 dB (decibels) per decade. Further processing of the speech signal then takes place by adding a bias level and taking a root of the predistorted waveform. The resultant signal is used to modulated an RF carrier in the AM fully suppressed carrier mode, with single or double sidebands.

The modulated RF signal is demodulated by an RF to acoustic demodulator that produces an intelligible acoustic replication of the original input speech.

The RF Hearing Effect is explained and analyzed as a thermal to acoustic demodulating process. Energy absorption in a medium, such as the head, causes mechanical expansion and contraction, and thus an acoustic signal.

When the expansion and contraction take place in the head of an animal, the acoustic signal is passed by conduction to the inner ear where it is further processed as if it were an acoustic signal from the outer ear.

The RF to Acoustic Demodulator thus has characteristics which permit the conversion of the RF energy input to an acoustic output.

Accordingly, it is an object of the invention to provide a novel technique for the intelligible encoding of signals. A related object is to provide for the intelligible encoding of speech.

Another object of the invention is to make use of the Radio Frequency ("RF") Hearing Effect in the intelligible demodulation of encoded signals, including speech.

Still another object of the invention is to suitably encode a pulsed RF carrier with an amplitude modulated ("AM") envelope such that the modulation will be intelligibly demodulated by means of the RF Hearing Effect. A related object is to permit a message to be identified and understood as speech when a listener does not know beforehand that the message is speech.

Other aspects of the invention will be come apparent after considering several illustrative embodiments, taken in conjunction with the drawings.

DESCRIPTION OF THE DRAWINGS

FIG. 1 is a block diagram model of RF to Acoustic Demodulation Process making use of the Radio Frequency ("RF") Hearing Effect;

FIG. 2 is a spherical demodulator and radiator having a specific acoustic impedance for demodulation using the RF Hearing Effect;

FIG. 3 is a diagram illustrating the overall process and constituents of the invention; and

FIG. 4 is an illustrative circuit and wiring diagram for the components of FIG. 3.

DETAINED DESCRIPTION OF THE PREFERRED EMBODIMENT

With reference to the drawings, FIG. 1 illustrates the RF to acoustic demodulation process of the invention. Ordinarily an acoustic signal A reaches the outer ear E of the head H and traverses first to the inner ear I and then to the acoustic receptors of the brain B. A modulated RF signal, however, enters a demodulator D, which is illustratively provided by the mass M of the brain, and is approximated, as shown in FIG. 2, by a sphere S of radius r in the head H. The radius

United States Patent [19]

Lenhardt et al.

[11] Patent Number: 5,047,994

[45] Date of Patent: Sep. 10, 1991

[54] SUPERSONIC BONE CONDUCTION HEARING AID AND METHOD

[75] Inventors: **Martin L. Lenhardt,** Hayes; **Alex M. Clarke; William Regelson,** both of Richmond, all of Va.

[73] Assignee: **Center for Innovative Technology,** Herndon, Va.

[21] Appl. No.: **608,429**

[22] Filed: **Nov. 2, 1990**

Related U.S. Application Data

[62] Division of Ser. No. 358,616, May 30, 1989, Pat. No. 4,982,434.

[51] Int. Cl.^{5} G01S 15/02
[52] U.S. Cl. **367/116**; 381/68.3
[58] Field of Search 367/116; 381/68.3, 68.1

[56] References Cited

U.S. PATENT DOCUMENTS

3,715,577	2/1973	Bohman	367/116
4,761,770	8/1988	Kim et al.	367/116

Primary Examiner—Daniel T. Pihulic
Attorney, Agent, or Firm—Rothwell, Figg, Ernst & Kurz

[57] **ABSTRACT**

A supersonic bone conduction hearing aid that receives conventional audiometric frequencies and converts them to supersonic frequencies for connection to the human sensory system by vibration bone conduction. The hearing is believed to use channels of communications to the brain that are not normally used for hearing. These alternative channels do not deteriorate significantly with age as does the normal hearing channels. The supersonic bone conduction frequencies are discerned as frequencies in the audiometric range of frequencies.

1 Claim, 2 Drawing Sheets

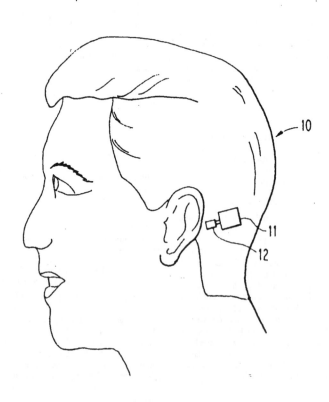

5,047,994

1

SUPERSONIC BONE CONDUCTION HEARING AID AND METHOD

This is a division of application Ser. No. 07/358,616, filed May 30, 1989 now U.S. Pat. No. 4,982,434.

This invention relates to hearing aids that shift the normal hearing frequencies to the supersonic range for transfer to the human sensory system by bone conduction and the like.

The traditional hearing aid is an air-conduction amplifying system such that a microphone picks up air conduction sounds, amplifies them and present them in the ear canals as an air conduction signal to the ear drum. These type of devices offer a small frequency range and also offer a small dynamic range of intensity.

Bone conduction hearing aids have also been developed for users where the conventional hearing aid is not satisfactory. A bone conduction device is attached to the head of the user and the output from a microphone pick-up is amplified and fed into this device which causes bone vibration. These devices operate over a small dynamic range and are designed principally for individuals whose middle ears could not be surgically repaired or for very young children who have abnormalities of the middle ear that cannot be surgically repaired until they are older. These bone conduction devices currently are rarely used.

Newer technology involves implanting rare earth magnets in the temporal bone and a microphone electronic coil system is used to cause the magnet to vibrate producing bone conduction hearing. These devices are also rarely used because of the surgery involved in drilling out the bone and putting the magnet in. However, their fidelity is reported to be very high.

There is no prior art showing the use of supersonic frequencies as a bone conducting hearing aid for normal hearing frequencies. There has been mention of supersonic frequency detection in the literature but not for hearing aids. All known textbooks suggests that hearing stops at 20,000 hertz.

The present invention involves transposing air conduction sounds in the conventional or audiometric range which is a frequency range of about 100 to about 10,000 hertz. These frequencies are shifted into the supersonic range which are frequencies above 20 kHz to about 108 kHz or higher and then transmit these supersonic frequencies by bone conduction or the like to the human sensory system. The hearing aid may transpose air conduction sound from the speech frequencies to the supersonic ranges in such a fashion that noise burst frequency modulated signals and quiet bursts that relate to speech frequencies will be shifted into the supersonic range. These signals are delivered by a bone conduction attachment such as a high fidelity electrical to vibrator transducer, preferably a piezoelectric type, functionally connected for bone conduction in the head.

While the inventors do not wish to be bound by any specific theory, it is hypothesized that the hearing aid and method of the present invention is based on a system of hearing quite distinct from normal hearing based on air conduction. It utilizes bone conduction and parallels the primary hearing response of reptiles. In reptiles, there is no air conduction hearing, but hearing is mediated via the saccule which, in man, has been considered an organ responsible for balance and determining acceleration and movement. In reptiles, this organ is a hear-

2

ing instrument and it possesses hearing potential in amphibia and in fish as well.

Phylogenetically, in evolution, hearing in fish, amphibia and reptiles is mediated by vibratory frequencies that work through vestibular systems. In amphibia, both bone and air conducted frequencies impinge on vestibular receptors. In reptiles, air conduction hearing is non-existent unless transduced via skin or bone to the vestibular saccule which is the primary hearing organ, as the cochlea does not exist. During evolution, as mammals evolved from reptiles, therapsids or amphibia, as gait, posture and skull evolved, so did the mammalian and avian cochlea which took over the role of the saccule as the primary hearing organ. The internal ear, or cochlea is now the primary mammalian acoustic contact with the external environment. The saccule, although equipped with the neuro-cortical functional capacity to ascertain sound became a back-up system of limited value, except for balance and motion detection. The awareness of the vestibular developmental role in evolutionary biology of hearing, was lost as physiologists expanded on our understanding of the role of air conduction with clinical emphasis on the physiology and pathology of the cochlea. Otolaryngologists, audiometrists, speech therapists, psychologists and physiologists look upon the saccule and utricular systems as accelerometers or motion detectors. The residual role of the saccule and vestibule in hearing perception is lost to current knowledge.

The hearing aid of the invention is believed to utilize direct bone transmission to the saccule and this enables hearing to be maintained via a system independent of air conduction and the inner ear although integrated with the air conduction system.

This provides a new device for allowing the nerve deaf to hear, but in addition, provides an alternative source of informational transfer independent of sounds moving through air. The sound is transmitted directly to the bones of the skull, and utilizes frequencies that are perceived by the saccule and not by the inner ear.

Apart from improving hearing in auditory nerve damaged users or hearing of those users suffering air conduction defects, this also permits the perfection of echo location devices for the blind that should perform better than those currently under development.

For echo location, dual electrical to vibration transducers are placed on separate designated locations on the cranium to provide stimulation to the saccules of each vestibule. This permits localized discernable signals returning from solid objects to enable the user to judge speed, distance and direction.

The echo location aspects of the invention are based on a determination that in the audiometric frequencies of 100 to 10,000 hertz the attenuation across the skull from one ear to the other is only in the range of zero to 20 decibels (dB) and even in the ultrasonic range of 10 to 20 kilohertz, there is only approximately 40 dB attenuation. However, in the supersonic range of over 20,000 hertz, the attenuation factor goes up and reaches 80 dB. Thus, when an audiometric tone is presented to one side of the skull, the propagation wave reaches the other side with little loss of energy, therefore, making echo location more difficult. However, in the supersonic range utilized by the present invention, there is a great loss of energy so that the hearing aid on one side can be distinguished from the hearing aid on the other side to give a far better capability at echo location both as to distance and direction. Bone conduction signals propa-

United States Patent [19]

Zink

[11] **3,766,331**

[45] **Oct. 16, 1973**

[54] **HEARING AID FOR PRODUCING SENSATIONS IN THE BRAIN**

[75] Inventor: **Henry R. Zink,** San Bernardino, Calif.

[73] Assignee: **ZCM Limited,** San Bernardino, Calif.

[22] Filed: **Nov. 24, 1971**

[21] Appl. No.: **201,831**

Related U.S. Application Data

[63] Continuation-in-part of Ser. No. 847,292, Aug. 4, 1969, abandoned.

[52] **U.S. Cl.** .... **179/107 R**
[51] **Int. Cl.** **H04r 25/00**
[58] **Field of Search** .... 128/2.1; 35/35 C; 179/107 R, 106 BC, 121 C, 15 A; 340/407

[56] **References Cited**
UNITED STATES PATENTS

3,629,521 12/1971 Puharich et al. .... 179/107 R

3,578,912	5/1971	Beavers, Jr.	169/15 A
3,170,993	2/1965	Puharich et al.	179/107 BC
3,497,637	2/1970	Puharich et al.	179/107 R
3,586,791	6/1971	Puharich et al.	179/107 R

FOREIGN PATENTS OR APPLICATIONS

278,833 10/1927 Great Britain .... 169/121 C

Primary Examiner—Kathleen H. Claffy
Assistant Examiner—Thomas L. Kundert
Attorney—Charles G. Lyon et al.

[57] **ABSTRACT**

A pulsed oscillator or transmitter supplies energy to a pair of insulated electrodes mounted on a person's neck. The transmitter produces pulses of intensity greater than a predetermined threshold value and of a width and rate so as to produce the sensation of hearing without use of the auditory canal thereby providing a hearing system enabling otherwise deaf people to hear.

19 Claims, 14 Drawing Figures

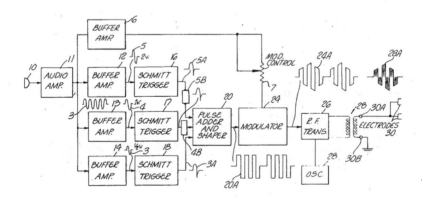

Chapter 9
Behavior Modification

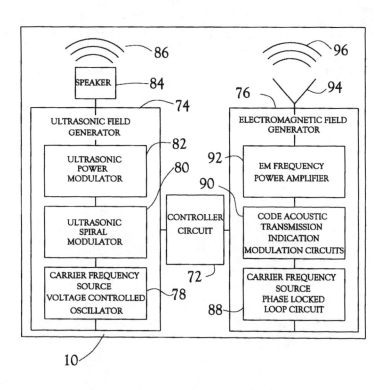

United States Patent [19]

Densky

[11] **Patent Number:** **4,717,343**

[45] **Date of Patent:** **Jan. 5, 1988**

[54] **METHOD OF CHANGING A PERSON'S BEHAVIOR**

[76] Inventor: **Alan B. Densky**

[21] Appl. No.: **880,551**

[22] Filed: **Jun. 30, 1986**

[51] Int. Cl.⁴ G09B 19/00
[52] U.S. Cl. .... 434/236; 434/262; 352/85; 352/91 R
[58] **Field of Search** .... 434/236–238, 434/262, 322, 333; 352/41, 42, 85, 91 R, 91 C, 91 S

[56] **References Cited**

U.S. PATENT DOCUMENTS

1,921,963	8/1933	Crabtree	369/285
2,133,085	10/1938	Draper	352/44
2,517,246	8/1950	Seitz	352/42
3,278,676	10/1966	Becker	358/142
3,545,849	12/1970	Miheles	352/45
3,782,006	1/1974	Symmes	434/234
3,905,701	9/1975	David	355/71
4,181,410	1/1980	Sicha et al.	352/91 R
4,200,364	4/1980	Borowski et al.	352/141
4,483,681	11/1984	Weinslatt	434/236

FOREIGN PATENT DOCUMENTS

1557773	2/1969	France	434/236

Primary Examiner—John E. Murtagh
Assistant Examiner—Andrew Joseph Rudy
Attorney, Agent, or Firm—Merrill N. Johnson

[57] **ABSTRACT**

A method of conditioning a person's unconscious mind in order to effect a desired change in the person's behavior which does not require the services of a trained therapist. Instead the person to be treated views a program of video pictures appearing on a screen. The program as viewed by the person's unconscious mind acts to condition the person's thought patterns in a manner which alters that person's behavior in a positive way.

7 Claims, No Drawings

METHOD OF CHANGING A PERSON'S BEHAVIOR

BACKGROUND OF THE INVENTION

The present invention relates to methods for conditioning a person's unconscious thought patterns by having the person view a program of video pictures projected upon a screen in order to alter that person's behavior.

It is well established in medicine and science that the human mind operates on two planes, the conscious and the unconscious. That part of the human mind used for reasoning and communicating with full awareness by the individual and which also controls voluntary behavior such as talking and walking is called the conscious mind. The unconscious mind, sometimes referred to as the subconscious, controls those functions which take place without the person's awareness such as heartbeat, breathing, glandular action, and such involuntary reactions as appetite, tension and pain.

Hypnosis was one of the first techniques used to reach a person's unconscious mind. In the late 1800's hypnosis was used to trigger the release of the endorphins, an opiate-like substance manufactured and stored within the brain, to serve as anesthesia during surgery. More recently, hypnosis has been used to effect appetite control, smoking abatement, reduction of stress and depression, and painless childbirth. During the first half of the 1900's Dr. Milton Erickson introduced the use of structured linguistic patterns in hypnotic therapy.

In the early 1970's Richard Bandler and John Grindler pioneered neuro-linguistic programming in which the therapist auditorially (by voice) tells the patient to complete a certain mental exercise in his mind's eye in order to bring about behavioral change at the unconscious and conscious levels of the patient's mind.

Both hypnosis and neuro-linguistic programming are methods of conditioning a person's thought processes through sounds transmitted by voice.

Another method of affecting an individual's unconscious thought processes is subliminal suggestion. Audio subliminals consist of a human voice repeating auditory suggestions over and over, and the voice is "covered over" by a sound such as ocean waves which is the only sound the conscious mind hears. But the unconscious hears the voiced suggestions. Video subliminals inject written messages (such as "buy popcorn") at a rate of about one frame per second into a moving picture film. There are 24 frames per second in the standard movie or video and thus the subliminal message registers only on the unconscious mind. One suggested use of video subliminal suggestion is set forth in U.S. Pat. No. 3,278,676 granted Oct. 11, 1966.

Suggestions have also been made to use visual displays projected upon a screen as an addition to audio signals, electric shock signals or other sensory messages to assist a person to build up an aversion to an undesirable habit. One such suggestion is set forth in U.S. Pat. No. 3,782,006 granted Jan. 1, 1974.

SUMMARY OF THE INVENTION

Most prior methods intended to reach a person's unconscious mind in order to effect a desired change in the person's habits require a trained therapist—a hypnotist or psychologist—to administer the program. Thus such methods are both expensive and limited by the number of specially trained therapists available to administer the programs.

I have invented a unique method for conditioning a person's unconscious mind in order to effect a desired change in the person's behavior which does not require a trained therapist. Instead, the person to be treated views a program of video pictures projected upon a screen. Although the pictures appearing on the screen are viewed by the person's conscious as well as unconscious mind, the program's images as viewed act to condition the person's unconscious thought patterns in a way which serves to alter that person's behavior.

Since it is usually a picture or image within a person's mind that creates the behavior and feeling a person will experience, my method programs the person's mind so that certain undesirable mental images in that person's conscious and/or unconscious mind (at the time of treatment and thereafter) will be automatically exchanged in the mind for a desirable mental image. When the mind thus exchanges mental images that person will experience a positive change in feelings and behavior.

My method of video programming uses two related but different techniques that I have named the Flash and the Chop, which are preferably viewed in sequence by the person being programmed.

The Flash is designed to set up new stimulus-response patterns in the brain. The person viewing the sequences of the Flash has his or her mind programmed to automatically replace a specific undesirable image when it appears with a desirable image. For example, should a stressful thought or mental image come into the person's mind, it will trigger a relaxing thought or a mental image of a relaxing scene.

By lengthy experimentation, I have determined the time of exposure and sequence of the scenes which comprise the Flash and which give it its power to program the human mind. The exact number of times the Flash is repeated will depend upon the nature of the program.

Basically, the sequence of views comprising the Flash includes two different pictures which I have named the cue picture and the outcome picture. The cue picture is a picture or image which may be either still or moving and which stimulates in the mind of the viewer an undesirable behavioral response. The outcome picture triggers a desired response.

The Flash comprises the following sequence of views:

1. Start with the cue picture in bright color, focused sharply and as large as possible. Hold the cue picture on the screen for a few seconds.

2. If the cue picture is a movie, have the movie go still and have the picture slowly recede (move away) gradually appearing smaller.

3. After a few seconds of the picture moving away, have the picture go from color to black and white.

4. After a few more seconds of the picture moving away, blur the picture.

5. After a few more seconds, the black and white blurred cue picture disappears by receding into the center of the screen.

6. Slowly bring the outcome picture into view from the same spot where the cue picture disappeared. The picture is still, small, blurred and in black and white but gradually gets larger and becomes sharply focused.

7. After a few more seconds, the picture gets larger and appears in color.

United States Patent [19]

D'Alitalia et al.

[11] **Patent Number:** **5,784,124**

[45] **Date of Patent:** **Jul. 21, 1998**

[54] **SUPRALIMINAL METHOD OF EDUCATION WITH PARTICULAR APPLICATION BEHAVIOR MODIFICATION**

[75] Inventors: **Joseph Anthony D'Alitalia; Talbert Mead**, both of El Paso County. Colo.

[73] Assignee: **Advanced Learning Corp.**, Colorado Springs, Colo.

[21] Appl. No.: **661,943**

[22] Filed: **Jun. 11, 1996**

Related U.S. Application Data

[63] Continuation-in-part of Ser. No. 410,275, Mar. 24, 1995, Pat. No. 5,644,363.

[51] Int. Cl.⁶ H04N 5/445
[52] U.S. Cl. 348/564; 348/553; 348/555
[58] Field of Search 378/563, 564, 378/578, 553, 555, 478, 473

[56] **References Cited**

U.S. PATENT DOCUMENTS

4,616,261 10/1986 Crawford et al. 348/564

5,027,208 6/1991 Dwyer, Jr. et al. 348/564
5,221,962 6/1993 Bachas et al. 348/564
5,270,800 12/1993 Sweet 348/564

Primary Examiner—Victor R. Kostak
Attorney, Agent, or Firm—Steven K. Barton

[57] **ABSTRACT**

A method of behavior modification involves having a patient view supraliminal video messages superimposed upon an underlying video presentation. The video messages incorporate messages wherein at least some of the messages link a desired modified behavior to positive feelings of the patient. A supraliminal message generator and superimposer iteratively selects individual messages for display from the sequence of messages, decompressing the messages as required, and places the selected messages in a buffer memory of a video generation device. A processor of the supraliminal message generator and superimposer then fades the selected message from an invisible level to a visible level on the video display, and then fades the selected message from the visible level back to the invisible level.

14 Claims, 6 Drawing Sheets

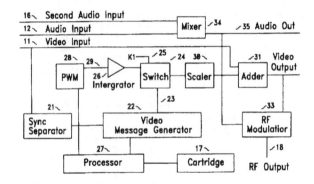

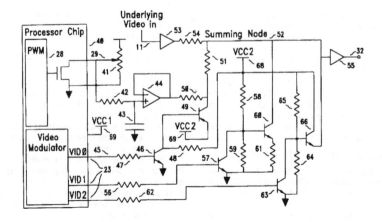

United States Patent [19]

Boyd

[11] **Patent Number:** **5,868,103**

[45] **Date of Patent:** **Feb. 9, 1999**

[54] **METHOD AND APPARATUS FOR CONTROLLING AN ANIMAL**

[75] Inventor: **Randal D. Boyd**, Knoxville, Tenn.

[73] Assignee: **Radio Systems Corporation**, Knoxville, Tenn.

[21] Appl. No.: **902,730**

[22] Filed: **Jul. 30, 1997**

[51] **Int. Cl.^{6}** **A01K 15/00**
[52] **U.S. Cl.** **119/719**; 119/720; 119/859; 119/908
[58] **Field of Search** 119/719, 720, 119/721, 859, 860, 908

[56] **References Cited**

U.S. PATENT DOCUMENTS

3,753,421	8/1973	Peck .	
4,627,385	12/1986	Vinci	119/908 X
4,652,261	3/1987	Mech et al.	119/859 X
4,898,120	2/1990	Brose	340/573 X
5,067,441	11/1991	Weinstein	340/573 X
5,381,129	1/1995	Boardman	340/573

Primary Examiner—Robert P. Swiatek
Attorney, Agent, or Firm—Pitts & Brittian, P.C.

[57] **ABSTRACT**

An apparatus for controlling an animal wherein the animal receives a control stimulus of the release of a substance having an adverse effect upon the animal as a corrective measure. The apparatus includes a transmitter for producing a transmitted field, and a releasable collar for attaching to the neck of the animal. The collar includes a receiver for receiving the transmitted field and for producing a received signal, a control circuit for determining when the received signal indicates that the animal requires a corrective measure and for producing a control signal, a container for containing the substance having an adverse effect upon the animal, and a mechanism for releasing the substance from the container into the presence of the animal upon the production of the control signal by the control circuit. In use, the transmitter is set to produce the transmitted field and the collar is attached to the neck of the animal. As the animal moves about, the receiver in the collar receives the transmitted field and produces a received signal. The control circuit determines when the received signal indicates that the animal requires a corrective measure. A control signal is produced by the control circuit when the determination is made that the animal requires a corrective measure. Upon the production of the control signal, the substance having an adverse effect upon the animal is released from the container and into the presence of the animal.

21 Claims, 6 Drawing Sheets

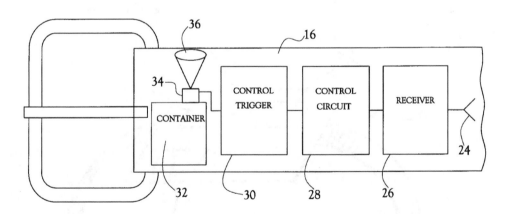

(12) **United States Patent**

Rose

(10) **Patent No.:** **US 6,258,022 B1**

(45) **Date of Patent:** **Jul. 10, 2001**

(54) **BEHAVIOR MODIFICATION**

(76) Inventor: **John Edward Rose**

(*) Notice: Subject to any disclaimer, the term of this patent is extended or adjusted under 35 U.S.C. 154(b) by 0 days.

(21) Appl. No.: **09/214,938**

(22) PCT Filed: **Jul. 14, 1997**

(86) PCT No.: **PCT/GB97/01898**

§ 371 Date: **Jan. 15, 1999**

§ 102(e) Date: **Jan. 15, 1999**

(87) PCT Pub. No.: **WO98/02200**

PCT Pub. Date: **Jan. 22, 1998**

(30) **Foreign Application Priority Data**

Jul. 16, 1996 (GB) 9614913

(51) Int. Cl.[7] **A61M 21/00**

(52) U.S. Cl. **600/26**; 600/27

(58) Field of Search 600/26, 27

(56) **References Cited**

U.S. PATENT DOCUMENTS

5,425,699   6/1995 Speigel .

5,518,497 * 5/1996 Widjaja et al. .

5,823,932 * 10/1998 Speigel 600/26

FOREIGN PATENT DOCUMENTS

0 195 254   9/1986 (EP) .

2 668 370   4/1992 (FR) .

* cited by examiner

Primary Examiner—Max Hindenburg
Assistant Examiner—Brian Szmal
(74) *Attorney, Agent, or Firm*—Smith-Hill and Bedell

(57) **ABSTRACT**

Behavior modification of a human subject takes place under hypnosis, when the subject is in a relaxed state. A machine plays back a video or audio recording, during which the subject is instructed to activate a device to create a perceptible stimulation which is linked, through the hypnosis, with a visualization of enhanced or improved performance. After the hypnosis, the user can reactivate the device at will, whenever the improved performance, such as an improved sporting performance, is desired. This will again create the perceptible stimulation and thus induce the required visualization.

10 Claims, 1 Drawing Sheet

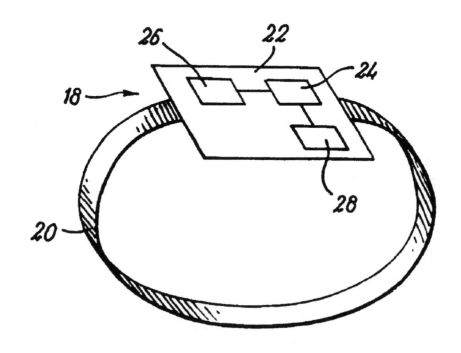

1

BEHAVIOR MODIFICATION

The present invention relates to behaviour modification in human subjects, and particularly, but not exclusively, to performance enhancement.

There are many situations in which the enhancement of human performance is important or desirable. For instance, many sportsmen wish to be able to enhance their performance in order to achieve greater success, but without making use of performance-enhancing drugs or other artificial aids which would infringe rules applicable to their sport or activity. Other desirable types of behaviour modification include overcoming phobias, fear, stress, road rage, insomnia, hypochondria and the like.

The present invention provides a method of behaviour modification of a human subject, in which a visualisation programme is undertaken by the subject under hypnosis and in association with a perceptible stimulation provided by stimulation means, the visualisation programme being so arranged as to enable the subject thereafter, in response to the perceptible stimulation, to visualise modified behaviour.

Preferably the method enhances performance.

The stimulation means is preferably adapted to be activated by the subject, and may be portable. Preferably the stimulation means may be carried or worn by the subject. The stimulation means may provide a stimulation which is perceptible by a part of the subject's body against which the stimulation means is worn or by which the stimulation means is carried or activated. The stimulation means may provide tactile or audible stimulation, such as noise, vibration, mechanical pulses or heat, or any other form of perceptible stimulation, such as trans-dermal, visual, smell, inhalation etc.

The hypnosis may be self-induced or induced externally.

Preferably the visualisation programme includes an induction phase to induce hypnosis, and one or more of the following components:

an ego boosting phase in which the subject is motivated;
a visualisation phase in which modified behaviour is visualised;
an anchoring phase in which a visualisation is anchored to the aforesaid perceptible stimulation; and
a trial phase in which the stimulation means is activated while under hypnosis to recreate a visualisation previously imparted.

Preferably the visualisation programme is pre-recorded, such as by audio or video recording.

The invention also provides stimulation apparatus for use in a method of modifying the behaviour of a human subject, comprising attachment means by which the apparatus may be attached to the body of the subject, and stimulation means operable to provide a stimulation which is perceptible to the subject.

The stimulation means is preferably adapted to be activated by the subject, and may be portable. Preferably the stimulation means may be carried or worn by the subject. The stimulation means may provide a stimulation which is perceptible by a part of the subject's body against which the stimulation means is worn or by which the stimulation means is carried or activated. The stimulation means may provide tactile or audible stimulation, such as noise, vibration, mechanical pulses or heat.

Preferably the stimulation means are mechanical or electrical and may be powered by electrical, mechanical, chemical or solar power means.

The attachment means may comprise a strap and/or adhesive means.

2

The invention also provides apparatus for behaviour modification, such as performance enhancement, comprising a pre-recorded visualisation programme which, in use, induces hypnosis in a human subject, and stimulation means operable to provide a perceptible stimulation to the human subject, the visualisation programme being so arranged as to enable the subject thereafter, in response to the perceptible stimulation, to visualise modified behaviour.

Preferably the stimulation means is in accordance with one or more definitions of the preceding aspects of the invention.

Preferably the visualisation programme includes an induction phase to induce hypnosis, and one or more of the following components:

an ego boosting phase in which the subject is motivated;
a visualisation phase in which modified behaviour is visualised;
an anchoring phase in which a visualisation is anchored to the aforesaid perceptible stimulation; and
a trial phase in which the stimulation means is activated while under hypnosis to recreate a visualisation previously imparted.

In a further aspect, the invention provides a method of using the apparatus of any of the definitions of the previous aspect of the invention, in which a subject plays back the pre-recorded visualisation programme while exposed to operation of the stimulation means, and wherein the stimulation means is operated by choice by the subject after the visualisation programme has been completed, to re-create, in response to the perceptible stimulation, a visualisation of modified behaviour.

Examples of the present invention will now be described in more detail, by way of example only and with reference to the accompanying drawings, in which:

FIG. 1 is a schematic diagram showing a subject under hypnosis in accordance with the invention; and

FIG. 2 is a schematic drawing of a stimulation means for use in accordance with the invention.

FIG. 1 shows a human subject 10 undergoing hypnosis in accordance with the present invention. The hypnosis may be self-induced or externally induced. The subject 10 is in a relaxed state, shown as lying down, preferably in quiet surroundings which may have subdued lighting. The subject 10 is near a machine 12 which can play back a video or audio recording shown schematically as a cassette 14. The cassette 14 is placed into the machine 12 (indicated schematically by the arrow 16) and the programme pre-recorded on the tape is then played back. It is to be appreciated that the recording medium could be any convenient medium, including software, tape, optical or other storage medium.

During playback, the subject 10 is exposed to operation of stimulation apparatus 18 shown generally in FIG. 2. The apparatus 18 has attachment means 20, shown as a strap, by which the apparatus may be attached to the body of the subject 10, such as by strapping the apparatus around the wrist of the subject. The strap 20 carries a capsule 22, preferably sealed against ingress of water, dirt etc. for longevity. Within the capsule 22, there is a power source 24 such as a battery, solar cell, chemical cell or electrical or mechanical power source. This may be renewable or not according to the desired longevity of the device and the capacity of the power source. It is envisaged that a small battery could provide adequate power for many months of normal use, in which case it is envisaged that replenishing the battery would not be necessary, but arrangements could be made for replacing the battery or replenished the power source, if appropriate.

Project MK-Ultra and Mind Control Technology

United States Patent [19]

Douglas et al.

[11] **Patent Number:** **6,039,688**

[45] **Date of Patent:** **Mar. 21, 2000**

[54] **THERAPEUTIC BEHAVIOR MODIFICATION PROGRAM, COMPLIANCE MONITORING AND FEEDBACK SYSTEM**

[75] Inventors: **Peter Douglas**, Montecito, Calif.; **Evan Dudik**, Vancouver, Wash.; **John Evans**, Pittstown, N.J.; **Alan Kritzer**, Van Nuys, Calif.

[73] Assignee: **Salus Media Inc.**, Sherman Oaks, Calif.

[21] Appl. No.: **08/962,238**

[22] Filed: **Oct. 31, 1997**

Related U.S. Application Data

[60] Provisional application No. 60/029,862, Nov. 1, 1996, and provisional application No. 60/052,222, Jul. 11, 1997.

[51] Int. Cl.⁷ **A61B 3/00**; G06F 15/00
[52] U.S. Cl. **600/300**; 128/921
[58] Field of Search 600/300, 301; 128/920, 921, 923, 897, 898

[56] **References Cited**

U.S. PATENT DOCUMENTS

4,712,562	12/1987	Ohayon et al.	128/672
4,731,726	3/1988	Allen, III	364/416
4,779,199	10/1988	Yoneda et al.	364/413.03
4,803,625	2/1989	Fu et al.	364/413.03
4,803,997	2/1989	Bowman	128/723
4,838,275	6/1989	Lee	128/670
4,933,873	6/1990	Kaufman et al.	364/513.5
4,951,197	8/1990	Mellinger	364/413.2
4,975,842	12/1990	Darrow et al.	364/413.02
5,012,411	4/1991	Policastro et al.	364/413.06
5,016,172	5/1991	Dessertine	364/413.02
5,018,067	5/1991	Mohlenbrock et al.	364/413.02
5,019,974	5/1991	Beckers	364/413.02
5,024,225	6/1991	Fang	128/630
5,036,852	8/1991	Leishman	128/630
5,142,484	8/1992	Kaufman et al.	222/638
5,263,491	11/1993	Thornton	128/774
5,301,105	4/1994	Cummings, Jr.	364/401
5,307,263	4/1994	Brown	364/413.09

(List continued on next page.)

Primary Examiner—Cary E. O'Connor
Assistant Examiner—Eric F. Winakur
Attorney, Agent, or Firm—Christie, Parker & Hale, LLP

[57] **ABSTRACT**

A therapeutic behavior modification program, compliance monitoring and feedback system includes a server-based relational database and one or more microprocessors electronically coupled to the server. The system enables development of a therapeutic behavior modification program having a series of milestones for an individual to achieve lifestyle changes necessary to maintain his or her health or recover from ailments or medical procedures. The program may be modified by a physician or trained case advisor prior to implementation. The system monitors the individual's compliance with the program by prompting the individual to enter health-related data, correlating the individual's entered data with the milestones in the behavior modification program and generating compliance data indicative of the individual's progress toward achievement of the program milestones. The system also includes an integrated system of graphical system interfaces for motivating the individual to comply with the program. Through the interfaces, the individual can access the database to review the compliance data and obtain health information from a remote source such as selected sites on the Internet. The system also provides an electronic calendar integrated with the behavior modification program for signaling the individual to take action pursuant to the behavior modification program in which the calendar accesses the relational database and integrates requirements of the program with the individual's daily schedule, and an electronic journal for enabling the individual to enter personal health-related information into the system on a regular basis. In addition, the system includes an electronic meeting room for linking the individual to a plurality of other individuals having related behavior modification programs for facilitating group peer support sessions for compliance with the program. The system enables motivational media presentations to be made to the individuals in the electronic meeting room as part of the group support session to facilitate interactive group discussion about the presentations. The entire system is designed around a community of support motif including a graphical electronic navigator operable by the individual to control the microprocessor for accessing different parts of the system.

34 Claims, 60 Drawing Sheets

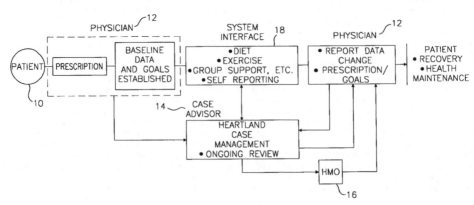

Chapter 10
Nervous System Manipulation

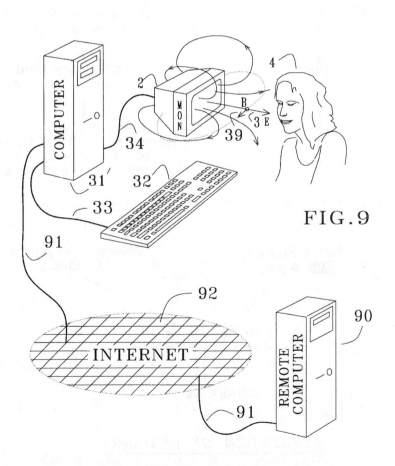

FIG.9

Aug. 8, 1961 H. K. PUHARICH ET AL **2,995,633**

MEANS FOR AIDING HEARING

Filed Sept. 25, 1958 2 Sheets—Sheet 1

FIG. 1

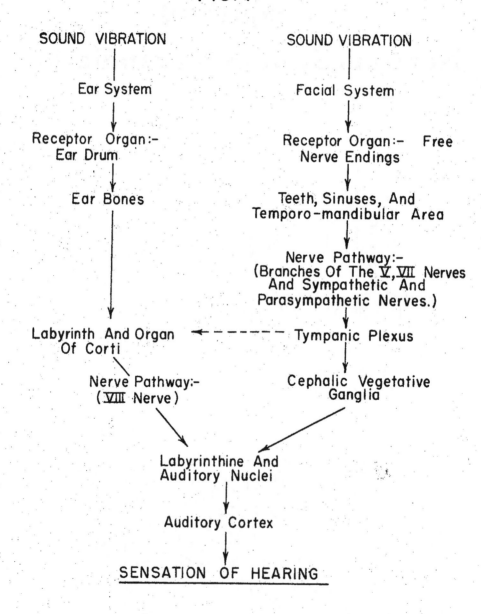

United States Patent Office

1

2,995,633
MEANS FOR AIDING HEARING

Henry K. Puharich, 30 East End Ave., and Joseph L. Lawrence, 570 Fort Washington Ave., both of New York, N.Y.
Filed Sept. 25, 1958, Ser. No. 763,406
5 Claims. (Cl. 179—107)

The present invention is directed to means for auxiliary hearing communication, useful for improving hearing, for example, and relates more specifically to novel and improved arrangements for auxiliary hearing communications by effecting the transmission of sound signals through the dental structure and facial nervous system of the user.

In the normal human hearing system, sound waves travelling through the air or through the bone structure are received in the ear and are transmitted, in a more or less mechanical manner, to the organ of Corti, which acts as a transducer to convert mechanical vibrations into electrical signals in the nervous system. These electrical signals are transmitted to the auditory centers of the brain and there give rise to sensations of sound.

In cases where hearing ability is subnormal, for example, it is frequently possible and desirable to employ a so-called hearing aid to assist in carrying out the functions of the hearing system. All such hearing aids, insofar as we are aware, function as amplifiers of sound waves travelling through the air and/or through the bone structure. And, while these devices may operate satisfactorily where the hearing deficiencies are substantially of a mechanical nature, there are certain hearing defects which are not correctible by mere amplification. For example, in cases of impairment or destruction of the organ of Corti, the system may be unable to translate the mechanical vibrations of sound into the proper electrical signals for transmissions to the auditory centers. In such cases mere amplification of the sound waves cannot give rise to sensations of sound in the brain.

Although, the normal facility for hearing in the human body is the above described system, which may be referred to as the ear system, there is present in the human body a second, dormant system, referred to herein as the facial system, which, if properly energized, will effect the transmission of signals to appropriate areas of the brain, sometimes referred to herein as auditory centers, to give rise to sensations of sound. The facial system, although coupled to the organ of Corti, is substantially parallel to the normal ear system, at least to the extent of having a branch bypassing the organ of Corti and apparently extending up to the point where signals are transmitted through the labyrinthine and auditory nuclei to the auditory centers. Substantially normal hearing is thus possible, even by persons whose normal or ear system has been substantially impaired or destroyed, upon proper energization of the facial system. Accordingly, the present invention, in its broadest aspects, provides a novel and wholly practical arrangement for artificially exciting or energizing the facial hearing system in the human body, to the end that substantially normal sensations of hearing may be realized by persons utilizing the invention, even though such persons may have substantial defects in their normal hearing systems.

In the facial hearing system of the human body there are included, as receptor elements, free nerve endings, such as those found in the teeth, sinuses and temporomandibular area. That is, these nerve endings, properly excited, are capable of transmitting the desired signals to the auditory centers of the brain. Accordingly, one of the more specific aspects of the invention resides in the aiding of hearing by, and in the provision of means for, controllably artificially exciting or stimulating the nerve

2

endings of the facial system, to the end that signals capable of producing sound sensations are transmitted through the facial system to the auditory centers of the brain. In its most advantageous and practical form, the device of the invention comprises means, in the form of a dental prosthetic device, for imparting or transmitting to viable nerves of a tooth electrical signals which, when transmitted to the brain, will give rise to sound sensations. Advantageously, the device or means of the invention comprises an element applied to a viable tooth, for receiving electromagnetic signals at radio frequency, and a transducer element coupled with the receiving element and with live nerve endings of the tooth for converting the electromagnetic signals to electric signals at audio frequency, and imparting the electrical signals to the nerve endings of the tooth for transmission to the brain.

In one practical form of the invention, a dental prosthetic device as described in the foregoing paragraph is utilized in combination with means, such as a microphone and radio transmitter positioned on or about the body of the user, for receiving sounds at audio frequency and translating such sound into electromagnetic energy at radio frequency for transmission to the receiving element of the prosthetic device. The prosthetic device, receiving the electromagnetic signals, translates or converts such signals to appropriate audio frequency electrical signals which are transmitted through the facial nervous system to the brain. The signals thus transmitted are of such a character as to provide the sensation of the sounds transmitted audibly to the microphone, so that the user of the device is able to hear as though through the regular ear system.

Where necessary or desirable, suitable arrangements may be provided for the amplification of the radio frequency electromagnetic signals. To this end, an auxiliary dental prosthetic device may be provided, which takes the form of a crystal diode receiver tuned sharply to the frequency of the transmitting set. Such an amplifying device may be housed in an enclosure having the form of a false tooth or a plurality of false teeth advantageously positioned immediately adjacent the viable tooth containing the transducer element.

In some advantageous forms of the invention, an element positioned in electrical contact with nerve endings of a tooth has piezoelectric properties and functions not only to impart the desirable electrical signals but to agitate the enrve endings and render them highly responsive to the electrical signals. This form of the invention may best be utilized in conjunction with an auxiliary prosthetic device housing a crystal diode receiver, since rectifying functions may be carried out by the receiver.

For a better understanding of the invention, reference should be made to the following detailed description and to the accompanying drawings, in which:

FIG. 1 is a simplified, diagrammatic representation of the ear and facial hearing systems found in the human body;

FIG. 2 is an enlarged representation of a viable tooth incorporating, as an insert, means for receiving radio frequency signals and for converting such signals to audio frequency electrical signals capable of producing sensations of sound in the brain;

FIG. 3 is an enlarged representation of a combination dental prosthetic device, including crystal diode amplifier means and means for converting amplified radio frequency signals to audio frequency electrical signals; and

FIG. 4 is a simplified, diagrammatic representation of a complete hearing aid system incorporating means of FIGS. 2 and 3.

Referring now to the drawing, and initially to FIG. 1 thereof, the normal or ear system for hearing in the human body is represented by the left hand column.

Nov. 10, 1964   H. K. PUHARICH ETAL   3,156,787

SOLID STATE HEARING SYSTEM

Filed Oct. 23, 1962

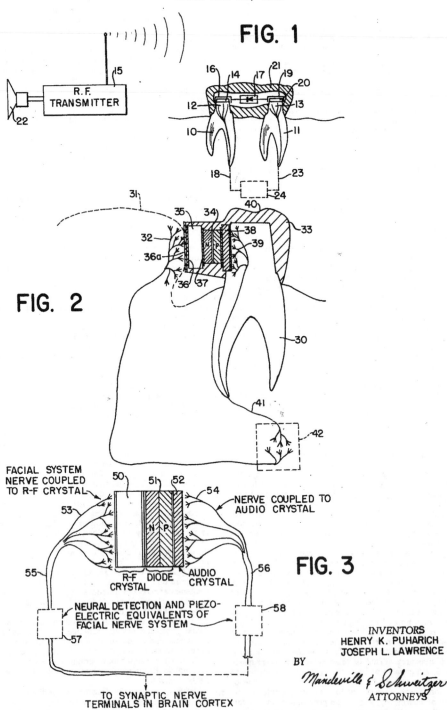

FIG. 1

FIG. 2

FIG. 3

R.F. TRANSMITTER

FACIAL SYSTEM NERVE COUPLED TO R-F CRYSTAL

NERVE COUPLED TO AUDIO CRYSTAL

R-F CRYSTAL   DIODE   AUDIO CRYSTAL

NEURAL DETECTION AND PIEZO-ELECTRIC EQUIVALENTS OF FACIAL NERVE SYSTEM

TO SYNAPTIC NERVE TERMINALS IN BRAIN CORTEX

INVENTORS
HENRY K. PUHARICH
JOSEPH L. LAWRENCE

BY

Mandeville & Schweitzer
ATTORNEYS

United States Patent Office

3,156,787
Patented Nov. 10, 1964

1

2

3,156,787
SOLID STATE HEARING SYSTEM
Henry K. Puharich, 87 Hawkes Ave., Ossining, N.Y., and
Joseph L. Lawrence, 570 Fort Washington Ave., New
York, N.Y.
Filed Oct. 23, 1962, Ser. No. 232,390
8 Claims. (Cl. 179—107)

The present invention relates to electronic hearing systems arranged for direct application to the nervous system of the human body, and is directed more particularly to specific improvement in the hearing system described and claimed in our prior United States Patent No. 2,995,633, granted August 8, 1961.

In the novel hearing system described and claimed in our before-mentioned patent, the sensation of hearing is induced in a human subject by applying modulated electrical signals to viable nerves of the facial system of the human subject, the "facial system" being a relatively specific network of nerves confined to facial areas of the human body and defined in more precise detail in our patent. The present invention, as its primary objective, provides an improved, highly simplified and wholly effective arrangement of physical and electrical components, enabling the system of our prior patent to be carried out in a highly reliable manner, at a minimum of cost and with components of minimum physical bulk.

A basic discovery incorporated in the system of our prior Patent No. 2,995,633 resides in the fact that modulated electromagnetic (i.e., radio) signals, when applied directly to the viable nerves of the facial system, can be converted to proper modulated electric signals which create a sensation of hearing in the human subject. In a most practical system for imparting the desired, modulated signals to the subject, an appliance is mounted on a viable tooth of the subject to receive transmitted radio input signals, convert them to usable form and apply the usable signals to the viable nerves of the tooth. In accordance with the present invention, an extremely simplified, reliable and economical appliance is provided for this purpose, which comprises essentially a piezoelectric crystal element, tuned sharply to the carrier frequency of the radio transmitter and connected to the negative terminal of a detector diode. This appliance is attached to the body of the subject in such a way that viable nerves of the facial system of the user are connected through one plate of the crystal to the negative terminal of the diode. The positive terminal of the diode is connected to the body of the subject in such a way as to complete an electrical circuit, through the nerve system of the subject, to the other plate of the crystal. The positive terminal of the diode need not necessarily be connected directly to an area of the facial nerve system of the subject, but it is advantageous to so connect the appliance, both for practical, physical reasons, and for most efficient performance.

In one of its advantageous forms, the appliance of the invention takes the form of a double-tooth bridge, which caps adjacent, denuded viable teeth of the subject, with connections being made to the viable nerves of each tooth to complete the desired circuit arrangements. In a second advantageous form, the appliance takes the form of a single tooth cap, with the terminals of the electrical components being connected at one side to viable nerves of the tooth and at the other side to viable nerves of other areas of the facial system, such as the tongue.

As a particularly advantageous aspect of the invention, the essential components of the appliance, namely, a tuned piezoelectric crystal and a simple diode, are arranged in a wafer-like arrangement of a practical minimum physical size, suitable for association with the teeth of a human subject.

In another specific, advantageous form of the invention, a second piezoelectric crystal element having a resonance in the audio frequency range, is electrically coupled to the positive terminal of the diode and arranged in physical and electrical contact with viable nerves of the facial system of the subject, in such a way that the electrical signals imparted to the nerves are accompanied by physical stimulation of the nerves for improved receptivity.

For a better understanding of the invention, reference should be made to the following detailed description and to the accompanying drawing, in which:

FIG. 1 is a simplified, schematic representation of one form of the invention;

FIG. 2 is a simplified, schematic representation of a second form of the invention, and

FIG. 3 is a schematic representation of the theorized circuit networks involved in the systems of FIGS. 1 and 2.

Referring now to the drawings, and initially to FIG. 1 thereof, the reference numerals 10, 11 designate viable teeth of a human subject which have been "denuded" by removal of their enamel covering and exposure of their respective nerve endings 12, 13.

In accordance with the invention, one of the denuded teeth, and specifically the tooth designated by the numeral 10 in the illustration of FIG. 1, has applied to the top thereof, in electrical and physical contact with the exposed nerve endings 12, a piezoelectric crystal element 14, which may be referred to herein as an R-F resonant crystal. The R-F resonant crystal 14, per se, may be of a conventional type, being advantageously formed of a lead zirconate titanate composition, polarized with its "plus" side against the nerve endings 12. Further, the R-F resonant crystal 14 is designed to be resonant over a predetermined, limited range of frequencies substantially inclusive of the carrier frequencies of a radio transmitter 15 associated near the body of the subject. Thus, for association with a typical R-F transmitter 15 having a carrier frequency on the order of four megacycles, the R-F resonant crystal 14 advantageously is tuned for resonance at or near four megacycles.

Connected to the R-F resonant crystal 14, advantageously by a metal conductor plate 16, is a diode 17, which may be a simple semi-conductor device for the detection of modulated alternating signals. In this respect, the term "diode" is not intended to be used in a limiting sense, but only to describe a non-linear element which performs a detecting and rectifying function.

In accordance with one aspect of the invention, the diode 17 has its negative terminal connected to the R-F resonant crystal 14 through the conductive plate 16. Thus, where the diode 17 is a simple semi-conductor device, having a single P-N junction, the N side of the semi-conductor is connected to the R-F resonant crystal. The positive or P side of the diode is, in accordance with the invention, connected to the body of the subject in such a way as to complete an electrical circuit back to the nerve system 18 serving the denuded tooth 10. While this circuit connection may be accomplished through various areas of the body (e.g., a finger) the connection advantageously is made to an adjacent, denuded tooth 11, substantially as shown in FIG. 1.

In the specific system illustrated in FIG. 1, the connection of the positive terminal of the diode 17 to the denuded tooth 11 is made through a conductive plate 19 and a piezoelectric crystal 20, the latter being in direct contact with the exposed nerve endings 13 of the tooth. The crystal element 20, while not necessary in a theoretical sense, is advantageous in that the appli-

Feb. 23, 1965   H. K. PUHARICH ETAL   **3,170,993**
                    MEANS FOR AIDING HEARING BY ELECTRICAL STIMULATION
                              OF THE FACIAL NERVE SYSTEM
Filed Jan. 8, 1962   4 Sheets—Sheet 1

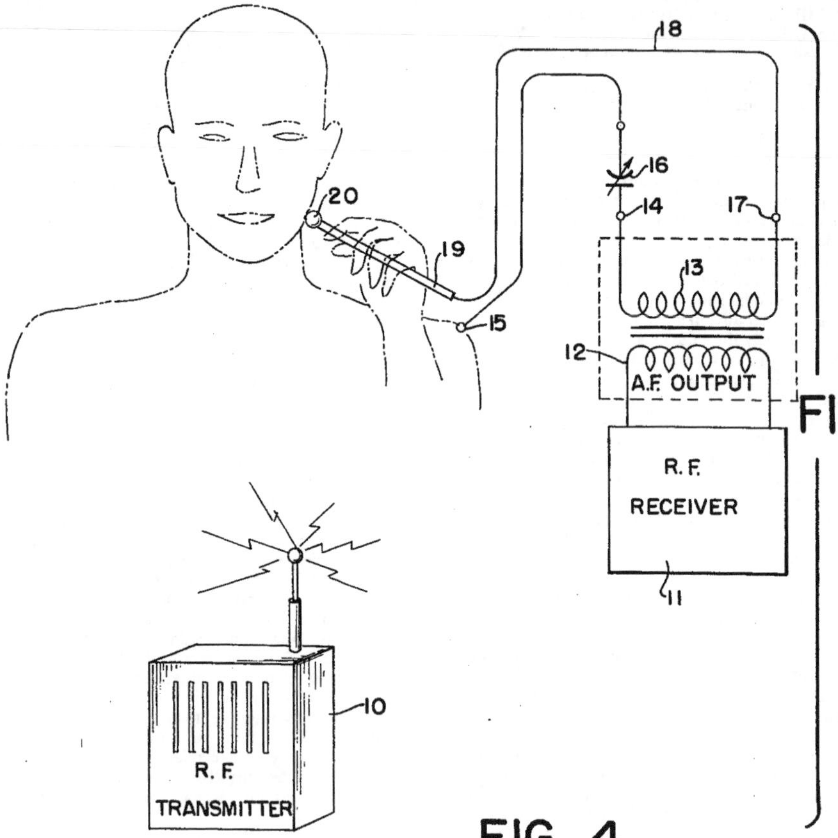

FIG. 1

FIG. 4

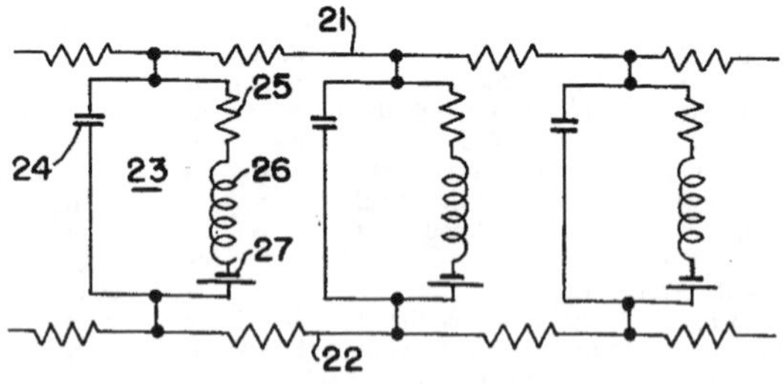

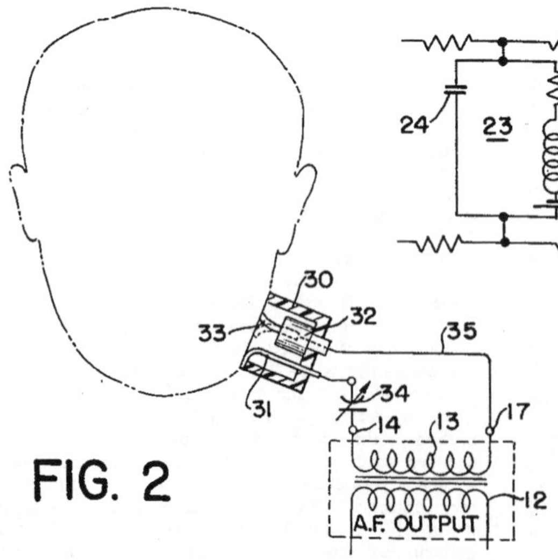

FIG. 2

INVENTORS
HENRY K. PUHARICH
JOSEPH L. LAWRENCE

184

United States Patent Office

3,170,993
Patented Feb. 23, 1965

1   2

3,170,993
MEANS FOR AIDING HEARING BY ELECTRICAL
STIMULATION OF THE FACIAL NERVE SYSTEM
Henry K. Puharich, 87 Hawkes Ave., Ossining, N.Y., and
Joseph L. Lawrence, 570 Fort Washington Ave., New
York, N.Y.
Filed Jan. 8, 1962, Ser. No. 164,882
24 Claims. (Cl. 179—107)

The present invention relates to facilities for use in conjunction with the human body for aiding hearing, and is directed more specifically to novel and improved arrangements for aiding hearing by electrical stimulation of the facial nerve system.

In our prior United States Patent No. 2,995,633, granted August 8, 1961, there is disclosed a fundamentally novel arrangement for assisting the hearing process of the human body through electrical stimulation of the facial nerve system of a user, employing modulated electrical signals corresponding to audible sounds. The basic discoveries described in our prior patent reside in the fact that the facial nerve system of the human body (the facial nerve system being a rather specifically defined nerve network, as will be described in more detail) is receptive to stimulation by electrical signals, corresponding to audible sounds, in such a way that modulated electrical signals are transmitted to produce sensations of sound equivalent to sounds received by the ear of a person having normal hearing capabilities.

Thus, in the normal hearing system of the human body, mechanisms in and associated with the ear seem to operate essentially as electromechanical transducers, converting the air pressure modulations constituting "sounds" into corresponding, modulated electrical signals, which are transmitted to hearing centers of the brain. It has been brought out by our prior discoveries, described in some detail in our prior patent, that the nerve network serving the ear mechanism is associated with the facial nerve system of the human body, which has nerve endings in the teeth and in other areas about the face and head, the association being such that modulated electrical signals of the proper type, applied to receptor nerve endings of the facial system in the teeth, bypass some of the usual mechanisms of the ear, or work in conjunction with them to produce sensations of sound which are largely indistinguishable from sensations derived through the usual hearing facilities. One of the significant consequences of the discovery resides in the fact that persons whose normal hearing mechanisms have been so damaged as to be partially or wholly unresponsive to conventional, essentially mechanical hearing aids, can be made to receive the usual sensations of sound by direct application of modulated electrical signals to the facial nerve system.

The present invention is directed specifically to the provision of improved facilities for imparting amplitude modulated electrical signals, corresponding to audible sounds, through the facial nerve system of the human body, to produce sensations of sound, with substantial fidelity and reliability. In particular, the improvement of the present invention resides in the discovery of, and the provision of means for applying in a practical way the principle of achieving especially advantageous electrical association between the facial nerve system of the body and a signal output appliance, by employing novel and improved coupling circuit arrangements.

In accordance with the invention, a novel and improved hearing aid system is provided, which includes a radio frequency receiver for receiving transmitted radio frequency signals and converting them to suitable audio modulated signals, the receiver being provided with a novel output circuit arrangement which, in conjunction with a portion of the facial nerve system to which it is coupled, constitutes a desirable and advantageous circuit. The improved arrangement is such that the audio modulated signals induced in the output circuit of the receiver are imparted to the facial nerve system in a desirable form, to which the facial nerve system is particularly receptive.

As a specific and significant aspect of the present invention, the improved audio modulated output circuit arrangement for imparting modulated electrical signals to the facial nerve system, incorporates capacitative coupling means for connecting a section of nerve "circuit" to the output of the radio frequency receiver, which supplies audio modulated electrical signals. The capacitative coupling means, in conjunction with the electrical parameters of the nerve "circuit" and the receiver output form a particularly advantageous operating circuit, which imparts to the nerve circuit the modulated output signals of the receiver in a desirable form, to which the facial nerve system has been found to be particularly responsive. As a result of the improved electrical association between the receiving appliance and the facial nerve system, the stimulations transmitted to hearing centers are of a form productive of particularly sharp and faithful sound sensations.

Although the desired capacitative coupling between the receiver output and the nerve circuit may be brought about effectively in a variety of ways, some of which will be described with particularity, the most advantageous, practical form of capacitative coupling presently known involves the use of one or more cup-shaped dental caps, which are electrically coupled to viable nerves of or normally serving the teeth, in a manner to provide an effective and desirable form of electrical capacity at each "terminal" of the nerve circuit.

The physical embodiment of the invention is capable of a substantial variety ranging from appliances adapted for application externally of the body to systems housed entirely within the oral cavity. In its most advantageous form, the means of the invention includes elements mounted on and electrically associated with one or more viable teeth of the user. However, provision is made for operatively installing an appliance according to the invention in the oral cavity of an edentulous person by incorporating the appliance within the structure of the dentures.

For a better understanding of the invention, reference should be made to the following detailed description and to the accompanying drawings, in which:

FIG. 1 is a simplified, schematic representation of an elementary form of hearing aid system according to the invention;

FIG. 2 is a simplified, schematic representation of a modification of the system shown in FIG. 1;

FIG. 3 is a further simplified, schematic representation of a circuit equivalent employed in the system of the invention, including a typical circuit equivalent representation for a nerve element;

FIG. 4 is a schematic representation, in more detailed form, of a circuit equivalent for a nerve section, as currently theorized from experimental data;

FIG. 5 is a simplified, schematic representation of a modified form of system incorporating the invention;

FIGS. 6 and 7 are further modified forms of the new system, in which circuit coupling appliances are mounted on two viable teeth of the user;

FIG. 8 is a simplified, schematic representation of the circuit equivalent for the systems of FIGS. 5–7;

FIG. 9 is a simplified, schematic representation of a further modified form of the invention adapted specifically for incorporation into a denture structure; and

FIG. 10 is a simplified, schematic representation of a circuit equivalent of the system of FIG. 9.

185

United States Patent [19]

Limoge

[11] **3,835,833**

[45] **Sept. 17, 1974**

[54] **METHOD FOR OBTAINING NEUROPHYSIOLOGICAL EFFECTS**

[76] Inventor: **Aime Limoge**

[22] Filed: **Sept. 21, 1972**

[21] Appl. No.: **290,804**

[30] **Foreign Application Priority Data**

Sept. 24, 1971 France 71.34365

[52] **U.S. Cl.**................. **128/1 C**, 128/420, 128/422
[51] **Int. Cl.**... **A61n 1/36**
[58] **Field of Search**........ 128/419 R, 420, 421, 422, 128/1 C

[56] **References Cited**
UNITED STATES PATENTS

3,648,708	3/1972	Haeri	128/1 C
3,712,292	1/1973	Zentmeyer, Jr. et al...........	128/1 C
3,727,616	4/1973	Lenzkes.............................	128/422

FOREIGN PATENTS OR APPLICATIONS

1,165,541	10/1969	Great Britain	128/1 C
1,554,569	12/1968	France	128/1 C
1,088,607	10/1967	Great Britain	128/1 C

OTHER PUBLICATIONS

Buchsbaum, "Electronics World," Sept. 1963, pp. 27–29.

Primary Examiner—William E. Kamm
Attorney, Agent, or Firm—Young & Thompson

[57] **ABSTRACT**

A method and apparatus for obtaining neurophysiological effects on the central and/or peripheral systems of a patient. Electrodes are suitably positioned on the body of the patient and a composite electric signal is applied at the electrodes. The composite signal is formed by the superpositioning of two signals: a first signal which is a rectified high-frequency carrier modulated in amplitude to about 100 percent by substantially square-shaped pulses whose duration, amplitude and frequency are chosen according to the neurophysiological effects desidered, and a second signal which has a relatively white noise spectrum. The mean value of the first electric signal has a predetermined sign which is opposite the sign of the mean value of the second electric signal.

5 Claims, 1 Drawing Figure

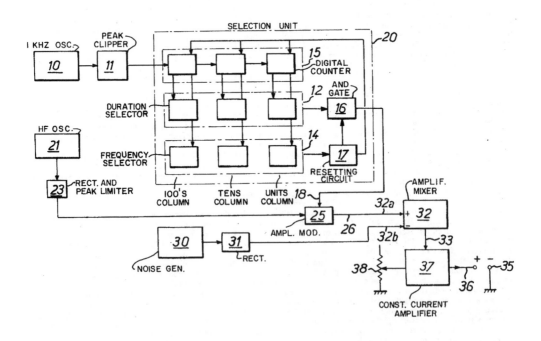

3,835,833

1

METHOD FOR OBTAINING NEUROPHYSIOLOGICAL EFFECTS

BACKGROUND OF THE INVENTION

The present invention concerns a method and apparatus for obtaining neurophysiological effects by the application of electric currents to the central and/or peripheral nervous systems of the human body.

It is known that the application of electrical signals at electrodes placed at suitably chosen points on the body of a patient is capable of causing various effects such as general or local anaesthesia, sleep or relaxion of the subject depending on the location of the electrodes and the parameters defining the signal.

Among the various types of signals for obtaining such results, it has been established that the use of square-shaped pulses of suitable amplitude, frequency and period is particularly effective.

Such signals, may, however, cause bothersome secondary phenomena such as contractures, polarization or electrolysis effects which could be redhibitory in numerous cases.

With regard to these drawbacks, it has been proposed to use for similar applications a complex signal consisting of a rectified high-frequency signal which is about 100 percent amplitude modulated by low frequency square-shaped pulses which in the majority of cases enables the total elimination of the contractures remaining when the low frequency pulses shapes a direct current signal instead of the envelope of a rectified high frequency signal.

The effects so obtained are clearly superior to those of the former technique. Nevertheless, the rectified high-frequency signals modulated by low-frequency square-shaped pulses is not entirely satisfactory in all applications, because they do not enable the complete elimination of undesirable phenomena such as local electrolysis, disagreeable tingling or other unacceptable reactions necessitating the reduction of the current of the applied signals or the shortening of the length of application thereof.

SUMMARY OF THE INVENTION

The present invention enables the reduction or even the complete elimination of undesirable secondary effects by reducing the mean value of the currents applied on which the said secondary effects directly depend, without substantially reducing the desired principal neurophysiological effects.

To this effect, the present invention provides a method for obtaining neurophysiological effects on the central and/or peripheral nervous systems of a patient, comprising positioning electrodes on the body of the patient, applying a composite electric signal at the electrodes formed by the superpositioning of a first and second electric signal, said first electric signal being a rectified high-frequency carrier modulated in amplitude to about 100 percent by substantially square-shaped pulses whose duration, amplitude and frequency are chosen according to the desired neurophysiological effects, the mean value of said first electric signal being of a predetermined signal said second signal having a relatively white noise spectrum, the sign of the mean value of said second electric signal being opposite that of the mean value of said first electric signal.

The white noise constituting the said second signal may have a substantially continuous spectrum ranging

2

from 1 KHz to 60 KHz and preferably between 20 and 60 KHz. Such a noise signal could be easily obtained by means of a gas discharge tube, a semi-conductor or other appropriate means.

As previously indicated, it has been observed throughout that the undesirable secondary effects of electrophysiological treatment are all the more accentuated when the average current passing through the electrodes applied to the body of the patient is increased.

In the method according to the invention, this average current intensity, whose value is the algebraic sum of the respective mean values of said first and second signals, is the difference between these mean values.

I was surprised to find that the presence of white noise which enables the reduction of the overall mean current strength, the electrolysis effects and the intolerance of the body, remains without any detriment to the effectiveness of the treatment. It is thought that this very advantageous property comes from the fact that the relatively continuous spectrum of the white noise signal avoids the generation of undesired possibly detrimental discrete beat frequencies from the pulse modulated carrier and the white noise signal, while being capable of bringing about by an appropriate choice of the limits of this continuous spectrum complementary neurophysiological effects resulting in a reinforcement of the principal desired effect.

According to the intended application, the relative proportion of the noise component and the modulated high-frequency component may be advantageous between one-fourth and one-half in the majority of cases, this proportion designating the ratio of the mean current strength of these components.

The method according to the invention is particularly applicable to obtaining neurophysiological effects such as relaxation, sleep, general analgesia, local-regional anaesthesia, and general anaesthesia.

Its use is particularly advantageous when the current strength of the pulse modulated high-frequency signal whose average value is the product of the r.m.s. value of the high-frequency carrier by the mark-to-space ratio of the square-shaped low-frequency pulses must be rather large, as for example in the case of electro-analgesia or electro-anaesthesia treatments.

Also disclosed is a device for carrying out the method described above comprising a high-frequency signal generator, a low-frequency pulse generator, means for modulating the amplitude of the said high-frequency signals by the low-frequency pulses, a noise generator adapted to generate electric signals having a relatively continuous frequency spectrum and mixing means adapted to superimpose the modulated high-frequency signal generated by said modulation means and the signals from the noise generator for providing a composite signal with a mean amplitude proportional to the difference between the respective mean amplitudes of the modulated high-frequency signal and said noise signal.

Preferably, the apparatus comprises control means selectively adjusting certain or all parameters defining the composite output signal, i.e., the peak amplitude of the modulated high-frequency signal, the amplitude of the noise signal, the frequency of the high-frequency signal, the length and the spacing of the low frequency modulation pukes, as well as the spectrum of the signal delivered by the noise generator.

United States Patent [19]

Ross

[11] **3,967,616**

[45] **July 6, 1976**

[54] **MULTICHANNEL SYSTEM FOR AND A MULTIFACTORIAL METHOD OF CONTROLLING THE NERVOUS SYSTEM OF A LIVING ORGANISM**

[76] Inventor: **Sidney A. Ross**

[22] Filed: **Sept. 5, 1974**

[21] Appl. No.: **503,468**

Related U.S. Application Data

[63] Continuation-in-part of Ser. No. 299,842, Oct. 24, 1972, Pat. No. 3,837,331.

[52] **U.S. Cl.** .... **128/1 C; 128/2.1 B**
[51] **Int. Cl.²** **A61B 5/05; A61B 19/00**
[58] **Field of Search** .... 128/2.1 B, 1 C, 2.1 R, 128/422

[56] **References Cited**
UNITED STATES PATENTS

2,501,808	3/1950	Brockway et al.	128/1 C
3,413,546	11/1968	Riehl et al.	128/2.1 B
3,495,596	2/1970	Condict	128/422
3,753,433	8/1973	Bakerich et al.	128/2.1 B
3,826,243	7/1974	Anderson	128/2.1 B
3,837,331	9/1974	Ross	128/1 C
3,841,309	10/1974	Salter	128/2.1 B
3,863,625	2/1975	Viglione et al.	128/2.1 B

OTHER PUBLICATIONS

Med. & Biol. Engng., vol. 8, No. 2, pp. 209–211, 1970.
The Washington Post, Apr. 30, 1972, Sec. D3.

Primary Examiner—Kyle L. Howell
Attorney, Agent, or Firm—Blakely, Sokoloff, Taylor & Zafman

[57] **ABSTRACT**

A novel method for controlling the nervous system of a living organism for therapeutic and research purposes, among other applications, and an electronic system utilized in, and enabling the practice of, the invented method. Bioelectrical signals generated in specifictopological areas of the organism's nervous system, typically areas of the brain, are processed by the invented system so as to produce a sensory stimulus if the system detects the presence or absence, as the case may be, of certain characteristics in the waveform patterns of the bioelectrical signals being monitored. The coincidence of the same or different characteristics in two or more waveform patterns, or the non-coincidence thereof, may be correlated with a certain desired condition of the organism's nervous system; likewise, with respect to the coincidence or non-coincidence of different characteristics of a single waveform pattern. In any event, the sensory stimulus provided by the invented system, typically an audio or visual stimulus, or combination thereof, is fed back to the organism which associates its presence with the goal of achieving the desired condition of its nervous system. Responding to the stimulus, the organism can be trained to control the waveform patterns of the monitored bioelectrical signals and thereby, control its own nervous system. The results of the coincidence function permit results heretofore unobtainable.

41 Claims, 2 Drawing Figures

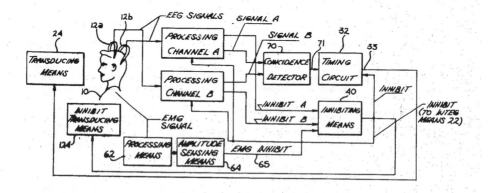

United States Patent [19]

Adams et al.

[11] **4,034,741**

[45] **July 12, 1977**

[54] **NOISE GENERATOR AND TRANSMITTER**

[75] Inventors: **Guy Emery Adams**, Monroe; **Jesse Carden, Jr.**, Piermont, both of N.Y.

[73] Assignee: **Solitron Devices, Inc.**, Tappan, N.Y.

[21] Appl. No.: **658,596**

[22] Filed: **Feb. 17, 1976**

[51] Int. Cl.² **A61B 19/00**
[52] U.S. Cl. .... **128/1 C; 307/240; 331/78; 332/31 T**
[58] Field of Search .... 128/1 C, 1 R; 331/78, 331/38 M; 307/239, 240, 304; 332/31 T

[56] **References Cited**

U.S. PATENT DOCUMENTS

2,304,095	12/1941	Hull	128/1 C
3,213,851	10/1965	Currea	128/1 R
3,219,028	11/1965	Giordano	128/1 C
3,404,235	10/1968	Goldberg	331/78
3,668,561	6/1972	Krupa et al.	332/31 T
3,712,292	1/1973	Zentmeyer, Jr.	128/1 C
3,718,987	3/1973	Carver	331/78
3,863,136	1/1975	Hanson	307/304

FOREIGN PATENT DOCUMENTS

1,165,541	10/1969	United Kingdom	128/1 C

Primary Examiner—William E. Kamm
Attorney, Agent, or Firm—Richard G. Geib

[57] **ABSTRACT**

An analgesic noise generator employs a circuit that can be switched to provide a variable waveform from an active noise source out of an integrated circuit amplifier.

4 Claims, 3 Drawing Figures

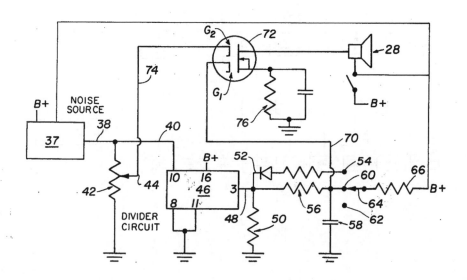

United States Patent [19]

Chang et al.

[11] **4,082,918**

[45] **Apr. 4, 1978**

[54] **AUDIO ANALGESIC UNIT**

[76] Inventors: **Roland Wan-chan Chang**

Charles A. Graves

[21] Appl. No.: **760,838**

[22] Filed: **Jan. 21, 1977**

[51] Int. Cl.^{2} **A61B 19/00; A61N 1/00**

[52] U.S. Cl. .... **179/1 AA**

[58] Field of Search .... 179/1 AA; 128/1 R

[56] **References Cited**

U.S. PATENT DOCUMENTS

2,986,140   5/1961   Gardner .... 128/1 R

3,213,851   10/1965   Currea .... 179/1 AA

Primary Examiner—Kathleen H. Claffy
Assistant Examiner—E. S. Kemeny

[57] **ABSTRACT**

An audio analgesic unit for use in masking sounds and substituting another sound which includes earmuffs to be used by a dental patient in which speakers are arranged and connected to a patient operated remote control unit to control the sound levels and a master control unit to override the patient remote control unit and operated by an operator, such as a dentist. A beeper indicates operation mode change.

2 Claims, 1 Drawing Figure

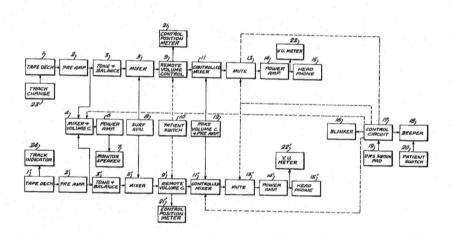

United States Patent [19]

Nagle

[11] **4,191,175**

[45] **Mar. 4, 1980**

[54] **METHOD AND APPARATUS FOR REPETITIVELY PRODUCING A NOISE-LIKE AUDIBLE SIGNAL**

[76] Inventor: **William L. Nagle,** c/o Seidel Gonda & Goldhammer

[21] Appl. No.: **870,050**

[22] Filed: **Jan. 16, 1978**

[51] Int. Cl.^{2} **A61B 19/00**
[52] U.S. Cl. .... **128/1 C**
[58] Field of Search .... 128/1 C, 2.1 B; 331/78

[56] **References Cited**

U.S. PATENT DOCUMENTS

3,576,185	4/1971	Schulz et al.	128/1 C
4,034,741	7/1977	Adams et al.	128/1 C

FOREIGN PATENT DOCUMENTS

1088607 10/1967 United Kingdom .... 128/1 C

OTHER PUBLICATIONS

Faran "The General Radio Experimenter" vol. 36, No. 7, Jul., 1962, pp. 4–5, 331/78.

Primary Examiner—William E. Kamm
Attorney, Agent, or Firm—Seidel, Gonda, Goldhammer & Panitch

[57] **ABSTRACT**

A digital pulse generator and shift register repetitively produce bursts of digital pulses at a first adjustable repetition frequency. The repetition frequency of the pulses in each burst is also adjustable. A pink noise filter accentuates the lower burst frequency components near 7 hz and substantially attenuates all frequency components of the bursts above a first cut-off point near 10 Khz. A tunable band pass amplifier having a center frequency adjustable over a preselected range of frequencies optimally detectable by the average human ear accentuates the pink noise filter output near 2.6 Khz. The tunable amplifier drives an audible signal source with noise-like pulses of varying amplitudes and frequency components. A low pass amplifier may be connected to the pink noise filter to generate a train of pulses having a repetition frequency near 7 hz which pulses a light source in synchronism with the audible noise-like signal.

10 Claims, 4 Drawing Figures

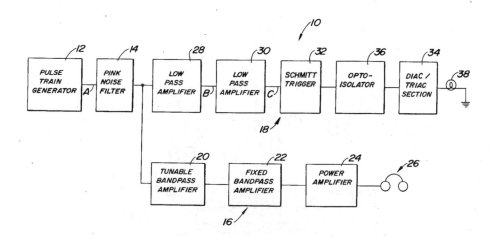

United States Patent [19]

Loos

[11] **Patent Number:**   **5,935,054**

[45] **Date of Patent:**   **Aug. 10, 1999**

[54] **MAGNETIC EXCITATION OF SENSORY RESONANCES**

[76] Inventor: **Hendricus G. Loos**

[21] Appl. No.: **08/486,918**

[22] Filed: **Jun. 7, 1995**

[51] **Int. Cl.⁶** **A61N 2/00**
[52] **U.S. Cl.** **600/9**
[58] **Field of Search** 600/9–15

[56] **References Cited**

U.S. PATENT DOCUMENTS

3,678,337	7/1972	Grauvogel	317/4
4,197,851	4/1980	Fellus	128/422
4,611,599	9/1986	Bentall	128/422
4,727,857	3/1988	Horl	600/15
5,667,469	9/1997	Zhang et al.	600/9

OTHER PUBLICATIONS

P. Lindemann, The Megabrain Report, vol. 1, #2, pp. 34–35 (1990).
P. Limdemann, The Megabrain Report, vol. 1, #1, pp. 30–31 (1990).

Primary Examiner—John P. Lacyk

[57] **ABSTRACT**

The invention pertains to influencing the nervous system of a subject by a weak externally applied magnetic field with a frequency near ½ Hz. In a range of amplitudes, such fields can excite the ½ sensory resonance, which is the physiological effect involved in "rocking the baby". The wave form of the stimulating magnetic field is restricted by conditions on the spectral power density, imposed in order to avoid irritating the brain and the risk of kindling. The method and apparatus can be used by the general public as an aid to relaxation, sleep, or arousal, and clinically for the control of tremors, seizures, and emotional disorders.

8 Claims, 4 Drawing Sheets

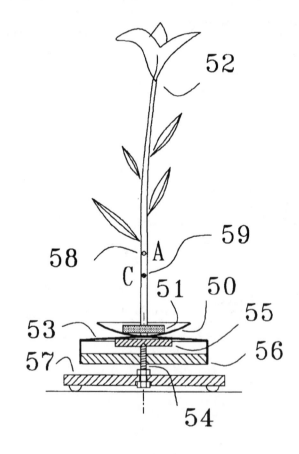

1

MAGNETIC EXCITATION OF SENSORY RESONANCES

BACKGROUND OF THE INVENTION

The human nervous system exhibits a sensitivity to certain low-frequency stimuli, as is evident from rocking a baby or relaxing in a rocking chair. In both cases, the maximum soothing effect is obtained for a periodic motion with a frequency near ½ Hz. The effect is here called "the ½ Hz sensory resonance". In the rocking response, the sensory resonance is excited principally by frequency-coded signals from the vestibular organ. However, the rocking motion also induces body strains, and these are detected by stretch receptors such as Ruffini corpuscules in the skin and muscle spindles throughout the body. In addition, signals may come from cutaneous cold and warmth receptors which report skin temperature variations caused by relative air currents induced by the rocking motion. All these receptors employ frequency coding in their sensory function, and it is believed that their signals are combined and compared with the vestibular nerve signals in an assessment of the somatic state. One may thus expect that the resonance can be excited separately not only through the vestibular nerve, but also through the other sensory modalities mentioned. This notion is supported by the observation that gently stroking of a child with a frequency near ½ Hz has a soothing effect as well. Appropriate separate stimulation of the other frequency-coding sensory receptors mentioned is expected to have a similar effect.

The notion has occurred that frequency-coding sensory receptors may perhaps respond to certain artificial stimulations, and that such stimulations could be used to cause excitation of the ½ Hz sensory resonance. This indeed can been done, by using externally applied weak electric fields as the artificial stimulus, as discussed in the U.S. patent application Ser. 08/447,394 [1]. Autonomic effects of this stimulation have been observed in the form of relaxation, drowsiness, sexual excitement, or tonic smile, depending on the precise electric field frequency near ½ Hz used. The question whether the effects are perhaps due to the direct action of the electric field on the brain has been settled by experiments in which localized weak electric fields are applied to areas of the skin away from the head; these experiments showed the same array of autonomic effects. It follows that the electric field acts on certain somatosensory nerves.

A major application of the electric exitation of the resonance is seen in the form of a sleeping aid. The method can further be used by the general public as an aid to relaxation and arousal, and clinically for the control of tremmors and seizures as well as disorders resulting from malfunctions of the autonomic nervous system, such as panic attacks.

Electric fields are subject to polarization effects that bar certain applications. These limitations would be circumvented if the excitation could be done by magnetic rather than electric fields. It is an object of the present invention to provide a method and apparatus for excitation of the ½ Hz sensory resonance by oscillatory magnetic fields.

An electromagnetic field apparatus for environmental control is discussed by Grauvogel in U.S. Pat. No. 3,678,337. The apparatus is to re-create indoors the electric and magnetic fields that occur naturally out-of-doors, in the interest of physical and mental well-being. In advancing this notion, Grauvogel overlooks the fact that the earth's magnetic field is not shielded by buildings; therefore, the magnetic part of his apparatus is superfluous in the context of his

2

objective. In Grauvogel's claims, the field of use is stated as "environmental control apparatus".

In U.S. Pat. No. 4,197,851 Fellus shows an apparatus for emitting high-frequency electromagnetic waves with a low intensity such as to avoid significant thermal effects in exposed tissue, employing an "antenna" which is applied closely to the skin via insulation material, in such a manner as to conform to body contours. Bentall, in U.S. Pat. No. 4,611,599 shows an electrical apparatus for influencing a metabolic growth characteristic, wherein a radio frequency electromagnetic field is applied to a subject at a low power level such as not to produce bulk heating of the exposed tissue. The high-frequencies used by Fellus and by Bentall are not suitable for exciting the ½ Hz sensory resonance.

A device for influencing subjects by means of pulsed electromagnetic fields has been discussed by Lindemann [2]. His "Centron" device comprises a square wave generator connected to an equiangular spiral coil with two branches. The pulse rate can be chosen from 12 discrete frequencies ranging from 1 to 18 Hz. Comments on the workings of the spiral coil are given by Lindeman [3] in the context of "scalar fields", a notion that happens to be in conflict with modern physics. According to Lindeman [3], the spiral coil of the Centron involves "a high degree of interaction between the inductance and capacitance, creating what is called a scalar". In spite of the erroneous physical basis presented, the Centron device may indeed affect the nervous system. However, several shortcomings are apparent in the design. First, the spiral coil is woefully inefficient and is therefore wasteful of electric current, a precious commodity in battery-operated devices. It may perhaps be thought that the spiral coil design provides localization of the magnetic field by clever cancellations, but that is not the case; a calculation of the steady asymptotic magnetic field induced by the coil shows that the far field is dominated by a dipole. Second, the frequency range of the device misses the ½ Hz sensory resonance alltogether, and the use of preset discrete frequencies hampers exploration of other resonances. Last but not least, the fundamental frequencies and some of the higher harmonics in the square wave produce nuisance signals in the brain, and pose a risk of kindling [4] in subjects with a disposition to epilepsy.

It is an object of the present invention to provide an efficient battery-powered device for inducing magnetic fields for the excitation of the ½ Hz sensory resonance without causing irritation to the brain or posing a threat of kindling.

Other devices that emit "scalar" fields for unspecified therapeutic purposes are the Teslar watch and the MicroHarmonizer, distributed by Tools For Exploration in San Rafael, Calif. The Teslar watch emits a pulsed magnetic field at a fixed frequency of 7.83 Hertz, and the MicroHarmonizer can be switched to either 7.83 Hz or 3.91 Hz. Neither device can be tuned to the ½ Hz sensory resonance.

There is much public concern about the health effects of low-frequency electromagnetic fields. In response, governments have issued guide lines for manufacturers of electronic equipment. Among these, the Swedish MPRII guide lines are the strictest in the world. For human exposure to low-frequency magnetic fields, MPRII calls for an upper limit of 250 nT in the frequency band from 5 Hz to 2 KHz, and 25 nT in the band from 2 KHz to 400 KHz. In the topical application of localized magnetic fields by coils placed close to the skin, compliance with the MPRII guidelines may require use of a distributed coil, in order to keep the spatial maximum of the field from exceeding the MPRII limit. It is

United States Patent [19]

Loos

[11] **Patent Number:** **6,091,994**

[45] **Date of Patent:** ***Jul. 18, 2000**

[54] **PULSATIVE MANIPULATION OF NERVOUS SYSTEMS**

[76] Inventor: **Hendricus G. Loos**

[*] Notice: This patent is subject to a terminal disclaimer.

[21] Appl. No.: **09/144,762**

[22] Filed: **Aug. 31, 1998**

Related U.S. Application Data

[63] Continuation-in-part of application No. 08/580,346, Dec. 28, 1995, Pat. No. 5,800,481.

[51] Int. Cl.[7] **A61F 2/00**
[52] U.S. Cl. **607/100**
[58] Field of Search 607/96–98, 100–102, 607/115, 148, 152; 600/552–558

[56] **References Cited**

U.S. PATENT DOCUMENTS

4,676,246	6/1987	Korenaga	128/399
4,763,666	8/1988	Strian et al.	600/557
4,860,748	8/1989	Chiurco et al.	607/96
5,315,994	5/1994	Guibert et al.	607/101
5,327,886	7/1994	Chiu	607/96
5,447,530	9/1995	Guibert et al.	607/107
5,800,481	9/1998	Loos	607/100

FOREIGN PATENT DOCUMENTS

9409850 5/1994 United Kingdom 607/88

Primary Examiner—Cary O'Connor
Assistant Examiner—Ryan Carter

[57] **ABSTRACT**

Method and apparatus for manipulating the nervous system by imparting subliminal pulsative cooling to the subject's skin at a frequency that is suitable for the excitation of a sensory resonance. At present, two major sensory resonances are known, with frequencies near ½ Hz and 2.4 Hz. The ½ Hz sensory resonance causes relaxation, sleepiness, ptosis of the eyelids, a tonic smile, a "knot" in the stomach, or sexual excitement, depending on the precise frequency used. The 2.4 Hz resonance causes the slowing of certain cortical activities, and is characterized by a large increase of the time needed to silently count backward from 100 to 60, with the eyes closed. The invention can be used by the general public for inducing relaxation, sleep, or sexual excitement, and clinically for the control and perhaps a treatment of tremors, seizures, and autonomic system disorders such as panic attacks. Embodiments shown are a pulsed fan to impart subliminal cooling pulses to the subject's skin, and a silent device which induces periodically varying flow past the subject's skin, the flow being induced by pulsative rising warm air plumes that are caused by a thin resistive wire which is periodically heated by electric current pulses.

12 Claims, 5 Drawing Sheets

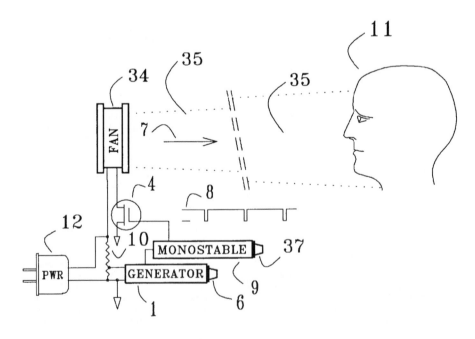

1

PULSATIVE MANIPULATION OF NERVOUS SYSTEMS

Continuation-in-part of application No. 580,346, Dec. 28, 1995, now U.S. Pat. No. 5,800,481, Sep. 1, 1998.

BACKGROUND OF THE INVENTION

The invention relates to influencing the nervous system of a subject by pulsative stimulation of sensory receptors, relying on the mechanisms of sensory resonance and frequency modulation of spontaneous spike patterns, as discussed in U.S. Pat. No. 5,782,874. [1]. In that patent, the stimulation is provided by an external electric field applied to the skin of the subject. The electric field appears to cause a modulation of the spiking patterns of certain cutaneous receptors, so that a pulsative field gives rise to a frequency modulation (fm) of the produced spike trains. Afferent nerves carry the frequency modulated spike trains to the brain, where in certain neural circuits the evoked fm signals cause excitation of a resonance with observable physiological consequences. One such "sensory resonance" that occurs near ½ Hz causes sleepiness, relaxation, a tonic smile, ptosis of the eyelids, a tense feeling in the stomach, or sexual excitement, depending on the precise pulse frequency used. The ½ Hz sensory resonance can also be excited by magnetic fields, as discussed in U.S. Pat. No. 5,935,054 [2].

Another known sensory resonance occurs near 2.4 Hz and causes a slowing of certain cortical activities.

SUMMARY

Experiments have shown that sensory resonances can be excited by imparting cooling pulses to the skin, when the pulse frequency is set to the resonance frequency of the sensory resonance, and the pulses have a proper subliminal amplitude. The sensory resonance near ½ Hz causes autonomic responses characterized by relaxation, sleepiness, ptosis of the eyelids, a tonic smile, a "knot" in the stomach, or sexual excitement, depending on the precise frequency used. The sensory resonance near 2.4 Hz causes slowing of certain cortical activities and is indicated by a large increase in the time needed to count silently backward from 100 to 60, with the eyes closed. The described effects occur only if the amplitude of the cooling pulses falls in a certain range called the effective intensity window.

The stimulation is thought to involve the following. The subliminal pulsative cooling of the skin causes a slight frequency modulation (fm) of the spike trains that are produced by cutaneous thermoreceptors. The spiking is transmitted to the brain by afferent nerves that report skin temperature. The frequency modulation of the spike train from a single thermoreceptor cannot be spotted by the brain, because the fm variations in the spike train are swamped by the much larger stochastic spiking variations. However, if afferents of a large number of affected thermoreceptors synapse on a single summing neuron, then the fm variations add coherently in the hillock potential, whereas the stochastic variations largely even out. Consequently, the signal to noise ratio for the fm signal is increased, and the more so the larger the skin area exposed to the cooling pulses. The fm signal is demodulated by further neural circuitry and the resulting signal can cause excitation of a resonance in certain subsequent processing circuits. The upper bound of the effective intensity window is thought to arise from the action of nuisance guarding neural circuits that block substantial repeditive nuisance signals from higher processing. The lower boundary of the window is simply due to a detection threshold.

2

Reliance on periodic frequency modulation of afferent spike trains, together with exploitation of the resonance phenomenon, leads to a method and apparatus for manipulation of nervous systems by imparting subliminal cooling pulses to the subject's skin. The invention can be used by the general public to induce relaxation, sleep, or sexual excitement, and clinically for control and perhaps a treatment of tremors and seizures, as well as autonomic disorders, such as panic attacks.

The cooling pulses may be imparted to the skin by convective or conductive means. In the latter case heat is extracted from the skin in pulsative fashion by a fast Peltier junction that is placed on the skin. In the convective method, cooling is provided through convective and evaporative heat transfer by means of a pulsed air jet aimed at the skin of the subject, or alternatively by a device wherein a periodic air sink draws atmospheric air past the skin of a nearby subject, the periodic air sink being induced by pulsative rising warm air plumes produced by a thin resistive wire that is heated by current pulses passed by a field effect transistor which is controlled by voltage pulses from a generator.

Using the latter device, the 2.4 Hz sensory resonance has been explored, employing the silent count from 100 to 60 as a resonance detector. The measured counting times define an excitation footprint in the plane which has pulse power and pulse frequency as coordinates.

A compact embodiment is shown in the form of a battery powered device, in which the resistive wire and the voltage generator are contained in a single small casing.

DESCRIPTION OF THE DRAWINGS

FIG. 1 shows a preferred embodiment where pulsative cooling of a subject's skin is achieved by a periodic air flow caused by a thermally induced air sink.

FIG. 2 shows an embodiment where pulsative cooling of the subject's skin is brought about by a fan powered by a voltage that is periodically interrupted.

FIG. 3 shows a voltage generator connected to a heatpatch for delivering heat pulses to the skin of a subject.

FIG. 4 depicts the delivery of heat pulses to the skin of a subject by an air jet with a periodic temperature.

FIG. 5 shows a circuit for producing a chaotic voltage.

FIG. 6 shows a circuit for generating a complex wave.

FIG. 7 shows an embodiment where pulsative cooling of a subject is obtained with a swiveling fan.

FIG. 8 shows an embodiment where pulsative cooling of a subject is obtained by an air jet that is periodically deflected by vanes.

FIG. 9 shows the results of experiments for excitation of the 2.4 Hz sensory resonance with the device of FIG. 1.

FIG. 10 depicts an embodiment wherein a thin resistive film is used to produce a periodic warm air plume which induces a periodic air sink that causes pulsative air flow past the subject.

FIG. 11 shows a Peltier junction for imparting pulsative cooling of a subject's skin by conduction.

FIG. 12 shows an embodiment wherein a generator and a thin resistive wire are contained in a single small casing.

DETAILED DESCRIPTION

In the excitation of sensory resonances by external electric [1] or magnetic [2] fields, the fields appear to induce in certain receptors a slight frequency modulation of their normal spontaneous stochastic spiking. Since cutaneous

United States Patent [19]

Loos

[11] **Patent Number:** **6,167,304**

[45] **Date of Patent:** **Dec. 26, 2000**

[54] **PULSE VARIABILITY IN ELECTRIC FIELD MANIPULATION OF NERVOUS SYSTEMS**

[76] Inventor: **Hendricus G. Loos**

[21] Appl. No.: **09/336,369**

[22] Filed: **Jun. 17, 1999**

Related U.S. Application Data

[63] Continuation-in-part of application No. 09/118,505, Jul. 17, 1998, Pat. No. 6,081,744, which is a continuation-in-part of application No. 08/788,582, Jan. 24, 1997, Pat. No. 5,782,874, which is a continuation-in-part of application No. 08/447,394, May 23, 1995, abandoned, which is a continuation of application No. 08/068,748, May 28, 1993, abandoned.

[51] **Int. Cl.^{7}** **A61N 1/40**
[52] **U.S. Cl.** **607/2**
[58] **Field of Search** 607/2, 39, 46

[56] **References Cited**

U.S. PATENT DOCUMENTS

1,973,911	9/1934	Ruben	607/152
3,678,337	7/1972	Graetzel	128/419 N
3,840,020	10/1974	Smith	128/419 N
3,886,932	6/1975	Suessmilch	128/908
3,941,136	3/1976	Bucalo	607/39
4,084,595	4/1978	Miller	128/422
4,197,851	4/1980	Fellus	128/422
4,297,980	11/1981	Suzuki	128/419 N
4,611,599	9/1986	Bentall et al.	178/422
4,856,526	8/1989	Liss et al.	128/422
5,169,380	12/1992	Brennan	600/26

FOREIGN PATENT DOCUMENTS

0285415	12/1965	Australia	607/2
3327126	4/1984	Germany	607/2
2164563	3/1986	United Kingdom	607/2

OTHER PUBLICATIONS

N. Wiener, Nonlinear Problems in Random Theory, 1958, p. 71,72 M. Hutchison, MegaBrain, 1991, p. 233,245.

Primary Examiner—William E. Kamm

[57] **ABSTRACT**

Apparatus and method for manipulating the nervous system of a subject by applying to the skin a pulsing external electric field which, although too weak to cause classical nerve stimulation, modulates the normal spontaneous spiking patterns of certain kinds of afferent nerves. For certain pulse frequencies the electric field stimulation can excite in the nervous system resonances with observable physiological consequences. Pulse variability is introduced for the purpose of thwarting habituation of the nervous system to the repetitive stimulation, or to alleviate the need for precise tuning to a resonance frequency, or to control pathological oscillatory neural activities such as tremors or seizures. Pulse generators with stochastic and deterministic pulse variability are disclosed, and the output of an effective generator of the latter type is characterized.

11 Claims, 5 Drawing Sheets

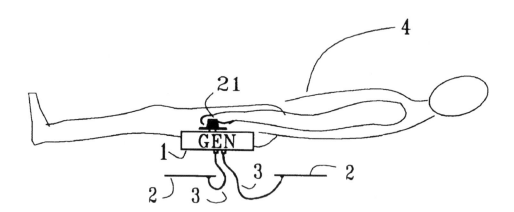

6,167,304

1

PULSE VARIABILITY IN ELECTRIC FIELD MANIPULATION OF NERVOUS SYSTEMS

This application is a Continuation-in-Part of Ser. No. 09/118,505, Jul. 17, 1998, U.S. Pat. No. 6,081,744 which is a Continuation-in-Part of Ser. No. 08/788,582, Jan. 24, 1997, U.S. Pat. No. 5,782,874, which is a Continuation-in-Part of Ser. No. 08/447,394, May 23, 1995, abandoned, which is a Continuation of Ser. No. 08/068,748, May 28, 1993, abandoned.

BACKGROUND OF THE INVENTION

The invention relates to the stimulation of the nervous system of humans by an electric field applied externally to the body. A neurological effect of external electric fields has been mentioned by Norbert Wiener [1], in discussing the bunching of brain waves through nonlinear interactions. The electric field was arranged to provide "a direct electrical driving of the brain" [1]. Wiener describes the field as set up by a 10 Hz alternating voltage of 400 V applied in a room between ceiling and ground.

Brennan [2] describes an apparatus for alleviating disruptions in circadian rythms of a mammal, in which an alternating electric field is applied across the head of the subject. The voltage applied to the electrodes is specified as at least 100 V, and the peak-to-peak value of the electric field as at least 590 V/m in free air before deploying the electrodes across the head of the subject. The frequency of the alternating electric field is in the range from 5 to 40 Hz. Brennan states that the method is aimed at subjecting at least part of the subject's brain to an alternating electric field. It should be noted that electric polarization of the head causes the field strength in the narrow space between electrode and skin to be about a factor h/2d larger than the free-air field strength, h being the distance between the electrodes and d the spacing between electrode and skin. For h=17 cm and d=5 mm the factor comes to 17, so that with the specified free-air field of at least 590 V/m the field in the gap between electrode and skin is at least 10 KV/m peak to peak.

A device involving a field electrode as well as a contact electrode is the "Graham Potentializer" mentioned in Ref. [3]. This relaxation device uses motion, light and sound as well as an alternating electric field applied predominantly to the head. The contact electrode is a metal bar in Ohmic contact with the bare feet of the subject; the field electrode is a hemispherical metal headpiece placed several inches from the subject's head. According to the brief description in [3], a signal less than 2 V at a frequency of 125 Hz is applied between the field electrode and the contact electrode. In this configuration the contact electrode supplies to the body the current for charging the capacitor formed by the field electrode and the apposing skin area. The resulting electric field stands predominantly in the space between the head piece and the scalp.

In the three external field methods mentioned, viz. Wiener [1], Brennan [2], and Graham [3], the electric field is applied to the head, and the brain is thereby exposed to polarization currents. These currents run through the brain in a broad swath, with a distribution influenced by nonuniformities of tissue conductivity and permittivity. The scale of the current density can be conveniently expressed over the skin of the head, of its component perpendicular to the local skin. This scale is easily calculated for sinusoidal fields as the product of radian frequency, vacuum permittivity, and maximum amplitude of the external field on the head. Using Brennan's [2] lowest frequency of 5 Hz,

2

his miniumum required free-air field strength of 590 V/m, and the factor 17 estimated above to account for the polarization of the head by the applied field, the scale of the polarization current density in the brain comes to about 280 pA/cm^2. Although such a current density would generally be considered very small in electrophysiology, a repetitive application at certain critical frequencies and along certain paths in the brain may perhaps cause kindling in individuals predisposed to epilepsy, and it is therefore deemed too large for use by the general public. Conservatively, we consider polarization current densities in the brain with a scale in excess of 70 fA/cm^2 to be substantial.

It is the object of the present invention to obtain a method and apparatus for manipulating the nervous system by externally applied electric fields without causing substantial polarization current densities in the brain.

The use of electric fields raises concerns about possible health effects. Such concerns have been widely discussed in the media in regard to electric power lines and electric apparatus [4]. Answering the pertinent questions by objective research will take time, but meanwhile governments have been setting guidelines for safe limits on field strengths. At present, the strictest limits of this sort are the Swedish MPRII guidelines. Magnetic fields are of no concern here, because the currents involved are so small. However, the electric field strengthy must be considered, since even at low voltages strong electric fields can result from electrodes placed close to the skin. For fields of extremely low frequency the MPRII guidelines limit the field strength to 25 V/m in the frequency range from 5 Hz to 2 KHz. In the Brennan patent [2] the minimum field strength of 590 V/m violates these guidelines by a factor 23; when the polarization effects are accounted for, the factor is about 400.

It is a further object of the present invention to manipulate the nervous system by external electric fields that are in compliance with the MPRII guidelines.

Brennan [2] stipulates voltages of at least 100 V, and as high as 600 V for his preferred embodiment. Generation of such voltages requires a voltage multiplier stage, if practical battery operation is desired. This increases the current drain and the size of the generator. The large voltages also raise safety concerns.

It is yet a further object of the present invention to manipulate the nervous system by external electric fields, using low voltages that are generated by small and safe battery-powered devices with low current consumption.

The nervous system generally habituates to repetitive stimuli. It is still a further object of the present invention to manipulate the nervous system by externally applied electric fields in such a manner as to thwart habituation.

SUMMARY

Experiments have shown that weak electric fields of frequency near ½ Hz applied externally to the skin of a subject can cause relaxation, doziness, ptosis of the eyelids, or sexual excitement, depending on the skin area of application and the precise frequency used. In these experiments the electric field was applied predominantly to selected skin areas away from the head, thereby avoiding substantial polarization current densities in the brain. Apparently, the external electric field influences somatosensory or visceral afferent nerves, which report the effect to the brain. Although the mechanism whereby the field acts on the afferents is unknown, the effect must take the form of a modulation of the spiking patterns of the nerves, because the electric

(12) **United States Patent**

Loos

(10) **Patent No.:** **US 6,238,333 B1**

(45) **Date of Patent:** **May 29, 2001**

(54) **REMOTE MAGNETIC MANIPULATION OF NERVOUS SYSTEMS**

(76) Inventor: **Hendricus G. Loos**

(*) Notice: Subject to any disclaimer, the term of this patent is extended or adjusted under 35 U.S.C. 154(b) by 0 days.

(21) Appl. No.: **09/371,289**

(22) Filed: **Aug. 10, 1999**

Related U.S. Application Data

(63) Continuation-in-part of application No. 08/486,918, filed on Jun. 7, 1995, now Pat. No. 5,935,054.

(51) **Int. Cl.**[7] **A61N 2/00**
(52) **U.S. Cl.** **600/9**
(58) **Field of Search** 600/9–15

(56) **References Cited**

U.S. PATENT DOCUMENTS

3,678,337	7/1972	Grauvogel	317/4
4,197,851	4/1980	Fellus	128/422
4,537,181 *	8/1985	Shalhoob et al.	600/9
4,611,599	9/1986	Bentall	128/422
4,727,857 *	3/1988	Horl	600/9
5,667,469 *	9/1997	Zhang et al.	600/9
6,001,055 *	12/1999	Souder	600/9

OTHER PUBLICATIONS

P. Lindemann, The Megabrain Report, vol. 1, #2, p. 34–35 (1990).
P. Limdemann, The Megabrain Report, vol. 1, #1, p. 30–31 (1990).

* cited by examiner

Primary Examiner—John P. Lacyk

(57) **ABSTRACT**

Apparatus and method for remote manipulation of nervous systems by the magnetic dipole field of a rotating bar magnet. Reliance on modulation of spontaneous spiking patterns of sensory nerve receptors, and exploitation of a resonance mechanism of certain neural circuits, allows the use of very weak magnetic fields. This, together with the large magnetic moments that can be obtained with a permanent bar magnet, makes it possible to effectively manipulate the nervous system of a subject over a distance of several hundred meters, using a small portable battery-powered device. The method can be used in law enforcement for standoff situations.

8 Claims, 3 Drawing Sheets

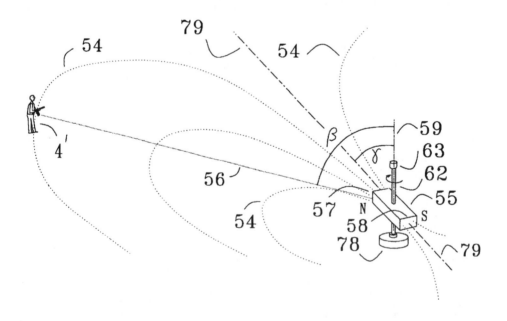

1

REMOTE MAGNETIC MANIPULATION OF NERVOUS SYSTEMS

Continuation in Part of application Ser. No. 08/486,918, Jun. 7, 1995, U.S. Pat. No. 5,935,054.

BACKGROUND OF THE INVENTION

The invention relates to stimulation of nerves by pulsed magnetic fields. Such fields induce in the body of an exposed subject eddy currents that are proportional to their rate of change. The currents may cause classical nerve stimulation wherein the nerve membrane is depolarized enough for the nerve to fire. At low frequencies, such a mechanism requires rather large magnetic fields. Fortunately, low-frequency magnetic manipulation of the nervous system is possible by another mechanism which allows the use of very much weaker fields. Instead of relying on causing the firing of normally quiescent nerves, the method uses modulation of the spiking patterns of spontaneously firing nerves. That this can be done with very small tissue electic fields was discussed more than four decades ago by C. A. Terzuolo and T. H. Bullock in "Measurement of Imposed Voltage Gradient Adequate to Modulate Neuronal Firing", Proceedings of the National Academy of Sciences U.S.A., Physiology, 42, 687 (1956). The effect can be exploited in magnetic as well as in electric stimulation, because the physiological effects of the former are solely due to the electric field that is induced by the rate of change of the magnetic field, and by the electric polarization that occurs as the consequence of the induced eddy currents.

The human nervous system exhibits a sensitivity to certain low-frequency stimuli, as is evident from rocking a baby or relaxing in a rocking chair. In both cases, the maximum soothing effect is obtained for a periodic motion with a frequency near ½ Hz. The effect is here called "the ½ Hz sensory resonance". In the rocking response, the sensory resonance is excited principally by frequency-coded signals from the vestibular end organ. However, the rocking motion also induces body strains, and these are detected by stretch receptors residing in the skin and elsewhere in the body. In addition, relevant signals may originate from thermal receptors which report skin temperature fluctuations caused by air currents that are induced by the rocking motion. All these receptors employ frequency coding in their sensory function, and it must be that their signals are combined and compared in the brain with the vestibular nerve signals in an assessment of the somatic state. One may thus expect that the sensory resonance can be excited not only through the vestibular nerve, but also separately through the other sensory modalities mentioned. This notion is supported by the observation that gently stroking of a child with a frequency near ½ Hz has a soothing effect. Further support derives from the successful excitation of the ½ Hz sensory resonance by weak external electric fields, as discussed in "Method and Apparatus for Manipulating Nervous Systems", U.S. Pat. No. 5,782,874. The ½ Hz sensory resonance involves the autonomic nervous system, and it can be used to induce relaxation, sleepiness, or sexual excitement, depending on the precise stimulation frequency and the affected afferent nerves. Another sensory resonance has been found at about 2.4 Hz; it involves the cortex since it can slow the speed of silently counting from 100 to 60, with the eyes closed, as discussed in the '874 patent and in U.S. Pat. No. 5,800,481. For both electric field and thermal stimulation, prolonged exposure to fluctuating electric fields near 2.4 Hz has been found to have a sleep-inducing and dizzying effect. The same physiological effect is expected

2

for pulsative magnetic stimulation, since electric fields are induced in the tissue by the changing magnetic field. When using the nerve modulation method, reliance on resonance mechanisms further reduces the stimulation strength required for manipulating the nervous system.

SUMMARY

Oscillatory magnetic fields induce electric fields in exposed biological tissue and can therefore act on nerves. Considerable tissue electric fields are needed to cause firing of otherwise quiescent nerves, but very much smaller fields suffice for modulation of spontaneous nerve spiking. Still weaker fields can be used for exciting resonances in certain neural circuits through evoked signals from afferent somatosensory nerves which carry the modulated spiking patterns to the brain.

It has been found that, in this manner, weak oscillatory magnetic fields with an amplitude between 5 femtotesla and 50 nanotesla can be used for manipulating the human nervous system, when the fields are tuned to certain frequencies near ½ Hz that cause excitation of sensory resonances. Observable physiological consequences of the resonance include ptosis of the eyelids, relaxation, sleepiness, and sexual excitement, depending on the precise frequency used, and on the location and duration of the magnetic field application.

Both topical and systemic field administration have been found effective. For the latter case the field can be produced over a considerable distance by a rotating permanent magnet that has a large magnetic moment. This makes it possible to manipulate a subject's nervous system over a range of several hundred meters, such as to cause relaxation and drowsiness. The method can be used in law enforcement for standoff situations.

Simple devices which use a rotating bar magnet are disclosed. Multiple rotating bar magnets can be used, and the phase angles of the magnets may then be arranged to cause constructive interference of the magnetic fields induced in the subject.

DESCRIPTION OF THE DRAWINGS

FIG. 1 illustrates an embodiment as a non-lethal weapon to be used in law enforcement, showing the dipole magnetic field projected upon a standoff site.

FIG. 2 shows how the dipole field of FIG. 1 has rotated in a a short time.

FIG. 3 illustrates the rotating magnet method of projecting a time-varying dipole field upon a remote subject.

FIG. 4 shows a drive circuit for the rotating magnet of FIG. 3.

FIG. 5 shows the preferred embodiment wherein the bar magnet rotation is caused by coils that induce magnetic fields which act directly on the bar magnet.

FIG. 6 illustrates an embodiment for topical application of an oscillating magnetic field for the excitation of a sensory resonance.

FIG. 7 shows a multipole coil for the generation of a localized magnetic field for topical field administration.

FIG. 8 shows a near-sine wave generator with automatic shutoff, suitable for driving magnetic coils.

DETAILED DESCRIPTION

It has been found in our laboratory that a weak oscillatory magnetic field can be used to excite the ½ Hz sensory

(12) **United States Patent**
Loos

(10) **Patent No.:** **US 6,506,148 B2**
(45) **Date of Patent:** **Jan. 14, 2003**

(54) **NERVOUS SYSTEM MANIPULATION BY ELECTROMAGNETIC FIELDS FROM MONITORS**

(76) Inventor: **Hendricus G. Loos**

(*) Notice: Subject to any disclaimer, the term of this patent is extended or adjusted under 35 U.S.C. 154(b) by 8 days.

(21) Appl. No.: **09/872,528**

(22) Filed: **Jun. 1, 2001**

(65) **Prior Publication Data**

US 2002/0188164 A1 Dec. 12, 2002

(51) **Int. Cl.^{7}** A61N 2/00; A61B 5/04; A61M 21/00
(52) **U.S. Cl.** **600/27**; 600/545
(58) **Field of Search** 600/9–27, 545; 313/419; 324/318; 378/901; 434/236

(56) **References Cited**

U.S. PATENT DOCUMENTS

3,592,965	A	*	7/1971	Diaz	313/419
4,800,893	A	*	1/1989	Ross et al.	600/545
5,169,380	A		12/1992	Brennan	600/26
5,304,112	A	*	4/1994	Mrklas et al.	434/236
5,400,383	A	*	3/1995	Yassa et al.	378/901
5,412,419	A	*	5/1995	Ziarati	324/318
5,450,859	A		9/1995	Litovitz	600/9
5,782,874	A		7/1998	Loos	607/2
5,800,481	A		9/1998	Loos	607/100
5,899,922	A		5/1999	Loos	607/2
5,935,054	A		8/1999	Loos	600/9
6,017,302	A		1/2000	Loos	600/28
6,081,744	A		6/2000	Loos	607/2
6,091,994	A		7/2000	Loos	607/100
6,167,304	A		12/2000	Loos	607/2
6,238,333	B1		5/2001	Loos	600/9

OTHER PUBLICATIONS

N.Wiener "Nonlinear problems in random theory" p.71–72 John Wiley New York 1958.
M.Hutchison "Megabrain" p.232–3 Ballantine Books New York 1991.
C.A.Terzuolo and T.H.Bullock "Measurement of imposed voltage gradient adequate to modulate neuronal firing" Proc. Nat. Acad. Sci, Physiology 42,687–94, 1956.
O.Kellogg"Foundations of Potential Theory"p. 191 Dover, 1953.
P.M.Morse and H.Feshbach"Methods of Theoretical Physics"p. 1267 McGraw-Hill New York, 1953.

* cited by examiner

Primary Examiner—Eric F. Winakur
Assistant Examiner—Nikita R Veniaminov

(57) **ABSTRACT**

Physiological effects have been observed in a human subject in response to stimulation of the skin with weak electromagnetic fields that are pulsed with certain frequencies near ½ Hz or 2.4 Hz, such as to excite a sensory resonance. Many computer monitors and TV tubes, when displaying pulsed images, emit pulsed electromagnetic fields of sufficient amplitudes to cause such excitation. It is therefore possible to manipulate the nervous system of a subject by pulsing images displayed on a nearby computer monitor or TV set. For the latter, the image pulsing may be imbedded in the program material, or it may be overlaid by modulating a video stream, either as an RF signal or as a video signal. The image displayed on a computer monitor may be pulsed effectively by a simple computer program. For certain monitors, pulsed electromagnetic fields capable of exciting sensory resonances in nearby subjects may be generated even as the displayed images are pulsed with subliminal intensity.

14 Claims, 9 Drawing Sheets

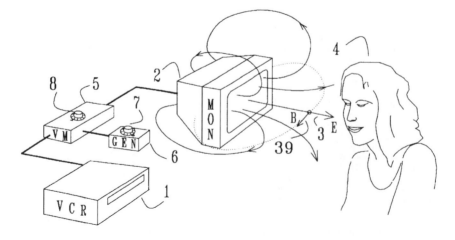

1

NERVOUS SYSTEM MANIPULATION BY ELECTROMAGNETIC FIELDS FROM MONITORS

BACKGROUND OF THE INVENTION

The invention relates to the stimulation of the human nervous system by an electromagnetic field applied externally to the body. A neurological effect of external electric fields has been mentioned by Wiener (1958), in a discussion of the bunching of brain waves through nonlinear interactions. The electric field was arranged to provide "a direct electrical driving of the brain". Wiener describes the field as set up by a 10 Hz alternating voltage of 400 V applied in a room between ceiling and ground. Brennan (1992) describes in U.S. Pat. No. 5,169,380 an apparatus for alleviating disruptions in circadian rythms of a mammal, in which an alternating electric field is applied across the head of the subject by two electrodes placed a short distance from the skin.

A device involving a field electrode as well as a contact electrode is the "Graham Potentializer" mentioned by Hutchison (1991). This relaxation device uses motion, light and sound as well as an alternating electric field applied mainly to the head. The contact electrode is a metal bar in Ohmic contact with the bare feet of the subject, and the field electrode is a hemispherical metal headpiece placed several inches from the subject's head.

In these three electric stimulation methods the external electric field is applied predominantly to the head, so that electric currents are induced in the brain in the physical manner governed by electrodynamics. Such currents can be largely avoided by applying the field not to the head, but rather to skin areas away from the head. Certain cutaneous receptors may then be stimulated and they would provide a signal input into the brain along the natural pathways of afferent nerves. It has been found that, indeed, physiological effects can be induced in this manner by very weak electric fields, if they are pulsed with a frequency near ½ Hz. The observed effects include ptosis of the eyelids, relaxation, drowziness, the feeling of pressure at a centered spot on the lower edge of the brow, seeing moving patterns of dark purple and greenish yellow with the eyes closed, a tonic smile, a tense feeling in the stomach, sudden loose stool, and sexual excitement, depending on the precise frequency used, and the skin area to which the field is applied. The sharp frequency dependence suggests involvement of a resonance mechanism.

It has been found that the resonance can be excited not only by externally applied pulsed electric fields, as discussed in U.S. Pat. Nos. 5,782,874, 5,899,922, 6,081,744, and 6,167,304, but also by pulsed magnetic fields, as described in U.S. Pat. Nos. 5,935,054 and 6,238,333, by weak heat pulses applied to the skin, as discussed in U.S. Pat. Nos. 5,800,481 and 6,091,994, and by subliminal acoustic pulses, as described in U.S. Pat. No. 6,017,302. Since the resonance is excited through sensory pathways, it is called a sensory resonance. In addition to the resonance near ½ Hz, a sensory resonance has been found near 2.4 Hz. The latter is characterized by the slowing of certain cortical processes, as discussed in the '481, '922, '302, '744, '944, and '304 patents.

The excitation of sensory resonances through weak heat pulses applied to the skin provides a clue about what is going on neurologically. Cutaneous temperature-sensing receptors are known to fire spontaneously. These nerves spike some-

2

what randomly around an average rate that depends on skin temperature. Weak heat pulses delivered to the skin in periodic fashion will therefore cause a slight frequency modulation (fm) in the spike patterns generated by the nerves. Since stimulation through other sensory modalities results in similar physiological effects, it is believed that frequency modulation of spontaneous afferent neural spiking patterns occurs there as well.

It is instructive to apply this notion to the stimulation by weak electric field pulses administered to the skin. The externally generated fields induce electric current pulses in the underlying tissue, but the current density is much too small for firing an otherwise quiescent nerve. However, in experiments with adapting stretch receptors of the crayfish, Terzuolo and Bullock (1956) have observed that very small electric fields can suffice for modulating the firing of already active nerves. Such a modulation may occur in the electric field stimulation under discussion.

Further understanding may be gained by considering the electric charges that accumulate on the skin as a result of the induced tissue currents. Ignoring thermodynamics, one would expect the accumulated polarization charges to be confined strictly to the outer surface of the skin. But charge density is caused by a slight excess in positive or negative ions, and thermal motion distributes the ions through a thin layer. This implies that the externally applied electric field actually penetrates a short distance into the tissue, instead of stopping abruptly at the outer skin surface. In this manner a considerable fraction of the applied field may be brought to bear on some cutaneous nerve endings, so that a slight modulation of the type noted by Terzuolo and Bullock may indeed occur.

The mentioned physiological effects are observed only when the strength of the electric field on the skin lies in a certain range, called the effective intensity window. There also is a bulk effect, in that weaker fields suffice when the field is applied to a larger skin area. These effects are discussed in detail in the '922 patent.

Since the spontaneous spiking of the nerves is rather random and the frequency modulation induced by the pulsed field is very shallow, the signal to noise ratio (S/N) for the fm signal contained in the spike trains along the afferent nerves is so small as to make recovery of the fm signal from a single nerve fiber impossibile. But application of the field over a large skin area causes simultaneous stimulation of many cutaneous nerves, and the fm modulation is then coherent from nerve to nerve. Therefore, if the afferent signals are somehow summed in the brain, the fm modulations add while the spikes from different nerves mix and interlace. In this manner the S/N can be increased by appropriate neural processing. The matter is discussed in detail in the '874 patent. Another increase in sensitivity is due to involving a resonance mechanism, wherein considerable neural circuit oscillations can result from weak excitations.

An easily detectable physiological effect of an excited ½ Hz sensory resonance is ptosis of the eyelids. As discussed in the '922 patent, the ptosis test involves first closing the eyes about half way. Holding this eyelid position, the eyes are rolled upward, while giving up voluntary control of the eyelids. The eyelid position is then determined by the state of the autonomic nervous system. Furthermore, the pressure exerted on the eyeballs by the partially closed eyelids increases parasympathetic activity. The eyelid position thereby becomes somewhat labile, as manifested by a slight flutter. The labile state is sensitive to very small shifts in

(12) **United States Patent**

Levin

(10) **Patent No.:** **US 6,939,288 B1**

(45) **Date of Patent:** **Sep. 6, 2005**

(54) **AUDITORY THERAPY SYSTEM FOR IMPACTING THE NERVOUS SYSTEM OF A LIVING ORGANISM**

(76) Inventor: **Yakov I. Levin**

(*) Notice: Subject to any disclaimer, the term of this patent is extended or adjusted under 35 U.S.C. 154(b) by 0 days.

(21) Appl. No.: **09/308,913**

(22) PCT Filed: **Dec. 26, 1996**

(86) PCT No.: **PCT/RU96/00364**

§ 371 (c)(1),
(2), (4) Date: **May 26, 1999**

(87) PCT Pub. No.: **WO98/19601**

PCT Pub. Date: **Mar. 14, 1998**

(51) **Int. Cl.**[7] **A61B 5/0432**
(52) **U.S. Cl.** **600/28**
(58) **Field of Search** 600/26, 27, 28

(56) **References Cited**

U.S. PATENT DOCUMENTS

5,267,942 A * 12/1993 Saperston 600/28

5,356,368 A * 10/1994 Monroe 600/28

* cited by examiner

Primary Examiner—George R. Evanisko
Assistant Examiner—Frances P. Oropeza
(74) *Attorney, Agent, or Firm*—I. Zborovsky

(57) **ABSTRACT**

A method of influencing the body has the steps of registering physical parameter biopotentials, transforming and processing of obtained data to calculate a biosignal characteristic generalized parameter, transforming the biosignal characteristic generalized parameter on the basis of detected criterial correspondence into a control signal and forming an external sound effect, implementing the external sound effect in the form of generation of musical sounds by a parametric variation tone, volume and duration thereof in criterial relation to variation of discrete current values of the characteristic generalized parameter of a frequency spectrum of the transformed biosignal.

2 Claims, 2 Drawing Sheets

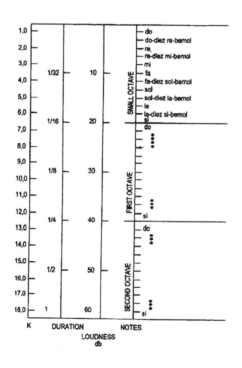

1

AUDITORY THERAPY SYSTEM FOR IMPACTING THE NERVOUS SYSTEM OF A LIVING ORGANISM

BACKGROUND OF THE INVENTION

The invention relates to the area of medicine and may be used for bioadaptive correction of man's functional condition.

Known from the level of technology are methods of influencing the body by biological feedback, where biopotentials, mainly of brain electrical activity are recorded, transformed and the obtained electroencephalogram (EEG) is processed to isolate, from the spectrum, a certain frequency band that corresponds to alpha-rhythm, and then a control signal is formed generating sound effect on the body with the level proportional to alpha-rhythm in the EEG spectrum (see USSR Authorship Certificate No. 1124922, class A 61 B May 4, 1998; USSR Authorship Certificate No. 1780716, class A 61 B May 4, 1992; U.S. Pat. No. 3,896,790, class A 61 B May 4, 1975).

Psychophysiological effect on man in the above methods, however, is limited by control of alpha activity which does not allow to effectively correct functional condition of the body.

Also known is the method of body functional condition correction with optimization of parameters of external effect on the body which includes recording of physiological parameter biopotentials, transformation and processing of the obtained information with calculation of a biosignal characteristic parameter which is transformed into a control signal, and external effect signals are formed on the basis of the data obtained (see USSR Authorship Certificate No. 1745204, class A 61 B May 4, 1992).

In this case the external effect, e.g. background sound, is selected from various prerecorded phonograms that differ in volume, rhythm, and tone, using biological feedback to optimize deviation of current characteristic value of the selected biosignal registered during correction of patient's functional condition from the estimated one determined in the preparatory mode. These prerecorded phonograms, however, are of random nature and may not fully correspond to individual features of the body, which reduces effectiveness of man's physiological condition psychophysiological correction by external effect of physical factors, e.g. sound.

SUMMARY OF THE INVENTION

The invention is aimed at creation of a method to influence the body by means of external physical factor—a sound in the form of a musical tune that adequately reflects man's psychophysiological condition.

Solution of the problem is provided by that the method of influencing the body which includes registration of physiological parameter biopotentials, transformation and processing of the obtained data with calculation of biosignal characteristic generalized parameter, which on the basis of detected criterial correspondence is transformed into a control signal and signals of external sound effect are formed, according to the invention, external sound effect is implemented as generation of musical sounds by parametric variation of their tone, volume, and duration in criterial dependence of variation of value of discrete current generalized parameter of transformed biosignal frequency spectrum, thus from the recorded graphic data isolated are time intervals of identical duration, which are transformed,

2

using the Fourier harmonic analysis, into a frequency spectrum, then a generalized characteristic dimensionless parameter is determined for each spectral interval, a proportional range of musical sound parameters is formed between minimum and maximum values of the generalized dimensionless parameter, appropriate values of sound tone, volume, and duration are determined for each spectral interval by numerical value of its generalized dimensionless parameter, which are then transformed by a synthesizer into sound signals formed in a sequence that corresponds to initially recorded discrete current alternation of time intervals.

The generalized dimensionless parameter is determined by ratio of power spectral density of at least two characteristic frequency bands isolated in each spectral interval.

A positive outcome of the claimed method is primarily provided by that sound reproduction of physiological activity biosignals is based on the analogy of oscillatory nature of recorded biosignal variation (electroencephalogram—EEG, electrocardiogram—ECG, electrogastrogram—EGG, electromyogram, electroretinogram, pulse wave oscillogram, etc.) and sound oscillatory nature, while suggested criterial dependence between characteristic generalized parameter of frequency spectrum of transformed biosignal and parameters of generated musical sound (tone, volume, and duration) most adequately reflects individual features of man's functional condition and allows to form sequence of sounds in the form of personality music which, if recorded in magnetic medium while the patient is in healthy condition, allows to effectively correct depressive conditions, sleep disturbance, anxiety and other psychophysiological disorders by music therapy.

BRIEF DESCRIPTION OF DRAWINGS

FIG. 1 shows the set of frequency spectra with discrete current alternation of time intervals.

FIG. 2 shows range of musical sound parameters.

DESCRIPTION OF THE PREFERRED EMBODIMENTS

The method suggested is implemented as follows.

Preliminary, during a satisfactory period of patient's healthy condition, physiological parameter biopotentials, e.g. bioelectric activity of brain, heart muscles, stomach, skeletal muscles, eye retina, pulse waves, etc., are recorded using well-known advanced instrumentation.

Electroencephalogram, EEG, is the most universal and adequately reflects individual functional condition; an example of EEG transformation into the "brain music" is given below.

EEG registered, e.g. within 10 seconds, is divided into equal time intervals of, e.g. 1 second duration; using harmonic analysis, a Fourier expansion, each interval is transformed into frequency spectrum (see FIG. 1), 4 common frequent ranges (Δ, θ, α, β) are isolated pursuant to the international standard:

Δ=0.1–3.9 Hz,

Θ=4.0–7.9 Hz,

α=8.0–12.9 Hz,

β=13.0–32.0 Hz,

and a dimensionless generalized characteristic parameter is determined for each spectral interval with respect to power spectral densities Θ and β intervals, namely:

United States Patent [19]

Ross et al.

[11] Patent Number: 4,800,893

[45] Date of Patent: Jan. 31, 1989

[54] **KINESTHETIC PHYSICAL MOVEMENT FEEDBACK DISPLAY FOR CONTROLLING THE NERVOUS SYSTEM OF A LIVING ORGANISM**

[76] Inventors: Sidney A. Ross; Mark J. Ross

[21] Appl. No.: 61,156

[22] Filed: Jun. 10, 1987

[51] Int. Cl.⁴ A61B 5/04

[52] U.S. Cl. 128/732; 128/905

[58] Field of Search 128/731-3, 128/905; 340/724-727

[56] **References Cited**

U.S. PATENT DOCUMENTS

3,837,331	9/1974	Ross	128/1 C
3,855,998	12/1974	Hidalgo-Briceno	128/732
3,893,450	7/1975	Ertl	128/731
3,967,616	7/1976	Ross	128/732 X
3,978,847	9/1976	Fehmi et al.	128/732
4,140,997	2/1979	Brady	128/732
4,354,505	10/1982	Shiga	128/732
4,632,126	12/1986	Aguilar	128/732

4,690,142	9/1987	Ross et al.	128/419 R

FOREIGN PATENT DOCUMENTS

8700746	12/1987	PCT Int'l Appl.	128/731

Primary Examiner—Max Hindenburg
Assistant Examiner—Angela D. Sykes
Attorney, Agent, or Firm—Blakely, Sokoloff, Taylor & Zafman

[57] **ABSTRACT**

A method and system for providing as a biofeedback signal a visual display showing kinesthetic physical movement to enable a subject to produce desired thought patterns. Sensors or electrodes are connected to the subject at one or more topological locations. The signals detected by the sensors are input to a conventional EEG device. The EEG output is processed into one or more analog voltage signals. These analog signals are input to a computer which generates a video display and audio if desired. The image on the display depicts kinesthetic physical movement as a function of the analog voltage.

56 Claims, 4 Drawing Sheets

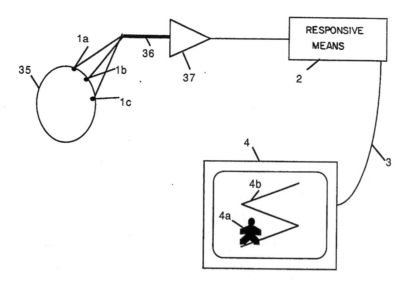

Chapter 11
Mind Manipulation

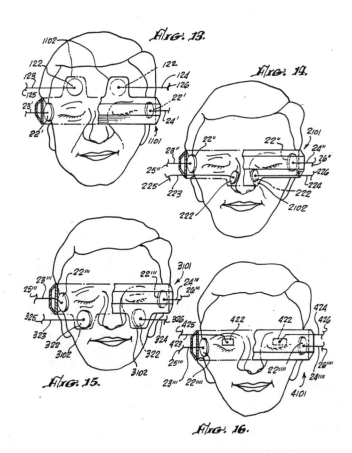

United States Patent [19]

Zentmeyer, Jr.

[11] **3,712,292**

[45] **Jan. 23, 1973**

[54] **METHOD AND APPARATUS FOR PRODUCING SWEPT FREQUENCY-MODULATED AUDIO SIGNAL PATTERNS FOR INDUCING SLEEP**

[75] Inventor: **John E. Zentmeyer, Jr.**, Charlottesville, Va.

[73] Assignee: **Karen V. Lafley**, Charlottesville, Va.

[22] Filed: **July 20, 1971**

[21] Appl. No.: **164,389**

[52] U.S. Cl. ....**128/1 C**
[51] Int. Cl. **A61n 1/34**
[58] Field of Search .... 128/1 C; 179/1 AA

[56] **References Cited**

UNITED STATES PATENTS

3,014,477	12/1961	Carlin	128/1 C
2,304,095	12/1942	Hull	128/1 C
3,140,709	7/1964	Weisz	128/1 R

FOREIGN PATENTS OR APPLICATIONS

| 1,165,541 | 10/1969 | Great Britain | 128/1 C |

Primary Examiner—William E. Kamm
Attorney—Thomas B. Van Poole et al.

[57] **ABSTRACT**

A method of producing sound signals for inducing sleep in a human being, and apparatus therefor together with REPRESENTATIONS thereof in recorded form, wherein an audio signal is generated representing a familiar, pleasing, repetitive sound, modulated by continuously sweeping frequencies in two selected frequency ranges having the dominant frequencies which occur in electrical wave patterns of the human brain during certain states of sleep. The volume of the audio signal is adjusted to mask the ambient noise and the subject can select any of several familiar, repetitive sounds most pleasing to him.

13 Claims, 2 Drawing Figures

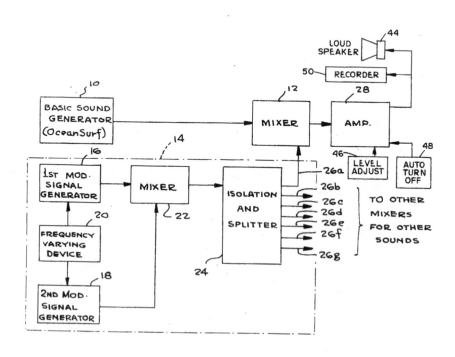

United States Patent [19]

Lenzkes

[11] **3,727,616**

[45] **Apr. 17, 1973**

[54] **ELECTRONIC SYSTEM FOR THE STIMULATION OF BIOLOGICAL SYSTEMS**

[75] Inventor: **Herbert H. Lenzkes,** Pomona, Calif.

[73] Assignee: **General Dynamics Corporation,** Pomona, Calif.

[22] Filed: **June 15, 1971**

[21] Appl. No.: **153,316**

[52] U.S. Cl. ....**128/422, 128/419 E**
[51] Int. Cl. **A61n 1/36**
[58] Field of Search......................128/419 C, 419 E, 128/419 P, 419 R, 420, 421, 422, 423, 2.1 A; 340/184

[56] **References Cited**

UNITED STATES PATENTS

3,236,240   2/1966   Bradley.............................128/419 E
3,195,540   7/1965   Waller...............................128/419 P
3,646,940   3/1972   Timm et al.......................128/419 E

3,662,758   5/1972   Glover...............................128/419 E

Primary Examiner—William E. Kamm
Attorney—Edward B. Johnson

[57] **ABSTRACT**

A receiver totally implanted within a living body is inductively coupled by two associated receiving coils to a physically unattached external transmitter which transmits two signals of different frequencies to the receiver via two associated transmitting coils. One of the signals from the transmitter provides the implanted receiver with precise control or stimulating signals which are demodulated and processed in a signal processor network in the receiver and then used by the body for stimulation of a nerve, for example, while the other signal provides the receiver with a continuous wave power signal which is rectified in the receiver to provide a source of electrical operating power for the receiver circuitry without need for an implanted battery.

9 Claims, 13 Drawing Figures

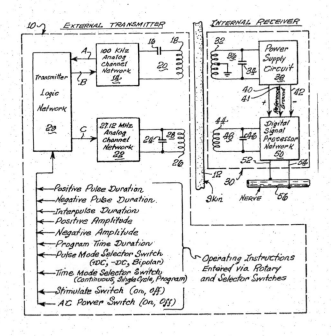

United States Patent [19]

Symmes

[11] **3,782,006**

[45] **Jan. 1, 1974**

[54] **MEANS AND METHODS TO ASSIST PEOPLE IN BUILDING UP AN AVERSION TO UNDESIRABLE HABITS**

[75] Inventor: **Eliot N. Symmes,** San Francisco, Calif.

[73] Assignee: **American Clinic, Inc.,** San Jose, Calif.

[22] Filed: **May 26, 1972**

[21] Appl. No.: **254,786**

[52] **U.S. Cl.**.. **35/22 R**
[51] **Int. Cl.** **G09b 19/00**
[58] **Field of Search**........................ 35/22 R, 21, 1; 128/1 C, 419 S; 272/10, 18, 8 R, 27 R; 273/1 E

[56] **References Cited**

UNITED STATES PATENTS

3,014,477 12/1961 Carlin .... 128/1 C

3,205,316	9/1965	Hechler	128/1 C UX
1,550,497	8/1925	Bray et al	272/27 R

FOREIGN PATENTS OR APPLICATIONS

1,557,773 1/1969 France .... 35/22 R

Primary Examiner—Wm. H. Grieb
Attorney—Edward M. Farrell

[57] **ABSTRACT**

Methods and means for assisting persons in breaking undesirable habits include means for projecting first and second images onto a screen. The first image is a fixation image to induce a person to concentrate in a small limited area. The second image relates to an object or message relating to the habits to be broken. Various additional sensory messages, such as electrical or audio signals, are communicated to the person while one or both of the images are being projected on the screen.

10 Claims, 2 Drawing Figures

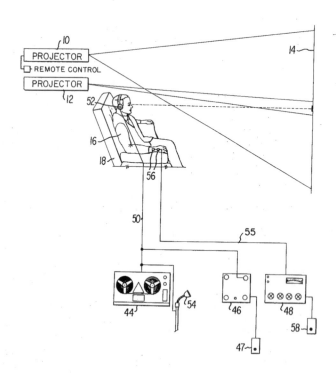

3,782,006

1

MEANS AND METHODS TO ASSIST PEOPLE IN BUILDING UP AN AVERSION TO UNDESIRABLE HABITS

It is well known that a person may develope undesirable habits which may adversely affect his health, state of mind or general well being. These habits generally originate from environmental conditions experienced during youth, the person's family life, his working conditions or from the many tensions resulting from pressures in a modern day society to which the person is exposed.

After an undesirable habit has been developed, it is very difficult for the average person to break it. This is especially true in cases where the habit has persisted over a number of years. Realization by the person involved that the habit may be detrimental to his health and general well being is often not sufficient to enable a person to break the habit.

Some of the habits developed by many people in our society involve smoking, over-eating, consumption of drugs and other habits which tend to cause physical and mental problems, which, in addition to causing general unhappiness, often lead to shorter life spans.

It is known that psychology and hypnotism, among other techniques, have been employed to assist persons to build up adversions to undesirable habits. In order to adequately treat different types of persons for different habits, different approaches must be employed by the psychologist, hypnotist or other trained personnel performing the treatments. It is often necessary to implement the words or suggestions of the individual administering the treatments with additional manifestations or suggestions from other sources.

It is known that, if a person starts to associate his habit with some unpleasant occurrence or experience, he will often associate the habit with the unpleasantness and build up an aversion to the habit.

While the words of the individual performing the treatment often carry a certain amount of persuasion to assist the person being treated to build up an aversion to a habit, it is desirable to supplement the words of the psychologist or hypnotist with additional manifestations. To achieve maximum results it is desirable to associate a maximum amount of unpleasantness with the habit to be broken in order to develope an aversion to the habit in a minimum amount of treatment time.

It is recognized that human beings experience and gain knowledge through all their senses, i.e., by seeing, hearing and feeling, for example. Ideally, if more than one or all of a person's senses could be used to receive messages which would associate unpleasantness towards a particular habit, the time taken to build up an aversion to that habit would be minimized.

It is an object of this invention to provide novel methods and means for treating a person to assist him in averting certain habits.

It is a further object of this invention to provide novel methods and means to assist persons to change undesirable habits, where the habits may involve a wide variety of different forms.

It is still a further object of this invention to provide novel methods and apparatus for treating persons to assist them in overcoming bad habits, in which the types of treatment available are widely variable to accommodate a wide variety of different people with different habits to be cured.

2

In accordance with the present invention, apparatus for assisting a person to build up an aversion to an undesirable habit includes visual displays for focusing his attention on a small area of a screen and then displaying a picture of an object or message relating to the habit on the screen. Additional means selectively provide audio signals, electrical shock signals, and/or other sensory messages to accompany the visual displays.

Other objects and advantages of the present invention will be apparent to those skilled in the art, from a reading of the following specification and claims, in conjunction with the accompanying drawing, in which:

FIG. 1 is a view, partly in block diagram form, illustrating a system for assisting a person to build up aversions to bad habits, in accordance with the present invention, and

FIG. 2 illustrates a slide for a projector which may be employed in the present invention.

Referring to the drawing, FIG. 1 illustrates an overall arrangement for treating a person and assisting him in building up an aversion to an undesirable habit. A pair of projectors 10 and 12 is disposed to project images onto a screen 14. FIG. 2 illustrates a series of images which may be projected onto a screen 14 by the projectors 10 and 12.

In treating a person 16 seated in a seat 18, a psychologist or other trained individual may go through a preliminary routine to put the person at ease. The individual giving the treatment then attempts to get the person to focus his attention on a relatively small area on the screen 14. While concentrating on the small area, the person tends to free his mind of extraneous thoughts. The projector 12 is used to project a relatively small image, illustrated in the form of small circles 20 or "X"'s 21 on a slide 22.

When the person is concentrating his attention on a relatively small circle 20 or "X" 21 projected onto the screen 14, the person being treated may be subjected to other induced sensory manifestations, as will be described.

When the person is concentrating his attention on the relatively small projected image on the screen, the projector 10 projects a second image onto the screen 14. The second image is associated with the habit for which the person is being treated. The second image may involve a number of different images sequentially presented as by a slide projector.

In FIG. 2 the slide 22 includes a number of different objects or messages. The particular slide 22 illustrated is used in connection with the habit of overeating. The various images are sequentially projected to induce a person to properly diet by building up an aversion to eating certain types of foods, notably calory rich desserts. Similar type slides to the slide 22 may be used in connection with building up aversions to smoking, drugs or other undesirable habits. In these cases, different images and messages would of course be included on the slides.

In FIG. 2, the circles 20 and "X"s 21 are illustrated to indicate how they are continuously projected along with the second image as the slide 22 is moved from frame to frame. In actual practice, the circles 20 and "X"s 21 would not actually be on the slide but rather super-imposed on the images or messages projected on the screen 14. The first images from the projector 12 are shown on the slide 22 merely for purposes of explanation.

United States Patent [19]

Monroe

[11] **3,884,218**

[45] **May 20, 1975**

[54] **METHOD OF INDUCING AND MAINTAINING VARIOUS STAGES OF SLEEP IN THE HUMAN BEING**

[75] Inventor: **Robert A. Monroe,** Charlottesville, Va.

[73] Assignee: **Monroe Industries, Inc.,** Charlottesville, Va.

[22] Filed: **Sept. 30, 1970**

[21] Appl. No.: **76,923**

[52] **U.S. Cl.** .... **128/1 C**
[51] **Int. Cl.** **A61b 19/00**
[58] **Field of Search** .... 128/1 C, 2.1 B, 422

[56] **References Cited**

UNITED STATES PATENTS

2,304,095	12/1942	Hull	128/1 C
3,032,029	5/1962	Cunningham	128/2.1 B
3,384,074	5/1968	Rautiola et al.	128/1 C
3,495,596	2/1970	Condict	128/422
3,576,185	4/1971	Schulz	128/1 C

FOREIGN PATENTS OR APPLICATIONS

211,752	4/1968	U.S.S.R.	128/1 C
1,165,541	10/1969	United Kingdom	128/1 C
1,183,607	12/1964	Germany	128/1 C

Primary Examiner—William E. Kamm
Attorney, Agent, or Firm—Sughrue, Rothwell, Mion, Zinn & Macpeak

[57] **ABSTRACT**

A method of inducing sleep in a human being wherein an audio signal is generated comprising a familiar pleasing repetitive sound modulated by an EEG sleep pattern. The volume of the audio signal is adjusted to overcome the ambient noise and a subject can select a familiar repetitive sound most pleasing to himself.

6 Claims, 8 Drawing Figures

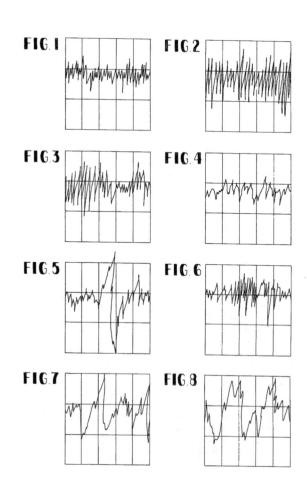

FIG. 1

FIG. 2

FIG. 3

FIG. 4

FIG. 5

FIG. 6

FIG. 7

FIG. 8

3,884,218

1

METHOD OF INDUCING AND MAINTAINING VARIOUS STAGES OF SLEEP IN THE HUMAN BEING

BACKGROUND OF THE INVENTION

1. Field of the Invention

This invention relates to a method of inducing sleep in a human being, and more particularly, to a method of inducing sleep by the generation of audio signals which are produced by the modulation of familiar repetitive noises with electroencephalographic (EEG) sleep patterns.

2. Description of the Prior Art

The use of audio generators to induce sleep is well known in the prior art, as exemplified by U.S. Pat. Nos. 2,711,165 and 3,384,074. The audio signals used include pleasing and harmonious steady sounds or vibrations, fixed frequency signals which are cyclicly varied as to amplitude, and repetitive sounds such as the falling of rain on a roof and the sighing wind through the trees.

The prior art also discloses, in U.S. Pat. No. 3,304,095, a method for inducing sleep by the generation of an audible or tactual signal which is related to the physiological processes of heartbeat and respiration. In this method, the pitch and amplitude of a pleasing audio signal are varied at a rate somewhat slower than either the rate of heartbeat or respiration. The heartbeat and respiration will tend to synchronize with the audio signal thereby lowering the heartbeat and respiration rate and inducing sleep.

SUMMARY OF THE INVENTION

The present invention comprises a method for inducing sleep wherein familiar, repetitive, pleasing sounds are modulated by predetermined EEG sleep signals to produce an audio signal which induces various stages of sleep.

It has been found through the use of an EEG that various patterns of electrical activity are associated with different states of consciousness. There are two primary states, waking and sleeping. Within the waking state, there are various degrees of alertness ranging from frantichyperalertness through relaxed attentiveness to drowsiness. There are also several stages of sleep ranging from a light to deep. All of the various states of alertness and sleep have EEG patterns which are characteristic of the state. These patterns tend to be basically similar for all normal human beings. It is well known in the prior art, as set forth above, that familiar, repetitive, pleasing sounds tend to produce drowsiness and sleep in an individual. In the method of this invention, however, the pleasing sounds are combined with the EEG sleep patterns by modulating the former with the latter. The audio signal thereby produced has been found to be a quick and efficient sleep inducing signal. In the method of this invention, the individual has the opportunity of selecting a signal most pleasing to himself for inducing sleep, and furthermore, he may determine the level of the sleep inducing signal in order to overcome ambient noise conditions.

In addition, the subject may time the sleep inducing signal such that upon completion of a predetermined time period the signal will stop and, he will drift back to wakefulness.

2

BRIEF DESCRIPTION OF THE DRAWINGS

FIG. 1 is a typical human EEG pattern of awakeness with eyes open.

FIG. 2 is an EEG pattern of awakeness with eyes closed.

FIG. 3 is an EEG pattern of drowsiness.

FIG. 4 is an EEG pattern of descending stage 1 sleep.

FIG. 5 is an EEG pattern of stage 2 sleep.

FIG. 6 is an EEG pattern of stage 2 sleep with sleep spindles.

FIG. 7 is an EEG sleep pattern of stage 3 sleep.

FIG. 8 is an EEG sleep pattern of stage 4 sleep.

DESCRIPTION OF THE PREFERRED METHOD

An electroencephalogram (EEG) is a device for measuring the fluctuation of electrical potentials due to the electrical activity of the brain. It has been found, through the use of the EEG, that various patterns are generated during different states of consciousness of the human being. This is the subject of the book *Electroencephalography: A Symposium In Its Various Aspects*, by Hill and Park. There are two primary states of consciousness, waking and sleeping. Within the waking state, there are various degrees of alertness ranging from frantic hyperalertness to drowsiness. Extreme alertness is associated with a low voltage, generally fast and irregular, of 10 to 20 microvolts amplitude and frequencies ranging from 10 to 40 cycles per second. Relaxed alertness is accompanied by an alpha rhythm, which is a regular sinusoidal rhythm with a frequency between 8 to 13 cps. As the state of consciousness changes from relaxed alertness to drowsiness, the alpha rhythm breaks up and tends to become less and less frequent.

The first stage of sleep or state 1 has an EEG pattern, as shown in FIG. 4, which consists of an irregular mixture of theta waves which are low in amplitude with a frequency of 4 to 8 cps, occasional alpha waves, and irregularly occurring alphoid waves which are similar to alpha waves but have a frequency of 1 to 2 cps lower than the alpha wave.

An individual progresses from stage 1 sleep to stage 2 sleep, the EEG pattern of which is shown in FIG. 5. The stage 2 pattern is similar to stage 1 except that sleep spindles begin to appear. The spindles are short bursts of waves at a frequency of about 14 cps. They start at low amplitude and build up very rapidly to an amplitude of 30 or 40 microvolts and then quickly taper off.

The individual then passes into stage 3 sleep, the EEG pattern of which is shown in FIG. 7. Stage 3 sleep is characterized by the appearance of delta waves which are waves of an amplitude of approximately 100 microvolts or more and a frequency of 1 cps. Stage 4 sleep which follows stage 3 sleep is characterized by a preponderance of delta waves as opposed to the occasional delta waves of stage 3 sleep. In sleep stages 3 and 4, the spindles and irregular theta waves appearing in stage 2 sleep still appear.

Stages 1 through 4 were initially conceived of as comprising a continuum from "light" to "deep" sleep, but many other measures of the depth of sleep contradict this ordering. Stage 1 sleep occurring later in the night seems to have very distinct characteristics which make it a distinct kind of sleep, while stages 2, 3 and

United States Patent [19]

Barbara

[11]   **4,141,344**

[45]   **Feb. 27, 1979**

[54] **SOUND RECORDING SYSTEM**

[76] Inventor: **Louis J. Barbara**

[21] Appl. No.: **882,777**

[22] Filed: **Mar. 2, 1978**

[51] Int. Cl.² **A61M 21/00**
[52] U.S. Cl. .... **128/1 C**
[58] Field of Search .... 128/1 C, 1 R, 2.1 B;
                                        328/158, 160; 360/18

[56]   **References Cited**

U.S. PATENT DOCUMENTS

3,400,333   9/1968   Inose 328/160

3,576,185	4/1971	Schulz et al.	128/1 C
3,712,292	1/1973	Zentmeyer, Jr.	128/1 C

Primary Examiner—William E. Kamm
Attorney, Agent, or Firm—Oltman and Flynn

[57]   **ABSTRACT**

In recording an audio program, such as music or voice, on a magnetic tape recorder an A.C. signal generator operating at a frequency below about 14 Hz. provides an A.C. baseline for the audio program signal. This 14 Hz. or lower A.C. signal is sensed by the listener's ear to create an Alpha or Theta state in his brain when the tape is played back.

9 Claims, 3 Drawing Figures

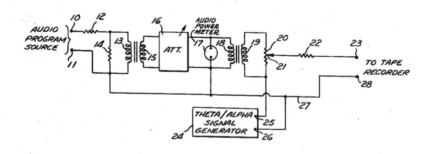

4,141,344

1

SOUND RECORDING SYSTEM

BACKGROUND OF THE INVENTION

Various methods have been used heretofore to put 5 the human brain into a Theta (below 7 Hz.) or Alpha (7–14 Hz.) brain wave state.

The Alpha state of the brain is considered desirable as promoting relaxation of the body, reducing or eliminating anxiety or mental stress, enhancing the brain's effi- 10 ciency and creativity, and promoting a feeling of peace and silence.

The Theta state of the brain is associated with peaceful sleep.

In considering the possibility of using conventional 15 magnetic tape recordings to induce the Theta or Alpha state, the first, seemingly insuperable problem is the low frequency limit of conventional tape recording/-playback instruments. Those in the low price range (e.g., below $60) typically are not designed for frequen- 20 cies below 200 Hz. Those in an intermediate price range (e.g., $95–175) typically can handle frequencies down to about 70 Hz. Even tape recorders/players in the price range above $1,000 cannot adequately record or repro- 25 duce signal frequencies below 20 Hz.

SUMMARY OF THE INVENTION

The present invention is directed to a novel apparatus and method which enables relatively inexpensive magnetic tape players to be used to stimulate Theta or 30 Alpha brain wave patterns in the listener.

In accordance with the present invention, an audio program is recorded on tape, consisting of signals completely or virtually completely within an audio frequency range substantially above 14 Hz. This audio 35 program may be music, voice, white noise, single frequency tones, or combinations of several different single frequency tones. During the recording of this audio program, which in and of itself would present no difficulty to the recording apparatus, the baseline of the 40 audio program is varied in accordance with a Theta or Alpha signal, which preferably is a single frequency signal, such as 10.53 Hz. Alpha signal. The Theta or Alpha signal provides a very low frequency A.C. base- 45 line for the audio program signal in place of the usual baseline at ground potential. Preferably, the amplitude of the Theta or Alpha baseline signal is about four times the maximum amplitude of the audio program signal, such as music or voice. 50

It has been found that magnetic tape recordings made this way, when played back, are effective in inducing a beneficial Theta or Alpha state in the listener's brain even though the listener may be only conscious of hearing the music, voice or other audio program from the 55 tape. Also, some listeners with hearing problems are better able to hear the music, voice or other audio program recorded this way.

Two presently preferred apparatus embodiments of this invention are illustrated in the accompanying draw- 60 ings in which:

FIG. 1 is a schematic electrical circuit diagram of a monaural recording arrangement in accordance with the present invention;

FIG. 2 shows the wave form of the output signal 65 from the Theta/Alpha signal generator in FIG. 1 and below it the wave form of the input signal to the tape recorder; and

2

FIG. 3 is a schematic electrical circuit diagram of a stereophonic (binaural) recording arrangement in accordance with this invention.

Before explaining the disclosed embodiments of the present invention in detail, it is to be understood that the invention is not limited in its application to the details of the particular arrangements shown since the invention is capable of other embodiments. Also, the terminology used herein is for the purpose of description and not of limitation.

Referring first to FIG. 1, the input terminals 10 and 11 of the present apparatus receive an audio program from a suitable source of music, speech, white noise, etc., which produces signals which are entirely or very predominantly within the audio frequency range substantially above 14 Hz. For purposes of this discussion, this audio program will be referred to hereinafter as music.

The upper audio program input terminal 10 is connected through a resistor 12 to the upper end of the primary 13 of a first stepdown transformer. The lower audio program input terminal 11 is connected directly to the lower end of the transformer primary 13. A shunt resistor 14 is connected across the transformer primary 13.

This transformer has a secondary winding 15 connected through an attenuator or adjustable volume control 16 and an audio power meter 17, both of known design, across the primary 18 of a step up transformer. This transformer has a secondary winding 19 connected across a potentiometer resistance 20. An adjustable tap 21 on the potentiometer is connected through a resistor 22 to a first input terminal 23 leading to the tape recorder.

A signal generator 24, which produces a sine wave falling somewhere within the Theta/Alpha frequency range below 14 Hz., has a first output terminal 25 connected to the lower end of the potentiometer 20 and the transformer secondary 19. This signal generator has a second output terminal 26 which is connected via line 27 to the remaining input terminal 28 for the tape recorder. Line 27 also is connected to the music program input terminal 11 and the lower end of the primary 18 of the second transformer. Line 27 may be grounded to the chasis of the signal generator 24 on the meter 17. Preferably, both the frequency and the amplitude of the output signal from the generator 24 are selectively adjustable.

In one practical embodiment of this circuit the ohmic value of each resistor 12, 14, 20 and 22, the first transformer primary 13 and the second transformer secondary 19 is 10,000 ohms, and the ohmic value of the first transformer secondary 15 and of the second transformer primary 18 is 500 ohms. In this embodiment, each transformer is designed for a frequency response of from 20 to 20,000 HZ. and has a power rating of 10 watts, and the generator 24 produces a 10.53 Hz. sine wave.

In the use of this recording arrangement, with the signal generator 24 disconnected or de-energized the attenuator 16 is adjusted to provide a zero decibel reading on the audio power meter 17. A cathode ray oscilloscope (not shown) is connected across the input terminals 23 and 28 for the tape recorder. With the time base of the oscilloscope adjusted to 1 millisecond, the adjustable potentiometer tap 21 is adjusted to provide a maximum input signal of 0.2 volt peak-to-peak on the oscilloscope. Then the oscilloscope time base is set for 10 milliseconds and its trigger level is set for one complete

United States Patent [19]

Meland et al.

[11] **4,227,516**

[45] **Oct. 14, 1980**

[54] **APPARATUS FOR ELECTROPHYSIOLOGICAL STIMULATION**

[76] Inventors: **Bruce C. Meland Bernard C. Gindes**, deceased, late of Los Angeles, Calif.; by Hanna Gindes, executrix

[21] Appl. No.: **969,104**

[22] Filed: **Dec. 13, 1978**

[51] Int. Cl.³ **A61M 21/00**
[52] U.S. Cl. .... **128/1 C**
[58] Field of Search .... 128/1 C, 1 R

[56] **References Cited**

U.S. PATENT DOCUMENTS

2,986,140	5/1961	Gardner et al.	128/1 R
3,255,753	6/1966	Wing	128/1 C
3,718,132	2/1973	Holt et al.	128/1 C
3,753,433	8/1973	Bakerich et al.	128/1 C
3,762,396	10/1973	Ballentine et al.	128/1 C
3,884,218	5/1975	Monroe	128/1 C
3,908,634	9/1975	Monaghan	128/1 C
4,047,377	9/1977	Banks, Jr.	128/1 C

Primary Examiner—William E. Kamm
Attorney, Agent, or Firm—Keith D. Beecher; Jessup & Beecher

[57] **ABSTRACT**

Apparatus for the electrophysiological stimulation of a patient is provided for creating an analgesic condition in the patient to induce sleep, treat psychosomatic disorders, and to aid in the induction of electrohypnosis and altered states of consciousness. The foregoing is achieved by repetitive stimuli in the patient for whom external influences, namely those of sight and sound, are intentionally excluded. The apparatus produces electrical stimulation of the patient in the form of a modulated wave which produces impulses in the delta, theta, alpha and beta regions of the brain's electrical activity, the electrical stimulation being accompanied by two sources of audio stimulation, one of which is a sinusoidal tone modulated by and synchronized with the electrical stimulation, and the other is derived from sound recordings.

15 Claims, 3 Drawing Figures

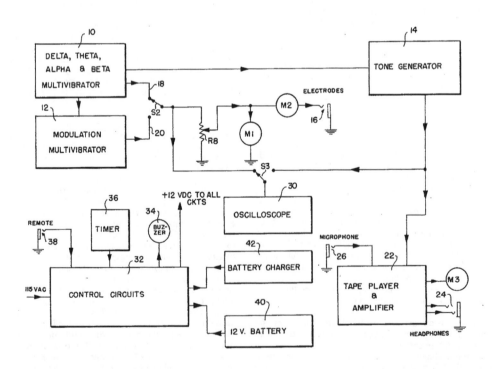

1

2

APPARATUS FOR ELECTROPHYSIOLOGICAL STIMULATION

BACKGROUND

Methods and apparatus are known for inducing sleep, treating psychosomatic disorders, and for aiding in the induction of hypnosis in a patient, the foregoing being achieved by passing a stimulation of electrical current pulses through the brain of the patient by electrodes attached, for example, to the back of the head and to the forehead. Such apparatus is described, for example, in U.S. Pat. No. 3,762,396. In the apparatus described in the patent, the electric current impulses of the stimulus have a frequency of 8–10 Hz. The apparatus described in the patent also passes a second stimulus of electric pulses to the brain of the patient having a frequency which is four times the frequency of the pulses of the first stimulus, the latter stimulus being introduced through the optic nerves of the patient by the electrodes attached to the temple and forehead. A third auditory stimulus is provided in the system described in the patent by way of sound attenuating chambers. The auditory stimulus is used acoustically to isolate the patient from a noise environment. The three stimuli are preferably synchronized with one another.

U.S. Pat. No. 3,908,634 describes a method and apparatus for inducing a vocalized analgesic condition in the patient by simulating the presence of a hypnotherapist. This is achieved by reproducing a recording of the speech that the hypnotherapist would normally make to the patient.

The apparatus of the present invention falls in the same general class as the apparatus described in the above-mentioned patents; and an objective of the apparatus of the invention, likewise, is to produce different states of consciousness in a patient by repetitive stimuli, with the patient being insulated from external influence. In the practice of the invention, the patient to all intents and purposes is placed in a closed chamber in which the apparatus is set to an operational mode which creates a sensory input; and impulses in the delta, theta, alpha and beta ranges are introduced to the optic cortex, each producing its specific state of consciousness in the patient.

The various ranges referred to above relate to the different rhythms in the brain's electrical activity. For example, the alpha rhythms have a pulse frequency in the 8–13 Hz range; the beta rhythms have a pulse frequency in the 13–30 Hz range; the theta rhythms have a pulse frequency in the 4–7 Hz range; and the delta rhythms are slow waves with pulse frequencies in the 0.5–3 Hz range. The alpha rhythms are customarily found in the normal human adult when he is relaxed and has his eyes closed; the beta rhythms are normally encountered when a person is aroused and anxious; the theta rhythms are often found in adolescents with behavior disorders; and the delta rhythms appear in the normal person when he is asleep.

Each impulse introduced to the patient by the apparatus of the invention is super-imposed on the brainwave activity, finally dominating it and thereby altering the patient's state of awareness. The result is light or deep sleep, somnolence, hypnosis, heightened awareness, or even agitation, depending upon the frequency of the pulses introduced to the patient.

The electrical stimulation is in the form of a modulated square wave accompanied by two sources of audio stimulation, one of which is a sinusoidal tone, modulated by and synchronized with the optical electrical stimulation. The other audio sound helps to overwhelm the circuits, minimizing internal and external inputs. The subject is restricted to the selective sensory impulses he is receiving, and he shuts out most of his internal and external environment, the result being that the impulses received alter the patterns of brain activity essentially bringing the brain into synchronism with the instrument.

Specifically, the present invention provides an improved instrument constructed for electrophysiological stimulation of a human being. The instrument is capable of inducing into the patient the effects produced by brainwave activity in the delta, theta, alpha and beta ranges. The apparatus uses a modulated square wave which creates the electrophysiological stimulation, and which is accompanied by two sources of audio stimulation, one being synchronized with the electrophysiological stimulation. The electrical stimulation is applied to the patient by means of electrodes attached to the forehead.

The audio stimulation is introduced to the patient by means of headphones. One of the audio stimuli is a sinusoidal tone modulated by and in synchronism with the electrophysiological stimulation. The other audio stimulus is derived from a cassette tape player, which plays pre-recorded tapes of special sound effects and hypnotic suggestions recorded for a specific patient.

The result of the foregoing three stimulating forces acting together enables the instrument to alter the mood or mental state of the patient so as to produce a variety of altered mental states. The instrument of the invention can be used, for example, for inducing sleep, inducing an hypnotic state, producing tranquility and relaxation, producing heightened awareness, increasing the ability of a person to concentrate, and for inducing other mental states. The instrument can also be used for treating psychosomatic disorders.

The instrument to be described is battery operated from a self-contained rechargeable 12-volt battery. Battery operation is used for electrical safety, since it completely eliminates the possibility of a patient being electrocuted, as could occur with alternating current line operated equipment.

BRIEF DESCRIPTION OF THE DRAWINGS

FIG. **1** is a block diagram of an instrument representing one embodiment of the invention; and

FIGS. **2** and **2A** represent a circuit diagram of the instrument of FIG. **1**.

DETAILED DESCRIPTION OF THE ILLUSTRATED EMBODIMENT

The system of the invention includes a block designated **10** which is the nucleus of the system. This block is an astable multivibrator which generates square waves of variable frequency and shape. The multivibrator of block **10** performs three functions: (1) it controls or synchronizes the output of a modulation multivibrator represented by block **12**; (2) it controls or synchronizes the output of a tone generator represented by block **14**; and (3) it produces square wave output pulses which can be used as the stimulating voltage applied to the patient by way of electrodes connected to a jack **16**.

The square wave output from the multivibrator of block **10** appears on a lead **18** which is connected to one

United States Patent [19]

Gorges

[11]   **4,315,502**

[45]   **Feb. 16, 1982**

[54] **LEARNING-RELAXATION DEVICE**

[76] Inventor: **Denis E. Gorges**

[21] Appl. No.: **84,051**

[22] Filed: **Oct. 11, 1979**

[51] Int. Cl.³ **A61N 1/34**
[52] U.S. Cl. .... **128/1 C**
[58] Field of Search .... 128/24 A, 24.1, 732,
       128/33, 1 R, 1 C, 630; 40/442, 455, 457; 35/22
       R; 350/145, 45; 351/158, 48

[56]   **References Cited**

U.S. PATENT DOCUMENTS

3,576,185	4/1971	Schulz et al.	128/1 C
3,612,651	10/1971	McCurdy	40/457
3,712,292	1/1973	Zentmeyer, Jr.	128/1 C
3,773,049	11/1973	Rabicher et al.	128/1 C
3,826,250	7/1974	Adams	128/33
3,857,383	12/1974	Sommerfeld et al.	128/630

FOREIGN PATENT DOCUMENTS

2314014	10/1974	Fed. Rep. of Germany	128/1 C
2846859	5/1979	Fed. Rep. of Germany	128/1 C
1165541	10/1969	United Kingdom	128/1 C
1422959	1/1976	United Kingdom	128/380
500802	4/1976	U.S.S.R.	128/1 C

OTHER PUBLICATIONS

Beck, R. C., "ELF Magnetic Fields and EEG Entrainment," Apha–Metrics Company Publication 1978.

Primary Examiner—Robert W. Michell
Assistant Examiner—Francis J. Jaworski
Attorney, Agent, or Firm—Yount & Tarolli

[57]   **ABSTRACT**

Disclosed is a device for relaxing, stimulating and/or driving brain wave form function in a human subject. The device comprises, in combination, an eye mask having independently controlled left and right eyepieces and a peripheral light array in each eyepiece, an audio headset having independently controlled left and right earpieces and a control panel which controls light and sound signals to the light arrays and earpieces, respectively. Various control functions allow simultaneous or alternating light and sound pulsations in the left and right light arrays and earpieces, as well as selective phasing between light and sound pulsations.

23 Claims, 8 Drawing Figures

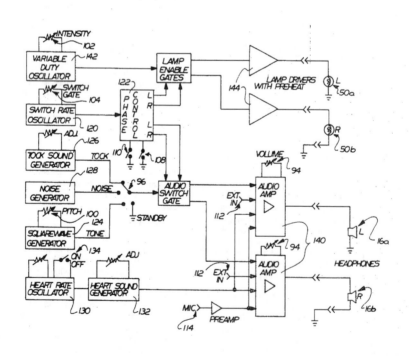

4,315,502

1

LEARNING-RELAXATION DEVICE

BACKGROUND OF THE INVENTION

This invention relates to the art of learning and relaxation aids and more particularly to a device which releases psychological and physiological stress and tension primarily by stimulating the senses of hearing and sight.

Various devices have been developed in recent years for use in both stimulating and patterning brain functions in both the fields of psychology and learning. Thus, the so-called bio-feedback devices utilize electrical signals from various sensors placed on the body of a subject which sense such variables as skin temperature, pulse rate, blood pressure and the like. From a summation of these various data, the subject is provided with some form of feedback which is indicative of these various conditions. By concentrating on particular symptoms, an alteration in one or more of the variables may be induced which in turn alters the feedback. Commonly, an audio tone is utilized to indicate a particular mental or physical state and variations in the tone indicate differing mental or physical states. Eventually, the subject "learns" how to induce changes in his physical state without feedback. A typical bio-feedback device is described in U.S. Pat. No. 3,942,516.

Subliminal stimulation is also known to impart knowledge to a subject through subconscious mental functioning. A tachistoscopic visual image impressed upon the field of vision of a subject, such as on a motion picture or a television screen, can stimulate and be retained by a subject's subconsciousness even when the stimulus is of such short duration that the subject's conscious mind is totally unaware of its presence. Similarly, it is also known that audio subliminal stimulation is possible by overlaying an audio signal onto a normal pattern of audio input. U.S. Pat. Nos. 3,060,795 and 3,278,676 are illustrative of these concepts.

In the field of learning, sensory isolation, wherein distracting sensory inputs are suppressed, is well known. The common study carrel which limits peripheral vision and usually incorporates sound deadening panels is typical of such devices. Also known is a learning aid which incorporates a pair of eye goggles which act in a manner similar to blinders to limit a subject's peripheral vision, and, as described in U.S. Pat. No. 3,534,484, may also incorporate a source of an audio signal which acts to block out other distracting audio inputs. This combination affords the user a reduction in distracting sensory inputs and thereby assists in the development of concentration on a particular subject matter.

Modern theories of psychology and learning have identified various functional areas in the physical structure of the brain and central nervous system. Thus, the so-called left hemisphere of the brain is thought to be the source of logical reasoning and rote functioning of the human consciousness. Conversely, the so-called right brain hemisphere is thought to be the source of artistic, creative and imaginative functioning within the brain.

A similar division has been noted in front and rear brain functioning. The rear portion of the brain controlling the instinctual function of the body such as the central nervous system, the limbic system, etc. while

2

human reasoning or social functioning is centered in the front portion of the brain.

Often the functioning of one hemisphere or portion is emphasized to the point of suppression of or conflict with the functioning of the other. Ideally, "whole" brain functioning would be utilized through a balancing of left and right, and front to back brain functions. In order to accomplish this, it is necessary to reduce the over-emphasized functioning and increase the under emphasized functioning to a point where there is cooperative functioning of both brain hemispheres, side to side and front to back.

It has been found that the brain utilizes wave patterns in order to function. It has also been found that light and sound stimuli can affect brain wave patterns and actually alter the flow of these brain wave patterns.

SUMMARY OF THE INVENTION

The present invention provides an apparatus for stimulating and coordinating whole brain wave function, which apparatus comprises in combination a source of pulsating light in an eye-covering mask which locates the light sources adjacent the left and right eyes of a subject and an audio headset which applies sound signals to the left and right ears of the subject.

In accordance with the invention, an eye mask generally in the form of goggles having left and right eyepieces includes a peripheral source of light for each eyepiece which may be independently controlled for pulsation frequency and light intensity. The mask incorporates a headband for securing the mask to the wearer's head and may also include integral air vents.

In a preferred embodiment of the invention, the eyepieces incorporate interchangeable lens and/or filter elements which may be colored lenses, prismatic lenses, mirrors and the like. Clear lenses may also be utilized.

In accordance with the preferred embodiment of the invention, the eye mask as above described, may further include a secondary pulsating light source located generally above and between the left and right eyepieces. A source of extremely low frequency (1-30 Hz) electromagnetic force fields may also be provided adjacent each eyepiece and electrically connected to pulse at the frequency and intensity of its associated light source and/or audio source.

The eye mask as above described is used in conjunction with an audio headset which is similar to a set of stereo headphones. Audio signals to left and right eyepieces are controlled independently along with light pulsations in the eye mask.

The eye mask and headset are connected, preferably through a single umbilical connector, to a control panel. The control panel incorporates controls for the intensity of both the light source and the sound volume. A pulsation frequency control is also utilized.

In the preferred embodiment, the control panel as above described may further include switching means which permits simultaneous left and right pulsations of both the light sources and sound outputs or may also permit alternating left and right pulsations in each mode. A second switching means may also be provided which alternates a light pulse with a sound pulse in one position and synchronizes light and sound pulses in a second position. Thus, in combination, the two switching means permit four possible combinations of alternating and synchronous pulsations between the left and right light and sound sources. Each of these switching

United States Patent [19]

Williamson

[11] **4,335,710**

[45] **Jun. 22, 1982**

[54] **DEVICE FOR THE INDUCTION OF SPECIFIC BRAIN WAVE PATTERNS**

[75] Inventor: **John D. Williamson,** North Canton, Ohio

[73] Assignee: **Omnitronics Research Corporation,** Akron, Ohio

[21] Appl. No.: **112,537**

[22] Filed: **Jan. 16, 1980**

[51] Int. Cl.^{3} **A61N 1/34**
[52] U.S. Cl. .... **128/1 C**
[58] Field of Search .... 128/1 C, 1 R

[56] **References Cited**

U.S. PATENT DOCUMENTS

2,466,054	4/1949	Siebel	128/1 R
3,160,159	12/1964	Hoody et al.	128/1C
3,576,185	4/1971	Schulz et al.	128/1 C
3,712,292	1/1973	Zentmeyer, Jr.	128/1 C
3,753,433	8/1973	Bakerich et al.	128/1 C
3,884,218	5/1975	Monroe	128/1 C
3,892,957	1/1975	Freeman	128/732
4,034,741	7/1977	Adams et al.	128/1 C

FOREIGN PATENT DOCUMENTS

1165541 10/1969 United Kingdom .... 128/1 C

Primary Examiner—William E. Kamm
Attorney, Agent, or Firm—Hamilton, Renner & Kenner

[57] **ABSTRACT**

Brain wave patterns associated with relaxed and meditative states in a subject are gradually induced without deleterious chemical or neurological side effects. A white noise generator (11) has the spectral noise density of its output signal modulated in a manner similar to the brain wave patterns by a switching transistor (18) within a spectrum modulator (12). The modulated white noise signal is amplified by output amplifier (13) and converted to an audio signal by acoustic transducer (14). Ramp generator (16) gradually increases the voltage received by and resultant output frequency of voltage controlled oscillator (17) whereby switching transistor (18) periodically shunts the high frequency components of the white noise signal to ground.

11 Claims, 2 Drawing Figures

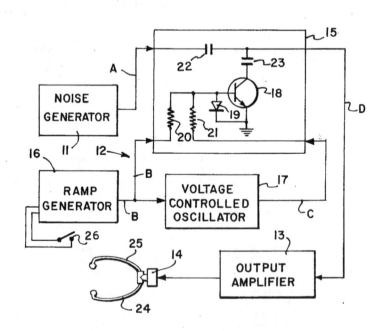

4,335,710

1

DEVICE FOR THE INDUCTION OF SPECIFIC BRAIN WAVE PATTERNS

TECHNICAL FIELD

The present invention relates generally to a device for effecting deep relaxation in a subject. More particular, the present invention relates to a device for the induction of brain wave patterns associated with relaxed and meditative states in a human subject, commonly known as a "brain driver".

BACKGROUND ART

It has long been recognized that most mammals and in particular humans exhibit distinct recurring electrical frequencies in their brain wave patterns, each of which is related to separately identifiable physiological states. Brain waves having dominant frequencies from approximately 8–13 Hz, inclusive, are known as Alpha frequency brain waves and are associated with relaxed and meditative states as would occur when a subject has his eyes closed but is conscious and not thinking.

Techniques and devices which attempt to promote natural relaxation may be generally classified as passive or active. Passive devices serve merely to mask out irritating external noises with more pleasant sounds or utilize random or "white noise" to psychologically distract the subject from events which inhibit natural relaxation. Active devices seek to intentionally induce Alpha frequency brain waves in the subject, a phenomena known as "brain driving". Irrespective of the manner in which such brain waves are induced, a subject whose brain waves are principally in the Alpha frequency range will become deeply relaxed and exhibit the same beneficial reduced muscular tension and lowered anxiety and adrenalin levels as are associated with a naturally occurring state of relaxation.

Typical of the numerous passive devices are those which vary the output signal from a "white noise" source and convert the same to an accoustical signal, resulting in pleasant masking sounds. In one device, the white noise source output has its amplitude varied by a saw tooth wave form to produce sounds similar to waves repeatedly breaking in a surf. In another device, the output signal from a "white noise" source has its spectral content and amplitude varied in direct response to a subject's instantaneous dominant brain wave frequency and amplitude, respectively, producing a feedback signal to be utilized by the subject to recognize his present physiological state. All passive devices suffer from a fundamental inadequacy in that they cannot actually induce Alpha frequency brain waves with its associated relaxed and meditative condition.

Currently only three basic techniques for forcing a subject into a state exhibiting Alpha frequency brain waves are known to exist. Perhaps the most widely used is chemical tranquilizers, always subject to potentially grave known and unknown negative side effects or contraindications. The other techniques for "brain driving" involve the use of very bright, quickly flashing lights, direct electrical pulse stimulation of the brain through skin electrodes, or some combination thereof. In either instance, the lights or electrical pulses are synchronized to occur at a rate within the Alpha frequency range, i.e., from about 8 to 14 Hz. However, such flashing lights are not only irritating but may likely initiate a seizure in epileptic individuals. Electrical pulses are not only irritating, but also may produce

2

unknown, deleterious side effects upon other parts of the brain or other neurological activity. Moreover, these devices attempt to very abruptly force the subject from an active and possibly highly emotional state to a highly relaxed and meditative state, thereby greatly increasing the likelihood of failure.

DISCLOSURE OF INVENTION

It is, therefore, an object of the invention to provide a device for the induction of brain wave patterns associated with relaxed and meditative states in a subject in a safe manner without deleterious or irritating side effects or contraindications.

It is a further object of the invention to provide a device for the induction of brain wave patterns associated with relaxed and meditative states in a subject, as above, which gradually induces such state in the subject.

It is yet a further object of the invention, to provide a device for the induction of brain wave patterns associated with relaxed and meditative states in a subject, as above, which utilizes a pleasing sound that is modulated and programmed in such manner as to induce Alpha frequency brain wave patterns only in those brain structures where it naturally occurs.

It is still a further object of the invention to provide a device for the induction of brain wave patterns associated with relaxed and meditative states in a subject, as above, which ultimately terminates all variations in modulation of the sound thereby freeing and encouraging the subject's brain to assume whatever somnolent brain wave patterns occur naturally to the subject.

It is still a further object of the invention to provide a device for the induction of brain wave patterns associated with relaxed and meditative states in a subject, as above, which includes a source of white noise and a circuit for modulating the spectral noise density of the white noise in a manner similar to the brain wave patterns associated with relaxed and meditative states so as to promote the gradual transition to an Alpha frequency brain wave condition and the continuous maintenance of the subject in that condition.

These and other objects and advantages of the present invention over existing prior art forms will become more apparent and fully understood from the following description in conjunction with the accompanying drawings.

In general, a device for the induction of brain wave patterns associated with relaxed and meditative states in a subject comprises a signal generator for generating a white noise signal having a uniform spectral noise density, a modulation circuit for receiving and modulating the white noise signal, and means for receiving the modulated noise signal and coupling it to the subject. The modulation circuit modulates the white noise signal in a manner similar to the brain wave patterns associated with relaxed and meditative states in the subject, thereby actively gradually inducing such state in the subject.

BRIEF DESCRIPTION OF THE DRAWINGS

FIG. 1 is a block diagram of an exemplary device according to the concept of the present invention, and depicts the spectral-noise density modulator schematically.

FIG. 2 is a somewhat schematic representation of the voltage waveforms at various points in the device

United States Patent [19]

Filley

[11] **4,388,918**

[45] **Jun. 21, 1983**

[54] **MENTAL HARMONIZATION PROCESS**

[76] Inventor: **Charles C. Filley**

[21] Appl. No.: **270,904**

[22] Filed: **Jun. 5, 1981**

[51] Int. Cl.³ A61B 19/00
[52] U.S. Cl. .... 128/1 C; 179/1 AA
[58] Field of Search .... 128/1 C; 179/1 AA

[56] **References Cited**

U.S. PATENT DOCUMENTS

2,843,111	7/1958	Roll	128/1 C
3,014,477	12/1961	Carlin	128/1 C
3,213,851	10/1965	Currea	179/1 AA
3,272,198	9/1966	Balkin	179/1 AA
3,773,049	11/1973	Rabichev et al.	128/1 C X
4,289,121	9/1981	Kuprinanovich	128/1 C
4,315,502	2/1982	Gorges	128/1 C

Primary Examiner—Kyle L. Howell
Assistant Examiner—John C. Hanley
Attorney, Agent, or Firm—Russell H. Schlattman

[57] **ABSTRACT**

A state of relaxation or mental harmonization in a subject is created by exposing a color solely to one field of vision of a subject and the complement of that color solely to the other field of vision of the subject while simultaneously exposing an audible tone solely to one ear of the subject and a harmonious tone solely to the other ear of the subject. The color and tones employed are subjectively comfortable and compatible. Preferably, the frequency difference between the two audible tones is one-half the frequency of the audible tone having the lowest frequency.

2 Claims, No Drawings

220

United States Patent [19]

Whitten et al.

[11] **Patent Number:** **4,508,105**

[45] **Date of Patent:** **Apr. 2, 1985**

[54] **SHADOW GENERATING APPARATUS**

[76] Inventors: **Glen A. Whitten; Lech Pisarski**

[21] Appl. No.: **464,970**

[22] Filed: **Feb. 8, 1983**

[51] Int. Cl.³ A61M 21/00
[52] U.S. Cl. .... 128/1 C
[58] Field of Search .... 128/1 C

[56] **References Cited**

U.S. PATENT DOCUMENTS

569,117	10/1896	Mosher	....	128/1 C
3,722,501	3/1973	Derouineau	....	128/1 C
3,972,319	8/1976	Dehlinger	....	128/1 C
4,315,502	2/1982	Gorges	....	128/1 C

FOREIGN PATENT DOCUMENTS

16357 of 1899 United Kingdom .... 128/1 C

Primary Examiner—William E. Kamm

Attorney, Agent, or Firm—Oldham, Oldham & Weber Co.

[57] **ABSTRACT**

Disclosed is an apparatus for inducing various brain wave patterns through visual stimulation. The apparatus comprises a pair of spectacles or other viewing apparatus having a liquid crystal display embedded in each lens. By repetitively activating and deactivating the liquid crystals, shadows are generated which are perceived by the subject individual wearing the viewing apparatus. Responding to the frequency of shadow generation, the subject's brain is thereby induced to generate sympathetic brain wave frequencies. The apparatus finds particular utility in the generation of alpha waves. Because learning is enhanced when the brain is in the alpha state, activities such as listening to tapes or lectures and the like can be carried out with greater facility. Shadow generation is accomplished through the use of a timing mechanism for each liquid crystal display and the frequency for each is adjustable over a wide range, permitting synchronous or asynchronous timing.

8 Claims, 5 Drawing Figures

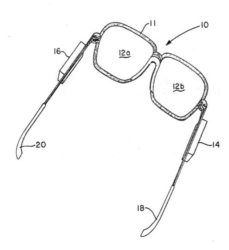

United States Patent [19]

Warnke

[11] **Patent Number:** **4,573,449**

[45] **Date of Patent:** **Mar. 4, 1986**

[54] **METHOD FOR STIMULATING THE FALLING ASLEEP AND/OR RELAXING BEHAVIOR OF A PERSON AND AN ARRANGEMENT THEREFOR**

[76] Inventor: **Egon F. Warnke**

[21] Appl. No.: **473,353**

[22] Filed: **Mar. 8, 1983**

[51] Int. Cl.⁴ A61N 1/34
[52] U.S. Cl. .... 128/1 C; 128/422
[58] Field of Search .... 128/1 C, 422

[56] **References Cited**

U.S. PATENT DOCUMENTS

3,712,292	1/1973	Zentmeyer, Jr.	128/1 C
3,835,833	9/1974	Limoge	128/1 C
3,884,218	5/1975	Monroe	128/1 C

FOREIGN PATENT DOCUMENTS

2536812	3/1977	Fed. Rep. of Germany	128/1 C
2385409	12/1978	France	128/1 C
2403802	5/1979	France	128/1 C

Primary Examiner—Kyle L. Howell
Assistant Examiner—Ruth S. Smith

[57] **ABSTRACT**

A method and apparatus is provided with which a person suffering from sleeplessness can be more easily relaxed and may more rapidly fall asleep. In particular, sound pulses are emitted by an electro-acoustic transducer, according to the cadence of which, the person seeking to fall asleep is induced to breathe in and out over a predetermined period of time. By suitably selecting the pulse sequence frequency, the pitch and the amplitude of the sound pulses may be adjusted thereby enhancing the process of falling asleep.

2 Claims, 3 Drawing Figures

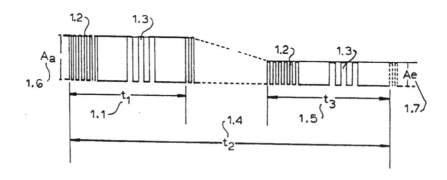

United States Patent [19]

Beck

[11] **Patent Number:** **4,664,117**

[45] **Date of Patent:** **May 12, 1987**

[54] **APPARATUS AND METHOD FOR GENERATING PHOSPHENES**

[76] Inventor: **Stephen C. Beck**

[21] Appl. No.: **658,888**

[22] Filed: **Oct. 9, 1984**

[51] Int. Cl.^{4} A61N 1/32
[52] U.S. Cl. .... 128/420 R
[58] Field of Search .... 128/1 R, 1 C, 419 R, 128/419 S, 420 AR, 421, 422, 423 R, 741, 791, 793

[56] **References Cited**

U.S. PATENT DOCUMENTS

2,703,344	3/1955	Anderson	3/1
2,721,316	10/1955	Shaw	128/419 R
3,376,870	4/1968	Yamamoto et al.	128/793
3,490,458	1/1970	Allison	128/421
3,594,823	7/1971	Collins et al.	3/1
4,140,133	2/1979	Kastrubin et al.	128/421
4,210,151	7/1980	Keller, Jr.	128/421
4,305,402	12/1981	Katims	128/421
4,390,756	6/1983	Hoffmann et al.	128/421

FOREIGN PATENT DOCUMENTS

1286316	8/1972	United Kingdom	3/1

Primary Examiner—William E. Kamm

Attorney, Agent, or Firm—Romney Golant Martin Seldon & Ashen

[57] **ABSTRACT**

The invention produces visual sensations by applying low voltages through conductive electrodes to the outside of a person's head, for transmission by natural mechanisms to the nervous system—to entertain or inform a sighted person, or to help a blind person to locate nearby objects.

As to entertainment, the apparatus generates various waveshapes, and an operator directs one or more to the electrodes. The operator also manually varies waveshape parameters such as frequency, amplitude, duty cycle and dc bias—or controls them with automatic sweep devices at selected sweep rates. Various wavetrains are combined at the electrodes or in the person's head for more-elaborate effects. The electrode wavetrains or necessary control signals are also recorded for playback.

As to information, the apparatus produces coded patterns or even rough analogs of normal visual scenes. As to aiding the blind, the apparatus responds to a sonar signal by placing phosphenes in the perceived visual field roughly where a normal person would see nearby objects.

15 Claims, 16 Drawing Figures

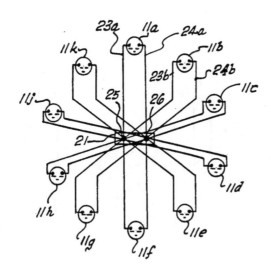

United States Patent [19]

Masaki

[11] **Patent Number:** **4,834,701**

[45] **Date of Patent:** **May 30, 1989**

[54] **APPARATUS FOR INDUCING FREQUENCY REDUCTION IN BRAIN WAVE**

[75] Inventor: **Kazumi Masaki**, Osaka, Japan

[73] Assignee: **Ken Hayashibara**, Okayama, Japan

[21] Appl. No.: **758,534**

[22] Filed: **Jul. 24, 1985**

[30] **Foreign Application Priority Data**

Aug. 24, 1984 [JP] Japan 59-175098

[51] Int. Cl.^{4} A61N 1/34
[52] U.S. Cl. 600/28
[58] Field of Search .... 128/731–732, 128/905, 1 C, 1 R; 600/26–28

[56] **References Cited**

U.S. PATENT DOCUMENTS

3,489,843	1/1970	Schrecongost	84/1.24
3,712,292	1/1973	Zentmeyer, Jr.	128/1 C
3,799,146	3/1974	John et al.	128/731
3,809,069	5/1974	Bennett	128/731
4,092,981	6/1978	Ertl	128/731
4,141,344	2/1979	Barbara	128/1 C
4,191,175	3/1980	Nagle	128/1 C
4,227,516	10/1980	Meland et al.	128/1 C
4,289,121	9/1981	Kupriyanovich	128/1 C
4,315,502	2/1982	Gorges	128/1 C
4,323,079	4/1982	Demetrescu	128/731
4,334,545	6/1982	Shiga	128/732
4,335,710	6/1982	Williamson	128/1 C
4,388,918	6/1983	Filley	128/1 C
4,550,736	11/1985	Broughton et al.	128/731
4,573,449	3/1986	Warncke	128/1 C

FOREIGN PATENT DOCUMENTS

1554569	1/1969	France	128/1 C
1392893	5/1975	United Kingdom .	
1451019	9/1976	United Kingdom .	
2067410	7/1981	United Kingdom .	
2124491	2/1984	United Kingdom .	

Primary Examiner—Kyle L. Howell
Assistant Examiner—Angela D. Sykes
Attorney, Agent, or Firm—Browdy and Neimark

[57] **ABSTRACT**

Frequency reduction in human brain wave is inducible by allowing human brain to perceive 4–16 hertz beat sound. Such beat sound can be easily produced with an apparatus, comprising at least one sound source generating a set of low-frequency signals different each other in frequency by 4–16 hertz. Electroencephalographic study revealed that the beat sound is effective to reduce beta-rhythm into alpha-rhythm, as well as to retain alpha-rhythm.

13 Claims, 3 Drawing Sheets

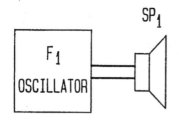

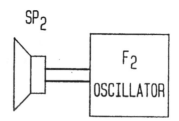

United States Patent [19]

Stocklin

[11] **Patent Number:** **4,858,612**

[45] **Date of Patent:** **Aug. 22, 1989**

[54] **HEARING DEVICE**

[76] Inventor: **Philip L. Stocklin**

[21] Appl. No.: **562,742**

[22] Filed: **Dec. 19, 1983**

[51] Int. Cl.[4] **A61N 1/36**
[52] U.S. Cl. .... **128/422;** 178/419 S
[58] **Field of Search** .... 128/419 R, 419 S, 422, 128/653, 771, 732, 741, 746, 791, 804; 340/407

[56] **References Cited**

U.S. PATENT DOCUMENTS

3,490,458	1/1970	Allison	128/421
3,751,605	8/1973	Michelson	128/1 R
3,951,134	4/1976	Malech	128/131
4,428,377	1/1984	Zollner et al.	128/419 R

FOREIGN PATENT DOCUMENTS

893311	2/1972	Canada	128/422
2811120	9/1978	Fed. Rep. of Germany ...	128/419 R
591196	1/1978	U.S.S.R.	128/419 R

OTHER PUBLICATIONS

Gerkin, G., "Electroencephalography & Clinical Neurophysiology", vol. 135, No. 6, Dec. 1973, pp. 652–653.
Frye et al., "Science", vol. 181, Jul. 27, 1973, pp. 356–358.
Bise, William, "Low Power Radio–Frequency and Microwave Effects on Human Electroencephalogram and Behavior", Physiol. Chem. & Physics 10 (1978).

Primary Examiner—William E. Kamm
Attorney, Agent, or Firm—Wegner & Bretschneider

[57] **ABSTRACT**

A method and apparatus for simulation of hearing in mammals by introduction of a plurality of microwaves into the region of the auditory cortex is shown and described. A microphone is used to transform sound signals into electrical signals which are in turn analyzed and processed to provide controls for generating a plurality of microwave signals at different frequencies. The multifrequency microwaves are then applied to the brain in the region of the auditory cortex. By this method sounds are perceived by the mammal which are representative of the original sound received by the microphone.

29 Claims, 7 Drawing Sheets

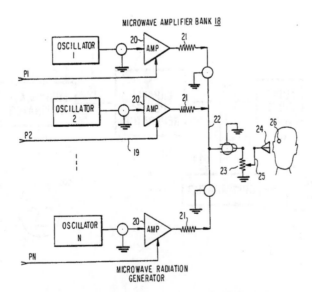

United States Patent [19]

Brunkan

[11] **Patent Number:** **4,877,027**

[45] **Date of Patent:** **Oct. 31, 1989**

[54] **HEARING SYSTEM**

[76] Inventor: **Wayne B. Brunkan,**

[21] Appl. No.: **202,679**

[22] Filed: **Jun. 6, 1988**

[51] Int. Cl.⁴ A61N 5/00
[52] U.S. Cl. 128/420.5
[58] Field of Search .... 128/420.5, 804, 419 R, 128/421, 422, 746; 381/68

[56] **References Cited**

U.S. PATENT DOCUMENTS

3,629,521	12/1971	Puharich et al.	128/402.5
3,766,331	10/1973	Zink	128/420.5

OTHER PUBLICATIONS

Cain et al, "Mammalian Auditory Responses . . . ", IEEE Trans Biomed Eng, pp. 288–293, 1978.
Frey et al, "Human Perception . . . Energy" Science, 181,356–358, 1973.

Jaski, "Radio Waves & Life", Radio–Electronics, pp. 45–45, Sep. 1960.
Microwave Auditory Effects and Applications, Lin, 1978, pp. 176–177.

Primary Examiner—Lee S. Cohen
Attorney, Agent, or Firm—Harry W. Brelsford

[57] **ABSTRACT**

Sound is induced in the head of a person by radiating the head with microwaves in the range of 100 megahertz to 10,000 megahertz that are modulated with a particular waveform. The waveform consists of frequency modulated bursts. Each burst is made up of ten to twenty uniformly spaced pulses grouped tightly together. The burst width is between 500 nanoseconds and 100 microseconds. The pulse width is in the range of 10 nanoseconds to 1 microsecond. The bursts are frequency modulated by the audio input to create the sensation of hearing in the person whose head is irradiated.

8 Claims, 1 Drawing Sheet

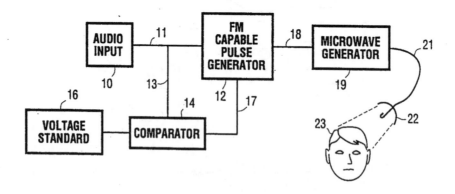

4,877,027

1

2

HEARING SYSTEM

This invention relates to a hearing system for human beings in which high frequency electromagnetic energy is projected through the air to the head of a human being and the electromagnetic energy is modulated to create signals that can be discerned by the human being regardless of the hearing ability of the person.

THE PRIOR ART

Various types of apparatus and modes of application have been proposed and tried to inject intelligible sounds into the heads of human beings. Some of these have been devised to simulate speech and other sounds in deaf persons and other systems have been used to inject intelligible signals in persons of good hearing, but bypassing the normal human hearing organs.

U.S. Pat. No. 3,629,521 issued Dec. 21, 1971 describes the use of a pair of electrodes applied to a person's head to inject speech into the head of a deaf person. An oscillator creates a carrier in the range of 18 to 36 KHz that is amplitude modulated by a microphone.

Science magazine volume 181, page 356 describes a hearing system utilizing a radio frequency carrier of 1.245 GHz delivered through the air by means of a waveguide and horn antenna. The carrier was pulsed at the rate of 50 pulses per second. The human test subject reported a buzzing sound and the intensity varied with the peak power.

Similar methods of creating "clicks" inside the human head are reported in I.E.E.E. Transactions of Biomedical Engineering, volume BME 25, No. 3, May 1978.

The transmission of intelligible speech by audio modulated Microwave is described in the book Microwave Auditory Effects and Applications by James C. Lin 1978 publisher Charles C. Thomas.

BRIEF SUMMARY OF THE INVENTION

I have discovered that a pulsed signal on a radio frequency carrier of about 1,000 megahertz (1000 MHz) is effective in creating intelligible signals inside the head of a person if this electromagnetic (EM) energy is projected through the air to the head of the person. Intelligible signals are applied to the carrier by microphone or other audio source and I cause the bursts to be frequency modulated. The bursts are composed of a group of pulses. The pulses are carefully selected for peak strength and pulse width. Various objects, advantages and features of the invention will be apparent in the specification and claims.

BRIEF DESCRIPTION OF THE DRAWINGS

In the drawings forming an integral part of this specification:

FIG. 1 is a block diagram of the system of the invention.

FIG. 2 is a diagram of an audio wave which is the input to be perceived by the recipient.

FIG. 3 is a diagram on the same time coordinate as FIG. 2 showing bursts that are frequency modulated by the wave form of FIG. 2.

FIG. 4 shows, on an enlarged time coordinate, that each vertical line depicted in FIG. 3 is a burst of pulses. (A burst is a group of pulses).

FIG. 5 shows, on a further enlarged time coordinate, a single continues pulse, Depicted as'a vertical line in FIG. 4.

DETAILED DESCRIPTION OF THE INVENTION

Inasmuch as microwaves can damage human tissue, any projected energy must be carefully regulated to stay within safe limits. The guideline for 1,000 MHz, set by the American Standards Institute, is 3.3 mw/cm2 (3.3 milliwatts per square centimeter). The apparatus described herein must be regulated to stay within this upper limit.

Referring to FIG. 1 a microphone 10 or other generator of audio frequencies, delivers its output by wire 11 to an FM capable pulse generator 12 and by branch wire 13 to a comparator 14. The comparator 14 also receives a signal from a voltage standard 16. When the peak voltage of the audio generator 10 falls below the standard 16 the comparator delivers a signal by wire 17 to the FM capable pulse generator 12 to shut down the pulse generator 12. This avoids spurious signals being generated. The output of the FM pulse generator 12 is delivered by wire 18 to a microwave generator 19 which delivers its output to the head of a human being 23. In this fashion the person 23 is radiated with microwaves that are in short bursts.

The microwave generator 19 operates at a steady frequency presently preferred at 1,000 megahertz (1,000 million). I presently prefer to pulse the microwave energy at pulse widths of 10 nanoseconds to 1 microsecond. For any one setting of the FM capable generator 12, this width is fixed. The pulses are arranged in bursts. The timing between bursts is controlled by the height of the audio envelope above the voltage standard line. In addition the bursts are spaced from one another at a non-uniform rate of 1 to 100 KHz. This non-uniform spacing of bursts is created in the FM capable generator 12.

Referring to FIG. 2 there is illustrated an audio wave 27 generated by the audio input 10 wherein the horizontal axis is time and the vertical axis is voltage. For illustrative purposes the wave 27 is shown as having a voltage peak 28 on the left part of FIG. 2 and a voltage peak 29 of the right side of FIG. 2. The voltage standard 16 of FIG. 1 generates a dc voltage designated at 31 in FIG. 2. This standard voltage is preferably at about 50% of the peak voltage 28. The comparator 14 of FIG. 1 actuates the FM capable generator 12 only when positive envelope of the audio wave 27 exceeds the voltage standard. The negative portions of the audio wave are not utilized.

Referring now to FIG. 3 there is illustrated two groups of bursts of microwave energy that are delivered by the antenna 22 of FIG. 1 to the head of the person 23. FIG. 3 has a horizontal time axis identical to the time axis of FIG. 2 and has a vertical axis that in this case represents the power of the microwaves from generator 19. At the left part of FIG. 3 are a plurality of microwave bursts 32 that occur on the time axis from the point of intersection of the standard voltage 31 with the positive part of the audio wave 27, designated as the time point 33 to time point 34 on FIG. 2. It will be noted in FIG. 3 that the bursts 32 are non-uniform in spacing and that they are closer together at the time of maximum audio voltage 28 and are more spread out toward the time points 33 and 34. This is the frequency modulation effected by the FM pulse generator 12.

United States Patent [19]

Rauscher et al.

[11] Patent Number: 4,889,526

[45] Date of Patent: Dec. 26, 1989

[54] **NON-INVASIVE METHOD AND APPARATUS FOR MODULATING BRAIN SIGNALS THROUGH AN EXTERNAL MAGNETIC OR ELECTRIC FIELD TO REDUCE PAIN**

[75] Inventors: **Elizabeth A. Rauscher; William L. Van Bise,** both of San Leandro, Calif.

[73] Assignee: **Magtech Laboratories, Inc.,** Reno, Nev.

[21] Appl. No.: **120,914**

[22] Filed: **Nov. 13, 1987**

Related U.S. Application Data

[60] Division of Ser. No. 775,100, Sep. 11, 1985, Pat. No. 4,723,536, which is a continuation-in-part of Ser. No. 644,148, Aug. 27, 1984, abandoned.

[51] Int. Cl.⁴ A61N 1/42; A61N 1/36;

[52] U.S. Cl. .... 600/14; 128/420 A; A61N/1/42; A61N/1/36

[58] Field of Search .... 128/419 R, 420 A, 421–422; 600/9–10, 13–14

[56] **References Cited**

U.S. PATENT DOCUMENTS

4,153,061	5/1979	Nemec	128/420 A
4,401,121	8/1983	Rodler	128/420 A
4,556,051	12/1985	Maurer	600/14
4,654,579	3/1987	Thaler	600/14 X
4,693,238	9/1987	Jenadek	600/14

Primary Examiner—Francis Jaworski
Attorney, Agent, or Firm—Thomas I. Rozsa

[57] **ABSTRACT**

This invention incorporates the discovery of new principles which utilize magnetic and electric fields generated by time varying square wave currents of precise repetition, width, shape and magnitude to move through coils and cutaneously applied conductive electrodes in order to stimulate the nervous system and reduce pain in humans. Timer means, adjustment means, and means to deliver current to the coils and conductive electrodes are described, as well as a theoretical model of the process. The invention incorporates the concept of two cyclic expanding an collapsing magnetic fields which generate precise wave forms in conjunction with each other to create a beat frequency which in turn causes the ion flow in the nervous system of the human body to be efficiency moved along the nerve path where the locus of the pain exists to thereby reduce pain. The wave forms are create either in one or more coils, one or more pairs of electrodes, or a combination of the two.

20 Claims, 6 Drawing Sheets

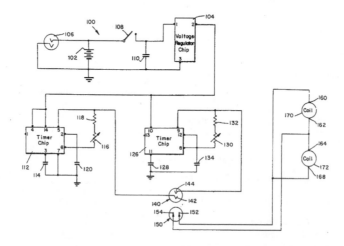

United States Patent [19]

Carter et al.

[11] Patent Number: 5,036,858

[45] Date of Patent: Aug. 6, 1991

[54] **METHOD AND APPARATUS FOR CHANGING BRAIN WAVE FREQUENCY**

[76] Inventors: John L. Carter

Harold L. Russell

[21] Appl. No.: 497,426

[22] Filed: Mar. 22, 1990

[51] Int. Cl.^{5} A61B 5/04
[52] U.S. Cl. 128/732; 600/27
[58] Field of Search 600/26, 27, 28; 128/732

[56] **References Cited**

U.S. PATENT DOCUMENTS

3,884,218	5/1975	Monroe	600/28
4,191,175	3/1980	Nagle	600/27
4,227,516	10/1980	Meland	600/26
4,228,807	10/1980	Yagi	128/732
4,315,502	2/1982	Gorges	600/27
4,834,701	5/1989	Masaki	600/28
4,883,067	11/1989	Knispel	600/28

OTHER PUBLICATIONS

Mind Power: Alpha, Radio Electronics, vol. 47, No. 7, pp. 36–39, 91, Jul. 1976, Gernsback Publications Inc., N.Y., N.Y.
Feedback Control of Amount and Frequency of Human Alpha Waves, Kobayashi et al., Jap. J. Medicene, vol. 14, No. 4, 8/1976.

Primary Examiner—Kyle L. Howell
Assistant Examiner—Robert L. Nasser, Jr.
Attorney, Agent, or Firm—Timmons & Kelly

[57] **ABSTRACT**

A method for changing brain wave frequency to a desired frequency determines a current brain wave frequency of a user, generates two frequencies with a frequency difference of a magnitude between that of the current actual brain wave frequency and the desired frequency but always within a predetermined range of the current actual brain wave frequency, and produces an output to the user corresponding to the two frequencies. One apparatus to accomplish the method has a computer processor, a computer memory, EEG electrodes along with an amplifier, a programmable timing generator responsive to the computer processor for generating the two frequencies, audio amplifiers and a beat frequency generator driving a visual frequency amplifier.

11 Claims, 1 Drawing Sheet

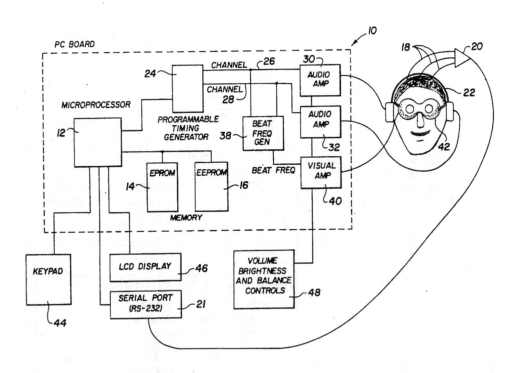

United States Patent [19]

Gavish

[11] **Patent Number:** 5,076,281

[45] **Date of Patent:** Dec. 31, 1991

[54] **DEVICE AND METHOD FOR EFFECTING RHYTHMIC BODY ACTIVITY**

[76] Inventor: **Benjamin Gavish**

[21] Appl. No.: **686,300**

[22] Filed: **Apr. 16, 1991**

Related U.S. Application Data

[63] Continuation of Ser. No. 358,146, May 30, 1989, abandoned.

[30] **Foreign Application Priority Data**

May 31, 1988 [IL] Israel 86582

[51] Int. Cl.^{5} A61B 5/00
[52] U.S. Cl. 128/721; 128/732; 128/905; 600/28
[58] Field of Search 128/716, 721, 731–732, 128/905; 600/26–28

[56] **References Cited**

U.S. PATENT DOCUMENTS

3,991,304	11/1976	Hillsman	128/905 X
4,063,550	12/1977	Tiep	128/905 X
4,282,864	8/1981	Pizer	600/26
4,289,121	9/1981	Kupriyanovich	600/27
4,454,886	6/1984	Lee	128/732
4,776,323	10/1988	Spector	128/905 X
4,798,538	1/1989	Yagi	128/721 X
4,883,067	11/1989	Knispel et al.	600/28

Primary Examiner—Ruth S. Smith
Attorney, Agent, or Firm—Nixon & Vanderhye

[57] **ABSTRACT**

A biorhythm modulator, consisting of a sensor for monitoring biorhythmic activity of the body of a user, a circuit for continuously analyzing the biorhythmic activity and producing parameter signals based upon a biorhythmic activity, a circuit for generating selectable sound-code pattern signals, a central processing unit (CPU) connected to receive signals from both the activity characteristic parameters producing circuit and the selected sound patterns generating circuit, and to feed the signals of the parameters and patterns to a sound pattern synthesizer for producing music-like sound pattern signals, transduceable into audible music-like patterns, and having a rhythm which is non-identical to the rhythm of the biorhythmic activity. A method for modulating biorhythmic activity is also described.

11 Claims, 2 Drawing Sheets

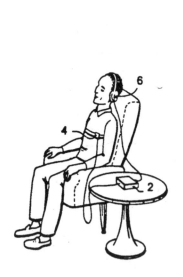

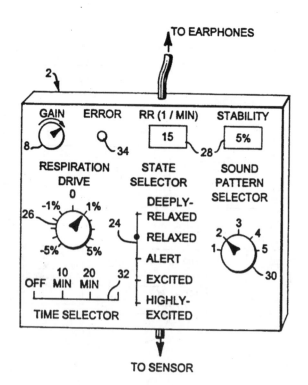

TO EARPHONES

GAIN   ERROR   RR (1 / MIN)   STABILITY

8   34   15   28   5%

RESPIRATION DRIVE   STATE SELECTOR   SOUND PATTERN SELECTOR

0
-1% 1%   DEEPLY-RELAXED
26   24   RELAXED
-5% 5%   ALERT
10 20 32   EXCITED
OFF MIN MIN   HIGHLY-
TIME SELECTOR   EXCITED

30

TO SENSOR

United States Patent [19]

Skille et al.

[11] **Patent Number:** **5,101,810**

[45] **Date of Patent:** **Apr. 7, 1992**

[54] **APPARATUS AND METHOD FOR THERAPEUTIC APPLICATION OF VIBRO-ACOUSTICAL ENERGY TO HUMAN BODY**

[75] Inventors: **Olav Skille**, Steinkjer; **Svein Sorsdal**, Trondheim, both of Norway

[73] Assignee: **Vibroacoustics A/S**, Trondheim, Norway

[21] Appl. No.: **508,543**

[22] · Filed: **Apr. 16, 1990**

Related U.S. Application Data

[60] Division of Ser. No. 255,827, Oct. 7, 1988, abandoned, which is a continuation-in-part of Ser. No. 124,848, Nov. 18, 1987, abandoned.

[51] Int. Cl.^{5} **A61H 1/00**
[52] U.S. Cl. **128/33; 128/64**
[58] Field of Search .... 128/33, 57, 64; 5/9 B; 84/651

[56] **References Cited**

U.S. PATENT DOCUMENTS

2,497,751	2/1950	Wettlaufer	128/33
3,235,891	2/1966	Chade et al. .	
3,446,204	5/1969	Murphy	128/33
3,556,088	1/1971	Leonardini	128/33
3,880,152	4/1975	Nohmura	128/33
4,023,566	5/1977	Martinmaas	128/33
4,046,081	9/1977	Gutridge et al.	5/9 B
4,055,170	10/1977	Nohmura	128/33
4,064,376	12/1977	Yamada	128/33
4,535,760	8/1985	Ikeda et al.	128/33
4,538,596	9/1985	Colasante	128/32
4,630,519	12/1986	Hirano et al.	84/651
4,721,100	1/1988	Hengl	128/57

FOREIGN PATENT DOCUMENTS

618053	1/1986	Japan	23/02
1165541	10/1969	United Kingdom .	
1251498	10/1971	United Kingdom .	

OTHER PUBLICATIONS

Wigram and Weeks, A Project Evaluating the Difference in Therapeutic Treatment Between the Use of Low Frequency Sound and Music, and Music Alone in Reducing High Muscle Tone in Multiply Handicapped People, and Oedema in Mentally Handicapped People, VibroAcoustics, 1989.
Skille, "Vibroacoustic Therapy", Music Therapy, 1989, vol. 8, No. 1, pp. 61–77.
A report from Haperbury Hospital, England.
A report from the insurance company Kansa in Finland.
A report from the Pedegogical Instittue of Tallinn in Esthonia.

Primary Examiner—Edgar S. Burr
Assistant Examiner—Aaron J. Lewis
Attorney, Agent, or Firm—Cushman, Darby & Cushman

[57] **ABSTRACT**

Apparatus for therapeutic application of vibro-acoustic energy to a human body, including a closed box with at least one sound opening in which is arranged a loudspeaker directed towards a part of the body. Upholstery is disposed between the box and the body at the location of the loudspeaker and has air passages. Low frequency signals are supplied to the loudspeaker and to one or a plurality of external loudspeakers. Music is supplied to the external loudspeakers. The low frequency signals are influenced either in step with the music, in a predetermined relation to the music, or in predetermined rhythm. As a storage medium for sound there may be used a tape cassette or compact disc in which at least one of the sound channels contains the influenced low frequency signal in the frequency range 30–120 Hz and the remaining sound channels contain pure music.

12 Claims, 6 Drawing Sheets

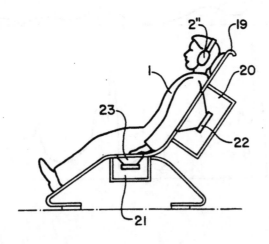

United States Patent [19]

Gall

[11] **Patent Number:**   **5,123,899**

[45] **Date of Patent:**   **Jun. 23, 1992**

[54] **METHOD AND SYSTEM FOR ALTERING CONSCIOUSNESS**

[76] Inventor: **James Gall**

[21] Appl. No.: **642,439**

[22] Filed: **Jan. 17, 1991**

[51] Int. Cl.⁵ **A61M 21/00**
[52] U.S. Cl. **600/28; 128/905**
[58] Field of Search 600/26–28; 128/731–732, 905

[56]   **References Cited**

U.S. PATENT DOCUMENTS

3,576,185	4/1971	Schulz	600/27
3,762,396	10/1973	Ballentine et al.	600/26
4,227,516	10/1980	Meland et al.	600/28
4,834,701	5/1989	Masaki	600/28

Primary Examiner—William E. Kamm

Assistant Examiner—J. P. Lacyk
Attorney, Agent, or Firm—Cahill, Sutton & Thomas

[57]   **ABSTRACT**

A system for altering the states of human consciousness involves the simultaneous application of multiple stimuli, preferable sounds, having differing frequencies and wave forms. The relationship between the frequencies of the several stimuli is exhibited by the equation

$$g = s^{n/4} \cdot f$$

where:
f = frequency of one stimulus;
g = frequency of the other stimuli of stimulus; and
n = a positive or negative integer which is different for each other stimulus.

4 Claims, 1 Drawing Sheet

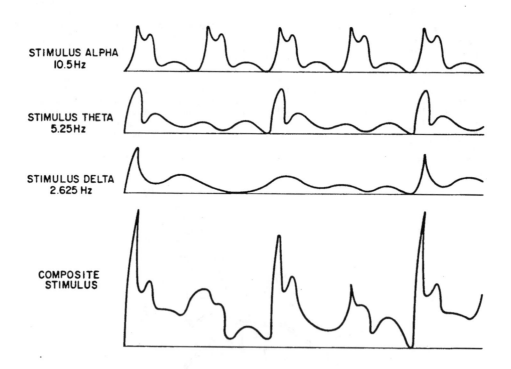

STIMULUS ALPHA
10.5 Hz

STIMULUS THETA
5.25 Hz

STIMULUS DELTA
2.625 Hz

COMPOSITE
STIMULUS

5,123,899

1

METHOD AND SYSTEM FOR ALTERING CONSCIOUSNESS

TECHNICAL FIELD

This invention is concerned with the application of stimuli to a human subject to induce different states of consciousness.

BACKGROUND ART

It is well accepted in scientific circles that there is a correlation between the electroencephalographic wave rhythms exhibited by the brain of a human and the state of consciousness of that being. Rhythms customarily found in the normal human adult when he is relaxed and his eyes closed have a pulse frequency in the seven-fourteen Hz. range and have come to be identified as "alpha" rhythms. Similarly, when a person is aroused and anxious, the rhythms exhibited fall in the 14–28 Hz. range and are known as "beta" rhythms. A normal person in sleep exhibits "delta" rhythms in the 1.75–3.5 Hz. range. Other brain wave rhythms which have been identified by researchers as being associated with various normal and abnormal states of consciousness are: "theta", 3.5–7.0 Hz. and "gamma", 28–56 Hz. Research by the applicant has led to the identification and naming of three additional rhythms, namely: "omega", 0.875–1.75 Hz.; "epsilon", 56–112 Hz.; and "zeta", 112–224 Hz.

Researchers have devised a variety of systems for stimulating the brain to exhibit specific brain wave rhythms and thereby alter the state of consciousness of the individual subject. Most of these efforts have been aimed at inducing an alpha, or relaxed, brain wave rhythm or a delta, or sleep, brain wave rhythm.

E.W. Ballentine and B.C. Gindes, in their U.S. Pat. No. 3,762,396, granted Oct. 2, 1973, for "Method and Apparatus for Inducing Sleep by Applying Electrical Pulses to Plural Portions of the Head", disclose a system for inducing sleep, treating psychosomatic disorders, and aiding the induction of hypnosis. With this system, the patient is subjected to three stimuli. The first stimulus is electrical current pulses having a frequency of 8–10 CPS applied by electrodes to the back of the head. A second stimulus of electrical current pulses having a frequency four times the frequency of the first stimulus is applied to the optic nerve through electrodes on the forehead. The third stimulus is a sound signal produced by the first stimulus and applied to the patient via sound attenuating chambers in order to isolate the patient from a noisy environment.

U.S. Pat. No. 3,576,185 was granted Apr. 27, 1971, to H. Shulz for "Sleep-Inducing Method and Arrangement Using Modulated Sound and Light". This patent describes an apparatus and a method for inducing sleep by directing at the subject two sound signals in the range of 40–80 Hz., free of overtones and amplitude modulated between the perceivable minimum and a perceivable maximum. The two signals differ in frequency by approximately 0.5–2 Hz. Optical stimuli may also be used.

K. Masaki in his U.S. Pat. No. 4,834,701, granted May 30, 1989, for "Apparatus for Inducing Frequency Reduction in Brain Wave" states his objective to be the reduction of beta-rhythm into alpha-rhythm as well as to retain alpha-rhythm. The subject is subjected to two sound signals which are each higher in frequency than 4–16 Hz. But are different and produce a beat signal

2

which is within the 4–16 Hz. range. It is represented that the subject exhibits improve ability in learning, researching and inventing.

B.C. Gindes also teamed with B.C. Meland to obtain U.S. Pat. No. 4,227,516, granted Oct. 14, 1980, for "Apparatus for Electrophysiological Stimulation". This patent discloses apparatus for stimulating the effects of brain wave activity in one of the delta, theta, alpha, and beta brain wave frequency ranges. A first wave is generated in a frequency range above the brain wave ranges. This first wave is then modulated by a second wave having a frequency within one of the brain wave frequencies. The modulated first waves are applied to the subject by means of electrodes on the forehead. The second wave may also be applied by sound through headphones. A third wave in a range 150–600 Hz. may be modulated by the second wave and the modulated tone that is produced applied to headphones worn by the subject. The system is represented as being able to, among other things, induce sleep, induce a hypnotic state, produce heightened awareness and increase the ability of a person to concentrate.

Each of the systems disclosed in these prior patents require that fairly complex apparatus be directly associated with the subject. And the systems of the two Gindes, et.al. patents hamper useful activity of the subject by the requirement that the subject be attached to electrodes and earphones.

There continues to be a need for a system for inducing brain wave rhythms which is inexpensive and easy to use from the subject's point of view.

DISCLOSURE OF THE INVENTION

This invention contemplates utilizing a plurality of brain wave rhythm stimuli simultaneously with each stimulus having a specific frequency relationship with every other stimulus That relationship is expressed in the following equation:

$$g = 2^{n/4} \cdot f$$

when f is the frequency of one stimulus, g is the corresponding frequency for each of the other stimulus or stimuli and n is a positive or negative integer. Although visual and electrical current stimuli can be employed in the system of this invention, aural stimuli are preferred. The latter can be recorded on small, convenient tape or disc records and played back by the subject on an inexpensive portable player.

BRIEF DESCRIPTION OF THE DRAWINGS

The invention is described in greater detail hereinafter by reference to the accompanying drawings, wherein:

FIG. 1 is a graphic presentation of the various types of brain wave rhythms with which this invention is concerned;

FIG. 2 illustrates graphically how a plurality of brain wave stimuli are combined to produce a brain wave rhythm according to the invention;

FIG. 3 is a block diagram of brain wave rhythm stimuli recording apparatus employed in the invention; and

FIG. 4 is a block diagram of brain wave rhythm stimuli playback apparatus employed in the invention.

United States Patent [19]

Meissner

[11] Patent Number: **5,135,468**

[45] Date of Patent: **Aug. 4, 1992**

[54] **METHOD AND APPARATUS OF VARYING THE BRAIN STATE OF A PERSON BY MEANS OF AN AUDIO SIGNAL**

[76] Inventor: **Juergen P. Meissner**

[21] Appl. No.: **561,776**

[22] Filed: **Aug. 2, 1990**

[51] Int. Cl.^{5} **A61M 21/00**
[52] U.S. Cl. **600/28**
[58] Field of Search 600/26–28; 128/731–732

[56] **References Cited**

U.S. PATENT DOCUMENTS

4,335,710	6/1982	Williamson	600/28
4,418,687	12/1983	Matsumoto et al.	600/26
5,036,858	8/1991	Carter et al.	600/27

FOREIGN PATENT DOCUMENTS

3626385	2/1988	Fed. Rep. of Germany	600/28
2165985	4/1986	United Kingdom	600/28

OTHER PUBLICATIONS

"A New Prescription: Mind over Malady" by Rob Welchsler, Discover Magazine, Feb. 1987.
"Physiology of Meditation", Scientific American, by Robert Keith Wallace and Herbert Bensen, Feb. 1972, vol. 226, No. 2, pp. 84–90.
Adler's Physiology of the Eye, Chapter 13, "Visual Pathways", p. 444.
"The Monroe Institute's Hemi–Sync Process—A Theoretical Perspective" by F. Holmes Atwater, Aug. 1988.
"Data Transformation explains the Basics of Neural Networks" by Doug Conner, EDN, May 12, 1988.
"The Mind within the Brain" by Gina Maranto, Discover Magazine, May, 1984, pp. 34–43.

Primary Examiner—Lee S. Cohen
Assistant Examiner—John P. Lacyk
Attorney, Agent, or Firm—Richard M. Goldberg

[57] **ABSTRACT**

A method of varying the brain state of a person includes the steps of supplying the first audio signal to one ear of the person, supplying a second audio signal to the other ear of the person, and substantially continuously varying the frequency of at least one of the first and second audio signals to vary the brain state of the person.

57 Claims, 9 Drawing Sheets

United States Patent [19]

Bick

[11] **Patent Number:** **5,151,080**

[45] **Date of Patent:** **Sep. 29, 1992**

[54] **METHOD AND APPARATUS FOR INDUCING AND ESTABLISHING A CHANGED STATE OF CONSCIOUSNESS**

[76] Inventor: **Claus Bick**

[21] Appl. No.: **490,552**

[22] PCT Filed: **Aug. 28, 1990**

[86] PCT No.: **PCT/CH89/00153**

§ 371 Date: **Apr. 27, 1990**

§ 102(e) Date: **Apr. 24, 1990**

[87] PCT Pub. No.: **WO90/01967**

PCT Pub. Date: **Mar. 8, 1990**

[30] **Foreign Application Priority Data**

Aug. 30, 1988 [CH] Switzerland 3219/88

[51] Int. Cl.⁵ **A61M 21/00**
[52] U.S. Cl. **600/28;** 600/26
[58] Field of Search 600/26, 27, 28; 381/54, 381/73.1, 61

[56] **References Cited**

U.S. PATENT DOCUMENTS

2,943,152	6/1960	Licklinder	381/54
3,712,292	1/1973	Zentmeyer	600/28
3,884,218	5/1975	Monroe	600/28
4,082,918	4/1978	Chang	600/28
4,717,343	1/1988	Densky	.

FOREIGN PATENT DOCUMENTS

3628420	2/1988	Fed. Rep. of Germany .
2124490	2/1984	United Kingdom .

Primary Examiner—William E. Kamm
Assistant Examiner—Scott R. Akers
Attorney, Agent, or Firm—Spencer, Frank & Schneider

[57] **ABSTRACT**

An electroacoustic device includes a sound generator as well as a system for producing synthetic human speech, connected to a modulation stage for superimposing the output signals thereof. The superimposed output signals are applied via an amplifier stage to one of a headphone system or loudspeaker system.

2 Claims, 1 Drawing Sheet

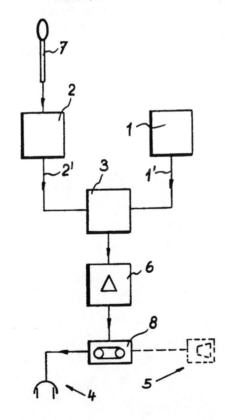

United States Patent [19]

Monroe

[11] **Patent Number:** **5,213,562**

[45] **Date of Patent:** **May 25, 1993**

[54] **METHOD OF INDUCING MENTAL, EMOTIONAL AND PHYSICAL STATES OF CONSCIOUSNESS, INCLUDING SPECIFIC MENTAL ACTIVITY, IN HUMAN BEINGS**

[75] Inventor: **Robert A. Monroe,** Nelson County, Va.

[73] Assignee: **Interstate Industries Inc.,** Faber, Va.

[21] Appl. No.: **514,460**

[22] Filed: **Apr. 25, 1990**

[51] Int. Cl.^{5} **A61M 21/00**
[52] U.S. Cl. **600/28**; 128/732
[58] Field of Search 600/26–28;
128/731–732, 905

[56] **References Cited**

U.S. PATENT DOCUMENTS

2,466,054	4/1949	Siebel .
3,160,159	12/1964	Hoody et al. .
3,576,185	4/1971	Schulz et al. .
3,712,292	1/1973	Zentmeyer, Jr. .
3,753,433	8/1973	Bakerich et al. .
3,826,243	7/1974	Anderson .
3,837,331	9/1974	Ross .
3,884,218	5/1975	Monroe 600/28
4,034,741	7/1977	Adams et al. .
4,141,344	2/1979	Barbara .
4,227,516	10/1980	Meland et al. .
4,335,710	6/1982	Williamson .
4,573,449	3/1986	Warnke .
4,834,701	5/1989	Masaki 600/28
5,036,858	8/1991	Carter et al. 128/732

Primary Examiner—Lee S. Cohen
Assistant Examiner—John P. Lacyk
Attorney, Agent, or Firm—Sughrue, Mion, Zinn, Macpeak & Seas

[57] **ABSTRACT**

A method having applicability in replication of desired consciousness states; in the training of an individual to replicate such a state of consciousness without further audio stimulation; and in the transferring of such states from one human being to another through the imposition of one individual's EEG, superimposed on desired stereo signals, on another individual, by inducement of a binaural beat phenomenon.

6 Claims, 5 Drawing Sheets

United States Patent [19]

Gall

[11] **Patent Number:** **5,289,438**

[45] **Date of Patent:** **Feb. 22, 1994**

[54] **METHOD AND SYSTEM FOR ALTERING CONSCIOUSNESS**

[76] Inventor: **James Gall**

[21] Appl. No.: **867,326**

[22] Filed: **Apr. 13, 1992**

Related U.S. Application Data

[62] Division of Ser. No. 642,439, Jan. 17, 1991, Pat. No. 5,123,899.

[51] Int. Cl.⁵ **G10F 1/00**
[52] U.S. Cl. **369/4; 600/28; 128/905**
[58] Field of Search 369/4, 127, 15; 360/5, 360/1; 600/28, 26; 128/905

[56] **References Cited**

U.S. PATENT DOCUMENTS

4,141,344	2/1979	Barbara	600/28
4,315,502	2/1982	Gorges	600/27
4,503,863	3/1985	Katims	600/26
4,883,067	11/1989	Knispel et al.	600/28
5,123,899	6/1993	Gall	600/28

Primary Examiner—Robert J. Pascal
Assistant Examiner—Tan Dinh
Attorney, Agent, or Firm—Cahill, Sutton & Thomas

[57] **ABSTRACT**

A system for altering the states of human consciousness involves the simultaneous application of multiple stimuli, preferable sounds, having differing frequencies and wave forms. The relationship between the frequencies of the several stimuli is exhibited by the equation

$$g = 2^{n/4} \cdot f$$

where:
  f=frequency of one stimulus;
  g=frequency of the other stimuli or stimulus; and
  n=a positive or negative integer which is different for each other stimulus.

2 Claims, 1 Drawing Sheet

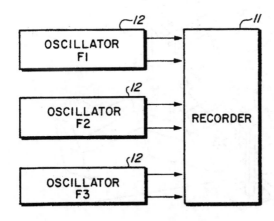

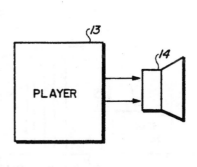

United States Patent [19]

Weathers

[11] **Patent Number:** 5,219,322

[45] **Date of Patent:** Jun. 15, 1993

[54] **PSYCHOTHERAPY APPARATUS AND METHOD FOR TREATING UNDESIRABLE EMOTIONAL AROUSAL OF A PATIENT**

[76] Inventor: **Lawrence R. Weathers**

[21] Appl. No.: **891,696**

[22] Filed: **Jun. 1, 1992**

[51] Int. Cl.⁵ **A61M 21/00**
[52] U.S. Cl. **600/27**
[58] Field of Search 600/26–28

[56] **References Cited**

U.S. PATENT DOCUMENTS

3,826,250	7/1974	Adams	600/28
4,140,997	2/1979	Brady	128/732
4,282,864	8/1981	Pizer	600/27
4,289,121	9/1981	Kupriyanovich	600/27
4,354,505	10/1982	Shiga	128/732
4,388,918	6/1983	Filley	600/27
4,640,266	2/1987	Levy	600/27
4,665,926	5/1987	Leuner et al.	600/26
4,777,937	10/1988	Rush et al.	600/27
4,902,274	2/1990	Gleeson, III	600/27
5,036,858	8/1991	Carter et al.	128/732

FOREIGN PATENT DOCUMENTS

0888601	9/1953	Fed. Rep. of Germany	600/27
3447105	7/1985	Fed. Rep. of Germany	600/27

Primary Examiner—Lee S. Cohen
Assistant Examiner—John P. Lacyk
Attorney, Agent, or Firm—John R. Flanagan

[57] **ABSTRACT**

A psychotherapy apparatus and method provides treating of an undesirable emotional arousal of a patient through coordinated and controlled presentation of visual and auditory stimuli to the patient. The operative steps of the psychotherapy apparatus and method include presenting visual stimuli observable by a stationarily-positioned patient at right and left extremes of the patient's range of eye movement, alternately switching the visual stimuli laterally between the right and left extremes of the patient's range of lateral eye movement, presenting auditory stimuli to the patient's ears, alternately switching the auditory stimuli between the patient's ears synchronously with alternately switching of the visual stimuli between the right and left extremes of the patient's range of lateral eye movement, monitoring physiological responses of the patient to the visual and auditory stimuli, and, in response to such monitoring, controlling the presenting and switching of the visual and auditory stimuli so as to elicit a mental imagery of a negative experience of the patient and to eliminate the undesirable emotional arousal evoked by the negative experience and to substitute a positive experience reinforcing a desired new behavior.

26 Claims, 2 Drawing Sheets

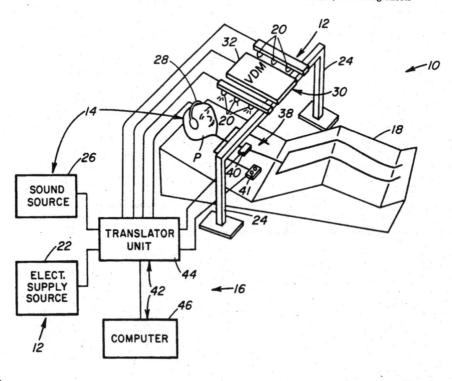

5,219,322

PSYCHOTHERAPY APPARATUS AND METHOD FOR TREATING UNDESIRABLE EMOTIONAL AROUSAL OF A PATIENT

BACKGROUND OF THE INVENTION

1. Field of the Invention

The present invention generally relates to psychotherapy techniques for treating emotional problems and, more particularly, to a psychotherapy apparatus and method for treating undesirable emotional arousal of a patient.

2. Description of the Prior Art

Many members of society currently demonstrating various undesirable (both pathological and non-pathological) behaviors are burdened with various emotional problems and emotionally-aggravated physical problems. Some examples of these problems are anxiety disorders, asthma, panic attacks, depression, anger, impotence, fears and phobias, grief, headaches, marriage problems, post Electro-Convulsive Therapy confusion, anxiety and memory loss, and post traumatic stress disorder (Vietnam and police service and child abuse and incest). The current undesirable behavior of a person provides connection of a current experience with a historical or more recent negative experience.

Heretofore, the primary mode of conducting psychotherapy for treatment of these problems has been by the use of one therapist with one patient or one or more therapists with a small group of patients. This mode of psychotherapy has been carried out mainly through verbal communication between therapists and patients. A significant drawback of relying primarily on verbal communication to conduct psychotherapy is that a large number of treatment sessions are needed to adequately deal with these problems. An unfortunate consequence of this is that the greater the overall quantity of time consumed in treatment the greater the cost and the fewer the number of persons that can be treated by a given population of therapists with proper qualification and clinical training. Another significant drawback is that some adults and many children are not verbal enough to successfully profit from verbal therapies.

Consequently, a need exists for a different approach to psychotherapy for treatment of emotional problems and emotionally-aggravated physical problems which approach will overcome the above-described drawbacks without introducing new ones in their place.

SUMMARY OF THE INVENTION

The present invention provides a psychotherapy apparatus and method being designed to satisfy the aforementioned needs. The psychotherapy apparatus and method of the present invention employ a sequence of operative steps which preferably are conducted in an automated manner so as to thereby reduce the number of treatment sessions and increase the number of patients that can be handled by a given therapist. The apparatus and method are designed for treating an undesirable emotional arousal of a patient through coordinated presentation of visual and auditory stimuli to the patient and through control of the visual and auditory stimuli. Preferably, although not necessarily, the visual and auditory stimuli is controlled in response to monitoring and measuring the physiological responses of the patient to the visual and auditory stimuli.

Accordingly, the present invention is directed to a psychotherapy apparatus for treating an undesirable

emotional arousal of a patient. The psychotherapy apparatus basically comprises: means for presenting visual stimuli so as to be observable by a stationarily-positioned patient substantially at predetermined opposite extremes of the patient's range of eye movement; means for presenting auditory stimuli to the ears of the patient; and control means connected to the visual stimuli presenting means and to the auditory stimuli presenting means for operating the visual stimuli presenting means to alternately switch the visual stimuli between the predetermined extremes of the patient's range of eye movement and for operating the auditory stimuli presenting means to alternately switch the auditory stimuli between the patient's ears. The control means is capable of operating the visual stimuli presenting means and the auditory stimuli presenting means to cause alternate switching of the visual stimuli and auditory stimuli in a predetermined coordinated synchronous relationship with respect to one another so as to elict in the patient a mental imagery of a given past negative experience of the patient and to eliminate the undesirable emotional arousal evoked in the patient by the given negative experience and to substitute a positive experience reinforcing a desired new behavior.

More particularly, the predetermined extremes are right and left lateral extremes of the patient's lateral eye movement. The visual stimuli presenting means includes a bank of lights located at each of the right and left lateral extremes of the patient's eye movement. The control means is operable to alternately blink the lights individually back and forth between the predetermined extremes of the patient's eye movement.

The auditory stimuli presenting means includes means for generating a sound and a pair of stereo headphones capable of being worn over the ears of the patient. The headphones are operable for receiving the sound and transmitting the sound to the patient's ears. The control means is connected between the headphones and the sound generating means and is operable to alternately switch the sound being transmitted through the headphones back and forth between the patient's ears.

The psychotherapy apparatus also comprises means disposed between the predetermined extemes of the patient's range of eye movement for displaying visual information toward the stationarily-positioned patient. The displaying means includes a video display monitor disposed between the predetermined extremes of the patient's range of eye movement. The control means is connected to the displaying means and is operable to cause the displaying means to display the visual information in a predetermined pattern.

Further, the control means includes means for monitoring and measuring at least one predetermined physiological response of the patient to the visual and auditory stimuli and producing an output representative of the response. The control means also includes means connected to the monitoring and measuring means for receiving the output thereof and for controlling, in response to the output, the visual stimuli presenting means and the auditory stimuli presenting means.

Also, the present invention is directed to a psychotherapy method for treating an undesirable emotional arousal of a patient. The psychotherapy method basically comprises the steps of: presenting visual stimuli so as to be observable by a stationarily-positioned patient substantially at predetermined opposite extremes of the

United States Patent [19]

Mrklas et al.

[11]	Patent Number:	**5,304,112**
[45]	Date of Patent:	**Apr. 19, 1994**

[54] **STRESS REDUCTION SYSTEM AND METHOD**

[75] Inventors: **Theresia A. Mrklas**

Maurice B. Daniel, Alexandria, Va.; **William B. Daniel**, Twinsburg, Ohio

[73] Assignee: **Theresia A. Mrklas**, North Olmsted, Ohio

[21] Appl. No.: **777,203**

[22] Filed: **Oct. 16, 1991**

[51] Int. Cl.⁵ **A61M 21/00**
[52] U.S. Cl. **600/27; 434/236; 601/15**
[58] Field of Search 434/236, 237, 238; 600/26, 27, 28, 21; 128/24.1, 24.2, 24.3, 33, 32

[56] **References Cited**

U.S. PATENT DOCUMENTS

3,014,477	12/1961	Carlin	600/27
3,278,676	10/1966	Becker .	
3,643,941	2/1972	Kashar	128/24.1
3,727,616	4/1973	Lenzkes .	
3,753,433	8/1973	Bakerich et al. .	
3,822,693	7/1974	King	600/27
3,826,250	7/1974	Adams .	
3,837,331	9/1974	Ross .	
3,967,616	7/1976	Ross .	
4,258,706	3/1981	Shank	128/24.1
4,315,502	2/1982	Gorges .	
4,335,710	6/1982	Williamson .	
4,388,918	6/1983	Filley .	
4,553,534	11/1985	Stiegler .	
4,640,266	2/1987	Levy .	
4,665,926	5/1987	Launer et al. .	
4,728,293	3/1988	Kole, Jr.	434/236
4,736,307	4/1988	Salb .	
4,893,615	1/1990	Khabirova	128/24.1
5,024,650	6/1991	Hagiwara et al.	128/24.1
5,036,858	8/1991	Carter et al.	600/27
5,076,281	12/1991	Gavish	600/28

FOREIGN PATENT DOCUMENTS

3447105	7/1985	Fed. Rep. of Germany	600/27
3823402	1/1990	Fed. Rep. of Germany	600/28
1119700	10/1984	U.S.S.R.	128/24.1
2201599	9/1988	United Kingdom	600/26
0004191	5/1989	World Int. Prop. O.	600/27

Primary Examiner—Jessica J. Harrison
Attorney, Agent, or Firm—Sixbey, Friedman, Leedom & Ferguson

[57] **ABSTRACT**

An integrated stress reduction system detects the stress level of a subject and displays a light pattern reflecting the relationship between the subject's stress level and a target level. At the same time, the system provides relaxing visual, sound, tactile, environmental, and other effects to aid the subject in reducing his or her stress level to the target level. In one preferred embodiment, the intensity, type, and duration of the relaxing effects are controlled by a computer program in response to the measured stress level. The light pattern stress level display uses a laser which is deflected on one axis by a measured stress level signal and on a second axis perpendicular to the first by a target signal representing the target stress level. The pattern produced is more complex when the two signals do not coincide, and becomes a less complex geometric figure as the subject's stress level approaches the target.

25 Claims, 9 Drawing Sheets

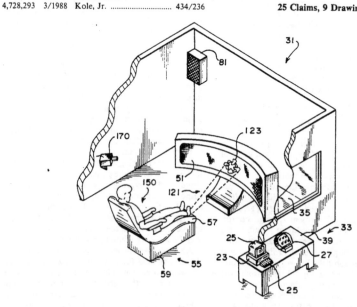

United States Patent [19]

Yasushi

[11] **Patent Number:** **5,330,414**

[45] **Date of Patent:** **Jul. 19, 1994**

[54] **BRAIN WAVE INDUCING APPARATUS**

[75] Inventor: **Mitsuo Yasushi**, Saitama, Japan

[73] Assignee: **Pioneer Electronic Corporation,** Tokyo, Japan

[21] Appl. No.: **833,937**

[22] Filed: **Feb. 11, 1992**

[30] **Foreign Application Priority Data**

May 23, 1991 [JP] Japan 3-118561

[51] Int. Cl.^{5} **A61M 21/00**
[52] U.S. Cl. **600/27**
[58] Field of Search 600/26–28; 128/731–732, 905

[56] **References Cited**

U.S. PATENT DOCUMENTS

3,837,331	9/1974	Ross	600/27
3,884,218	5/1975	Monroe	600/28
3,893,450	7/1975	Ertl .	
4,195,626	4/1980	Schweizer .	
4,334,545	6/1982	Shiga	128/732

FOREIGN PATENT DOCUMENTS

0375106 6/1990 European Pat. Off. 128/732

412629	2/1991	European Pat. Off. .	
2713891	10/1978	Fed. Rep. of Germany .	
62-87165	4/1987	Japan .	
1088607	10/1967	United Kingdom	600/28
2067410	7/1981	United Kingdom	600/28

Primary Examiner—Kyle L. Howell
Assistant Examiner—J. P. Lacyk
Attorney, Agent, or Firm—Sughrue, Mion, Zinn, Macpeak & Seas

[57] **ABSTRACT**

A random signal generator outputs a random noise signal to a band pass filter which selectively passes frequency components in the frequency range of a desired brain wave from a subject. The output of the band pass filter is supplied to an automatic level controller. The automatic level controller sets the output of band pass filter to a predetermined amplitude. Then, the output of the automatic level controller is fed to a stimulating light generator, which converts the output of the automatic level controller into a light signal for stimulating the subject in order to induce the desired brain wave from the subject. The light signal is then emitted into the subject's eyes.

10 Claims, 1 Drawing Sheet

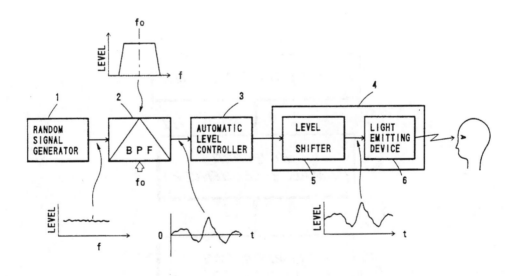

United States Patent [19]

Davis

[11] **Patent Number:** **5,352,181**

[45] **Date of Patent:** **Oct. 4, 1994**

[54] **METHOD AND RECORDING FOR PRODUCING SOUNDS AND MESSAGES TO ACHIEVE ALPHA AND THETA BRAINWAVE STATES AND POSITIVE EMOTIONAL STATES IN HUMANS**

[76] Inventor: **Mark E. Davis**

[21] Appl. No.: **939,088**

[22] Filed: **Sep. 2, 1992**

[51] Int. Cl.^{5} **A61M 21/00**
[52] U.S. Cl. **600/28**
[58] Field of Search 600/26–28; 128/731–732, 897–898; 84/611–612, 635–636, 651–652, 667–668, 713–714

[56] **References Cited**

U.S. PATENT DOCUMENTS

3,060,795	10/1962	Corrigan et al.	88/16.6
3,278,676	10/1966	Corrigan et al.	178/6
4,141,344	2/1979	Barbara	600/28
4,227,516	10/1980	Meland et al.	600/26
4,395,600	7/1983	Lundy et al.	179/1.5 M
4,777,529	10/1988	Schultz et al.	358/143
5,123,899	6/1992	Gall	600/28
5,128,765	7/1992	Dingwall et al.	358/182
5,135,468	8/1992	Meissner	600/28
5,151,080	9/1992	Bick	600/26 X

OTHER PUBLICATIONS

Ostrander & Schroeder, *Super–Learning*, Feb. 1981, pp. 49, 64, 68–69, 114–115, 312–315.
Prevention Magazine, Healthy Pleasures, Jun. 1989, pp. 97–101.
Fast Track Magazine, See Me, Feel Me, Touch Me, Heal Me, Feb. 1991, p. 26.
American Journal of Nursing, Forty–five Minutes of Mozart, BID, Feb. 1992, p. 13.
Journal of American Medical Assoc., Medical News and Perspectives, Music Aids Elderly, Sep. 1991, pp. 1323–1329.
Moss & Webster, Nations Business Magazine, Music & Wellness, May, 1986, p. 1.

Primary Examiner—Angela D. Sykes
Attorney, Agent, or Firm—Walter A. Hackler

[57] **ABSTRACT**

A method and recording for use in achieving Alpha and Theta brain wave states and effecting positive emotional states in humans to enhance learning and self-improvement, is provided which includes a medium having a musical composition recorded thereon with an initial tempo decreasing to a final tempo and verbal phrases, comprising between approximately 4 and approximately 8 words, recorded in synchrony with the decreasing initial tempo.

10 Claims, 1 Drawing Sheet

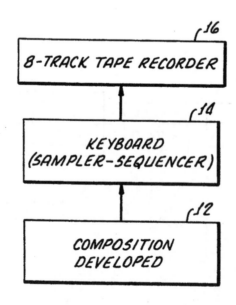

United States Patent [19]

Monroe

[11] **Patent Number:** **5,356,368**

[45] **Date of Patent:** *Oct. 18, 1994

[54] **METHOD OF AND APPARATUS FOR INDUCING DESIRED STATES OF CONSCIOUSNESS**

[75] Inventor: **Robert A. Monroe,** Nelson County, Va.

[73] Assignee: **Interstate Industries Inc.,** Faber, Va.

[*] Notice: The portion of the term of this patent subsequent to May 25, 2010 has been disclaimed.

[21] Appl. No.: **664,176**

[22] Filed: **Mar. 1, 1991**

[51] Int. Cl.⁵ **A61M 21/00**
[52] U.S. Cl. **600/28;** 128/732
[58] Field of Search 600/26–28; 128/731–732

[56] **References Cited**

U.S. PATENT DOCUMENTS

2,466,054	4/1949	Siebel .
3,160,159	12/1964	Hoody et al. .
3,576,185	4/1971	Schulz et al. .
3,712,292	1/1973	Zentmeyer, Jr. .
3,753,433	8/1973	Bakerich et al. .
3,826,243	7/1974	Anderson .
3,837,331	9/1974	Ross .
3,884,218	5/1975	Monroe .
4,034,741	7/1977	Adams et al. .
4,141,344	2/1979	Barbara .

4,227,516	10/1980	Meland et al. .
4,335,710	6/1982	Williamson .
4,573,449	3/1986	Warnke .
4,834,701	5/1989	Masaki .
4,883,067	11/1989	Knispel et al. 600/28
5,036,858	8/1991	Carter et al. .
5,101,831	4/1992	Koyama et al. 600/26

Primary Examiner—Lee S. Cohen
Assistant Examiner—J. P. Lacyk
Attorney, Agent, or Firm—Sughrue, Mion, Zinn, Macpeak & Seas

[57] **ABSTRACT**

Improved methods and apparatus for entraining human brain patterns, employing frequency following response (FFR) techniques, facilitate attainment of desired states of consciousness. In one embodiment, a plurality of electroencephalogram (EEG) waveforms, characteristic of a given state of consciousness, are combined to yield an EEG waveform to which subjects may be susceptible more readily. In another embodiment, sleep patterns are reproduced based on observed brain patterns during portions of a sleep cycle; entrainment principles are applied to induce sleep. In yet another embodiment, entrainment principles are applied in the work environment, to induce and maintain a desired level of consciousness. A portable device also is described.

28 Claims, 21 Drawing Sheets

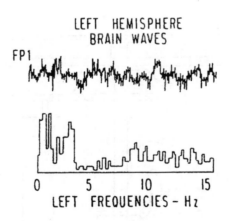

LEFT HEMISPHERE
BRAIN WAVES

FP1

0   5   10   15
LEFT FREQUENCIES – Hz

United States Patent [19]

Harner

[11] **Patent Number:**   **5,479,941**

[45] **Date of Patent:**   **Jan. 2, 1996**

[54] **DEVICE FOR INDUCING ALTERED STATES OF CONSCIOUSNESS**

[75] Inventor: **Michael Harner**, Norwalk, Conn.

[73] Assignee: **Foundation of Shamanic Studies**, Norwalk, Conn.

[21] Appl. No.: **138,343**

[22] Filed: **Oct. 18, 1993**

[51] **Int. Cl.**[6] **A61G 15/00**; A61G 7/04
[52] **U.S. Cl.** **128/845**; 5/616
[58] **Field of Search** 128/845, 846;
606/237, 239, 240, 241, 242, 245; 5/600,
601, 613; 297/DIG. 10

[56]   **References Cited**

                U.S. PATENT DOCUMENTS

715,668	12/1902	Kiddie .	
1,044,391	11/1912	Jones	472/2
1,106,255	8/1914	Thompson .	
1,553,528	9/1925	Hartong .	
2,671,898	3/1954	Wada	128/858
2,869,538	1/1959	Hawk .	
3,558,129	1/1971	Curry .	
3,646,896	3/1972	Derujinsky .	
4,101,165	7/1978	Hammer	297/273
4,379,588	4/1983	Speice .	
4,544,202	10/1985	Keaton .	
4,597,119	7/1986	Padgett .	
4,720,140	1/1988	Change, III .	

4,841,165	6/1989	Bowles	307/132
4,862,530	9/1989	Chen	5/616
4,934,997	6/1990	Skakas .	
5,044,377	9/1991	Stillman	128/845
5,072,462	12/1991	Attison	5/600
5,078,451	1/1992	Sobel .	
5,095,561	3/1992	Green	5/161

OTHER PUBLICATIONS

Eliade, M. (1964) in "Shamanism, Archaic Techniques of Ecstasy", (Panther Books) p. 130.
F. Andres (1939), "Die Himmelsreise der Caraibischen Medizinmanner", ZE, LXX, 3–5, p. 340.
Metraux (1944), "Le Shamanisme chez les Indiens de l'Amerique du Sud Tropicale", p. 208.
H. Kalweit (1988), "Dreamtime and Inner Space, The World of the Shaman", Shambhala Press, pp. 163–165.
Carlos Castaneda (1981), in "The Eagle's Gift," Washington Square Press, New York, N.Y., at pp. 61–62.
Bridwell et al. (1990), "Climbing Big Walls," pp. 58–59.

Primary Examiner—Michael A. Brown
Attorney, Agent, or Firm—Greenlee and Winner

[57]   **ABSTRACT**

A rotating device for producing altered states of consciousness in a subject is provided. The subject's body rotates about a point in the center of the body support means at a speed between about 10 and about 60 revolutions per minute. In a preferred embodiment the direction of rotation is periodically reversed.

19 Claims, 4 Drawing Sheets

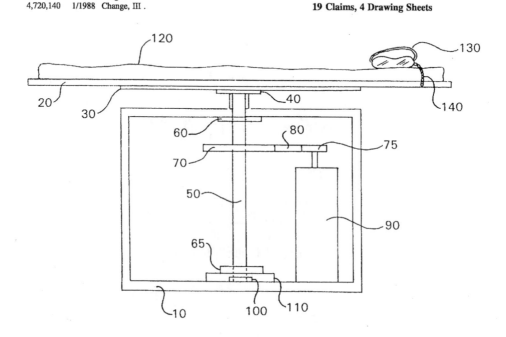

5,479,941

1

DEVICE FOR INDUCING ALTERED STATES OF CONSCIOUSNESS

FIELD OF THE INVENTION

This invention is a device for producing altered states of consciousness and comprises means for rotating the subject's body.

BACKGROUND OF THE INVENTION

Shamans in all cultures from ancient times until the present have employed means for altering their states of consciousness so as to induce visions and become conscious of non-ordinary realities where information helpful in healing illnesses and performing divinations may be available. Such means include the ingestion of psychotropic plant substances, the use of rhythmic and monotonous sound such as drumming and chanting, and dancing such as the Sufi whirling dervish dances.

Mircea Eliade (1964) in "Shamanism, Archaic Techniques of Ecstasy", (Panther Books) p.130 describes a practice of shamans of the Carib Indians of South America who place apprentices on "a platform suspended from the ceiling of the hut by a number of cords twisted together, which, as they unwind, make the platform revolve with increasing speed. The novice sings: 'The platform of the pujai will carry me to the sky . . . ' and he enters the various celestial spheres one after the other and sees the spirits in a vision . . . Finally, the apprentice feels that he is carried into the sky and enjoys celestial visions." [Citing F. Andres (1939), "Die Himmelsreise der Caraibischen Medizinmanner" ZE LXX 3–5 p.340; and Metraux, "Le Shamanisme chez les Indiens de l'Amerique du Sud Tropicale", p.208.]

H. Kalweit (1988), "Dreamtime and Inner Space, The World of the Shaman", Shambhala Press, pp. 163–165 also describes this device and states that Robert Masters and Jean Houston have developed a similar device and found that a person being subjected to vertical or horizontal movements would, after about twenty minutes, experience an altered state of consciousness marked by highly realistic fantasies. The Masters and Houston device is described by its developers as similar to the European "witches' cradle", essentially a swing. Best results were achieved with the subject standing up with the eyes covered. A similar device was displayed at Essalen Institute in California during the 1960's, comprising a swing in which the subject could sit and swing and spin. The subject's entire body was covered and bound in canvas.

In none of these devices were means provided for controlling the speed of rotation or continuing the rotation over a period of up to thirty minutes with periodic reversal of the direction of rotation.

Carlos Castaneda (1981), in "The Eagle's Gift," Washington Square Press, New York, N.Y., at page 61–62 describes a harness device for a game in which the subject is suspended in a harness and must keep his balance as antagonists pull the ropes suspending the subject. The game is for sharpening visual prowess and gaining access to "memory of the body".

Devices which rotate the human body for purposes other than trance induction are known to the art. A number of such devices are designed for holding the subject in a seated rather than a reclining position, as shown in the following U.S. Patents: Kiddie U.S. Pat. No. 715,668 for "Pleasure Device" shows a swing which is hung on a rotatable mount

2

to convert it into a carousel. Jones U.S. Pat. No. 1,044,391 for Roundabout Swing shows a rotating swing with a center post. A platform rotates about a shaft piercing its middle, suspending on ropes or wires which wind up around the shaft as the platform turns and cause reversal of its motion when unwinding. Curry U.S. Pat. No. 3,558,129 for "Children's Merry-Go-Round" shows a merry-go-round having retractable seat arms and powered by an electric motor. Keaton U.S. Pat. No. 4,544,202 shows a rotatable, manually powered lounge chair pivoted on a base. It has a gear connection to control the amount of rotation and to position the chair. Change U.S. Pat. No. 4,720,140 discloses a rotating platform for a sunbather having a chair mounted upon the platform. It has a center pivot about which the platform will rotate and the platform also has rollers at its end. The platform may be motor-powered. Sobel U.S. Pat. No. 5,078,451 discloses a manually rotatable chaise lounge in which the body support has a base element which is pivotally supported on the base frame. There are roller bearings between the base and the rotatable support.

U.S. Patents which disclose rotating display devices are as follows: Thompson U.S. Pat. No. 1,106,255 for Spectacular Display Apparatus shows a display device useful for stage productions with a sling for suspending the article to be displayed, such as a grand piano, which can be both rotated and moved vertically. The device may be rotated by pulling a rope attached to a pulley. Hartong U.S. Pat. No. 1,553,528 for "Display Device," shows a device for merchandise display having a circular platform rotated by means of an electric motor beneath the platform powering peripheral drive means.

Rotatable platforms on which sunbathers may lie supine are as follows: Derujinsky U.S. Pat. No. 3,646,896 for Sunbather's Rotatable Platform shows a sunbather's platform for two individuals who lie on it in a supine position. The platform is manually rotated. Speice U.S. Pat. No. 4,379,588 for Revolving Solar Lounger shows a chaise-type lounger which rotates on a base only in response to energization from the sun's rays. When the sun is covered by clouds, the lounge does not rotate. Padgett U.S. Pat. No. 4,597,119 for Suntanning Device, shows a rotatable sunbathing lounge which is pivotally supported on the pivot base and has an adjustable braking device to slow down the rotation to a desired speed, and is rotated by a spring or an electric motor, or gravity. This device is believed to provide rotational speeds considerably slower than required for trance induction.

A climber's device in which the subject may lie supine on a platform suspended on straps is the Portaledge by A-5 Company of Phoenix Ariz., depicted in Bridwell, et al. (1990), "Climbing Big Walls," pages 58–59. This device is not designed to rotate.

None of the foregoing disclose or suggest a rotating device upon which the subject may lie supine, suitable for trance induction. Nor has any rotating device been taught adapted to automatically rotate at a speed suitable for trance induction.

SUMMARY OF THE INVENTION

The device of this invention causes the occupant (called the "subject" herein) to enter a state of extreme relaxation in an altered state of consciousness which, in a darkened room or with the eyes closed or blindfolded, leads to an experience of weightlessness as though flying through space, stimulating dream-like imagery and out-of-body sensations. The

United States Patent [19]

Van Dick

[11] **Patent Number:**   **5,480,374**

[45] **Date of Patent:**   **Jan. 2, 1996**

[54] **METHOD AND APPARATUS FOR REDUCING PHYSIOLOGICAL STRESS**

[76] Inventor: **Robert C. Van Dick**

[21] Appl. No.: **219,088**

[22] Filed: **Mar. 28, 1994**

[51] **Int. Cl.⁶** **A61B 17/52**
[52] **U.S. Cl.** **600/26**; 600/9; 600/14
[58] **Field of Search** 600/9, 10, 11, 600/12, 13, 14, 15, 26; 128/731, 722; 607/72

[56] **References Cited**

U.S. PATENT DOCUMENTS

3,773,049	11/1973	Rabichev et al.	128/362
3,882,850	5/1975	Bailin et al.	128/2.1
3,884,218	5/1975	Monroe	128/1
3,951,134	4/1976	Malech	128/2.1
4,187,506	2/1980	Dickinson	343/100
4,388,918	6/1983	Filley	128/1
4,444,199	4/1984	Shafer	128/691
4,838,850	6/1989	Rosengart	600/14
4,846,178	7/1989	Fuxue et al.	128/419
4,998,532	3/1991	Griffith	128/419
5,066,272	11/1991	Eaton et al.	600/9
5,092,835	3/1992	Schurig et al.	600/9
5,213,338	5/1993	Brotz	273/460
5,269,746	12/1993	Jacobson	600/13

Primary Examiner—Lee S. Cohen
Assistant Examiner—Stephen Huang
Attorney, Agent, or Firm—Kennedy & Kennedy

[57] **ABSTRACT**

Physiological stress in a human subject is treated by generating a weak electromagnetic field about a grounded electrode by the application of pulses of between 5 and 50 microseconds each at a pulse rate of between 0.5K and 10K pulses per second to a power electrode, the power electrode and grounded electrode being coupled to high voltage pulse generation means. A subject is positioned within the weak electromagnetic field for a period of time sufficient to cause an increase in his or her alpha or theta brain wave levels.

10 Claims, 5 Drawing Sheets

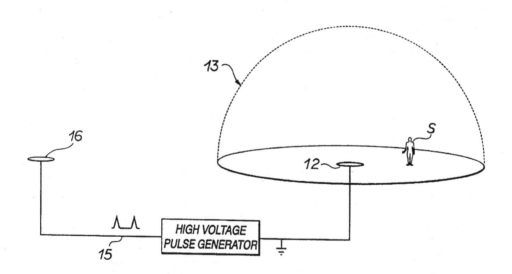

5,480,374

1

METHOD AND APPARATUS FOR REDUCING PHYSIOLOGICAL STRESS

TECHNICAL FIELD

The present invention relates to methods and apparatuses for reducing physiological stress in humans. More particularly, the invention relates to methods of reducing physiological stress by increasing an individual's alpha and theta brain waves amplitudes without the need for conscious mental effort or the attachment of devices to the body.

BACKGROUND OF THE INVENTION

The human brain produces electrical brain waves at frequencies ranging from 0 to 64 Hertz (Hz). Within this range are delta waves from 0 to 3 Hz, theta waves from 3 to 8 Hz, alpha waves from 8 to 13 Hz, and beta waves from 13 to 64 Hz. These brain waves are usually present at any given time but in varying magnitudes depending on an individual's thought processes. Beta levels dominate during the alert awakened state. Alpha levels rise and beta levels fall in the light sleep state. Theta levels increase while alpha and beta levels decrease during the deep sleep state. Delta levels rise during a deep-deep sleep state.

It is known that an increase in physiological stress is manifested by low levels of alpha and theta brain waves. An increase in theta frequency levels produce the best physiological stress reduction results, yet they are the most difficult for individuals consciously to produce. While it has been found that an increase in theta frequency levels correspondingly increases alpha frequency levels, the reverse is not true. The more readily increased alpha brain waves do not correspondingly increase theta brain wave levels.

Current techniques used to reduce psychological stress are essentially limited to conscious mental efforts. This is sometimes achievable through pure meditation and sometimes not. Such technique is thus often unreliable. Physiological stress reduction can also be achieved by mental exercises in association with electronic bio-feedback instruments that inform individuals of their success or failure in controlling brain wave frequencies, and which assist in altering brain wave frequencies. These bio-feedback instruments typically employ sensors that are attached to the individual's skull and which are electrically coupled with analytic and display apparatuses. Since the individual is physically attached to the instrument, limitations in movement exist which can inhibit the ability of the individual to increase his or her alpha and theta brain wave frequencies and to maintain such increases for a sufficiently period of time to achieve therapeutic results.

Thus, there remains a need for a method of reducing physiological stress that does not require conscious mental effort by individuals and which does not require the attachment of devices to the persons. Accordingly, it is to the provision of such physiological stress that the present invention is primarily directed.

SUMMARY OF THE INVENTION

It has now been discovered that physiological stress reduction can also be achieved with the use of electrical means without the need for conscious effort nor the attachment of devices to persons. By merely exposing a person or persons to a weak electromagnetic field produced in a certain manner, the person's alpha and theta brain wave levels may be increased and thereby reduce physiological stress.

2

The weak electromagnetic field is produced about a grounded electrode that is coupled with a high voltage pulse generator. The generator transmits pulses of between 5 and 50 microseconds each, at a pulse repetition rate of between 0.5K and 10K pulses per second, to a power electrode, the power electrode and grounded electrode being coupled to a high voltage pulse generator. The subject is positioned within the weak electromagnetic field for a period of time sufficient to cause an increase in alpha and/or theta brain wave levels of the subject.

The method may be practiced with a therapeutic unit that has a treatment space of a size sufficient to accommodate one or more human subjects positioned within the weak electromagnetic field about the grounded electrode. The weak electromagnetic field itself may be specifically prescribed by monitoring brain wave levels of the subject while varying an electrical parameter of the pulse trains generated by the high voltage pulse generator and identifying that parameter which produces a desirable increase in alpha and/or theta brain wave levels for the individual.

BRIEF DESCRIPTION OF THE DRAWING

FIG. 1 is a schematic diagram of a therapeutic unit that embodies principles of the present invention.

FIG. 2 is a graphic representation of a pulse train generated for use in practicing the method of the present invention.

FIG. 3A represents brain wave patterns of a Subject A before utilizing the method of the present invention while FIG. 3B represents the brain wave patterns of subject A after utilizing the method of the present invention.

FIG. 4A represents the brain wave patterns of a Subject B before utilizing the method of the present invention while FIG. 4B represents the brain wave patterns of the Subject B after utilizing the method of the present invention.

DETAILED DESCRIPTION OF THE DRAWINGS

With reference next to the drawing, there is schematically shown in FIG. 1 a therapeutic unit for the treatment of physiological stress in a human subject. The unit has means for generating a weak electromagnetic field about a grounded electrode 12 of generally semi-spherical spatial shape as indicated at 13, there of course being no sharply defined boundary of such. A human subject S is shown positioned within this weak electromagnetic field for treatment which may, for example, be in a room of a building.

The weak electromagnetic field is generated by the use of a high voltage pulse generator that is connected via a well insulated conductor to both the grounded electrode 12 and to earth ground. The generator is also connected via another insulated conductor 15 to a power electrode 16 that is located outside of the weak electromagnetic field.

The high voltage pulse generator is capable of generated pulses of between 0.5 KV to 30 KV of variable pulse widths and pulse repetition rates. It has been found that pulse widths of between 5 and 50 microseconds as measured at 50% of peak voltage and of a pulse repetition rate of between 500 Hz and 10K Hz, peak to peak, as shown in FIG. 2, produces a weak electromagnetic field that is of substantial therapeutic value here. Moreover, it has been determined that different pulse repetition frequencies or rates within this overall range provide better benefits for different individuals than others. Thus by observing alpha and theta levels in an individual while varying the pulse repetition rate, an opti-

US005495853A

United States Patent [19]

Yasushi

[11] **Patent Number:** **5,495,853**

[45] **Date of Patent:** **Mar. 5, 1996**

[54] **SYSTEM FOR EVOKING ELECTROENCEPHALOGRAM SIGNALS**

[75] Inventor: **Mitsuo Yasushi**, Kawagoe, Japan

[73] Assignee: **Pioneer Electronic Corporation,** Tokyo, Japan

[21] Appl. No.: **305,755**

[22] Filed: **Sep. 14, 1994**

Related U.S. Application Data

[63] Continuation of Ser. No. 498,671, Mar. 26, 1990, abandoned.

[30] **Foreign Application Priority Data**

Aug. 10, 1989 [JP] Japan 1-205780

[51] **Int. Cl.⁶** **A61B 5/04**
[52] **U.S. Cl.** **128/732**; 600/27
[58] **Field of Search** 128/731–732; 600/26–28

[56] **References Cited**

U.S. PATENT DOCUMENTS

3,255,753	6/1966	Wing	600/26
3,388,699	6/1968	Webb	600/26
3,753,433	8/1973	Bakerich et al.	128/732
3,837,331	9/1974	Ross .	
3,882,850	5/1975	Bailin et al.	128/732
3,893,450	7/1975	Ertl .	
3,896,790	7/1975	Dikmen	128/732
4,227,516	10/1980	Meland et al. .	
4,228,807	10/1980	Yagi et al. .	

4,315,502	2/1982	Gorges	600/27
4,462,411	7/1984	Rickards .	
4,595,013	7/1986	Jones et al.	128/644
4,697,598	10/1987	Bernard et al.	128/644
4,777,937	10/1988	Rush et al.	600/27
4,858,609	8/1989	Cole	600/26
4,902,274	2/1990	Gleeson, III	600/27
5,036,858	8/1991	Carter et al.	600/27
5,241,967	9/1993	Yasushi et al.	128/732
5,356,368	10/1994	Monroe	128/732

Primary Examiner—Angela D. Sykes
Assistant Examiner—Robert L. Nasser, Jr.
Attorney, Agent, or Firm—Sughrue, Mion, Zinn, Macpeak & Seas

[57] **ABSTRACT**

A system for evoking an electroencephalogram (EEG) signal from the brain of a user has a brain wave evoking terminal unit which includes a headgear for being mounted on the head of the user, a light emitter, mounted on the headgear, for applying an EEG signal evoking photic stimulus to the eyes of the user, and electrodes, mounted on the headgear, for detecting brain waves produced by the user. The system also has a brain wave signal processor, responsive to brain wave signals from the electrodes, for generating a stimulating signal having a frequency corresponding to a brain wave to be evoked, and for applying the stimulating signal to the light emitter. The brain wave to be evoked is extracted and fed back as stimulating light to the user, who can be rapidly and strongly brought into a desired brain wave condition. The brain wave signal processor may be combined with the brain wave evoking terminal unit, so that the system is small in size, simple in arrangement, and can be carried and mounted on the user's head with ease.

5 Claims, 5 Drawing Sheets

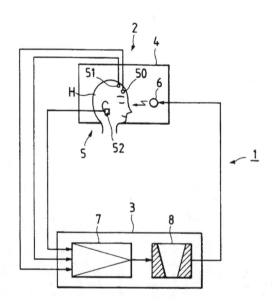

United States Patent [19]

Raynie et al.

[11]	Patent Number: 5,551,879
[45]	Date of Patent: Sep. 3, 1996

[54] **DREAM STATE TEACHING MACHINE**

[75] Inventors: **Arthur D. Raynie; Raul G. Rodriguez; Gary L. Forister; Alexander B. Crawford**, all of San Antonio, Tex.

[73] Assignee: **Dream Weaver J.V.**, San Antonio, Tex.

[21] Appl. No.: **307,324**

[22] Filed: **Sep. 16, 1994**

[51] Int. Cl.^{6} **A61M 21/00**
[52] U.S. Cl. **434/236**; 600/26; 600/27
[58] Field of Search 434/236–238; 446/419; 600/26–28; 128/731, 732

[56] **References Cited**

U.S. PATENT DOCUMENTS

3,884,218	5/1975	Monroe .
4,735,199	4/1988	DiLullo .
4,832,050	5/1989	DiLullo .... 446/419 X
4,863,259	9/1989	Schneider et al. .
5,219,322	6/1993	Weathers 600/27

OTHER PUBLICATIONS

Kaser, Vaughn A. "The Effects of an Auditory Subliminal Message Upon the Production of Images and Dreams", *The Journal of Nervous and Mental Disease*, vol. 174, No. 7 (1986), 397–407.
LaBerge, Stephen P. "Lucid Dreaming as a Learnable Skill: A Case Study", *Perceptual and Motor Skills*, 51 (1980), 1039–1042.

LaBerge, Stephen P., Lynn E. Nagel, William C. Dement, and Vincent P. Zarcone, Jr. "Lucid Dreaming Vertified by Volitional Communication During REM Sleep", *Perceptual and Motor Skills*, 52 (1981), 727–732.
LaBerge, Stephen, Ph.D. *Lucid Dreaming* (New York: Ballantine Books, 1986), pp. 161–162.
LaBerge, Stephen, Ph.D. and Howard Rheingold. *Exploring the World of Lucid Dreaming* (New York: Ballantine Books, 1990).
Sergio, W. "Use of DMAE (2–dimethylaminoethanol) in the Induction of Lucid Dreams", *Medical Hypotheses* 26 (1988), 255–257.
Tholey, Paul. "Techniques for Inducing and Manipulating Lucid Dreams", *Perceptual and Motor Skills*, 57 (1983), 79–90.

Primary Examiner—Richard J. Apley
Assistant Examiner—Glenn E. Richman
Attorney, Agent, or Firm—Gunn, Lee & Miller, PC

[57] **ABSTRACT**

A device for enhancing lucidity in the dream state of an individual. The device includes electronic circuitry incorporated into a headband for the user to wear while sleeping. The circuitry includes a detector for fitting adjacent to the eye of the sleeping individual, for detecting Rapid Eye Movement (REM), which occurs during the dream state. The detector emits a signal that is evaluated by additional circuitry to determine whether or not REM sleep is occurring. If REM sleep is occurring, a signal is generated to operate a recorded, which typically plays prerecorded messages through the headphones engaging the ear of the sleeping individual.

23 Claims, 6 Drawing Sheets

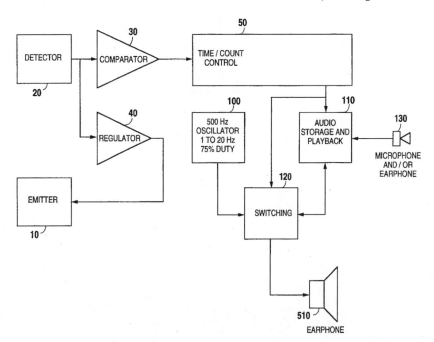

United States Patent [19]

Van Dick

[11] **Patent Number:** 5,562,597

[45] **Date of Patent:** Oct. 8, 1996

[54] **METHOD AND APPARATUS FOR REDUCING PHYSIOLOGICAL STRESS**

[76] Inventor: **Robert C. Van Dick**

[21] Appl. No.: **509,813**

[22] Filed: **Aug. 1, 1995**

Related U.S. Application Data

[63] Continuation-in-part of Ser. No. 219,088, Mar. 28, 1994, Pat. No. 5,480,374.

[51] **Int. Cl.^{6}** **A61B 17/52**
[52] **U.S. Cl.** **600/26**; 600/9; 600/14
[58] **Field of Search** 600/9–15, 26; 607/1, 2

[56] **References Cited**

U.S. PATENT DOCUMENTS

4,441,498 4/1984 Nordling 607/32
4,838,850 6/1989 Rosengart 600/14
4,846,178 7/1989 Fuxue et al. 607/2

Primary Examiner—Angela D. Sykes
Assistant Examiner—Stephen Huane
Attorney, Agent, or Firm—Kennedy & Kennedy

[57] **ABSTRACT**

Physiological stress in a human subject is treated by generating a weak electromagnetic field about a quartz crystal. The crystal is stimulated by applying electrical pulses of pulse widths between 0.1 and 50 microseconds each at a pulse repetition rate of between 0.5K and 10K pulses per second to a conductor positioned adjacent to the quartz crystal thereby generating a weak electromagnetic field. A subject is positioned within the weak electromagnetic field for a period of time sufficient to reduce stress.

17 Claims, 6 Drawing Sheets

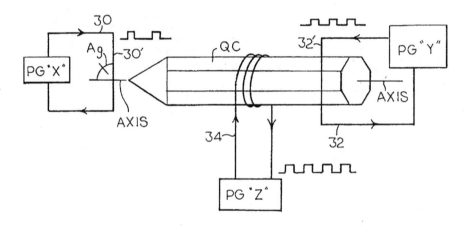

5,562,597

1

METHOD AND APPARATUS FOR REDUCING PHYSIOLOGICAL STRESS

REFERENCE TO RELATED APPLICATION

This is a continuation-in-part of application Ser. No. 08/219,088 filed Mar. 28, 1994, now issued Jan. 2, 1996 U.S. Pat. No. 5,480,374.

TECHNICAL FIELD

The present invention relates to methods and apparatuses for reducing physiological stress in humans. More particularly, the invention relates to methods of reducing physiological stress by increasing an individual's alpha and theta brain waves amplitudes without the need for conscious mental effort or the attachment of devices to the body.

BACKGROUND OF THE INVENTION

The human brain produces electrical brain waves at frequencies ranging from 0 to 64 Hertz (Hz). Within this range are delta waves from 0 to 3 Hz, theta waves from 3 to 8 Hz, alpha waves from 8 to 13 Hz, and beta waves from 13 to 64 Hz. These brain waves are usually present at any given time but in varying magnitudes depending on an individual's thought processes. Beta levels dominate during the alert awakened state. Alpha levels rise and beta levels fall in the light sleep state. Theta levels increase while alpha and beta levels decrease during the deep sleep state. Delta levels rise during a deep-deep sleep state.

It is known that an increase in physiological stress is manifested by low levels of alpha and theta brain waves. An increase in theta frequency levels produce the best physiological stress reduction results, yet they are the most difficult for individuals consciously to produce. While it has been found that an increase in theta frequency levels correspondingly increases alpha frequency levels, the reverse is not true. The more readily increased alpha brain waves do not correspondingly increase theta brain wave levels.

Current techniques used to reduce psychological stress are essentially limited to conscious mental efforts. This is sometimes achievable through pure meditation and sometimes not. Such technique is thus often unreliable. Physiological stress reduction can also be achieved by mental exercises in association with electronic biofeedback instruments that inform individuals of their success or failure in controlling brain wave frequencies, and which assist in altering brain wave frequencies. These bio-feedback instruments typically employ sensors that are attached to the individual's skull and which are electrically coupled with analytic and display apparatuses. Since the individual is physically attached to the instrument, limitations in movement exist which can inhibit the ability of the individual to increase his or her alpha and theta brain wave frequencies and to maintain such increases for a sufficiently period of time to achieve therapeutic results.

Thus, there remains a need for a method of reducing physiological stress that does not require conscious mental effort by individuals and which does not require the attachment of devices to the persons. Accordingly, it is to the provision of such physiological stress that the present invention is primarily directed.

SUMMARY OF THE INVENTION

It has now been discovered that physiological stress reduction can also be achieved with the use of electrical means without the need for conscious effort nor the attach-

2

ment of devices to persons. By merely exposing a person or persons to a weak electromagnetic field produced in a certain manner, the person's alpha and theta brain wave levels may be increased and thereby reduce physiological stress.

The weak electromagnetic field is produced about a grounded electrode that is coupled with a high voltage pulse generator. The generator transmits pulses of between 5 and 50 microseconds each, at a pulse repetition rate of between 0.5K and 10K pulses per second, to a power electrode, the power electrode and grounded electrode being coupled to a high voltage pulse generator. The subject is positioned within the weak electromagnetic field for a period of time sufficient to cause an increase in alpha and/or theta brain wave levels of the subject.

The method may be practiced with a therapeutic unit that has a treatment space of a size sufficient to accommodate one or more human subjects positioned within the weak electromagnetic field about the grounded electrode. The weak electromagnetic field itself may be specifically prescribed by monitoring brain wave levels of the subject while varying an electrical parameter of the pulse trains generated by the high voltage pulse generator and identifying that parameter which produces a desirable increase in alpha and/or theta brain wave levels for the individual.

In an alternative form of the invention a human subject is treated for physiological stress by stimulating a quartz crystal by applying electrical pulses of pulse widths between 0.1 and 50 microseconds each at a pulse repetition rate of between 0.5K and 10K pulses per second to a conductor positioned adjacent to the quartz crystal thereby generating a weak electromagnetic field about the crystal, and positioning the subject within the weak electromagnetic field. Apparatus for use in this treatment method comprises a quartz crystal, an electrical conductor mounted adjacent the quartz crystal, and means for applying to the conductor electrical pulses of pulse widths of between 0.1 and 50 microseconds each at a pulse repetition rate of between 0.5K and 10K pulses per second.

BRIEF DESCRIPTION OF THE DRAWING

FIG. 1 a schematic diagram of a therapeutic unit that embodies principles of the present invention.

FIG. 2 is a graphic representation of a pulse train generated for use in practicing the method of the present invention.

FIG. 3A represents brain wave patterns of a Subject A before utilizing the method of the present invention while

FIG. 3B represents the brain wave patterns of Subject A after utilizing the method of the present invention.

FIG. 4A represents the brain wave patterns of a Subject B before utilizing the method of the present invention while FIG. 4B represents the brain wave patterns of the Subject B after utilizing the method of the present invention.

FIG. 5 is a schematic diagram of a therapeutic unit that embodies principles of the invention in another form.

FIG. 6 is a graphic representation of a pulse train generated for use in practicing the method of the invention with the unit shown in FIG. 5.

DETAILED DESCRIPTION OF THE DRAWINGS

With reference next to the drawing, there is schematically shown in FIG. 1 a therapeutic unit for the treatment of physiological stress in a human subject. The unit has means

United States Patent [19]

Davis

[11] **Patent Number:** **5,586,967**

[45] **Date of Patent:** *Dec. 24, 1996**

[54] **METHOD AND RECORDING FOR PRODUCING SOUNDS AND MESSAGES TO ACHIEVE ALPHA AND THETA BRAINWAVE STATES AND POSITIVE EMOTIONAL STATES IN HUMANS**

[76] Inventor: **Mark E. Davis**

[*] Notice: The term of this patent shall not extend beyond the expiration date of Pat. No. 5,352,181.

[21] Appl. No.: **267,149**

[22] Filed: **Jun. 27, 1994**

Related U.S. Application Data

[63] Continuation-in-part of Ser. No. 939,088, Sep. 2, 1992, Pat. No. 5,352,181.

[51] Int. Cl.⁶ **A61M 21/00**
[52] U.S. Cl. **600/28**
[58] Field of Search 600/26–28; 128/731, 128/732, 897, 898

[56] **References Cited**

U.S. PATENT DOCUMENTS

4,141,344	2/1979	Barbara	600/28
4,227,516	10/1980	Meland et al.	600/26
4,834,701	5/1989	Masaki	600/28
5,123,899	6/1992	Gall	600/28
5,135,468	8/1992	Meissner	600/28
5,151,080	9/1992	Bick	600/26 X

OTHER PUBLICATIONS

Ostrander & Schroeder, Super–Learning, Feb. 1981, pp. 49,64,68–69, 114–115, 312–315.

Prevention Magazine, Healthy Pleasures, Jun. 1989, pp. 97–101.

Primary Examiner—Angela Sykes
Assistant Examiner—Stephen D. Huane
Attorney, Agent, or Firm—Walter A. Hackler

[57] **ABSTRACT**

A method and recording for the use in achieving alpha and theta brainwave states and effecting positive emotional states in humans, is provided which includes a medium having a musical composition thereon with an initial tempo decreasing to a final tempo and verbal phrases recorded in synchrony with the decreasing tempo.

5 Claims, 1 Drawing Sheet

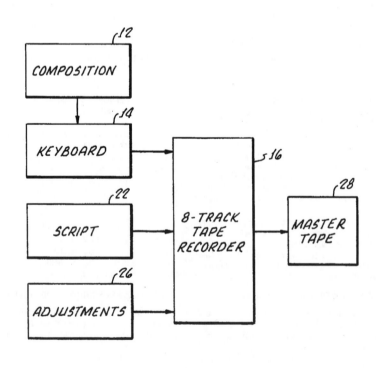

United States Patent [19]

Gozlan et al.

[11] **Patent Number:** **5,595,488**

[45] **Date of Patent:** **Jan. 21, 1997**

[54] **APPARATUS AND METHOD FOR MONITORING AND IMPROVING THE ALERTNESS OF A SUBJECT**

[75] Inventors: **Eli Gozlan**, Kiryat Motzkin; **Shlomo Breznitz**, Haifa; **Dan Nir**, Haifa; **Sharon Erlich**, Haifa, all of Israel

[73] Assignee: **Vigilant Ltd.**, Israel

[21] Appl. No.: **285,688**

[22] Filed: **Aug. 4, 1994**

[51] Int. Cl.^{6} **G09B 19/00**
[52] U.S. Cl. **434/236**; 434/237; 434/258
[58] Field of Search 434/236–238, 434/258

[56] **References Cited**

U.S. PATENT DOCUMENTS

4,006,539 2/1977 Slomoki 434/258
5,344,324 9/1994 O'Donnell et al. 434/258

Primary Examiner—Richard J. Apley
Assistant Examiner—Glenn E. Richman
Attorney, Agent, or Firm—Mark M. Friedman

[57] **ABSTRACT**

Apparatus and method for monitoring and for improving the state of alertness of a subject while he continues to perform a primary task, driving a vehicle, operating machinery, etc. The apparatus includes stimulation apparatus for issuing stimuli to the subject and response apparatus for enabling the subject to reply to the stimuli. The stimuli can be audible, visual or tactile. Test results are processed and compared to baseline values taken when the subject is displaying a normal state of alertness. The rate of activation of the stimulation apparatus increases inversely with a deteriorating state of alertness of the subject to improve the state of alertness of the subject. The apparatus can be fashioned in a wide range of devices including a hand-held portable device, a wristwatch, a behind-the-ear (BTE) clip, a pair of spectacles, and for installation in a steering wheel.

9 Claims, 11 Drawing Sheets

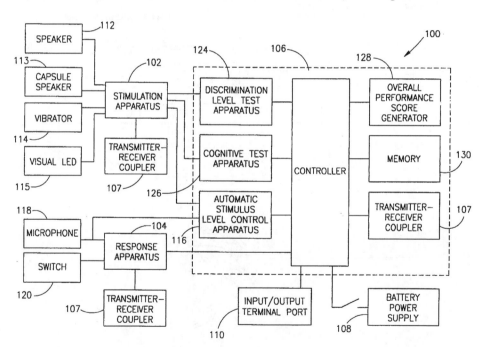

United States Patent [19]

Yanagidaira et al.

[11] **Patent Number:**	**5,954,629**
[45] **Date of Patent:**	***Sep. 21, 1999**

[54] **BRAIN WAVE INDUCING SYSTEM**

[75] Inventors: **Masatoshi Yanagidaira; Yuichi Kimikawa; Takeshi Fukami; Mitsuo Yasushi,** all of Saitama-ken, Japan

[73] Assignee: **Pioneer Electronic Corporation,** Tokyo, Japan

[*] Notice: This patent issued on a continued prosecution application filed under 37 CFR 1.53(d), and is subject to the twenty year patent term provisions of 35 U.S.C. 154(a)(2).

[21] Appl. No.: **08/797,655**

[22] Filed: **Jan. 31, 1997**

[30] **Foreign Application Priority Data**

Feb. 21, 1996 [JP] Japan 8-033848

[51] **Int. Cl.^{6}** **A61M 21/00**
[52] **U.S. Cl.** **600/27**; 600/26; 600/28
[58] **Field of Search** 600/26–28, 544, 600/545, 558; 128/731, 732, 745

[56] **References Cited**

U.S. PATENT DOCUMENTS

5,241,967	9/1993	Yasushi et al.	.... 600/27
5,495,853	3/1996	Yasushi	.... 600/27
5,613,498	3/1997	Yasushi et al.	.... 600/27

Primary Examiner—Linda C. M. Dvorak
Assistant Examiner—Rosiland Kearney
Attorney, Agent, or Firm—Nikaido, Marmelstein, Murray & Oram LLP

[57] **ABSTRACT**

Sensors are provided for detecting brain waves of a user, and a band-pass filter is provided for extracting a particular brain waves including an α wave included in a detected brain wave. The band-pass filter comprises a first band-pass filter having a narrow pass band, and a second band-pass filter having a wide pass band. One of the first and second band-pass filters is selected, and a stimulation signal is produced in dependency on an α wave extracted by a selected band-pass filter. In accordance with the stimulation signal, a stimulation light is emitted to the user in order to induce the user to relax or sleeping state.

6 Claims, 12 Drawing Sheets

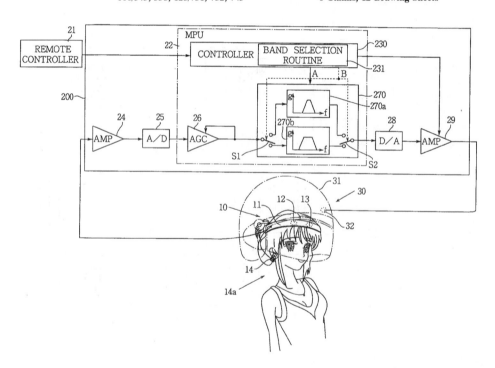

United States Patent [19]

Masaki et al.

[11] **Patent Number:** **5,954,630**

[45] **Date of Patent:** **Sep. 21, 1999**

[54] **FM THETA-INDUCING AUDIBLE SOUND, AND METHOD, DEVICE AND RECORDED MEDIUM TO GENERATE THE SAME**

[75] Inventors: **Kazumi Masaki**, Osaka; **Osamu Matsuda**, Okayama, both of Japan

[73] Assignee: **Ken Hayashibara**, Okayama, Japan

[21] Appl. No.: **08/305,834**

[22] Filed: **Sep. 14, 1994**

[30]   **Foreign Application Priority Data**

Sep. 16, 1993	[JP]	Japan	....	5-252124
Sep. 24, 1993	[JP]	Japan	....	5-258973
Sep. 24, 1993	[JP]	Japan	....	5-258993

[51] **Int. Cl.^{6}** **A61M 21/00**

[52] **U.S. Cl.** **600/28**

[58] **Field of Search** 600/26–28

[56]   **References Cited**

U.S. PATENT DOCUMENTS

4,141,344	2/1979	Barbara	600/28
4,227,516	10/1980	Meland et al.	600/28
4,335,710	6/1982	Williamson	600/28
5,123,899	6/1992	Gall .	

FOREIGN PATENT DOCUMENTS

2569348	2/1986	France .	

4003476	8/1991	Germany	600/28
61-56653	3/1986	Japan .	
61-131757	6/1986	Japan .	
61-159970	7/1986	Japan .	
2124491	2/1984	United Kingdom	600/28

OTHER PUBLICATIONS

Agu, M. et al., "1/f fluctuation with pleasant human sensation and its application to household appliances." (abstract) Journal of the Institute of Elecetrical Engineers of Japan, vol. 113, No. 1 (Jan. 1993).

Inouye, Tsuyoshi et al. "EEG Characteristics of Frontal Midline Theta Activity." The EEG of Mental Activities pp. 136–148 (1988).

Primary Examiner—John P. Lacyk
Attorney, Agent, or Firm—Browdy and Neimark

[57]   **ABSTRACT**

An audible sound of modulated wave where a very low-frequency wave of about 20 hertz or lower is superposed on an audio low-frequency wave effectively stimulates Fm theta in human brain waves to improve attention and concentration during mental tasks when auditorily administered. The audible sound is also effective in stimulation of human alpha wave when the very low-frequency wave lies within the range of about 2–10 hertz. Such audible sound is artificially obtainable by generating an electric signal which contains such a modulated wave, and transducing it into audible sound wave.

20 Claims, 8 Drawing Sheets

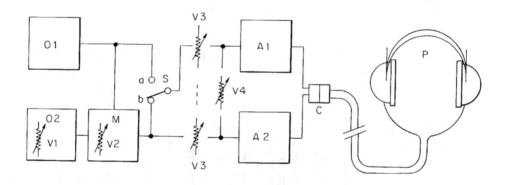

United States Patent [19]

Bowman et al.

[11] Patent Number: 6,135,944

[45] Date of Patent: Oct. 24, 2000

[54] METHOD OF INDUCING HARMONIOUS STATES OF BEING

[75] Inventors: **Gerard D. Bowman**, West Boylston; **Edward M. Karam**, Springfield; **Steven C. Benson**, Watertown, all of Mass.

[73] Assignee: **Zebedee Research, Inc.**, West Boylston, Mass.

[21] Appl. No.: **09/187,591**

[22] Filed: **Nov. 6, 1998**

Related U.S. Application Data

[60] Provisional application No. 60/065,851, Nov. 14, 1997.

[51] Int. Cl.^{7} **A61M 21/00**
[52] U.S. Cl. **600/27**; 600/28
[58] Field of Search 600/27, 28, 26

[56] **References Cited**

U.S. PATENT DOCUMENTS

4,834,701 5/1989 Masaki 600/28

4,883,067	11/1989	Knispel et al.	600/28
5,036,858	8/1991	Carter et al.	600/27
5,135,468	8/1992	Meissner	600/28
5,213,562	5/1993	Monroe	600/28
5,289,438	2/1994	Gall	600/28
5,356,368	10/1994	Monroe	600/28

OTHER PUBLICATIONS

"Chaos—Making A New Science", 1987 by James Gleick p. 293.

Primary Examiner—Max Hindenburg
Assistant Examiner—Brian Szmal

[57] **ABSTRACT**

A method of inducing harmonious states of being using vibrational stimuli, preferably sound, comprised of a multitude of frequencies expressing a specific pattern of relationship. Two base signals are modulated by a set of ratios to generate a plurality of harmonics. The harmonics are combined to form a "fractal" arrangement.

15 Claims, 6 Drawing Sheets

[Carrier]
Base
Frequency 1

$$10 \left[FC \right]$$

$$\left[FC1' \right] 20$$

[Carrier]
Base
Frequency 1'

*   *

$$\left[R_1 \quad R_2 \quad R_3 \ldots R_N \right] 30$$

[Modulation]
Multiplication
Array

$$-$$

$$\parallel \qquad \parallel$$

$$\begin{bmatrix} FC1 * R_1 & FC1' * R_1 \\ FC1 * R_2 & FC1' * R_2 \\ FC1 * R_3 & FC1' * R_3 \\ \cdot & \cdot \\ \cdot & \cdot \\ \cdot & \cdot \\ FC1 * R_N & FC1' * R_N \end{bmatrix} 40$$

Harmonic
Fractal
Matrix

(12) **United States Patent**

Hatayama

(10) **Patent No.:** **US 6,219,657 B1**

(45) **Date of Patent:** **Apr. 17, 2001**

---

(54) **DEVICE AND METHOD FOR CREATION OF EMOTIONS**

(75) Inventor: **Akemi Hatayama**, Tokyo (JP)

(73) Assignee: **NEC Corporation**, Tokyo (JP)

(*) Notice: Subject to any disclaimer, the term of this patent is extended or adjusted under 35 U.S.C. 154(b) by 0 days.

(21) Appl. No.: **09/041,658**

(22) Filed: **Mar. 13, 1998**

(30) **Foreign Application Priority Data**

Mar. 13, 1997 (JP) 9-078918

(51) **Int. Cl.^{7}** **G06F 15/18**; G06E 1/00; G06E 3/00

(52) **U.S. Cl.** **706/14**; 706/18; 706/20; 706/26

(58) **Field of Search** 706/14, 18, 26, 706/20

(56) **References Cited**

U.S. PATENT DOCUMENTS

5,497,430	*	3/1996	Sadovnik et al. 382/156
5,724,484	*	3/1998	Kagami et al. 706/50
5,774,591	*	6/1998	Black et al. 382/236

FOREIGN PATENT DOCUMENTS

7-72900	3/1995	(JP) .
7-104778	4/1995	(JP) .
8-339446	12/1996	(JP) .
10-49188	2/1998	(JP) .

OTHER PUBLICATIONS

Avent et al, "Machine Vision Recognition of Facial Affect Using Backpropagation Neural Networks", IEEE Proceedings of the 16th Annual International Conference on New Opportunities for Biomedical Engineers, Engineering in Medicine and Biology Society, Nov. 1994.*

Yamada et al, "Pattern Recognition of Emotion with Neural Network", IEEE International Conference on Industrial Electronics, Control and Instrumentation, Nov. 1995.*

Sato et al, "Emotion Modeling in Speech Production Using Emotion Space", IEEE 5th International Workshop on Robot and Human Communication, Nov. 1996.*

Pramadihanto et al, "Face Recognition from a Single View Based on Flexible Neural Network Matching", IEEE 5th International Workshop on Robot and Human Communication, Nov. 1996.*

Ding et al, "Neural Network Structures for Expression Recognition", Proceeding of IEEE 1993 International Conference on Neural Networks, 1993.*

(List continued on next page.)

Primary Examiner—George B. Davis

(74) *Attorney, Agent, or Firm*—Foley & Lardner

(57) **ABSTRACT**

A device and a method for creation of emotions are provided for an interface of information, such as an artificial agent and a personified agent, intervened between a human being (i.e., user) and an electronic apparatus. For instance, an emotion creating device is configured by a neural network, a behavior determination engine and a feature determination engine. The neural network inputs user information, representing conditions of the user, and apparatus information, representing conditions of the apparatus, so as to produce emotional states. Herein, a present set of emotional states are produced in consideration of a previous set of emotional states. The emotional states represent prescribed emotions such as pleasure, anger, sadness and surprise. The behavior determination engine refers to a behavior determination database using the user information and the emotional states of the neural network so as to determine a behavior of the interface. The feature determination engine refers to a database using the emotional states of the neural network to determine a feature of the interface, which corresponds to a facial feature.

11 Claims, 11 Drawing Sheets

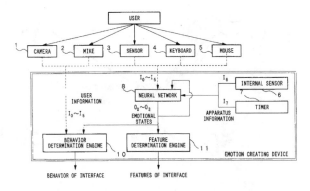

(12) **United States Patent**
    Karell

(10) **Patent No.:** **US 6,430,443 B1**
(45) **Date of Patent:** **Aug. 6, 2002**

(54) **METHOD AND APPARATUS FOR TREATING AUDITORY HALLUCINATIONS**

(76) Inventor: **Manuel L. Karell**

(*) Notice: Subject to any disclaimer, the term of this patent is extended or adjusted under 35 U.S.C. 154(b) by 0 days.

(21) Appl. No.: **09/551,154**

(22) Filed: **Mar. 21, 2000**

Related U.S. Application Data

(63) Continuation-in-part of application No. 08/899,472, filed on Mar. 21, 2000, now abandoned.

(51) Int. Cl.[7] A61N 1/32
(52) U.S. Cl. 607/55; 607/57
(58) Field of Search 607/2, 3, 45, 46, 607/55–58, 72–76

(56) **References Cited**

U.S. PATENT DOCUMENTS

4,702,254 A	10/1987	Zabara
4,867,164 A	9/1989	Zabara
4,988,333 A	1/1991	Engebretson
5,025,807 A	6/1991	Zabara
5,231,988 A	8/1993	Wernicke
5,269,303 A	12/1993	Wernicke
5,299,569 A	4/1994	Wernicke
5,540,734 A	7/1996	Zabara
5,549,658 A	8/1996	Shannon
5,975,085 A	11/1999	Rise

Primary Examiner—Jeffrey R. Jastrzab

(57) **ABSTRACT**

Stimulating one or more vestibulocochlear nerves or cochlea or cochlear regions will treat, prevent and control auditory hallucinations.

23 Claims, 11 Drawing Sheets

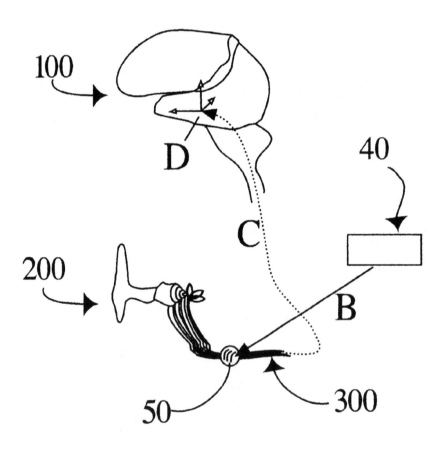

US 6,430,443 B1

1

METHOD AND APPARATUS FOR TREATING AUDITORY HALLUCINATIONS

This is a C.I.P application of application Ser. No. 08/899, 472 filing date Jul. 23, 1997 now abandoned.

FIELD OF THE INVENTION

The present invention generally relates to method and apparatus for treating, controlling or preventing auditory hallucinations by the application of modulating electrical signals to a vestibulocochlear cranial nerve or cochlea or cochlear region and/or by the application of audio signals through an ear.

BACKGROUND OF THE INVENTION

Scientific advances have revealed that schizophrenia is primarily organic and not psychological in nature. Scrambled language, distorted thoughts, and auditory hallucinations are the hallmarks of schizophrenia and have been linked to abnormal physical changes in specific areas of the human brain that begin during pregnancy. Auditory hallucinations are a prominent symptom and present in nearly all schizophrenic patients. Hallucinations are defined as sensory perceptions without environmental stimuli and occur as simple experiences of hearing, tasting, smelling, touching, or seeing what is not physically present; they also occur as mixed or complex experiences of more than one simple experience. When these experiences take the form of "voices" arising internally, the subjective experience is of "hearing" the voice of another, an auditory hallucination.

Theories of the etiology of hallucinations include (1) stimulation and/or (2) inhibition. Examples of stimulation are neurochemical (for example, the neurotransmitter dopamine) changes, electrical discharges, and seizure episodes. An example of inhibition causing an hallucination is when there is destruction of normally inhibitory functions, resulting in disinhibition, as in the phantom limb syndrome. Auditory hallucinations arising from the disordered monitoring of inner speech (thinking in words) may be mixed stimulation and inhibition. Other theories of the etiology of schizophrenia include infection, autoimmune or immune dysfunction, and environmental.

Hallucinations occur in a wide range of human experiences. For example, there are physician prescribed medications known to cause hallucinations; and there are drugs of abuse such as alcohol and LSD that are also known to cause hallucinations. Auditory hallucinations may occur in organic brain disorders such as epilepsy, Parkinson's and Alzheimer's disease. Hallucinations may occur to bilingual schizophrenics; for example, they can be perceived in English even though his/her mother tongue may be Spanish.

Hearing impairment (acute or chronic) combined with stress may lead to pseudo-hallucinations in normal persons. Auditory hallucinations may occur in diseases not involving the brain, such as otosclerosis (where the bones in the ear do not move freely); in this case the auditory hallucinations may be cured with surgery.

The brain activity of schizophrenics who hear imaginary voices has been found to be similar to the brain activity of people that are hearing real voices. Schizophrenia may be the result of dysfunction of neurons utilizing dopamine as a neurotransmitter; the antipsychotic (neuroleptic) drugs block dopamine. Auditory hallucinations found in disorders such as schizophrenia are associated with an abnormal pattern of brain activation, as can be seen with brain imaging, such as positron emission tomography (PET), and by other means, such as encephalographic methods.

2

Auditory hallucinations involve language regions of the cortex in a pattern similar to that seen in normal subjects listening to their own voices but different in that left prefrontal regions are not activated. The striatum plays a critical role in auditory hallucinations. Magnetic resonance imaging (MRI) has shown that the hippocampal-amygdala complex and the parahippocampal gyrus (areas in the temporal lobe) are reduced in schizophrenic patients. Schizophrenics have increased levels of dopamine in the left amygdala. When using functional MRI brain imaging, a patient is positioned within an imaging apparatus; protons within the brain are then made to radiate a signal, which can be picked up with a radio antenna. Active areas of the brain will radiate a different signal than areas of the brain that are at rest; scanning schizophrenics while they are hallucinating is possible.

Magnetic resonance spectroscopy has found that schizophrenic patients have lower levels of several nucleic acids in the brain, including phosphomonoesters and inorganic phosphate and higher levels of phosphodiesters and adenosine triphosphate. Neurotransmitters such as dopamine, serotonin (5-HT), norepinephrine and glutamates are involved. It has been postulated that loss of input to the prefrontal cortex results in lack of feedback to other circuits of the limbic regions which leads to hyperactivity of the dopamine pathways.

Computed tomography (CT) studies have repeatedly shown that the brains of schizophrenic patients have lateral and third ventricular enlargement and some degree of reduction in cortical volume. Other CT studies have reported abnormal cerebral asymmetry, reduced cerebellar volume, and brain density changes.

Changes in the bioelectrical brain activity are recorded in electroencephalography (EEG). The changes for schizophrenic patients are: (1) "choppy activity"—prominent low voltage, with desynchronized fast activity—considered as highly specific for schizophrenia; (2) intermittent occurrence of slow, high amplitude waves; (3) waves most prominent in the frontal region for delta, and in the occipital region for the theta; (4) pattern of increased slow activity; (5) decrease in alpha peak frequencies; (6) increased beta power; (7) increased left frontal delta power; (8) more anterior and superficial equivalent-dipoles in the beta bands. Some EEG changes are best noted during transition from wake to sleep.

In general, there are three changes in the EEG recordings: (i) spontaneous EEG, (ii) Event-Related Potentials and (iii) event-related EEG changes known as Event-Related Desynchronization and Event-Related Synchronization. Both real and imagined movement and both real and imagined voices may cause changes in these three types of EEG recording.

Hallucinations effect evoked potentials and alpha frequency which are noted when using quantitative EEG (qEEG).

Normal brain structures related to language tend to be larger on the left side; however, schizophrenic patients have the asymmetry reversed. Persons who have epilepsy of the left temporal lobe of the brain exhibit symptoms resembling schizophrenia. The brain activity of schizophrenics who hear imaginary voices has been found to be similar to the brain activity of people that are hearing real voices; however, the initiation of this brain activity arises from within rather than from external sources.

The planum temporale is associated with comprehending language, and if one stimulates this area electrically, a person hears complex sounds similar to a schizophrenic's auditory hallucinations.

(12) **United States Patent**
Katz

(10) **Patent No.:** **US 6,488,617 B1**
(45) **Date of Patent:** **Dec. 3, 2002**

(54) **METHOD AND DEVICE FOR PRODUCING A DESIRED BRAIN STATE**

(75) Inventor: **Bruce F. Katz**, Haverford, PA (US)

(73) Assignee: **Universal Hedonics**, Haverford, PA (US)

(*) Notice: Subject to any disclaimer, the term of this patent is extended or adjusted under 35 U.S.C. 154(b) by 6 days.

(21) Appl. No.: **09/687,599**

(22) Filed: **Oct. 13, 2000**

(51) Int. Cl.[7] **A61M 21/00**; A61B 5/04
(52) U.S. Cl. **600/26**; 600/544
(58) Field of Search 600/9–15, 300, 600/544, 545, 26–27, 409; 128/897; 607/45

(56) **References Cited**

U.S. PATENT DOCUMENTS

3,882,850 A		5/1975	Bailin et al.
4,227,516 A		10/1980	Meland et al.
4,700,135 A		10/1987	Hoenig
4,736,751 A	*	4/1988	Gevins et al. 600/545
4,940,453 A		7/1990	Cadwell
5,036,858 A		8/1991	Carter et al.
5,092,835 A	*	3/1992	Schurig et al. 600/9
5,215,086 A		6/1993	Terry, Jr. et al.
5,280,793 A		1/1994	Rosenfeld
5,309,923 A	*	5/1994	Leuchter et al. 600/544
5,356,368 A		10/1994	Monroe
5,495,853 A		3/1996	Yasushi
5,732,702 A		3/1998	Mueller
5,743,854 A	*	4/1998	Dobson et al. 600/409
5,769,778 A		6/1998	Abrams et al.
5,813,993 A	*	9/1998	Kaplan et al. 600/544
5,954,629 A		9/1999	Yanagidaira et al.
6,266,556 B1		7/2001	Ives et al.
6,304,775 B1	*	10/2001	Iasemidis et al. 600/544

OTHER PUBLICATIONS

John R. Hughes, et al; "Conventional and Quantitative Electroencephalography in Psychiatry"; *The Journal of Neuropsychiatry and Clinical Neuroscience,* 1999; 11:2 190–208.
Daniel L. Menkes et al., "Right frontal lobe slow frequency repetitive transcranial magnetic stimulation (SF r–TMS) is an effective treatment for depression: a case–control pilot study of safety and efficacy;" *J. Neurol Neurosurgery Psychiatry* 1999; 67:113–115.
Andreas Killen; "Magnetic headbangers"; www.salon.com, Oct. 3, 2000.

* cited by examiner

Primary Examiner—Kevin Shaver
Assistant Examiner—Nikita R Veniaminov
(74) *Attorney, Agent, or Firm*—Wolf, Block, Schorr and Solis-Cohen LLP; Robert F. Zielinski; Eric A. Dichter

(57) **ABSTRACT**

A method and device for the production of a desired brain state in an individual contain means for monitoring and analyzing the brain state while a set of one or more magnets produce fields that alter this state. A computational system alters various parameters of the magnetic fields in order to close the gap between the actual and desired brain state. This feedback process operates continuously until the gap is minimized and/or removed.

30 Claims, 2 Drawing Sheets

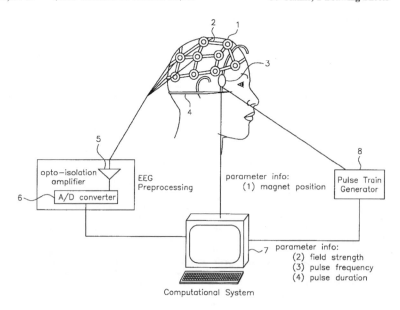

(12) **United States Patent**   (10) **Patent No.:**   **US 8,636,640 B2**

Chang   (45) **Date of Patent:**   **Jan. 28, 2014**

(54) **METHOD AND SYSTEM FOR BRAIN ENTERTAINMENT**

(75) Inventor: **Daniel Wonchul Chang**, Arcadia, CA (US)

(73) Assignee: **Brain Symphony LLC**, Los Angeles, CA (US)

(*) Notice: Subject to any disclaimer, the term of this patent is extended or adjusted under 35 U.S.C. 154(b) by 1155 days.

(21) Appl. No.: **12/386,006**

(22) Filed: **Apr. 11, 2009**

(65) **Prior Publication Data**

US 2010/0056854 A1   Mar. 4, 2010

Related U.S. Application Data

(60) Provisional application No. 61/123,832, filed on Apr. 11, 2008, provisional application No. 61/188,421, filed on Aug. 8, 2008.

(51) **Int. Cl.**
A61M 21/00   (2006.01)
(52) **U.S. Cl.**
USPC **600/28**
(58) **Field of Classification Search**
USPC 600/26–28; 128/897–899
See application file for complete search history.

(56) **References Cited**

U.S. PATENT DOCUMENTS

2,304,095 A	*	12/1942	Hull	600/28
3,712,292 A	*	1/1973	Zentmeyer, Jr.	600/28
5,213,562 A	*	5/1993	Monroe	600/28
6,017,302 A	*	1/2000	Loos	600/28
6,687,193 B2	*	2/2004	Jung	369/4
2005/0049452 A1	*	3/2005	Lawlis et al.	600/28
2007/0084473 A1	*	4/2007	Hewett	128/898
2008/0101621 A1	*	5/2008	Zimmerman	381/61

OTHER PUBLICATIONS

Transparentcorp.com website dated Dec. 30, 2006, accessed on archive.org, describing Brain Sound Studio.
Pages from Brain Sound Studio product reflecting sample transforms; the Brain Sound Studio product containing these pages was on-sale in 2006.

* cited by examiner

Primary Examiner — Charles A Marmor, II
Assistant Examiner — Shannon McBride
(74) *Attorney, Agent, or Firm* — Steven E. Shapiro

(57) **ABSTRACT**

The present invention is a method of modifying music files to induce a desired state of consciousness. First and second modulations are introduced into a music file such that, when the music file is played, both of the modulations occur simultaneously. Additional modulations can be introduced, as well as sound tones at window frequencies.

16 Claims, 4 Drawing Sheets

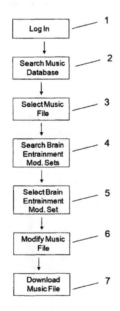

(12) **United States Patent**

Dawson

(10) Patent No.: **US 6,729,337 B2**

(45) **Date of Patent:** **May 4, 2004**

(54) **METHOD AND SYSTEM FOR GENERATING SENSORY DATA ONTO THE HUMAN NEURAL CORTEX**

(75) Inventor: **Thomas P. Dawson**, Escondido, CA (US)

(73) Assignees: **Sony Corporation**, Tokyo (JP); **Sony Electronics Inc.**, Park Ridge, NJ (US)

(*) Notice: Subject to any disclaimer, the term of this patent is extended or adjusted under 35 U.S.C. 154(b) by 0 days.

(21) Appl. No.: **10/353,225**

(22) Filed: **Jan. 28, 2003**

(65) **Prior Publication Data**

US 2003/0145864 A1 Aug. 7, 2003

Related U.S. Application Data

(62) Division of application No. 09/690,571, filed on Oct. 17, 2000, now Pat. No. 6,536,440.

(51) Int. Cl.^{7} **A61B 19/00**
(52) U.S. Cl. **128/898**
(58) Field of Search 128/897, 898, 128/24; 607/54

(56) **References Cited**

U.S. PATENT DOCUMENTS

3,848,608 A	11/1974	Leonard
4,343,301 A	8/1982	Indech
4,611,596 A	9/1986	Wasserman
4,628,933 A	12/1986	Michelson
4,664,117 A	5/1987	Beck
4,883,067 A	11/1989	Knispel et al.
4,979,508 A	12/1990	Beck
5,031,154 A	7/1991	Watanabe
5,097,326 A	3/1992	Meijer
5,109,844 A	5/1992	de Juan, Jr. et al.

5,159,927 A	11/1992	Schmid	
5,179,455 A	1/1993	Garlick	
5,651,365 A	7/1997	Hanafy et al.	
5,738,625 A	4/1998	Gluck	
5,853,370 A	12/1998	Chance et al.	
5,935,155 A	8/1999	Humayun et al.	
5,956,292 A	9/1999	Bernstein	
5,971,925 A	10/1999	Hossack et al.	
6,017,302 A	1/2000	Loos	
6,400,989 B1 *	6/2002	Eckmiller	607/54
6,536,440 B1 *	3/2003	Dawson	128/897
6,584,357 B1 *	6/2003	Dawson	607/54

OTHER PUBLICATIONS

Department pf Molecular and Cell Biology, Division of Neurobiology, University of California. Garrett B. Stanley, Fei F. Li, and Yang Dan. "Reconstruction of Natural Scenes from Ensemble Responses in the Lateral Geniculate Nucleus" The Journal of Neuroscience, pp. 8036–8042; 1999.

Ultrasonics Fundamentals, Technology, Applications. Dale Ensminger, Columbus, Ohio. (pp. 373–376).

(List continued on next page.)

Primary Examiner—Samuel G. Gilbert

(57) **ABSTRACT**

A non-invasive system and process for projecting sensory data onto the human neural cortex is provided. The system includes a primary transducer array and a secondary transducer array. The primary transducer array acts as a coherent signal source, and the secondary transducer array acts as a controllable diffraction pattern that focuses energy onto the neural cortex in a desired pattern. In addition, the pattern of energy is constructed such that each portion projected into the neural cortex may be individually pulsed at low frequency. This low frequency pulsing is formed by controlling the phase differences between the emitted energy of the elements of primary and secondary transducer arrays.

8 Claims, 3 Drawing Sheets

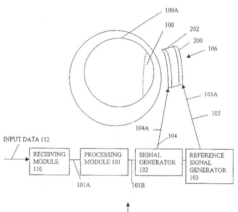

US 6,729,337 B2

1

METHOD AND SYSTEM FOR GENERATING SENSORY DATA ONTO THE HUMAN NEURAL CORTEX

CROSS REFERENCE TO RELATED APPLICATION

This application is a division of U.S. patent application Ser. No. 09/690,571 entitled "Method And System For Generating Sensory Data Onto The Human Neural Cortex" filed on Oct. 17, 2000 and now U.S. Pat. No. 6,536,440.

FIELD OF THE INVENTION

The present invention relates to non-invasive methods and systems for generating sensory experiences within the human neural cortex.

BACKGROUND OF THE INVENTION

A conventional technique for generating neural activity in the human nervous system requires surgical implants. The implants may comprise wires that cause electronic impulses to interact with some portion of the human nervous system, such as the human neural cortex, and thereby cause neural activity in the human neural cortex. Researchers have successfully mapped audio sensory data to the cochlear channel, and visual data to the visual cortex.

Conventional invasive techniques have several drawbacks. First, surgical implants may cause patient trauma and medical complications during and/or after surgery. Second, additional or on-going surgery may be required, particularly if new technology is developed.

SUMMARY OF THE INVENTION

The present invention solves the foregoing drawbacks by providing a non-invasive system and process for generating/projecting sensory data (visual, audio, taste, smell or touch) within/onto the human neural cortex.

One embodiment of the system comprises a primary transducer array and a secondary transducer array. The primary transducer array acts as a coherent or nearly-coherent signal source. The secondary transducer array acts as a controllable, acoustical diffraction pattern that shapes, focuses and modulates energy from the primary transducer onto the neural cortex in a desired pattern. The secondary transducer emits acoustical energy that may be shifted in phase and amplitude relative to the primary array emissions.

The pattern of energy is constructed such that each portion of the pattern projected into the neural cortex may be individually pulsed at low frequency. The system produces low frequency pulsing by controlling the phase differences between the emitted energy of the primary and secondary transducer array elements. The pulsed ultrasonic signal alters the neural firing timing in the cortex. Changes in the neural firing timing induce various sensory experiences depending on the location of the firing timing change in the cortex. The mapping of sensory areas of the cortex is known and used in current surgically invasive techniques. Thus, the system induces recognizable sensory experiences by applying ultrasonic energy pulsed at low frequency in one or more selected patterns on one or more selected locations of the cortex.

One of the advantages of the present system is that no invasive surgery is needed to assist a person, such as a blind person, to view live and/or recorded images or hear sounds.

This brief summary has been provided so that the nature of the invention may be understood quickly. A more complete understanding of the invention can be obtained by reference to the following detailed description of the preferred embodiments thereof in connection with the attached drawings.

2

BRIEF DESCRIPTION OF THE DRAWINGS

FIG. 1 illustrates one embodiment of a system in accordance with the present invention.

FIG. 2 illustrates one embodiment of a transducer system within the system of FIG. 1.

FIG. 3 illustrates one embodiment of a process in accordance with the present invention.

Use of the same reference symbols in different figures indicates similar or identical items.

DETAILED DESCRIPTION

FIG. 1 illustrates one embodiment of a system 120 in accordance with the present invention. FIG. 1 shows a visual portion 100 of the human cortex located in a person's brain 100A, such as for example, a vision-impaired person's brain. The system 120 of FIG. 1 is used with the visual cortex 100 merely as an example and is not intended to limit the scope of the invention. Instead of or in addition to the visual cortex 100, the system 120 may be used to stimulate neural activity in other areas of the nervous system. For example, the system 120 may be used as is or modified to generate audio, taste, smell or touch sensations within the brain 100A.

In FIG. 1, the system 120 comprises a receiving module 110, a processing module 101, a signal generator 102, a reference signal generator 103, a transducer system 106, a first signal line 104 and a second signal line 105. The receiving module 110, processing module 101, signal generator 102, and reference signal generator 103, may be referred to as, alone or in combination, a sensory data processing system. Various configurations of the system 120 may be configured in accordance with the present invention. The system 120 may comprise other modules and components in addition to or instead of the modules and components shown in FIG. 1.

In general, the system 120 receives, analyzes and transfers the sensory data 112 to the human brain 100A. The receiving module 110 receives sensory input data 112. Such data 112 may comprise live video data captured by a video camera (not shown) which a vision-impaired person may not be able to see. The sensory data 112 may be live or recorded. The data 112 may be generated by other sources, such as for example a VCR, a DVD player, a cable broadcast, a satellite broadcast, an Internet connection, etc.

The processing module 101 receives input data 101A from the receiving module 110 and formats or converts the data 101A. For example, analog input data from the receiving module 110 may be digitized and/or converted into a neural firing time difference pattern. In one embodiment, the system 120 uses a technique that is reversed from a technique disclosed in "Reconstruction of Natural Scenes from Ensemble Responses in the Lateral Geniculate Nucleus" by Garrett B. Stanley et al. in the Sep. 15, 1999 issue of the Journal of Neuroscience, which is hereby incorporated by reference in its entirety.

Processed data 101B is transferred to the signal generator 102. Based upon the data 101B, the signal generator 102 generates a first signal 104A on the first line 104. The reference signal generator 103 generates a reference signal 105A on the second line 105. Both signals 104A and 105A are transferred to a transducer system 106.

(12) **United States Patent**

Becker

(10) **Patent No.:** **US 7,988,613 B2**

(45) **Date of Patent:** **Aug. 2, 2011**

(54) **METHOD AND APPARATUS FOR THE TREATMENT OF PHYSICAL AND MENTAL DISORDERS WITH LOW FREQUENCY, LOW FLUX DENSITY MAGNETIC FIELDS**

(76) Inventor: **Paul F. Becker**, Stuart, FL (US)

(*) Notice: Subject to any disclaimer, the term of this patent is extended or adjusted under 35 U.S.C. 154(b) by 0 days.

(21) Appl. No.: **12/760,391**

(22) Filed: **Apr. 14, 2010**

(65) **Prior Publication Data**

US 2010/0298624 A1   Nov. 25, 2010

Related U.S. Application Data

(60) Division of application No. 11/095,612, filed on Apr. 1, 2005, now Pat. No. 7,819,794, which is a continuation-in-part of application No. 10/927,840, filed on Aug. 27, 2004, now Pat. No. 7,276,020, which is a continuation-in-part of application No. 10/278,109, filed on Oct. 21, 2002, now Pat. No. 6,899,667.

(51) **Int. Cl.**
 A61N 1/00   (2006.01)
(52) **U.S. Cl.** **600/14**; 600/26
(58) **Field of Classification Search** 600/9–15, 600/26–28; 128/897–898; 607/50–51; 336/90, 336/122, 230

See application file for complete search history.

(56) **References Cited**

U.S. PATENT DOCUMENTS

4,266,533 A	5/1981	Ryaby et al.
4,428,366 A	1/1984	Findl et al.
4,548,208 A	10/1985	Niemi
4,550,714 A	11/1985	Talish et al.
4,587,957 A	5/1986	Castel
4,616,629 A	10/1986	Moore
4,674,482 A	6/1987	Waltonen et al.
4,889,526 A	12/1989	Rauscher et al.
4,940,453 A	7/1990	Cadwell
5,014,699 A	5/1991	Pollack et al.
5,030,196 A	7/1991	Inoue
5,063,912 A *	11/1991	Hughes 601/47
5,116,304 A	5/1992	Cadwell
5,192,263 A	3/1993	Kraus
5,195,941 A	3/1993	Erickson et al.

(Continued)

FOREIGN PATENT DOCUMENTS

EP	018053	5/1986

(Continued)

Primary Examiner — John P Lacyk

(74) *Attorney, Agent, or Firm* — Pillsbury Winthrop Shaw Pittman LLP

(57) **ABSTRACT**

A method and apparatus for generating electromagnetic fields for healing. A device preferably includes a microcontroller and associated memory, a wire coil in electrical communication with a driving circuit that is controlled by the microcontroller in accordance with a program stored in the associated memory, wherein the driving circuit is effective to produce a pulsed DC output having a frequency in the range of about 0-45 Hz, more preferably in the range of 0.5-14.1 Hz and most preferably around 9.6 Hz. A user interface is provided for selecting one of a plurality of modes of operation and a port (e.g., a USB port) is provided to allow the program stored in the associated memory to be modified by way of a computer, memory card or the Internet. In another embodiment, the apparatus takes the form of a medallion that can be worn around a user's neck or strategically placed on a user's body or embedded in other user hardware such as a combat or racing helmet.

33 Claims, 9 Drawing Sheets

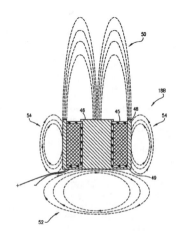

US 7,988,613 B2

1

METHOD AND APPARATUS FOR THE TREATMENT OF PHYSICAL AND MENTAL DISORDERS WITH LOW FREQUENCY, LOW FLUX DENSITY MAGNETIC FIELDS

This application is a divisional application of U.S. patent application Ser. No. 11/095,612, filed Apr. 1, 2005 now U.S. Pat. No. 7,819,794, which is a continuation-in-part of U.S. patent application Ser. No. 10/927,840, filed Aug. 27, 2004 now U.S. Pat. No. 7,276,020, which is a continuation-in-part of U.S. patent application Ser. No. 10/278,109, filed Oct. 21, 2002 now U.S. Pat. No. 6,899,667, the contents of each of which are hereby incorporated by reference herein in their entireties.

BACKGROUND

1. Field of the Invention

This invention relates generally to a method and apparatus for the treatment of physical and mental disorders, and, more particularly, to a portable device capable of being operated safely and effectively by patients which produces a time varying, magnetic field having a low frequency and low flux density effective in the treatment of a wide variety of physical and mental disorders.

2. Background of the Invention

Magnetic fields have long been used for the treatment of physical injuries and chronic pain. Early magnetic therapy involved the use of static magnetic fields produced by permanent magnets incorporated into items such as bracelets, belts, back pads, mattress pads and mattresses. It is believed that static magnetic fields have some efficacy in the treatment of broken bones and soft tissue injuries, and tend to promote the circulation of blood as well as relieve stiffness in muscles. The effectiveness of such treatments in human and veterinary applications has been the subject of debate.

More recent attempts to employ the therapeutic effects of magnetic fields have focused on devices which generate an electromagnetic field, and the methods of treatment employing such devices. Although a variety of designs have been proposed in the prior art, electromagnetic devices generally comprise a power supply coupled to a circuit capable of producing an AC or DC output which is transmitted to an inductor coil. One form of inductor coil consists of a number of wire windings wrapped about a coil body with an open or air center, or, alternatively, a ferrous core wrapped with wire windings. In response to the output from the circuit, an electromagnetic field is generated by the inductor coil which is then directed toward the area(s) of the body of a patient to be treated.

In many instances, the circuit of electromagnetic devices produces a pulsed or time-varying output in the shape of a square wave, sine wave, triangular wave or the like. Such output can be at essentially any selected frequency and voltage. A pulsed output from the circuit results in the production of a time-varying or pulsed magnetic field by the inductor coil. If the circuit emits an AC signal, the position of the north and south poles of the resulting magnetic field from the inductor coil changes with each cycle, whereas a DC output produces an electromagnetic field in which the position of the magnetic poles remains constant.

The application of the general concepts of the formation of electromagnetic fields noted above to the treatment of physical and mental disorders has resulted in a widely varying array of devices and treatment methods. Prior art devices operate at completely different ends of the spectrum in terms of field strength and frequency. The predominant approach

2

appears to follow the adage that "more is better." U.S. Pat. Nos. 6,425,852; 6,132,361; 5,813,970 and 5,769,778, for example, teach electromagnetic devices which produce a magnetic field having a flux density in range of up to 10,000 to 20,000 gauss. Devices of this type are used for therapies such as transcranial magnetic brain stimulation for the treatment of neurological and mental disorders. On the other end of the spectrum, devices have been developed for the treatment of various conditions using a magnetic field having a flux density in the range of 10 nanogauss to 10 milligauss, applied at frequencies in the range of 0 to 1000 Hz. See, for example, U.S. Pat. Nos. 6,099,459 and 5,496,258.

There appears to be no consensus whatsoever as to what flux density levels or frequencies should be employed in electromagnetic therapy. Although proposed as a non-invasive alternative to pharmacological and nutritional solutions, it is believed that electromagnetic therapy conducted at the high flux density and/or high frequency levels noted above may, in fact, be harmful whereas treatment at the lower end of the spectrum as suggested in U.S. Pat. No. 6,099,459 will have little, if any, therapeutic effect without extensive technical expertise. None of these treatment methods are reflective of the magnetic field density levels and frequencies which occur naturally within a patient, or are produced naturally within the ionosphere and by the earth.

Other significant limitations of many prior art therapeutic electromagnetic devices are their lack of portability, their complexity and the need for relatively skilled medical personnel to operate them effectively. For example, U.S. Pat. Nos. 6,280,376; 6,099,459; 6,210,317 and application US 2002/0103411 disclose devices which are not portable and require a skilled technician or physician to operate. In order to receive treatment, patients must undertake the time and expense of traveling to the office where the machine is located during normal business hours. Other devices, while they may be more portable, permit a relatively wide range of adjustment of field strength and/or frequency. Allowing patients and practitioners to control these parameters, even with prior instruction, can lead to ineffective or potentially harmful treatment.

BRIEF SUMMARY OF THE INVENTION

It is therefore among the objectives of this invention to provide a method and apparatus for the treatment of physical and mental disorders with electromagnetic therapy which does not require skilled personnel to administer, which is portable, which operates at naturally occurring magnetic field strengths and frequencies, which limits the extent of operating adjustments permitted on the part of a patient or practitioner and which is capable of treating a wide variety of physical and mental disorders in human or animal subjects.

These objectives are accomplished in the instant method and apparatus comprising a circuit adapted to be coupled to a power supply which produces a pulsed DC output, and a magnetic field generating coil coupled to the output of the circuit which is effective to produce a time varying magnetic field having a flux density in the range of about 0.0001 to 90 gauss, and greater, at only specific frequencies which occur naturally within the patient or are naturally occurring terrestrially in the range of about 0 to 45 Hz, and most preferably to no more than about 20 Hz. The coil is positioned at or near the site on the body of the patient to be treated, or, alternatively, beneath the patient's sleeping surface, for a period ranging from about one-half hour to several hours depending upon the condition or method used for treatment.

An important aspect of this invention is predicated upon the concept that naturally occurring magnetic fields, both in

(19) **United States**

(12) **Patent Application Publication** (10) Pub. No.: **US 2003/0171688 A1**

Yoo et al. (43) Pub. Date: **Sep. 11, 2003**

(54) **MIND CONTROLLER**

(76) Inventors: **Jae Sup Yoo**, Seoul (KR); **Jae Chun Yoo**, Seoul (KR)

(21) Appl. No.: **10/199,346**

(22) Filed: **Jul. 19, 2002**

(30) **Foreign Application Priority Data**

Mar. 6, 2002 (KR) 2002-11846

Publication Classification

(51) Int. Cl.^{7} **A61B 5/04**
(52) U.S. Cl. **600/544**

(57) **ABSTRACT**

A mind controller is disclosed. The mind controller can induce a user's brain waves into an alpha wave state or a theta wave state by sensing and analyzing human brain waves and then transmitting a mind control audio message suitable for the analyzed human brain waves to the user, so that the user can improve mental concentration power or memory for himself/herself. The mind controller for activating brain waves generated from the user's brain, includes: an EEG(Electroencephalogram) sensor for sensing frequency band corresponding to alpha waves and theta waves from the brain waves generated from the user's brain; an MCU(Memory Control Unit) for analyzing whether the brain waves sensed by the EEG sensor are alpha waves or theta waves through a built-in program of a brain wave analysis program pack and controlling output of a message, which corresponds to the alpha waves or the theta waves, out of mind control audio messages of an MP3 pack; an audio decoder for demodulating signal converted into data in the MP3 pack by control signal output from the MCU; a D/A converter for receiving signal provided from the audio decoder and converting the signal into analog audio signal; and audio output means for converting and providing the analog audio signal into sound.

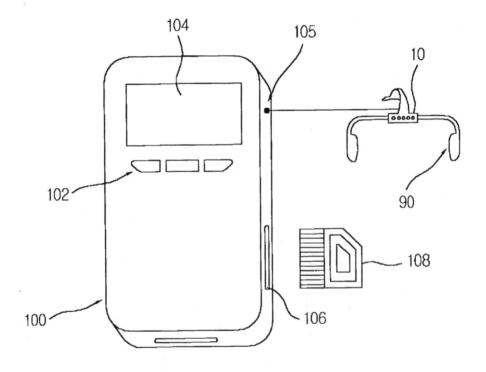

Chapter 12
Mental Monitoring

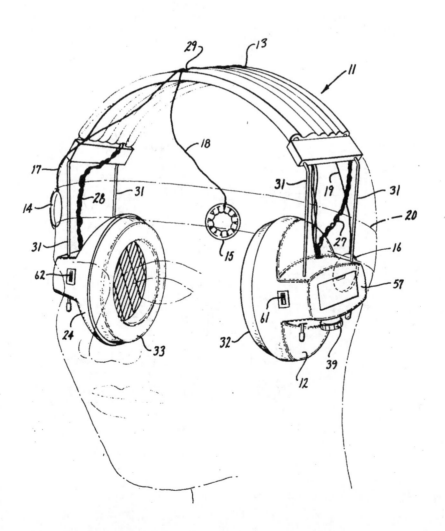

United States Patent [19]

Bakerich et al.

[11] **3,753,433**

[45] **Aug. 21, 1973**

[54] **ELECTROENCEPHALOPHONE AND FEEDBACK SYSTEM**

[75] Inventors: **Frank Bakerich; Robert T. Scully,** both of Mendocino, Calif.

[73] Assignee: **Aquarius Electronics,** Mendocino, Calif.

[22] Filed: **Jan. 18, 1971**

[21] Appl. No.: **107,215**

[52] **U.S. Cl.** .... **128/2.1 B,** 128/1 C
[51] **Int. Cl.** **A61b 5/05**
[58] **Field of Search** .... 128/2.1 A, 2.1 B, 128/2.1 R, 2.06 R, 1 C, 422

[56] **References Cited**
UNITED STATES PATENTS

3,032,029	5/1962	Cunningham	128/2.1 B
3,488,586	1/1970	Watrous et al.	128/2.1 A
3,565,058	2/1971	Mansfield	128/2.06 R
3,195,533	7/1965	Fischer	128/2.1 B
3,495,596	2/1970	Condict	128/1 C

3,413,546	11/1968	Riehl et al.	128/2.1 B

Primary Examiner—William E. Kamm
Attorney—Warren, Rubin, Brucker & Chickering

[57] **ABSTRACT**

An electroencephalophone which is battery operated and completely self-contained in a headset to be worn by the user and having a plurality of scalp electrodes carried on flexible leads permitting placement of the electrodes on the user's head when the headset is mounted thereon and having an electronic circuit and transducer for converting brain wave signals picked up by the electrodes into recognizable audio tones enabling the user to listen to his own brain wave generation. The scalp electrode signals are amplified and chopped by an audible oscillator signal the frequency of which is controlled by the scalp electrode signals. The resulting combined amplitude and frequency modulation of the audible generator tone provides a distinctive sound for brain wave recognition.

19 Claims, 7 Drawing Figures

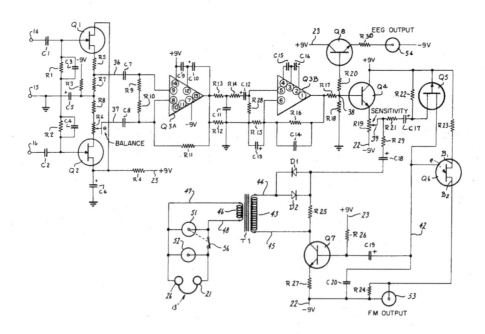

United States Patent [19]

Shiga

[11] **4,354,505**

[45] **Oct. 19, 1982**

[54] **METHOD OF AND APPARATUS FOR TESTING AND INDICATING RELAXATION STATE OF A HUMAN SUBJECT**

[75] Inventor: **Kazumasa Shiga**, Kawasaki, Japan

[73] Assignee: **Matsushita Electric Industrial Company, Limited**, Osaka, Japan

[21] Appl. No.: **183,750**

[22] Filed: **Sep. 3, 1980**

[30] **Foreign Application Priority Data**

Sep. 4, 1979 [JP] Japan 54-113744

[51] Int. Cl.³ A61B 5/04
[52] U.S. Cl. 128/732; 128/905
[58] Field of Search 128/731, 732, 733, 905

[56] **References Cited**

U.S. PATENT DOCUMENTS

3,837,331	9/1974	Ross	128/905 X
3,967,616	7/1976	Ross	128/905 X
3,978,847	9/1976	Fehmi et al.	128/732
4,031,883	6/1977	Fehmi et al.	128/732

OTHER PUBLICATIONS

Winson, J., "A Simple Sleep Stage Detector for the Rat", Electroencephalograph and Clin. Neureophys., vol. 41, No. 2, pp. 179–182, Aug. 1976.
Sciarretta et al., Med. & Biol. Engng., vol. 8, No. 5, pp. 517–519.
Cohen et al., Med. & Biol. Eng. & Comput., vol. 15, Jul. 1977, pp. 431–437.

Primary Examiner—Kyle L. Howell
Assistant Examiner—John C. Hanley
Attorney, Agent, or Firm—Lowe, King, Price & Becker

[57] **ABSTRACT**

In a self-training biofeedback system, a physiological signal representing the state of relaxation of a person using the system is applied to a time counter to generate a binary count output representing the relaxation period. A visual indicator connected to the time counter provides the self trained person with a quick display of the measured time period so he can gauge the depth of his relaxation.

20 Claims, 6 Drawing Figures

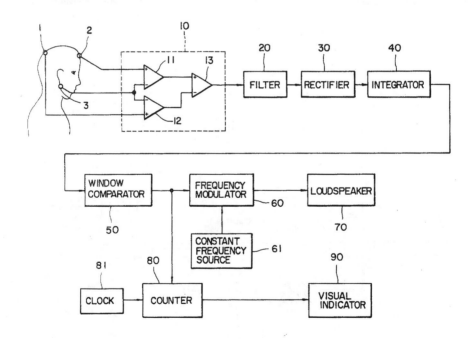

United States Patent [19]

Malech

[11] **3,951,134**

[45] **Apr. 20, 1976**

[54] **APPARATUS AND METHOD FOR REMOTELY MONITORING AND ALTERING BRAIN WAVES**

[75] Inventor: **Robert G. Malech**, Plainview, N.Y.

[73] Assignee: **Dorne & Margolin Inc.**, Bohemia, N.Y.

[22] Filed: **Aug. 5, 1974**

[21] Appl. No.: **494,518**

[52] U.S. Cl. .... **128/2.1 B**
[51] Int. Cl.² **A61B 5/04**
[58] Field of Search .... 128/1 C, 1 R, 2.1 B, 128/2.1 R, 419 R, 422 R, 420, 404, 2 R, 2 S, 2.05 R, 2.05 V, 2.05 F, 2.06 R; 340/248 A, 258 A, 258 B, 258 D, 229

[56] **References Cited**

UNITED STATES PATENTS

2,860,627	11/1958	Harden et al.	128/2.1 B
3,096,768	7/1963	Griffith, Jr.	128/420
3,233,450	2/1966	Fry	128/2.1 R
3,483,860	12/1969	Namerow	128/2.05 F
3,495,596	2/1970	Condict	128/1 C
3,555,529	1/1971	Brown et al.	128/2.1 R
3,773,049	11/1973	Rabichev et al.	128/1 C
3,796,208	3/1974	Bloice	128/2 S

Primary Examiner—William E. Kamm
Attorney, Agent, or Firm—Darby & Darby

[57] **ABSTRACT**

Apparatus for and method of sensing brain waves at a position remote from a subject whereby electromagnetic signals of different frequencies are simultaneously transmitted to the brain of the subject in which the signals interfere with one another to yield a waveform which is modulated by the subject's brain waves. The interference waveform which is representative of the brain wave activity is re-transmitted by the brain to a receiver where it is demodulated and amplified. The demodulated waveform is then displayed for visual viewing and routed to a computer for further processing and analysis. The demodulated waveform also can be used to produce a compensating signal which is transmitted back to the brain to effect a desired change in electrical activity therein.

11 Claims, 2 Drawing Figures

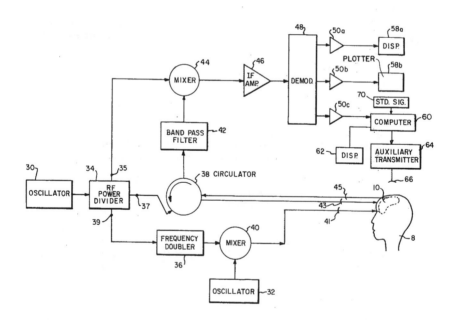

3,951,134

1

2

APPARATUS AND METHOD FOR REMOTELY MONITORING AND ALTERING BRAIN WAVES

BACKGROUND OF THE INVENTION

Medical science has found brain waves to be a useful barometer of organic functions. Measurements of electrical activity in the brain have been instrumental in detecting physical and psychic disorder, measuring stress, determining sleep patterns, and monitoring body metabolism.

The present art for measurement of brain waves employs electroencephalographs including probes with sensors which are attached to the skull of the subject under study at points proximate to the regions of the brain being monitored. Electrical contact between the sensors and apparatus employed to process the detected brain waves is maintained by a plurality of wires extending from the sensors to the apparatus. The necessity for physically attaching the measuring apparatus to the subject imposes several limitations on the measurement process. The subject may experience discomfort, particulary if the measurements are to be made over extended periods of time. His bodily movements are restricted and he is generally confined to the immediate vicinity of the measuring apparatus. Furthermore, measurements cannot be made while the subject is conscious without his awareness. The comprehensiveness of the measurements is also limited since the finite number of probes employed to monitor local regions of brain wave activity do not permit observation of the total brain wave profile in a single test.

SUMMARY OF THE INVENTION

The present invention relates to apparatus and a method for monitoring brain waves wherein all components of the apparatus employed are remote from the test subject. More specifically, high frequency transmitters are operated to radiate electromagnetic energy of different frequencies through antennas which are capable of scanning the entire brain of the test subject or any desired region thereof. The signals of different frequencies penetrate the skull of the subject and impinge upon the brain where they mix to yield an interference wave modulated by radiations from the brain's natural electrical activity. The modulated interference wave is re-transmitted by the brain and received by an antenna at a remote station where it is demodulated, and processed to provide a profile of the suject's brain waves. In addition to passively monitoring his brain waves, the subject's neurological processes may be affected by transmitting to his brain, through a transmitter, compensating signals. The latter signals can be derived from the received and processed brain waves.

OBJECTS OF THE INVENTION

It is therefore an object of the invention to remotely monitor electrical activity in the entire brain or selected local regions thereof with a single measurement.

Another object is the monitoring of a subject's brain wave activity through transmission and recception of electromagnetic waves.

Still another object is to monitor brain wave activity from a position remote from the subject.

A further object is to provide a method and apparatus for affecting brain wave activity by transmitting electromagnetic signals thereto.

DESCRIPTION OF THE DRAWINGS

Other and further objects of the invention will appear from the following description and the accompanying drawings, which form part of the instant specification and which are to be read in conjunction therewith, and in which like reference numerals are used to indicate like parts in the various views;

FIG. 1 is a block diagram showing the interconnection of the components of the apparatus of the invention;

FIG. 2 is a block diagram showing signal flow in one embodiment of the apparatus.

DESCRIPTION OF THE PREFERRED EMBODIMENT

Referring to the drawings, specifically FIG. 1, a high frequency transmitter 2 produces and supplies two electromagnetic wave signals through suitable coupling means 14 to an antenna 4. The signals are directed by the antenna 4 to the skull 6 of the subject 8 being examined. The two signals from the antenna 4, which travel independently, penetrate the skull 6 and impinge upon the tissue of the brain 10.

Within the tissue of the brain 10, the signals combine, much in the manner of a conventional mixing process technique, with each section of the brain having a different modulating action. The resulting waveform of the two signals has its greatest amplitude when the two signals are in phase and thus reinforcing one another. When the signals are exactly 180° out of phase the combination produces a resultant waveform of minimum amplitude. If the amplitudes of the two signals transmitted to the subject are maintained at identical levels, the resultant interference waveform, absent influences of external radiation, may be expected to assume zero intensity when maximum interference occurs, the number of such points being equal to the difference in frequencies of the incident signals. However, interference by radiation from electrical activity within the brain 10 causes the waveform resulting from interference of the two transmitted signals to vary from the expected result, i.e., the interference waveform is modulated by the brain waves. It is believed that this is due to the fact that brain waves produce electric charges each of which has a component of electromagnetic radiation associated with it. The electromagnetic radiation produced by the brain waves in turn reacts with the signals transmitted to the brain from the external source.

The modulated interference waveform is re-transmitted from the brain 10, back through the skull 6. A quantity of energy is re-transmitted sufficient to enable it to be picked up by the antenna 4. This can be controlled, within limits, by adjusting the absolute and relative intensities of the signals, originally transmitted to the brain. Of course, the level of the transmitted energy should be kept below that which may be harmful to the subject.

The antenna passes the received signal to a receiver 12 through the antenna electronics 14. Within the receiver the wave is amplified by conventional RF amplifiers 16 and demodulated by conventional detector and modulator electronics 18. The demodulated wave, representing the intra-brain electrical activity, is amplified by amplifiers 20 and the resulting information in electronic form is stored in buffer circuitry 22. From the buffers 22 the information is fed to a suitable visual

United States Patent [19]

Sharpe et al.

[11] **Patent Number:** **4,958,638**

[45] **Date of Patent:** **Sep. 25, 1990**

[54] **NON-CONTACT VITAL SIGNS MONITOR**

[75] Inventors: **Steven M. Sharpe**, Atlanta; **Joseph Seals**, Stone Mountain; **Anita H. MacDonald**, Tucker; **Scott R. Crowgey**, Avondale Estates, all of Ga.

[73] Assignee: **Georgia Tech Research Corporation**, Atlanta, Ga.

[21] Appl. No.: **213,783**

[22] Filed: **Jun. 30, 1988**

[51] Int. Cl.^{5} **A61B 5/02; A61B 5/08**
[52] U.S. Cl. .... **128/653 R; 128/671; 128/721**
[58] Field of Search 128/653, 716, 721, 670, 128/671, 782

[56] **References Cited**

U.S. PATENT DOCUMENTS

3,483,860	12/1969	Namerow	128/653 R
3,951,134	4/1976	Malech	128/653 R
4,085,740	4/1978	Allen, Jr.	128/653 R
4,488,559	12/1984	Iskander	128/653 R
4,638,808	1/1987	Mawhinney	128/653 R

Primary Examiner—Kyle L. Howell
Assistant Examiner—K. M. Pfaffle
Attorney, Agent, or Firm—Hurt, Richardson, Garner, Todd & Cadenhead

[57] **ABSTRACT**

An apparatus for measuring simultaneous physiological parameters such as heart rate and respiration without physically connecting electrodes or other sensors to the body. A beam of frequency modulated continuous wave radio frequency energy is directed towards the body of a subject. The reflected signal contains phase information representing the movement of the surface of the body, from which respiration and heartbeat information can be obtained. The reflected phase modulated energy is received and demodulated by the apparatus using synchronous quadrature detection. The quadrature signals so obtained are then signal processed to obtain the heartbeat and respiratory information of interest.

21 Claims, 6 Drawing Sheets

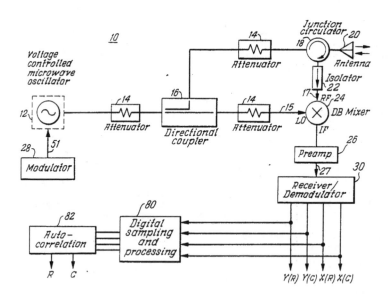

4,958,638

1

NON-CONTACT VITAL SIGNS MONITOR

GOVERNMENT INTEREST

This invention was made with Government support under contract No. N 00014-82C-0930 awarded by the Department of the Navy and under Contract No. F 33615-83D-0601 awarded by the Department of the Air Force. The Government has certain rights in the invention.

BACKGROUND OF THE INVENTION

This invention relates in general to the use of radar techniques to detect minute body movements which are associated with cardiac and respiratory activity. The invention is based on the principle that breathing and heartbeat produce measurable phase changes in electromagnetic waves as they reflect off of a living person. The invention offers significant advantages over other similar and earlier approaches, including greater sensitivity, lower radiated power, improved reliability and lower cost.

Functionally, the non-invasive, electromagnetically-based Vital Signs Monitor (VSM) is an extremely sensitive motion detection system capable of detecting small body motions produced by respiratory and cardiac functioning. Motion detection is achieved by transmitting an interrogating electromagnetic field at the target of interest, and then measuring the time-delay of the return signal reflected back from the surface of the target. When the target surface is moving, as does the surface of the chest in conjunction with respiratory and cardiac activities, corresponding variations will be observed in the measured time delay. The observed variations can be used to determine motion-related target parameters such as displacement and velocity.

In the medical field, it is essential that a subject's respiration and heartbeat be capable of being measured. The medical profession is accustomed to voltage-derived electrocardiogram waveforms for monitoring heartbeat. Most respiration monitors also require physical connection to the subject's body. Many commercially-available devices are available for measuring heart and respiration rates, but most of them are electrode-based requiring physical contact with the subject. Devices requiring physical contact, however, are difficult to use on children susceptible to sudden infant death syndrome (SIDS) or burn patients who cannot tolerate the touch of electrodes. Many infants wear sensors while they sleep that trigger an alarm if their breathing stops, but electrodes attached to the child can be jarred loose as the infant tosses and turns.

The invention has similarities with motion-detection systems based on ultrasonic or optical techniques. However, an electromagnetically-based approach offers several advantages for monitoring of vital signs-related motions. For example, with proper antenna design, an interrogating electromagnetic field will suffer minimal attenuation while propagating in air (unlike ultrasonic signals which propagate poorly in air). Thus, the electromagnetically-based Vital Signs Monitor can easily be used in a completely non-contacting mode and can, in fact, be placed an appreciable distance from the test subject if required. Electromagnetic signals in the microwave band are also capable of penetrating through heavy clothing. This offers advantages over optical techniques which would have a difficult time of detecting motion through even thin clothing. Another feature

2

of an electromagnetically-based approach is that the system could be designed to simultaneously interrogate the entire chest surface and provide information pertaining to any respiratory or cardiac function manifested as chest wall motions. Conversely, by modifying the antenna design, a localized region of the chest surface could be interrogated to obtain information about some specific aspect of respiratory or cardiac function. Such versatility would be difficult to achieve with other motion detection techniques.

In the prior art the patent to Allen, U.S. Pat. No. 4,085,740 discloses a method for measuring physiological parameters such as pulse rate and respiration without electrodes or other sensors being connected to the body. A beam of electromagnetic energy is directed at the region of interest which undergoes physical displacement representing variations in the parameter to be measured. The phase of the reflected energy when compared with the transmitted energy indicates the amount of actual physical movement of the body region concerned. The method does disclose simultaneous detection and processing of respiration and heart beat; however, frequency modulation is not used, therefore and the subject must be reasonably still. The receiver includes two channels and in one of them the received signal is mixed with a signal substantially in quadrature with the transmitted signal to maximize amplitude output in those cases in which the received signal is 180° out of phase with the transmitted signal.

The patent to Kaplan, et al., U.S. Pat. No. 3,993,995 discloses an apparatus for monitoring the respiration of a patient without making physical contact. A portion of the patient's body is illuminated by a transmitted probe signal with the reflected echo signal detected by a monitor. The phase difference between the transmitted and reflected signals is determined in a quadrature mixer which generates outputs indicative of the sine and cosine of the difference signal. These two outputs are coupled to differentiators and when both time derivatives are substantially zero an x-ray unit is triggered since it represents an instant of respiration extrema (apnea). The outputs of the quadrature mixer are also coupled to a direction of motion detector which indicates inhalation or exhalation.

The patent to Kearns, U.S. Pat. No. 4,289,142 discloses a respiration monitor and x-ray triggering apparatus in which a carrier signal is injected into the patient's thorax which is indicative of the transthoracic impedance of the patient. This impedance changes as a function of the respiration cycle. The carrier signal is injected through electrodes coupled to the patient's thorax. The transthoracic impedance has an alternating current component having a respiratory component between 0.2 to 5 ohms and a cardiac component varying between 0.02 to 0.2 ohms.

The patent to Robertson et al., U.S. Pat. No. 3,524,058 discloses a respiration monitor which uses body electrodes to direct an electric current to a particular part of the patient's body where changes in electrical impedance provide output signals that vary with respiration.

The patent to Bloice, U.S. Pat. No. 3,796,208 discloses an apparatus for monitoring movements of a patient including a microwave scanner (doppler radar) which creates a movement sensitive field surrounding part of the patient. Movements of the patient create

United States Patent [19]

Shevrin et al.

[11] **Patent Number:** **4,699,153**

[45] **Date of Patent:** **Oct. 13, 1987**

[54] **SYSTEM FOR ASSESSING VERBAL PSYCHOBIOLOGICAL CORRELATES**

[75] Inventors: Howard Shevrin; William J. Williams; Robert E. Marshall, all of Ann Arbor, Mich.

[73] Assignee: The University of Michigan, Ann Arbor, Mich.

[21] Appl. No.: 726,056

[22] Filed: Apr. 23, 1985

[51] Int. Cl.⁴ A61B 5/04

[52] U.S. Cl. 128/731; 128/745

[58] Field of Search 128/731–732, 128/733, 745

[56] **References Cited**

PUBLICATIONS

Williams et al.; "A Transinformation Measure of Word Meaning in Evoked Potentials"; 4–1984.

Shevrin; "Unconscious Conflict: A Convergent Psychodynamic and Electrophysiological Approach"; *Emotional & Cognitive Factors in Unconscious Processes*, Stanford, Calif., 7–1984.

Boudrot et al.; "A Clinical Feedback EEG System"; *Am. J. EEG Technol.*, No. 3, 9–1976, pp. 117–127.

"A Continuous Information Theoretic Approach . . . ", by Fuller and Williams, Biological Cybernetics, Jun. 20, 1982.

"Cortical Response to Tactile Stimulus . . . ", by Shevrin and Rennick, Psychophysiology, vol. 3, No. 4, 1967.

"Visual Evoked Response Correlates . . . ", by Shevrin and Fritzler, Science, vol. 161, pp. 295–298, Jul. 19, 1968.

"Brain Response Correlates of Repressiveness", by Shevrin and Fritzler, Psychological Reports, 1968, 887–92, 12/68.

"Repressiveness as a Factor in the Subliminal . . . ", by Shevrin, Smith, and Fritzler, The Journal of Nervous and Mental Disease, vol. 149, No. 3, 1969.

Published comments of Dr. Shevrin, Psychological Variables in AEP Experiment (Average Evoked Potentials).

"Subliminally Stimulated Brain and Verbal Responses . . . ", by Shevrin and Smith, Journal of Abnormal Psychology, 1970, vol. 75, No. 1, 39–46.

"Direct Measurement of Unconscious Mental Processes: . . . ", by Shevrin, Smith, and Hoobler, Proceedings, 78th Annual Convention, APA 1970.

"Average Evoked Response and Verbal Correlates . . .

", by Shevrin and Smith, Psychophysiology, vol. 8, No. 2, 1971.

"Brain Wave Correlates of Subliminal Stimulation . . . ", by Shevrin, Psychological Issues Monograph 30, Psychoanalytic Research, vol. III, No. 2, 1973.

"Neurophysiological Correlates of Psychodynamic Unconscious Processes", by Shevrin, Symposium on the Unconscious under the auspices of the Georgian Academy of Sciences, Tbilisi, USSR, 1978.

"Evoked Potential Evidence for Unconscious Mental Processes: A Review of the Literature", by Shevrin, International Symposium on the Unconscious, Tsibili, Georgia, USSR, 1978.

"Some Assumptions of Psychoanalytic Communication: . . . ", by Shevrin, Communicative Structures and Psychic Structures, 1977.

"Glimpses of the Unconscious", by Shevrin, Psychology Today, Apr. 1980.

Primary Examiner—Kyle L. Howell
Assistant Examiner—Angela D. Sykes
Attorney, Agent, or Firm—Rohm & Monsanto

[57] **ABSTRACT**

A system for assessing psychobiological conditions of a subject utilizes a plurality of words which are selected to be in four categories as critical stimuli. The words are presented by a tachistoscope to the subject in subliminal and supraliminal modes of operation. Subliminal stimulation of the subject is achieved by presenting the selected words for an exposure period of approximately one millisecond. The supraliminal exposure time is approximately thirty milliseconds. Prior to stimulation, the subject is diagnosed in accordance with conventional psychoanalytical techniques to establish the presence and nature of a pathological condition. The words are selected and categorized in four groups: pleasant words, unpleasant words, words related to a diagnosed conscious pathological condition, and words related to a diagnosed unconscious pathological condition. The brain wave responses which are evoked by the stimulation are collected via electrodes and analyzed in accordance with a transinformation technique which is based on information signal theory for establishing a probabilistic value which corresponds to the information content of the evoked responses.

23 Claims, 4 Drawing Figures

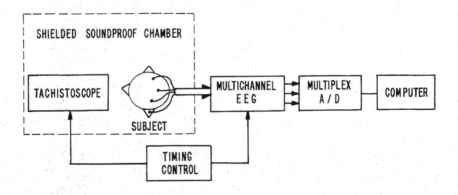

4,699,153

1

SYSTEM FOR ASSESSING VERBAL PSYCHOBIOLOGICAL CORRELATES

BACKGROUND OF THE INVENTION

This invention relates generally to systems for examining brain wave responses to stimulation of a subject, and more particularly to a system wherein evoked potentials responsive to selected critical verbal stimuli are analyzed mathematically to establish a probabilistic value corresponding to the information content of the evoked signal responses.

It has long been proposed that the unconscious mind is psychologically meaningful in that there exists a psychic continuity whereby seemingly discontinuous psychological patterns are actually continuous, but certain psychological events are unknown and in the unconscious. It has therefore been reasoned that the existence of an unconscious must be assumed in psychoanalysis, but methods other than the clinical methods of psychoanalysis must be employed to demonstrate the unconscious. The experimental stimulus used in some experimental efforts to demonstrate the unconscious is a picture of a pen pointing at a knee. By tracing the conceptual associations of pen and knee, by words such as "ink," "paper," "foot," and "leg," rational, secondary process thinking was sampled. However, if clang associations were to be traced, then the experiment would be sampling primary process ideation. Examples of such clangs would be "pennant pennant," "happen," "nei ther," and "any." Finally, two clangs can combine or condense to form a new word, "penny,"which is entirely unrelated in meaning to its components. Associations to this clang condensation can be traced in the form of words such as "coin," "nickel, " "Lincoln," etc. The penny combination is another level of primary-process ideation based on the fact that the stimulus is a pictorial representation of a word, or a rebus, one of the oldest forms of writing and closely allied to dream thinking. Aside from the theoretical relevance of the stimulus, it has the technical advantage of involving no clinical judgment in scoring. Lists of associations based on normative data can be used by assistants with an error rate which is consistently less than 3%.

The rebus method of analysis has been used successfully in various studies. For example, in one experiment, it was shown that pen and knee clang associations and penny rebus associations appeared more often in associations following Stage I, rapid eye movement awakenings, than after Stage II awakenings. On the other hand, pen and knee conceptual associations appeared more frequently following Stage II awakenings than after Stage I, rapid eye movement awakenings. Primary process thought was prominent following dream arousals and secondary-process thought was prominent following one type of non-dream arousal.

It was not, however, until the rebus method was combined with the method of average evoked responses that it became possible to detect directly brain responses to subliminal stimuli and to discover the usefulness of these waves as indicators of complex dynamic and cognitive processes. The average evoked response is based upon the sampling of short periods of the EEG immediately following a given stiumlus. Ordinarily, it is difficult to detect a specific stimulus-locked response in the EEG beacause the EEG reflects so many other simultaneous responses to internal and external stimuli. However, by repeatedly sampling the EEG, a pattern

2

emerges which is directly related to a selected stimulus. It has now been shown that EEG amplitudes within the first 300 milliseconds after stimulation are associated with attention.

In one well known experiment, it was postulated that attentional and perceptual processes were subliminal. This could be tested by presenting two matched stimuli, one of which could be more interesting than the other, and to predict that the more interesting stimulus would elicit a larger brain response. Thus, a matched pair of stimuli were presented in a series of experiments. The experimental stimulus was the fountain pen pointing at a knee, while a controlled stimulus, which matches the experimental one in size, configuration, color, and contour, lacks conventional meaning. FIG. 1A is the experimental stimulus and is a picture of a fountain pen pointed at a leg which is prominently flexed at the knee. FIG. 1B is the control stimulus which is made up of two nonsense figures matching the experimental stimulus in configuration, shape, color, and contour. It was found that one millisecond of exposure of the stimuli to a subject resulted in consistent discrimination between the two stimuli in favor of the rebus. Such discrimination took the form of a larger amplitude in the brain wave with a latentcy of approximately 170 milliseconds.

FIG. 2 is a schematic representation of an averaging method of an EEG signal for the same time epoch. As shown, each response appears different from the other. However, if the different segments are added algebraically, then a consistency emerges reflected in a sizable amplitude. The average evoked response curve shows the appearance of this amplitude. This curve is a total algebraic sum for the amplitude increment, which is then divided by the total number of responses to give the averages.

It therefore has been established by experimentation that a brain wave in the form of an average evoked response discriminates between two subliminal stimuli. Such discrimination is attributable to an amplitude component associated with attention which occurs at approximately between 140 and 80 milliseconds post-stimulus; less than a quarter of a second. Associations to the subliminal rebus stimulus are activated and can be elicited by a free association method. Such free association confirms that thought processes are activated by a subliminal stimulus and persist unconsciously. During such association, the subject is totally unaware of associating more of one category of words than another. The conceptual, secondary-process associations, such as the knee associations, are positively correlated with the size of the discriminating average evoked response amplitude. In other words, the larger the average evoked response amplitude to the rebus stimulation, the more frequently will conceptual secondary-process associations be elicited. This relationship establishes a link between a truly neurophysiological event and an unconscious thought process, for the subjects can in no way be aware of this relationship. However, primary-process associations (clang and rebus words) are not correlated with this amplitude component. Rather, the incidence of primary-process associations is contingent upon the appearance of bursts of rhythmic activity in the alpha range.

Repressiveness, as rated independently on the Rorschach test, is negatively correlated with the magnitude of the discriminating amplitude for the subliminal stimuli. Thus, the more repressive the person is judged on

United States Patent [19]

Zanakis et al.

[11] **Patent Number:** **4,951,674**

[45] **Date of Patent:** **Aug. 28, 1990**

[54] **BIOMAGNETIC ANALYTICAL SYSTEM USING FIBER-OPTIC MAGNETIC SENSORS**

[76] Inventors: **Michael F. Zanakis**; **Philip A. Femano**

[21] Appl. No.: **325,942**

[22] Filed: **Mar. 20, 1989**

[51] Int. Cl.^{5} **A61B 5/04**

[52] U.S. Cl. .... **128/653 R**; 128/731; 324/244.1

[58] Field of Search .... 324/244 OP; 128/653 R, 128/639, 630, 731, 732

[56] **References Cited**

U.S. PATENT DOCUMENTS

4,591,787 5/1986 Hoening 324/260
4,771,239 9/1988 Hoenig .... 128/653 R

OTHER PUBLICATIONS

"Introduction to Magnetoencephalography—A New Window on the Brain", Biomagnetic Technologies, Inc., San Diego, Calif., undated.
Kersey et al., Journal of Lightwave Technology, vol. LT-3, No. 4, Aug. 1985, pp. 836–840.
Enokiharae et al., Journal of Lightwave Technology, vol. LT-5, No. 11, Nov. 1987, pp. 1584–1590.
Mermelstein, Journal of Lightwave Technology, vol. LT-4, No. 9, Sep. 1986, pp. 1376–1380.
Koo et al., Journal of Lightwave Technology, vol. LT-5, No. 12, Dec. 1987, pp. 1680–1684.

Yariv et al., Optics Letters, vol. 5, No. 3, Mar. 1980, pp. 87–89.
Koo et al., Optics Letters, vol. 7, No. 7, Jul. 1982, pp. 334–336.
Koo et al., J. Lightwave Tech., vol. LT-1, No. 3, Sep. 1983, pp. 524–525.

Primary Examiner—Lee S. Cohen
Assistant Examiner—John C. Hanley
Attorney, Agent, or Firm—Michael Ebert

[57] **ABSTRACT**

A biomagnetic analytical system for sensing and indicating minute magnetic fields emanating from the brain or from any other tissue region of interest in a subject under study. The system includes a magnetic pick-up device constituted by an array of fiber-optic magnetic sensors mounted at positions distributed throughout the inner confines of a magnetic shield configured to conform generally to the head of the subject or whatever other body region is of interest. Each sensor yields a light beam whose phase or other parameter is modulated in accordance with the magnetic field emanating from the related site in the region. The modulated beam from each sensor is compared in an interferometer with a reference light beam to yield an output signal that is a function of the magnetic field being emitted at the related site. The output signals from the interferometer are processed to provide a display or recording exhibiting the pattern or map of magnetic fields resulting from emanations at the multitude of sites encompassed by the region.

8 Claims, 2 Drawing Sheets

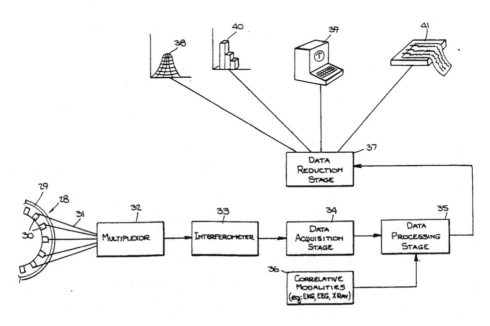

4,951,674

1

BIOMAGNETIC ANALYTICAL SYSTEM USING FIBER-OPTIC MAGNETIC SENSORS

BACKGROUND OF INVENTION

1. Field of Invention

This invention relates generally to biomagnetic analytic systems for sensing and indicating minute magnetic fields emanating from the brain and other tissue regions of the human body, and more particularly to a system using fiber-optic magnetic sensor pick-up devices for this purpose.

2. Status of Prior Art

Biomagnetic fields arise from three principal sources, the first being electric currents produced by the movement of ions. The second source is remanent magnetic movement of contaminants, and the third is paramagnetic or diamagnetic constituents of the body.

The first source is of primary significance in human brain activity in which the currents creating the magnetic fields result from signals generated by neurons as they communicate with each other and with sensory organs of the body. The intensity of extracranial magnetic field produced by such currents is extremely minute, having a strength no more than about a billionth of the magnetic field at the earth's surface. It is usually measured in terms of tesla (T) or gauss (G), one T being equal to 10^4 G.

The magnetic field arising from spontaneous brain activity (alpha waves) is about one picotesla ($1pT = 10^{-12}T$), whereas the magnetic field at the earth's surface is about $6 \times 10^{-5}T$. The magnetic field emanating from the brain has a strength much below that emitted by the heart. Hence monitoring of brain magnetic activity presents formidable difficulties.

A major concern of the present invention is magnetoencephalography (also commonly referred to as MEG). This is the recording of magnetic fields emanating from the brain resulting from neuronal electric currents, as distinguished from an electroencephalogram (EEG) in which electric potentials originating in the brain are recorded. With an EEG measurement, it is difficult to extract the three-dimensional distribution of electrically active brain sites from potentials developed at the scalp. While this difficulty can be overcome by inserting electrodes through apertures bored in the skull, this invasive technique is not feasible in the study of normal brain functions or to diagnose functional brain disorders or brain dysfunctions. Thus ionic currents associated with the production of electrically measurable epileptic seizures generate detectable extracranial magnetic fields, and these can be detected externally without invading the skull.

Non-invasive MEG procedures are currently used in epilepsy research to detect the magnetic field distribution over the surface of the head of a patient with a view to localizing the seizure foci and spread patterns. This analysis serves as a guide to surgical intervention for the control of intractable seizures. (See: "Magnetoencephalography and Epilepsy Research"—Rose et al.; Science—16 Oct. 1987—Volume 238, pp. 329–335.)

MEG procedures have been considered as a means to determine the origin of Parkinson's tremor, to differentiate at the earliest possible stage Alzheimer's disease from other dementias, and to localize the responsible cortical lesions in visual defects of neurological origin. MEG procedures are also of value in classifying active drugs in respect to their effects on specific brain structures, and to in this way predict their pharmaceutical efficacy. And with MEG, one can gain a better understanding of the recovery process in head trauma and strokes by observing the restoration of neurological functions at the affected site.

2

But while MEG holds great promise in the above-noted clinical and pharmaceutical applications, practical considerations, mainly centered on limitations inherent in magnetic sensors presently available for this purpose, have to a large degree inhibited these applications.

The characteristics of biomagnetic activity that are measurable are the strength of the field, the frequency domain and the nature of the field pattern outside of the body. In magnetoencephalography, measurement of all three of these components are important. Ideally, simultaneous measurement of three orthogonal components of the magnetic field provides a complete description of the field as a function of space and time. Coincident measurement of the magnetic field along the surface of the skull can provide a magnetic field map of the cortical and subcortical magnetic activity. With spontaneous activity, the brain emits magnetic fields of about 10^{-8} to 10^{-9} Gauss, compared with approximately 10^{-6} Gauss emitted by the heart. Thus, monitoring of the brain's magnetic activity places heavy demand upon the required hardware.

In brain activity, the current dipole or source is generated by the current flow associated within a neuron or group of neurons. Volume current is analogous to the extracellular component of the current source. In MEG, the net magnetic field measured depends on the magnetic field generated by the current dipole itself. The contribution from volume conduction is small in which approximations to spherical symmetry are made. However, there are tangential magnetic components originating from secondary sources representing perturbations of the pattern by the volume current at boundaries between regions of different conductivity. Contributions from these secondary sources to the tangential component of the field become relatively more pronounced with distance from the current dipole. But there is no interference from these secondary sources when measurement is confined to the magnetic fields perpendicular to the skull.

In biomagnetic analysis, three types of magnetic sensors are known to have adequate sensitivy and discrimination against ambient noise for this purpose. (See: "Magnetoencephalography"—Sato et al.—Journal of Clinical Neurophysiology—Vol. 2, No. 2—1985.) The first is the induction coil. But because of Nyquist noise associated with the resistance of the windings and its loss of sensitivity at frequencies below a few Herz, the induction coil is rarely used in MEG studies.

The second is the Fluxgate magnetometer; and while this has been used in geophysical studies, it has certain drawbacks when used in MEG applications. It is for this reason that the third type, the SQUID system, is presently used almost exclusively in MEG applications.

A SQUID (Superconducting QUantum Interference Device) comprises a superconducting loop incorporating a "weak link" highly sensitive to the magnetic field encompassed within the area of the loop. While the loop itself can act as a magnetic field sensor, use is made of a detection coil tightly coupled to the superconducting loop, the coil acting as a flux transformer. Both the coil and the loop are immersed in a bath of liquid helium contained within a dewar.

United States Patent [19]

Hudspeth

[11] **Patent Number:** **5,392,788**

[45] **Date of Patent:** **Feb. 28, 1995**

[54] **METHOD AND DEVICE FOR INTERPRETING CONCEPTS AND CONCEPTUAL THOUGHT FROM BRAINWAVE DATA AND FOR ASSISTING FOR DIAGNOSIS OF BRAINWAVE DISFUNCTION**

[76] Inventor: **William J. Hudspeth**

[21] Appl. No.: **13,026**

[22] Filed: **Feb. 3, 1993**

[51] Int. Cl.^{6} **A61B 5/0476**
[52] U.S. Cl. **128/731**
[58] Field of Search 128/731

[56] **References Cited**

U.S. PATENT DOCUMENTS

3,087,487	3/1961	Clynes .
3,705,297	12/1972	John .
3,901,215	8/1975	John 128/731
4,188,956	2/1980	John .
4,201,224	5/1980	John .
4,279,258	7/1981	John .
4,408,616	10/1983	Duffy et al. 128/731
4,411,273	10/1983	John .
4,417,592	11/1983	John .
4,421,122	12/1983	Duffy .
4,462,411	7/1984	Rickards .
4,493,327	1/1985	Bergelson et al. .
4,503,863	3/1985	Katims .
4,545,388	10/1985	John .
4,651,145	3/1987	Sutter .
4,676,611	6/1987	Nelson et al. .
4,705,049	11/1987	John .
4,815,474	3/1989	Duffy .
4,841,943	6/1989	Favreau et al. .
4,844,086	7/1989	Duffy .
4,846,190	7/1989	John .
4,913,160	4/1990	John .
4,926,968	5/1990	Wright et al. .
4,926,969	5/1990	Wright et al. 128/731
4,928,704	5/1990	Hardt .
4,941,477	7/1990	Farwell 128/731
4,949,725	8/1990	Raviv et al. 128/731
4,953,968	9/1990	Sherwin et al. .
4,987,903	1/1991	Keppel et al. 128/731
5,003,986	4/1991	Finitzo et al. .
5,113,870	5/1992	Rossenfeld 128/731
5,230,346	7/1993	Leuchter et al. 128/731
5,243,517	9/1993	Schmidt et al. 128/731

OTHER PUBLICATIONS

Klein, "IEEE Transactions on Biomedical Engineering" vol. BME 2343, May, 1976, pp. 246–252.
Walter, "Electronic Engineering", Nov. 1943, pp. 236–240.
Neuropsychologia, 1978, vol. 16, pp. 201 to 212, Neural Models for Short–Term Memory: A Quantitative Study of Average Evoked Potential Waveform, William J. Hudspeth and G. Brian Jones.
The Geometric Representation of Some Simple Structures, Richard L. Degerman pp. 193–211.
A Taxonomy of Some Principal Types of Data and of Multidimensional Methods for Their Analysis, Roger N. Shepard, pp. 21–47.
VEPs and Dimensions of Perception, William J. Hudsepth, Center for Brain Research, Radford University, Radford, Va. (USA), p. 132 of Abstracts submitted to 5th Intl. Conference of Psychology, Budapest, Jul. 1990.
Newspaper article, Fujitsu Labs Tries 'Silent Speech' Input, Dec. 08, 1992.

Primary Examiner—William E. Kamm
Attorney, Agent, or Firm—Oblon, Spivak, McClelland, Maier & Neustadt

[57] **ABSTRACT**

A system for acquisition and decoding of EP and SP signals is provided which comprises a transducer for presenting stimuli to a subject, EEG transducers for recording brainwave signals from the subject, a computer for controlling and synchronizing stimuli presented to the subject and for concurrently recording brainwave signals, and either interpreting signals using a model for conceptual perceptional and emotional thought to correspond EEG signals to thought of the subject or comparing signals to normative EEG signals from a normative population to diagnose and locate the origin of brain dysfunctional underlying perception, conception, and emotion.

18 Claims, 10 Drawing Sheets

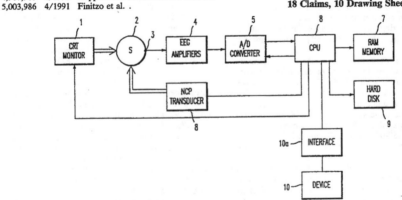

5,392,788

1

METHOD AND DEVICE FOR INTERPRETING CONCEPTS AND CONCEPTUAL THOUGHT FROM BRAINWAVE DATA AND FOR ASSISTING FOR DIAGNOSIS OF BRAINWAVE DISFUNCTION

BACKGROUND OF THE INVENTION

1. Field of the Invention

This invention relates to the field of neuroscience and more particularly relates to the application of human brain wave analysis including quantitative electroencephalography. More particularly, the present invention relates to conceptual interpreters and conceptually driven interfaces.

2. Discussion of the Background

Electrical brain activity can be detected using electrodes placed on the scalp of a human subject. An electroencephalogram (EEG) is a recording of a time-varying spontaneous potential (SP) that is obtained from an alert and resting subject. When a subject is presented brief sensory stimuli (e.g., a flash, a click, a mild shock to the skin), a time-varying evoked potential (EP) is superimposed upon the normally present SP so that the EEG voltage includes both SP and EP components. The EP waveform begins within a few milliseconds after receipt of a sensory stimulus, and continues with a decreasing oscillatory magnitude so that it can be distinguished from the SP for as long as one second.

Previous investigations of EP signals have been directed toward methods and devices for distinguishing between normal subjects and subjects with various brain dysfunctions and for use of EP signals to control hardware devices.

Various regions of the brain have different functions and some of those regions are responsible for different types of conceptual functions, such as spatial relationship and word interpretation. When one of those areas of the brain dysfunctions, the specific mental functions associated therewith are impaired.

U.S. Pat. No. 3,901,215 discloses selection of stimuli that are intended to generate different levels of brain function, such as sensory, perceptual, and conceptual function. A neurometric test battery is disclosed in the '215 patent. That test battery includes several stimulus conditions that represent different levels of stimulus complexity. For each stimulus condition, the disclosed neurometric test battery attempts to determine whether the brain of a subject, as indicated by EP waveforms, distinguishes between two exemplars of a similar type. The model used in the '215 patent assumes, however, only that a difference in EP signals received from the brain of a subject while that subject senses different stimuli indicates that the brain of the subject has distinguished between those stimuli. Therefore, the only answer obtainable based upon the model disclosed in the '215 patent is that two stimulus conditions are either the same or different.

U.S. Pat. No. 4,926,969 discloses an EP based control device in which a subject must focus attention on one checkerboard stimulus among a panel of such stimuli. Those stimuli are used to stimulate the receptor system of a subject at different frequencies. When the subject focuses attention on one of the panels, the unique frequency associated with that panel generates a unique EP waveform from the brain of the subject. The unique frequency dependence generated thereby is used to selectively control a hardware device. Different commands may be issued to the device depending upon

2

which checkerboard the subject stares at. Using that system, the subject must attend to a computer display representing a desired control command. The '969 patent explicitly (see column 8, lines 34–41) avoids using complex stimuli such as size, color, and shape.

SUMMARY OF THE INVENTION

Accordingly, one object of this invention is to provide a novel system that can be used to determine from brainwave recordings from a subject whether translation of external stimuli has occurred.

Another object of this invention is to provide a novel system for determining from the brain waves of a subject whether conception, perception, or emotion has occurred in that subject.

Another object of the invention is to provide a novel system for determining functionally damaged areas of the brain of a subject and to determine what type of functional damage has occurred.

Another object of the invention is to provide a novel hardware control device that can be regulated by brain waveforms corresponding to predetermined thoughts.

Another object of the invention is to provide a hardware control device than can be regulated by EP waveforms induced by either external stimuli or by imagination of a subject.

These and other objects of the invention are provided by a novel system for the acquisition and decoding of EP and SP signals, which comprises a transducer for presenting stimuli to a subject, EEG sensors for recording brainwave signals from the subject, a computer for controlling and synchronizing stimuli presented to the subject and for concurrently recording brainwave signals. The computer also provides means to decode the content of the brainwave signals according to a stimulus model for perceptual, conceptual, and emotional translations.

The invention also provide a novel SP source locator method for determining whether regions of the brain of a subject are functional or dysfunctional, by recording a plurality of SP waveforms from a plurality of scalp locations, determining three basis waveforms from the SP waveforms, along three orthogonal axes. Each of the basis waveforms provide a best fit to the variation in SP waveform along one of the orthogonal axes so that the most complete representation of all the SP waveforms by linear combinations of the three basis waveforms is provided. A coordinate for each SP waveform consisting of the three coefficients for the three basis waveforms representing that SP waveform is plotted, forming a three dimensional plot. That plot is compared with a similar plot representing normative values obtained from a large population of subjects, wherein deviations of the position of a coordinate corresponding to an electrode from a normative value position indicates that a functional region of the brain adjacent to said electrode position is dysfunctional.

I have discovered that the brain interprets sensory stimuli to have perceptual conceptual or emotional meaning, that according to certain rules which indicate whether the stimuli have perceptual, conceptual, or emotional meaning, that EEG signals from the brain encode the type of interpretation of stimuli which the brain has made, and that similar EEG signals occur if an individual imagines an interpreted stimulus instead of experiencing that stimulus. Certain terms must be defined to adequately describe the discoveries and the

United States Patent [19]

Farmer et al.

[11] **Patent Number:** 5,458,142

[45] **Date of Patent:** Oct. 17, 1995

[54] **DEVICE FOR MONITORING A MAGNETIC FIELD EMANATING FROM AN ORGANISM**

[76] Inventors: **Edward J. Farmer; Diane J. Hovey**

[21] Appl. No.: **33,900**

[22] Filed: **Mar. 19, 1993**

[51] Int. Cl.^{6} **A61B 5/00**
[52] U.S. Cl. **128/653.1**; 128/905; 324/260
[58] Field of Search 128/653.1, 905;
600/9, 10, 11; 324/244, 260

[56] **References Cited**

U.S. PATENT DOCUMENTS

3,721,230	3/1973	Ziernicki .	
3,727,604	4/1973	Sidwell et al. .	
3,951,134	4/1976	Malech .	
4,134,395	1/1979	Davis .	
4,557,271	12/1985	Stoller et al.	128/734
4,602,639	7/1986	Hoogendoorn et al.	128/639
4,625,732	12/1986	Kasa et al.	128/670
4,688,580	8/1987	Ko et al.	128/734
4,690,149	9/1987	Ko	128/653
4,697,599	10/1987	Woodley et al. .	
4,719,425	1/1988	Ettinger	324/316
4,864,282	9/1989	Toeg	340/573
4,930,516	6/1990	Alfano et al.	128/665
4,940,058	7/1990	Taff et al.	128/653.1
4,951,674	8/1990	Zanakis et al.	128/653 R
4,961,428	10/1990	Nikias et al.	128/699
5,003,979	2/1991	Merickel et al. .	
5,020,538	6/1991	Morgan et al.	128/653.1
5,092,835	3/1992	Schurig et al.	600/9
5,152,288	10/1992	Hoenig et al.	128/653.1
5,183,456	2/1993	Liboff et al.	600/9
5,261,405	11/1993	Fossel	128/653.2
5,307,807	5/1994	Valdes Sosa et al.	128/653.1

Primary Examiner—Ruth S. Smith
Attorney, Agent, or Firm—Bernhard Kreten

[57] **ABSTRACT**

A diagnostic and therapeutic instrument for use in the treatment of living organisms is provided including a sensor for detecting magnetic fields emanating from the living organism. The sensor is located proximate to the organism and is formed from a ferromagnetic core surrounded by a multi-turn fine wire coil. The sensor is coupled to signal processing which amplifies a signal from the sensor and filters out portions of the signal which represent background magnetic fields emanating from other sources. The signal from the sensor is utilizable to detect abnormalities in the field emanating from the organism indicative of the organism's well-being. The signal can also be utilized to excite a magnetic field radiator which outputs a field complementary to the field emanating from the organism.

7 Claims, 5 Drawing Sheets

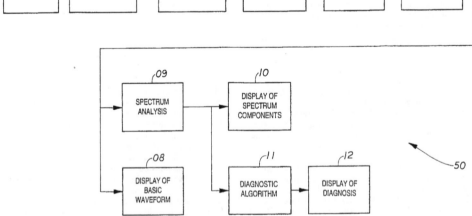

5,458,142

1

DEVICE FOR MONITORING A MAGNETIC FIELD EMANATING FROM AN ORGANISM

FIELD OF THE INVENTION

The present invention relates to the systems, methods, and apparatus by which the electromagnetic emissions of a living organism may be monitored. Specifically, the present invention relates to the systems, methods, and means whereby the physical state and emotional state of an organism and the changes in the physical and emotional state of the organism can be monitored.

It also provides a means of altering the physical state and emotional state of an organism by the introduction of specific compensatory and corrective electromagnetic patterns associated with the physical and emotional condition of the organism.

BACKGROUND OF THE INVENTION

The concept of an energy field around a living organism that reflects its physical condition is a central concept in Aurvedic medicine dating back 5,000 years. The idea has appeared multiple times in different cultures and at different times in history. It provides the foundation for healing practices in Tibetan, Chinese, and Hawaiian medicine. The energy field is seen as having multiple layers ranging from a greater density near the body to a rarefied layer encircling the body and extending a greater distance therefrom. In all of the aforementioned philosophies, the layer closest to the body is believed to reflect its physical condition while those extending outward represent emotional and spiritual conditions. In Sanskrit, the word describing the energy field is "prana," in Chinese it is called "chi" and Hawaiian it is called "aka." It has also been called the etheric field or aura. In all philosophies, illness is believed to be the result of a lack of or imbalance in the energy field around the body and can be observed by examining the field. Healing and regeneration can only take place when the energy field is balanced and strong.

The validity and acceptability of these ancient philosophies are of present interest and are being tested with traditional western medicine. Dr. Deepak Chopra, M.D., FACS, former chief of staff of New England Memorial Hospital in Stoneham, Mass. has devoted considerable attention to combining traditional western medicine with Aurvadic philosophy. Dr. Chopra has chosen to use the term "Ayurveda" (instead of the more common "Aurvada") because in his judgement this spelling more properly reflects the Sanskrit roots of this philosophy. In his books, which include *Perfect Health, Creating Health,* and *Quantum Healing,* he provides many case histories to support his concept of Ayurvedic medicine. He characterizes the Ayurvedic field with an analogy with quantum mechanics which he expresses thus:

"In Ayurveda, the physical body is the gateway to what I call the "quantum mechanical human body." Physics informs us that the basic fabric of nature lies at the quantum level, far beyond atoms and molecules. A quantum, defined as the basic unit of matter or energy, is from 10,000,000 to 100,000,000 times smaller than the smallest atom. At this level, matter and energy become interchangeable. All quanta are made of invisible vibrations—ghosts of energy—waiting to take physical form. Ayurveda says that the same is true of the human body—it first takes form as intense but invisible vibrations, called quantum fluctuations, before it proceeds to

2

coalesce into impulses of energy and particles of matter.

The quantum mechanical body is the underlying basis for everything we are: thoughts, emotions, proteins, cells, organs-any visible or invisible part of ourselves. At the quantum level, your body is sending out all kinds of invisible signals, waiting for you to pick them up."

Dr. Delores Krieger, RN researched the energy fields described in these ancient philosophies and through rigorous controlled experiments documented the healing that resulted from manipulating these energy fields. She continued this research and taught the technique she named "Therapeutic Touch" throughout her 20 year tenure as professor of neurophysiology at the New York University School of Nursing until her recent retirement. She now teaches and speaks on the subject at medical and nursing schools across the country.

During Dr. Krieger's research she met and continued to work with one of the few individuals who profess to be able to actually see this energy field, Dora Van Gelder Kunz. As part of Dr. Krieger's establishment of an experimentally documented baseline that would establish credibility with mainstream medicine, both women participated in a study arranged by Elmer Green, Ph.D., Director of Research at the Menniger Foundation. The study was conducted during a Council Grove Conference during which a patient was brought in from another state along with his physician and a complete set of lab reports. Each woman was allowed to examine the patient over a 15 minute period, but were not permitted to talk with the person. At the end of their examination each woman presented her findings to a panel of five physicians and the patient's physician. Dora Kunz's diagnosis was rated at 100 percent while Dr. Krieger received a rating of 80 percent.

A Therapeutic Touch practitioner that is unable to see the etheric field around the body assesses the patient's condition by moving both hands over the energy field surrounding the patient's body. The perceived differences in the field indicate injury or disease in the underlying body structure. The assessment has been described by many experienced practitioners as the most difficult part of the process because it is frequently very difficult to feel the differences in the field of a very ill patient, or a child.

The present invention has demonstrated a high degree of correlation with the impressions of practitioners trained and experienced in therapeutic touch. It serves to augment therapeutic touch as a diagnostic tool. It also serves as a training aid in teaching therapeutic touch.

Tests with the apparatus have also established predictable electromagnetic field variations resulting from changes in mental activity level. For example, the waveform emitted by the subject becomes significantly more complex when responding to a command question requiring the subject to generate a specific type of visual image. The increase in complexity occurs in the absence of speech and when speech is required, precedes verbalization of the response and decays rapidly when the verbal response is complete.

Tests involving stress, including situations in which the subject attempts to provide false answers to questions, produce more complex and higher amplitude responses than situations in which the subject experiences less stress.

Others have addressed the concept of diagnosis through external measurements by monitoring skin potential using various techniques. These techniques use contacting sensors and monitor direct current flow on the surface of the body, and hence do not monitor fields about the body or emissions therefrom. They demonstrate the state of the art in non-

United States Patent [19]

Stirbl et al.

[11] **Patent Number:**   **5,507,291**

[45] **Date of Patent:**   **Apr. 16, 1996**

[54] **METHOD AND AN ASSOCIATED APPARATUS FOR REMOTELY DETERMINING INFORMATION AS TO PERSON'S EMOTIONAL STATE**

[76] Inventors: **Robert C. Stirbl**

Peter J. Wilk,

[21] Appl. No.: **222,835**

[22] Filed: **Apr. 5, 1994**

[51] Int. Cl.^{6} **A61B 5/04**

[52] U.S. Cl. **128/653.1**; 128/661.08; 128/691; 128/745; 128/660.02

[58] **Field of Search** 128/653.1, 660.01, 128/660.02, 661.08, 691, 736, 745, 664

[56] **References Cited**

U.S. PATENT DOCUMENTS

3,483,860	12/1969	Namerow	128/653.1
3,598,107	8/1971	Ishikawa et al.	128/653.1
3,875,929	4/1975	Grant	128/653.1
3,951,134	4/1976	Malech	128/653.1
3,993,995	11/1976	Kaplan et al.	128/653.1
4,048,986	9/1977	Ott	128/653.1
4,085,740	4/1978	Allen, Jr.	128/653.1
4,365,637	12/1982	Johnson	128/734
4,509,531	4/1985	Ward	128/736
4,556,057	12/1985	Hiruma et al.	.
4,569,354	2/1986	Shapiro et al.	.
4,981,139	1/1991	Pfohl	.
4,991,585	2/1991	Mawhinney	128/653.1
4,998,533	3/1991	Winkelman	128/653.1
5,022,405	6/1991	Hök et al.	.
5,099,852	3/1992	Meister et al.	128/691
5,137,027	8/1992	Rosenfeld	128/745
5,305,748	4/1994	Wilk	.
5,360,005	11/1994	Wilk	128/653.1

Primary Examiner—Krista M. Zele
Attorney, Agent, or Firm—R. Neil Sudol; Henry D. Coleman

[57] **ABSTRACT**

In a method for remotely determining information relating to a person's emotional state, an waveform energy having a predetermined frequency and a predetermined intensity is generated and wirelessly transmitted towards a remotely located subject. Waveform energy emitted from the subject is detected and automatically analyzed to derive information relating to the individual's emotional state. Physiological or physical parameters of blood pressure, pulse rate, pupil size, respiration rate and perspiration level are measured and compared with reference values to provide information utilizable in evaluating interviewee's responses or possibly criminal intent in security sensitive areas.

33 Claims, 4 Drawing Sheets

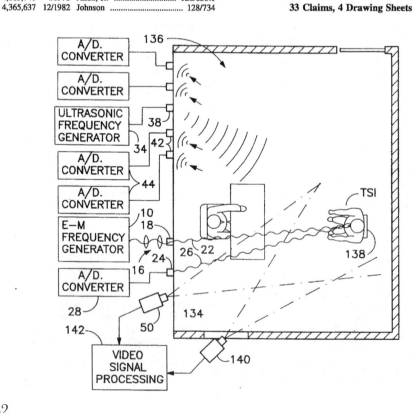

5,507,291

1

METHOD AND AN ASSOCIATED APPARATUS FOR REMOTELY DETERMINING INFORMATION AS TO PERSON' S EMOTIONAL STATE

BACKGROUND OF THE INVENTION

This invention relates to a method and an associated apparatus for remotely determining information pertaining to an individual's emotional and/or metabolic state.

In many situations, to make decisions it would be helpful to have objective information regarding a person's emotional state. Such information is useful in ascertaining the person's thoughts and intentions. For example, in an interview situation, objective information as to the interviewee's emotional state provides a better basis on which to judge the truthfulness of the interviewee's responses to questions. Such information has been conventionally obtained, in certain applications, by so-called lie detectors. A problem with such devices is that the interviewee is necessarily aware of the testing. This introduces a complication in evaluating the results of the lie detector testing. Accordingly, it would be desirable to provide a means for objectively determining emotional state parameters without the knowledge of the subject.

Such technology would also be useful for medical purposes, to determine, for example, whether a person is in danger of a life-threatening heart attack. Some of the physiological parameters which indicate emotional stress are also indicative of the physical stress of a heart condition. Such physiological parameters include blood pressure and pulse rate. An irregular pulse is especially indicative of a cardiac arrythmia which may be a prelude to myocardial infarction.

Technology which serves to objectively identify emotional state without the knowledge of the subject is also useful in security applications. It would be beneficial, for example, to detect an individual contemplating a robbery or hijacking prior to entry of that individual into a bank or an airplane.

OBJECTS OF THE INVENTION

An object of the present invention is to provide a method for obtaining information pertinent to a person's emotional state, without the person's knowledge.

Another object of the present invention is to provide such a method for use in determining the truthfulness or sincerity of the person during an interview.

An alternative object of the present invention is to provide such a method for use in checking the health of the person.

Another alternative object of the present invention is to provide such a method for use in detecting those contemplating a criminal act.

Another, more particular, object of the present invention is to provide such a method which is implemented remotely, without touching the subject.

Yet another object of the present invention is to provide an associated apparatus or system for obtaining information pertinent to a person's emotional state, without the person's knowledge.

These and other objects of the present invention will be apparent from the drawings and detailed descriptions herein.

SUMMARY OF THE INVENTION

A method for remotely determining information relating to a person's emotional state, comprising the steps of (a) generating waveform energy having a predetermined frequency and a predetermined intensity, the step of generating being implemented at a location remotely spaced from a target individual, (b) wirelessly transmitting the waveform energy towards the individual, (c) detecting energy emitted or reflected from the individual in response to the waveform energy, and (d) automatically analyzing the emitted or reflected energy to derive information relating to the individual's emotional state.

According to another feature of the present invention, the step of analyzing includes the steps of determining a value related to a physiological parameter taken from the group consisting of blood pressure, pulse rate, respiration rate, pupil size, and perspiration, and comparing the value with a stored reference value to identify a change in the parameter.

Where the parameter is respiration rate and the detected energy is reflected from the individual's chest wall, the method further comprises the steps of processing the reflected energy to determine location of the individual's chest wall, and automatically monitoring the individual's position and compensating for changes in the individual's position in determining changes in location of the individual's chest wall.

Alternatively, respiration rate may be determined by monitoring the differential remote absorption of the individual subject's exhalation gases. Invisible electromagnetic radiation from a source such as a light emitting diode (e.g., a laser diode) is directed towards the subject's mouth. The diode generated radiation is modulated at a high rate with a phase-locked component. Radiation returning from the subject and particularly from gases at the subject's mouth are filtered via an electro-optical modulating polarization component. This polarization component may take the form of a filter wheel rotating, for example, at a speed between 300 and 1,000 Hz. An opto-electric detector senses the radiation penetrating the filter wheel. An amplifier phase-locked with the modulator component serves to detect signals only at the frequency of modulation. Any ambient constant energy which is not part of the measuring signal is filtered out.

In remotely monitoring a person's respiration rate, the waveform energy may be modulated electromagnetic radiation or ultrasonic or subsonic pressure waves. Where the measuring waveform is electromagnetic, the measurement may be effectuated using the principles of differential backscatter absorption or interferometery to detect phase changes owing to a change in position of the subject surface (the individual's chest wall). The wavelength or frequency of the modulated electromagnetic radiation is selected from the infrared and near-millimeter portions of the spectrum so as to penetrate clothing material and be reflected from the underlying skin surface. Where the measuring waveform is an ultrasonic or subsonic pressure wave, changes in position of the chest wall may be detected via phase changes and/or by changes in travel time.

Where the monitored parameter is pulse rate, the measuring energy may be modulated electromagnetic radiation, in the near-ultraviolet, infrared or near-millimeter ranges. A collimated beam of radiation is generated and directed or aimed towards a predetermined point on the individual overlying or on a blood vessel. The emitted or reflected energy is processed to determine (1) intensity, change in intensity or change in polarization or fluorescence of the emitted or reflected energy and (2) amount of transdermal absorption. Changes in transdermal absorption can be tracked to determine changes in volume of blood and, accordingly, the pulse of the target individual. If necessary,

United States Patent [19]

Lerner

[11] **Patent Number:** **5,522,386**

[45] **Date of Patent:** **Jun. 4, 1996**

[54] **APPARATUS PARTICULARLY FOR USE IN THE DETERMINATION OF THE CONDITION OF THE VEGETATIVE PART OF THE NERVOUS SYSTEM**

[76] Inventor: **Eduard N. Lerner**

[21] Appl. No.: **140,056**

[22] PCT Filed: **Apr. 29, 1992**

[86] PCT No.: **PCT/NL92/00079**

§ 371 Date: **Nov. 24, 1993**

§ 102(e) Date: **Nov. 24, 1993**

[87] PCT Pub. No.: **WO92/19192**

PCT Pub. Date: **Nov. 12, 1992**

[30]   **Foreign Application Priority Data**

Apr. 29, 1991 [NL] Netherlands 9100740

[51] **Int. Cl.^{6}** **A61B 5/00**
[52] **U.S. Cl.** **128/630**; 128/745; 128/746; 128/744; 128/741
[58] **Field of Search** 128/731–4, 736, 128/739–42, 744, 745–6

[56]   **References Cited**

U.S. PATENT DOCUMENTS

3,837,331	9/1974	Ross	128/732 X
3,893,450	7/1975	Ertl	128/731
4,131,113	12/1978	Fender et al.	
4,201,224	5/1980	John	
4,462,411	7/1984	Rickards	128/731 X
4,557,271	12/1985	Stoller et al.	
4,561,449	12/1985	Hu et al.	
4,570,640	2/1986	Barsa	
4,987,903	1/1991	Keppel et al.	128/731 X
5,036,858	8/1991	Carter et al.	128/732
5,191,894	3/1993	Yasushi	128/733
5,291,894	3/1994	Nagy	128/732 X
5,331,969	7/1994	Silberstein	128/731

FOREIGN PATENT DOCUMENTS

0208007	1/1987	European Pat. Off. .
2113846	8/1983	United Kingdom .
WO90/14794	12/1990	WIPO .

OTHER PUBLICATIONS

By Y. Kosugi et al., "Quantitive Evaluation of Saccadic Eye Movement Disorders Under Random Visual Stimuli on CRT", Mar. 1982, vol. BME–29, No. 3, pp. 184–192, New York.
By K. Plattig, "Gustatory and Olfactory Evoked Potentials In Man", 1987, vol. 2, pp. 961–962.

Primary Examiner—Angela D. Sykes
Attorney, Agent, or Firm—Young & Thompson

[57]   **ABSTRACT**

Apparatus for use in the determination of the condition of the vegetative part of the nervous system and/or of sensory functions of an organism, i.e. a human being or animal. The apparatus comprises devices for generating and supplying to said organism at least one sensory stimulus chosen from a group of sensory stimuli, such as visual, sound, olfactory, gustatory, tactile or pain stimuli, and devices for measuring the skin potential and the evoked response of the organism to a stimulus. The measured data are processed by processing devices for automatically controlling the supply of at least one stimulus for providing a non-rhythmical sequence of stimuli. Preferably, pairs of stimuli are supplied for developing a conditioned reflex.

20 Claims, 1 Drawing Sheet

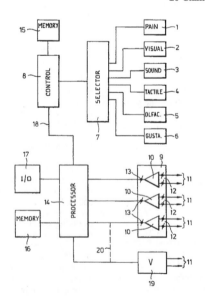

5,522,386

1

APPARATUS PARTICULARLY FOR USE IN THE DETERMINATION OF THE CONDITION OF THE VEGETATIVE PART OF THE NERVOUS SYSTEM

FIELD OF THE INVENTION

The invention relates to an apparatus for use in the determination of the condition of the vegetative part of the nervous system and/or of sensory functions of an organism, i.e. a human being or animal, comprising:

means for measuring the skin or organ surface potential of the organism;

means for generating and supplying to the organism at least one sensory stimulus chosen from a group of sensory stimuli;

means for measuring the evoked response of the organism to the at least one sensory stimulus, and

processing means, for processing the skin or organ surface potential and the evoked response values measured by the measuring means.

BACKGROUND OF THE INVENTION

Examination of the vegetative part of the nervous system or the sensory functions is carried out by supplying sensory stimuli to the organism under examination and by measuring the response to such a stimulus. The evoked response to a stimulus can be obtained from several variables of an organism, for example, skin potential, skin impedance, skin temperature, electrical signals from deep tissue e.g. muscle potentials, changes in the fluid production, e.g. the water production i.e. the water secretion or water content of tissue cells etc.

International patent application WO-A-9,014,749 discloses a method and an apparatus of the type mentioned above for analyzing neural sickness from the vegetative part of the nervous system of an organism, in response to sensory stimuli supplied to the organism under examination. Said stimuli can be chosen from a group of sensory stimuli, such as visual stimuli, sound stimuli, olfactory stimuli, gustatory stimuli, tactile stimuli or pain stimuli. The neural signals are achieved from measuring the evoked response of the organism to such a stimulus.

The results of said measurements can be evaluated and classified into different types, i.e. hypersympatheticotonia, pre-sympatheticotonia, vegetative normotonia (eutonia), preparasympatheticotonia and hyperparasympatheticotonia. By correlation of said types and other medical data, diagnosis on existing diseases or the probability of falling ill with a specific disease in future can be estimated.

International patent application PCT/NL91/00071, not a prior publication, discloses a method for measuring sensory functions of an organism, such as hearing, sight, smell, touch and pain, providing an objective assessment of the functioning of the sense organs, i.e. without the need for report by the organism under examination. In this method, specific stimuli are supplied to the organism, adapted to the sense under investigation i.e. auditory, visual, olfactory, gustatory, tactile, or pain stimuli. The reaction to such a specific stimulus is determined by measuring the evoked response of the organism.

It has been found that the evoked response by a sequence of stimuli of a certain type, e.g. light or sound, applied in a rhythmical manner is not stable over time. It is to say, as the time of stimulation increases, the response of the nervous system to said sequence of stimuli undesirable alters and/or decreases. Further, repeated investigation of the organs of sense, for example on the next day, can also have an adverse effect on the response of the organism to a specific stimulus or sequence of stimuli.

SUMMARY OF THE INVENTION

The invention now provides an improved apparatus for use in the determination of the condition of the vegetative part of the nervous system and/or of sensory functions of an organism, characterized by;

control means, for controlling the supply of the at least one stimulus in terms of its' type, intensity, duration and/or repetition rate subject to the skin or organ surface potential and the evoked response values measured by said measuring means and processed by said processing means, for automatically providing a non-rhythmical sequence of stimuli.

With the apparatus according to the invention the vegetative nervous system and/or sensory functions of an organism, i.e. a human being or an animal, can be examined, wherein the evoked response of the nervous system to a sequence of stimuli is essentially independent over time providing reliable, satisfactory results. For example, compared to a rhythmical, repeatedly applied sequence of stimuli, an improvement in the accuracy of the determination of the condition of the vegetative part of the nervous system of a factor 3 to 5 is obtained. The stimulation pattern is automatically selected and controlled by the individual state of the vegetative nervous system of the organism, by analysis of the measured skin or organ surface potential of the organism.

It is noted that many different apparatuses for providing stimuli to an organism are known in the state of the art.

U.S. Pat. No. 4,131,113 discloses means for examining the human eye by analysis of electrical signals generated by the retinal of an eye in response to a quasi-random light stimulus. The stimulus applied is a bend-limited white-noise light intensity signal, projected onto the human eye through a cup electrode. However, the band-limited white-noise generator disclosed is not equipped for providing a controllable non-rhythmical sequence of stimuli, having adjustable parameters such as duration, intensity, repetition rate etc. Automatically controlling the sequence of stimuli subject to the state of the vegetative part of the nervous system of the organism is not disclosed nor suggested.

In a publication by Y. Kosugi et al. "Quantitative Evaluation of Saccadic Eye Movement Disorders Under Random Visual Stimuli on CRT" in IEEE Transactions on Biomedical Engineering, Vol. BME 29, no. 3. March 1982 a computer aided examination system is presented, in which a pseudo-random binary sequence is used for moving a target on a screen, in order to evoke saccadic eye movements. Controlling the supplied stimuli in terms of type, intensity, duration and repetition rate, subject to the state of the vegetative part of the nervous system and the evoked response of the organism is not described nor suggested.

U.S. Pat. No. 4,570,640 discloses an apparatus for monitoring the sensory system of a patient to enable determination of the level and depth of spinal and epidural nerve blocks affecting the sympathetic and motor nervous system. An electric stimulator is provided which can be manually or automatically activated. By comparing the response due to an applied stimulus against the response obtained from a reference level, the strength of the stimulus is controlled by

United States Patent [19] **Bowman et al.**

[11] **Patent Number: 5,557,199**

[45] **Date of Patent: Sep. 17, 1996**

[54] **MAGNETIC RESONANCE MONITOR**

[75] Inventors: **Joseph D. Bowman**, Cincinnati; **Daniel P. Engel, III**, Cheviot, both of Ohio

[73] Assignee: **The United States of America as represented by the Department of Health and Human Services**, Washington, D.C.

[21] Appl. No.: **235,833**

[22] Filed: **Apr. 29, 1994**

[51] **Int. Cl.**[6] **G01V 3/00**

[52] **U.S. Cl.** **324/301**; 324/322

[58] **Field of Search** 324/300, 301, 324/306, 307, 309, 318, 322, 244, 248; 128/653.5

[56] **References Cited**

U.S. PATENT DOCUMENTS

4,591,788	5/1986	Mohri et al.	324/260
4,771,239	9/1988	Hoenig	324/248
4,791,368	12/1988	Tsuzuki	324/301
4,793,355	12/1988	Crum et al.	128/653
4,801,882	1/1989	Daalmans	324/248
4,827,217	5/1989	Paulson	324/248
4,864,238	9/1989	Seitz	324/253
4,931,152	6/1990	Naik et al.	204/38.5
4,951,674	8/1990	Zanakis et al.	128/653 R
4,977,896	12/1990	Robinson et al.	128/653 R
4,994,739	2/1991	Honda et al.	324/207.14
4,994,742	2/1991	Lowther	324/251
5,015,953	5/1991	Ferguson et al.	324/244
5,018,724	5/1991	Naser et al.	272/73
5,020,538	6/1991	Morgan et al.	128/653 R
5,027,819	7/1991	Crum	128/653
5,136,242	8/1992	Abraham-Fuchs	324/301
5,198,766	3/1993	Spraul et al.	324/300

OTHER PUBLICATIONS

Bartington Instruments Ltd. (1993): Operation/Service Manual for the MAG-03MC Three Axis Magnetic Field Sensor and MAG-03MC Power Supply Unit. Oxon, England. Mo. of Pub. unknown.

Bierbaum P J, Peters J M (1991): Proceedings of the Scientific Workshop on the Health Effects of Electric and Magnetic Fields on Workers. DHHS (NIOSH) Publication No. 91-111. Cincinnati, OH: National Institute for Occupational Safety and Health. Mo. of Pub. unknown.

Blackman C F (1990): ELF effects on calcium homeostasis. In Wilson B W, Stevens R G, Anderson L E, (eds.): Extremely Low Frequency Electromagnetic Fields: The Question of Cancer. Columbus, OH: Battelle, pp. 187–208. Mo of Pub. unknown.

Bowman J D, Sobel E, London S J, Thomas D C, Garabrant D H, Pearce N, Peters J M (1992): Electric and Magnetic Field Exposure, Chemical Exposure, and Leukemia Risk in "Electrical" Occupations. EPRI Report TR-101723. Palo Alto, CA: Electric Power Research Institute. Mo. of Pub. unknown.

(List continued on next page.)

Primary Examiner—Louis M. Arana

Attorney, Agent, or Firm—Lowe, Price, LeBlanc & Becker

[57] **ABSTRACT**

A magnetic resonance monitor measures static and extremely low frequency magnetic fields in order to determine the degree of magnetic resonance with the magnetic moments of a biological substrate, more particularly resonance with the magnetic moments of a human body. A digital bandpass filter varies in response to the magnitude of the static magnetic field so that it selects frequencies of the oscillating magnetic field in accordance with the gyromagnetic equation. A spatial analyzer determines the three spatial components of the filtered signals representing the magnetic field oscillating parallel to the static magnetic field vector and the two circularly-polarized components rotating perpendicular to the static field with helicities opposite to each other. A resonance analyzer evaluates accurately the resonance yield which is the change in biochemical processes due to magnetic field exposures. The magnetic resonance monitor can measure from magnetic fields in residential and workplace environments, either for research studies or for the routine evaluations of health hazards.

16 Claims, 7 Drawing Sheets

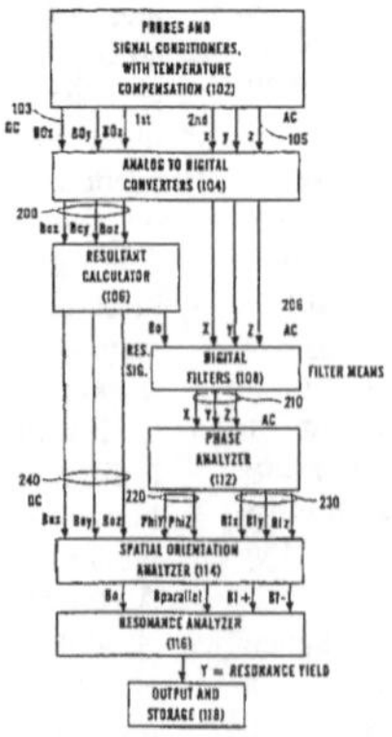

5,557,199

1

MAGNETIC RESONANCE MONITOR

TECHNICAL FIELD

This invention relates to measurement instruments for magnetic fields, and more particularly to instruments for measuring combined static and extremely low frequency magnetic fields in the environment. Still more specifically, the invention relates to instruments for measurement of environmental magnetic fields which are in magnetic resonance with magnetic moments in a biological organism, particularly the human body.

BACKGROUND ART

Research has recently been undertaken on the possibility that magnetic fields may cause cancer, reproductive abnormalities, or psychoneurological disorders [Bierbaum and Peters, 1991]. Research emphasis is being placed on possible effects of magnetic fields produced by AC electric power transmission facilities and electric appliances, although other sources may be involved. In order to carry out such research more effectively and accurately, there is a requirement for instrumentation for measuring magnetic fields with frequencies below 3000 Hz. Moreover, it is necessary to make such measurements in workplaces, homes and other environments so that compact, transportable, instruments are required.

Although many instruments are available for measuring magnetic fields in the environment, such instruments do not distinguish between those magnetic fields which may interact with a biological organism and those which may not. Thus, in order to obtain meaningful research results, it is necessary to be able to identify and measure magnetic fields which may have biological effects on the human body.

To explain the biological effects of interest, it has been proposed that ions important to cell functioning may experience "cyclotron resonance" [Liboff et al., 1990] or "parametric resonance" [Lednev, 1991]. Other forms of magnetic resonance with the magnetic fields in the environment are being investigated for potential chemical effects produced thereby [Grundler, et al., 1992]. For example, electron spin resonance is known to enhance the production of "free radical" molecules [Steiner and Ulrich, 1989; McLaughlin, 1992], and magnetic field interactions with magnetosomes (biological magnetic crystals) are being studied [Kirschvink, 1992].

The magnetic field combinations that cause nuclear magnetic resonance and electron spin resonance are well known [Macomber, 1976], and laboratory studies now suggest that magnetic resonance principles may apply to magnetic moments from electron spin, ferromagnetic crystals, or ionic motion in biological substrates. These hypotheses imply that biological processes can be affected by combinations of oscillating and static magnetic fields which are in resonance with magnetic moments in the human body.

In order to determine resonance conditions, it is necessary to measure both static and oscillating magnetic fields, and to provide output data more detailed than an average magnitude of either (or both) the static and oscillating fields. It is also necessary to identify the frequency components of the oscillating field as well as the relative spatial orientation of the two fields.

More specifically, it is necessary to monitor all the temporal, spatial and frequency characteristics of a magnetic field which may have biological effects on the human body.

2

It is moreover necessary to analyze the measured magnetic field characteristics in order to provide a quantity indicative of such resonance. It is particularly desirable to measure and identify magnetic field components capable of resonance with a predetermined magnetic moment, such as a magnetic moment indicative of biological resonance and more specifically indicative of resonance with the human body. Preferably, such measurement, analysis and identification should be performed in accordance with known theories of magnetic resonance.

Indeed, in some laboratory experiments [Blackman, 1990; Liboff et al., 1990], biological changes attributed to magnetic fields have been found to depend on a relation between the frequency and orientation of a oscillating field produced by AC electricity and a static magnetic field originating in the earth (the geomagnetic field).

To determine a linkage or causal relationship between magnetic resonances and cancer, spontaneous abortions or other health disorders associated with magnetic fields in epidemiological studies, instruments are thus needed to measure and monitor magnetic resonance conditions in the environment. Such instruments would be used in epidemiological studies to measure exposures to magnetic resonances of subjects in their homes, workplaces and other environments.

Moreover, if it is established that exposure to magnetic resonances is a risk factor for diseases, then magnetic resonance monitors will also be required to measure exposure to resonance conditions in order to evaluate health risks and control devices thereof.

The present invention is thus provided to permit measurement of magnetic field combinations which are, or may be, in resonance with magnetic moments in a biological organism, such as the human body.

Many systems are known for measuring exposures to magnetic fields with extremely low frequencies. However, the known systems are not suited for measuring human exposures to magnetic resonance conditions in health studies. The deficiencies of the prior art are based on the following.

1. Many systems only measure a oscillating magnetic field in frequency bandwidths which include the electric power frequency (60 Hz in North America and 50 Hz in the rest of the world). Frequencies from 30–3000 Hz is called the extremely low frequency (ELF) range. The most common sensor for measuring ELF magnetic fields is an induction coil, which responds to the oscillating fields but not to the static fields also needed for consideration in determining resonance conditions. Such common sensor systems are available from various sources, such as AJM Electronics, Electric Field Measurements, Enertech Consultants, Holaday Industries, and Positron Industries.

2. Most systems which measure both static and oscillating magnetic fields use either Hall-effect probes or fluxgate probes. Such systems are also limited, and can only determine the average magnitude of the field's component, either static or ELF. These instruments often label these two frequency modes as the "DC" and "AC" modes. Such systems are available from companies such as Bartington Instruments, F. W. Bell, Holaday Industries, and Schoenstedt Instrument Company. The magnetic field instruments with an ELF output usually determine the root-mean-squared (rms) magnitude of that field component through a frequency filter with a fixed bandwidth. Since resonance occurs at

United States Patent [19]

Smyth

[11]	**Patent Number:**	**5,649,061**
[45]	**Date of Patent:**	**Jul. 15, 1997**

[54] **DEVICE AND METHOD FOR ESTIMATING A MENTAL DECISION**

[75] Inventor: **Christopher C. Smyth**, Fallston, Md.

[73] Assignee: **The United States of America as represented by the Secretary of the Army**, Washington, D.C.

[21] Appl. No.: **439,392**

[22] Filed: **May 11, 1995**

[51] **Int. Cl.⁶** **A61B 3/14**; A61B 5/05

[52] **U.S. Cl.** **395/20**; 351/210; 250/221; 128/731; 395/21

[58] **Field of Search** 128/731, 745; 351/218, 209; 395/20

[56]   **References Cited**

U.S. PATENT DOCUMENTS

3,986,030	10/1976	Teltscher .	
4,109,145	8/1978	Graf .	
4,474,186	10/1984	Ledley	128/733
4,610,259	9/1986	Cohen	128/731
4,648,052	3/1987	Friedman et al. .	
4,859,050	8/1989	Borah	351/210
4,973,149	11/1990	Hutchinson .	
5,092,343	3/1992	Spitzer	128/733
5,218,530	6/1993	Jastrzebski	364/413.05
5,417,211	5/1995	Abraham-Fuchs	128/653.1
5,447,166	9/1995	Gevins	128/731
5,481,622	1/1996	Gerhardt	382/103
5,491,492	2/1996	Knapp	345/8
5,517,021	5/1996	Kaufman	20/221

FOREIGN PATENT DOCUMENTS

301790	2/1989	European Pat. Off.	A61B 5/04
6-266497	9/1994	Japan	B42F 21/06

OTHER PUBLICATIONS

Adams, C. "If Looks Could Kill: The Eyes Have It." *Military & Aerospace Electronics* (1990): 35–37.

Box, G. and G. Jenkins. *Time Series Analysis, Forecasting, and Control.* Holden–Day, 1976.

Calhoun, G.; W. Janson and C. Arbak. "Use Of Eye Control To Select Switches." *Proceedings of the Human Factors Society 30th Annual Meeting* (1986).

Carpenter, P. and M. Just. "Eye Fixations During Menta Rotations." in *Eye Movements and the Higher Psychological Functions.* Edited by, J. Senders, D. Fisher and R. Monty. Lawrence Erlbaum Associates, 1978, pp. 115–133.

(List continued on next page.)

Primary Examiner—David K. Moore
Assistant Examiner—Jeffrey S. Smith
Attorney, Agent, or Firm—Freda L. Krosnick; Muzio B. Roberto

[57]   **ABSTRACT**

A device and method for estimating a mental decision to select a visual cue from the viewer's eye fixation and corresponding single event evoked cerebral potential. The device comprises an eyetracker, an electronic biosignal processor and a digital computer. The eyetracker determines the instantaneous viewing direction from oculometric measurements and a head position and orientation sensor. The electronic processor continually estimates the cerebral electroencephalogramic potential from scalp surface measurements following corrections for electrooculogramic, electromyogramic and electrocardiogramic artifacts. The digital computer analyzes the viewing direction data for a fixation and then extracts the corresponding single event evoked cerebral potential. The fixation properties, such as duration, start and end pupil sizes, end state (saccade or blink) and gaze fixation count, and the parametric representation of the evoked potential are all inputs to an artificial neural network for outputting an estimate of the selection interest in the gaze point of regard. The artificial neural network is trained off-line prior to application to represent the mental decisions of the viewer. The device can be used to control computerized machinery from a video display by ocular gaze point of regard alone, by determining which visual cue the viewer is looking at and then using the estimation of the task-related selection as a selector switch.

5 Claims, 7 Drawing Sheets

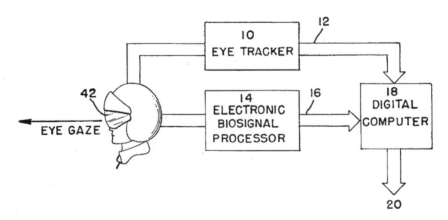

5,649,061

1

DEVICE AND METHOD FOR ESTIMATING A MENTAL DECISION

BACKGROUND OF THE INVENTION

1. Field of the Invention

The present invention relates to estimating a mental decision to activate a task related function which is selected by a visual cue and, therefore, can be used to control machines from a visual display by eye gaze alone.

The present invention has many potential applications in the medical, scientific, engineering, manufacturing, military, entertainment, and other fields. The present invention may be used as a tool for medical diagnosis of ocular functions, as an aid to the paraplegic handicapped, as an instrument for providing measurement of ocular functions and workload in human factors studies, as a measure of subject training, as a tool for fatigue monitoring, as part of an electronic safety net to detect performance degradation due to pilot incapacitation in piloted and teleoperated vehicles, as a component of an electronic intelligent pilot-vehicle interface used for situation awareness aiding in piloted and teleoperated vehicles, as a tool for task scan analysis including situation awareness measuring, as a controller of machines and computer games, and for advertisement and usability analysis.

Particularly, the present invention is utilized to control computerized machines from an electronic video display by the ocular gaze point of regard alone. Examples of machine control by ocular functions are: (1) updating computer generated information displays, (2) selecting panel switches and instruments, (3) controlling the fidelity of computer generated imagery scene inserts in simulations, (4) controlling the viewing direction of remotely located cameras, (5) controlling the movement of teleoperated robotics platforms or vehicles, (6) selecting display subareas for automated scene analysis in aided target recognition, (7) designating targets from direct sight or from a sensor display, and (8) weapon system pointing.

The present invention has particular applications to time shared concurrent tasks where hands are involved in a continual time critical pilotage task and eyes are used intermittently to control a discrete task. The present invention enables both tasks to share a common visual working area with overlaid visual images. Therefore, the present invention allows task interference to be reduced by dedicating eye-movements and visual attention to the same working surface.

An example of such an application would be single pilot nap-of-earth low-level helicopter flight while updating on-board heads-up displays. A similar application is teleoperations of remote vehicles from video displays with camera control. Another such application is to the operation of completely enclosed armored vehicles with "transparent" or "see through" armor. There the operator would see a video projection of the outside scene, recorded by externally mounted cameras and relayed to internal monitors. The operator would use the present invention to control displays overlaid on the scene projection while concurrently performing the vehicle pilotage task. Similar comments apply to the piloting of "glass cockpit" designs for completely enclosed, high performance aircraft.

The present invention with a properly designed oculometer can also be used with head-mounted video displays in many application fields. The head-mounted video displays, such as those developed for virtual reality, stereographic displays, monocular or binocular vision helmet mounted displays, and night vision goggles used in piloted

2

helicopters, vehicles, and teleoperated robotics control stations are all suitable.

2. Description of the Background Art

The conventional method of decision estimation for control of machines by ocular functions is based on measuring the eye gaze fixation duration, which commonly is longer for a visual cue of task interest than for a visual cue of disinterest. However, the statistical distributions of the interest and disinterest fixation durations tend to overlap and are clearly not separable. In practice, the user must extend the gaze duration with an unnaturally directed stare to designate a cue of interest. Usually, the user follows the display response to the cue selection with a motor action like a button push to confirm the visual selection. In some designs the user must execute an extended stare for cue selection in conjunction with the motor action to indicate a selection. This need for an extensively forced gaze tends to interrupt the task flow since any naturally occurring visual search patterns are momentarily suppressed. It can also increase ocular fatigue due to the corresponding reduction in eye blinks and the associated reductions in corneal lubrication and oxygenation. Furthermore, the need for a confirming motor action increases the workload of the viewer.

SUMMARY OF THE INVENTION

The present invention estimates a mental decision to select a visual cue of task related interest, from both eye fixation and the associated single event evoked cerebral potential. The invention uses the start of the eye fixation to trigger the computation of the corresponding evoked cerebral potential.

The design of the invention is based on the physiological evidence for the relationships existing between eye movements, evoked visual potentials and human visual information processing. This evidence is summarized as follows:

(1) While a visual cue is acquired by a rapid eye-movement known as a saccade, the cue can only be studied during a fixation lasting typically from 200 to 600 milliseconds;

(2) Simple target cues at known locations are identified within several fixations, which taken together define a gaze with the first fixation locating a critical feature of the cue and the second fixation being longer in time during which the critical feature is mentally compared;

(3) The duration of an eye fixation occurring during a mental comparison tends to be longer for a visual cue of task-interest than for a visual cue of disinterest;

(4) The evoked visual potential generated during a fixation period has waveform components which correspond to the stages of visual information processing;

(5) The amplitude of the evoked potential component occurring about 250 to 300 milliseconds is greater for a visual cue of task-interest than for a visual cue of disinterest;

(6) The eye pupil of an alert viewer in constant illumination tends to dilate at the start of information processing reaching its maximum just before decision is made, and contracts at the moment of decision making; and

(7) Eye blinks appear to mark brief breaks that the brain takes at the end of each phase of a mental task, and in this way punctuate the sequence of mental events involved in acquiring and processing information.

A preferred embodiment of the present invention is directed to a device for estimating a mental decision, com-

United States Patent [19]

Wagner

[11] **Patent Number:**	**5,922,016**
[45] **Date of Patent:**	***Jul. 13, 1999**

[54] **APPARATUS FOR ELECTRIC STIMULATION OF AUDITORY NERVES OF A HUMAN BEING**

[75] Inventor: **Hermann Wagner**, Berlin, Germany

[73] Assignees: **Ingeborg Hochmair; Erwin Hochmair**, both of Axams/Tirol, Austria

[*] Notice: This patent issued on a continued prosecution application filed under 37 CFR 1.53(d), and is subject to the twenty year patent term provisions of 35 U.S.C. 154(a)(2).

[21] Appl. No.: **08/590,567**

[22] Filed: **Jan. 26, 1996**

[51] Int. Cl.^{6} **A61F 2/18**
[52] U.S. Cl. **607/137**; 600/559; 128/898
[58] Field of Search 607/55, 56, 136, 607/137; 128/898; 381/312, 60; 600/559

[56] **References Cited**

U.S. PATENT DOCUMENTS

3,799,146	3/1974	John et al.	.... 128/2.1
4,535,785	8/1985	Van Den Honert et al.	.... 128/746
4,577,641	3/1986	Hochmair et al.	.... 128/746
4,858,612	8/1989	Stocklin	.... 607/136
5,119,826	6/1992	Baart De La Faille	.... 128/746
5,291,785	3/1994	Downs	.... 73/585
5,395,301	3/1995	Russek	.... 601/41

Primary Examiner—Jack W. Lavinder
Assistant Examiner—David M Ruddy
Attorney, Agent, or Firm—Henry M. Feiereisen

[57] **ABSTRACT**

Apparatus for electric stimulation and diagnostics of auditory nerves of a human being, e.g. for determination of sensation level (SL), most conformable level (MCL) and uncomfortable level (UCL) audibility curves, includes a stimulator detachably secured to a human being for sending a signal into a human ear, and an electrode placed within the human ear and electrically connected to the stimulator by an electric conductor for conducting the signals from the stimulator into the ear. A control unit is operatively connected to the stimulator for instructing the stimulator as to characteristics of the generated signals being transmitted to the ear.

9 Claims, 8 Drawing Sheets

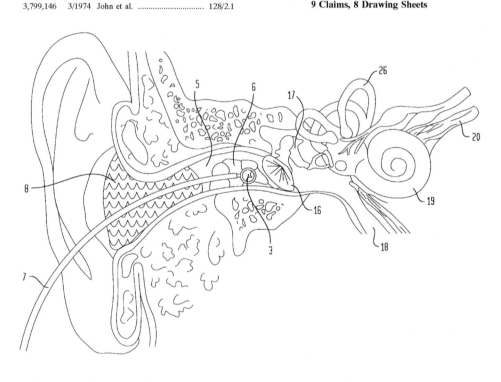

United States Patent [19]

Bogdashevsky et al.

[11] **Patent Number:** **6,006,188**

[45] **Date of Patent:** **Dec. 21, 1999**

[54] **SPEECH SIGNAL PROCESSING FOR DETERMINING PSYCHOLOGICAL OR PHYSIOLOGICAL CHARACTERISTICS USING A KNOWLEDGE BASE**

[75] Inventors: **Rostislav Bogdashevsky; Vladimir Alexeev; Vitaly Yarigin**, all of Moscow, Russian Federation; **George Baker**, Los Alamos, N.Mex.; **Harrison Stanton**, Henderson, Nev.

[73] Assignee: **Dendrite, Inc.**, Las Vegas, Nev.

[21] Appl. No.: **08/820,566**

[22] Filed: **Mar. 19, 1997**

[51] **Int. Cl.**[6] **G01L 5/06**; G01L 9/00

[52] **U.S. Cl.** **704/270**; 706/50

[58] **Field of Search** 704/270; 434/236, 434/262; 706/50

[56] **References Cited**

U.S. PATENT DOCUMENTS

3,855,416	12/1974	Fuller	704/272
3,855,417	12/1974	Fuller	704/272
3,855,418	12/1974	Fuller	704/272
3,971,034	7/1976	Bell, Jr. et al.	346/33 R

(List continued on next page.)

FOREIGN PATENT DOCUMENTS

0424071 A2	4/1991	European Pat. Off.	G10L 5/06
94/04072	3/1994	WIPO	A61B 5/00
95/20216	7/1995	WIPO	G10L 9/00
WO 95/20216	7/1995	WIPO	G10L 9/00

OTHER PUBLICATIONS

Toyotoshi Yamada, et al. "Pattern recognition of emotion with Neural Network," Proc. IEEE IECON, vol. 1, p. 183–187, Nov. 1995.

Tsuyoshi Moriyama, et al. "Evaluation of the Relationship Between Emotional Concepts and Emotional Parameters of Speech," Proc. ICASSP, p. 1431–1434, Apr. 1997.

Alan A. Wrench, et al. "Objective Speech Quality Assessment in Patients With Intra–Oral Cancers: Voiceless Fricatives", International Conference on Spoken Language Processing ICSLP, Oct. 1992.

Alan A. Wrench, et al. "A Speech Therapy Workstation Providing Visual Feedback of Segmental Quality," ESCA Workshop on Technology for Disabled Persons, Jun. 1993.

(List continued on next page.)

Primary Examiner—David R. Hudspeth
Assistant Examiner—Tálivaldis Ivars Šmits
Attorney, Agent, or Firm—Morrison & Foerster

[57] **ABSTRACT**

A speech-based system for assessing the psychological, physiological, or other characteristics of a test subject is described. The system includes a knowledge base that stores one or more speech models, where each speech model corresponds to a characteristic of a group of reference subjects. Signal processing circuitry, which may be implemented in hardware, software and/or firmware, compares the test speech parameters of a test subject with the speech models. In one embodiment, each speech model is represented by a statistical time-ordered series of frequency representations of the speech of the reference subjects. The speech model is independent of a priori knowledge of style parameters associated with the voice or speech. The system includes speech parameterization circuitry for generating the test parameters in response to the test subject's speech. This circuitry includes speech acquisition circuitry, which may be located remotely from the knowledge base. The system further includes output circuitry for outputting at least one indicator of a characteristic in response to the comparison performed by the signal processing circuitry. The characteristic may be time-varying, in which case the output circuitry outputs the characteristic in a time-varying manner. The output circuitry also may output a ranking of each output characteristic. In one embodiment, one or more characteristics may indicate the degree of sincerity of the test subject, where the degree of sincerity may vary with time. The system may also be employed to determine the effectiveness of treatment for a psychological or physiological disorder by comparing psychological or physiological characteristics, respectively, before and after treatment.

63 Claims, 29 Drawing Sheets

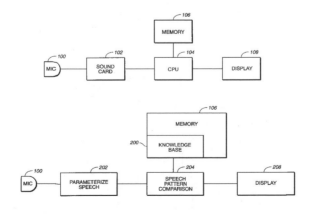

United States Patent [19]

Mardirossian

[11] **Patent Number:** **6,011,991**

[45] **Date of Patent:** **Jan. 4, 2000**

[54] **COMMUNICATION SYSTEM AND METHOD INCLUDING BRAIN WAVE ANALYSIS AND/ OR USE OF BRAIN ACTIVITY**

[75] Inventor: **Aris Mardirossian**, Germantown, Md.

[73] Assignee: **Technology Patents, LLC**, Derwood, Md.

[21] Appl. No.: **09/206,365**

[22] Filed: **Dec. 7, 1998**

[51] Int. Cl.⁷ **A61N 5/00**
[52] U.S. Cl. **600/544**; 600/545
[58] Field of Search 600/300, 544–545;
128/897–898, 904, 905

[56] **References Cited**

U.S. PATENT DOCUMENTS

5,059,814	10/1991	Mead et al. .
5,118,606	6/1992	Lynch et al. .
5,136,687	8/1992	Edelman et al. .
5,224,203	6/1993	Skeirik .
5,303,705	4/1994	Nenov .
5,325,862	7/1994	Lewis et al. .
5,461,699	10/1995	Arbabi et al. .
5,522,863	6/1996	Spano et al. .
5,640,493	6/1997	Skeirik .
5,715,821	2/1998	Faupel .
5,719,561	2/1998	Gonzales .
5,722,418	3/1998	Bro 128/905
5,730,146	3/1998	Itil et al. 600/544
5,736,543	4/1998	Rogers et al. .
5,737,485	4/1998	Flanagan et al. .
5,747,492	5/1998	Lynch et al. .
5,791,342	8/1998	Woodard 600/544
5,816,247	10/1998	Maynard .

Primary Examiner—Cary O'Connor
Assistant Examiner—Michael Astorino
Attorney, Agent, or Firm—Joseph A. Rhoa

[57] **ABSTRACT**

A system and method for enabling human beings to communicate by way of their monitored brain activity. The brain activity of an individual is monitored and transmitted to a remote location (e.g. by satellite). At the remote location, the monitored brain activity is compared with pre-recorded normalized brain activity curves, waveforms, or patterns to determine if a match or substantial match is found. If such a match is found, then the computer at the remote location determines that the individual was attempting to communicate the word, phrase, or thought corresponding to the matched stored normalized signal.

8 Claims, 3 Drawing Sheets

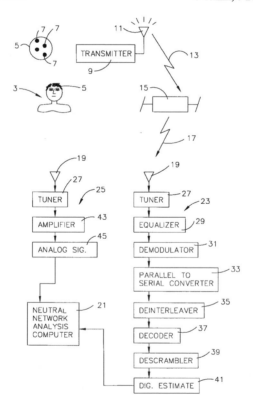

6,011,991

1

COMMUNICATION SYSTEM AND METHOD INCLUDING BRAIN WAVE ANALYSIS AND/ OR USE OF BRAIN ACTIVITY

This invention relates to a system and method for enabling human beings to communicate with one another by monitoring brain activity. In particular, this invention relates to such a system and method where brain activity of a particular individual is monitored and transmitted in a wireless manner (e.g. via satellite) from the location of the individual to a remote location so that the brain activity can be computer analyzed at the remote location thereby enabling the computer and/or individuals at the remote location to determine what the monitored individual was thinking or wishing to communicate.

In certain embodiments this invention relates to the analysis of brain waves or brain activity, and/or to the remote firing of select brain nodes in order to produce a predetermined effect on an individual.

BACKGROUND OF THE INVENTION

It is known to monitor brain activity by way of electro-encephalograph (EEG) methods, magnetoencephalograph (MEG) methods, and the like. For example, see U.S. Pat. Nos. 5,816,247 and 5,325,862, the disclosures of which are both hereby incorporated herein by reference. As discussed in the '247 patent, an EEG may be recorded from a number of pairs of scalp electrodes and processed according to known software. Such software and/or hardware acquires both processed and unprocessed EEG data and may record it on a disk. The records may be replayed and statistics of the on-line measures made on suitable sections placed in categories predefined by a user. This may utilize the form of database of statistical measures of brain activity. Unfortunately, neither the '862 nor the '247 patents disclose or suggest any methods by which humans can communicate with one another by way of monitoring brain activity.

U.S. Pat. No. 5,719,561 discloses a communications device and method, the entire disclosure of the '561 patent hereby being incorporated herein by reference. The '561 patent discusses a method and device for vibromechanical tactile communications adaptable for use by individuals to recognize alpha numeric messages in a language or in other symbols known to them. The '561 patent discusses using a series of sequentially firing vibromechanical stimulators vibrating against a suitably tactile sensitive surface of the wearer (e.g. skin) to induce a phenomenon of illustration of linear continuity. Unfortunately, the '561 patent requires the use of burdensome and complex vibromechanical tactile devices, and is not suitable for long distance communication.

It is a purpose of this invention to address any or all of the above-identified problems in the prior art, as well as other problems which will become apparent to the skilled artisan from the following detailed description of this invention.

SUMMARY OF THE INVENTION

Generally speaking, this invention fulfills the above described needs in the art by providing a method of communicating comprising the steps of:

providing a first human being at a first location;

providing a computer at a second location that is remote from the first location;

providing a satellite;

providing at least one sensor (preferably a plurality—e.g. tens, hundreds, or thousands, with each sensor moni-

2

toring the firing of one or more brain nodes or synapse type members) on the first human being;

detecting brain activity of the first human being using the at least one sensor, and transmitting the detected brain activity to the satellite as a signal including brain activity information;

the satellite sending a signal including the brain activity information to the second location;

a receiver at the second location receiving the signal from the satellite and forwarding the brain activity information in the signal to the computer;

comparing the received brain activity information of the first human being with normalized or averaged brain activity information relating to the first human being from memory; and

determining whether the first human being was attempting to communicate particular words, phrases or thoughts, based upon the comparing of the received brain activity information to the information from memory.

In certain embodiments, the invention includes the following step: asking the first human being a plurality of questions and recording brain activity of the first human being responsive to the plurality of questions in the process of developing said normalized or averaged brain activity information relating to the first human being stored in the memory. A database in a memory may include, for each of a plurality (e.g. one hundred or thousands) of individuals, a number of prerecorded files each corresponding to a particular thought, attempt to communicate a word, attempt to communicate a phrase or thought, or mental state. Measured brain activity of a given individual may be compared to files from that database of that individual to determine what the individual is attempting to communicate or what type of mental state the individual is in.

In certain embodiments, the plurality of questions are the same question.

In certain embodiments, the plurality of questions are different questions.

In certain embodiments, the invention includes the step of normalizing or averaging recorded brain activity responsive to a given question or set of questions in developing the normalized or averaged brain activity information relating to the first human being.

It is an object of this invention to enable brain activity of a first human being to be monitored, with the activity being transmitted to a remote location so that individuals and/or a computer at the remote location can determine what the first human being was thinking or intending to communicate. In such a manner, human beings can communicate with one another via monitoring of brain activity, and transmission of the same.

It is another object of this invention to communicate monitored brain activity from one location to another in a wireless manner, such as by IR, RF, or satellite.

It is another object of this invention to provide a system capable of identifying particular nodes in an individual's brain, the firings of which affect characteristics such as appetite, hunger, thirst, communication skills (e.g. which nodes are utilized to communicate certain words such as "yes", "no", or phrases such as "I don't know", "I'm not sure", or numbers such as "one", "two", "ten", "one hundred" and the like), thought processes, depression, and the like). When such nodes are identified, they may be specifically monitored by one or more sensors to analyze behavior or communication or words, phrases, or thoughts. In other

(12) **United States Patent**

Patton

(10) **Patent No.:** **US 6,292,688 B1**

(45) **Date of Patent:** **Sep. 18, 2001**

(54) **METHOD AND APPARATUS FOR ANALYZING NEUROLOGICAL RESPONSE TO EMOTION-INDUCING STIMULI**

(75) Inventor: **Richard E. Patton**, Colorado Springs, CO (US)

(73) Assignee: **Advanced Neurotechnologies, Inc.**, Colorado Springs, CO (US)

(*) Notice: Subject to any disclaimer, the term of this patent is extended or adjusted under 35 U.S.C. 154(b) by 732 days.

(21) Appl. No.: **08/608,440**

(22) Filed: **Feb. 28, 1996**

(51) Int. Cl.[7] **A61B 5/04**
(52) U.S. Cl. **600/544**; 600/545; 600/300
(58) Field of Search 128/731, 732, 128/630; 600/544, 545, 300

(56) **References Cited**

U.S. PATENT DOCUMENTS

Re. 34,015	* 8/1992	Duffy	.... 128/731
4,649,482	* 3/1987	Raviv et al.	.... 128/731
4,736,307	* 4/1988	Salb	.... 128/731
4,744,029	* 5/1988	Raviv et al.	.... 128/731
4,789,235	12/1988	Borah et al. .	
4,794,533	12/1988	Cohen .	
4,815,474	* 3/1989	Duffy	.... 128/731
4,862,359	* 8/1989	Trivedi et al.	.... 128/731
4,955,388	9/1990	Silberstein .	

5,024,235	6/1991	Ayers .	
5,113,870	5/1992	Rossenfeld .	
5,137,027	8/1992	Rosenfeld .	
5,230,346	7/1993	Leuchter et al. .	
5,243,517	9/1993	Schmidt et al. .	
5,331,969	* 7/1994	Siberstein	.... 128/731
5,339,826	8/1994	Schmidt et al. .	
5,392,788	2/1995	Hudspeth .	

* cited by examiner

Primary Examiner—Michael Peffley
(74) *Attorney, Agent, or Firm*—Vedder Price Kaufman & Kammholz

(57) **ABSTRACT**

A method of determining the extent of the emotional response of a test subject to stimului having a time-varying visual content, for example, an advertising presentation. The test subject is positioned to observe the presentation for a given duration, and a path of communication is established between the subject and a brain wave detector/analyzer. The intensity component of each of at least two different brain wave frequencies is measured during the exposure, and each frequency is associated with a particular emotion. While the subject views the presentation, periodic variations in the intensity component of the brain waves of each of the particular frequencies selected is measured. The change rates in the intensity at regular periods during the duration are also measured. The intensity change rates are then used to construct a graph of plural coordinate points, and these coordinate points graphically establish the composite emotional reaction of the subject as the presentation continues.

22 Claims, 4 Drawing Sheets

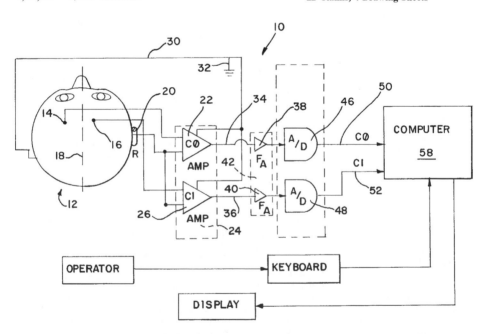

1

METHOD AND APPARATUS FOR ANALYZING NEUROLOGICAL RESPONSE TO EMOTION-INDUCING STIMULI

BACKGROUND OF THE INVENTION

The present invention relates generally to methods and apparatus for neurological testing, and more particularly, to methods and apparatus for determining the emotional state of an individual over the period of time during which that individual is being exposed to time-varying stimuli. While in one respect the invention applies to determining the neurological, psychological, or emotional response of an individual to test stimuli, in many instances, the invention is applicable to using individuals to test a program containing certain stimuli, in order to determine whether such a program will subsequently create favorable responses in other individuals of similar sociocultural-economic makeup.

One of the most practical applications of the method and apparatus with which the invention is presently concerned is that of consumer response testing. Accordingly, this aspect of the method will be discussed immediately herein, while a discussion of other applications and purposes implicit in the invention will be set out elsewhere herein.

In the United States, and elsewhere throughout the world, advertising is heavily used to promote consumer, commercial and industrial products. It is almost universally accepted that, as between or among products which are generally similar to one another in content, price, or quality, successful advertising can help a particular product achieve much greater market penetration and financial success than an otherwise similar product. Advertising, and particularly consumer advertising, although a multi-billion dollar industry in the United States alone, is an area wherein workers find it extremely difficult to create and reproduce what prove to be consistently successful advertising campaigns, themes, or other materials. It is likewise accepted that while it is often easy to predict that response to a particular proposed advertisement or campaign will be unfavorable, it is not known how to create individual advertisements and/or campaigns which can virtually be assured of success on a consistent basis.

Moreover, while it is not always difficult to discover how to make advertising which may simply interest or amuse potential consumers, or to create advertising that consumers will remember, it is often quite another thing to create an advertisement or campaign which succeeds in actually motivating potential consumers to become actual consumers. There are numberless instances known to the advertising community wherein advertising for a particular product is well recognized, is associated with the product and creates a lasting and favorable impression on the consumer as regards the manner in which the advertisement is presented. Yet, as far as can be accurately measured, many such ads fail to impel viewers to use more of such product, or favor it over that of a competitor.

The advertising industry has also recognized that an advertisement must serve the functions referred to above and that this is normally done in individual stages. Thus, the agencies realize that the creative message must attract the user in some way, and preferably, convey a message or impression about the product as well as contain a command or "call to action." However, the particular emotion required to secure attention may defeat the purpose of the message or compromise the call to action portion. Likewise, a part of the message, in an attempt to be clever, may offend some viewers or, in an attempt to gain attention, may appear more frivolous than intended.

2

Hence, it is very difficult on a prospective basis to predict whether a viewer will see a commercial as imaginative and clever on the one hand or frivolous and incredible on the other, when the differences in such presentation are very slight. Similarly, an overly detailed message may appear to be too clinical or perhaps worse, condescending, while another message may be non-offensive but also non-informing. The differences in comprehensional and emotional states of advertising material viewers may be slight but extremely important.

Hence, among all the possible advertisements that might be produced in the hopes of generating a successful consumer response, even where a large number of efforts are summarily dismissed or weeded out, the persons preparing the advertising and the companies using the advertising for promotional purposes simply cannot be sure within narrow limits as to whether particular advertising material will be a success in the marketplace. Accordingly, it is common to find that long after decisions are made and expenditures incurred in pursuit of presenting a particular advertisement (or theme or campaign of advertisements), that such efforts have simply not been successful, in that the campaign failed to produce sales in amounts proportionate to the expenditure of effort and money.

It is believed that an ideal advertisement is one which can be comprehended by the viewer or listener, which contains an inherently credible message, and which contains an imperative or call to action which will stimulate the viewer or listener to purchase the product in question. The advertising industry has for decades accepted the principle that a simple presentation of an advertising message in cold, hard, clear and logical terms is usually insufficient to induce a prospective purchaser to buy a particular product.

Even if viewers were highly analytical, (and it is accepted that most consumers are not), there is still the problem of differentiation between products whose characteristics are either highly subjective or whose quantitative differences are very minute vis-a-vis those of a competitor. Thus, the flavor of a beer or a hamburger, or the appearance of an article of clothing, is simply incapable of being quantified and presented in analytical terms. Even if such were the case, the question of motivation to buy a selected product would still remain.

Consequently, it has come to be accepted that in a great majority of cases, with a few possible exceptions not pertinent here, the decision to buy products is an emotional one in one sense or another. The presence of such emotion does not imply that the choice is irrational, but merely that it meets a need that the subject perceives himself to have, or will have, at the time of purchase. Whether the emotional response is one of self-satisfaction, one of belief that an intelligent choice has been made or that the choice will create a favorable appearance, image or other response in the buyer is not particularly important. According to the invention, it is believed that discovering and qualitatively and quantitatively analyzing the actual emotional response of a subject is the key to correlation between an advertising presentation and a successful sale of the product.

Referring again to the subject of advertising response, it would be ideal if people preparing advertisements were able to put themselves in the shoes, so to speak, of the particular customer. However, while certain advertising agencies are able to use the talents of creative personnel who are successful more often than not, a high degree of correspondence between choosing and presenting a particular ad and achieving product sales is simply not available on a consistent basis.

(12) **United States Patent**
Tsukada et al.

(10) **Patent No.:** US 6,842,637 B2
(45) **Date of Patent:** *Jan. 11, 2005

(54) **MAGNETIC FIELD MEASUREMENT APPARATUS**

(75) Inventors: **Keiji Tsukada**, Kashiwa (JP); **Akihiko Kandori**, Hachioji (JP); **Tsuyoshi Miyashita**, Kokubunji (JP); **Hiroyuki Suzuki**, Hitachinaka (JP); **Hitoshi Sasabuchi**, Mito (JP)

(73) Assignee: **Hitachi, Ltd.**, Tokyo (JP)

(*) Notice: Subject to any disclaimer, the term of this patent is extended or adjusted under 35 U.S.C. 154(b) by 305 days.

This patent is subject to a terminal disclaimer.

(21) Appl. No.: **09/948,857**

(22) Filed: **Sep. 10, 2001**

(65) **Prior Publication Data**

US 2002/0019589 A1 Feb. 14, 2002

Related U.S. Application Data

(63) Continuation of application No. 09/176,767, filed on Oct. 22, 1998, now Pat. No. 6,424,853.

(30) **Foreign Application Priority Data**

Oct. 24, 1997 (JP) 9-292025

(51) **Int. Cl.^{7}** A61B 5/05
(52) **U.S. Cl.** 600/409; 600/407; 600/410; 600/422; 600/423; 323/43
(58) **Field of Search** 600/409, 407, 600/410, 422, 423, 523, 524, 440, 569, 509; 323/43

(56) **References Cited**

U.S. PATENT DOCUMENTS

4,324,255 A * 4/1982 Barach et al. 600/300
4,793,355 A * 12/1988 Crum et al. 600/409

(List continued on next page.)

FOREIGN PATENT DOCUMENTS

JP	2-116767	5/1990
JP	5-146416	6/1993
JP	05-196711	8/1993
JP	7-148131	6/1995
JP	08-071051	3/1996

OTHER PUBLICATIONS

Review of Scientific Instruments, vol. 66, No. 10, Oct. 1995, "Multi–channel SQUID system detecting tangential components of the cardiac magnetic field", K. Tsukada et al, pp. 5085–5091.
10th International Conference on Biomagnetism BIOMAG96, 1996, "A 129 Channel Vector Neuromagnetic Imaging System", Y. Yoshida et al, p. 351.

Primary Examiner—Angela D. Sykes
Assistant Examiner—William C. Jung
(74) *Attorney, Agent, or Firm*—Mattingly, Stanger & Malur, P.C.

(57) **ABSTRACT**

A magnetic field measurement apparatus includes a plurality of magnetometers each having SQUID's and three detection coils, one of which detects each of three orthogonal directional magnetic field components (B_x, B_y, B_z) of a magnetic field generated from a subject to be inspected, a display which displays time variation of waveforms of the magnitude ($\sqrt{(B_x^2+B_y^2+B_z^2)}$) of magnetic field synthesized by square sum of each of the three orthogonal directional magnetic field components of the magnetic field generated from the subject to be inspected, a holder for holding a Dewar's vessel for arranging magnetometers therein, and a controller for controlling a positional relationship between the subject to be inspected and the Dewar's vessel. Accurate time variation of the magnetic field generated from the subject to be inspected can be detected without influence of positional change of the subject to be inspected, by simultaneously measuring each of the three orthogonal directional magnetic field components (B_x, B_y, B_z) of the magnetic field generated from current sources in the subject to be inspected.

4 Claims, 15 Drawing Sheets

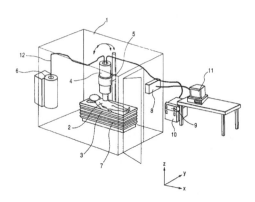

1

MAGNETIC FIELD MEASUREMENT APPARATUS

This is a continuation application of U.S. Ser. No. 09/176,767, filed Oct. 22, 1998 now U.S. Pat. No. 6,424, 853.

BACKGROUND OF THE INVENTION

1. Field of the Invention

The present invention relates to a magnetic field measurement apparatus consisting of a magnetometer comprised of a Superconductive Quantum Interferometer Device (SQUID) for measuring magnetic fields generated by the nervous activity of the brain of humans or animals or myocardial activity or magnetic substances contained in the subject to be inspected.

2. Description of Related Art

In measurements of very weak magnetic fields in the conventional art using equipment such as SQUID for measuring biomagnetic fields, generally the magnetic field on the surface of a living body is capable of being measured. Such measurements can be just the vertical components of a magnetic field with the head regarded as a sphere, for instance the polar coordinates (r, ϕ, θ) in the case of the head, and the magnetic field component Br in the vertical r direction on the head surface, or in the case of the heart, the orthogonal coordinates (X, Y, Z), of the chest section when measured on the flat planes X and Y, and the magnetic field component B_z. in the vertical Z direction on the X and Y planes.

On the other hand while few in number, there is literature reporting on measurement apparatus for measuring magnetic components of a biomagnetic field in a plurality of directions. For instance, the simultaneous measurement of the magnetic component B_X in the X direction and the magnetic component B_Y in the Y direction on the orthogonal coordinates (X, Y, Z); as well as the display of magnitude $\sqrt{(B_X^2 + B_Y^2)}$ synthesized by magnetic component B_X in the X direction and magnetic component B_Y in the Y direction have been reported (K. Tsukada et. al., Rev. Sci. Instrum., 66 (10), pp 5085–5091(1995)).

Further, though not the three directions B_r, B_ϕ, B_θ of the polar coordinates (r, ϕ, θ) of the magnetic components B_X, B_Y and B_Z in the three directions of the orthogonal coordinates (X, Y, Z); a method has been reported for measuring the three components of each intersecting magnetic field, finding the magnetic components B_r, B_ϕ, B_θ in the three directions on the polar coordinates (r, ϕ, θ) and displaying a waveform showing the time variation of each magnetic component in three directions on polar coordinates (r, ϕ, θ) on a CRT screen (Y. Yoshida et. al., 10th Int'l Conf. on Biomagnetisim (1996)).

Also, in the conventional art, not only a waveform showing time variations in a magnetic field strength but also the distribution of the magnitude of a magnetic field can be found from results of magnetic measurements of a plurality of points in an organism utilizing a plurality of magnetometers and the result displayed as a magnetic field magnitude contour map. Factors such as the position, magnitude and direction of electrical current sources in an organism can be analyzed over desired periods of time on a magnetic field contour map and changes over time in the electrical physiological phenomenon in the organism thus discovered. In the conventional art, changes in electrical physiological phenomenon in a dynamic organism can therefore be revealed by utilizing these magnetic field contour maps to aid in the diagnosis of disease.

2

In the method used in the conventional art, the heart of the child or adult which is the subject of measurement is fixed in a constant position and direction versus the magnetic plane of the magnetic field of the magnetometer. However, there is the problem that when measuring the magnetic field of the heart of a fetus, an accurate measurement of the heart's magnetic field cannot be made since the position and direction of the fetus cannot be fixed since the fetus is constantly moving within the body of the mother. In other words, even if there is no change in the electrical current source within the heart of the fetus the position and direction will change versus the magnetic plane of the magnetic field generated in the magnetometer by the heart of the fetus creating the problem that the time waveform and the components of the magnetic field being measured cannot be fixed. Another problem in the conventional art, is that a standardized waveform cannot be obtained due to variations in the magnetic field waveform due to changes in the body position of the fetus within the body of the mother, making an accurate diagnosis of the heart disease of the fetus difficult. Further, when the position of the Dewar's vessel housing the magnetometer is moved in order to increase the magnetic signal to measure the component in just one direction of the magnetic field, the magnetic signal reaches a maximum and the measurement range narrows so that setting an ideal position and direction for measurement with the Dewar's vessel is difficult creating the problem that a long time is required. A still further problem is that a large drift occurs in the magnetic signal being detected when moving the Dewar's vessel to an optimal position versus the subject being measured and a long time is thus required to stabilize the magnetic signal being detected.

Yet another problem is that high sensitivity non-destructive inspection of minute impurities having magnetic properties within a nonmagnetic substance is difficult and furthermore the investigation cannot be conducted with high speed.

SUMMARY OF THE INVENTION

In order to resolve the above mentioned problems, it is therefore an object of this invention to provide a magnetic field measurement apparatus and a magnetic field measurement method for accurately measuring the electrical physiological phenomenon within the heart of a fetus without affecting a change in the status of the fetus even when the direction and position of the fetus changes within the body of the mother. It is a further object of the invention to provide a magnetic field measurement apparatus and a magnetic field measurement method for accurately detecting changes over time in the magnetic field from the subject of inspection even in cases where a position change has occurred in the subject for inspection while placed in an environment for inspection or the subject for inspection is placed inside a special material for inspection.

The magnetic field measurement apparatus of this invention is comprised of a detection coils for detecting magnetic fields of three directions and a superconductive quantum interferometer device (SQUID) connected to these detection coils; a single or a plurality of vector magnetometers are provided for isolating and measuring each of the magnetic components for the three directions. The magnetic components of the intersecting three directions measured with the single or plurality of vector magnetometers are synthesized by the square sum method and a time waveform of the resulting magnitude of the magnetic field is shown on a display means (monitor).

In the magnetic field measurement apparatus of this invention, a holding means and control means for storing

(19) **United States**

(12) **Patent Application Publication** (10) Pub. No.: **US 2010/0234697 A1**
Walter et al. (43) **Pub. Date:** **Sep. 16, 2010**

(54) **SYSTEMS, DEVICES, AND METHODS FOR MONITORING A SUBJECT**

(75) Inventors: **Timothy J. Walter**, Upper Arlington, OH (US); **Uma Marar**, Blacklick, OH (US)

(73) Assignee: **Lotus Magnus, LLC**, Grove City, OH (US)

(21) Appl. No.: **12/438,273**

(22) PCT Filed: **Apr. 29, 2008**

(86) PCT No.: **PCT/US08/61889**

§ 371 (c)(1),
(2), (4) Date: **Feb. 20, 2009**

Publication Classification

(51) **Int. Cl.**
A61B 5/0476 (2006.01)
A61B 5/0488 (2006.01)
A61B 5/0496 (2006.01)

(52) **U.S. Cl.** **600/301**

(57) **ABSTRACT**

Systems, devices, and methods for monitoring a subject using a monitoring patch that may include electroencephalography apparatus, electromyography apparatus, and electrooculography apparatus.

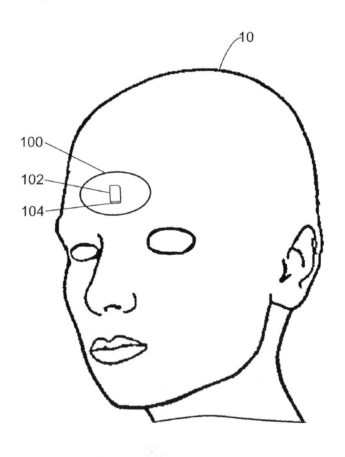

SYSTEMS, DEVICES, AND METHODS FOR MONITORING A SUBJECT

[0001]   The present invention relates generally to systems, devices, and methods for monitoring a subject (e.g., monitoring a subject's various states of sleep and wakefulness). More specifically, the present invention relates to systems, devices, and methods that may monitor the neural, muscular, and/or ocular activity of a subject with a small portable device to determine the amount and/or quality of the sleep the subject undergoes and/or the vigilance of the subject while the subject is awake.

[0002]   Electroencephalography (EEG) records the neural activity of electrical potential across cell membranes, which are detected through the cerebral cortex and recorded by a plurality of electrodes. The changes in electrical potential in the cortex contain rhythmical activity, which typically occur at frequencies of about 0.5 to about 70 cycles per second (hertz). While awake, fast, random signals are predominately generated at low voltage and mixed frequency. While asleep, more predictable signals are generated at a low voltage and predictable frequencies over predictable periods.

[0003]   Five distinct brain wave patterns that are commonly detected during an EEG recording are delta waves (e.g., about 0.5-3 hertz), theta waves (e.g., about 3-8 hertz), alpha waves (e.g., about 8-12 hertz), beta waves (e.g., about 13-20 hertz), and gamma waves (e.g., about 26-70 hertz). Many of these frequencies may be observed in a subject's sleep cycle. A sleep cycle may be defined as a progression of brainwave patterns that may be seen while a subject is sleeping. Generally, subjects undergo several sleep cycles per night, each lasting around ninety minutes. Each progression of brainwave patterns during the sleep cycle may be referred to as a stage of the sleep cycle. Generally, each sleep cycle progresses consecutively through stage I sleep, stage II sleep, stage III sleep, stage IV sleep (stage III sleep and stage IV sleep may be grouped together and refereed to as slow wave sleep), briefly back to stage II sleep, and then rapid eye movement (REM) sleep.

[0004]   Waking consciousness is generally experienced neurophysiologically at a brainwave frequency of about forty hertz.

[0005]   Electrooculography (EOG) records the ocular activity of the electrical potential from the retina, which consists of an electrically-charged nerve membrane. EOG signals can be measured by placing electrodes near an eye. Motion of an eye may cause a measurable change of electrical potential between two or more surface electrodes.

[0006]   Electromyography (EMG) records the muscular activity of electrical potential across muscular membranes, which range between about 50 microvolts to about 30 millivolts (depending on the muscle under observation). Typical repetition rate of muscle unit firing is about 7 hertz to about 20 hertz, depending on the size of the muscle, the type of muscle, etc. EMG signals may be recorded within a muscle (i.e., intramuscular EMG) or on the surface a subject's skin outside of a muscle.

[0007]   Sleep may be characterized by specific patterns in a subject's EEG and/or EMG. Analysis of EEG and/or EMG recordings may be performed to, e.g., diagnose various sleep disorders such as, circadian rhythm disorders (e.g., advanced sleep phase syndrome, delayed sleep phase syndrome, free-running type, jet lag, and shift work sleep disorder), disorders of REM sleep (e.g., REM Sleep Behavior Disorder). Further, analysis of EEG and/or EMG recordings may be performed to calculate the amount of sleep a subject obtains in regards to insomnia (e.g., inadequate sleep hygiene, paradoxical insomnia, primary insomnia, secondary insomnia, psychophysiological insomnia) in a way that would be more objective and more accurate than the currently used modalities of actigraphy and/or a sleep diary, hypersomnia (narcolepsy, idiopathic hypersomnia, Klein-Levin Syndrome, and menstrual related hypersomnia) or to measure the effects of sleep promoting and alertness promoting pharmaceuticals on the state of vigilance of the subject, etc.

[0008]   Sleep onset is characterized by specific changes in a subject's EEG and/or EMG data. As such, signal data recorded by EEG and/or EMG apparatus may be utilized to determine how long an individual subject has slept. For example, a skilled practitioner may analyze the data for patterns of sleep and wakefulness that would provide diagnostic support for the various sleep and wakefulness disorders described herein. The data would be analyzed to determine how long a subject has slept. Also, for example, a computer may analyze the data using pre-existing algorithms and software (e.g., Polysmith 2003) to score the various stages of sleep and wakefulness to determine how long a subject as slept.

[0009]   The determination of how long an individual subject has slept over a given or selected time period has a number of commercial applications. Such a determination may be important for shift workers, truck drivers, train operators, air traffic controllers, airplane pilots, and other subjects whose work could be dangerous if they become too drowsy. In addition, many of these workers and others may be required by governmental entities (e.g., the National Transportation Safety Board or the Federal Motor Carrier Administration), worker unions, employers, etc. to sleep a minimum number of hours per work week.

[0010]   Sleep may be an important factor in determining vigilance of a subject. Vigilance may be characterized by specific changes in a subject's EEG and/or EMG data. As such, signal data recorded by EEG and/or EMG may be utilized to determine the vigilance of a subject. Such signal data may be monitored in real-time to determine the vigilance of a subject. For example, devices exist that analyze EEG or EMG data to determine if a truck driver is becoming drowsy, and subsequently alerts the driver to increase his/her vigilance (e.g., using an alarm). Such data may also be recorded and then analyzed offline.

[0011]   Further, collecting EEG and/or EMG data is useful for various sleep disorder testing. For example, EEG and/or EMG data may be collected during a Multiple Sleep Latency Test (MSLT). Typically, a MSLT is conducted the day following an overnight sleep. The purpose of this test is to objectively measure daytime sleepiness and to look for REM sleep during daytime naps. Although REM sleep may be seen in normal subjects during the day under special circumstances, often, REM sleep during day is indicative of narcolepsy (i.e., a disorder of REM sleep).

[0012]   Also further, for example, collecting EEG data is useful in determining the duration and/or timing of sleep periods in patients with circadian rhythm disorders and insomnia. Often, circadian rhythm disorders and insomnia are determined by actigraphy and/or sleep logs, which may be inherently inaccurate.

United States Patent [19]

Duffy et al.

[11] **4,408,616**

[45] **Oct. 11, 1983**

[54] **BRAIN ELECTRICAL ACTIVITY MAPPING**

[75] Inventors: **Frank H. Duffy,** Brookline, Mass.; **Norman D. Culver,** Spotswood, N.J.

[73] Assignee: **The Children's Medical Center Corporation,** Boston, Mass.

[21] Appl. No.: **264,043**

[22] Filed: **May 15, 1981**

[51] Int. Cl.³ **A61B 5/04**
[52] U.S. Cl. **128/731**
[58] Field of Search 128/731–733, 128/905

[56] **References Cited**

U.S. PATENT DOCUMENTS

2,928,189	3/1960	Molner et al.	35/22
3,696,808	10/1972	Roy et al.	128/2.1 B
3,705,297	12/1972	John	235/150.53
3,706,308	12/1972	John et al.	128/2.06 R
3,707,147	12/1972	Sellers	128/2.06 G
3,717,141	2/1973	Krohn et al.	128/2.66 R
3,780,724	12/1973	John	128/2.1 B
3,799,146	3/1974	John et al.	128/2.1 B
3,837,331	9/1974	Ross	128/732 X
3,901,215	8/1975	John	128/2.1 B
3,958,563	5/1976	Fernandez et al.	128/731
4,094,307	6/1978	Young	128/2.1 B
4,171,696	10/1979	John	128/731
4,201,224	5/1980	John	128/731
4,214,591	7/1980	Sato et al.	128/731

OTHER PUBLICATIONS

Duffy et al.; *Significance Probability Mapping: An Aid in the Topographic Analysis of Brain Electrical Activity;* EEG and Clin. and Neurophysiology, 1981; pp. 1–8.
Duffy et al.; "Quantification of Focal Abnormalities in Beam Data by Grid Sector Analysis".
Duffy et al.; "Dyslexia: Automated Diagnosis of Computerized Classif. of Brain Electrical Activity"; *Annals of Neur.,* vol. 7, No. 5, 5–1980, pp. 421–428.
Duffy et al.; "Dyslexia: Regional Diff. in Brain Electri-

cal Activity by Topographic Mapping"; *Annals of Neur.,* vol. 7, No. 5, 5–1980, pp. 412–420.
Ueno et al., Topographic Computer Display of Abnormal EEG Activities in Patients with CNS Diseases, Memoirs of the Faculty of Engineering, Kyushu University, vol. 34, No. 3, (Feb., 1975) pp. 195–209.
Marguerite Zientara (CW Staff) Multiple Personalities 'Mapped' by Computer, Computer World Publication, Jan. 24, 1983, p. 14.
Duffy et al., "Brain Electrical Activity Mapping (BEAM): A Method for Extending the Clinical Utility of EEG and Evoked Potential Data," *Annals of Neurology,* vol. 5, No. 4 (Apr., 1979) pp. 309–321.

Primary Examiner—Lee S. Cohen
Assistant Examiner—Angela D. Sykes

[57] **ABSTRACT**

Topographic displays of brain electrical activity are produced from matrices of data derived from evoked potential (EP) and steady-state responses of skull transducers. In different aspects, EP responses are displayed at a variable frame rate, the rate of data sampling is sufficient to capture rapid transient events, difference matrices are derived as the difference between matrices corresponding to two different brain conditions, the baseline of the EP responses is zeroed based on the average prestimulus response, and the steady-state response is analyzed by Fourier transforms. In other aspects, statistical comparison matrices representing statistical differences between corresponding elements in two matrices are generated, a coefficient-of-variance matrix is generated, additional display matrices are temporally interpolated, response waveforms are previewed and tagged for elimination from further processing, the topographic maps are displayed on a video monitor with appropriate scaling of the data to the tones of the display, and additional display points are interpolated between the measured data points for display.

82 Claims, 32 Drawing Figures

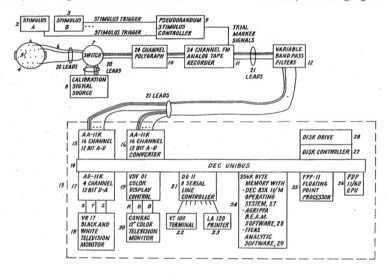

Chapter 13
Directed Energy Weapons

The personnel halting and stimulation response rifle (PHASR) is a prototype
non-lethal laser dazzler developed by the Air Force Research Laboratory's
Directed Energy Directorate, U.S. Department of Defense.

Feb. 23, 1971　　　　A. E. FLANDERS　　　　**3,566,347**

PSYCHO-ACOUSTIC PROJECTOR

Filed April 27, 1967　　　　　　　　　　　2 Sheets—Sheet 1

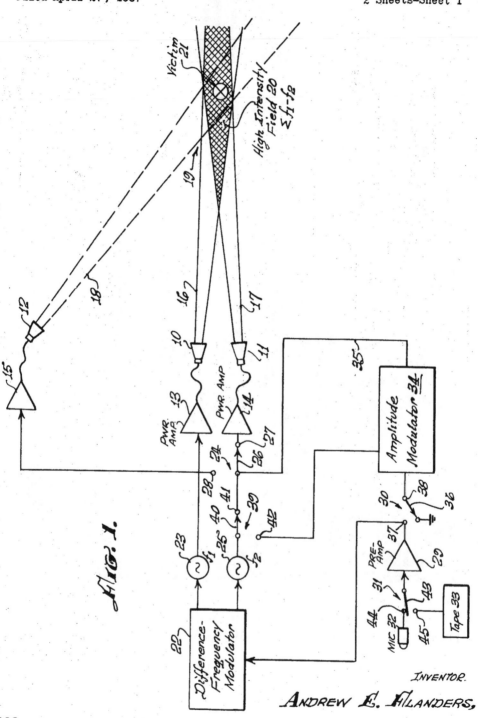

INVENTOR.

ANDREW E. FLANDERS,

United States Patent Office

3,566,347
Patented Feb. 23, 1971

1

3,566,347
PSYCHO-ACOUSTIC PROJECTOR
Andrew E. Flanders, Pomona, Calif., assignor to General
Dynamics Corporation, a corporation of Delaware
Filed Apr. 27, 1967, Ser. No. 634,348
Int. Cl. H04b 11/00
U.S. Cl. 340—15   7 Claims

ABSTRACT OF THE DISCLOSURE

Broadly, this disclosure is directed to a system for producing aural psychological disturbances and partial deafness of the enemy during combat situations. Essentially, a high directional beam is radiated from a plurality of distinct transducers and is modulated by a noise, code or speech beat signal. The invention may utilize various forms and may include movable radiators mounted on a vehicle and oriented to converge at a desired point, independently positioned vehicles with a common frequency modulator, or means employed to modulate the acoustical beam with respect to a fixed frequency. During combat, friendly forces would be equipped with a reference generator to provide aural demodulation of the projected signal, thereby yielding an intelligible beat signal while enemy personnel would be rendered partially deaf by the projected signal as well as being unable to perceive any intelligence transmitted in the form of a modulated beat signal.

BACKGROUND OF THE INVENTION

This invention is directed to means for producing undesirable noise, and more particularly to a means for providing intense aural psychological disturbance and temporary partial deafness as an aid in personal type combat while additionally providing long distance voice communication.

Many prior devices have been developed wherein physically damaging noises are employed to rid a given area of undesirable pests as exemplified by U.S. Pats. 2,922,999; 3,058,103; and 3,113,304. Other prior efforts have been directed to providing ear filters which are employed to block damaging signals while allowing desired signals to be heard as illustrated by U.S. Pat. 3,098,121, while other prior efforts have been directed to ambient noise reduction systems such as found in U.S. Pats. 3,057,960 and 3,133,990. However, no known prior effort has been directed to the modulation of an undesirable, unwanted or noise signal by a desired intelligible signal nor the use of such a system in a combat environment.

SUMMARY OF THE INVENTION

The present invention advances the state of the art by providing a means for producing intense aural psychological disturbance and temporary partial deafness as an aid in personal type combat, while being utilized for voice communication by properly equipped friendly personnel.

Therefore, it is an object of this invention to provide a system capable of producing aural psychological disturbance while simultaneously providing voice communication.

A further object of the invention is to provide a means for radiating a highly directional beam from a plurality of distant transducers which is modulated by a noise, discretely coherent tone or beat, code or speech beat signal.

Another object of the invention is to provide intense aural psychological disturbance and temporary partial deafness as an aid in personal type combat.

Another object of the invention is to provide intense aural psychological disturbance to certain individuals

2

while simultaneously providing effective communication with other individuals (while maintaining radio silence).

Other objects of the invention will become readily apparent from the following description and accompanying drawing wherein:

BRIEF DESCRIPTION OF THE DRAWING

FIG. 1 is a view illustrating an embodiment of a system for carrying out the invention;

FIG. 2 is a block diagram illustrating an embodiment of the circuitry which composes the FIG. 1 difference frequency modulator; and

FIG. 3 is a schematic illustration of an embodiment of the FIG. 2 paraphase inverter.

As illustrated in the drawings, a highly directional acoustic beam is provided by a plurality of moderately high frequency, high power radiators. Each one of the radiators may consist of an array of transducers operating on an acoustical "carrier" frequency in the vicinity, for example, of 5 or 6 kc. The carrier frequency region of operation is selected to provide a maximum of directivity with a minimum of attenuation with distance. One carrier frequency differs from the other by the amount desired to convey the signal of interest. The resulting "beat" or combination frequencies supplied by virtue of ear non-linearity may be irritating noise, code or speech. Amplitude modulation may also be employed as desired.

Referring now to FIG. 1, the illustrated embodiment comprises three (3) high power radiators or speaker units 10, 11 and 12 operating in the frequency range, for example, of 5 to 6 kc. and with a difference frequency of about 100 c.p.s. Units 10, 11 and 12 are operatively connected to power amplifiers 13, 14 and 15, respectively, and positioned so as to direct acoustic beams 16, 17 and 18, respectively, to a single area indicated generally at 19 to provide a high intensity field 20 within which the person or victim indicated at 21 is located. Each of the power amplifiers 13, 14 and 15 are electrically connected to a difference-frequency modulator 22, while the input to pre-amplifier 29 is connected via a switch generally indicated at 31 to either of a pair of transducers, such as a microphone 32 or a tape recorder unit 33. An amplitude modulator 34 is positioned such that it is adapted to be connected intermediate the difference-frequency modulator 22 and the power amplifiers 14 and 15, and to the pre-amplifier 29. The output of the amplitude modulator 34 indicated at 35 is operatively connected to switch 24. Switch 30 is constructed such that the blade 36 thereof is movable to interconnect a terminal 37 connected to difference-frequency modulator 22 and a terminal 38 connected to the amplitude modulator 34, such that the output of pre-amplifier 29 may be operatively connected to both modulators 22 and 34. The amplitude modulator 34 may also be connected to the output signal 25 of difference-frequency modulator 22 via a switch generally indicated at 39 which includes a blade element 40 movable between a terminal 41 connected to switch 24 and a terminal 42 connected to the input of modulator 34. Switch 31 includes a blade 43 which is movable between a terminal 44 connected to microphone 32 and a terminal 45 connected to tape recorder 33.

While not shown, it is within the scope of this invention to gang the switches 30 and 39 such that the output signal 25 from the difference-frequency modulator 22 and the output from the pre-amplifier 29 may be simultaneously directed into the amplitude modulator 34. Also, switch 24 may be modified such that the output from either the amplitude modulator 34 and/or the output signal 25 from the difference-frequency modulator 22 may be directed simultaneously to radiators 14 and 15. While the switches have been illustrated and described

United States Patent [19]

Drewes et al.

[11] **4,349,898**

[45] **Sep. 14, 1982**

[54] **SONIC WEAPON SYSTEM**

[75] Inventors: **William Drewes**
Edward M.
Vlicki

[73] Assignee: **William Drewes, Bronxville, N.Y.**

[21] Appl. No.: **959,302**

[22] Filed: **Nov. 9, 1978**

[51] Int. Cl.^{3} H04B 1/02
[52] U.S. Cl. 367/138; 367/92;
367/139
[58] Field of Search 367/92, 137, 138, 139

[56] **References Cited**

U.S. PATENT DOCUMENTS

3,612,211 10/1971 Clark .... 367/139 X
3,613,069 10/1971 Cary, Jr. et al. 367/92

OTHER PUBLICATIONS

Rudenko et al., "TheoreticalFoundations of Nonlinear
Acoustics", (English Translation) Consultant's Bureau,
New York, 1977, pp. 145–147.

Primary Examiner—Richard A. Farley
Attorney, Agent, or Firm—Hubbell, Cohen, Stiefel &
Gross

[57] **ABSTRACT**

A system for transmitting a parametrically pumped
sonic signal through a transmission medium to a remote
location is disclosed. The preferred system, which is
particularly intended for use as a sonic weapon, comprises a sound source; means for separating the sound
into a plurality of discrete frequency components including a fundamental component and at least one additional component, each additional component having a
frequency twice that of the next lowest frequency component; means for adjusting the phase difference between each frequency component and the next lowest
frequency component to substantially 90°; means for
colinearly focusing the components on the remote location; and means for rendering the transmission medium
nonlinear between the focusing means and the remote
location.

36 Claims, 11 Drawing Figures

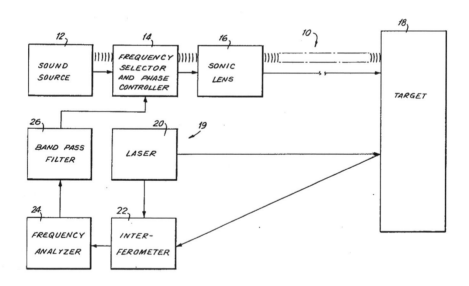

Directed Energy Weapons

United States Patent [19]

Kreithen

[11] **Patent Number:** **5,774,088**

[45] **Date of Patent:** **Jun. 30, 1998**

[54] **METHOD AND SYSTEM FOR WARNING BIRDS OF HAZARDS**

[75] Inventor: **Melvin L. Kreithen**, Pittsburgh, Pa.

[73] Assignee: **The University of Pittsburgh**, Pittsburgh, Pa.

[21] Appl. No.: **852,915**

[22] Filed: **May 8, 1997**

Related U.S. Application Data

[63] Continuation of Ser. No. 598,093, Feb. 7, 1996, abandoned, which is a continuation of Ser. No. 280,287, Jul. 26, 1994, abandoned.

[51] **Int. Cl.⁶** **G01S 13/93**
[52] **U.S. Cl.** **342/22**
[58] **Field of Search** .... 342/22; 367/139; 116/22 A

[56] **References Cited**

U.S. PATENT DOCUMENTS

3,717,802	2/1973	Plevy et al.	174/117 FF
4,109,605	8/1978	Bachli	116/22 A
4,562,212	12/1985	Tomlinson, Sr. et al.	514/690
4,656,770	4/1987	Nuttle	116/22 A
4,736,907	4/1988	Steffen	244/1 R
4,769,794	9/1988	Beuter et al.	367/139
5,181,338	1/1993	Chatten	43/58
5,270,707	12/1993	Schulte et al.	340/981

OTHER PUBLICATIONS

Behavioral Energetics: The Cost of Survival in Vertebrates, by Melvin L. Kreithen, Ohio State University Press, 1983, pp. 3–28.
Frequency Shift Discrimination: Can Homing Pigeons Locate Infrasounds by Doppler Shifts?, by Douglas Quine and Melvin Kreithen; Journal of Comparative Physiology 141, pp. 153–155.
Infrasound Detection by the Homing Pigeon: A Behavioral Audiogram, The Journal of Comparative Physiology, 129, pp. 1–4, (1979).

Homing Pigeons:, Their Navigation and Sensory Abilities, by Melvin L. Kreithen, New York's Food and Life Sciences, vol. 12, No. 1, 1979, p. 13–15.

Sensory Mechanisms for Animal Orientation—Can Any New Ones Be Discovered?, by Melvin L. Kreithen, Springer Verlag, Berlin Heidelberg 1978, pp. 25–34.

(List continued on next page.)

Primary Examiner—Ian J. Lobo
Attorney, Agent, or Firm—Flehr Hohbach Test Albritton & Herbert LLP

[57] **ABSTRACT**

A hazard warning system radiates pulses of microwave energy in the frequency range of 1 GHz to about 40 GHz to alert and warn target flying birds of the presence of wind turbine electrical generators, power distribution systems, aircraft, and other protected areas from hazardous intrusion. The warning system includes a control unit governing pulse control circuitry that outputs pulses ranging from about 5 μs to about 25 μs in duration. These pulses trigger a pulsed source of microwave energy that is coupled to a microwave antenna that emanates the warning radiation. The radiation is sensed by the birds auditory system, attaining their attention to the presence of the protected area. The sensed radiation itself may cause the birds to veer from a collision course, or supplemental hazard-warning radiation including ultraviolet light and infrasound may also be employed. A proximity detector can enhance operating efficiency by steering the antenna toward a detected target. Further, the warning system can remain in a standby mode until alerted by the proximity detector to the presence of target birds, whereupon the warning system begins to output pulsed microwave energy. The pulse control circuitry may be caused to generate complex pulse trains that can preferably evoke a biologically significant response within recipient birds. The warning system operates at the speed of light, and can transmit a benign warning, transparently to humans. Not only is an area protected by the system, but the birds themselves can be protected from the area.

1 Claim, 3 Drawing Sheets

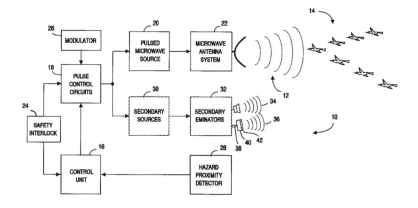

United States Patent [19]

Ziolkowski

[11] **Patent Number:** **4,959,559**

[45] **Date of Patent:** **Sep. 25, 1990**

[54] **ELECTROMAGNETIC OR OTHER DIRECTED ENERGY PULSE LAUNCHER**

[75] Inventor: **Richard W. Ziolkowski**, Livermore, Calif.

[73] Assignee: **The United States of America as represented by the United States Department of Energy**, Washington, D.C.

[21] Appl. No.: **331,141**

[22] Filed: **Mar. 31, 1989**

[51] Int. Cl.^{5} H01Q 3/26; H04B 1/12; H01S 3/23; H01S 3/30

[52] U.S. Cl. 307/425; 307/510; 307/522; 342/14; 342/13; 342/81; 364/822; 315/409

[58] Field of Search 342/13–20, 342/81, 378, 379–391; 364/724.16, 725–727, 819–824, 841–849; 328/168–171, 233; 307/425, 430, 510, 511, 515, 522, 527; 350/96.11; 315/409

[56] **References Cited**

U.S. PATENT DOCUMENTS

4,032,922	6/1977	Provencher	.... 342/81 X
4,216,475	8/1980	Johnson	.... 364/725 X
4,270,223	5/1981	Marston	.... 328/169 X
4,321,550	3/1982	Evtuhov	.... 307/425 X
4,342,949	8/1982	Harte et al.	.... 315/409
4,595,994	6/1986	Verber et al.	.... 364/841
4,641,259	2/1987	Shan et al.	.... 364/724.16
4,656,601	4/1987	Merritt et al.	.... 364/821
4,779,984	10/1988	Cook	.... 350/96.11 X
4,806,888	2/1989	Salvage et al.	.... 307/511 X

Primary Examiner—Stanley D. Miller
Assistant Examiner—David R. Bertelson
Attorney, Agent, or Firm—Henry P. Sartorio; L. E. Carnahan; William R. Moser

[57] **ABSTRACT**

The physical realization of new solutions of wave propagation equations, such as Maxwell's equations and the scaler wave equation, produces localized pulses of wave energy such as electromagnetic or acoustic energy which propagate over long distances without divergence. The pulses are produced by driving each element of an array of radiating sources with a particular drive function so that the resultant localized packet of energy closely approximates the exact solutions and behaves the same.

20 Claims, 11 Drawing Sheets

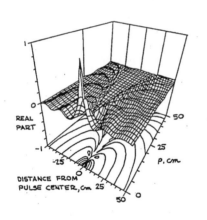

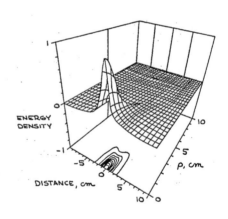

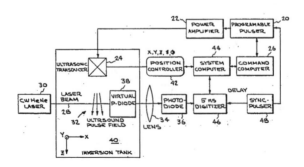

4,959,559

1

ELECTROMAGNETIC OR OTHER DIRECTED ENERGY PULSE LAUNCHER

The U.S. Government has rights to this invention pursuant to Contract No. W-7405-ENG-48 between the U.S. Department of Energy and the University of California, for the operation of Lawrence Livermore National Laboratory.

BACKGROUND OF THE INVENTION

The invention relates generally to transmission of pulses of energy, and more particularly to the propagation of localized pulses of electromagnetic or acoustic energy over long distances without divergence.

As the Klingon battle cruiser attacks the Starship Enterprise, Captain Kirk commands "Fire photon torpedoes". Two darts or blobs of light speed toward their target to destory the enemy spaceship. Stardate 1989, Star Trek reruns, or 3189, somewhere in intergalactic space. Fantasy or reality. The ability to launch localized packets of light or other energy which do not diverge as they travel great distances through space may incredibly be at hand.

Following the pioneering work of J. N. Brittingham, various groups have been actively pursuing the possibility that solutions to the wave equation can be found that allow the transmission of localized, slowly decaying pulses of energy, variously described as electromagnetic missiles or bullets, Bessel beams, transient beam fields, and splash pulses. These efforts have in common the space-time nature of the solutions being investigated and their potential launching mechanisms, pulse-driven antennas.

Brittingham's original work involved a search, over a period of about 15 years, for packet-like solutions of Maxwell's equations (the equations that describe how electromagnetic waves propagate). The solutions sought were to be continuous and nonsingular (well-behaved, realizable), three-dimensional in pulse structure (localized), and nondispersive for all time (faithfully maintaining their shape). They were also to move at the velocity of light in straight lines and carry finite electromagnetic energy. The solutions discovered, termed focus wave modes (FWMs), had all the aforementioned properties except the last; like plane-wave solutions to the same equations, they were found to have finite energy density but infinite energy, despite all attempts to remove this deficiency, and thus are not physically realizable.

Conventional methods for propagation of energy pulses are based on simple solutions to Maxwell's equations and the wave equation. Spherical or planar waveforms are utilized. Beams of energy will spread as they propagate as a result of diffraction effects. For a source of diameter D and wavelength of λ the distance to which a pulse will propagate without substantial spread is the Rayleigh length D^2/λ.

Present arrays are based on phasing a plurality of elements, all at the same frequency, to tailor the beam using interference effects. In a conventional antenna system, such as a phased array driven with a monochromatic signal, only spatial phasing is possible. The resulting diffraction-limited signal pulse begins to spread and decay when it reaches the Rayleigh length L_R. For an axisymmetric geometry, an array of radius a, and a driving wavelength of λ, L_R is about a^2/λ.

2

There have been several previous attempts to achieve localized transmission beyond this Rayleigh distance with conventional systems. The best known of these are the super-gain or super-directive antennas, where the goal was to produce a field whose amplitude decays as one over the distance from the antenna, but whose angular spread can be as narrow as desired. There are theoretical solutions to this problem, but they turn out to be impractical; the smallest deviation from the exact solution completely ruins the desired characteristics.

The original FWMs can be related to exact solutions of the three-dimensional scalar wave equation in a homogeneous, isotropic medium (one that has the same properties at any distance in all directions). This equation has solutions that describe, for example, the familiar spherical acoustic waves emanating from a sound source in air.

The FWMs are related to solutions that represent Gaussian beams propagating with only local deformation, i.e., a Gaussian-shaped packet that propagates with changes only within the packet. Such a pulse, moving along the z axis, with transverse distance denoted by ρ,

$$\Phi_k(r,t) = e^{ik(z+ct)}\left[\frac{e^{-k\rho^2/[z_0 + i(z-ct)]}}{4\pi i[z_0 + i(z-ct)]}\right]$$

is an exact solution of the scalar wave equation developed by applicant. This fundamental pulse is a Gaussian beam that translates through space-time with only local variations. These pulses can also form components of solutions to Maxwell's equations.

These fundamental Gaussian pulses have a number of interesting characteristics. They appear as either a transverse plane wave or a particle, depending on whether k is small or large. Moreover, for all k they share with plane waves the property of having finite energy density but infinite total energy.

Thus traditional solutions to the wave equation and Maxwell's equations do not provide a means for launching pulses from broadband sources which can travel desirable distances without divergence problems. The laser is a narrowband light source which has a relatively low divergence over certain distances (i.e. relatively long Rayleigh length). However, acoustic and microwave sources, because of longer wavelengths, are more severely limited. Phased arrays do not provide the solution.

Accordingly, it is an object of the invention to provide method and apparatus for launching electromagnetic and acoustic pulses which can travel distances much larger than the Rayleigh length without divergence.

It is also an object of the invention to provide method and apparatus for launching pulses which approximate new solutions to the scalar wave and Maxwell's equations.

It is another object of the invention to physically realize new solutions to the scalar wave and Maxwell's equations which provide localized packets of energy which transverse large distances without divergence.

It is a further object of the invention to provide compact arrays for launching these pulses.

United States Patent [19]

Hinkey et al.

[11] **Patent Number:** **5,864,517**

[45] **Date of Patent:** **Jan. 26, 1999**

[54] **PULSED COMBUSTION ACOUSTIC WAVE GENERATOR**

[75] Inventors: **John B. Hinkey**; **Joseph T. Williams**, both of Seattle; **Thomas R.A. Bussing**, Issaquah, all of Wash.

[73] Assignee: **Adroit Systems, Inc.**, Bellevue, Wash.

[21] Appl. No.: **820,882**

[22] Filed: **Mar. 21, 1997**

[51] **Int. Cl.⁶** **G01V 1/00**

[52] **U.S. Cl.** .... **367/145**; 181/116; 181/117; 116/23; 116/137 R; 116/137 A

[58] **Field of Search** .... 367/145; 181/116, 181/117, 118; 116/23, 137 R, 137 A

[56] **References Cited**

U.S. PATENT DOCUMENTS

2,766,837	10/1956	McCollum	367/145
2,831,666	4/1958	Compton	367/145
3,048,816	8/1962	Lubnow	367/145
3,064,619	11/1962	Fortman	367/145
3,064,753	11/1962	McClure	367/145
4,189,026	2/1980	Elliot et al.	181/118
4,642,611	2/1987	Koemer	340/385
4,896,502	1/1990	Ravel et al.	60/270.1
5,345,758	9/1994	Bussing	60/39.38
5,353,588	10/1994	Bussing	60/39.38

OTHER PUBLICATIONS

Sutton, G.P., "Rocket Propulsion Elements: An Introduction to the Engineering of Rockets," Wiley–Interscience Publications, New York, New York, 1992.
Mattingly, J.D., Heiser, W.H., and Daley, D.H., "Aircraft Engine Design," AIAA Education Series, AIAA, Washington, DC, 1987.
Oates, G.C., Editor, "Aircraft Propulsion Systems Technology and Design," AIAA Education Series, AIAA, Washington, DC, 1989.
Johnson, W., "Analytical and Experimental Study of the Pulsejet Ejector," Ph.D. Dissertation, Department of Mechanical Engineering, University of Clemson, 1967.
Heiser, W.H. "Thrust Augmentation." Paper No. 66–GT–116, American Society of Mechanical Engineers. 1966.
Lockwood, R.M. "Interim Summary Report on Investigation of the Process of Energy Transfer from an Intermittent Jet to a Secondary Fluid in an Ejector–type Thrust Augmentor." Hiller Aircraft Corp. Report No. ARD–286, Mar. 31, 1961.
Lockwood, R.M. "Interim Summary Report on Investigation of the Process of Energy Transfer from an Intermittent Jet to a Secondary Fluid in an Ejector–type Thrust Augmentor." Hiller Aircraft Corp. Report No. ARD–305, Jun. 30, 1962.
Clark, L.T., "Aplication of Compound Flow Analysis to Supersonic Ejector–Mixer Performance Prediction," AIAA Paper 95–0645, 1995.
Bernstein, A., Heiser, W., and Hevenor, C., "Compound–Compressible Nozzle Flow," AIAA Paper 66–663, 1966.
FOA, J.V., "Intermittant Jets", vol. XII High Speed Aerodynamics and Jet Propulsion, 1959.
O'Brien, J.G. "The Pulse Jet Engine A Review of Its Development Potential", Naval Postgraduate School, Jun. 1974.

Primary Examiner—J. Woodrow Eldred
Attorney, Agent, or Firm—Christensen O'Connor Johnson & Kindness PLLC

[57] **ABSTRACT**

A pulsed combustion acoustic wave generator includes a tubular barrel having an inlet end and an open outlet end, a fuel controller for metering a controlled quantity of fuel into the inlet end of the barrel, an oxidant controller for metering a controlled quantity of oxidant into the inlet end of the barrel and an igniter extending into the inlet end of the barrel that is controllable by an operator to ignite a mixture of fuel and oxidant in the inlet end.

19 Claims, 7 Drawing Sheets

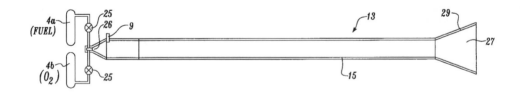

5,864,517

1

PULSED COMBUSTION ACOUSTIC WAVE GENERATOR

FIELD OF THE INVENTION

The subject invention pertains to a compact device designed to generate repetitive high amplitude acoustic pulses or pressure waves which may be utilized in a variety of applications.

BACKGROUND OF THE INVENTION

A device to produce high amplitude impulsive pressure waves may be based on several different schemes. Electrical energy may be utilized to produce sound waves through loudspeakers or piezoelectric devices, but high power requirements may result in energy storage difficulties as well as problems with the large physical dimensions necessary to produce high acoustic intensities (low power densities). Mechanical devices may be used to produce repetitive loud sounds, but would be inefficient and unwieldy. Methods which convert chemical energy to acoustical energy are ideal because of the high power densities which may be achieved. Solid explosives have very high energy densities and are capable of producing extremely high peak pressure levels (i.e., blast waves from bombs), but are dangerous to work with and are not practical to use if a repetitive impulse is required. Gaseous and liquid chemicals can be easily stored, are typically quite safe when fuels and oxidizers are separately stored, and can be mixed and combusted in a very rapid manner. Although not as high in energy density as solid explosives, gaseous or liquid combustible mixtures provide reasonable energy densities which may be quickly converted to pressure or acoustical energy. Repetitive release of stored chemical energy (via an energetic chemical reaction) to produce high amplitude pressure/acoustic waves can be achieved through pulsed combustion technology. Pulse combustion includes two different modes of burning: detonation and deflagration. Detonative combustion is characterized by an extremely fast flame speed (2,000 to 4,000 m/s) and very high amplitude pressure waves, while deflagrative combustion typically exhibits a much slower flame speed (generally less than about 200 m/s) and significantly lower amplitude pressure waves.

Repetitive, high amplitude pressure or acoustic waves can be utilized as a non-lethal effects device. The detrimental effects on humans of continuous exposure to high levels of "noise" (broad band and discrete frequency) are well studied and have been known for many years. These detrimental effects are usually long term in nature and consist of symptoms such as permanent hearing loss, general fatigue, elevated stress levels, and other physiological effects. The sound pressure and corresponding sound pressure levels (SPLs) of continuous exposure with which the average person is familiar are shown in Table 1.

TABLE 1

Examples of typical sound pressure levels (SPLs) and sound pressures for common environments.

Sound Pressure Pa(N/m^2)	Sound Pressure Level dB (2 × 10^{-5} Pa ref.)	Typical Environment
0.000020	0	Threshold of Hearing
0.000063	10	Rustle of Leaves
0.00020	20	Broadcast Studio
0.00063	30	Bedroom at Night

2

TABLE 1-continued

Examples of typical sound pressure levels (SPLs) and sound pressures for common environments.

Sound Pressure Pa(N/m^2)	Sound Pressure Level dB (2 × 10^{-5} Pa ref.)	Typical Environment
0.0020	40	Library
0.0063	50	Quiet Office
0.02	60	Conversational Speech
0.063	70	Average Radio
0.1	74	Light Traffic Noise
0.2	80	Typical Factory
0.63	90	Subway Train
2.0	100	Symphony Orchestra
6.3	110	Rock Band
20.	120	Aircraft Takeoff
200	140	Threshold of pain

Sensations of feeling or tickle commence at approximately 130 dB (0.009 psi rms) while significant discomfort occurs at approximately 120 dB (0.003 psi rms). Thus a pressure rise as small as 0.003 psi may cause considerable discomfort.

Non-continuous tone (impulsive noises) may have different effects on an individual, especially if the impulses are unexpected. An impulsive noise is one which has a high peak pressure acting over a short duration. The form of the impulses can be high amplitude sound waves suddenly switched on which then rapidly decay in amplitude or discrete pressure pulses which may contain many frequencies.

The physiological effects of low amplitude impulsive noise consists mainly of the startle response if the peak amplitude is not excessive. At higher peak amplitudes, in addition to the startle response, temporary threshold shift (TTS) occurs. TTS is the temporary increase in the threshold of hearing (the minimum sound level which evokes an auditory response) as a result of exposure to noise. TTS generally occurs at a minimum sound pressure level of 140 dB for gunfire and 130 dB for impact noise in an enclosed space (TTS is reported to increase when exposure occurs in an enclosed space). In general the amount of TTS increases with peak sound pressure level, but as the duration of the impulse decreases below 5 milliseconds, the effect is lessened for a given peak amplitude. In addition, the amount of TTS increases approximately linearly with exposure time, resulting in an increase in TTS with the total number of repetitive pulses one is exposed to (not the total exposure time). Upon cessation of exposure to repetitive impulsive noise. the threshold shift immediately begins a rapid recovery and reaches a minimum after approximately 1 minute, but then rebounds to a maximum at approximately 2 min. This is known as the bounce effect and may be useful in attempts at incapacitation/impairment using repetitive impulsive noise.

The threshold of pain normally associated with continuous exposure (non-impulsive noise) cannot be used to predict the risk of damage due to non-continuous sounds (impulsive noise). In fact intermittent noise has been observed to be less hazardous than steady-state noise for an equivalent amount of sound energy delivered to the ear.

Eye and hand coordination are particularly affected by impulsive noise, with significant impairment lasting from a typical 2 to 3 seconds to as much as 30 seconds in some individuals.

At still higher peak pressures, the physiological effects are centered mainly on damage to the structures of the ear. Peak

United States Patent [19]

Naff et al.

[11]	**Patent Number:**
[45]	**Date of Patent:**

5,973,999

Oct. 26, 1999

[54] **ACOUSTIC CANNON**

[75] Inventors: **John T. Naff**, Pleasanton; **James H. Shea**, Castro Valley, both of Calif.

[73] Assignee: **Maxwell Technologies Systems Division, Inc.**, San Diego, Calif.

[21] Appl. No.: **08/939,265**

[22] Filed: **Sep. 29, 1997**

[51] **Int. Cl.^{6}** **H04B 1/034**; G08B 15/00

[52] **U.S. Cl.** **367/139**; 181/142

[58] **Field of Search** .... 367/137, 138, 367/139; 181/142, 144, 145; 381/161, 337, 338, 339; 89/1.1, 1.11; 116/22 A; 43/124

[56] **References Cited**

U.S. PATENT DOCUMENTS

2,552,970	5/1951	Horsley et al. .
3,039,559	6/1962	Ellsworth .
3,410,142	11/1968	Daiber et al. .
3,557,899	1/1971	Longinette et al. .
3,756,344	9/1973	Daiber et al. .
3,804,021	4/1974	McGirr .
4,287,768	9/1981	Hayakawa et al. 73/626
4,349,898	9/1982	Drewes et al. .
4,757,227	7/1988	Danley et al. .
4,769,794	9/1988	Beuter et al. .
4,882,974	11/1989	Reuter et al. .
4,912,869	4/1990	Govett .
5,081,900	1/1992	Buntzen et al. .
5,225,638	7/1993	Quint .
5,259,289	11/1993	Peries et al. .
5,269,214	12/1993	Badura et al. .
5,473,836	12/1995	Liu .
5,606,297	2/1997	Phillips 381/159

Primary Examiner—Ian J. Lobo
Attorney, Agent, or Firm—Gregory S. Rosenblatt; Wiggin & Dana

[57] **ABSTRACT**

An acoustic cannon has a plurality of acoustic sources with output ends symmetrically arranged in a planar array about a central point. Pressure pulses are generated in each acoustic source at substantially the same time. The pressure pulses exit the output ends as sonic pulses. Interaction of the sonic pulses generates a Mach disk, a non-linear shock wave that travels along an axis perpendicular to the planar array with limited radial diffusion. The Mach disk retains the intensity of the sonic pulses for a time and a distance significantly longer than that achievable from a single sonic source. The acoustic cannon is useful as a non-lethal weapon to disperse crowds or disable a hostile target.

15 Claims, 5 Drawing Sheets

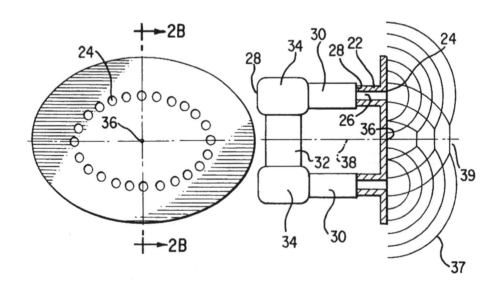

1

ACOUSTIC CANNON

BACKGROUND OF THE INVENTION

1. Field of the Invention

This invention relates to an acoustic device that emits repetitive sonic pulses capable of dispersing or incapacitating a biological target. More particularly, a planar array of multiple acoustic pulse sources cooperates to generate highly focused pulses of high intensity sonic energy over a small area.

2. Description of the Related Art

Military and law enforcement personnel have a need for non-lethal weapons. Such weapons are useful in riot control to disperse a hostile crowd. In sniper and hostage situation, a non-lethal weapon provides a means to neutralize a hostile target without collateral damage to hostages, bystanders or property. In combat, a non-lethal weapon is useful to neutralize sentries and warning devices. Since the weapon produces casualties, rather than fatalities, each hit removes three opponents, the injured and a two-person rescue squad, from the combat zone instead of the one person removed by a fatality.

High intensity sound pulses have a debilitating effect on biological targets. Humans become disoriented by exposure to sonic pulses exceeding a threshold of pain of about 150 decibels (dB). Eardrum rupture occurs at about 190 dB, the threshold for pulmonary injury is about 200 dB and the onset of lethality is about 220 dB.

U.S. Pat. No. 3,557,899 to Longinette et al. discloses a parabolic reflector that focuses and transmits a continuous sound at a frequency of between 8 kilohertz (kHz) and 13 kHz. Within this frequency range, sound attenuates rapidly and the disclosed device is believed effective only at close ranges. The U.S. Pat. No. 3,557,889 patent discloses utilizing the device in close proximity to a riot or in enclosed areas, such as a bank vault.

U.S. Pat. No. 4,349,898 to Drewes et al. discloses a sonic weapon to destroy buildings and disable personnel. A plurality of tubes each conduct a continuous sound generated by a jet engine. Rotating fans at the ends of the tubes create pulsed sound of a desired frequency. The fan speeds are set such that each tube has a pulse sound frequency two times the frequency of a preceding tube leading to an additive effect of sound waves referred to as a parametric pump. The disclosed device appears heavy and requires careful alignment of a number of large apparatus for operation.

There remains, therefore, a need for a portable acoustic weapon capable of dispersing or disabling biological targets at distances of up to 100 meters that does not suffer from the disadvantages of the prior art discussed above.

SUMMARY OF THE INVENTION

Accordingly, it is an object of the invention to provide an acoustic device capable of dispersing or incapacitating a biological target. One feature of the invention is that the device has a planar array of simultaneously actuated acoustic pulse sources. Interaction between the sonic pulses forms a Mach disk. A second feature of the invention is that the device is actuated by either a shock tube or detonation of an explosive chemical mix.

Among the advantages of the invention are that the Mach disk is a compact packet of sound that may be accurately fired to minimize harm to hostages, bystanders and property. The Mach disk effectively incapacitates or disperses a biological target with a minimal threat of lethality. The

2

acoustic device is relatively lightweight and is readily transported by an infantry vehicle and operated by a single person.

In accordance with the invention, there is provided an acoustic cannon that has a plurality of acoustic sources arranged in a planar array about a central point. Each of the plurality of acoustic sources has an input end and an output end. The input end receives a sonic pulse and the output end transmits a sonic output. A sonic pulse generator is coupled to each of the input ends and a timing mechanism is coupled to the sonic pulse generator such that the sonic pulse is received by each of the input ends at substantially the same time and is of substantially the same frequency and duration. The combination of the planar array and the parameters of the sonic output effectively generates a Mach disk.

The above stated objects, features and advantages will become more apparent from the specification and drawings that follows.

IN THE DRAWINGS

FIG. 1 shows in cross-sectional representation a single sonic source as known from the prior art.

FIGS. 2A and 2B illustrate the acoustic cannon of the invention.

FIG. 3 illustrates in cross-sectional representation an acoustic cannon in accordance with a first embodiment of the invention

FIGS. 4A through 4E graphically illustrate the generation of a sonic pulse through the use of a shock tube.

FIG. 5 illustrates in cross-sectional representation an acoustic cannon in accordance with a second embodiment of the invention.

FIG. 6 graphically illustrates the relationship between frequency content of the sonic pulse and directivity.

FIG. 7 graphically illustrates the relationship between frequency contained in the sonic pulse and attenuation.

FIG. 8 graphically illustrates the relationship between pulse range and peak pressure measured in decibels.

DETAILED DESCRIPTION

FIG. 1 illustrates in cross-sectional representation a muzzle portion 12 of an acoustic device 10 as known from the prior art. A sonic source (not shown) generates a pressure wave 16 that is transmitted along an interior bore 14 and emitted from an output end 18 as spherically expanding sound waves 20. The spherically expanding sound waves 20 diffuse rapidly. The prior art acoustic device has limited value as a weapon. The strength of the pressure wave 16 drops to below useful values within a very short distance and time. Additionally, the spherically expanding sound waves 20 diffuse over a broad area rendering target selectivity difficult or impossible.

The disadvantages of the prior art are resolved by an acoustic cannon in accordance with the present invention. FIG. 2 schematically illustrates a portion of the acoustic cannon of the invention in Front (FIG. 2A) and Side (FIG. 2B) Views. Acoustic sources 22 terminate at an output end 24. Interior bores 26 extend from output ends 24 to input ends 28 that are adjacent to a sonic pulse generator 30. A timing mechanism 32 controls the rate and duration of generated sonic pulses. In a first embodiment of the invention, the sonic pulses are generated by detonation of an explosive mix and a fuel storage chamber 34 is provided to house required quantities of the additional explosive mix, or explosive mix precursors.

(12) **United States Patent**

Brown

(10) **Patent No.:** **US 8,049,173 B1**

(45) **Date of Patent:** **Nov. 1, 2011**

(54) **DUAL USE RF DIRECTED ENERGY WEAPON AND IMAGER**

(75) Inventor: **Kenneth W. Brown**, Yucaipa, CA (US)

(73) Assignee: **Raytheon Company**, Waltham, MA (US)

(*) Notice: Subject to any disclaimer, the term of this patent is extended or adjusted under 35 U.S.C. 154(b) by 1202 days.

(21) Appl. No.: **11/750,292**

(22) Filed: **May 17, 2007**

(51) **Int. Cl.**
  G01J 5/02 (2006.01)
(52) **U.S. Cl.** **250/341.7**
(58) **Field of Classification Search** 250/341.1, 250/341.6, 341.7, 393, 370.09; 89/1.11; 342/13, 22
  See application file for complete search history.

(56) **References Cited**

U.S. PATENT DOCUMENTS

5,089,828 A	2/1992	Moss	
5,214,438 A	5/1993	Brusgard	
5,612,503 A *	3/1997	Sepp	89/1.11
6,204,762 B1	3/2001	Dering	
6,487,950 B2 *	12/2002	Samland	89/1.13
6,799,499 B2 *	10/2004	Seregelyi et al.	89/1.13
6,967,612 B1	11/2005	Gorman	
7,126,477 B2	10/2006	Gallivan	
7,490,538 B2 *	2/2009	Lowell et al.	89/1.11
7,784,390 B1 *	8/2010	Lowell et al.	89/1.11
2007/0040725 A1	2/2007	Lowell	
2007/0076774 A1	4/2007	Brown	
2008/0304549 A1 *	12/2008	Calico et al.	375/131
2009/0146907 A1	6/2009	Brown	
2010/0117885 A1 *	5/2010	Holbrook et al.	342/22

FOREIGN PATENT DOCUMENTS

WO WO 2007022339 2/2007

OTHER PUBLICATIONS

Riu et al., "A thermal model for human thresholds of microwave-evoked warmth sensation," 1996.
Blick et al., "Thresholds of microwave-evoked warmth sensation in human skin," 1997.
Walters et al., "Effects of blood flow on skin heating induced by millimeter wave irradiation in humans," 2004.
Walters et al., "Heating and pain sensation produced in human skin by millimeter waves: comparison to a simple thermal model," 2000.
U.S. Appl. No. 11/300,876, filed Dec. 15, 2005, Brown.
Delisio & York, "Quasi optical and spatial power combining," IEEE Trans. Microwave Theory and Techniques, v. 50, No. 3, Mar. 2002.
Raytheon Company, Silent Guardian Protection System Datasheet, Jun. 2006.
Wikipedia, "Active Denial System", http://en.wikipedia.org/wiki/Active_Denial_System.
Malibu Research, "Technology—Introduction to FLAPS", http://www.maliburesearch.com/technology.htm.
Kelkar, FLAPS: Conformal phased reflecting surfaces, Mar. 1991, pp. 1-6.
European Patent Office, European Search Report for European Application No. 08836387.4, Mail Date Apr. 28, 2011, pp. 1-9.

* cited by examiner

Primary Examiner — David Porta
Assistant Examiner — Marcus Taningco
(74) *Attorney, Agent, or Firm* — SoCal IP Law Group LLP; John E. Gunther; Steven C. Sereboff

(57) **ABSTRACT**

There is disclosed an dual use RF directed energy weapon and imager. A generator may provide a first beam of RF electromagnetic energy which may be directed to an object by a beam director. An imager may form an image of the object. The imager may share an aperture defined by the beam director.

31 Claims, 7 Drawing Sheets

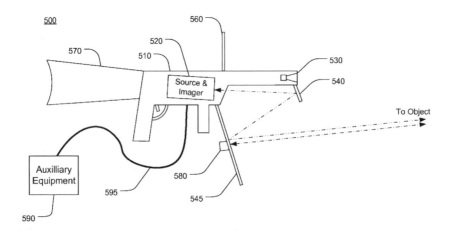

1

DUAL USE RF DIRECTED ENERGY WEAPON
AND IMAGER

NOTICE OF COPYRIGHTS AND TRADE DRESS

BACKGROUND

1. Field

This disclosure relates to non-lethal weapon systems and to non-lethal weapons systems utilizing directed microwave energy in particular.

2. Description of the Related Art

Non-lethal weapons employing directed microwave energy are a known method to deter or discourage an intruder or other target individual from entering a controlled area or from continuing some undesired action. Example microwave directed energy weapons, also termed "active denial" systems, are described in U.S. Pat. No. 7,126,477 B2 and US 2007/0040725 A1.

DESCRIPTION OF THE DRAWINGS

FIG. 1 is a block diagram of a dual use directed energy weapon and imager.

FIG. 2 is a block diagram of a dual use directed energy weapon and imager.

FIG. 3A and FIG. 3B are schematic diagrams of an optical system.

FIG. 4 is a schematic diagram of an optical system.

FIG. 5 is a conceptual elevational view of a hand-held dual use directed energy weapon and imager.

FIG. 6 is a conceptual elevational view of a vehicle-mounted dual use directed energy weapon and imager.

DETAILED DESCRIPTION

Throughout this description, the embodiments and examples shown should be considered as exemplars, rather than limitations on the apparatus and methods disclosed or claimed.

Description of Apparatus

Referring now to FIG. 1, a dual use directed energy weapon and imager 100 may include a generator 110 for generating a first beam of electromagnetic energy 114, a beam director 120 for directing the first beam of electromagnetic energy 114 to an object 190, and an imager 140 to capture an image of the object 190. The dual use directed energy weapon and imager 100 may optionally include an illuminator 130 for illuminating the object 190 with a second beam of electromagnetic energy 132. The imager 140 may capture an image of the object 190 using at least a portion of the second beam of electromagnetic energy 132 that is reflected from the object 190 as image beam 134. The generator 110 may include an electromagnetic energy source 112 which may be supported by a power conditioner 116 and a cooling subsystem 118. The electromagnetic energy source 112 may be a solid-state source, a vacuum tube source, or another source. The electromagnetic energy source 112 may include an array of solid

2

state sources, such as a planar reflect-array, a grid oscillator array, a grid amplifier array, or another form of amplifier array. The outputs of the array of solid state sources may be spatially combined, or combined using a conventional waveguide power combiner, stripline power combiner, or another power combining technique. The electromagnetic energy source 112 may generate W-band millimeter wave (MMW) electromagnetic energy, which may have a frequency of 75 to 110 GHz. The electromagnetic energy source 112 may generate microwave energy, terahertz energy, or other electromagnetic energy.

The power conditioner 116 may convert power from a primary power source to one or more power forms required by the electromagnetic energy source 112. The primary power source may be a battery, a vehicle generator or other generator, or a conventional 120-volt or other AC power supply.

The cooling subsystem 118 may remove heat generated by the electromagnetic energy source 112 and power conditioner 116. The cooling subsystem may incorporate a coolant which may be air or another gas, a liquid, or a phase change material. The cooling system may use cryogenic gas from a gas bottle as a coolant. The cooling system may include one or more heat exchangers to transfer heat from the electromagnetic energy source 112 to the coolant, and/or from the coolant to the surrounding air or to another medium.

The beam director 120 may include at least one optical element 125 which may define an aperture through which the first beam of electromagnetic energy 114 must pass. While the optical element 125 is shown schematically in FIG. 1 as a curved mirror, the beam director 120 may include multiple optical elements which may include spherical, parabolic, aspheric or other curved mirrors, flat mirrors, spherical and aspheric lenses, and passive reflect-arrays which, although physically flat, function similar to a curved mirror.

The beam director 120 may also include an aperture-sharing element 128 to separate the image beam 134 used for imaging from the first beam of electromagnetic energy 114. Many configurations of an aperture-sharing element are known. In the example of FIG. 1, the aperture-sharing element 128 transmits the first beam of electromagnetic energy 114 but reflects the image beam 134 from the object 190. To allow separation at the aperture-sharing element 128, the first beam of electromagnetic energy 114 and the image beam 134 may differ in frequency, polarization state, or both frequency and polarization.

The illuminator 130 may be a continuous-wave (CW) or modulated source of millimeter wave or other electromagnetic energy. As will be discussed, the imager 140 may capture an image of the object 190 using a portion of the energy from the illuminator 130 which is reflected from the object 190. The illuminator 130 and the imager 140 do not constitute a Radar sensor, since no attempt is made to determine the range to the object or to otherwise form a three-dimensional image. In order to allow the reflected beam 134 to be separated from the first beam of electromagnetic energy 114 at the aperture-sharing element 128, the illuminator 130 may generate an illumination beam 132 that has a different frequency, or a different polarization, or both, from the first beam of electromagnetic energy 114.

The imager 140 for capturing an image of object 190 may include an image detector array 142 that receives the image beam 134 from the aperture-sharing element 128. Within this document, the phrase "capture an image" is intended to mean optically forming an image at a focal plane and detecting the image with an array of detectors to form an electronic image signal representative of the image. The captured image may be displayed and/or recorded. Within this document, an

A Long-Range Acoustic Device (LRAD) in use on the USS Blue Ridge.

The U.S. military's "Pain Ray," officially named the Active Denial System (ADS). The weapon emits 95 GHz waves that heat flesh, penetrating the outermost layer of human skin.

Chapter 14
Electronic Surveillance

United States Patent [19]

Loeb et al.

[11] **Patent Number:** **5,551,016**

[45] **Date of Patent:** **Aug. 27, 1996**

[54] **MONITORING SYSTEM AND INTERFACE APPARATUS THEREFOR**

[75] Inventors: **Gerald E. Loeb**, Kingston; **Roy A. Young**, Odessa; **Kevin H. Hood**, Kingston, all of Canada

[73] Assignee: **Queen's University at Kingston,** Kingston, Canada

[21] Appl. No.: **84,928**

[22] Filed: **Jul. 1, 1993**

[51] Int. Cl.^{6} **G06F 3/05**

[52] U.S. Cl. **395/550**

[58] Field of Search 395/550; 348/537; 364/556, 566, 569; 341/122, 123; 375/355

[56] **References Cited**

U.S. PATENT DOCUMENTS

3,900,721	8/1975	Speiser et al.	235/156
3,900,887	8/1975	Soga et al.	
4,053,708	10/1977	Hotchkiss	178/69.1
4,291,299	9/1981	Hinz et al.	340/347 AD
4,416,015	11/1983	Gitlin	375/14
4,630,139	12/1986	Dickens	
4,905,085	2/1990	Faulhaber	348/537
4,970,582	11/1990	Scott	
5,027,208	6/1991	Dwyer, Jr. et al.	
5,045,940	9/1991	Peters et al.	
5,255,289	10/1993	Tomita	375/86

OTHER PUBLICATIONS

M. J. Bak and G. E. Loeb "A Pulsed Integrator for EMG Analysis" Electroencephalography and Clinical Neurophysiology, 1979, 47: 738–741.

Primary Examiner—Thomas M. Heckler
Attorney, Agent, or Firm—Richard J. Hicks

[57] **ABSTRACT**

In monitoring systems for acquiring data about a subject, such as are used, for example, in the medical, scientific and engineering fields, determination of temporal relationships between data acquired from multiple monitoring devices is facilitated by means of an interface unit which interconnects the monitoring devices with tape recorders for storing the data and a computer for processing the data. The interface unit generates various timing and control signals including a time code signal. The interface unit supplies the time code signal to the recording devices for recording simultaneously with the data. The time code signal may be a linear time code (LTC) derived from a video sync signal generated by the interface unit for synchronizing a camera. A sampling clock signal for controlling digitizing of the analog data acquired by the system is derived from the time code signal. The time code signal may comprise a common temporal reference signal, for example the SMPTE used with NTSC format video or its European equivalent EBU used with the PAL format. The video synchronization signal may itself be synchronized to and external timing signal, perhaps derived from one of the monitoring devices.

54 Claims, 7 Drawing Sheets

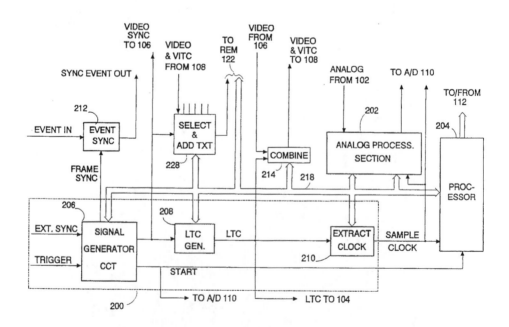

(12) **United States Patent**

Hind et al.

(10) **Patent No.:** **US 7,076,441 B2**

(45) **Date of Patent:** **Jul. 11, 2006**

(54) **IDENTIFICATION AND TRACKING OF PERSONS USING RFID-TAGGED ITEMS IN STORE ENVIRONMENTS**

(75) Inventors: **John R. Hind**, Raleigh, NC (US); **James M. Mathewson, II**, Chapel Hill, NC (US); **Marcia L. Peters**, Durham, NC (US)

(73) Assignee: **International Business Machines Corporation**, Armonk, NY (US)

(*) Notice: Subject to any disclaimer, the term of this patent is extended or adjusted under 35 U.S.C. 154(b) by 1059 days.

(21) Appl. No.: **09/847,889**

(22) Filed: **May 3, 2001**

(65) **Prior Publication Data**

US 2002/0165758 A1   Nov. 7, 2002

(51) **Int. Cl.**
   G06Q 99/00   (2006.01)
(52) **U.S. Cl.** **705/10**
(58) **Field of Classification Search** 705/10
   See application file for complete search history.

(56) **References Cited**

U.S. PATENT DOCUMENTS

5,995,015	A *	11/1999	DeTemple et al.	..... 340/825.49
6,294,999	B1 *	9/2001	Yarin et al.	.... 340/573.1
6,484,148	B1 *	11/2002	Boyd	.... 705/14
6,563,423	B1 *	5/2003	Smith	.... 340/572.1
6,577,275	B1 *	6/2003	Turner	.... 342/465
6,659,344	B1 *	12/2003	Otto et al.	.... 235/381
6,700,960	B1 *	3/2004	Kaufman et al.	...... 379/112.01
6,865,546	B1 *	3/2005	Song	.... 705/26

2003/0040922	A1 *	2/2003	Bodin	.... 705/1

FOREIGN PATENT DOCUMENTS

JP		2002-319001 A	* 10/2002

OTHER PUBLICATIONS

Jones, Working Without Wires, Industrial Distribution, Aug. 1999, p. M6, M8-M9 [PROQUEST].*

Welling, Unveiling AIM's store of the future, part I, Apparel Industry Magazine, vol. 6, No. 2, Feb. 2000, p. 24-31 [DIALOG: file 15].*

Quinlan, Radio Tags—The New Identifier, Handling & Shipping Management, vol. 26, Apr. 1985, start p. 90 [DIALOG: file 148].*

(Continued)

Primary Examiner—Susanna M. Diaz
(74) *Attorney, Agent, or Firm*—Synnestvedt & Lechner LLP; Martin J. McKinley

(57) **ABSTRACT**

A method and system for identifying and tracking persons using RFID-tagged items carried on the persons. Previous purchase records for each person who shops at a retail store are collected by POS terminals and stored in a transaction database. When a person carrying or wearing items having RFID tags enters the store or other designated area, a RFID tag scanner located therein scans the RFID tags on that person and reads the RFID tag information. The RFID tag information collected from the person is correlated with transaction records stored in the transaction database according to known correlation algorithms. Based on the results of the correlation, the exact identity of the person or certain characteristics about the person can be determined. This information is used to monitor the movement of the person through the store or other areas.

27 Claims, 4 Drawing Sheets

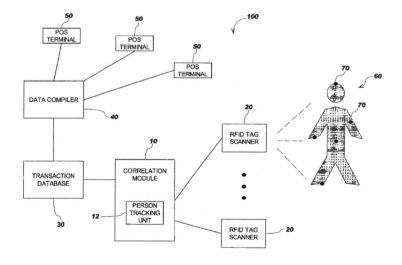

(12) **United States Patent**
Huffman et al.

(10) **Patent No.:** **US 6,947,978 B2**
(45) **Date of Patent:** **Sep. 20, 2005**

(54) **METHOD FOR GEOLOCATING LOGICAL NETWORK ADDRESSES**

(75) Inventors: **Stephen Mark Huffman**, Sandy Spring, MD (US); **Michael Henry Reifer**, Columbia, MD (US)

(73) Assignee: **The United States of America as represented by the Director, National Security Agency**, Washington, DC (US)

(*) Notice: Subject to any disclaimer, the term of this patent is extended or adjusted under 35 U.S.C. 154(b) by 990 days.

(21) Appl. No.: **09/752,898**

(22) Filed: **Dec. 29, 2000**

(65) **Prior Publication Data**

US 2002/0087666 A1 Jul. 4, 2002

(51) **Int. Cl.**[7] **G06F 15/177**
(52) **U.S. Cl.** **709/220**; 709/219; 709/225; 370/455; 370/456; 455/456.1
(58) **Field of Search** 709/220, 219, 709/225; 370/455, 456; 455/456.1

(56) **References Cited**

U.S. PATENT DOCUMENTS

6,243,746 B1	*	6/2001	Sondur et al.	709/220
6,671,514 B1	*	12/2003	Cedervall et al.	455/456.1
6,684,250 B2	*	1/2004	Anderson et al.	709/225
2002/0016831 A1	*	2/2002	Peled et al.	709/219
2004/0203851 A1	*	10/2004	Vetro et al.	455/456.1
2004/0203866 A1	*	10/2004	Sahinoglu et al.	455/456.1

OTHER PUBLICATIONS

Beongku et al., "A Cellular Architecture For Supporting Geocast Services", VTC 2000, IEEE, pp. 1452–1459.*
Beongku et al., "A Geocast Architecture For Mobile Cellular Networks", NJ Institute Of Technology, 2000 ACM, pp. 59–67.*
Bhasker et al., "Employing User Feedback For Fast, Accurate Low–Maintenance Geolocationing", UCSD technical report #CS2003–0765, pp. 1–16.*
Cook, Peter, "A Systems Approach to Base Stations", Oct. 19, 2000, Base Station Working group, Software Defined Radio Forum Contribution, 11 pages.*

* cited by examiner

Primary Examiner—Jack B. Harvey
Assistant Examiner—Hai V. Nguyen
(74) *Attorney, Agent, or Firm*—Stephen M. Bloor; Robert D. Morelli

(57) **ABSTRACT**

Method for geolocating logical network addresses on electronically switched dynamic communications networks, such as the Internet, using the time latency of communications to and from the logical network address to determine its location. Minimum round-trip communications latency is measured between numerous stations on the network and known network addressed equipment to form a network latency topology map. Minimum round-trip communications latency is also measured between the stations and the logical network address to be geolocated. The resulting set of minimum round-trip communications latencies is then correlated with the network latency topology map to determine the location of the network address to be geolocated.

11 Claims, 3 Drawing Sheets

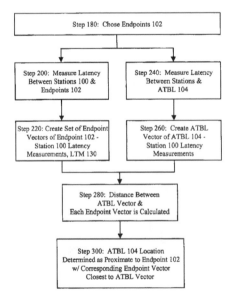

US 6,947,978 B2

1

METHOD FOR GEOLOCATING LOGICAL NETWORK ADDRESSES

FIELD OF THE INVENTION

The present invention, a Method for Geolocating Logical Network Addresses, relates to networked communications, and more particularly to a method for determining or verifying the physical location of a logical network address.

BACKGROUND OF THE INVENTION

As more of the nation's commerce and communication have moved from traditional fixed-point services to electronically switched networks the correlation between who you are communicating or doing business with and where they are physically located no longer exists. In the past, communication and commerce took place between parties at known physical locations, whether across a store counter or between post office addressees. Even telephone numbers correlated, more or less, to a permanent fixed location.

There are still many advantages to knowing the physical location of a party one is dealing with across electronically switched networks. For example, in the realm of advertising, knowing the geographic distribution of sales or inquires can be used to measure the effectiveness of advertising across geographic regions. As another example, logon IDs and passwords can only go so far in providing security when a remote user is logging into a system. If stolen, they can be easily used to masquerade as valid users. But if an ability to check the location were part of the security procedure, and the host machine knew the physical location of the remote user, a stolen logon/password could be noted or disabled if not used from or near the appropriate location. Network operators could benefit from knowing the location of a network logon to ensure that an account is being accessed from a valid location and logons from unexpected locations could be brought to the network operator's attention.

Methods of locating electronic emitters to a point on the earth, or geolocating emitters, have been used for many years. These methods include a range of techniques from high-frequency direction finding triangulation techniques for finding a ship in distress to quickly locating the origin of an emergency "911" call on a point-to-point wireline telephone system. These techniques can be entirely passive and cooperative, such as when geolocating oneself using the Global Positioning System or active and uncooperative, such as a military targeting radar tracking its target.

These geolocation techniques may be targeted against a stationary or moving target but most of these direction finding and geolocation techniques start with the assumption they are working with signals in a linear medium. For example, in radio triangulation, several stations each determine the direction from which a common signal was intercepted. Because the assumption can be made that the intercepted signal traveled in a straight line, or at least on a known line of propagation, from the transmitter to each station, lines of bearing can be drawn from each station in the direction from which the signal was intercepted. The point where they cross is the point at which the signal source is assumed to be located.

In addition to the direction of the signal, other linear characteristics can be used to geolocate signals, including propagation time and Doppler shift, but the underlining tenets that support these geolocation methodologies are not applicable to a network environment. Network elements are not connected via the shortest physical path between them,

2

data transiting the network is normally queued and later forwarded depending on network loading causing the data to effectively propagate at a non-constant speed, and switching elements within the network can cause the data to propagate through non-constant routing. Thus, traditional time-distance geolocation methodologies are not effective in a network environment.

In his book "The Cuckoo's Egg" (Doubleday 1989, Ch. 17), Clifford Stoll recounted his difficulties in using simple echo timing on a network to determine the distance from his computer to his nemesis, a computer hacker attacking a University of California at Berkeley computer. Network switching and queuing delays produced echo distance results several orders of magnitude greater than the actual distance between the computers.

In a fully meshed network, every station, from which a geolocation in initiated, is directly connected to every endpoint from which an "echo timing" is measured. The accuracy results of geolocation using round-trip echo timing are dependent on: the degree to which the network is interconnected or "meshed," the specific web of connectivity between the stations and endpoints, the number and deployment of stations, and the number and deployment of endpoints chosen.

Fortunately many of the survivability concerns for which the original ARPAnet was designed, and the commercial forces which gave rise to the expansion of the follow-on Internet and continue to fuel its growth, are also forces and concerns which drive it not only to be more interconnected and meshed but are also working to minimize the effects of latency due to line speed, queue size, and switching speeds. As a result there is a reasonable expectation that forces will continue to work toward the development of a highly meshed Internet.

There are other methods for physically locating a logical network address on the Internet that do not rely on the physics of electronic propagation. One method currently in use for determining the location of a network address relies on network databases. This method of network geolocation looks up the IP address of the host computer to be located, retrieves the physical address of a point of contact for that logical network address from the appropriate registry and then cross-references that physical address to a latitude and longitude. An example of an implementation of such a method can be found at the University of Illinois web site: http://cello.cs.uiuc.edu/cgi-bin/slamm/ip2ll. This implementation uses the Internic registry and the listed technical point of contact to report the physical location of the logical address.

There are a number of shortcomings to this method. First, the level of resolution to which the address is resolved is dependent on the level of resolution of the information in the registry. Second, there is an assumption that the supplied data in the registry correctly and properly identifies the physical location of the logical network address. It is entirely possible the host associated with the logical address is at a completely different physical location than the physical address given for the technical point of contact in registry. Third, if the supplied physical address given cannot be cross-referenced to a physical location no geolocation is possible. Geolocation information is often available from network databases but access to and the veracity of this information is uncertain. An independent method is needed to geolocate network addresses.

SUMMARY OF THE INVENTION

In consideration of the problems detailed above and the discrepancies enumerated in the partial solutions thereto, an

(12) **United States Patent**
Berkowitz

(10) **Patent No.:** **US 7,805,291 B1**
(45) **Date of Patent:** **Sep. 28, 2010**

(54) **METHOD OF IDENTIFYING TOPIC OF TEXT USING NOUNS**

(75) Inventor: **Sidney Berkowitz**, Baltimore, MD (US)

(73) Assignee: **The United States of America as represented by the Director National Security Agency**, Washington, DC (US)

(*) Notice: Subject to any disclaimer, the term of this patent is extended or adjusted under 35 U.S.C. 154(b) by 1272 days.

(21) Appl. No.: **11/137,594**

(22) Filed: **May 25, 2005**

(51) **Int. Cl.**
G06F 17/27 (2006.01)
(52) **U.S. Cl.** **704/9**
(58) **Field of Classification Search** 704/4, 704/7, 10
See application file for complete search history.

(56) **References Cited**

U.S. PATENT DOCUMENTS

5,418,951	A	5/1995	Damashek	
5,937,422	A	8/1999	Nelson et al.	
6,122,647	A *	9/2000	Horowitz et al.	715/205
6,199,034	B1 *	3/2001	Wical	704/9
6,638,317	B2	10/2003	Nakao	
2003/0167252	A1	9/2003	Odom et al.	
2003/0182631	A1	9/2003	Tsochantaridis et al.	
2004/0029085	A1 *	2/2004	Hu et al.	434/178

2004/0122657	A1	6/2004	Brants et al.
2004/0205457	A1	10/2004	Bent et al.

OTHER PUBLICATIONS

Lin et al, "Identifying Topics by Position", 1997, In Proc. of the Applied Natural Language Processing Conf., pp. 283-290.*
Lin et al , "Knowledge Based Automatic Topic Identification", 1995, In Proc. of the 33rd Annual Meeting of the ACL, pp. 308-310.*
Clifton et al, "TopCat: Data Mining for Topic Identification in a Text Corpus", 1999, In Proc. of the 3rd European Conf. of Principles and Practice of knowledge Discovery in Databases, pp. 1-33.*

* cited by examiner

Primary Examiner—James S Wozniak
Assistant Examiner—Olujimi A Adesanya
(74) *Attorney, Agent, or Firm*—Robert D. Morelli

(57) **ABSTRACT**

A method of identifying a topic of a text. Text is received. Then, the nouns in the text are identified. The singular form of each identified noun is determined. Combinations are created of the singular form of the identified nouns, where the number of singular forms of the nouns in the combinations is user-definable. The frequency of occurrence in the text of each noun that corresponds to its singular form is determined. Each frequency of occurrence is assigned as a score to its corresponding singular form noun. Each combination of singular form nouns is assigned a score that is equal to the sum of the scores of its constituent singular form nouns. The user-definable number of top scoring singular form nouns and combinations of singular form nouns are selected as the topic of the text.

2 Claims, 1 Drawing Sheet

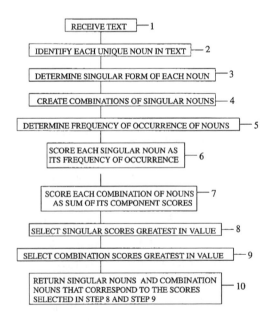

1

METHOD OF IDENTIFYING TOPIC OF TEXT USING NOUNS

FIELD OF INVENTION

The present invention relates, in general, to data processing of a document and, in particular, to topic identification.

BACKGROUND OF THE INVENTION

There is continuing research in the area of topic identification. Previous methods in this area are based on the use of keywords. A disadvantage of such a method is that any variation in the spelling of a keyword without any significant change in meaning might cause the performance of the method to degrade. One proposed solution to this problem is to use a dictionary, thesaurus, or semantic index to generate variations of the keyword. This suggestion improves performance when there is a spelling variation without a change in meaning, but causes further performance degradation when there is a change in meaning in the presence of similar spelling.

U.S. Pat. No. 5,418,951, entitled "METHOD OF RETRIEVING DOCUMENTS THAT CONCERN THE SAME TOPIC," discloses a method of identifying the topic of a document using segments of text called n-grams, where ~1 indicates the number of characters in the textual segment. The present invention does not use n-grams to identify the topic of text as does U.S. Pat. No. 5,418,951. U.S. Pat. No. 5,418,951 is hereby incorporated by reference into the specification of the present invention.

U.S. Pat. No. 5,937,422, entitled "AUTOMATICALLY GENERATING A TOPIC DESCRIPTION FOR TEXT AND SEARCHING AND SORTING TEXT BY TOPIC USING THE SAME," discloses a method of identifying a topic of text by using the definition of each word in the text. The present invention does not require the use of the definition of each word in a text as does U.S. Pat. No. 5,937,422. U.S. Pat. No. 5,937,422 is hereby incorporated by reference into the specification of the present invention.

U.S. Pat. No. 6,638,317, entitled "APPARATUS AND METHOD FOR GENERATING DIGEST ACCORDING TO HIERARCHICAL STRUCTURE OF TOPIC," discloses a method of calculating a lexical cohesion degree at each position in a document and extracting key sentences and generates a digest based on the relationship between a target passage and a passage containing the target passage. The present invention neither extracts sentences nor compares a target passage to another passage containing the target passage as does U.S. Pat. No. 6,638,317. U.S. Pat. No. 6,638,317 is hereby incorporated by reference into the specification of the present invention.

U.S. Pat. Appl. No. 20030167252, entitled "TOPIC IDENTIFICATION AND USE THEREOF IN INFORMATION RETRIEVAL SYSTEMS," discloses a method of identifying a topic of text by identifying the most frequently occurring combinations of words in the text. The present invention does not identify the topic of text by identifying the most frequently occurring combination of words in a text as does U.S. Pat. Appl. No. 20030167252. U.S. Pat. Appl. No. 20030167252 is hereby incorporated by reference into the specification of the present invention.

U.S. Pat. Appl. No. 20030182631, entitled "SYSTEMS AND METHODS FOR DETERMINING THE TOPIC STRUCTURE OF A PORTION OF TEXT," discloses a method of identifying a topic of text using a Probabilistic Latent Semantic Analysis. The present invention does not

2

identify the topic of text by using a Probabilistic Latent Semantic Analysis as does U.S. Pat. Appl. No. 20030182631. U.S. Pat. Appl. No. 2003018263 1 is hereby incorporated by reference into the specification of the present invention.

U.S. Pat. Appl. No. 20040122657, entitled "SYSTEMS AND METHODS FOR INTERACTIVE TOPIC-BASED TEXT SUMMARIZATION," discloses a method of identifying a topic of text using key phrases, n-grams, and sentences. The present invention does not identify the topic of text by using key phrases, n-grams, and sentences as does U.S. Pat. Appl. No. 20040122657. U.S. Pat. Appl. No. 20040122657 is hereby incorporated by reference into the specification of the present invention.

U.S. Pat. Appl. No. 20040205457, entitled "AUTOMATIC SUMMARISING TOPICS IN A COLLECTION OF ELECTRONIC DOCUMENTS," discloses a method of identifying a topic of text using vectors of terms and sentences to create a correlation matrix. The present invention does not identify the topic of text by using vectors of terms and sentences to create a correlation matrix as does U.S. Pat. Appl. No. 20040205457. U.S. Pat. Appl. No. 20040205457 is hereby incorporated by reference into the specification of the present invention.

SUMMARY OF THE INVENTION

It is an object of the present invention to identify the topic of text.

It is another object of the present invention to identify the topic of text using nouns that occur in the text.

The present invention is a method of identify the topic of text using nouns that occur in the text.

The first step of the method is receiving the text.

The second step of the method is identifying each unique word in the text that is a noun.

The third step of the method is determining a singular form of each identified noun.

The fourth step of the method is creating combinations of the singular forms of the identified nouns, where the number of singular forms of the nouns in each combination is user-definable.

The fifth step of the method is determining a frequency of occurrence in the text of each identified noun.

The sixth step of the method is assigning a score to each singular form noun, where the score of each singular form noun is the frequency of occurrence of the corresponding noun determined in the fifth step.

The seventh step of the method is assigning a score to each combination of singular form nouns, where the score of each combination is a sum of the scores of the singular form nouns in the combination.

The eighth step of the method is selecting a user-definable number of scores of singular form nouns that are greatest in value.

The ninth step of the method is selecting a user-definable number of scores of combinations of singular form nouns that are greatest in value.

The tenth, and last, step of the method is returning the singular forms of nouns and the combinations of singular form nouns that correspond to the scores selected in the eighth and ninth steps as the topic of the text.

BRIEF DESCRIPTION OF THE DRAWINGS

FIG. **1** is a flowchart of the steps of the present invention.

(12) **United States Patent**
Covell et al.

(10) **Patent No.:** US 8,479,225 B2
(45) **Date of Patent:** Jul. 2, 2013

(54) **SOCIAL AND INTERACTIVE APPLICATIONS FOR MASS MEDIA**

(75) Inventors: **Michele Covell**, Palo Alto, CA (US); **Shumeet Baluja**, Santa Clara, CA (US); **Michael Fink**, Brookline, MA (US)

(73) Assignee: **Google Inc.**, Mountain View, CA (US)

(*) Notice: Subject to any disclaimer, the term of this patent is extended or adjusted under 35 U.S.C. 154(b) by 521 days.

(21) Appl. No.: **11/563,661**

(22) Filed: **Nov. 27, 2006**

(65) **Prior Publication Data**

US 2007/0130580 A1   Jun. 7, 2007

Related U.S. Application Data

(60) Provisional application No. 60/740,760, filed on Nov. 29, 2005, provisional application No. 60/823,881, filed on Aug. 29, 2006.

(51) **Int. Cl.**

H04H 60/32	(2008.01)
G06F 3/00	(2006.01)
G06F 13/00	(2006.01)
H04N 5/445	(2011.01)
H04H 60/58	(2008.01)
H04N 21/439	(2011.01)
H04N 21/462	(2011.01)

(52) **U.S. Cl.**
CPC *H04H 60/58* (2013.01); *H04N 21/4394* (2013.01); *H04N 21/4622* (2013.01)
USPC **725/18**; 725/40; 725/51

(58) **Field of Classification Search**
USPC 725/37
See application file for complete search history.

(56) **References Cited**

U.S. PATENT DOCUMENTS

4,811,399	A	3/1989	Landell et al.
5,706,364	A	1/1998	Kopec et al.
5,870,744	A	2/1999	Sprague
6,023,693	A	2/2000	Masuoka et al.
6,044,365	A	3/2000	Cannon et al.
6,236,758	B1	5/2001	Sodagar et al.
6,494,720	B1	12/2002	Meyrowitsch
6,529,526	B1	3/2003	Schneidewend
6,563,909	B2	5/2003	Schmitz
6,585,521	B1	7/2003	Obrador
6,704,920	B2	3/2004	Brill et al.
6,751,601	B2	6/2004	Zegers
6,754,667	B2	6/2004	Kim et al.
6,763,339	B2	7/2004	Fu et al.

(Continued)

FOREIGN PATENT DOCUMENTS

EP	1524857	4/2005
JP	2002-209204	7/2002
JP	2004049438	2/2004

OTHER PUBLICATIONS

Yang, Chen. "MACS: Music Audio Characteristic Sequence Indexing for Similarity Retrieval". Oct. 21-24, 2001, New Paltz, New York.*

(Continued)

Primary Examiner — Bennett Ingvoldstad
(74) *Attorney, Agent, or Firm* — Fish & Richardson P.C.

(57) **ABSTRACT**

Systems, methods, apparatuses, user interfaces and computer program products provide social and interactive applications for mass media based on real-time ambient-audio and/or video identification.

39 Claims, 7 Drawing Sheets

Ambient-Audio Identification System (Client-Side)
200

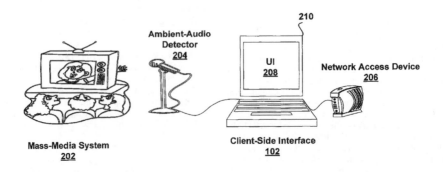

Ambient-Audio Detector
204

210

UI
208

Network Access Device
206

Mass-Media System
202

Client-Side Interface
102

1

SOCIAL AND INTERACTIVE APPLICATIONS FOR MASS MEDIA

RELATED APPLICATIONS

This application claims the benefit of priority from U.S. Provisional Patent Application No. 60/740,760, for "Environment-Based Referrals," filed Nov. 29, 2005, which application is incorporated by reference herein its entirety.

This application claims the benefit of priority from U.S. Provisional Patent Application No. 60/823,881, for "Audio Identification Based on Signatures," filed Aug. 29, 2006, which application is incorporated by reference herein its entirety.

This application is related to U.S. patent application Ser. No. 11/563,653, for "Determining Popularity Ratings Using Social and Interactive Applications For Mass Media," filed Nov. 27, 2006, and U.S. patent application Ser. No. 11/563,665, for "Detecting Repeating Content In Media," filed Nov. 27, 2006. Each of these patent applications is incorporated by reference herein in its entirety.

TECHNICAL FIELD

The disclosed implementations are related to social and interactive applications for mass media.

BACKGROUND

Mass media channels (e.g., television and radio broadcasts) typically provide limited content to a large audience. By contrast, the World Wide Web provides vast amounts of information that may only interest a few individuals. Conventional interactive television attempts to bridge these two communication mediums by providing a means for viewers to interact with their televisions and to receive content and/or services related to television broadcasts.

Conventional interactive television is typically only available to viewers through cable or satellite networks for a subscription fee. To receive interactive television service the viewer has to rent or buy a set-top box and have it installed by a technician. The viewer's television is connected to the set-top box, which enables the viewer to interact with the television using a remote control or other input device, and to receive information, entertainment and services (e.g., advertisements, online shopping, forms and surveys, games and activities, etc.).

While conventional interactive television can improve the viewer's television experience, there remains a need for social and interactive applications for mass media that do not rely on significant additional hardware or physical connections between the television or radio and a set-top box or computer.

One social and interactive television application that is lacking with conventional and interactive television systems is the ability to provide complementary information to the mass media channel in an effortless manner. With conventional systems, a user would have to log-on to a computer and query for such information which would diminish the passive experience offered by mass media. Moreover, conventional television systems cannot provide complementary information in real-time while the user is watching a broadcast.

Another social and interactive television application that is lacking with conventional interactive television systems is the ability to dynamically link a viewer with an ad hoc social peer community (e.g., a discussion group, chat room, etc.) in real-time. Imagine that you are watching the latest episode of

2

"Friends" on television and discover that the character "Monica" is pregnant. You want to chat, comment or read other viewers' responses to the scene in real-time. One option would be to log on your computer, type in the name of "Friends" or other related terms into a search engine, and perform a search to find a discussion group on "Friends." Such required action by the viewer, however, would diminish the passive experience offered by mass media and would not enable the viewer to dynamically interact (e.g., comment, chat, etc.) with other viewers who are watching the program at the same time.

SUMMARY

The deficiencies described above are addressed by the disclosed systems, methods, apparatuses, user interfaces and computer program products for providing social and interactive applications based on real-time ambient-audio and/or video identification.

In some implementations, a method includes: receiving a descriptor identifying ambient audio associated with a media broadcast; comparing the descriptor to reference descriptors associated with the media broadcast; and aggregating personalized information related to the media broadcast based on the result of the comparison.

In some implementations, a method includes: receiving a first descriptor identifying ambient audio associated with a first media broadcast; receiving a second descriptor identifying ambient audio associated with a second media broadcast; comparing the first and second descriptors to determine if the first and second media broadcasts are the same; and aggregating personalized information based on the result of the comparison.

In some implementations, a method includes: detecting ambient audio associated with a media broadcast; generating descriptors identifying the media broadcast; transmitting the descriptors to a network resource; and receiving aggregated personalized information from the network resource based on the descriptors.

In some implementations, a system includes a database of reference descriptors. A database server is operatively coupled to the database and to a client system. The database server is configurable to receive a descriptor from the client system for identifying ambient audio associated with a media broadcast, comparing the received descriptor with one or more reference descriptors, and aggregating personalized information related to the media broadcast based on the result of the comparison.

In some implementations, a system includes an audio detector configurable for sampling ambient audio. A client interface is operatively coupled to the audio detector and configurable to generate descriptors identifying a media broadcast. The client interface is configurable for transmitting the descriptors to a network resource, and for receiving aggregated personalized information from the network resource based on the descriptors.

Other implementations are directed to systems, methods, apparatuses, user interfaces, and computer program products.

DESCRIPTION OF DRAWINGS

FIG. **1** is a block diagram of one embodiment of a mass personalization system.

FIG. **2** illustrates one embodiment of an ambient-audio identification system, including the client-side interface shown in FIG. **1**.

Project MK-Ultra and Mind Control Technology

(12) **United States Patent**
Smith et al.

(10) Patent No.: **US 8,959,573 B2**
(45) **Date of Patent:** **Feb. 17, 2015**

(54) **NOISE, ENCRYPTION, AND DECOYS FOR COMMUNICATIONS IN A DYNAMIC COMPUTER NETWORK**

(75) Inventors: **Wayne B. Smith**, Melbourne Beach, FL (US); **Charles Powers**, Melbourne, FL (US); **Ellen K. Lin**, West Melbourne, FL (US); **Christopher T. Dowin**, Melbourne, FL (US); **Ryan E. Sharpe**, Indialantic, FL (US)

(73) Assignee: **Harris Corporation**, Melbourne, FL (US)

(*) Notice: Subject to any disclaimer, the term of this patent is extended or adjusted under 35 U.S.C. 154(b) by 152 days.

(21) Appl. No.: **13/461,057**

(22) Filed: **May 1, 2012**

(65) **Prior Publication Data**
US 2013/0298181 A1   Nov. 7, 2013

(51) **Int. Cl.**
G06F 17/00 (2006.01)
H04L 29/06 (2006.01)

(52) **U.S. Cl.**
CPC *H04L 63/20* (2013.01)
USPC **726/1**

(58) **Field of Classification Search**
CPC H04L 63/20; H04L 63/102
USPC 726/1, 4; 713/189
See application file for complete search history.

(56) **References Cited**

U.S. PATENT DOCUMENTS

5,734,649 A   3/1998 Carvey et al.
6,052,064 A *   4/2000 Budnik et al. 340/7.24

6,646,989 B1   11/2003 Khotimsky et al.
6,917,974 B1   7/2005 Stytz et al.
6,981,146 B1   12/2005 Sheymov
7,010,604 B1   3/2006 Munger et al.
7,043,633 B1   5/2006 Fink et al.
7,085,267 B2   8/2006 Carey et al.
7,133,930 B2   11/2006 Munger et al.
7,216,359 B2   5/2007 Katz et al.
7,236,598 B2   6/2007 Sheymov et al.
7,382,778 B2   6/2008 Chari et al.
7,469,279 B1   12/2008 Stamler et al.

(Continued)

FOREIGN PATENT DOCUMENTS

JP   2008177714 A   7/2008

OTHER PUBLICATIONS

U.S. Appl. No. 13/369,424, filed Feb. 9, 2012 Dynamic Computer Network With Variable Identity Parameters.

(Continued)

Primary Examiner — Anthony Brown
(74) *Attorney, Agent, or Firm* — Fox Rothschild, LLP; Robert J. Sacco

(57) **ABSTRACT**

A method and apparatus for processing data messages in a dynamic computer network is disclosed. The method includes implementing a mission plan specifying a message type, a message generation location, and a message distance vector for false messages, receiving a data message that includes a plurality of identity parameters, and determining a message type and a message distance vector for the received message. The network device is configured to generate false messages and process received messages. If the message type is a false message and the distance vector of the false message has been exhausted, the data message is dropped. If the distance vector of the false message has not been exhausted, transmitting the false message in accordance with the mission plan.

20 Claims, 13 Drawing Sheets

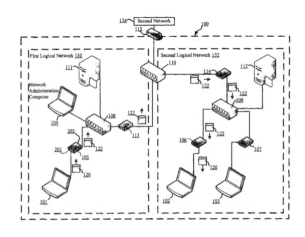

324

1

NOISE, ENCRYPTION, AND DECOYS FOR COMMUNICATIONS IN A DYNAMIC COMPUTER NETWORK

BACKGROUND OF THE INVENTION

1. Statement of the Technical Field

The inventive arrangements relate to computer network security, and more particularly to systems for generating noise, decoys, and encryption where the network is dynamically maneuverable to defend against malicious attacks.

2. Description of the Related Art

The central weakness of current cyber infrastructure is its static nature. Assets receive permanent or infrequently-changing identifications, allowing adversaries nearly unlimited time to probe networks, map and exploit vulnerabilities. Additionally, data traveling between these fixed entities can be captured and attributed. The current approach to cyber security places technologies such as firewalls and intrusion detection systems around fixed assets, and uses encryption to protect data en route. However, this traditional approach is fundamentally flawed because it provides a fixed target for attackers. In today's globally connected communications infrastructure, static networks are vulnerable networks.

The Defense Advanced Research Projects Agency (DARPA) Information Assurance (IA) Program has performed initial research in the area of dynamic network defense. A technique was developed under the Information Assurance Program to dynamically reassign Internet protocol (IP) address space feeding into a pre-designated network enclave for the purpose of confusing any would-be adversaries observing the network. This technique is called dynamic network address transformation (DYNAT). An overview of the DYNAT technology was presented in a published paper by DARPA entitled Dynamic Approaches to Thwart Adversary Intelligence (2001).

SUMMARY OF THE INVENTION

A method of processing data messages in a dynamic computer network is disclosed. The method includes implementing a mission plan specifying a message type, a message generation location, and a message distance vector for false messages. The method includes receiving a data message generated in accordance with the mission plan that includes a plurality of identity parameters. A message type and a message distance vector is determined for the received message. On a condition that the message type is a false message and the distance vector of the false message has been exhausted, the data message is dropped. On a condition that the distance vector of the false message has not been exhausted, transmitting the false message in accordance with the mission plan.

A network device for processing data messages is disclosed. The network device is connected to a first network. A plurality of ports on the network device are configured to receive and transmit data messages that include a plurality of identity parameters. A memory is configured to store a mission plan that specifies a message type, a message generation location, and a message distance vector for false messages. The device also includes at least one processing unit configured to generate a false message based on the mission plan. The processing unit is also configured to determine a message type and a message distance vector of a received data message. If the message type is a false message and the distance vector of the false message has been exhausted, the processing unit is configured to drop the data message. On the other

2

hand, if the distance vector of the data message has not been exhausted, transmit the data message in accordance with the mission plan.

BRIEF DESCRIPTION OF THE DRAWINGS

Embodiments will be described with reference to the following drawing figures, in which like numerals represent like items throughout the figures, and in which:

FIG. **1** is an example of a computer network that is useful for understanding the present invention.

FIG. **2** is an example of a module that can be used in the present invention for performing certain manipulations of identity parameters.

FIG. **3** is a drawing that is useful for understanding a tool that can be used to help characterize the network in FIG. **1**.

FIG. **4**, is an example of a dialog box of a graphical user interface that can be used to select dynamic settings for modules in FIG. **1**.

FIG. **5** is an example of a dialog box of a graphical user interface that can be used to select a sequence of active states and bypass states associated with each module in FIG. **1**.

FIG. **6** is a diagram that is useful for understanding the way in which a mission plan can be communicated to a plurality of modules in the network in FIG. **1**.

FIG. **7** is an example of a dialog box of a graphical user interface that can be used to select a mission plan and communicate the mission plan to the modules as shown in FIG. **6**.

FIG. **8** is a flowchart that is useful for understanding the operation of a module in FIG. **1**.

FIG. **9** is a flowchart that is useful for understanding the operation of a network control software application (NCSA) in relation to creating and loading mission plans.

FIG. **10** is a block diagram of a computer architecture that can be used to implement the modules in FIG. **1**.

FIG. **11** is a block diagram of a computer architecture that can be used to implement the network administration computer (NAC) in FIG. **1**.

FIG. **12** is a flowchart that is useful for understanding the operation of a network device that processes noise and decoy messages.

FIG. **13** is a table that is useful for understanding some of the types of identity parameters that can be modified.

DETAILED DESCRIPTION

The invention is described with reference to the attached figures. The figures are not drawn to scale and they are provided merely to illustrate the instant invention. Several aspects of the invention are described below with reference to example applications for illustration. It should be understood that numerous specific details, relationships, and methods are set forth to provide a full understanding of the invention. One having ordinary skill in the relevant art, however, will readily recognize that the invention can be practiced without one or more of the specific details or with other methods. In other instances, well-known structures or operations are not shown in detail to avoid obscuring the invention. The invention is not limited by the illustrated ordering of acts or events, as some acts may occur in different orders and/or concurrently with other acts or events. Furthermore, not all illustrated acts or events are required to implement a methodology in accordance with the invention.

It should also be appreciated that the terminology used herein is for the purpose of describing particular embodiments only and is not intended to be limiting of the invention. As used herein, the singular forms "a", "an" and "the" are

(19) **United States**

(12) **Patent Application Publication** (10) Pub. No.: **US 2008/0220749 A1**
Pridmore et al. (43) **Pub. Date:** **Sep. 11, 2008**

(54) **ACQUIRING IDENTITY PARAMETERS BY EMULATING BASE STATIONS**

(75) Inventors: **Andrew Paul Pridmore**, Hampshire (GB); **Paul Maxwell Martin**, Hampshire (GB); **Riki Benjamin Dolby**, Hampshire (GB)

(73) Assignee: **M.M.I. RESEARCH LIMITED**, Hampshire (UK)

(21) Appl. No.: **11/996,230**

(22) PCT Filed: **Jul. 17, 2006**

(86) PCT No.: **PCT/GB06/02639**

§ 371 (c)(1),
(2), (4) Date: **Jan. 18, 2008**

(30) **Foreign Application Priority Data**

Jul. 22, 2005 (GB) 0515125.3
Jan. 31, 2006 (GB) 0601956.6

Publication Classification

(51) **Int. Cl.**
$H04Q\ 7/20$ (2006.01)
$H04Q\ 7/34$ (2006.01)
$H04Q\ 7/38$ (2006.01)

(52) **U.S. Cl.** **455/414.1**; 455/500; 455/425

(57) **ABSTRACT**

A method of acquiring the identity parameters of two or more mobile devices (**20**), the method comprising: obtaining a list of two or more base stations (**1, 2, 3**); and acquiring identity parameters from the devices (**20**) by emulating each base station in the list. Two or more base stations may be simultaneously emulated, and the list of two or more base stations may be obtained by simultaneously interrogating two or more base stations (**1, 2, 3**). The identity parameters may be IMSI and/or IMEI and/or TMSI codes.

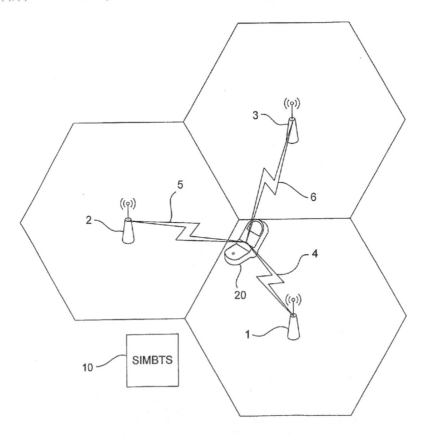

NSA Headquarters in Fort Meade, Maryland

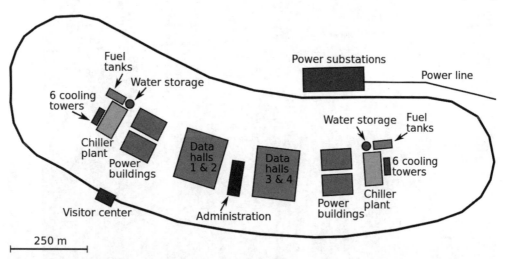

The NSA's Data Center at Camp Williams near Bluffdale, Utah

Officially known as the Intelligence Community Comprehensive National Cybersecurity Initiative Data Center, the Utah Data Center's mission is classified. It is a data storage facility used by the United States Intelligence Community designed to store an unfathomable amount of data – some trillions of terabytes.

The NSA's Utah Data Center. Photo: Electronic Frontier Foundation - EFF.org

Chapter 15
Implants and Nanotech

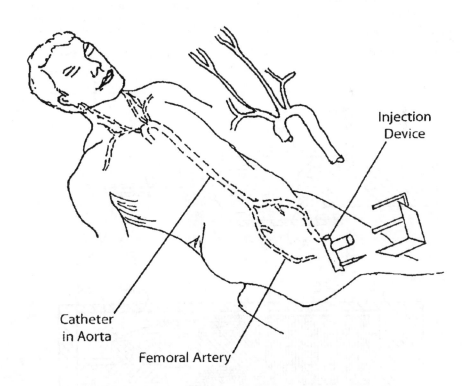

Injection
Device

Catheter
in Aorta

Femoral Artery

United States Patent [19]

Taylor et al.

[11] Patent Number: 5,211,129

[45] Date of Patent: May 18, 1993

[54] SYRINGE-IMPLANTABLE IDENTIFICATION TRANSPONDER

[75] Inventors: **Vern Taylor**, Broomfield, Calif.; **Daniel Koturov; John Bradin**, both of Colo.; **Gerald E. Loeb**, Clarksburg, Md.

[73] Assignees: **Destron/IDI, Inc.; Hughes Aircraft Co.**, both of Boulder, Colo.

[21] Appl. No.: **647,617**

[22] Filed: **Jan. 25, 1991**

Related U.S. Application Data

[63] Continuation of Ser. No. 267,726, Oct. 26, 1988, abandoned, which is a continuation of Ser. No. 135,563, Dec. 24, 1987, abandoned, which is a continuation of Ser. No. 832,684, Feb. 25, 1986, abandoned.

[51] Int. Cl.⁵ **A01K 61/00; A61M 5/00**

[52] U.S. Cl. **119/3; 606/117; 128/655; 128/899**

[58] Field of Search 128/654, 655, 656, 899; 606/116, 117; 119/3

[56] **References Cited**

U.S. PATENT DOCUMENTS

4,065,753	12/1977	Paul, Jr.	606/116 X
4,909,250	3/1990	Smith	606/117
4,920,670	5/1990	Amick	119/3 X
4,955,396	9/1990	Fralick et al.	606/117 X

Primary Examiner—Robert P. Swiatek
Attorney, Agent, or Firm—Earl C. Hancock

[57] **ABSTRACT**

An improved transponder for transmitting an identification of an animal or the like is described which is sufficiently miniaturized to be syringe-implantable, thus avoiding the necessity of surgical procedures. The transponder comprises a coil which receives an interrogation signal and transmits an identification signal in response thereto. The transponder receives the energy required for transmission by inductive coupling to an interrogator. A single integrated circuit chip is provided which detects the interrogation signal, rectifies it to generate power needed for transmission, stores an identification of the transponder and hence of the animal in which it is implanted, and generates a frequency-shift-keyed, Manchester encoded identification signal in response to the interrogation signal. The device transmits the identification signal in real time, that is, immediately upon commencement of the interrogation signal, such that no discrete elements for energy storage are required. The transmission frequency and the bit rate are both determined by integer division of the interrogation signal such that no discrete elements such as crystal oscillators are required for signal generation.

27 Claims, 6 Drawing Sheets

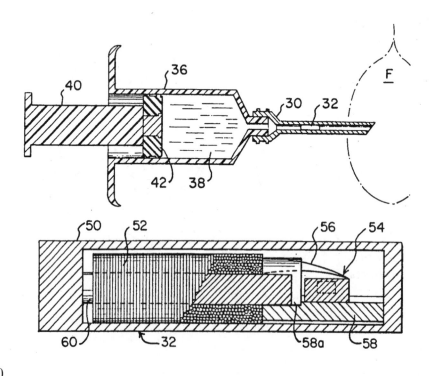

5,211,129

1

SYRINGE-IMPLANTABLE IDENTIFICATION TRANSPONDER

This application is a continuation of U.S. patent application Ser. No. 07/267,726, filed Oct. 26, 1988, which is a continuation of U.S. Pat. Application, Ser. No. 07/135,563, filed Dec. 24, 1987, which is a continuation of U.S. patent application Ser. No. 07/832,684, filed Feb. 25, 1986, all three of which are now abandoned.

FIELD OF THE INVENTION

This invention relates to identification transponders for implantation into animals for their identification, useful in monitoring migratory patterns and for other purposes. More particularly, this invention relates to an identification transponder which is passive, meaning that it receives all its operating power from an interrogator device, which is sufficiently small as to be implanted by a syringe, thus avoiding the necessity of a surgical procedure, and which, upon interrogation, provides a signal indicative of the identity of the particular animal, and which is durable and reliable over a period of years.

BACKGROUND OF THE INVENTION

There are many applications in which a transponder which can be carried by an animal for automatic identification of the animal would be useful. Typical uses include monitoring migratory patterns of wild animals, for studying their habits, and for providing automatic identification of domestic animals, for controlling automatic feeding devices and the like, and for verifying their identity, e.g., in connection with racehorses. Automatically operated transponders would also be useful in connection with the monitoring of laboratory animals, for a wide variety of experimental purposes.

The prior art shows a number of transponders which provide identification of animals. However, no prior art device of which the inventors are aware includes all the attributes which would be desirable. See, for example, Fathauer U.S. Pat. No. 3,541,995 which shows a transponder which can be affixed to an animal's collar or the like for identifying it as belonging to a particular class. The Fathauer device is relatively large and bulky and not suitable for identification of wild animals.

Particularly in connection with the tracking of the movements of wild animals, it is desirable that transponders be provided which are extremely small and which can be readily implanted in the animals. An implantable transponder offers the advantage that it is not susceptible to loss and does not impede the motion of the animal. In particular, it would be desirable to provide transponders which are implantable in animals without the requirement of surgical procedures. To this end, Jefferts et al. U.S. Pat. No. 3,313,301 shows injection of a length of wire having magnetic properties into an animal by means of a syringe or generally similar device. See generally Jefferts et al. U.S. Pat. Nos. 3,128,744, 4,233,964, 3,820,545 and 3,545,405.

The presence of an animal having had a sliver of wire implanted therein can be detected automatically by an inductive coil or the like; however, the animal cannot be specifically identified in such an arrangement. Thus, it is not possible to track the movements of an individual animal, but only of a large number of them. Jefferts et al. U.S. Pat. No. 4,233,964 shows a similarly implantable tag which has grooves formed into its outer surface

2

such that an individual animal can be identified by x-raying it and analyzing the groove pattern. This is obviously a very awkward system in use and does not lend itself readily to automatic monitoring of the movements of specific animals.

The prior art also includes transponders which provide an indication of the identity of a particular animal upon interrogation by an automatic interrogator device. Animal identification thus does not require operator intervention. See Hanton et al. U.S. Pat. No. 4,262,632 which shows a transponder for retention in the second stomach of a ruminant animal. The Hanton et al. transponder is adapted to be interrogated by an interrogator, to receive all operating power from the interrogator by means of an inductive coupling, and to transmit an identification signal in response to the interrogation. Hanton et al. also teach that such a transponder can be suitably encapsulated in glass for durability, another important aspect of devices of this type. However, the transponder of Hanton et al. is stated to be approximately three-quarters of an inch in diameter by three inches long. Such a transponder can only be implanted in an animal by a surgical procedure or by causing the animal to swallow it, e.g., by use of a conventional veterinary "balling gun." Such a transponder is not suitable for use in connection with wildlife, since it would be unduly complicated to apply these procedures to a large number of animals, such as fish, whose migratory patterns are to be studied. Not only is the Hanton et al. transponder too large for convenient implantation by means of a syringe or an automatic machine such as shown in some of the Jefferts et al. patents, but it is physically too large to be implanted into a relatively small animal such as a fish, a laboratory mouse, or the like.

A need therefore exists in the art for a transponder which is small enough to be syringe- or machine-implantable into a relatively small animal such as a fish, yet which provides an identification of the individual animal when interrogated by a suitable interrogator, such that the movements of individual animals can be studied by means of interrogators which record the animal's position without the intervention of a human operator.

It is therefore an object of the invention to provide a transponder which provides identification of an individual animal when it is interrogated, yet which is small enough to be syringe- or machine- implantable into an animal such as a fish.

It will be appreciated by those of skill in the art that it is important that a transponder for animal identification be durable in service, and it is accordingly an object of the invention to provide a transponder which is durable and reliable in service over a period of years, yet which is syringe-implantable and which provides an identification of the specific animal when interrogated.

Certain prior art transponders have relied on batteries for transmission of the identification signal. Other prior art transponders are powered by the interrogator itself by way of an inductive coupling. This is shown in Hanton et al. However, no reference known to the applicants shows a syringe-implantable transponder which is adapted to be powered by means of an inductive coupling to an interrogator, nor one in which the transponder additionally transmits an identification of an individual animal, and to provide the same is therefore an object of the present invention.

United States Patent [19]

Bucalo

[11] **3,951,132**

[45] **Apr. 20, 1976**

[54] **IMPLANT AND IMPLANTING METHOD**

[75] Inventor: **Louis Bucalo,** Holbrook, N.Y.

[73] Assignee: **Investors in Ventures, Inc.,** New York, N.Y.

[22] Filed: **Apr. 15, 1974**

[21] Appl. No.: **461,009**

Related U.S. Application Data

[63] Continuation-in-part of Ser. No. 359,429, May 11, 1973, Pat. No. 3,815,578.

[52] **U.S. Cl.** .... **128/1 R;** 128/334 R
[51] **Int. Cl.²** **A61B 19/00**
[58] **Field of Search** .... 128/1 R, 334 R, 334 C; 3/1

[56] **References Cited**

UNITED STATES PATENTS

2,453,056	11/1948	Zack	128/334
3,123,077	3/1964	Alcamo	128/335.5
3,221,746	12/1965	Noble	128/334 R
3,308,819	3/1967	Arp	128/215
3,646,615	3/1972	Ness	3/1
3,699,957	10/1972	Robinson	128/1 R

Primary Examiner—Dalton L. Truluck
Attorney, Agent, or Firm—Steinberg and Blake

[57] **ABSTRACT**

An implant which includes an elongated member to be situated in the interior of a tubular body organ and carrying at its exterior a structure for promoting the ingrowth of tissue, this structure being situated inwardly from a free end of the elongated member which enters the tubular organ in advance of the ingrowth structure. Between this free end of the elongated member and the ingrowth structure are barbs which are fixed to the elongated member, which are circumferentially distributed about the latter, and which are inclined away from the free end of the elongated member and extend over the ingrowth structure. These barbs are flexible so that they are capable of being radially deflected toward the elongated member. When the elongated member is to be introduced into the tubular organ, the latter is gripped with tweezers which have teeth which engage the tubular organ and which are circumferentially distributed about the latter. The tweezer teeth are out of longitudinal alignment with the barbs so that when the teeth and barbs pass each other during introduction of the implant into the tubular organ, while the latter is pulled onto the elongated member with the tweezers, the tweezer teeth will be aligned with spaces between the barbs.

10 Claims, 11 Drawing Figures

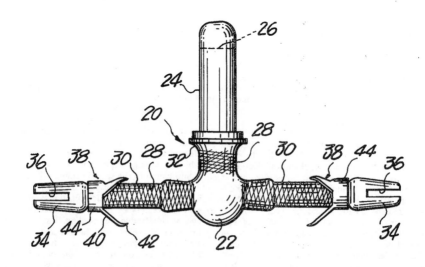

United States Patent [19]

Schulman et al.

[11] **Patent Number:** **5,522,865**

[45] **Date of Patent:** **Jun. 4, 1996**

[54] **VOLTAGE/CURRENT CONTROL SYSTEM FOR A HUMAN TISSUE STIMULATOR**

[75] Inventors: **Joseph H. Schulman**, Santa Clarita; **John C. Gord**, Venice; **Primoz Strojnik**, Granada Hills; **David I. Whitmoyer**, Los Angeles; **James H. Wolfe**, Canyon Country, all of Calif.

[73] Assignee: **Alfred E. Mann Foundation for Scientific Research**, Sylmar, Calif.

[21] Appl. No.: **322,068**

[22] Filed: **Oct. 12, 1994**

Related U.S. Application Data

[63] Continuation-in-part of Ser. No. 23,584, Feb. 26, 1993, which is a continuation of Ser. No. 752,069, Aug. 29, 1991, abandoned, which is a continuation-in-part of Ser. No. 411,563, Sep. 22, 1989, abandoned.

[51] Int. Cl.^{6} **H04R 25/00**; A61N 1/36
[52] U.S. Cl. **607/56**; 607/55; 607/57; 607/60; 607/32
[58] Field of Search 607/55, 56, 57, 607/32, 60

[56] **References Cited**

U.S. PATENT DOCUMENTS

3,742,947	7/1973	Hashem	128/696
3,942,536	3/1976	Mirowski et al.	607/17
4,267,410	5/1981	Forster et al.	607/57
4,428,377	1/1984	Zollner et al.	128/419
4,532,930	8/1985	Crosby et al.	128/419
4,592,359	6/1986	Galbraith	607/57
4,612,934	9/1986	Borkan	607/60
4,868,908	9/1989	Pless et al.	323/267
4,918,745	4/1990	Hutchison	455/41
4,947,844	8/1990	McDermott	607/57
5,285,779	2/1994	Cameron et al.	607/5

OTHER PUBLICATIONS

Medical Progress Through Technology; vol. 5:3, pp. 127–140 (Jul. 1977).

Primary Examiner—William E. Kamm
Assistant Examiner—Carl H. Layno
Attorney, Agent, or Firm—Fitch, Even, Tabin & Flannery

[57] **ABSTRACT**

A tissue stimulating system includes an external transmitter for transmitting a data signal to an implanted stimulator. The implanted stimulator includes a processor for generating stimulation signals for application to a plurality of tissue stimulating electrodes through respective isolated output channels. The implanted stimulator also includes a power supply that extracts a raw power signal from the data signal. A voltage downconverter generates at least four separate voltages from the extracted raw power signal by alternately connecting at least four capacitors in series across the raw power signal, thereby providing at least four output voltages, and then connecting the capacitors in parallel to transfer the charge stored thereon to a storage capacitor, which serves as the power source for portions of the stimulator. A selected one of the output voltages from the voltage downconverter is applied to an isolated refresh voltage capacitor in each output channel, where it controls a voltage controlled current source. The processor selectively monitors the electrodes and/or voltages generated in the stimulator and generates status indicating/measurement signals for transmission to the external transmitter. The external processor receives and processes the status indicating/measurement signals and uses the information therefrom to control the amount of power transmitted to the stimulator.

21 Claims, 15 Drawing Sheets

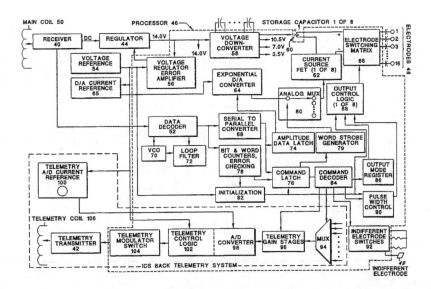

United States Patent [19]

Gargano et al.

[11] Patent Number:	5,629,678
[45] Date of Patent:	May 13, 1997

[54] **PERSONAL TRACKING AND RECOVERY SYSTEM**

[75] Inventors: **Paul A. Gargano**
David H. Gilmore, Cayman Kai, Cayman Islands; **Frank A. Pace**, Ballston Spa, N.Y.; **Lee Weinstein**, Somerville, Mass.

[73] Assignee: **Paul A. Gargano**, Belmont, Mass.

[21] Appl. No.: **371,089**

[22] Filed: **Jan. 10, 1995**

[51] Int. Cl.⁶ **G08B 23/00**

[52] U.S. Cl. **340/573**; 128/903; 340/539; 340/825.49; 342/357; 455/100

[58] Field of Search 340/573, 574, 340/572, 539, 825.49; 455/100; 379/37–38; 342/450, 357, 44, 42, 51; 128/774, 903, 653.1, 696

[56] **References Cited**

U.S. PATENT DOCUMENTS

3,618,059	11/1971	Allen	340/572 X
3,815,611	6/1974	Denniston, III	607/17 X
4,453,537	6/1984	Spitzer	623/3
4,594,997	6/1986	Hakky	600/40
4,602,621	7/1986	Hakky	600/40
4,706,689	11/1987	Man	340/539 X
4,713,054	12/1987	Kelly et al.	604/89
5,007,927	4/1991	Badylak et al.	623/3
5,051,741	9/1991	Wesby	340/825.49

5,318,501	6/1994	Lee et al.	600/16
5,342,408	8/1994	de Coriolis et al.	607/32
5,456,715	10/1995	Liotta	623/3
5,461,365	10/1995	Schlager et al.	340/573
5,461,390	10/1995	Hoshen	340/573 X
5,476,488	12/1995	Morgan et al.	128/903 X

OTHER PUBLICATIONS

Dialog OneSearch Results, May 13, 1994.

Primary Examiner—Thomas Mullen
Attorney, Agent, or Firm—Hamilton, Brook, Smith & Reynolds, P.C.

[57] **ABSTRACT**

Apparatus for tracking and recovering humans utilizes an implantable transceiver incorporating a power supply and actuation system allowing the unit to remain implanted and functional for years without maintenance. The implanted transmitter may be remotely actuated, or actuated by the implantee. Power for the remote-activated receiver is generated electromechanically through the movement of body muscle. The device is small enough to be implanted in a child, facilitating use as a safeguard against kidnapping, and has a transmission range which also makes it suitable for wilderness sporting activities. A novel biological monitoring feature allows the device to be used to facilitate prompt medical dispatch in the event of heart attack or similar medical emergency. A novel sensation-feedback feature allows the implantee to control and actuate the device with certainty.

19 Claims, 2 Drawing Sheets

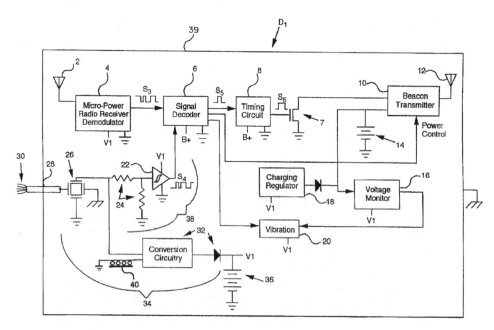

1

PERSONAL TRACKING AND RECOVERY SYSTEM

BACKGROUND OF THE INVENTION

The present invention relates, in general, to tracking and recovery systems and systems for tracking and recovering humans. More particularly, it discloses a system employing a self-powered, self-maintained transceiver, small enough to be implanted in a human, for locating, tracking, and recovering persons in distress, such as kidnap victims, people encountering adverse circumstances while in the wilderness, victims of heart attacks and the like.

BACKGROUND OF THE INVENTION

Various apparatus and techniques for tracking and locating animate and inanimate objects are known in the art. Recently, international legislation has established a satellite tracking system for locating downed aircraft and distressed seagoing vessels. This system utilizes user-activated transmitters operating at a frequency of 460 MHz, as spelled out in the Code of Federal Regulations chapter 47 part 90. These inexpensive transmitters are known as Emergency Position Indicating Radio Beacons (EPIRB's). The associated satellite network is capable of locating a transmitting EPIRB anywhere on the face of the globe. By international agreement, this system is used only for distressed aircraft and seagoing vessels, and all other potential uses are forbidden.

U.S. Pat. No. 4,818,998 describes a vehicle tracking and recovery system employing a transceiver (to be hidden within a motor vehicle), and a network of fixed and mobile ground transmitters and receivers to facilitate tracing and recovery of stolen vehicles. This system is presently in wide use by LoJack Corporation in the United States. The system operates at a frequency of 173.075 MHz, permanently assigned as a police radio service frequency in 1992. The unit, mounted in an automobile, is continuously operated as a receiver until such time as it is remotely activated, at which time it transmits a radio beacon (similarly to the EPIRB system), facilitating tracking and recovery. The tracking and recovery in the LoJack system is accomplished through a network of ground based fixed and mobile receiver units, which utilize field strength measurements and directional receivers to locate the transmitter, as opposed to the timing and triangulation methods used by the EPIRB system. The receiver in the automobile-mounted unit draws its power from the vehicle battery, and utilizes a small local rechargeable battery that powers the unit should the vehicle battery be disconnected.

U.S. Pat. No. 4,706,689, Issued to Daniel Man on Nov. 17th, 1987, describes a device designed to be implantable behind the ear of a human. The device transmits a coded signal intended to enable tracking of the person outfitted with the implanted device. The device operates continuously, and is designed to be recharged through external contacts. It is also designed to incorporate a biological monitoring function, such as might facilitate out-patient monitoring.

The above described devices all have limitations making them unsuitable as systems for the widespread tracking and recovery of humans. The EPIRB transmitter and Lojack transceiver are not miniaturized to the point where implantation is practical. The techniques for manually activating the EPIRB unit also make it unsuited for implantation. The LoJack unit requires substantial power to be supplied con-

2

tinually from a vehicle battery system, and unsuited for implantation from this point of view as well.

Daniel Man's implantable device is designed for continuous operation, which places severe constraints on its transmission range, even if it is only to be operated for a day at a time between battery recharges. With a given level of background radio frequency noise, communication theory can be used to calculate the minimum power consumption needed for detection of an event within a given time to within a given certainty, at a given distance from an omnidirectional transmitter. The resultant average transmission power is independent of whether the transmitter is pulsed or continuous. Further problems arise with Man's system when a number of units are in use in the same area. The tracking problem becomes prohibitively expensive for many simultaneous units, and the malfunction of any unit can mask the detectability of other units, or require significantly increased transmission power levels for all units. Such a system would require a very expensive closely spaced network of permanent tracking receivers with very costly hardware capable of tracking multiple units at one time. A system where transmitters are active all the time requires n times more bandwidth in the radio spectrum than minimal-bandwidth system with only one transmitter transmitting at one time. The availability of bandwidth could become quite a problem if the Man system were put into wide use.

In addition, the implanted unit would need to be recharged (probably daily) through contacts brought out through the person's skin. Such an arrangement presents a significant health hazard. In addition, the need for regular recharging puts significant restraints on the person using the device and also heightens the users awareness of the implanted device, resulting in a less "free and natural" state of mind. The complexity of the Man system could result in a significant level of false alarms, and/or prohibitively high cost.

The present invention contemplates improving upon the features available in the aforementioned devices and makes possible a widespread tracking and recovery system for humans in distress. The present invention will benefit from novel features allowing it to remain implanted and functional for many years. The device will remain in a dormant state until activated, either by the person in whom it is implanted, or by remote means. Novel means for powering and triggering the device will make recharging and battery replacement unnecessary. The device meets the growing demand for a new level of safety and peace of mind.

Consequently, it is a general object of this invention to provide a new means and method for locating, tracking, and recovering humans in distress. Ideally, the device will bring peace of mind and an increased quality of life for those who use it, and for their families, loved ones, and associates who depend on them critically. Adults who are at risk due to their economic or political status, as well as their children who may be at risk of being kidnapped, will reap new freedoms in their every-day lives by employing the device. Law enforcement agencies will be able to more economically protect those at risk, those who would potentially perpetrate acts of violence against individuals will be more effectively deterred. Those who enjoy wilderness sports such as mountain climbing, skiing, hang gliding, etc. will enjoy new freedom knowing that a rescue mission can be dispatched to their exact location if they encounter trouble.

A specific object of the invention is the rapid effective recovery of individuals who have been kidnapped. A further object of this invention is to afford peace of mind and increased quality of life to those utilizing the invention, and

United States Patent [19]

Marsh

[11] **Patent Number:** **5,868,100**

[45] **Date of Patent:** **Feb. 9, 1999**

[54] **FENCELESS ANIMAL CONTROL SYSTEM USING GPS LOCATION INFORMATION**

[75] Inventor: **Robert E. Marsh**, Kansas City, Mo.

[73] Assignee: **AgriTech Electronics L.C.**, Chanute, Kans.

[21] Appl. No.: **885,572**

[22] Filed: **Jun. 30, 1997**

Related U.S. Application Data

[60] Provisional application No. 60/021,342, Jul. 8, 1996.

[51] **Int. Cl.** [6] **A01K 15/02**; G08B 23/00

[52] **U.S. Cl.** **119/421**; 119/721; 340/573

[58] **Field of Search** 119/718, 719, 119/720, 721

[56] **References Cited**

U.S. PATENT DOCUMENTS

4,399,821	8/1983	Bowers .
4,910,500	3/1990	Carr .
5,067,441	11/1991	Weinstein .
5,241,923	9/1993	Janning .
5,307,759	5/1994	Rose .
5,379,224	1/1995	Brown et al. .
5,408,956	4/1995	Quigley .
5,512,902	4/1996	Guthrie et al. .
5,570,655	11/1996	Targa .
5,575,242	11/1996	Davis .
5,742,233	4/1998	Hoffman et al. 340/573

Primary Examiner—Thomas Price
Attorney, Agent, or Firm—Hovey,Williams,Timmons & Collins

[57] **ABSTRACT**

A fenceless animal confinement system comprising portable units attached to the animal and including means for receiving GPS signals and for providing stimulation to the animal. The GPS signals are processed to provide location information which is compared to the desired boundary parameters. If the animal has moved outside the desired area, the stimulation means is activated. The signal processing circuitry may be included either within the portable unit or within a separate fixed station.

18 Claims, 4 Drawing Sheets

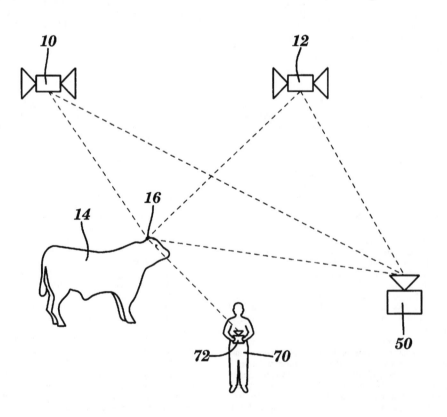

1

FENCELESS ANIMAL CONTROL SYSTEM USING GPS LOCATION INFORMATION

RELATED APPLICATIONS

This application claims the benefit of copending provisional application number 60/021,342, filed Jul. 8, 1996.

FEDERALLY SPONSORED RESEARCH OR DEVELOPMENT

Not applicable.

MICROFICHE APPENDIX

Not applicable.

BACKGROUND OF THE INVENTION

1. Field of the Invention

This invention relates to the fenceless control of animals, and more particularly, to the control of livestock utilizing a receiver attached to the animal that receives data identifying the location of the animal and administers appropriate control stimuli to the animal based on the location of the animal relative to the desired location.

2. Description of the Prior Art

Animal Confinement

Various conventional fencing systems are currently used to control the location of livestock. These systems include barrier fencing (such as barbed wire fencing) that physically blocks the movement of the animal and electric fencing that utilizes an electric shock to control the animal. The use of electric fencing has become more widespread because of its lower cost and ease of relocation.

Electric fencing has particular application in managed intensive grazing in which a large number of animals are confined to a smaller pasture area for a relatively short duration. Studies have shown that this higher stocking density followed by a longer period of no grazing yields significantly increased pasture productivity. This method more closely replicates the movement of an unrestrained herd of grazing animals and is more consistent with the evolutionary development of both grasses and grazing animals. Unfortunately, this method is labor intensive and requires substantial investment in electric fencing materials.

It is well established that animals respond to electrical stimuli, as evidenced by the effectiveness of electric fencing. A more recent development is the use of electrical stimulation via a stimulation device attached to the animal. Pet confinement systems have been developed that utilize an animal-attached receiver that applies an electrical shock when the animal approaches the proximity of a buried, current conducting, wire. Recent research has established that such a system also has application to livestock control. U.S. Pat. No. 5,408,956, incorporated herein by reference as part of the disclosure hereof, describes a system in which animals wear small ear tag receivers that are activated when the animal enters an exclusion zone defined by stationary field transmitters. This system has particular application for locations in which traditional fencing is impractical and it is necessary to permanently exclude animals from sensitive areas.

Various methods have been developed for applying aural and electrical stimulus, including the ear tag described in U.S. Pat. No. 5,408,956 and the electronic nose clip described in U.S. Pat. No. 5,307,759, incorporated herein by reference as part of the disclosure hereof. Collar-mounted units are widely used in dog and other appropriate confine-

2

ment applications. It is desirable to provide an audible signal prior to applying any electrical shock to allow the animal time to move and avoid the shock. In practice, the audible signal is generally sufficient to cause the desired animal movement.

Position Determination

Significant advancements have been made in the technology available to precisely determine the location of an object. The United States government has placed in operation a multiple satellite global positioning system ("GPS"). A GPS receiver receives signals from multiple satellites and calculates the position of the receiver based on the signal data. The method of operation of GPS systems is well known. For example, U.S. Pat. No. 5,379,224, incorporated herein by reference as part of the disclosure hereof, describes GPS system operation in detail. Even greater accuracy is possible with a "differential" GPS method that determines a correction factor based on the difference between the GPS-determined location of a fixed station and the actual known location of that station.

Many types of GPS receivers are available. Most include components to perform the processing functions necessary to convert the GPS satellite data into location information. Some receivers simply retransmit the data received from the GPS satellite to a central processing unit that converts that data into location information, in an effort to reduce the cost of the receiver components.

SUMMARY OF THE INVENTION

The present invention enables an animal confinement system that does not require physical fencing and that permits virtually labor-free redefinition of the confinement boundaries.

In the preferred embodiment a portable unit is attached to each animal that includes a GPS receiver and a means for providing an audible signal and an electrical shock. Each portable unit further includes a suitable battery and appropriate electrical circuitry.

In one embodiment, the portable unit also contains signal processing components necessary to convert the GPS signal into location information and a remotely programmable memory to receive and store the desired boundary parameters. Circuitry within the portable unit compares the GPS-defined location information with the defined boundary parameters and activates the audible signal, and if necessary, the electrical shock circuitry, when the portable unit approaches the defined boundary. For increased precision, a fixed station may also be used with this arrangement for differential GPS positioning.

In another embodiment, the portable unit receives the GPS signal and retransmits it to a fixed station. The fixed station receives and stores the desired boundary parameters, performs the necessary signal processing to convert the GPS data to location information, and performs the necessary comparison of the unit location and the defined boundary. The fixed station then, if necessary, transmits to the portable unit appropriate signals activating the audible warning and, if necessary, the electrical shock circuitry located in the portable unit.

Another aspect of this invention is to provide specific location information with respect to each animal to facilitate animal location, counting and the monitoring of individual animal behavior.

BRIEF DESCRIPTION OF THE DRAWINGS

FIG. 1 is a block diagram illustrating the primary physical elements of the present invention;

United States Patent [19]

Layson, Jr.

[11] **Patent Number:** **6,014,080**

[45] **Date of Patent:** **Jan. 11, 2000**

[54] **BODY WORN ACTIVE AND PASSIVE TRACKING DEVICE**

[75] Inventor: **Hoyt M. Layson, Jr.,** Palm Harbor, Fla.

[73] Assignee: **Pro Tech Monitoring, Inc.,** Palm Harbor, Fla.

[21] Appl. No.: **09/181,244**

[22] Filed: **Oct. 28, 1998**

[51] Int. Cl.[7] **G08B 23/00**
[52] U.S. Cl. **340/573.1**; 340/573.4; 340/539; 342/357.07; 701/212
[58] Field of Search 340/573.1, 573.3, 340/573.4, 539, 825.36, 825.46, 825.49, 357.02, 357.07, 357.08, 357.09; 342/357; 701/211, 212, 213

[56] **References Cited**

U.S. PATENT DOCUMENTS

4,438,491	3/1984	Constant	701/106
5,345,244	9/1994	Gildea et al.	342/357
5,373,531	12/1994	Kawasaki	375/1
5,497,149	3/1996	Fast	340/988
5,504,684	4/1996	Lau et al.	340/988
5,528,248	6/1996	Steiner et al.	342/357
5,535,237	7/1996	LaPadula, III et al.	375/200
5,625,668	4/1997	Loomis et al.	455/456
5,627,548	5/1997	Woo et al.	342/357
5,652,570	7/1997	Lepkofker	340/573.4
5,663,734	9/1997	Krasner	342/357
5,712,619	1/1998	Simkin	340/539

5,714,931	2/1998	Petite et al.	340/539
5,731,757	3/1998	Layson, Jr.	340/573.1
5,731,785	3/1998	Lemelson et al.	342/357
5,742,233	4/1998	Hoffman et al.	340/573.1
5,742,509	4/1998	Goldberg et al.	701/211
5,773,993	6/1998	Trimberger	326/38
5,825,327	10/1998	Krasner	342/357.09
5,831,574	11/1998	Krasner	342/357.8
5,838,237	11/1998	Revell et al.	340/573.1
5,867,103	2/1999	Taylor, Jr.	340/573.4
5,884,214	3/1999	Krasner	701/207
5,905,461	5/1999	Neher	342/357.07

OTHER PUBLICATIONS

U.S. application No. 09/082,313, Layson, Jr., filed May 20, 1998.

Primary Examiner—Jeffery A. Hofsass
Assistant Examiner—Van T. Trieu
Attorney, Agent, or Firm—Larson & Larson, P.A.; James E. Larson

[57] **ABSTRACT**

Tamper resistant body-worn tracking device to be worn by offenders or potential victims for use in a wireless communication system receiving signals from a global positioning system (GPS). The tracking device directly communicates spacial coordinates to multiple remote sites. The tracking device is an enclosed case worn on a limb of a person. The case contains a battery, a signaling device, and a circuit board containing a field programmable gate array, a wireless data modem, a conventional GPS receiver, and a matched filtering GPS receiver.

16 Claims, 4 Drawing Sheets

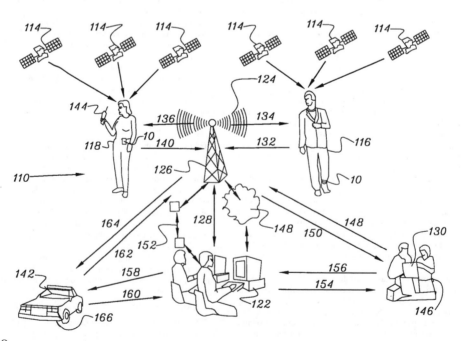

United States Patent [19]

Schulman et al.

[11] **Patent Number:** **6,067,474**

[45] **Date of Patent:** **May 23, 2000**

[54] **IMPLANTABLE DEVICE WITH IMPROVED BATTERY RECHARGING AND POWERING CONFIGURATION**

[75] Inventors: **Joseph H. Schulman**, Santa Clarita; **Robert Dan Dell**, Canyon Country; **Alfred E. Mann**, Beverly Hills; **Michael A. Faltys**, Northridge, all of Calif.

[73] Assignees: **Advanced Bionics Corporation; Alfred E. Mann Foundation for Scientific Research**, both of Sylmar, Calif.

[21] Appl. No.: **09/126,615**

[22] Filed: **Jul. 31, 1998**

Related U.S. Application Data

[60] Provisional application No. 60/054,480, Aug. 1, 1997.

[51] **Int. Cl.**^{7} **A61N 1/34**
[52] **U.S. Cl.** **607/57**; 607/33
[58] **Field of Search** 607/55, 56, 57, 607/33

[56] **References Cited**

U.S. PATENT DOCUMENTS

3,942,535	3/1976	Schulman .
4,006,748	2/1977	Schulman .
4,041,955	8/1977	Kelly et al. .
4,134,408	1/1979	Brownlee et al. .
4,495,917	1/1985	Byers .
4,516,820	5/1985	Kuzma 339/48
4,991,582	2/1991	Byers et al. .
5,314,451	5/1994	Mulier 607/33
5,314,457	5/1994	Jeutter et al. 607/116
5,411,537	5/1995	Munshi et al. 607/33
5,411,538	5/1995	Lin 607/33
5,603,726	2/1997	Schulman et al. 607/57
5,626,629	5/1997	Faltys et al. 607/57
5,702,431	12/1997	Wang et al. 607/33

FOREIGN PATENT DOCUMENTS

0499939	8/1992	European Pat. Off. .
1197468	9/1968	Germany .
9837926	2/1998	WIPO .

Primary Examiner—Scott M. Getzow
Attorney, Agent, or Firm—Bryant R. Gold

[57] **ABSTRACT**

An implantable system, such as a neural stimulator or a cochlear implant system, includes a rechargeable battery configuration having improved recharging and lifetime characteristics. The battery is housed within the implant's case and has first and second electrode plates. Each electrode plate has a plurality of slits that extend across a substantial portion of the plate's surface area. The slits in the electrode plates reduce the magnitude of eddy currents induced in the plates by external ac magnetic fields allowing faster battery recharging times. Alternatively, the electrode plates are wrapped in a spiral configuration such that, in the plane of the spiral, the electrode plates have a small cross-sectional area and no closed current loops. Additionally, the implant device may be housed in a case formed of a high-resistivity material and a circuit included in the implant device is configured to avoid large current loops that would result in eddy current heating. As a backup option, the circuitry of the implant device may optionally be powered from an external battery that inductively couples energy to the same coil that is used to charge the internal battery. In one embodiment, the implantable system is partitioned into first and second implantable cases, each having electrical circuitry therein, and only one having a rechargeable power source therein, facilitating its subsequent replacement for repair or upgrading purposes. The two cases are coupled together when the system is in use. Coupling is achieved either magnetically and/or with a detachable electrical cable. In one embodiment, power is transferred from one implant case to the other using a 3-phase transmission scheme.

59 Claims, 9 Drawing Sheets

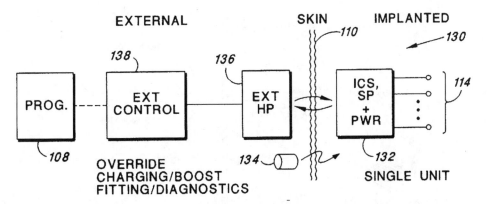

United States Patent [19]

Schulman et al.

[11] **Patent Number:**   **6,164,284**

[45] **Date of Patent:**   **Dec. 26, 2000**

5,766,231	6/1998	Erickson et al.	128/903 X
5,810,735	9/1998	Halperin et al.	128/899 X

[54] **SYSTEM OF IMPLANTABLE DEVICES FOR MONITORING AND/OR AFFECTING BODY PARAMETERS**

[76] Inventors: **Joseph H. Schulman**

Robert Dan Dell,

John C. Gord,

[21] Appl. No.: **09/048,827**

[22] Filed: **Mar. 25, 1998**

Related U.S. Application Data

[60] Provisional application No. 60/042,447, Mar. 28, 1997, and provisional application No. 60/039,164, Feb. 26, 1997.

[51] **Int. Cl.**[7] **A61B 19/00**

[52] **U.S. Cl.** **128/899**

[58] **Field of Search** 600/300; 128/899, 128/897, 898, 903, 904

[56] **References Cited**

U.S. PATENT DOCUMENTS

4,543,955	10/1985	Schroeppel .	
4,888,064	12/1989	Strandberg .	
5,113,859	5/1992	Funke .	
5,411,535	5/1995	Fujii et al.	128/903
5,481,262	1/1996	Urbas et al.	128/903 X
5,694,952	12/1997	Lidman et al.	128/899
5,725,559	3/1998	Alt et al.	128/903 X
5,728,154	3/1998	Crossett et al.	623/3

Primary Examiner—Samuel G. Gilbert

Attorney, Agent, or Firm—Freilich, Hornbaker & Rosen

[57]   **ABSTRACT**

A system for monitoring and/or affecting parameters of a patient's body and more particularly to such a system comprised of a system control unit (SCU) and one or more other devices, preferably battery-powered, implanted in the patient's body, i.e., within the envelope defined by the patient's skin. Each such implanted device is configured to be monitored and/or controlled by the SCU via a wireless communication channel. In accordance with the invention, the SCU comprises a programmable unit capable of (1) transmitting commands to at least some of a plurality of implanted devices and (2) receiving data signal from at least some of those implanted devices. In accordance with a preferred embodiment, the system operates in closed loop fashion whereby the commands transmitted by the SCU are dependent, in part, on the content of the data signals received by the SCU. In accordance with the invention, a preferred SCU is similarly implemented as a device capable of being implanted beneath a patient's skin, preferably having an axial dimension of less than 60 mm and a lateral dimension of less than 6 mm. Wireless communication between the SCU and the implanted devices is preferably implemented via a modulated sound signal, AC magnetic field, RF signal, or electric conduction.

21 Claims, 14 Drawing Sheets

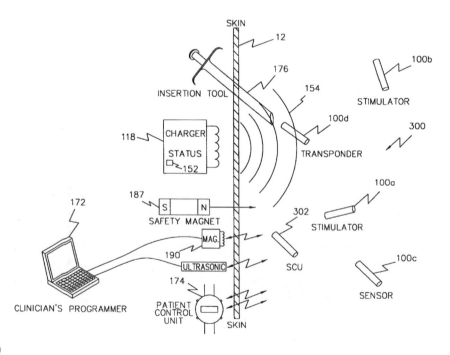

1

SYSTEM OF IMPLANTABLE DEVICES FOR MONITORING AND/OR AFFECTING BODY PARAMETERS

This application claims the benefit of U.S. Provisional Application No. 60/042,447 filed Mar. 27, 1997 and U.S. patent application Ser. No. 09/030,106 filed Feb. 25, 1998 entitled "Battery-Powered Patient Implantable Device" which in turn claims the benefit of U.S. Provisional Application No. 60/039,164 filed Feb. 26, 1997.

BACKGROUND OF THE INVENTION

The present invention relates to systems for monitoring and/or affecting parameters of a patient's body for the purpose of medical diagnosis and/or treatment. More particularly, systems in accordance with the invention are characterized by a plurality of devices, preferably battery-powered, configured for implanting within a patient's body, each device being configured to sense a body parameter, e.g., temperature, O_2 content, physical position, etc., and/or to affect a parameter, e.g., via nerve stimulation.

Applicants' parent application No. 09/030,106 entitled "Battery Powered Patient Implantable Device", incorporated herein by reference, describes devices configured for implantation within a patient's body, i.e., beneath a patient's skin, for performing various functions including: (1) stimulation of body tissue, (2) sensing of body parameters, and (3) communicating between implanted devices and devices external to a patient's body.

SUMMARY OF THE INVENTION

The present invention is directed to a system for monitoring and/or affecting parameters of a patient's body and more particularly to such a system comprised of a system control unit (SCU) and one or more devices implanted in the patient's body, i.e., within the envelope defined by the patient's skin. Each said implanted device is configured to be monitored and/or controlled by the SCU via a wireless communication channel.

In accordance with the invention, the SCU comprises a programmable unit capable of (1) transmitting commands to at least some of a plurality of implanted devices and (2) receiving data signals from at least some of those implanted devices. In accordance with a preferred embodiment, the system operates in closed loop fashion whereby the commands transmitted by the SCU are dependent, in part, on the content of the data signals received by the SCU.

In accordance with a preferred embodiment, each implanted device is configured similarly to the devices described in Applicants' parent application 09/030,106 and typically comprises a sealed housing suitable for injection into the patient's body. Each housing preferably contains a power source having a capacity of at least 1 microwatt-hour, preferably a rechargeable battery, and power consuming circuitry preferably including a data signal transmitter and receiver and sensor/stimulator circuitry for driving an input/output transducer.

In accordance with a significant aspect of the preferred embodiment, a preferred SCU is also implemented as a device capable of being injected into the patient's body. Wireless communication between the SCU and the other implanted devices can be implemented in various ways, e.g., via a modulated sound signal, AC magnetic field, RF signal, or electrical conduction.

In accordance with a further aspect of the invention, the SCU is remotely programmable, e.g., via wireless means, to

2

interact with the implanted devices according to a treatment regimen. In accordance with a preferred embodiment, the SCU is preferably powered via an internal power source, e.g., a rechargeable battery. Accordingly, an SCU combined with one or more battery-powered implantable devices, such as those described in the parent application, form a self-sufficient system for treating a patient.

In accordance with a preferred embodiment, the SCU and other implanted devices are implemented substantially identically, being comprised of a sealed housing configured to be injected into the patient's body. Each housing contains sensor/stimulator circuitry for driving an input/output transducer, e.g., an electrode, to enable it to additionally operate as a sensor and/or stimulator.

Alternatively, the SCU could be implemented as an implantable but non-injectable housing which would permit it to be physically larger enabling it to accommodate larger, higher capacity components, e.g., battery, microcontroller, etc. As a further alternative, the SCU could be implemented in a housing configured for carrying on the patient's body outside of the skin defined envelope, e.g., in a wrist band.

In accordance with the invention, the commands transmitted by the SCU can be used to remotely configure the operation of the other implanted devices and/or to interrogate the status of those devices. For example, various operating parameters, e.g., the pulse frequency, pulse width, trigger delays, etc., of each implanted device can be controlled or specified in one or more commands addressably transmitted to the device. Similarly, the sensitivity of the sensor circuitry and/or the interrogation of a sensed parameter, e.g., battery status, can be remotely specified by the SCU.

In accordance with a significant feature of the preferred embodiment, the SCU and/or each implantable device includes a programmable memory for storing a set of default parameters. In the event of power loss, SCU failure, or any other catastrophic occurrence, all devices default to the safe harbor default parameters. The default parameters can be programmed differently depending upon the condition being treated. In accordance with a further feature, the system includes a switch preferably actuatable by an external DC magnetic field, for resetting the system to its default parameters.

In an exemplary use of a system in accordance with the present invention, a patient with nerve damage can have a damaged nerve "replaced" by an implanted SCU and one or more implanted sensors and stimulators, each of which contains its own internal power source. In this exemplary system, the SCU would monitor a first implanted sensor for a signal originating from the patient's brain and responsively transmit command signals to one or more stimulators implanted past the point of nerve damage. Furthermore, the SCU could monitor additional sensors to determine variations in body parameters and, in a closed loop manner, react to control the command signals to achieve the desired treatment regimen.

The novel features of the invention are set forth with particularity in the appended claims. The invention will be best understood from the following description when read in conjunction with the accompanying drawings.

BRIEF DESCRIPTION OF THE DRAWINGS

FIG. 1 is a simplified block diagram of the system of the present invention comprised of implanted devices, e.g., microstimulators, microsensors and microtransponders, under control of an implanted system control unit (SCU);

(12) United States Patent
Kuzma et al.

(10) Patent No.: **US 6,205,361 B1**
(45) Date of Patent: **Mar. 20, 2001**

(54) **IMPLANTABLE EXPANDABLE MULTICONTACT ELECTRODES**

(75) Inventors: **Janusz A. Kuzma**, Englewood, CO (US); **Carla M. Mann**, Beverly Hills, CA (US)

(73) Assignee: **Advanced Bionics Corporation**, Sylmar, CA (US)

(*) Notice: Subject to any disclaimer, the term of this patent is extended or adjusted under 35 U.S.C. 154(b) by 0 days.

(21) Appl. No.: **09/239,927**

(22) Filed: **Jan. 28, 1999**

Related U.S. Application Data

(60) Provisional application No. 60/074,198, filed on Feb. 10, 1998.

(51) Int. Cl.^{7} **A61N 1/05**
(52) U.S. Cl. **607/116**; 607/117; 607/152
(58) Field of Search 607/116, 117, 607/119, 129, 152

(56) **References Cited**

U.S. PATENT DOCUMENTS

3,724,467 * 4/1973 Avery et al. .
4,379,462 4/1983 Borkan et al. .
4,989,617 2/1991 Memberg et al. .
5,143,067 9/1992 Rise et al. .
5,282,468 2/1994 Klepinski .
5,391,200 * 2/1995 KenKnight et al. 607/129
5,397,342 * 3/1995 Heil, Jr. et al. .
5,417,719 * 5/1995 Hull et al. .
5,458,629 10/1995 Baudino et al. .
5,634,462 6/1997 Tyler et al. .
5,643,330 7/1997 Holsheimer et al. .
5,733,322 3/1998 Starkebaum .

* cited by examiner

Primary Examiner—Carl H. Layno
(74) Attorney, Agent, or Firm—Bryant R. Gold

(57) **ABSTRACT**

A paddle-type electrode or electrode array is implantable like a percutaneously inserted lead, i.e., without requiring major surgery, but once inserted, expands to provide a platform for many electrode configurations. The electrode array is provided on a flexible, foldable, subcarrier or substrate. Such subcarrier or substrate is folded, or compressed. during implantation, thereby facilitating its insertion using simple, well-known percutaneous implantation techniques. Once implanted, such subcarrier or substrate expands, thereby placing the electrodes in a desired spaced-apart positional relationship, and thus achieving a desired electrode array configuration. A memory element is used within the subcarrier or substrate which causes the electrode array to expand or unfold to a desired unfolded or expanded state after it has been implanted while in a folded up or compressed state. Further, the electrode array includes a membrane as an integral part thereof that prevents ingrowth of tissue inside the electrode array, thereby facilitating repositioning, removal, and/or reinsertion of the electrode array, as required.

8 Claims, 7 Drawing Sheets

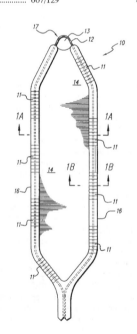

US 6,205,361 B1

1

IMPLANTABLE EXPANDABLE MULTICONTACT ELECTRODES

This application claims the benefit of U.S. Provisional Application Serial No. 60/074,198, filed Feb. 10, 1998.

BACKGROUND OF THE INVENTION

The present invention relates to implantable, expandable, multicontact electrodes. In a preferred embodiment, such electrodes comprise deployable, paddle-type, multicontact electrodes useful for spinal stimulation.

There are two major types of electrodes used for spinal stimulation: (1) percutaneously implanted in-line electrodes/leads requiring local anesthesia for implant, and (2) paddle-shaped electrodes requiring major surgery for implantation.

The first type of electrodes, i.e., the in-line electrodes, comprise thin, rod-type electrodes. Such in-line or rod-type electrodes are easy and less invasive to implant, typically requiring only local anesthesia and the use of a large gauge needle. Disadvantageously, such in-line electrodes are not as stable as paddle leads, and are prone to migration.

The second type of electrodes, i.e., the paddle-shaped electrodes, provide a large-area electrode surface to contact the body tissue, much like a miniature ping-pong paddle. Advantageously, such paddle-type electrodes are more effective and stable than in-line electrodes. Moreover, such paddle-type electrodes provide a platform for multiple electrodes in many possible configurations to thereby optimize electrode programming and clinical results. In contrast, the percutaneous in-line electrodes can only combine electrodes in a vertical row. Disadvantageously, however, the paddle-type electrodes require complex major surgery for implantation, along with all the attendant risks associated with major complex surgery.

It is thus evident, that there is a need in the art for an electrode which can deliver the maximum advantages of the paddle-type electrodes, but without requiring extensive surgery for implantation.

SUMMARY OF THE INVENTION

The present invention addresses the above and other needs by combining the advantages of both the paddle-type electrode and the in-line (rod-type) electrode. That is, the present invention provides an implantable electrode or electrode array that may be implanted like a percutaneously inserted lead, i.e., without requiring major surgery, but once inserted, expands to provide a platform for many electrode configurations.

In accordance with one important aspect of the invention, an electrode array is provided on a flexible, foldable, subcarrier or substrate. Such subcarrier or substrate is folded, or compressed. during implantation, thereby facilitating its insertion using simple, well-known percutaneous implantation techniques. Once implanted, such subcarrier or substrate expands, thereby placing the electrodes in a desired spaced-apart positional relationship, and thus achieving a desired electrode array configuration.

In accordance with another aspect of the invention, the substrate or subcarrier of the electrode array includes a memory element which causes the electrode array to expand or unfold to a desired configuration after the electrode array has been implanted while in a folded up or compressed state.

In accordance with yet another aspect of the invention, the electrode array includes a membrane as an integral part thereof that prevents ingrowth of tissue inside the electrode

2

array, thereby facilitating repositioning, removal, and/or reinsertion of the electrode array, as required.

In one embodiment, the invention may be characterized as a system for implanting an expandable electrode array. Such system includes an electrode array and an insertion tool. The electrode array comprises (a) a flexible substrate, (b) a plurality of parallel columns of spaced-apart electrodes integrally formed on a surface of the flexible substrate, and (c) means for making electrical contact with each electrode in each of the plurality of parallel columns of electrodes. The flexible substrate normally assumes a planar flat shape, but is configured so that it may be collapsed or folded so as to assume a folded or compressed state. The insertion tool comprises a hollow tube or hollow needle wherein the electrode array may be placed while in its folded or compressed state.

In order to implant the electrode array, the hollow tube or needle (with the folded or compressed electrode array therein) is injected into the living tissue of the desired implant site. The folded electrode array is then expelled from the hollow tube and allowed to assume its expanded or unfolded state within the tissue.

It is thus a feature of the present invention to provide a foldable, paddle-type electrode which can be implanted using a simple, needle-type tool without major surgical intervention.

It is a further feature of the invention to provide a loading tool that assists with the folding and inserting of the paddle-type electrode into an insertion tool.

It is yet another feature of the invention to provide a simple method of implanting a foldable, paddle-type electrode that does not require major surgical intervention.

BRIEF DESCRIPTION OF THE DRAWINGS

The above and other aspects, features and advantages of the present invention will be more apparent from the following more particular description thereof, presented in conjunction with the following drawings wherein:

FIG. 1 shows a planar view of an implantable, foldable, collapsible electrode array made in accordance with one embodiment of the invention;

FIG. 1A is a sectional view of the electrode array of FIG. 1 taken along the line 1A—1A of FIG. 1;

FIG. 1B is a partial sectional view of the electrode array of FIG. 1 taken along the line 1B—1B of FIG. 1;

FIG. 2 illustrates one manner in which the electrode array of FIG. 1 may be implanted using an insertion stylet;

FIG. 2A depicts the manner in which the distal tip of the electrode array of FIG. 1 is held by the distal tip of the insertion stylet of FIG. 2 during the implantation process;

FIG. 2B is a side schematic diagram that illustrates the manner in which a releasable holding string may be threaded through the insertion stylet in order to hold the distal tip of the electrode array in a desired position within a groove of the insertion stylet during the implantation process;

FIG. 3 shows a slitted insertion needle into which the foldable electrode array of FIG. 1 and the insertion stylet of FIG. 2 may be placed;

FIG. 3A depicts the manner in which the folded electrode array and insertion stylet fit within the lumen of the needle of FIG. 3;

FIG. 4 illustrates an alternative embodiment of an implantable, foldable electrode array made in accordance with the invention;

(12) **United States Patent**

Loeb et al.

(10) Patent No.: **US 6,175,764 B1**

(45) Date of Patent: **Jan. 16, 2001**

(54) **IMPLANTABLE MICROSTIMULATOR SYSTEM FOR PRODUCING REPEATABLE PATTERNS OF ELECTRICAL STIMULATION**

(75) Inventors: **Gerald E. Loeb; Frances J. R. Richmond**, both of Kingston (CA)

(73) Assignee: **Advanced Bionics Corporation**, Sylmar, CA (US)

(*) Notice: Under 35 U.S.C. 154(b), the term of this patent shall be extended for 0 days.

(21) Appl. No.: **09/490,921**

(22) Filed: **Jan. 25, 2000**

Related U.S. Application Data

(62) Division of application No. 09/077,662, filed on May 29, 1998, now Pat. No. 6,051,017.

(60) Provisional application No. 60/011,870, filed on Feb. 20, 1996, provisional application No. 60/012,019, filed on Feb. 20, 1996, provisional application No. 60/011,868, filed on Feb. 20, 1996, and provisional application No. 60/011,869, filed on Feb. 20, 1996.

(51) **Int. Cl.^{7}** **A61N 1/00**

(52) **U.S. Cl.** **607/3**

(58) **Field of Search** 607/1–3, 46, 48–52, 607/59–61; 128/899; 600/559, 302, 377

(56) **References Cited**

U.S. PATENT DOCUMENTS

3,971,388		7/1976	Cowdery .
4,026,304	*	5/1977	Levy 607/51
4,041,955		8/1977	Kelly et al. .
4,524,774		6/1985	Hildebrandt .
4,991,582		2/1991	Byers et al. .
5,094,242		3/1992	Gleason et al. .
5,167,229	*	12/1992	Peckham et al. 607/48
5,193,539	*	3/1993	Schulman et al. 607/61
5,193,540	*	3/1993	Schulman et al. 607/61
5,312,439		5/1994	Loeb .

5,324,316	6/1994	Schulman et al. .
5,405,367	4/1995	Schulman et al. .
5,482,008	1/1996	Stafford et al. .
5,814,089	9/1998	Stokes et al. .

FOREIGN PATENT DOCUMENTS

0047013	10/1982	(EP) .
2107826	9/1971	(FR) .
9200747	1/1992	(WO) .
9405361	3/1994	(WO) .
9729802	8/1997	(WO) .

* cited by examiner

Primary Examiner—George R. Evanisko

(74) *Attorney, Agent, or Firm*—Bryant R. Gold; Kenneth L. Green

(57) **ABSTRACT**

Improved implantable microstimulators are covered with a biocompatible polymeric coating in order to provide increased strength to the capsule and to capture fragments of the microstimulator should it become mechanically disrupted. Such coating also makes the microstimulator safer and easier to handle. The coating may include one or more diffusible chemical agents that are released in a controlled manner into the surrounding tissue. The chemical agents, such as trophic factors, antibiotics, hormones, neurotransmitters and other pharmaceutical substances, are selected to produce desired physiological effects, to aid, support or to supplement the effects of the electrical stimulation. Further, microstimulators in accordance with the invention provide systems that prevent and/or treat various disorders associated with prolonged inactivity, confinement or immobilization of one or more muscles. Such disorders include pressure ulcers, venous emboli, autonomic dysreflexia, sensorimotor spasticity and muscle atrophy. The microstimulator systems include external control for controlling the operation of the microstimulators. The control include memory for programming preferred stimulation patterns for later activation by the patient or caregiver.

6 Claims, 5 Drawing Sheets

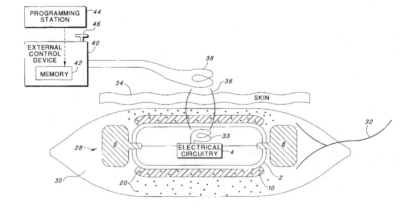

(12) **United States Patent**

Loeb et al.

(10) **Patent No.:** **US 6,214,032 B1**

(45) **Date of Patent:** **Apr. 10, 2001**

(54) **SYSTEM FOR IMPLANTING A MICROSTIMULATOR**

(75) Inventors: **Gerald E. Loeb; Frances J. R. Richmond**, both of Kingston (CA)

(73) Assignee: **Advanced Bionics Corporation,** Sylmar, CA (US)

(*) Notice: Subject to any disclaimer, the term of this patent is extended or adjusted under 35 U.S.C. 154(b) by 0 days.

(21) Appl. No.: **09/490,922**

(22) Filed: **Jan. 25, 2000**

Related U.S. Application Data

(62) Division of application No. 09/077,662, filed as application No. PCT/US97/02576 on Feb. 19, 1997, now Pat. No. 6,051,017.

(60) Provisional application No. 60/011,870, filed on Feb. 20, 1996, provisional application No. 60/012,019, filed on Feb. 20, 1996, provisional application No. 60/011,868, filed on Feb. 20, 1996, and provisional application No. 60/011,869, filed on Feb. 20, 1996.

(51) **Int. Cl.[7]** **A61N 1/00**

(52) **U.S. Cl.** **607/1**

(58) **Field of Search** 607/1–3, 48–52, 607/59–61, 46; 128/877; 600/554, 302, 377

(56) **References Cited**

U.S. PATENT DOCUMENTS

3,971,388	7/1976	Cowdery .
4,026,304	5/1977	Levy .
4,041,955	8/1977	Kelly et al. .
4,524,774	7/1985	Hildebrandt .
4,824,433 *	4/1989	Marz et al. 600/554
4,991,582	2/1991	Byers et al. .
5,007,902 *	4/1991	Witt 600/554
5,094,242	3/1992	Gleason et al. .
5,193,539	3/1993	Schulman et al. .
5,193,540	3/1993	Schulman et al. .
5,312,439	5/1994	Loeb .
5,324,316	6/1994	Schulman et al. .
5,405,367	4/1995	Schulman et al. .
5,482,008	1/1996	Stafford et al. .
5,814,089	9/1998	Stokes et al. .

FOREIGN PATENT DOCUMENTS

0047013	10/1982	(EP) .
2107826	9/1971	(FR) .
9200747	1/1992	(WO) .
9405361	3/1994	(WO) .
9729802	8/1997	(WO) .

* cited by examiner

Primary Examiner—George R. Evanisko

(74) *Attorney, Agent, or Firm*—Bryant R. Gold; Kenneth L. Green

(57) **ABSTRACT**

Improved implantable microstimulators are covered with a biocompatible polymeric coating in order to provide increased strength to the capsule and to capture fragments of the microstimulator should it become mechanically disrupted. Such coating also makes the microstimulator safer and easier to handle. The coating may include one or more diffusible chemical agents that are released in a controlled manner into the surrounding tissue. The chemical agents, such as trophic factors, antibiotics, hormones, neurotransmitters and other pharmaceutical substances, are selected to produce desired physiological effects, to aid, support or to supplement the effects of the electrical stimulation. Further, microstimulators in accordance with the invention provide systems that prevent and/or treat various disorders associated with prolonged inactivity, confinement or immobilization of one or more muscles. Such disorders include pressure ulcers, venous emboli, autonomic dysreflexia, sensorimotor spasticity and muscle atrophy. The microstimulator systems include external control for controlling the operation of the microstimulators. The control includes memory for programming preferred stimulation patterns for later activation by the patient or caregiver.

5 Claims, 5 Drawing Sheets

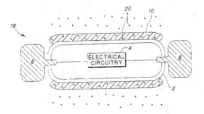

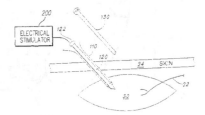

(12) **United States Patent**

Glen

(10) **Patent No.:** **US 6,239,705 B1**

(45) **Date of Patent:** **May 29, 2001**

(54) **INTRA ORAL ELECTRONIC TRACKING DEVICE**

(76) Inventor: **Jeffrey Glen**

(*) Notice: Subject to any disclaimer, the term of this patent is extended or adjusted under 35 U.S.C. 154(b) by 0 days.

(21) Appl. No.: **09/552,324**

(22) Filed: **Apr. 19, 2000**

(51) **Int. Cl.**[7] **H04Q 1/30**

(52) **U.S. Cl.** **340/573.1**; 340/572.8; 340/573.4

(58) **Field of Search** 340/573.1, 573.4, 340/572.8; 433/8, 37, 38, 80

(56) **References Cited**

U.S. PATENT DOCUMENTS

3,034,356	5/1962	Bieganski et al. .	
3,297,021	* 1/1967	Davis et al.	128/2
3,852,713	12/1974	Roberts et al. .	
4,629,424	* 12/1986	Lauks et al.	433/6
4,706,689	* 11/1987	Man .	
5,383,915	* 1/1995	Adams .	
5,476,488	* 12/1995	Morgan et al.	607/30
5,629,678	* 5/1997	Gargano et al. .	
5,760,692	* 6/1998	Block	340/573
5,954,673	* 9/1999	Staehlin et al.	600/590

OTHER PUBLICATIONS

Personal Satellite Tracking Applications. Protect your child, via satellite.

* cited by examiner

Primary Examiner—Jeffery Hofsass
Assistant Examiner—Son Tang
(74) Attorney, Agent, or Firm—McNees, Wallace & Nurick; Mitchell A. Smolow; Carmen Santa Maria

(57) **ABSTRACT**

An improved stealthy, non-surgical, biocompatable electronic tracking device is provided in which a housing is placed intraorally. The housing contains microcircuitry. The microcircuitry comprises a receiver, a passive mode to active mode activator, a signal decoder for determining positional fix, a transmitter, an antenna, and a power supply. Optionally, an amplifier may be utilized to boost signal strength. The power supply energizes the receiver. Upon receiving a coded activating signal, the positional fix signal decoder is energized, determining a positional fix. The transmitter subsequently transmits through the antenna a position locating signal to be received by a remote locator. In another embodiment of the present invention, the microcircuitry comprises a receiver, a passive mode to active mode activator, a transmitter, an antenna and a power supply. Optionally, an amplifier may be utilized to boost signal strength. The power supply energizes the receiver. Upon receiving a coded activating signal, the transmitter is energized. The transmitter subsequently transmits through the antenna a homing signal to be received by a remote locator.

20 Claims, 4 Drawing Sheets

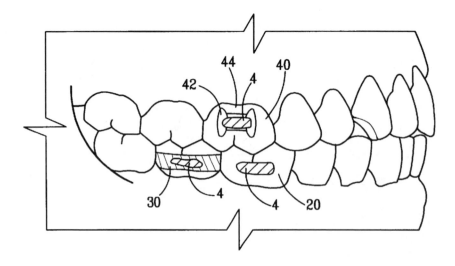

1

INTRA ORAL ELECTRONIC TRACKING DEVICE

FIELD OF THE INVENTION

The present invention relates generally to an electronic tracking and locating system, and more specifically, to an improved system whereby a transducer is placed intraorally.

BACKGROUND OF THE INVENTION

Numerous electronic devices have been introduced to track and locate mobile assets, such as for example, trucks, rail cars, and shipping containers. Hundreds of thousands of these assets have been equipped with tracking and locating transducers. The most sophisticated systems permit location of an asset to within a few feet.

More recently, systems to track and locate people have been developed. These tracking and locating devices are useful in managing persons who may be incapable or unable to seek assistance, such as for example, people with Alzheimer's disease, prisoners, children, and military personnel. Additional systems have been proposed to track pets and other animals.

Transmitters and transceivers utilized in locating and tracking humans have been worn as bracelets, sewn into clothing, placed in backpacks, implanted behind the ear of a human, and implanted, generally, under the skin.

One such system utilizes global positioning satellite technology to track and locate inanimate objects, animals, and humans. In one form, a bracelet containing a receiver is worn by a child. Utilizing the known location of three orbiting satellites and the time it takes for a signal to travel between the transducer and each of the three satellites, a three-dimensional position of the transducer is able to be calculated.

In addition to a receiver being worn as a bracelet, systems have been used employing a self-powered self-maintained transceiver, small enough to be implanted under the skin, for locating, tracking and recovering persons in distress such as for example, kidnap victims, people encountering adverse circumstances while in the wilderness, victims of heart attacks, and the like.

Other systems have been used which remain passive until remotely activated. For example, one recovery system employs a transceiver hidden within a motor vehicle and a network of fixed and mobile ground transmitters and receivers to facilitate tracking and recovery of stolen vehicles. The unit is continuously operated as a receiver until it is remotely activated. Once activated, it transmits a radio beacon facilitating tracking and recovery. Ground based fixed and mobile receiver units utilizing field strength measurements and directional receivers then are able to locate the transmitter.

Location and recovery systems have also been developed using timing and triangulation methods, such as that used by the Emergency Position Indicating Radio Beacons (EPIRB). Using the global positioning satellite system, once the user activates a transmitter, the associated satellite network is capable of locating a transmitting EPIRB anywhere on the face of the globe.

Receivers and transceivers worn as jewelry or sewn into clothing are easily found and removed, limiting their usefulness for military, intelligence and personal protection applications. Receivers and transceivers implantable under the skin require an invasive surgical procedure to implant these devices, and additional invasive surgical procedures to repair or remove the device. In addition, surgically

2

implanted devices are susceptible to infection and may be rejected by the body's autoimmune defense system. For these reasons, implanted devices have a low acceptance rate among potential users, particularly, children.

What is needed is a stealthy, non-surgical, biocompatable way to attach a transducer to a living organism such as an animal or human being which can be utilized for tracking and locating a human being or animal.

SUMMARY OF THE INVENTION

In accordance with an aspect of the present invention, an improved stealthy, non-surgical, biocompatable electronic tracking device is provided in which a housing is placed intraorally. The housing contains microcircuitry. The microcircuitry comprises a receiver, a passive mode to active mode activator, a signal decoder for determining positional fix, a transmitter, an antenna, and a power supply. Optionally, an amplifier may be utilized to boost signal strength.

The power supply energizes the receiver. The receiver is in a passive mode until it is activated, to conserve power. Upon receiving a coded activating signal, the positional fix signal decoder is energized, determining a positional fix. The transmitter subsequently transmits through the antenna a position locating signal to be received by a remote locator.

In another embodiment of the present invention, the microcircuitry comprises a receiver, a passive mode to active mode activator, a transmitter, an antenna and a power supply. Optionally, an amplifier may be utilized to boost signal strength. The power supply energizes the receiver. Upon receiving a coded activating signal, the transmitter is energized. The transmitter subsequently transmits through the antenna a homing signal to be received by a remote locator.

In still another embodiment of the present invention, the power supply is replaced by a power storage device. Power is supplied to the storage device by establishing an intraoral galvanic reaction utilizing saliva and differing metals placed within the oral cavity, or alternatively, by collecting and storing RF energy.

The transmitter may be activated by the user or activation may be triggered by an external event, such as for example, a received coded RF signal or coded electromagnetic signal from, for example, a global positioning satellite ("GPS") signal. The tracking device is preferably capable of being programmed to remain in a dormant or passive mode until receiving an activating signal.

The tracking device can be affixed to the external surface of a tooth or teeth through the use of dental adhesives, bonding agents and/or ligation, or it may be incorporated completely within a dental restoration, endodontically prepared root canal system, a prosthetic tooth or denture.

One advantage of the present invention is that placement of the tracking device intraorally does not require an invasive procedure. In this manner, the device may be stealthy, yet still maintain non-surgical accessibility for maintenance and repair.

Another advantage of the present invention is the ease of removal when the device is meant to be utilized only for a short period of time.

Still another advantage of the present invention is the ability to utilize the galvanic potential of the oral cavity to power the device, eliminating or reducing the need for a separate power supply.

When an internal power supply is utilized, the intra oral location makes for easy accessibility to recharge the power supply without removing the device.

(12) **United States Patent**
Llinas

(10) **Patent No.:** **US 8,447,392 B2**
(45) **Date of Patent:** **May 21, 2013**

---

(54) **BRAIN-MACHINE INTERFACE SYSTEMS AND METHODS**

(75) Inventor: **Rodolfo R. Llinas**, New York, NY (US)

(73) Assignee: **New York University**, New York, NY (US)

(*) Notice: Subject to any disclaimer, the term of this patent is extended or adjusted under 35 U.S.C. 154(b) by 1682 days.

(21) Appl. No.: **11/776,278**

(22) Filed: **Jul. 11, 2007**

(65) **Prior Publication Data**

US 2008/0015459 A1   Jan. 17, 2008

Related U.S. Application Data

(63) Continuation of application No. 10/645,328, filed on Aug. 21, 2003, now Pat. No. 7,257,439.

(60) Provisional application No. 60/405,192, filed on Aug. 21, 2002.

(51) **Int. Cl.**
A61B 5/04   (2006.01)

(52) **U.S. Cl.**
USPC **600/544**; 600/377; 600/378; 600/381

(58) **Field of Classification Search**
USPC 600/544, 545, 373, 377, 378, 381, 600/509, 513, 38
See application file for complete search history.

(56) **References Cited**

U.S. PATENT DOCUMENTS

3,826,244	A	*	7/1974	Salcman et al. 600/377
4,341,221	A	*	7/1982	Testerman 600/377

4,852,573	A		8/1989	Kennedy 600/378
4,913,160	A	*	4/1990	John 600/544
4,959,130	A	*	9/1990	Josowicz et al. 205/210
4,967,038	A	*	10/1990	Gevins et al. 600/383
5,143,089	A	*	9/1992	Alt 607/121
5,201,903	A	*	4/1993	Corbett et al. 29/872
5,391,147	A	*	2/1995	Imran et al. 604/528
5,411,527	A	*	5/1995	Alt 607/5

(Continued)

FOREIGN PATENT DOCUMENTS

JP	62-022626	1/1987
JP	4501214	3/1992

(Continued)

OTHER PUBLICATIONS

Rodolfo R. Llinas et al., "Brain-Machine Interface Via a Neurovascular Approach", Converging Technologies for Improving Human Performance, Jun. 2002, pp. 244-251.

(Continued)

Primary Examiner — Navin Natnithithadha
(74) *Attorney, Agent, or Firm* — Foley & Lardner LLP

(57) **ABSTRACT**

A system and method for interfacing a brain with a machine. An exemplary embodiment of the present invention employs a vascular approach in which one or more nano-electrodes are deployed in vasculature having a close geometric relationship with proximal innervation. Each nano-electrode is preferably deployed in a blood vessel so that its sensing end is at or near a nerve passing close to or intersecting the blood vessel. The sensing end of each nano-electrode is adapted so as to be carried along in the blood stream so as to position the sensing end at a desired point within the blood vessel. An array of nano-electrodes of varying lengths can be used to monitor multiple nerves or neurons along a blood vessel.

19 Claims, 5 Drawing Sheets

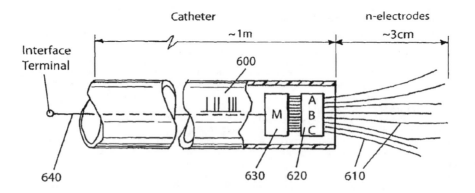

1

BRAIN-MACHINE INTERFACE SYSTEMS AND METHODS

PRIORITY DATA

This application is a Continuation of U.S. patent application Ser. No. 10/645,328, filed Aug. 21, 2003, which claims priority from U.S. Provisional Application Ser. No. 60/405, 192, filed Aug. 21, 2002, both of which is are incorporated herein by reference as if set forth in their entirety.

FIELD OF THE INVENTION

The present invention relates to systems and methods for providing an interface between a brain and a machine.

BACKGROUND INFORMATION

When considering the role of neuroscience in modern society, the issue of a brain-machine interface (e.g., between a human brain and a computer) is one of the central problems to be addressed. Indeed, the ability to design and build new information analysis and storage systems that are light enough to be easily carried, has advanced exponentially in the last few years. Ultimately, the brain-machine interface will likely become the major stumbling block to robust and rapid communication with such systems.

To date, developments towards a brain-machine interface have not been as impressive as the progress in miniaturization or computational power expansion. Indeed, the limiting factor with most modern devices relates to the human interface. For instance, buttons must be large enough to manipulate and displays large enough to allow symbol recognition. Clearly, establishing a more direct relationship between the brain and such devices is desirable and will likely become increasingly important.

With conventional means, brain activity can be recorded from the surface of the skull. In the case of electro-encephalography (EEG), electrodes are placed on the skull and record activity occurring on the surface of the brain. In the case of magneto-encephalography (MEG), recording probes are also placed on the surface, but through triangulation brain activity can be mapped in three dimensions.

Such methods as EEG and MEG, while minimally invasive, suffer from poor resolution and distortion due to the deformation of electromagnetic fields caused by the scalp and skull. To overcome these limitations with known technology requires the much more invasive option of opening the skull and inserting electrodes into the brain mass. Similarly, to stimulate the brain as is done therapeutically for some patients with Parkinson's disease or the like, the skull must be opened and electrodes inserted.

As the need for a more direct relationship between the brain and machines becomes increasingly important, a revolution is taking place in the field of nanotechnology (n-technology). Nanotechnology deals with manufactured objects with characteristic dimensions of less than one micrometer. It is the inventors' belief that the brain-machine bottleneck will ultimately be resolved through the application of nanotechnology. The use of nanoscale electrode probes coupled with nanoscale electronics seems promising in this regard.

To date, the finest electrodes have been pulled from glass. These microelectrodes have tips less than a micron in diameter and are filled with a conductive solution. They are typically used for intracellular recordings from nerve and muscle cells. A limitation is that activity is recorded from only one cell at a time. It has been possible, however, to obtain record-

2

ings from over 100 individual cells using multi-electrode arrays. Nonetheless, this is an invasive procedure as the electrodes are lowered into the brain from the surface of the skull.

In addition to probing large numbers of points in the brain, the need also exists for processing the large number of signals thus captured and analyzing them in a meaningful way. Methods for processing and displaying signals from multiple sites within the brain have been developed for multi-electrode work with animals and for MEG work with human subjects

What is required is a robust and non-invasive way to tap, address and analyze brain activity that is optimized for future brain-machine interaction.

In addition to serving as a means of interacting with machines, a brain-machine interface could also be useful in the diagnosis and treatment of many neurological and psychiatric conditions.

SUMMARY OF THE INVENTION

The present invention relates to a brain-machine interface which is secure, robust and minimally invasive. In accordance with a first aspect of the present invention, a vascular-based brain-machine interface is disclosed.

The fact that the nervous system parenchyma is permeated by a rich vascular bed makes this space a very attractive area for a brain-machine interface. Gas exchange and nutrient delivery to the brain mass occur in the brain across 25,000 meters of capillaries having diameters of approximately 10 microns. Moving towards the heart, the vessels increase rapidly in diameter with a final diameter of over 20 millimeters.

The present invention employs nano-wire technology coupled with nanotechnology electronics to record activity and/or stimulate the brain or spinal cord through the vascular system. The present invention allows the nervous system to be addressed by a large number of isolated nano-probes that are delivered to the brain via the vascular bed through catheter technology used extensively in medicine and particularly in interventional neuroradiology.

In accordance with the present invention, an exemplary embodiment of a recording device comprises a set of nanowires (n-wires) tethered to electronics in a catheter such that they spread in a "bouquet" arrangement into a particular portion of the brain's vascular system. Such an arrangement can support a very large number of probes (e.g., several million). Each n-wire is used to record the electrical activity of a single neuron, or small group of neurons, without invading the brain parenchyma. An advantage of such an n-electrode array is that its small size does not interfere with blood flow, gas or nutrient exchange and it does not disrupt brain activity.

The techniques of the present invention are also applicable to the diagnosis and treatment of abnormal brain function. Such technology allows constant monitoring and functional imaging as well as direct modulation of brain activity. For instance, an advanced variation of conventional deep brain stimulation can be implemented in accordance with the present invention.

With the present invention, intravascular neuronal recordings can be amplified, processed, and used to control computer interfaces or artificial prostheses. In controlling computational devices, neuronal activity becomes the user input, very much like the manipulation of devices such as keyboards and mice is today. Such input signals could also be used to control the movement of natural limbs that have been separated from their nerve supply through spinal cord or other injury. Thus while direct interface with "intelligent" devices can significantly improve the quality of life for normal indi-

Microwave magenetic nanotechnology

Self-assembled carbon structures containing billions of nanotubes

Chapter 16
Subliminal Messaging

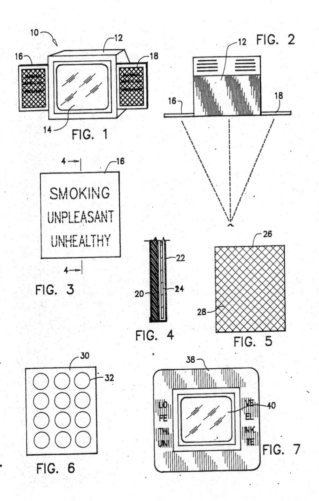

FIG. 1

FIG. 2

SMOKING
UNPLEASANT
UNHEALTHY

FIG. 3

FIG. 4

FIG. 5

FIG. 6

FIG. 7

United States Patent [19]

Lundy et al.

[11]   **4,395,600**

[45]   **Jul. 26, 1983**

[54] **AUDITORY SUBLIMINAL MESSAGE SYSTEM AND METHOD**

[76] Inventors: **Rene R. Lundy**   **David L. Tyler**

[21] Appl. No.:   **210,645**

[22] Filed: **Nov. 26, 1980**

[51] Int. Cl.^{3} **H04M 15/00; H04K 1/02**
[52] U.S. Cl. .... **179/1.5 M; 340/348 E; 179/1 AA**
[58] Field of Search .... 179/1 AA, 1 P, 1.5 M; 340/348 E; 358/183, 22; 430/9; 178/17.5; 250/214 R; 352/130, 131, 201, 81

[56]   **References Cited**

U.S. PATENT DOCUMENTS

625,627	5/1899	Woody	353/81
711,440	10/1902	Relchenbach	352/201
1,356,223	10/1920	Sawyer	352/55
2,073,370	3/1937	Goldsmith et al.	178/17.5
2,338,551	1/1944	Stanko	179/1 P
2,409,058	10/1946	Mitchell	179/1 P
2,501,327	3/1950	Good	179/1 P
2,609,294	9/1952	Prentice	430/9
2,706,218	4/1955	Wootten	352/131
2,730,565	1/1956	Owens	358/183
2,784,246	3/1957	Hurford	358/183
2,788,386	4/1957	Purington	174/153 R
2,808,455	10/1957	Moore	358/22
2,809,298	10/1957	Cawein	250/214 R
2,931,857	4/1960	Hammond, Jr. et al.	352/130
2,941,044	6/1960	Volkmann	179/1 P
2,969,428	1/1961	Wittlig	179/7.1 R
3,060,795	10/1962	Corrigan et al.	352/131
3,173,136	3/1965	Atkinson	340/384 E
3,278,676	10/1966	Becker	358/142
3,410,958	11/1968	Cohen	179/1 P
3,579,233	5/1971	Raschke	340/384 E
3,934,084	1/1976	Munson et al.	179/1 P
3,934,085	1/1976	Munson et al.	179/1 P
4,052,720	10/1977	McGregor et al.	179/1 P
4,059,726	11/1977	Watters et al.	179/1.5 M
4,061,874	12/1977	Fricke et al.	179/1 A

OTHER PUBLICATIONS

Brit. Journal of Psychology, (1979), 254–258, Mykel et al., Emergence of Unreported Stimuli in Imagery as a Function of Laterality . . . .
Perceptual and Motor Skill, pp. 375–378, (1974), Zenhausern et al., "Differential Effect of Subliminal . . . ".
Proc. of 1978 IEEE, Region 3 Conf., 4/10–12/78, Atlanta, Becker et al., "Subliminal Communication: . . . ".
Applications of Subliminal Video and Audio Stimuli in . . . Commercial Settings, 3/28/80, Becker et al.
The Living Brain, W. Grey Walter, W. W. Norton and Co., 1953, pp. 83–113.
The Human Brain, John Pfeiffer, Harper Bros., 1955, pp. 156–161.
Strobe–The Lively Light, Howard Luray, Camera Craft Publishing, 1949, pp. 11–15.
"Electronic Magic", H. W. Secor, Radio Electronics, Jun. 1949, pp. 20–22.
"TV Video Switching", John Brush, Television Eng., Jul. 1951, pp. 12–15, 29.
"Fighting the Five Finger Discount", American Way, American Airlines, 11/80, pp. 72 et seq.
"Application of Signal Detection Theory to Subliminal and Supraliminal Accessory Stimulation", Zwosta and Zenhausern, Perceptual and Motor Skills, 1969, pp. 699–704.

Primary Examiner—Sal Cangialosi
Attorney, Agent, or Firm—Klarquist, Sparkman, Campbell, Leigh, Whinston & Dellett

[57]   **ABSTRACT**

Ambient audio signals from the customer shopping area within a store are sensed and fed to a signal processing circuit that produces a control signal which varies with variations in the amplitude of the sensed audio signals. A control circuit adjusts the amplitude of an auditory subliminal anti-shoplifting message to increase with increasing amplitudes of sensed audio signals and decrease with decreasing amplitudes of sensed audio signals. This amplitude controlled subliminal message may be mixed with background music and transmitted to the shopping area. To reduce distortion of the subliminal message, its amplitude is controlled to increase at a first rate slower than the rate of increase of the amplitude of ambient audio signals from the area. Also, the amplitude of the subliminal message is controlled to decrease at a second rate faster than the first rate with decreasing

4,395,600

1

AUDITORY SUBLIMINAL MESSAGE SYSTEM AND METHOD

BACKGROUND OF THE INVENTION

The present invention relates to a system and method for providing subliminal auditory signals to an area such as a customer shopping area within a store. More particularly, the invention relates to such a system and method in which the amplitude of the subliminal signal is adjusted in response to the amplitude of ambient audio signals from the customer shopping area.

It has been established that auditory subliminal signals, that is, those presented below the conscious recognition level of the listener, can be used to influence the listener's behavior to some degree. Some early research into visual and auditory subliminal stimulation effects are exemplified in U.S. Pat. Nos. 3,060,795 of Corrigan, et al. and 3,278,676 of Becker.

In addition, Becker is understood to have experimented with the use of auditory subliminal messages to deter shoplifting by retail store customers. Although applicants have not seen or studied Mr. Becker's device, it is believed to combine an auditory subliminal message with background music. However, during non-peak shopping and other times when the store area is exceptionally quiet, the background music signal component in Becker must be much louder than the subliminal signal as otherwise the subliminal signal would be at a level such that it may be consciously recognized by a listener. In addition, as a result of this large difference between the amplitude of the background music and that of the subliminal message signal, the effectiveness of the Becker subliminal message is reduced. Also, Becker is understood to maintain his combined background music and subliminal message at a level sufficiently high enough to enable the music to be heard even under noisy store conditions. However, when the ambient audio signal level drops, such as during non-peak store traffic times, the combined background music and subliminal signal would remain the same and seem overly loud. Thus, Becker is simply not understood to control the amplitude of a subliminal message in response to ambient audio signals from an area.

Accordingly, there is a need for an auditory subliminal message system and method which solves these and other problems.

SUMMARY OF THE INVENTION

The present invention is a method and system for adjusting the amplitude of an auditory subliminal message in response to the amplitude of ambient audio signals from an area to which the subliminal message is to be transmitted. In accordance with one aspect of the invention, an audio signal processing circuit means receives signals representing the amplitude of audio signals in the area, such as a retail shopping area of a store. This processing circuit means produces a control signal for an amplitude adjustment or control circuit means which adjusts the amplitude or volume of an auditory subliminal signal which is to be transmitted to the area. The amplitude of the auditory subliminal signal is adjusted to increase with increasing sensed ambient audio signals and decrease with decreasing sensed ambient audio signals.

As a more specific aspect of the invention, a masking signal is generated and fed to the area. This masking signal has frequency and amplitude characteristics

2

which cover or render the subliminal signal inperceptible to the conscious recognition level of a listener. In the preferred embodiment, the amplitude of this masking signal is also controlled in response to the sensed ambient audio signals so that its amplitude follows the amplitude of the adjusted subliminal message signal. The masking signal may be combined with the subliminal signal to provide a composite signal having an amplitude controlled by the control circuit in response to the control signal.

As a more specific feature of the invention, to reduce distortion of the subliminal message signal, the processing circuit means produces a control signal which causes the control circuit means to increase the amplitude of the auditory subliminal message signal slowly at a rate slower than the rate of change of the ambient audio signals at times when the ambient audio signals are increasing in magnitude. In addition, at times when the ambient audio signals are decreasing to minimize the possibility of conscious perception of the subliminal message signal, the processing circuit means produces a control signal which causes the control circuit means to decrease the amplitude of the subliminal signal at a fast rate.

It is accordingly one object of the invention to provide an improved auditory subliminal message system and method.

Another object of the invention is to provide an auditory subliminal message having an amplitude which is adjusted in response to ambient noise levels within an area to which the auditory subliminal message is to be transmitted.

A further object of the invention is to provide a method and system which adjusts the amplitude of an auditory subliminal message at one rate with increasing ambient audio signal levels in the area and at another, faster rate with decreasing ambient audio signal levels.

A still further object of the invention is to provide such a method and system in which the amplitude of an auditory subliminal signal is adjusted to rise at a rate slower than the rate of increases in ambient audio signal levels.

Another object of the invention is to provide an auditory subliminal message which is continuously maintained below the conscious perception level.

A further object of the invention is to provide an auditory subliminal message which is maintained below the conscious perception level of listeners in an area and which is adjusted in response to ambient audio signals in the area so as to remain close to the level of conscious perception.

Still another object of the invention is to provide an auditory masking signal for an auditory subliminal message, the masking signal having an amplitude which is adjusted in response to ambient noise levels in an area to which the auditory subliminal message is to be transmitted.

A more specific object of the invention is to provide an auditory subliminal message anti-shoplifting system and method.

These and other objects, features and advantages of the invention will become apparent with reference to the following drawings and description.

United States Patent [19]

Crawford et al.

[11] **Patent Number:** **4,616,261**

[45] **Date of Patent:** **Oct. 7, 1986**

[54] **METHOD AND APPARATUS FOR GENERATING SUBLIMINAL VISUAL MESSAGES**

[75] Inventors: **James R. Crawford,** Lainsburg; **Jerald L. Winegeart,** Niles; **Michael H. Erb,** DeWitt, all of Mich.

[73] Assignee: **Stimutech, Inc.,** Ann Arbor, Mich.

[21] Appl. No.: **542,467**

[22] Filed: **Oct. 17, 1983**

Related U.S. Application Data

[63] Continuation-in-part of Ser. No. 491,612, May 4, 1983, abandoned.

[51] Int. Cl.⁴ H04N 5/262; H04N 13/02
[52] U.S. Cl. **358/181**; 358/92; 358/142; 358/183
[58] Field of Search 358/181, 183, 92, 142, 358/236

[56] **References Cited**

U.S. PATENT DOCUMENTS

4,006,291	2/1977	Imsand	358/92
4,151,557	4/1979	Iida	358/181
4,424,591	1/1984	Boardman	358/181

Primary Examiner—Tommy P. Chin
Attorney, Agent, or Firm—Krass & Young

[57] **ABSTRACT**

A system for generating a subliminal message during the display of a normal television program on a television receiver utilizes a personal computer to generate an RF carrier modulated with video signals encoding the subliminal message. The computer runs under the control of an application program which stores the subliminal message and also controls the computer to cause it to generate timing signals that are provided to a single pole double-throw switch. The source of the normal television program and the video output of the computer are connected to the two switch inputs and the switch output is connected to the television receiver antenna system. The timing signals cause the switch to normally display the conventional television program and to periodically switch to the computer output to generate the subliminal message. The video output of the computer includes horizontal and vertical synchronizing signals which are of substantially the same frequency as the synchronizing signals incorporated within the normal program source but of an arbitrary phase.

22 Claims, 3 Drawing Figures

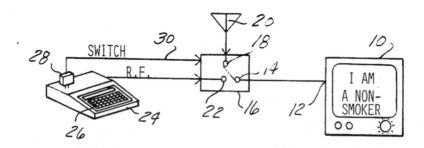

1

METHOD AND APPARATUS FOR GENERATING SUBLIMINAL VISUAL MESSAGES

This application is a continuation-in-part of application Ser. No. 491,612, filed May 4, 1983 abnd.

FIELD OF THE INVENTION

This invention relates to a method and apparatus for causing the generation of a subliminal message superimposed on a supraliminal program being displayed on a television receiver.

BACKGROUND OF THE INVENTION

A substantial body of scientific evidence exists to support the proposition that a human subject may be influenced by visual messages generated at intensity and duration levels sufficiently low that they are not consciously perceived by the subject. U.S. Pat. Nos. 3,060,795 and 3,278,676 disclose a variety of systems adapted to display a supraliminally perceptible visual image having a subliminally perceptible message superimposed thereon. These patents disclose motion picture and television systems for displaying conventional programs along with secondary visual signals that have such low levels of intensity and/or duration that they are not consciously perceptible by a human observer but are capable of impressing themselves upon the subconscious mind of the observer to influence behavior.

The systems disclosed in these patents as well as the subsequent subliminal visual message system disclosed in U.S. Pat. No. 4,006,291 all involve arrangements wherein both the source of the supraliminal program signal and subliminal message signal are under control of the system's operator. In the motion picture version disclosed in U.S. Pat. No. 3,060,795, a pair of separate motion picture projectors employ mechanism connecting them so that they operate in synchronism to generate the supraliminal program signal and the superimposed subliminal mesasge. In the television versions disclosed in the above-noted patents, pairs of television cameras are used to generate the two signals and their outputs are synchronized to provide a combined signal suitable for use directly by a television receiver or for radio transmission to remote receivers.

The highly specialized apparatus required for these prior art systems has severely limited their application. If a subliminal mesasge system could be formed with readily available equipment, such as a home television receiver, which could use conventionally broadcast programs as the supraliminal program source, it would have great utility for impressing the observer with subliminal message that might educate the observer or direct him or her toward desirable action.

SUMMARY OF THE INVENTION

The present invention is accordingly directed toward a method and apparatus for superimposing subliminally perceptible messages on a conventional television receiver which is displaying normal program sources derived from broadcast or cable TV, a video record or the like. The system is intended to be attached to an entertainment television receiver without the necessity of any mechanical or electrical modification of the television set. It utilizes as its primary components apparatus often available in the home for other purposes.

Broadly, the present invention provides means for generating a video signal encoded with a subliminal

2

message and horizontal and vertical synchronizing signals which are of substantially the same frequency as those forming part of the supraliminal signal source connected to the receiver but have an artibrary phase with respect to the supraliminal synchronizing signal. The present invention further contemplates a single pole double-throw RF switching device having inputs from the supraliminal program source and the subliminal message source and having an output to the television receiver. The switch is controlled so that it normally is connected to the supraliminal program source causing the receiver to display that program under control of the horizontal and vertical synchronizing signals forming part of the program composite signal. At regular intervals the switch is controlled to disconnect the program source from the television receiver and supply the subliminal signal with its independent synchronizing signals. The subliminal signal may be applied to the receiver for as little as 500 microseconds, but, in the preferred embodiment, it is generated for the time required to display one full raster field on the television screen, normally about 1/60th of a second. During this time, the synchronization generators of the television receiver are under the control of the synchronizing signals forming part of the subliminal program source and will switch the phase of the generated raster scan to match these new synchronizing signals. The subliminal message will, therefore, be generated on the TV screen during one raster scan or field.

In order to assure synchronization of the vertical and horizontal synch signals as well as synchronization of color signals, AFG and AGC, display of the subliminal message is delayed from one to 24 picture fields following switching off from the supraliminal program source. During this delay, a completely black or blue field is displayed so that the synchronization is not perceived by the viewer. The delay is not visually objectionable and does not negatively affect the device as a subliminal generator.

In the preferred embodiment of the present invention a subliminal video signal is generated by a general purpose computer, preferably of the "home" or "personal" type, running an application program which causes repeated generation of the subliminal video message, once for each raster field, at the video output of the computer. The application program also causes the generation of two-level switching signals for the antenna switch and also synchronizes display of the subliminal program material with vertical retrace signals so that the program material or "message" is displayed at a predetermined position in each picture field. In one embodiment of the invention, which will subsequently be disclosed in detail, the application program for the computer takes the form of a module, including a read-only memory (ROM), adapted to be connected to the computer. The module may also contain a bistable switching device (flip-flop) for generating the timing signals. Alternatively, the application program may make use of a flip-flop and an output port available on the computer to generate the timing signals. The application program stored in the ROM causes the computer to generate logic level signals which are applied to the flip-flop and cause it to provide a higher power output switching signal. This switching signal is coupled to the RF switch, along with the subliminal RF signal, and controls its operation.

In an alternative embodiment of the invention, the subliminal message is not encoded in the application

United States Patent [19]

Mould

[54] **VIDEO SUBCONSCIOUS DISPLAY ATTACHMENT**

[76] Inventor: **Richard E. Mould**

[21] Appl. No.: **823,456**

[22] Filed: **Jan. 28, 1986**

[51] **Int. Cl.⁴** **G09B 19/00**
[52] **U.S. Cl.** **434/236; 40/584**
[58] **Field of Search** 434/236, 346; 40/427, 40/584, 579, 580

[56] **References Cited**

U.S. PATENT DOCUMENTS

2,822,634 2/1958 Salyers et al. 40/584

[11] **Patent Number:** **4,692,118**

[45] **Date of Patent:** **Sep. 8, 1987**

3,055,117 9/1962 Bernstein et al. 434/346

Primary Examiner—William H. Grieb
Attorney, Agent, or Firm—Baker, Maxham & Jester

[57] **ABSTRACT**

An apparatus and method for introducing messages to the subconscious mind is disclosed, which includes a panel positioned adjacent a television screen, with the panel having non-distractive messages imprinted thereon, such that as the subject consciously focuses his attention on the video screen, his subconscious mind records the message from the panel that is within his peripheral vision.

17 Claims, 10 Drawing Figures

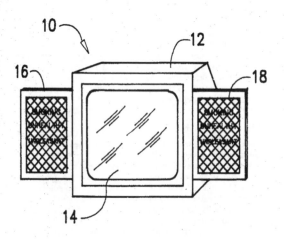

4,692,118

1

VIDEO SUBCONSCIOUS DISPLAY ATTACHMENT

BACKGROUND OF THE INVENTION

The present invention relates to self-improvements, methods and apparatus, and pertains particularly to methods and apparatus for the introduction of messages to the subconscious mind.

It is known to introduce subliminal messages to the subconscious mind by way of video recordings wherein the subliminal message is presented below the conscious level of the observer. Tehcniques of subliminal application of messages employ electronic devices which flash messages onto a video or projection screen that are below the conscious level of the observer during the conscious viewing of a movie or the like. These messages, however, are typically employed for the sale of and marketing of goods. Moreover, they are not typically within the control of the observer.

These prior art approaches to the introduction of subliminal messages to the subconscious mind require the use of complicated and expensive equipment. Such equipment and techniques are not readily available to the ordinary consumer. Moreover, such message devices are not available which enable the consumer to control the message introduced or received.

It is, therefore, desirable that a simple and inexpensive means for the introduction of desirable messages to the subconscious mind be available.

SUMMARY AND OBJECTS OF THE INVENTION

It is the primary object of the present invention to provide a simple and inexpensive method and apparatus for the introduction of selected messages to the subconscious mind.

In accordance with the primary aspect of the present invention, apparatus for the introduction of messages to the subconscious mind includes one or more panels on which are disposed a non-distractive expression of a selected message to be positioned adjacent to a video screen or the like for being within the periphreal vision of the observer.

Another aspect of the invention comprises panels of planar surfaces having non-distractive messages thereon for positioning adjacent to objects of primary focused interest such as a video or television screen.

BRIEF DESCRIPTION OF THE DRAWINGS

The above and other objects and advantages of the present invention will become apparent from the following description when read in conjunction with the drawings wherein:

FIG. 1 is a perspective view of a preferred embodiment of the invention;

FIG. 2 is a top plan view of the embodiment of FIG. 1;

FIG. 3 is a front elevation view of an exemplary embodiment of the message panel;

FIG. 4 is a detailed side elevation view in section showing details of the construction of the preferred panel;

FIG. 5 is front elevation view illustrating an embodiment obscuring means of the panel;

FIG. 6 is a view like FIG. 5 of an alternate embodiment;

2

FIG. 7 is a front elevation view of a still further embodiment;

FIG. 8 is a front elevation view of an alternate arrangement of the message of the system;

FIG. 9 is a view like FIG. 8 showing an alternate embodiment of the invention; and,

FIG. 10 is a top plan view of the embodiment of FIG. 9.

DETAILED DESCRIPTION OF PREFERRED EMBODIMENTS

Referring to the drawings, particularly FIGS. 1 and 2, there is illustrated an embodiment of an apparatus or system for carrying out the present invention. In accordance with the invention, means are provided for introducing a message to the subconscious mind. This means provides a nondistracting form of the message, which is introduced to the subconscious mind while the conscious mind is focused on some normal activity, such as viewing a video screen or the like.

In the illustrated embodiment, a system, designated generally by the numeral 10, comprises a video system, such as a standard television set or the like 12 having a screen 14 on which the normal video image is projected. The invention contemplates means, such as one or more panels or the like 16 and 18 which are disposed within the peripheral vision of one who is concentrating his vision on a point or area of interest, such as watching the video screen 14. In the illustrated embodiment, these panels are positioned to either side of the screen, and preferably within the basic plane of the screen, as can be seen in FIG. 2. This positioning adjacent the screen is believed to be the best position to achieve the maximum benefit of the peripheral vision and the other aspects of the invention. The positioning can be just slightly to the side of the screen, and the images on the panel are preferably of a nondistracting form, such that the observer is not distracted from his attention to the video screen.

It has been found that an angle off the center of focus of perhaps between two and five degrees and possibly up to thirty degrees can still be within the peripheral vision of the observer, yet be sufficiently out of the primary focus of attention such that the message thereon is not distracting to the observer.

Messages on the panel are preferably in a form that can be seen by conscious observation but are not so obvious as to be distracting from the primary focus of attention. The message then imposes its primary influence on the subconscious mind, thereby introducing the message into the subconscious mind during other normal activities of the observer.

The subconscious mind is known to take in information on a subconscious level without interfering with the conscious attention of the observer. In this manner, a system in accordance with the invention permits the individual to control the information that is submitted to his subconscious mind. He may selectively program his subconscious mind in the desired fashion to achieve various self-improvement objectives.

By way of example, a panel for mounting adjacent the screen of a television set may take the form, such as basically illustrated in FIGS. 3 and 4, with a support panel or structure 20 being attached by suitable bracket means or thelike to the television chassis, and having transparent cover 22 forming an envelope or pocket within which is inserted a message panel 24. The support panel 20 is preferably light in weight and substan-

357

United States Patent [19]

McClure

[11] Patent Number: **4,734,037**

[45] Date of Patent: **Mar. 29, 1988**

[54] **MESSAGE SCREEN**

[76] Inventor: **J. Patrick McClure**

[21] Appl. No.: **832,464**

[22] Filed: **Feb. 21, 1986**

[51] Int. Cl.⁴ G09B 19/00
[52] U.S. Cl. 434/236; 40/427;
434/307
[58] Field of Search 434/236, 307; 40/427

[56] **References Cited**

U.S. PATENT DOCUMENTS

2,969,531	1/1961	Stewart	340/347 R
3,014,724	12/1961	Cryder et al.	273/DIG. 28 X
3,060,795	10/1962	Becker	434/236 X
3,278,676	10/1966	Becker	434/236 X
3,542,365	11/1970	Gantz	273/DIG. 28 X
3,568,356	3/1971	Berman	273/DIG. 28 X
3,728,480	4/1973	Baer	273/DIG. 28 X

FOREIGN PATENT DOCUMENTS

1198344 6/1959 France 434/307

Primary Examiner—William H. Grieb
Attorney, Agent, or Firm—Fliesler, Dubb, Meyer & Lovejoy

[57] **ABSTRACT**

A transparent sheet is disclosed having a message thereon. The sheet has a first side adapted to be attached facing a plate which is normally viewed by a viewer and a second side facing the viewer. The message is arranged to be readably intelligible from the second side but is not liminally visible to the viewer when viewed from a normal viewing distance from the second side under normal viewing conditions. The message has a subliminal effect upon the viewer when viewed from the normal viewing distance from the second side under normal viewing conditions. A viewer can electively subject him or herself to subliminal messages while viewing television at leisure.

9 Claims, 1 Drawing Figure

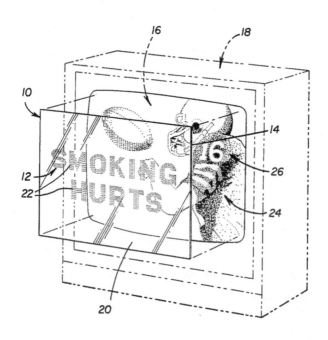

United States Patent [19]

Schultz et al.

[11] **Patent Number:** **4,777,529**

[45] **Date of Patent:** **Oct. 11, 1988**

[54] **AUDITORY SUBLIMINAL PROGRAMMING SYSTEM**

[75] Inventors: **Richard M. Schultz,** Marengo; **Raymond Dolejs,** Arlington Heights, both of Ill.

[73] Assignee: **R. M. Schultz & Associates, Inc.,** McHenry, Ill.

[21] Appl. No.: **76,113**

[22] Filed: **Jul. 21, 1987**

[51] Int. Cl.⁴ H04N 5/92
[52] U.S. Cl. 358/143; 358/341; 380/23; 381/73.1; 381/105; 381/124; 434/307; 434/319
[58] Field of Search 358/93, 143, 341; 380/23; 381/73.1, 105, 124; 434/307, 319

[56] **References Cited**

U.S. PATENT DOCUMENTS

2,338,551	7/1942	Stanko .
2,409,058	12/1944	Mitchell .
2,501,327	3/1950	Good .
2,941,044	6/1980	Volkmann .
3,060,795	10/1962	Corrigan et al. .
3,173,136	3/1965	Atkinson .
3,278,676	10/1966	Becker .
3,410,958	11/1968	Cohen .
3,579,233	5/1971	Raschke .
3,934,084	1/1976	Munson et al. .
3,934,085	1/1976	Munson et al. .
4,052,720	10/1977	McGregor et al. .
4,061,874	12/1977	Frick et al. .
4,124,943	11/1978	Mitchell 434/307
4,230,990	10/1980	Lert 358/84
4,270,284	6/1981	Skellings 434/169
4,315,502	3/1982	Gorges .
4,373,918	2/1983	Berman 434/307
4,395,600	7/1983	Lundy 381/73.1
4,396,946	9/1983	Bond .
4,699,153	10/1987	Shevrin 128/731
4,717,343	1/1988	Densky 434/262

Primary Examiner—Howard W. Britton
Attorney, Agent, or Firm—Willian Brinks Olds Hofer Gilson & Lione Ltd.

[57] **ABSTRACT**

An auditory subliminal programming system includes a subliminal message encoder that generates fixed frequency security tones and combines them with a subliminal message signal to produce an encoded subliminal message signal which is recorded on audio tape or the like. A corresponding subliminal decoder/mixer is connected as part of a user's conventional stereo system and receives as inputs an audio program selected by the user and the encoded subliminal message. The decoder/mixer filters the security tones, if present, from the subliminal message and combines the message signals with selected low frequency signals associated with enhanced relaxation and concentration to produce a composite auditory subliminal signal. The decoder/mixer combines the composite subliminal signal with the selected audio program signals to form composite signals only if it detects the presence of the security tones in the subliminal message signal. The decoder/mixer outputs the composite signal to the audio inputs of a conventional audio amplifier where it is amplified and broadcast by conventional audio speakers.

21 Claims, 2 Drawing Sheets

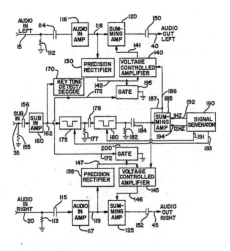

United States Patent [19]

MacLeod

[11] **Patent Number:** **4,821,326**

[45] **Date of Patent:** **Apr. 11, 1989**

[54] **NON-AUDIBLE SPEECH GENERATION METHOD AND APPARATUS**

[75] Inventor: **Norman MacLeod,** Sunnyvale, Calif.

[73] Assignee: **Macrowave Technology Corporation,** San Jose, Calif.

[21] Appl. No.: **121,659**

[22] Filed: **Nov. 16, 1987**

[51] Int. Cl.⁴ G10L 7/02
[52] U.S. Cl. **381/51;** 381/70; 364/513.5; 623/9
[58] Field of Search 381/36–40, 381/51, 70, 86; 364/513.5; 623/9

[56] **References Cited**

U.S. PATENT DOCUMENTS

3,914,550	10/1975	Cardwell, Jr.	381/70
4,292,472	9/1981	Lennox	381/70
4,338,488	7/1982	Lennox	381/70
4,473,905	9/1984	Katz et al.	381/70
4,502,150	2/1985	Katz et al.	381/70
4,550,427	10/1985	Katz et al.	381/70
4,571,739	2/1986	Resnick	381/70
4,612,664	9/1986	Walsh et al.	381/70
4,627,095	12/1986	Thompson	381/70
4,633,864	1/1987	Walsh	623/9 X
4,672,673	6/1987	Katz et al.	381/70

Primary Examiner—Peter S. Wong
Assistant Examiner—Emanuel T. Voeltz
Attorney, Agent, or Firm—Rosenblum, Parish & Bacigalupi

[57] **ABSTRACT**

A non-audible speech generation apparatus and method for producing non-audible speech signals which includes an ultrasonic transducer or vibrator for projecting a series of glottal shaped ultrasonic pulses to the vocal track of a speaker. The glottal pulses, in the approximate frequency spectrum extending from fifteen kilohertz to one hundred five kilohertz, contain harmonics of approximately 30 times the frequency of the acoustical harmonics generated by the vocal cords, but which may nevertheless be amplitude modulated to produce non-audible speech by the speaker's silently mouthing of words. The ultrasonic speech is then received by an ultrasonic detector disposed outside of the speaker's mouth and electrically communicated to a translation device which down converts the ultrasonic signals to corresponding signals in the audible frequency range and synthesizes the signals into artificial speech.

26 Claims, 4 Drawing Sheets

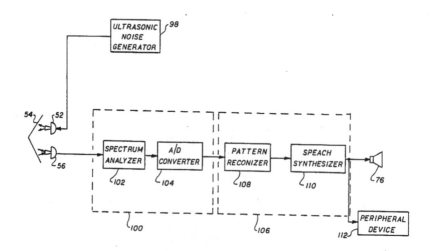

United States Patent [19]

Yamamura

[11]	Patent Number:	4,924,744
[45]	Date of Patent:	May 15, 1990

[54] **APPARATUS FOR GENERATING SOUND THROUGH LOW FREQUENCY AND NOISE MODULATION**

[75] Inventor: **Kimio Yamamura**, Tokyo, Japan

[73] Assignee: **Hudson Soft Co., Ltd.**, Hokkaido, Japan

[21] Appl. No.: **230,342**

[22] Filed: **Aug. 9, 1988**

[30]   **Foreign Application Priority Data**

Aug. 27, 1987 [JP]	Japan	62-213978
Aug. 27, 1987 [JP]	Japan	62-213979
Aug. 27, 1987 [JP]	Japan	62-213980
Aug. 27, 1987 [JP]	Japan	62-213981
Aug. 27, 1987 [JP]	Japan	62-213982
Aug. 27, 1987 [JP]	Japan	62-213983

[51] Int. Cl.^{5} G10H 7/00; G10H 1/06; G10H 1/04; G10H 1/08

[52] U.S. Cl. **84/601;** 84/602; 84/622; 84/624; 84/625

[58] Field of Search .... 84/1.22, 1.23, 1.25, 84/DIG. 12, DIG. 27, DIG. 1 Z, 1.27, 600–602, 604, 615, 617, 624, 625, 647, 655, 659, 660, 678, 682, 694, 697, 1.03; 381/1, 17, 51–53, 62; 369/4

[56]   **References Cited**

U.S. PATENT DOCUMENTS

3,795,756	3/1974	Suzuki	84/1.22
3,878,472	4/1975	Osakabe	84/DIG. 27
4,258,602	3/1981	Niimi et al.	84/1.22 X
4,300,225	11/1981	Lambl	369/4 X
4,347,405	8/1982	Davis	84/DIG. 1
4,402,243	9/1983	Deforeit	84/624 X
4,419,919	12/1983	Kashio	84/1.25 X
4,554,854	11/1985	Kato	84/1.27 X
4,577,540	3/1986	Yamana	381/1 X
4,648,115	3/1987	Sakashita	381/17
4,685,134	8/1987	Wine	381/17
4,747,332	5/1988	Uchiyama et al.	84/655
4,754,680	7/1988	Morikawa et al.	84/1.22
4,821,326	4/1989	MacLeod	381/51

Primary Examiner—A. T. Grimley
Assistant Examiner—Matthew S. Smith
Attorney, Agent, or Firm—Lowe, Price, Leblanc, Becker & Shur

[57]   **ABSTRACT**

In an apparatus for generating sound, there are provided a plurality of channels for generating sounds. Each of the channels includes a memory for storing waveform data, and at least one of the channels includes a noise generator so that various kinds of sounds including rhythm sound-effects sound, effects sound-vibrato etc. are generated. There is further provided a controller by which voice sound signal is passed through the channels so that artificial sound, voice sound etc. are generated. There is still further provided a circuit for adjusting an amplitude level of a whole sound which is obtained by mixing output sounds of the channels so that far and near sound is produced. Further, each of the channels includes left and right attenuators which divide a channel sound into left and right channel sounds. Still further, the apparatus comprises a low frequency oscillator for controlling a depth of frequency modulation, and a controller for writing sampling data of a predetermined waveform into serial addresses of a memory.

2 Claims, 7 Drawing Sheets

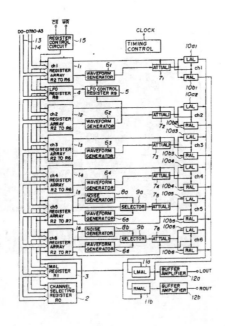

United States Patent [19]

Backus et al.

[11] **Patent Number:** **5,017,143**

[45] **Date of Patent:** **May 21, 1991**

[54] **METHOD AND APPARATUS FOR PRODUCING SUBLIMINAL IMAGES**

[75] Inventors: **Alan Backus**, Los Angeles; **Ronald Popeil**, Beverly Hills, both of Calif.

[73] Assignee: **Popeil Industries, Inc.,** Beverly Hills, Calif.

[21] Appl. No.: **333,423**

[22] Filed: **Apr. 4, 1989**

[51] **Int. Cl.⁵** **G09B 19/00**
[52] **U.S. Cl.** **434/236; 434/307;** 358/22; 358/92; 358/142; 358/182; 358/183
[58] **Field of Search** 434/236, 307, 308, 309; 358/92, 93, 142, 22, 182, 183

[56] **References Cited**

U.S. PATENT DOCUMENTS

3,278,676	10/1966	Becker	434/236 X
3,782,006	1/1974	Symmes	434/236
4,616,261	10/1986	Crawford et al.	358/142 X
4,717,343	1/1988	Densky	434/236

Primary Examiner—Richard J. Apley
Assistant Examiner—J. L. Doyle
Attorney, Agent, or Firm—Lyon & Lyon

[57] **ABSTRACT**

A method and apparatus to produce more effective visual subliminal communications. Graphic and/or text images, presented for durations of less than a video frame, at organized rhythmic intervals, the rhythmic intervals intended to affect user receptivity, moods or behavior. Subliminal graphic images having translucent visual values locally dependent on background values in order to maintain desired levels of visual contrast.

5 Claims, 1 Drawing Sheet

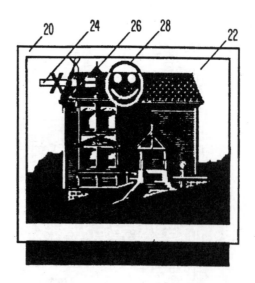

(12) **United States Patent**

Gerosa

(10) **Patent No.:** **US 6,426,919 B1**

(45) **Date of Patent:** **Jul. 30, 2002**

(54) **PORTABLE AND HAND-HELD DEVICE FOR MAKING HUMANLY AUDIBLE SOUNDS RESPONSIVE TO THE DETECTING OF ULTRASONIC SOUNDS**

(76) Inventor: **William A. Gerosa**, 12-6 Foxwood Dr., Pleasantville, NY (US) 10570

(*) Notice: Subject to any disclaimer, the term of this patent is extended or adjusted under 35 U.S.C. 154(b) by 0 days.

(21) Appl. No.: **09/754,543**

(22) Filed: **Jan. 4, 2001**

(51) **Int. Cl.^{7}** **H04B 11/00**
(52) **U.S. Cl.** **367/132**
(58) **Field of Search** 367/132, 134, 367/135, 137

(56) **References Cited**

U.S. PATENT DOCUMENTS

4,039,999 A	8/1977	Weston
4,821,326 A	4/1989	MacLeod 381/51
5,539,705 A	7/1996	Akerman et al. 367/132
5,661,699 A	8/1997	Sutton 367/132

FOREIGN PATENT DOCUMENTS

DE 29714812 U1 * 10/1997

* cited by examiner

Primary Examiner—Daniel T. Pihulic
(74) *Attorney, Agent, or Firm*—Richard L. Miller

(57) **ABSTRACT**

A portable and hand-held device for making humanly audible sounds responsive to the detecting of ultrasonic sounds. The device includes a hand-held housing and circuitry that is contained in the housing. The circuitry includes a microphone that receives the ultrasonic sound, a first low voltage audio power amplifier that strengthens the signal from the microphone, a second low voltage audio power amplifier that further strengthens the signal from the first low voltage audio power amplifier, a 7-stage ripple carry binary counter that lowers the frequency of the signal from the second low voltage audio power amplifier so as to be humanly audible, a third low voltage audio power amplifier that strengthens the signal from the 7-stage ripple carry binary counter, and a speaker that generates a humanly audible sound from the third low voltage audio power amplifier.

15 Claims, 1 Drawing Sheet

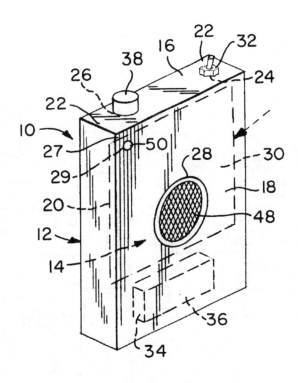

United States Patent [19]

Dwyer, Jr. et al.

[11] Patent Number: **5,027,208**

[45] Date of Patent: **Jun. 25, 1991**

[54] **THERAPEUTIC SUBLIMINAL IMAGING SYSTEM**

[75] Inventors: **Joseph J. Dwyer, Jr.; Loy R. White,** both of Newton, N.H.; **Matthew K. Haggerty,** Medford; **John A. Purbrick,** Arlington, both of Mass.

[73] Assignee: **Sub-Tv Limited Partnership,** Newton Junction, N.H.

[21] Appl. No.: **464,906**

[22] Filed: **Jan. 16, 1990**

Related U.S. Application Data

[63] Continuation-in-part of Ser. No. 260,738, Oct. 21, 1988, abandoned.

[51] Int. Cl.⁵ H04W 5/04
[52] U.S. Cl. 358/148; 358/149; 358/142; 358/183
[58] Field of Search 358/148, 158, 149, 142, 358/183

[56] **References Cited**

U.S. PATENT DOCUMENTS

3,278,676	10/1966	Becker	358/142
4,346,407	8/1982	Bear et al.	358/149
4,425,581	1/1984	Schweppe et al.	358/148
4,864,401	9/1989	Kawata et al.	358/148

Primary Examiner—Howard W. Britton
Assistant Examiner—David E. Harvey
Attorney, Agent, or Firm—Hamilton, Brook, Smith & Reynolds

[57] **ABSTRACT**

A therapeutic subliminal imaging system wherein a selected subliminal message is synchronized with and added to an existing video signal containing a supraliminal message. A television receiver or video recorder can be used to provide the supraliminal message and a video processing circuit varies the intensity of that perceptible message to incorporate one or more subliminal images.

16 Claims, 3 Drawing Sheets

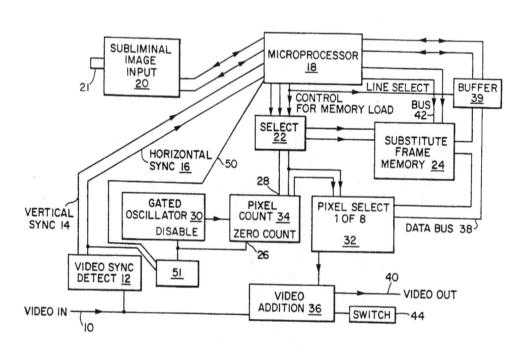

5,027,208

1

THERAPEUTIC SUBLIMINAL IMAGING SYSTEM

BACKGROUND OF THE INVENTION

This is a Continuation-In-Part of U.S. patent application Ser. No. 07/260,738 filed Oct. 21, 1988, which is incorporated herein by reference now abandoned.

The present invention relates to systems for generating subliminal messages synchronously added to selected supraliminal messages where the combined image is displayed for the purpose of therapeutically influencing behavior.

The behavior of individuals may be influenced by visual messages generated at intensity or duration levels sufficiently low that they are not consciously perceived. A variety of systems have been developed to display a supraliminally perceptible visual image having a subliminally perceptible message presented in conjunction therewith. These systems typically use motion picture or television systems for displaying conventional programs along with a therapeutic message that is not consciously perceptible by a human observer but is capable of influencing the subconscious mind of the observer in such a way as to influence behavior.

The systems typically involve arrangements wherein both the source of the supraliminal video signal and subliminal video signal are under the control of the system's operator. In a motion picture version, a pair of separate motion picture projectors employ a mechanism connecting them so that they operate in synchrony to generate the supraliminal program signal along with the superimposed subliminal message. Alternatively, pairs of television cameras have been used to separately generate two signals which are synchronized to provide a combined signal suitable for use with a television receiver.

The apparatus required for most existing systems has severely limited their application. However, some subliminal message systems have utilized readily available equipment and conventionally broadcast programs for the supraliminal program source and simply switch to a subliminal signal at short intervals to impress the observer with a subliminal message that might direct the observer to undertake desirable action.

SUMMARY OF THE INVENTION

The invention relates to portable systems for implementing behavior modification therapy wherein a subliminal message is added to a preexisting supraliminal message and the combined image is displayed on a video screen.

A television receiver or video recorder can be used to provide the supraliminal message. The desired subliminal message or image is provided by a preprogrammed chip that is inserted by the user into a compact video processing circuit that combines the two signals for viewing.

The video processing system of a preferred embodiment of the invention synchronizes the video signal containing the supraliminal message with a signal containing the desired subliminal message. The system then either lightens or darkens portions of the supraliminal message, in a manner that is not consciously perceptible to the viewer, to present the subliminal message. Thus an optical characteristic of a portion of the supraliminal message is altered slightly to incorporate the subliminal message.

2

This embodiment utilizes an analog oscillator in conjunction with a digital circuit to synchronize the subliminal message signal with the existing video signal. A video synchronization detector circuit receives the supraliminal video signal and generates digital outputs that mark the beginning of each vertical and horizontal line within the two dimensional image. These vertical and horizontal synchronization signals are used to instruct a microprocessor, which accesses a digital memory in which the subliminal message has been stored, to deliver the contents of each line of the subliminal message for addition to the appropriate line of the supraliminal image. An analog oscillator is used rather than a crystal clock because it can be stopped by a composite synchronization pulse and re-started, thereby starting each line at exactly the same time interval following the synchronization pulse. This results in improved stability of the subliminal message relative to the supraliminal message during one scan of the screen and between successive scans.

A monostable ("one shot") multivibrator is gated by the microprocessor to produce pulses so that only selected portions of each supraliminal image are altered to incorporate the subliminal message. The oscillator is controlled directly by the one-shot's output and is stopped only for the duration of the one-shot pulse.

A counter is used to control delivery of the subliminal message for each screen line. The counter does not depend on the stopping of the oscillator to control counting. Rather, the counter disables itself after counting the pixels on each line of the subliminal image and allows the oscillator to run. The one-shot is used to both stop the oscillator and zero the counter. This video mixer thus uses a simple control circuit to provide placement of the subliminal message anywhere on the supraliminal image. The system avoids the use of noisy analog differentiation circuits to provide pulse signals which control circuit operation.

The above, and other features of the invention, including various novel details of construction and combination of parts, will now be more particularly described with reference to the accompanying drawings and pointed out in the claims. It will be understood that the particular therapeutic subliminal imaging system embodying the invention is shown by way of illustration only and not as a limitation of the invention. The principle features of this invention may be employed in various embodiments without departing from the scope of the invention.

BRIEF DESCRIPTION OF THE DRAWINGS

FIG. 1 is a schematic diagram of the processing circuit for a preferred embodiment of the invention.

FIG. 2 is a process flow diagram illustrating a method of subliminal therapy embodying the invention.

DETAILED DESCRIPTION

A preferred embodiment of the invention is a device for implementing behavior modification therapy in either a clinical or home setting. The types of behavior being treated include, but are not limited to, self-destructive habits and addictions such as over-eating, smoking, alcohol and drug dependencies. The system can also be employed for the presentation of performance enhancing, or stress reducing messages useful in a wide variety of applications.

The method employed involves the presentation of a subliminal message imposed on an existing television

United States Patent [19]

Dingwall et al.

[11] **Patent Number:**   **5,128,765**

[45] **Date of Patent:**   **Jul. 7, 1992**

[54] **SYSTEM FOR IMPLEMENTING THE SYNCHRONIZED SUPERIMPOSITION OF SUBLIMINAL SIGNALS**

[75] Inventors: **Robert T. Dingwall,** Clinton Corners; **Howard T. Bellin,** New York, both of N.Y.

[73] Assignee: **Visual Subliminal Technologies, Inc.,** New York, N.Y.

[21] Appl. No.:   **277,293**

[22] Filed: **Nov. 29, 1988**

[51] **Int. Cl.⁵** H04N 5/262
[52] **U.S. Cl.** **358/182**
[58] **Field of Search** 358/181, 92, 142, 183, 358/143, 341, 182; 380/23; 381/73.1, 105, 125; 434/307, 319

[56]   **References Cited**

U.S. PATENT DOCUMENTS

4,230,990 10/1980 Lert, Jr. et al. 358/84
4,616,261 10/1986 Crawford et al. 358/142
4,777,529 10/1988 Schultz et al. 358/143
4,807,031   2/1989 Broughton et al. 358/146

Primary Examiner—Donald McElheny, Jr.
Attorney, Agent, or Firm—Hopgood, Calimafde, Kalil, Blaustein & Judlowe

[57]   **ABSTRACT**

An apparatus and system for the controlled delivery of a subliminal video and/or audio message on to a source signal from a video tape player or similar. The source signal is divided into audio and video portions. A video processor reads sychronization information from the source signal. A controller transmits a stored subliminal image at designated times to a mixer amplifier fully synchronized with the source signal. Concurrently, an audio subliminal message is applied to the source audio at a volume level regulated at some fraction to the source audio. The combined signals are transmitted to a monitor for undistracted viewing.

1 Claim, 3 Drawing Sheets

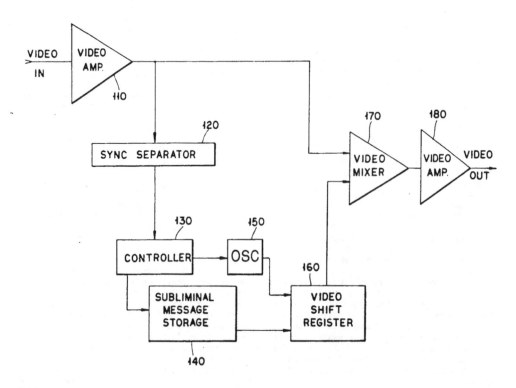

5,128,765

1

SYSTEM FOR IMPLEMENTING THE SYNCHRONIZED SUPERIMPOSITION OF SUBLIMINAL SIGNALS

This invention generally relates to a system for processing a subliminal message signal. More particularly, this invention relates to a process and apparatus for superimposing a subliminal signal onto a continuous composite source signal at controlled intervals.

The human cognitive process is often broken down into discrete levels of perception. These range from conscious recognition of outside events down through varying degrees of semi- or unconscious levels of recognition. The factors that contribute to the level of event recognition or perception are numerous and include the duration of the event and the degree of autonomous processing normally associated with the event. For example, many activities reach such a level of instinctive behavior that conscious thought is no longer involved in the individual's reaction to the event; in appearance the reaction process becomes automated. In fact, the individual's reaction to the event is often relegated to subconscious control, as the individual is not consciously aware of his reaction to the event. In this context "event" is used to describe external stimuli to an individual, as perceived by the individual's senses, e.g., sight, hearing, touch, etc.

Subliminal perception involves the recognition by the individual of an event on an unconscious or semi-conscious level, i.e., the individual is conscious, but the level of sensory perception of the event is so low as to only register on the individual's subconscious memory. An example of a subliminal event would be a short duration image of a soft drink presented during an engrossing visual presentation, such as a movie. Since the image of the soft drink is provided for a fraction of a second, the viewer does not consciously perceive the image and continues to focus on the movie. But, the split-second soft drink image is perceived "subconsciously" and initiates a thirst drive in the individual. It is this potential commercial exploitation of subliminal perception that has evoked significant regulation on its use.

The use of subliminal perception has extended into the medical field and is applied for beneficial behavioral modification. For example, instead of an image of a soft drink, the subliminal message may include anti-smoking, or anti-eating symbols or statements. In the case of treating anorexia nervosa, the subliminal symbols will contain enticing visions of food in an attempt to stimulate a subconscious hunger drive. These symbols, received on the subconscious level, will contribute to behavior modification in accordance with an overall treatment. Furthermore, the subliminal message can be applied as an image, a low volume audio, or a combination of both image and audio. Low volume audio, as with the short duration image, is perceived on a lower order of memory and, therefore, not consciously recognized by the recipient.

Television/video systems are ideally suited for subliminal message conduits. In practice the problems involved in adapting the standard video/TV system for medical application of subliminal perception are numerous. To preclude improper use of the subliminal process, the insertion of the subliminal message must be a decentralized operation, i.e., it cannot be part of a central broadcast signal sent to many users. Moreover, the

2

individual must have control of the message for proper application. Inserting the subliminal message locally, as a separate signal to the receiver, has remained troublesome, as the insertion process itself often distorts the source signal. For example, in U.S. Pat. No. 4,616,261, a personal computer is used to turn off the source (i.e., broadcast) signal, insert a subliminal image and then reconnect the source signal. This interference with the source signal will invariably distort the resulting video image in a manner cognizable by the viewer.

It is, therefore, an object of the present invention to provide a subliminal message in the form of a short duration image, as applied during the normal use of a conventional video system.

It is another object of the present invention to provide a simplified apparatus adaptable to a home video system for superimposing a subliminal message locally controlled by the user.

Yet another object of the present invention is to provide an integrated system for superimposing a subliminal image at controlled intervals and a subliminal audio signal at controlled volume onto a source signal.

Still another object of the present invention is to provide a system for superimposing a short duration synchronized subliminal image onto a source video signal without distorting the source signal.

The above and other objects are realized in an apparatus and system for superimposing a subliminal message onto a source signal. The source signal is taken from a suitable discrete device, i.e., television receiver, video cassette recorder, laser disk, etc., in the form of separate audio and video signals. The video signal is processed for horizontal and vertical synchronization information. A controller recalls a video subliminal message from integrated memory and superimposes this message as a video signal, fully synchronized, onto the existing video source signal. In addition, the controller optionally feeds a low volume audio message into the source audio signal, wherein the volume level is regulated at some fractional value of the source audio.

The foregoing features of the present invention may be more fully understood from the following detailed discussion of a specific illustrative embodiment thereof, presented hereinbelow in conjunction with the accompanying drawing, in which:

FIG. 1 is a block diagram of the various subsystems of the present invention;

FIG. 2 is a schematic diagram of the video processing subsystem of the present invention; and

FIG. 3 is a schematic diagram of the audio processing subsystem of the present invention.

Referring to FIG. 1, the various components of the operative subliminal system are presented. Signal Source 10 represents a source of composite audio/video signal and can be selected from a number of possible devices, including video tape recorders, laser disk players, television receivers, and personal computers. The output signal from Signal Source 10, is a divisible audio/video transmission, carrying the source image and sound information. The video portion of this source signal is transmitted to the video processor, 100, while the audio portion is transmitted to the audio processor, 300. Video and audio processors, are shown in more detail in FIGS. 2 and 3, respectively.

Referring now to FIG. 2, the video signal is transmitted to buffer amplifier 110, split into parallel paths, and directed to the video mixer 170 and sync separator 120.

United States Patent [19]

Willson

[11] **Patent Number:** **5,134,484**

[45] **Date of Patent:** **Jul. 28, 1992**

[54] **SUPERIMPOSING METHOD AND APPARATUS USEFUL FOR SUBLIMINAL MESSAGES**

[75] Inventor: Joseph Willson, Newtown Square, Pa.

[73] Assignee: MindsEye Educational Systems, Inc., Strafford, Pa.

[21] Appl. No.: 359,974

[22] Filed: Jun. 1, 1989

[51] Int. Cl.⁵ H04N 5/272; H04N 5/45
[52] U.S. Cl. 358/183; 358/160
[58] Field of Search 358/22, 183, 160

[56] **References Cited**

U.S. PATENT DOCUMENTS

4,616,261	10/1986	Crawford	358/183
4,644,399	2/1987	McCord et al.	358/142
4,675,737	6/1987	Fujino et al.	358/183
4,748,504	5/1988	Ikeda et al.	358/183 X
4,777,529	10/1988	Schultz et al.	358/142 X
4,855,827	8/1989	Best	358/142 X
4,864,399	9/1989	Romesburg et al.	358/148
4,891,705	1/1990	Suzuki et al.	358/22 X
4,899,139	2/1990	Ishimochi	358/183 X
4,907,086	3/1990	Truong	358/183

Primary Examiner—James J. Groody
Assistant Examiner—Mark R. Powell

Attorney, Agent, or Firm—Louis Weinstein

[57] **ABSTRACT**

Data to be displayed is combined with a composite video signal. The data is stored in a memory in digital form. Each byte of the data is read out in sequential fashion to determine: the recurrence display rate of the data according to the frame sync pulses of the video signal; the location of the data within the video image according to the line sync pulses of the video signal; and the location of the data display within the video image according to the position information. Synchronization of the data with the video image is derived from the sync pulses of the composite video signal. A similar technique is employed to combine sound data with an audio signal. Data to be displayed may be presented as a subliminal message or may persist for a given time interval. The data may be derived from a variety of sources including a prerecorded or live video signal. The message may be a reminder message displayed upon a television screen to remind the viewer of an appointment. The data may be stored in a variety of different memory devices capable of high speed data retrieval. The data may be generated locally on-line or off-line and transferred to memory which stores the data necessary to create the message.

109 Claims, 18 Drawing Sheets

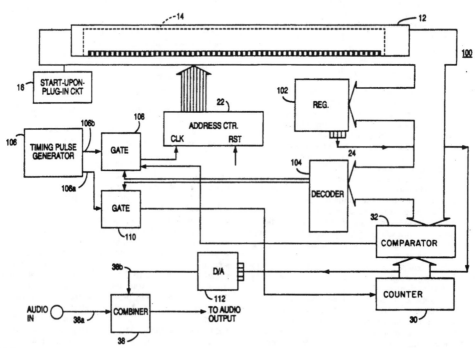

1

SUPERIMPOSING METHOD AND APPARATUS USEFUL FOR SUBLIMINAL MESSAGES

FIELD OF THE INVENTION

The present invention relates to apparatus for combining video signals with additional information, and more particularly to a novel method and apparatus for superimposing messages, graphic information and the like to video signals and/or audio signals and which is uniquely adapted to provide both static and dynamic information for either normal or subliminal presentation.

BACKGROUND OF THE INVENTION

A variety of different applications exist wherein it is desirable to combine information signals. For example, one typical application is the provision of subliminal messages. In order to present a subliminal message upon a television screen, it is necessary to provide apparatus for producing the data in the form of signals which are capable of being processed by a standard television receiver and to synchronize the signals with the R.F. signals being broadcast to the television receiver such as, for example, a transmission from a local or network television station to a television in a viewer's residence.

The transmitted video signal is typically comprised of synchronizing signals, namely, frame and line synchronizing signals also referred to as vertical and horizontal sync signals, respectively. The sync signals are combined with the image information to form a composite video signal which is transmitted to a television receiver by way of a carrier frequency signal which is modulated by the composite video signal.

The modulated carrier is processed at the television receiver to remove the composite video signal from the carrier frequency signal whereupon the video display is generated in accordance with the information signals and the corresponding synchronizing signals.

Heretofore, conventional techniques for displaying information such as messages, graphic and pictorial images and the like, utilize synchronizing signals which are generated specifically for the data to be superimposed, which signals are generated totally independently of the synchronizing signals forming part of the composite video signal.

One such conventional prior art technique is described in U.S. Pat. No. 4,616,261 in which switching means is provided for alternately switching between the composite video signal and the information to be combined therewith. This system has the disadvantages of cutting out the composite video signal during the time that the message, such as a subliminal message, is being introduced, and further requires separate, independent sync signals for the subliminal message, which switching system is thus incapable of precisely synchronizing the subliminal message with the video image as regards its rate of occurrence and precise location upon the screen.

•BRIEF DESCRIPTION OF THE INVENTION

The present invention is characterized by comprising a system in which the synchronizing signals for the overlay message are derived from the composite video signal, thus assuring perfect synchronism of the overlay message with the video image and further assuring the precise location of the overlay message according to the desires of the particular application. An overlay mes-

2

sage (or messages) may be a subliminal or a persistent image or combinations thereof.

The present invention is characterized by comprising an electronic solid state system in which a memory source which may, for example, be a READ ONLY MEMORY (ROM) contains information relating to the refresh rate, the line position and the location on each line at which the message is to be displayed, as well as information representing the message.

The present invention is characterized by comprising a method and apparatus for extracting a composite video signal from a modulated carrier, extracting the frame and line signals from the composite video signal, examining a memory device in which data representing the frame count, line count and placement information are stored in a predetermined arrangement within the memory whereby a frame count is utilized to initiate the regeneration of message signals and to determine the refresh rate therefor, a line count is utilized to determine the line or lines which are to receive information and the position information is utilized to determine the location of the display data on each line of the video image, as well as the arrangement of the data or message on each line. The line (i.e., line sync pulse) count is extracted from memory and compared with the count of accumulated line sync pulses derived from the composite video signal. When the number of line sync pulses accumulated compares with (i.e. is equal to) the line count extracted from the memory, the line position count is then extracted from memory and the pulses generated by a timing pulse generator are counted and the count of the line position is compared with the timing pulses accumulated from the timing pulse generator. When these two counts compare, the data in the next memory location is extracted, which data represents the display information, and may be in the form of the presence or absence of a dot or the presence or absence of a dot of a predetermined brightness. For each location along the line which is to contain a dot, a dot production signal is combined with the composite video signal to produce a composite video plus message signal which is then preferably modulated with the channel 3 or channel 4 carrier, for example, for coupling to the television receiver for presentation of the video image and overlay message information upon the television screen, which may be a subliminal and/or a persistent message.

Each line making up the television display, which may, for example, be a 525 line screen, is divided into a precise number of data (i.e. dot) positions according to a precision timing pulse generator. The timing pulse generator generates pulses at a rate to precisely create the number of data positions per line, and which is the same for each line. The accuracy of the timing pulse generator is enhanced by automatically restarting the timing pulse generator each time a line sync signal is produced to assure initiation of the first timing pulse with a line sync signal and further to assure that the precise number of pulses are produced for each line making up the video display. Thus, the data on each line is precisely located relative to the left-hand edge of the display screen, for example.

The information to be displayed per line may necessitate a storage capacity of one or a plurality of binary bytes. The bytes are sequentially withdrawn from the memory, which is preferably a READ ONLY MEM-

United States Patent [19]

Lowery

[11] **Patent Number:** **5,159,703**

[45] **Date of Patent:** **Oct. 27, 1992**

[54] **SILENT SUBLIMINAL PRESENTATION SYSTEM**

[76] Inventor: **Oliver M. Lowery**

[21] Appl. No.: **458,339**

[22] Filed: **Dec. 28, 1989**

[51] Int. Cl.^{5} **H04B 7/00; H04R 25/00; H04R 3/02**

[52] U.S. Cl. **455/42;** 455/46; 455/66; 381/73.1; 128/420.5

[58] Field of Search 455/46, 47, 66, 109, 455/110, 42–43; 381/73.1, 105, 124; 358/141–143; 600/28; 128/420.5; 380/38

[56] **References Cited**

U.S. PATENT DOCUMENTS

3,060,795	10/1962	Corrigan et al.	352/131
3,278,676	10/1966	Becker	358/142
3,393,279	7/1968	Flanagan	128/420.5
3,712,292	1/1973	Zentmeyer, Jr.	600/28
4,141,344	2/1979	Barbara	600/28
4,395,600	7/1983	Lundy et al.	381/73.1
4,463,392	7/1984	Fischer et al.	360/30
4,777,529	10/1988	Schultz et al.	381/73.1
4,834,701	5/1989	Masaki	600/28
4,877,027	10/1989	Brunkan	128/420.5

Primary Examiner—Reinhard J. Eisenzopf
Assistant Examiner—Andrew Faile

[57] **ABSTRACT**

A silent communications system in which nonaural carriers, in the very low or very high audio frequency range or in the adjacent ultrasonic frequency spectrum, are amplitude or frequency modulated with the desired intelligence and propagated acoustically or vibrationally, for inducement into the brain, typically through the use of loudspeakers, earphones or piezoelectric transducers. The modulated carriers may be transmitted directly in real time or may be conveniently recorded and stored on mechanical, magnetic or optical media for delayed or repeated transmission to the listener.

3 Claims, 3 Drawing Sheets

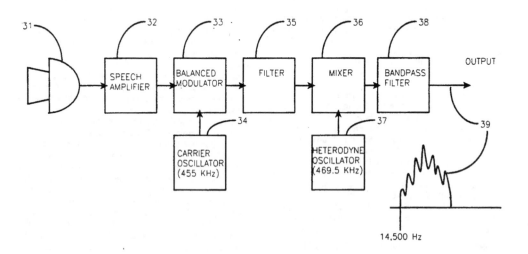

370

United States Patent [19]

Taylor et al.

[11] **Patent Number:** **5,170,381**

[45] **Date of Patent:** **Dec. 8, 1992**

[54] **METHOD FOR MIXING AUDIO SUBLIMINAL RECORDINGS**

[76] Inventors: **Eldon Taylor**

James R. **Woodhams**

[21] Appl. No.: **440,244**

[22] Filed: **Nov. 22, 1989**

[51] Int. Cl.⁵ H04M 15/00; H04B 1/20
[52] U.S. Cl. 369/4; 369/1;
381/73.1; 381/104
[58] Field of Search 381/73.1, 104, 1031;
369/1, 3, 4, 292, 84, 85; 358/22, 181, 183;
380/19, 22

[56] **References Cited**

U.S. PATENT DOCUMENTS

2,825,755	3/1958	Baracket	358/181
3,278,676	10/1966	Becker	358/142
3,493,681	2/1970	Richards	369/3
3,673,324	6/1972	Ito	358/183
4,064,364	12/1977	Veale	369/4
4,201,895	5/1980	Hill	369/4
4,360,114	12/1981	Callahan	369/3
4,395,600	7/1983	Lundy	381/73.1
4,438,526	3/1984	Thomalla	381/73.1
4,551,688	11/1985	Craiglow	330/280
4,777,529	10/1988	Schultz	381/105

FOREIGN PATENT DOCUMENTS

2123251	1/1984	United Kingdom	369/1

OTHER PUBLICATIONS

Electronics Today Article, vol. 10, No. 11 (Nov. 1981) p. 57.
Electronics Today Article, vol. 10, No. 12 (Dec. 1981) p. 74.
Schematic Diagram, Tandy Dual Tape Deck, Model #SCT-45-METAL, available from Radio Shack, National Parts Dept. Fort Worth Tex. 76101.

Primary Examiner—Stuart S. Levy
Assistant Examiner—Joseph A. Rhoa
Attorney, Agent, or Firm—John Edward Roethel

[57] **ABSTRACT**

Audio subliminal recordings are made in which in addition to using a primary carrier, such as music, two audio channels are used to deliver subliminal messages to the brain. On one channel, accessing the left brain hemisphere, the message delivered is meaningfully spoken, forward-masked, permissive affirmations delivered in a round-robin manner by a male voice, a female voice and a child's voice. On the other channel, accessing the right brain, directive messages, in the same voices, are recorded in backward-masked (or meta-contrast). The three voices are recording in round-robin fashion with full echo reverberation. The audio tracks are mixed using a special processor which converts sound frequencies to electrical impulses and tracks the subliminal message to synchronize the subliminal message in stereo with the primary carrier. The processor maintains constant gain differential between the primary carrier and the subliminal verbiage and, with the subliminal verbiage being recorded with round-robin, full echo reverberation, ensures that none of a message is lost. The primary carrier should be continuous music without breaks or great differences in movements.

48 Claims, 14 Drawing Sheets

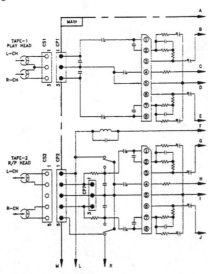

United States Patent [19]

Tanefsky et al.

[11] **Patent Number:** **5,175,571**

[45] **Date of Patent:** **Dec. 29, 1992**

[54] **GLASSES WITH SUBLIMINAL MESSAGE**

[76] Inventors: **Faye Tanefsky**
Michael R. McCaughey

[21] Appl. No.: **640,224**

[22] Filed: **Jan. 11, 1991**

[30] **Foreign Application Priority Data**

Jan. 11, 1990 [CA] Canada 2007611

[51] **Int. Cl.⁵** G02C 1/00
[52] **U.S. Cl.** 351/158; 351/49
[58] **Field of Search** 351/41, 47, 45, 46, 351/158

[56] **References Cited**

U.S. PATENT DOCUMENTS

3,597,054	8/1971	Winter	351/158
4,163,607	8/1979	Nannini	351/47
4,329,378	5/1982	Tarumi et al.	351/165
4,338,004	7/1982	Visper	351/47
4,414,431	11/1983	McCartney	351/47
4,715,702	12/1987	Dillon	351/44
4,938,582	7/1990	Leslie	351/158

Primary Examiner—Paul M. Dzierzynski

[57] **ABSTRACT**

A pair of subliminal imaging spectacles is provided with a matched pair of visual subliminal images designed and placed so as to merge into one image due to the stereoscopic effect of human vision and thus to impart a subliminal message to the wearer.

7 Claims, 2 Drawing Sheets

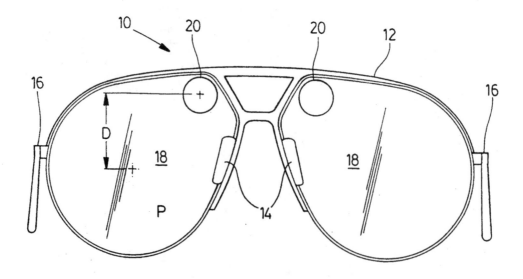

United States Patent [19]

Mohan et al.

[11] **Patent Number:** **5,194,008**

[45] **Date of Patent:** **Mar. 16, 1993**

[54] **SUBLIMINAL IMAGE MODULATION PROJECTION AND DETECTION SYSTEM AND METHOD**

[75] Inventors: **William L. Mohan; Samuel P. Willits,** both of Barrington; **Steven V. Pawlowski,** Hanover Park, all of Ill.

[73] Assignee: **Spartanics, Ltd.,** Rolling Meadows, Ill.

[21] Appl. No.: **858,196**

[22] Filed: **Mar. 26, 1992**

[51] Int. Cl.^{5} F41G 3/76
[52] U.S. Cl. 434/22; 434/20; 273/316; 358/93
[58] Field of Search 434/16, 17, 19, 20–23, 434/27; 358/93, 142, 146; 273/310–316, 358; 353/10, 30, 42; 250/493.1, 495.1

[56] **References Cited**

U.S. PATENT DOCUMENTS

4,065,860	1/1978	Linton et al.	434/22
4,079,525	3/1978	Linton et al.	434/18
4,177,580	12/1979	Marshall et al.	434/22
4,210,329	7/1980	Steiger et al.	273/312 X
4,290,757	9/1981	Marshall et al.	434/20 X
4,336,018	6/1982	Marshall et al.	434/22
4,553,943	11/1985	Ahola et al.	434/22
4,583,950	4/1986	Schroeder	434/22
4,608,601	8/1986	Shreck et al.	358/146
4,619,616	10/1986	Clarke	434/22
4,640,514	2/1987	Myllyla et al.	273/310
4,804,325	2/1989	Willits et al.	434/22
4,824,374	4/1989	Hendry et al.	434/22

Primary Examiner—Richard J. Apley
Assistant Examiner—Joe H. Cheng
Attorney, Agent, or Firm—Robert A. Brown

[57] **ABSTRACT**

Weapon training simulation system including a computer operated video display scene whereon is projected a plurality of visual targets. The computer controls the display scene and the targets, whether stationary or moving, and processes data of a point of aim sensor apparatus associated with a weapon operated by a trainee. The sensor apparatus is sensitive to non-visible or subliminal modulated areas having a controlled contrast of brightness between the target scene and the targets. The sensor apparatus locates a specific subliminal modulated area and the computer determines the location of a target image on the display scene with respect to the sensor apparatus.

36 Claims, 12 Drawing Sheets

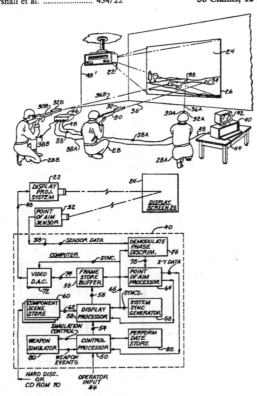

United States Patent [19]

Lauffer et al.

[11] Patent Number:	**5,215,468**
[45] Date of Patent:	**Jun. 1, 1993**

[54] **METHOD AND APPARATUS FOR INTRODUCING SUBLIMINAL CHANGES TO AUDIO STIMULI**

[76] Inventors: **Martha A. Lauffer; Donald K. Lauffer**

[21] Appl. No.: **667,490**

[22] Filed: **Mar. 11, 1991**

[51] Int. Cl.⁵ **G09B 19/00; G09B 5/04**
[52] U.S. Cl. **434/236; 434/319; 482/3; 482/148**
[58] Field of Search 434/307, 319, 236, 179, 434/178; 360/74, 72, 73.8, 73.01, 73.08, 73.06; 84/484, 612, 636, 652, 668, 714; 369/189

[56] **References Cited**

U.S. PATENT DOCUMENTS

3,231,282	1/1966	Dennis	369/189
3,695,553	10/1972	Everett	360/134 X
4,296,446	10/1981	Zorbalas	360/73.08
5,033,966	7/1991	Behunin	434/178
5,103,348	4/1992	Sasho et al.	360/73.08 X

Primary Examiner—Richard J. Apley
Assistant Examiner—John Pleubecker
Attorney, Agent, or Firm—Gregory P. Gadson

[57] **ABSTRACT**

A method and apparatus for introducing gradual changes to an audio signal so that the changes are subliminal. The changes can involve tempo and volume, for example, and can take the form of a gentle gradient having ever increasing/decreasing ramp-like changes over a sufficient duration, or a more complex program involving several gentle gradients. In the preferred embodiment, an enhanced audio play-back device such as a portable audio cassette recorder can be programmed to subliminally alter the characteristics of a standard pre-recorded tape containing music, for example. As a motivational tool during walking, jogging or other repetitive exercise, the tempo is gradually increased over a period of time to encourage a corresponding gradual (and subliminal) increase in physical exertion by a user whose rate of movement is proportional to the tempo of the music. The tempo can be either manually changed in conjunction with a subliminal program, or by itself in an override mode, or by itself in a version of the present-inventive audio play-back device which allows only manual tempo alternation. In an alternate embodiment, a special pre-recorded tape contains subliminal changes in tempo, for example, for play-back on a standard audio cassette recorder (which operates at one speed, only) to cause the same effect as the preferred embodiment.

22 Claims, 5 Drawing Sheets

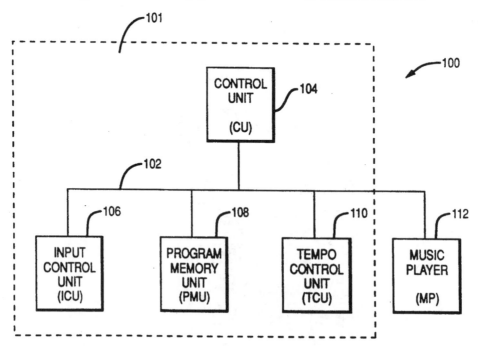

United States Patent [19]

Backus et al.

[11] **Patent Number:** **5,221,962**

[45] **Date of Patent:** **Jun. 22, 1993**

[54] **SUBLIMINAL DEVICE HAVING MANUAL ADJUSTMENT OF PERCEPTION LEVEL OF SUBLIMINAL MESSAGES**

[75] Inventors: **Alan L. Backus; Ronald Popeil,** both of Beverly Hills, Calif.; **Casey Walsh,** Medford, Oreg.; **Jerry Lawson,** Santa Clara, Calif.

[73] Assignee: **Popeil Industries, Inc.,** Beverly Hills, Calif.

[21] Appl. No.: **567,376**

[22] Filed: **Aug. 14, 1990**

Related U.S. Application Data

[63] Continuation-in-part of Ser. No. 252,667, Oct. 3, 1988, abandoned.

[51] Int. Cl.⁵ H04N 5/445
[52] U.S. Cl. 358/183; 434/236; 434/307
[58] Field of Search 434/236, 262, 307, 319, 434/433; 358/183, 182, 22, 198

[56] **References Cited**

U.S. PATENT DOCUMENTS

3,060.795	10/1962	Corrigan et al. .
3,278,676	10/1966	Becker .
3,585.991	6/1971	Balamoth .
3,782,006	1/1974	Symmes .
4,006,291	2/1977	Imsand .
4,395,600	7/1983	Lundy .
4,616,261	10/1986	Crawford et al. .
4,692,118	9/1987	Mould .
4,717,343	1/1988	Densky .
4,734,037	3/1988	McClure .
4,777,529	10/1988	Schultz et al. .

Primary Examiner—James J. Groody
Assistant Examiner—Mark R. Powell
Attorney, Agent, or Firm—Keck, Mahin & Cate

[57] **ABSTRACT**

A method and apparatus for presenting subliminal visual and/or audio messages which allows user verification of message content and presence, as well as proper adjustment of message obviousness while accounting for ambient conditions and user sensitivities is disclosed. This method and apparatus also presents synchronized reinforced sensory input of subliminal messages. This is performed by simultaneously overlaying images received from a VCR over a plurality of television signals. This apparatus directs overlay images over RF television signals having both audio and video components.

15 Claims, 4 Drawing Sheets

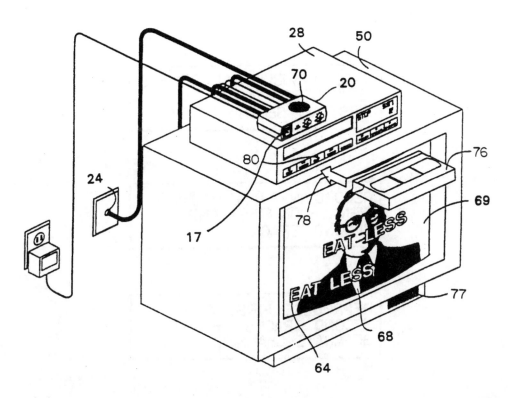

United States Patent [19]

Vavagiakis

[11] **Patent Number:** **5,224,864**

[45] **Date of Patent:** **Jul. 6, 1993**

[54] **METHOD OF RECORDING AND REPRODUCING SUBLIMINAL SIGNALS THAT ARE 180 DEGREES OUT OF PHASE**

[76] Inventor: **Steven Vavagiakis**

[21] Appl. No.: **674,138**

[22] Filed: **Mar. 25, 1991**

[51] Int. Cl.^{5} **G09B 5/04; G09B 19/00; A61M 21/00; H04R 3/02**

[52] U.S. Cl. **434/319; 434/236; 600/28; 381/73.1**

[58] Field of Search 434/307, 319, 236, 262; 360/90, 22, 18, 20; 352/131; 358/142; 73/156; 381/73.1, 105, 124, 51, 71, 74, 97; 395/2; 346/1.1; 600/28, 27

[56] **References Cited**

U.S. PATENT DOCUMENTS

4,315,502 2/1982 Gorges 600/27

4,395,600 7/1983 Lundy et al. 381/73.1
4,658,306 4/1987 Daigaku et al. 360/22
4,777,529 10/1988 Schultz et al. 434/307

Primary Examiner—Richard J. Apley
Assistant Examiner—John P. Leubecker

[57] **ABSTRACT**

A subliminal recording includes both subliminal message and mask signals applied to both tracks of a two track recording medium. The subliminal message signals are identical in content, and are recorded in an out-of-phase relationship. The mask signals are recorded in phase. The resulting recording may be utilized in the conventional manner for subliminal recordings. By combining the composite signals in an inverted relationship, the mask signals cancel while the subliminal message signals are additive, thus allowing the presence of the subliminal message signal to be confirmed on the recording.

1 Claim, 3 Drawing Sheets

RECORD SUBLIMINAL SIGNALS 180° OUT-OF-PHASE ON FIRST AND SECOND TRACKS

RECORD IN-PHASE MASKING SIGNALS ON FIRST AND SECOND TRACKS

REPRODUCE FIRST AND SECOND TRACKS THROUGH SEPARATE CHANNELS

United States Patent [19]

Mikell

[11] **Patent Number:** **5,245,666**

[45] **Date of Patent:** **Sep. 14, 1993**

[54] **PERSONAL SUBLIMINAL MESSAGING SYSTEM**

[76] Inventor: **Bruce T. Mikell**

[21] Appl. No.: **711,933**

[22] Filed: **Jun. 6, 1991**

[51] Int. Cl.^{5} H03G 3/20
[52] U.S. Cl. 381/73.1; 381/57; 381/108
[58] Field of Search 381/73.1, 57, 108

[56] **References Cited**

U.S. PATENT DOCUMENTS

3,160,707	12/1964	Meyers	381/57
4,395,600	7/1983	Lundy et al.	381/73.1
4,553,257	11/1985	Mori et al.	381/57
4,628,526	12/1986	Germer	381/57
4,777,529	10/1988	Schultz et al.	381/73.1

OTHER PUBLICATIONS

H. A. Beagley, Audiology and Audiological Medicine, vol. 1, p. 125, 1981.

J. V. Tobias, Foundations of Modern Auditory Theory, vol. 1, 1970, pp. 90–94.
H. Davis and S. R. Silverman, Hearing and Deafness, 1978, p. 41.
Katz et al, eds., Handbook of Clinical Audiology, pp. 170–176 and 1077.

Primary Examiner—Forester W. Isen

[57] **ABSTRACT**

A personal subliminal messaging system includes a wide range linear subliminal modulator (43), a digital audio recording or play device (46), a microphone (51) to pick up the sound at the ear, and an earpiece (50) to deliver the subliminal message. The sound level at the user's ear is detected and measured. After risetime and decay conditioning of the varying dc control signal, the wide range linear modulator (43) uses this signal to control the level of the message to the earpiece (50). The user adjusts the system for a liminal of a subliminal level. The psychoacoustic phenomena of Post Masking is used to increase the integrity of the message in subliminal messaging systems.

17 Claims, 3 Drawing Sheets

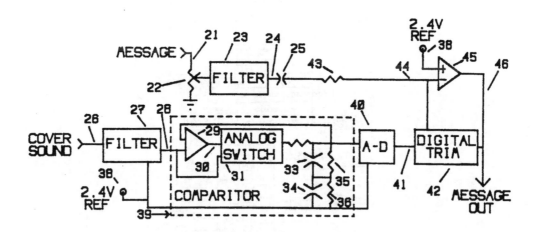

United States Patent [19]

Sweet

[11]   **Patent Number:**   **5,270,800**

[45]   **Date of Patent:**   **Dec. 14, 1993**

[54] **SUBLIMINAL MESSAGE GENERATOR**

[76] Inventor: **Robert L. Sweet**

[21] Appl. No.: **574,432**

[22] Filed: **Aug. 28, 1990**

[51] Int. Cl.⁵ H04N 7/08; H04N 5/40
[52] U.S. Cl. 358/22; 358/142;
                                                                          358/183
[58] Field of Search 358/141–142,
                                                                    358/188, 183, 22

[56]   **References Cited**

U.S. PATENT DOCUMENTS

3,278,676	10/1966	Becker	358/142
4,279,088	7/1981	Hyre	40/442
4,616,261	10/1986	Crawford et al.	358/181
4,692,118	9/1987	Mould	434/236
4,733,301	3/1988	Wright	358/181
4,734,037	3/1988	McClure	434/236
4,777,529	10/1988	Schutz et al.	
4,897,726	1/1989	Morton et al.	358/183
5,017,143	5/1989	Backus	358/183
5,027,208	6/1991	Dwyer, Jr. et al.	358/149

Primary Examiner—James J. Groody
Assistant Examiner—David E. Harvey
Attorney, Agent, or Firm—Krass & Young

[57]   **ABSTRACT**

A combined subliminal and supraliminal message generator for use with a television receiver permits complete control of subliminal messages and their manner of presentation. A video synchronization detector enables a video display generator to generate a video message signal corresponding to a received alphanumeric text message in synchronism with a received television signal. A video mixer selects either the received video signal or the video message signal for output. The messages produced by the video message generator are user selectable via a keyboard input. A message memory stores a plurality of alphanumeric text messages specified by user commands for use as subliminal messages. This message memory preferably includes a read only memory storing predetermined sets of alphanumeric text messages directed to differing topics. The sets of predetermined alphanumeric text messages preferably include several positive affirmations directed to the left brain and an equal number of positive affirmations directed to the right brain that are alternately presented subliminally. The left brain messages are presented in a linear text mode, while the right brain messages are presented in a three dimensional perspective mode. The user can control the length and spacing of the subliminal presentations to accommodate differing conscious thresholds. Alternative embodiments include a combined cable television converter and subliminal message generator, a combine television receiver and subliminal message generator and a computer capable of presenting subliminal messages.

8 Claims, 8 Drawing Sheets

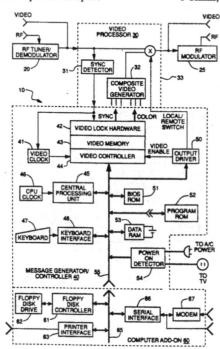

United States Patent [19]

Mead

[11] **Patent Number:** **5,644,363**

[45] **Date of Patent:** **Jul. 1, 1997**

[54] **APPARATUS FOR SUPERIMPOSING VISUAL SUBLIMINAL INSTRUCTIONAL MATERIALS ON A VIDEO SIGNAL**

[75] Inventor: **Talbert Mead**, Colorado Springs, Colo.

[73] Assignee: **The Advanced Learning Corp.**, Colorado Springs, Colo.

[21] Appl. No.: **410,275**

[22] Filed: **Mar. 24, 1995**

[51] Int. Cl.^{6} **H04N 5/445**
[52] U.S. Cl. **348/563**; 348/473
[58] Field of Search 348/473, 589, 348/563, 584, 600, 598, 525, 521; H04N 5/445

[56] **References Cited**

U.S. PATENT DOCUMENTS

3,278,676 10/1966 Becker .

3,742,125	6/1973	Siegel	348/729
4,872,054	10/1989	Gray et al.	348/553
5,128,765	7/1992	Dingwall et al.	348/729
5,134,484	7/1992	Willson	348/564
5,221,962	6/1993	Backus et al.	348/563
5,227,863	7/1993	Bilbrey et al.	348/578

Primary Examiner—Victor R. Kostak
Attorney, Agent, or Firm—Steven K. Barton

[57] **ABSTRACT**

A subliminal video instructional device comprises circuitry for receiving an underlying video signal and presenting this signal to horizontal and vertical synchronization detection circuits, circuitry for generating a subliminal video message synchronized to the underlying video signal, and circuitry for adding the subliminal video message to the underlying video signal to create a combination video signal.

4 Claims, 4 Drawing Sheets

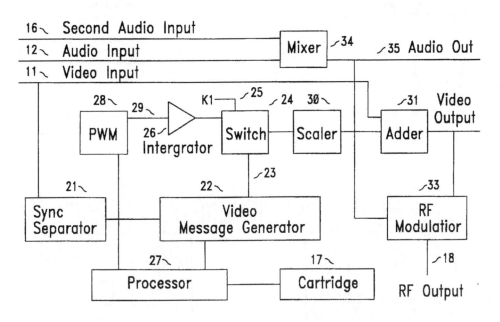

United States Patent [19]

Akerman et al.

[11] Patent Number: 5,539,705

[45] Date of Patent: Jul. 23, 1996

[54] **ULTRASONIC SPEECH TRANSLATOR AND COMMUNICATIONS SYSTEM**

[75] Inventors: **M. Alfred Akerman**, Knoxville; **Curtis W. Ayers**, Clinton; **Howard D. Haynes**, Knoxville, all of Tenn.

[73] Assignee: **Martin Marietta Energy Systems, Inc.**, Oak Ridge, Tenn.

[21] Appl. No.: **329,889**

[22] Filed: **Oct. 27, 1994**

[51] Int. Cl.^{6} **H04B 11/00**
[52] U.S. Cl. **367/132**
[58] Field of Search 367/132, 131, 367/133, 134, 7

[56] **References Cited**

U.S. PATENT DOCUMENTS

3,662,371	5/1972	Lee et al.	367/93
3,688,029	8/1972	Bartoc Jr. et al.	367/7
3,790,891	2/1974	Bjelvert	367/132
3,828,336	8/1974	Massa	367/94
3,867,715	2/1975	Geil	367/132
3,942,176	3/1976	Bright	367/191
3,967,260	6/1976	Massa	367/901
3,980,954	9/1976	Whyte	455/45
4,039,999	8/1977	Weston	367/132
4,068,093	1/1978	Fidi	367/128
4,206,449	6/1980	Galvin et al.	340/505
4,236,665	4/1981	Watts	367/94
4,310,854	1/1982	Baer	358/143
4,319,349	3/1982	Hackett	367/94
4,367,458	1/1983	Hackett	340/539
4,432,079	2/1984	Mackelburg et al.	367/132
4,711,152	12/1987	Fortunko	89/6.5
4,821,326	4/1989	MacLeod	381/51
5,136,555	8/1992	Gardos	367/132
5,159,703	10/1992	Lowery	455/42

Primary Examiner—Daniel T. Pihulic
Attorney, Agent, or Firm—J. S. Spicer; A. S. Neely; H. W. Adams

[57] **ABSTRACT**

A wireless communication system undetectable by radio frequency methods for converting audio signals, including human voice, to electronic signals in the ultrasonic frequency range, transmitting the ultrasonic signal by way of acoustical pressure waves across a carrier medium, including gases, liquids, or solids, and reconverting the ultrasonic acoustical pressure waves back to the original audio signal. The ultrasonic speech translator and communication system (20) includes an ultrasonic transmitting device (100) and an ultrasonic receiving device (200). The ultrasonic transmitting device (100) accepts as input (115) an audio signal such as human voice input from a microphone (114) or tape deck. The ultrasonic transmitting device (100) frequency modulates an ultrasonic carrier signal with the audio signal producing a frequency modulated ultrasonic carrier signal, which is transmitted via acoustical pressure waves across a carrier medium such as gases, liquids or solids. The ultrasonic receiving device (200) converts the frequency modulated ultrasonic acoustical pressure waves to a frequency modulated electronic signal, demodulates the audio signal from the ultrasonic carrier signal, and conditions the demodulated audio signal to reproduce the original audio signal at its output (250).

32 Claims, 6 Drawing Sheets

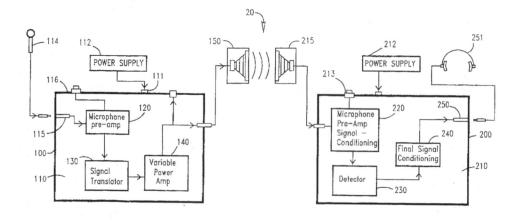

5,539,705

1

ULTRASONIC SPEECH TRANSLATOR AND COMMUNICATIONS SYSTEM

This invention was made with Government support under Contract DE-AC05-840R21400 awarded by the U.S. Department of Energy to Martin Marietta Energy Systems Inc., the Government has certain rights to this invention.

BACKGROUND OF THE INVENTION

The present invention relates generally to the art of wireless communication and, more particularly, to a system which utilizes ultrasonic acoustical pressure waves to transmit and receive audio signals across a medium such as gas, liquid, or solid material. The invention further relates to the art of modulation of audio signals to the ultrasonic frequency range, and to the art of demodulation of audio signals from frequency modulated ultrasonic carrier signals. The invention further relates to the art of inaudible communication, whereby the information contained in the signals is secure and undetectable by radio frequency monitoring.

Radio frequency waves , or electromagnetic radiation in the frequency range of approximately 10 kilohertz to 100 gigahertz, has been utilized for wireless communication systems by civilian and military personnel for decades. Numerous applications of radio frequency communication methods include, to name a few, radio broadcasting, air traffic control, and cellular telecommunications. Radio frequency communication is limited, for practical purposes, to operation within mediums such as air and space. Furthermore, radio frequency methods are inappropriate in some circumstances where communication is required, such as within blasting zones where explosives may be susceptible to unplanned detonation due to radio interference. In addition, radio frequency methods are limited in their ability to provide a secure system to ensure confidentiality of information, which is required by many applications for communication.

Sound waves, or acoustical pressure waves, have likewise been successfully employed as a method of wireless ultrasonic communication across various mediums. Ultrasonic communication is most often utilized in underwater applications because the physical properties of solids and liquids tend to allow waves traveling via molecular vibrations to cover relatively long distances, on the order of the kilometer range. It has been similarly employed for communication over structural matter such as beams or pipes. Ultrasonic communication has generally not been utilized in air for long range communication because radio frequency methods are particularly suitable in air for long range communication, offering suitable and efficient means for most applications.

Some applications, however, require security and inaudibility by radio detectors. Examples of these applications include undercover operations where it is necessary not only that the communication be uninterpretable, but also that the communication be undetectable so as not to alert the presence of such communication. Other applications requiring inaudibility include situations where radio frequency methods are inappropriate, such as, for example, in a blasting zone where the presence of radio frequency waves could unexpectedly set off a detonator or in a factory with sensitive electronics or other components sensitive to electromagnetic radiations.

In applications requiring confidentiality and a high degree of security, numerous schemes have been employed to minimize detection and eavesdropping. These schemes often

2

include scrambling a signal prior to broadcasting and then unscrambling the signal after reception, as well as continual switching from frequency to frequency. The main problem with these existing techniques is that the simple detection of any radio frequency transmission whatsoever, even if the transmitted signals are not decoded or interpreted, indicates the presence of existing communication. Thus, such schemes may not provide sufficient security in operations requiring complete inaudibility. It is desirable, therefore, to provide a communication system which is inaudible by radio frequency detectors.

The invention is disclosed herein in the context of utilizing ultrasonic waves for relatively long range, secure, wireless communication through air. However, by way of example, and not limitation, the disclosed invention is useful in a variety of applications including undercover operations, industrial applications, and many commercial uses in various media.

Prior art ultrasonic communication systems involving the conversion of audio signals to ultrasonic acoustical pressure waves encompass a variety of methods and applications. In the context of the present invention, it may be noted that there are no known prior art communication systems which employ ultrasonic acoustical pressure waves for signal transmission through air for relatively long distances.

Prior art ultrasonic communication systems employ a means of carrying a modulated ultrasonic frequency signal from a transmitter to a receiver. One approach has been disclosed for use in electrical power networks, whereby a two-tone control signal frequency modulates an ultrasonic subcarrier which is then used to frequency modulate the broadcast of a local FM station. The frequency modulated ultrasonic signal is demodulated from the FM broadcast program on the receiving end by receiver circuitry. In this particular approach, however, communication is entirely through radio frequency waves and telephone lines, whereby although a signal is used to modulate an ultrasonic subcarrier, the modulated ultrasonic subcarrier is never transformed from radio frequency signals to acoustical pressure waves. The communication thus remains detectable by radio frequency detectors. It is desirable to employ an alternate communication carrier other than radio frequency waves such that the system is not limited to the use of radio facilities or wire lines.

Another prior art approach for transmitting a modulated ultrasonic frequency signal across a medium is through the conversion of the electronic audio signals to acoustical pressure waves. This technique is employed in many communication systems where radio waves cannot travel useful distances due to the attenuation caused by the properties of the carrier medium, as in underwater communication.

Prior art ultrasonic communication systems employ a means of modulating an ultrasonic frequency signal with an audio frequency signal. Methods utilized have included both amplitude modulation and angle modulation, which encompasses both frequency and phase modulation.

The amplitude modulation techniques used in prior art have encountered the inherent limitation that medium disturbance, e.g. air or water currents, causes additional amplitude modulation of a carrier signal. Thus, unwanted signals from medium disturbance become superimposed on the amplitude modulated carrier, which often results in difficulty recovering a clean original audio signal. Furthermore, amplitude modulation, even when superimposed on a carrier of ultrasonic frequency, may still be audible.

Another prior art approach for modulating an ultrasonic frequency signal with an audio signal is through frequency

United States Patent [19]

Lowrey, III

[11] **Patent Number:** **6,052,336**

[45] **Date of Patent:** **Apr. 18, 2000**

[54] **APPARATUS AND METHOD OF BROADCASTING AUDIBLE SOUND USING ULTRASONIC SOUND AS A CARRIER**

[76] Inventor: **Austin Lowrey, III**

[21] Appl. No.: **09/070,850**

[22] Filed: **May 1, 1998**

Related U.S. Application Data

[60] Provisional application No. 60/046,803, May 2, 1997.

[51] **Int. Cl.⁷** **H01M 29/02; H04R 25/00**
[52] **U.S. Cl.** **367/139**; 367/137; 367/134
[58] **Field of Search** 367/137, 139, 367/134; 381/77; 455/46; 607/56

[56] **References Cited**

U.S. PATENT DOCUMENTS

5,159,703 10/1992 Lowery 455/42

5,889,870 3/1999 Norris 381/77

OTHER PUBLICATIONS

"In The Audio Spotlight" by David Schneider; Scientific American, News and Analysis (Oct. 1998); pp. 40–41.

Primary Examiner—Daniel T. Pihulic
Attorney, Agent, or Firm—Staas & Halsey LLP

[57] **ABSTRACT**

An ultrasonic sound source broadcasts an ultrasonic signal which is amplitude and/or frequency modulated with an information input signal originating from an information input source. If the signals are amplitude modulated, a square root function of the information input signal is produced prior to modulation. The modulated signal, which may be amplified, is then broadcast via a projector unit, whereupon an individual or group of individuals located in the broadcast region detect the audible sound.

21 Claims, 4 Drawing Sheets

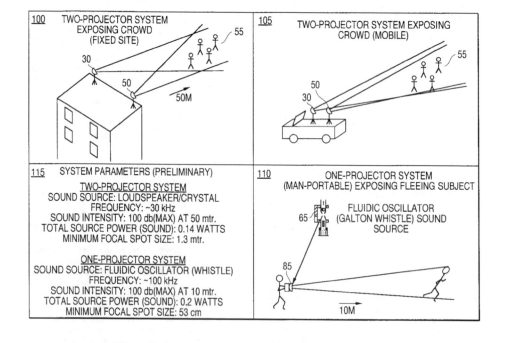

382

6,052,336

1

APPARATUS AND METHOD OF BROADCASTING AUDIBLE SOUND USING ULTRASONIC SOUND AS A CARRIER

CROSS REFERENCE TO RELATED APPLICATION

This application claims the benefit of U.S. provisional application Ser. No. 60/046,803, filed May 2, 1997, entitled A METHOD FOR TRANSMITTING AUDIBLE SOUNDS THROUGH THE AIR USING ULTRASONIC SOUND AS A CARRIER by Austin Lowrey, III and incorporated by reference herein.

BACKGROUND OF THE INVENTION

1. Field of the Invention

The present invention is directed to an apparatus and method of broadcasting an audible sound, and in particular, to an apparatus and method of broadcasting an audible sound using an ultrasonic sound as a carrier modulated by the audible sound as an input signal.

2. Description of the Related Art

Over the past few years, several situations have arisen in military and civil areas where crowds, with or without leaders, have posed a serious problem to Government forces.

For example, in Somalia, leader General Aideed would almost never remain outside unless surrounded by a crowd of sympathizers. Troops attempting to seize or capture the leader would have to engage the crowd, probably killing or injuring some, in order to get close enough to capture him. Hence, forces were not likely to attempt to capture the leader.

Another example is the U.S. invasion of Haiti, where a ship with troops was sent to perform various actions that would have been helpful to the population living there. The landing of these troops was, however, opposed by a crowd on the dock. Hence, in order to land, the crowd on the dock must first be disposed of. Again, crowd members would likely be hurt, resulting in the troops deciding not to act.

Still another example is any situation where an angry crowd gathers. In this situation, the crowd frequently turns to looting and destruction of property. It is a constant challenge for, for example, police to disperse such a crowd without causing casualties, perhaps fatal ones.

All of these examples have a common theme, namely a crowd or leader that one would like to influence such that they leave or stop their hostile activities.

SUMMARY OF THE INVENTION

It is an object of the present invention to provide a nonlethal individual or crowd control device which uses an audible sound broadcasted using an ultrasonic sound as a carrier.

It is another object of the present invention to provide a device that will allow the hearing impaired to hear speech.

It is still another object of the present invention to provide a device that will emit audible sound to listeners located in a defined area.

It is yet another object of the present invention to provide a low frequency sound, either audible or sub-audible frequency, in the heads of listeners.

In one embodiment of the present invention, there is provided an apparatus including a unit amplitude modulating an ultrasonic signal with a square root of an information signal to produce a modulated signal, and a projector coupled to the unit and projecting the modulated signal to a listener.

2

In one aspect of the embodiment, the apparatus further includes a circuit producing the square root of the information signal, a modulator amplitude modulating the ultrasonic signal with the square root of the information signal, a first sound source outputting the information signal, and a second sound source outputting the ultrasonic signal.

In another aspect of the embodiment, the information signal is a voice signal from, for example, a microphone.

In another embodiment of the invention, there is provided a method of modulating an ultrasonic signal with a square root of an information signal to produce a modulated signal, and projecting the modulated signal to a listener.

In one aspect of the embodiment, the method further includes producing a square root signal from the information signal, modulating the ultrasonic signal with the square root of the information signal to produce the modulated signal, amplifying the modulated signal, and transmitting the amplified modulated signal.

In another aspect of the embodiment, the modulating is an amplitude modulation.

In yet another embodiment of the present invention, there is provided an apparatus including a first modulator frequency modulating a first ultrasonic signal with a first input signal to produce a first modulated signal, an ultrasonic signal source providing a second ultrasonic signal, and a broadcasting system, coupled to the first modulator and the ultrasonic signal source, broadcasting the first modulated signal and the second ultrasonic signal to a listener.

In one aspect of the embodiment, the apparatus further includes a first projector projecting the modulated signal, a second projector projecting the second ultrasonic signal, a first input sound source outputting the first input signal, a second ultrasonic signal source providing the first ultrasonic signal, a second modulator amplitude modulating the second ultrasonic signal with a second input signal to produce a second modulated signal, a second input sound source outputting the second input signal, and an amplifier amplifying the amplitude modulated signal.

In another aspect of the embodiment, the first and second ultrasonic signals produce a difference signal for the listener in an audible range of the listener.

In yet another aspect of the embodiment, the input signal is a square root of an information signal.

In still another aspect of the embodiment, the information signal is a voice from, for example, a microphone.

In still another embodiment of the present invention, there is provided a method of frequency modulating a first ultrasonic signal with a first input signal to produce a first modulated signal, providing a second ultrasonic signal, and broadcasting the first modulated signal and the second ultrasonic signal to a listener.

In one aspect of the embodiment, the method includes amplitude modulating the second ultrasonic signal with a second input signal to produce a second modulated signal, amplifying the amplitude modulated signal, and projecting the first and second modulated signals in the audible range of the listener.

In yet another embodiment of the present invention, there is provided an apparatus including a unit modulating an ultrasonic signal with an information signal to produce a modulated signal in which the information signal is completely intelligible to a listener, and a projector coupled to the unit and projecting the modulated signal to the listener.

These together with other objects and advantages which will be subsequently apparent, reside in the details of

383

United States Patent [19]

Jändel

[11]   **Patent Number:**   **6,122,322**

[45]   **Date of Patent:**   **Sep. 19, 2000**

[54]   **SUBLIMINAL MESSAGE PROTECTION**

[75]   Inventor: **Magnus Jändel**, Upplands Väsby, Sweden

[73]   Assignee: **Telefonaktiebolaget LM Ericsson,** Stockholm, Sweden

[21]   Appl. No.: **09/310,739**

[22]   Filed: **May 13, 1999**

Related U.S. Application Data

[63]   Continuation of application No. PCT/SE97/01909, Nov. 13, 1997.

[30]   **Foreign Application Priority Data**

Nov. 19, 1996   [SE]   Sweden 9604241

[51]   **Int. Cl.**^{7} **H04N 5/14; H04N 9/64**

[52]   **U.S. Cl.** **375/240.13**; 348/154; 348/473; 348/699; 358/908

[58]   **Field of Search** 346/46, 94; 358/908; 348/699, 700, 473, 475, 553, 154, 155; H04N 5/14, 9/64

[56]   **References Cited**

U.S. PATENT DOCUMENTS

5,099,322   3/1992   Gove 358/105

5,642,174	6/1997	Kazui et al.	348/700
5,644,363	7/1997	Mead	348/563
5,719,643	2/1998	Nakajima	348/700
5,751,378	5/1998	Chen et al.	348/700
5,801,765	9/1999	Gotoh et al.	348/155
5,929,920	10/1999	Sizer, II	348/473
5,969,755	10/1999	Courtney	348/155

FOREIGN PATENT DOCUMENTS

4106246 C1	3/1992	Germany	.
95/06985 A1	3/1995	WIPO	.

Primary Examiner—Howard Britton
Assistant Examiner—Nhon T Diep
Attorney, Agent, or Firm—Nixon & Vanderhye, PC

[57]   **ABSTRACT**

The present invention relates to a method and to a system for detecting a first context change between two frames. When a second context change between a further two frames occurs within a predetermined time interval, the frames accommodated within the two context changes are defined as a subliminal message. An alarm is sent to an observer upon detection of a subliminal message.

19 Claims, 8 Drawing Sheets

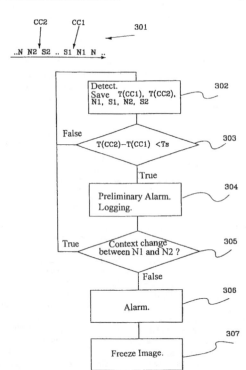

VIMANA:
Flying Machines of the Ancients
by David Hatcher Childress

According to early Sanskrit texts the ancients had several types of airships called vimanas. Like aircraft of today, vimanas were used to fly through the air from city to city; to conduct aerial surveys of uncharted lands; and as delivery vehicles for awesome weapons. David Hatcher Childress, popular *Lost Cities* author and star of the History Channel's long-running show Ancient Aliens, takes us on an astounding investigation into tales of ancient flying machines. In his new book, packed with photos and diagrams, he consults ancient texts and modern stories and presents astonishing evidence that aircraft, similar to the ones we use today, were used thousands of years ago in India, Sumeria, China and other countries. Includes a 24-page color section.

408 Pages. 6x9 Paperback. Illustrated. $22.95. Code: VMA

QUEST FOR ZERO-POINT ENERGY
Engineering Principles for "Free Energy"
by Moray B. King

King expands, with diagrams, on how free energy and anti-gravity are possible. The theories of zero point energy maintain there are tremendous fluctuations of electrical field energy embedded within the fabric of space. King explains the following topics: Tapping the Zero-Point Energy as an Energy Source; Fundamentals of a Zero-Point Energy Technology; Vacuum Energy Vortices; The Super Tube; Charge Clusters: The Basis of Zero-Point Energy Inventions; Vortex Filaments, Torsion Fields and the Zero-Point Energy; Transforming the Planet with a Zero-Point Energy Experiment; Dual Vortex Forms: The Key to a Large Zero-Point Energy Coherence. Packed with diagrams, patents and photos. With power shortages now a daily reality in many parts of the world, this book offers a fresh approach very rarely mentioned in the mainstream media.

224 PAGES. 6x9 PAPERBACK. ILLUSTRATED. $14.95. CODE: QZPE

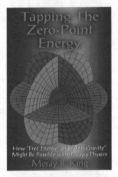

TAPPING THE ZERO POINT ENERGY
Free Energy & Anti-Gravity in Today's Physics
by Moray B. King

King explains how free energy and anti-gravity are possible. The theories of the zero point energy maintain there are tremendous fluctuations of electrical field energy imbedded within the fabric of space. This book tells how, in the 1930s, inventor T. Henry Moray could produce a fifty kilowatt "free energy" machine; how an electrified plasma vortex creates anti-gravity; how the Pons/Fleischmann "cold fusion" experiment could produce tremendous heat without fusion; and how certain experiments might produce a gravitational anomaly.

180 PAGES. 5x8 PAPERBACK. ILLUSTRATED. $12.95. CODE: TAP

THE FREE-ENERGY DEVICE HANDBOOK
A Compilation of Patents and Reports
by David Hatcher Childress

A large-format compilation of various patents, papers, descriptions and diagrams concerning free-energy devices and systems. *The Free-Energy Device Handbook* is a visual tool for experimenters and researchers into magnetic motors and other "over-unity" devices. With chapters on the Adams Motor, the Hans Coler Generator, cold fusion, superconductors, "N" machines, space-energy generators, Nikola Tesla, T. Townsend Brown, and the latest in free-energy devices. Packed with photos, technical diagrams, patents and fascinating information, this book belongs on every science shelf. With energy and profit being a major political reason for fighting various wars, free-energy devices, if ever allowed to be mass distributed to consumers, could change the world! Get your copy now before the Department of Energy bans this book!

292 PAGES. 8x10 PAPERBACK. ILLUSTRATED. BIBLIOGRAPHY. $16.95. CODE: FEH

BEYOND EINSTEIN'S UNIFIED FIELD
Gravity and Electro-Magnetism Redefined
By John Brandenburg, Ph.D.

Brandenburg reveals the GEM Unification Theory that proves the mathematical and physical interrelation of the forces of gravity and electromagnetism! Brandenburg describes control of space-time geometry through electromagnetism, and states that faster-than-light travel will be possible in the future. Anti-gravity through electromagnetism is possible, which upholds the basic "flying saucer" design utilizing "The Tesla Vortex." Chapters include: Squaring the Circle, Einstein's Final Triumph; A Book of Numbers and Forms; Kepler, Newton and the Sun King; Magnus and Electra; Atoms of Light; Einstein's Glory, Relativity; The Aurora; Tesla's Vortex and the Cliffs of Zeno; The Hidden 5th Dimension; The GEM Unification Theory; more. Includes an 8-page color section.

312 Pages. 6x9 Paperback. Illustrated. $18.95. Code: BEUF

DEATH ON MARS
The Discovery of a Planetary Nuclear Massacre
By John E. Brandenburg, Ph.D.

New proof of a nuclear catastrophe on Mars! In an epic story of discovery, strong evidence is presented for a dead civilization on Mars and the shocking reason for its demise: an ancient planetary-scale nuclear massacre leaving isotopic traces of vast explosions that endure to our present age. The story told by a wide range of Mars data is now clear. Mars was once Earth-like in climate, with an ocean and rivers, and for a long period became home to both plant and animal life, including a humanoid civilization. Then, for unfathomable reasons, a massive thermo-nuclear explosion ravaged the centers of the Martian civilization and destroyed the biosphere of the planet. But the story does not end there. This tragedy may explain Fermi's Paradox, the fact that the cosmos, seemingly so fertile and with so many planets suitable for life, is as silent as a graveyard.

278 Pages. 6x9 Paperback. Illustrated. Bibliography. Color Section. $19.95. Code: DOM

THE A.T. FACTOR
A Scientists Encounter with UFOs: Piece For A Jigsaw Part 3
by Leonard Cramp
British aerospace engineer Cramp began much of the scientific anti-gravity and UFO propulsion analysis back in 1955 with his landmark book *Space, Gravity & the Flying Saucer* (out-of-print and rare). His next books (available from Adventures Unlimited) *UFOs & Anti-Gravity: Piece for a Jig-Saw* and *The Cosmic Matrix: Piece for a Jig-Saw Part 2* began Cramp's in depth look into gravity control, free-energy, and the interlocking web of energy that pervades the universe. In this final book, Cramp brings to a close his detailed and controversial study of UFOs and Anti-Gravity.
324 PAGES. 6x9 PAPERBACK. ILLUSTRATED. BIBLIOGRAPHY. INDEX. $16.95. CODE: ATF

COSMIC MATRIX
Piece for a Jig-Saw, Part Two
by Leonard G. Cramp

Leonard G. Cramp, a British aerospace engineer, wrote his first book *Space Gravity and the Flying Saucer* in 1954. Cosmic Matrix is the long-awaited sequel to his 1966 book *UFOs & Anti-Gravity: Piece for a Jig-Saw*. Cramp has had a long history of examining UFO phenomena and has concluded that UFOs use the highest possible aeronautic science to move in the way they do. Cramp examines anti-gravity effects and theorizes that this super-science used by the craft—described in detail in the book—can lift mankind into a new level of technology, transportation and understanding of the universe. The book takes a close look at gravity control, time travel, and the interlocking web of energy between all planets in our solar system with Leonard's unique technical diagrams. A fantastic voyage into the present and future!
364 PAGES. 6x9 PAPERBACK. ILLUSTRATED. BIBLIOGRAPHY. $16.00. CODE: CMX

UFOS AND ANTI-GRAVITY
Piece For A Jig-Saw
by Leonard G. Cramp
Leonard G. Cramp's 1966 classic book on flying saucer propulsion and suppressed technology is a highly technical look at the UFO phenomena by a trained scientist. Cramp first introduces the idea of 'anti-gravity' and introduces us to the various theories of gravitation. He then examines the technology necessary to build a flying saucer and examines in great detail the technical aspects of such a craft. Cramp's book is a wealth of material and diagrams on flying saucers, anti-gravity, suppressed technology, G-fields and UFOs. Chapters include Crossroads of Aerodymanics, Aerodynamic Saucers, Limitations of Rocketry, Gravitation and the Ether, Gravitational Spaceships, G-Field Lift Effects, The Bi-Field Theory, VTOL and Hovercraft, Analysis of UFO photos, more.
388 PAGES. 6x9 PAPERBACK. ILLUSTRATED. $16.95. CODE: UAG

THE TESLA PAPERS
Nikola Tesla on Free Energy & Wireless Transmission of Power
by Nikola Tesla, edited by David Hatcher Childress

David Hatcher Childress takes us into the incredible world of Nikola Tesla and his amazing inventions. Tesla's rare article "The Problem of Increasing Human Energy with Special Reference to the Harnessing of the Sun's Energy" is included. This lengthy article was originally published in the June 1900 issue of *The Century Illustrated Monthly Magazine* and it was the outline for Tesla's master blueprint for the world. Tesla's fantastic vision of the future, including wireless power, anti-gravity, free energy and highly advanced solar power. Also included are some of the papers, patents and material collected on Tesla at the Colorado Springs Tesla Symposiums, including papers on: •The Secret History of Wireless Transmission •Tesla and the Magnifying Transmitter •Design and Construction of a Half-Wave Tesla Coil •Electrostatics: A Key to Free Energy •Progress in Zero-Point Energy Research •Electromagnetic Energy from Antennas to Atoms •Tesla's Particle Beam Technology •Fundamental Excitatory Modes of the Earth-Ionosphere Cavity
325 PAGES. 8x10 PAPERBACK. ILLUSTRATED. $16.95. CODE: TTP

THE FANTASTIC INVENTIONS OF NIKOLA TESLA
by Nikola Tesla with additional material by David Hatcher Childress
This book is a readable compendium of patents, diagrams, photos and explanations of the many incredible inventions of the originator of the modern era of electrification. In Tesla's own words are such topics as wireless transmission of power, death rays, and radio-controlled airships. In addition, rare material on German bases in Antarctica and South America, and a secret city built at a remote jungle site in South America by one of Tesla's students, Guglielmo Marconi. Marconi's secret group claims to have built flying saucers in the 1940s and to have gone to Mars in the early 1950s! Incredible photos of these Tesla craft are included. The Ancient Atlantean system of broadcasting energy through a grid system of obelisks and pyramids is discussed, and a fascinating concept comes out of one chapter: that Egyptian engineers had to wear protective metal head-shields while in these power plants, hence the Egyptian Pharoah's head covering as well as the Face on Mars! •His plan to transmit free electricity into the atmosphere. •How electrical devices would work using only small antennas. •Why unlimited power could be utilized anywhere on earth. •How radio and radar technology can be used as death-ray weapons in Star Wars.
342 PAGES. 6x9 PAPERBACK. ILLUSTRATED. CODE: FINT

ANCIENT ALIENS ON THE MOON
By Mike Bara
What did NASA find in their explorations of the solar system that they may have kept from the general public? How ancient really are these ruins on the Moon? Using official NASA and Russian photos of the Moon, Bara looks at vast cityscapes and domes in the Sinus Medii region as well as glass domes in the Crisium region. Bara also takes a detailed look at the mission of Apollo 17 and the case that this was a salvage mission, primarily concerned with investigating an opening into a massive hexagonal ruin near the landing site. Chapters include: The History of Lunar Anomalies; The Early 20th Century; Sinus Medii; To the Moon Alice!; Mare Crisium; Yes, Virginia, We Really Went to the Moon; Apollo 17; more. Tons of photos of the Moon examined for possible structures and other anomalies.
248 Pages. 6x9 Paperback. Illustrated.. $19.95. Code: AAOM

ANCIENT ALIENS ON MARS
By Mike Bara
Bara brings us this lavishly illustrated volume on alien structures on Mars. Was there once a vast, techno-logically advanced civilization on Mars, and did it leave evidence of its existence behind for humans to find eons later? Did these advanced extraterrestrial visitors vanish in a solar system wide cataclysm of their own making, only to make their way to Earth and start anew? Was Mars once as lush and green as the Earth, and teeming with life? Chapters include: War of the Worlds; The Mars Tidal Model; The Death of Mars; Cydonia and the Face on Mars; The Monuments of Mars; The Search for Life on Mars; The True Colors of Mars and The Pathfinder Sphinx; more. Color section.
252 Pages. 6x9 Paperback. Illustrated. $19.95. Code: AMAR

ANCIENT ALIENS ON MARS II
By Mike Bara
Using data acquired from sophisticated new scientific instruments like the Mars Odyssey THEMIS infrared imager, Bara shows that the region of Cydonia overlays a vast underground city full of enormous structures and devices that may still be operating. He peels back the layers of mystery to show images of tunnel systems, temples and ruins, and exposes the sophisticated NASA conspiracy designed to hide them. Bara also tackles the enigma of Mars' hollowed out moon Phobos, and exposes evidence that it is artificial. Long-held myths about Mars, including claims that it is protected by a sophisticated UFO defense system, are examined. Data from the Mars rovers Spirit, Opportunity and Curiosity are examined; everything from fossilized plants to mechanical debris is exposed in images taken directly from NASA's own archives.
294 Pages. 6x9 Paperback. Illustrated. $19.95. Code: AAM2

ANCIENT ALIENS & SECRET SOCIETIES
By Mike Bara
Did ancient "visitors"—of extraterrestrial origin—come to Earth long, long ago and fashion man in their own image? Were the science and secrets that they taught the ancients intended to be a guide for all humanity to the present era? Bara establishes the reality of the catastrophe that jolted the human race, and traces the history of secret societies from the priesthood of Amun in Egypt to the Templars in Jerusalem and the Scottish Rite Free-masons. Bara also reveals the true origins of NASA and exposes the bizarre triad of secret societies in control of that agency since its inception. Chapters include: Out of the Ashes; From the Sky Down; Ancient Aliens?; The Dawn of the Secret Societies; The Fractures of Time; Into the 20th Century; The Wink of an Eye; more.
288 Pages. 6x9 Paperback. Illustrated. $19.95. Code: AASS

THE CRYSTAL SKULLS
Astonishing Portals to Man's Past
by David Hatcher Childress and Stephen S. Mehler
Childress introduces the technology and lore of crystals, and then plunges into the turbulent times of the Mexican Revolution form the backdrop for the rollicking adventures of Ambrose Bierce, the renowned journalist who went missing in the jungles in 1913, and F.A. Mitch-ell-Hedges, the notorious adventurer who emerged from the jungles with the most famous of the crystal skulls. Mehler shares his extensive knowledge of and experience with crystal skulls. Having been involved in the field since the 1980s, he has personally examined many of the most influential skulls, and has worked with the leaders in crystal skull research, including the inimitable Nick Nocerino, who developed a meticulous methodology for the purpose of examining the skulls.
294 pages. 6x9 Paperback. Illustrated. Bibliography. $18.95. Code: CRSK

ARK OF GOD
The Incredible Power of the Ark of the Covenant
By David Hatcher Childress
Childress takes us on an incredible journey in search of the truth about (and science behind) the fantastic biblical artifact known as the Ark of the Covenant. This object made by Moses at Mount Sinai—part wooden-metal box and part golden statue—had the power to create "lightning" to kill people, and also to fly and lead people through the wilderness. The Ark of the Covenant suddenly disappears from the Bible record and what happened to it is not mentioned. Was it hidden in the underground passages of King Solomon's temple and later discovered by the Knights Templar? Was it taken through Egypt to Ethiopia as many Coptic Christians believe? Childress looks into hidden history, astonishing ancient technology, and a 3,000-year-old mystery that continues to fascinate millions of people today. Color section.
420 Pages. 6x9 Paperback. Illustrated. $22.00 Code: AOG

THE ANTI-GRAVITY HANDBOOK
edited by David Hatcher Childress, with Nikola Tesla, T.B. Paulicki, Bruce Cathie, Albert Einstein and others

The new expanded compilation of material on Anti-Gravity, Free Energy, Flying Saucer Propulsion, UFOs, Suppressed Technology, NASA Cover-ups and more. Highly illustrated with patents, technical illustrations and photos. This revised and expanded edition has more material, including photos of Area 51, Nevada, the government's secret testing facility. This classic on weird science is back in a 90s format!
- **How to build a flying saucer.**
- **Arthur C. Clarke on Anti-Gravity.**
- **Crystals and their role in levitation.**
- **Secret government research and development.**

230 PAGES. 7x10 PAPERBACK. ILLUSTRATED. $16.95. CODE: AGH

ANTI–GRAVITY & THE WORLD GRID

Is the earth surrounded by an intricate electromagnetic grid network offering free energy? This compilation of material on ley lines and world power points contains chapters on the geography, mathematics, and light harmonics of the earth grid. Learn the purpose of ley lines and ancient megalithic structures located on the grid. Discover how the grid made the Philadelphia Experiment possible. Explore the Coral Castle and many other mysteries, including acoustic levitation, Tesla Shields and scalar wave weaponry. Browse through the section on anti-gravity patents, and research resources.

274 PAGES. 7x10 PAPERBACK. ILLUSTRATED. $14.95. CODE: AGW

ANTI–GRAVITY & THE UNIFIED FIELD
edited by David Hatcher Childress

Is Einstein's Unified Field Theory the answer to all of our energy problems? Explored in this compilation of material is how gravity, electricity and magnetism manifest from a unified field around us. Why artificial gravity is possible; secrets of UFO propulsion; free energy; Nikola Tesla and anti-gravity airships of the 20s and 30s; flying saucers as superconducting whirls of plasma; anti-mass generators; vortex propulsion; suppressed technology; government cover-ups; gravitational pulse drive; spacecraft & more.

240 PAGES. 7x10 PAPERBACK. ILLUSTRATED. $14.95. CODE: AGU

THE MYSTERY OF THE OLMECS
by David Hatcher Childress

Lost Cities author Childress takes us deep into Mexico and Central America in search of the mysterious Olmecs, North America's early, advanced civilization. The Olmecs, now sometimes called Proto-Mayans, were not acknowledged to have existed as a civilization until an international archeological meeting in Mexico City in 1942. At this time, the megalithic statues, large structures, ceramics and other artifacts were acknowledged to come from this hitherto unknown culture that pre-dated all other cultures of Central America. But who were the Olmecs? Where did they come from? What happened to them? How sophisticated was their culture? How far back in time did it go? Why are many Olmec statues and figurines seemingly of foreign peoples such as Africans, Europeans and Chinese? Is there a link with Atlantis? In this heavily illustrated book, join Childress in search of the lost cites of the Olmecs!

432 Pages. 6x9 Paperback. Illustrated. Bibliography. $20.00. Code: MOLM

THE TIME TRAVEL HANDBOOK
A Manual of Practical Teleportation & Time Travel
edited by David Hatcher Childress

The Time Travel Handbook takes the reader beyond the government experiments and deep into the uncharted territory of early time travellers such as Nikola Tesla and Guglielmo Marconi and their alleged time travel experiments, as well as the Wilson Brothers of EMI and their connection to the Philadelphia Experiment—the U.S. Navy's forays into invisibility, time travel, and teleportation. Childress looks into the claims of time travelling individuals, and investigates the unusual claim that the pyramids on Mars were built in the future and sent back in time. A highly visual, large format book, with patents, photos and schematics. 316 PAGES. 7x10 PAPERBACK. ILLUSTRATED. $18.95. CODE: TTH

MAPS OF THE ANCIENT SEA KINGS
Evidence of Advanced Civilization in the Ice Age
by Charles H. Hapgood

Charles Hapgood's classic 1966 book on ancient maps produces concrete evidence of an advanced world-wide civilization existing many thousands of years before ancient Egypt. He has found the evidence in the Piri Reis Map that shows Antarctica, the Hadji Ahmed map, the Oronteus Finaeus and other amazing maps. Hapgood concluded that these maps were made from more ancient maps from the various ancient archives around the world, now lost. Not only were these unknown people more advanced in mapmaking than any people prior to the 18th century, it appears they mapped all the continents. The Americas were mapped thousands of years before Columbus. Antarctica was mapped when its coasts were free of ice!

316 PAGES. 7x10 PAPERBACK. ILLUSTRATED. BIBLIOGRAPHY & INDEX. $19.95. CODE: MASK

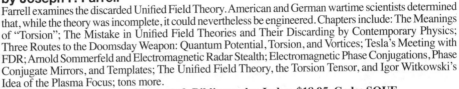

SECRETS OF THE UNIFIED FIELD
The Philadelphia Experiment, the Nazi Bell, and the Discarded Theory
by Joseph P. Farrell

Farrell examines the discarded Unified Field Theory. American and German wartime scientists determined that, while the theory was incomplete, it could nevertheless be engineered. Chapters include: The Meanings of "Torsion"; The Mistake in Unified Field Theories and Their Discarding by Contemporary Physics; Three Routes to the Doomsday Weapon: Quantum Potential, Torsion, and Vortices; Tesla's Meeting with FDR; Arnold Sommerfeld and Electromagnetic Radar Stealth; Electromagnetic Phase Conjugations, Phase Conjugate Mirrors, and Templates; The Unified Field Theory, the Torsion Tensor, and Igor Witkowski's Idea of the Plasma Focus; tons more.

340 pages. 6x9 Paperback. Illustrated. Bibliography. Index. $18.95. Code: SOUF

REICH OF THE BLACK SUN
Nazi Secret Weapons and the Cold War Allied Legend
by Joseph P. Farrell

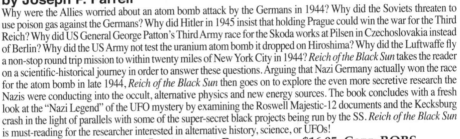

Why were the Allies worried about an atom bomb attack by the Germans in 1944? Why did the Soviets threaten to use poison gas against the Germans? Why did Hitler in 1945 insist that holding Prague could win the war for the Third Reich? Why did US General George Patton's Third Army race for the Skoda works at Pilsen in Czechoslovakia instead of Berlin? Why did the US Army not test the uranium atom bomb it dropped on Hiroshima? Why did the Luftwaffe fly a non-stop round trip mission to within twenty miles of New York City in 1944? *Reich of the Black Sun* takes the reader on a scientific-historical journey in order to answer these questions. Arguing that Nazi Germany actually won the race for the atom bomb in late 1944, *Reich of the Black Sun* then goes on to explore the even more secretive research the Nazis were conducting into the occult, alternative physics and new energy sources. The book concludes with a fresh look at the "Nazi Legend" of the UFO mystery by examining the Roswell Majestic-12 documents and the Kecksburg crash in the light of parallels with some of the super-secret black projects being run by the SS. *Reich of the Black Sun* is must-reading for the researcher interested in alternative history, science, or UFOs!

352 PAGES. 6x9 PAPERBACK. ILLUSTRATED. BIBLIOGRAPHY. $16.95. CODE: ROBS

THE GIZA DEATH STAR
The Paleophysics of the Great Pyramid & the Military Complex at Giza
by Joseph P. Farrell

Physicist Joseph Farrell's amazing book on the secrets of Great Pyramid of Giza. *The Giza Death Star* starts where British engineer Christopher Dunn leaves off in his 1998 book, *The Giza Power Plant*. Was the Giza complex part of a military installation over 10,000 years ago? Chapters include: An Archaeology of Mass Destruction; Thoth and Theories; The Machine Hypothesis; Pythagoras, Plato, Planck, and the Pyramid; The Weapon Hypothesis; Encoded Harmonics of the Planck Units in the Great Pyramid; High Freqquency Direct Current "Impulse" Technology; The Grand Gallery and its Crystals: Gravito-acoustic Resonators; The Other Two Large Pyramids; the "Causeways," and the "Temples"; A Phase Conjugate Howitzer; Evidence of the Use of Weapons of Mass Destruction in Ancient Times; more.

290 PAGES. 6x9 PAPERBACK. ILLUSTRATED. $16.95. CODE: GDS

THE GIZA DEATH STAR DEPLOYED
The Physics & Engineering of the Great Pyramid
by Joseph P. Farrell

Farrell expands on his thesis that the Great Pyramid was a chemical maser, designed as a weapon and eventually deployed—with disastrous results to the solar system. Includes: Exploding Planets: The Movie, the Mirror, and the Model; Dating the Catastrophe and the Compound; A Brief History of the Exoteric and Esoteric Investigations of the Great Pyramid; No Machines, Please!; The Stargate Conspiracy; The Scalar Weapons; Message or Machine?; A Tesla Analysis of the Putative Physics and Engineering of the Giza Death Star; Cohering the Zero Point, Vacuum Energy, Flux: Synopsis of Scalar Physics and Paleophysics; Configuring the Scalar Pulse Wave; Inferred Applications in the Great Pyramid; Quantum Numerology, Feedback Loops and Tetrahedral Physics; and more.

290 PAGES. 6x9 PAPERBACK. ILLUSTRATED. BIBLIOGRAPHY. $16.95. CODE: GDSD

THE GIZA DEATH STAR DESTROYED
The Ancient War For Future Science
by Joseph P. Farrell

Recapping his earlier books, Farrell moves on to events of the final days of the Giza Death Star and its awesome power. These final events, eventually leading up to the destruction of this giant machine, are dissected one by one, leading us to the eventual abandonment of the Giza Military Complex—an event that hurled civilization back into the Stone Age. Chapters include: The Mars-Earth Connection; The Lost "Root Races" and the Moral Reasons for the Flood; The Destruction of Krypton: The Electrodynamic Solar System, Exploding Planets and Ancient Wars; Turning the Stream of the Flood: the Origin of Secret Societies and Esoteric Traditions; The Quest to Recover Ancient Mega-Technology; Non-Equilibrium Paleophysics; Monatomic Paleophysics; Frequencies, Vortices and Mass Particles: The Topology of the Aether; "Acoustic" Intensity of Fields; The Pyramid of Crystals; tons more.

292 pages. 6x9 paperback. Illustrated. $16.95. Code: GDES

ANCIENT TECHNOLOGY IN PERU & BOLIVIA
By David Hatcher Childress
Childress speculates on the existence of a sunken city in Lake Titicaca and reveals new evidence that the Sumerians may have arrived in South America 4,000 years ago. He demonstrates that the use of "keystone cuts" with metal clamps poured into them to secure megalithic construction was an advanced technology used all over the world, from the Andes to Egypt, Greece and Southeast Asia. He maintains that only power tools could have made the intricate articulation and drill holes found in extremely hard granite and basalt blocks in Bolivia and Peru, and that the megalith builders had to have had advanced methods for moving and stacking gigantic blocks of stone, some weighing over 100 tons.
340 Pages. 6x9 Paperback. Illustrated.. $19.95 Code: ATP

SAUCERS, SWASTIKAS AND PSYOPS
A History of a Breakaway Civilization: Hidden Aerospace Technologies and Psychological Operations
By Joseph P. Farrell
Farrell discusses George Adamski; the alleged Hannebu and Vril craft of the Third Reich; The Strange Case of Dr. Hermann Oberth; Nazis in the US and their connections to "UFO contactees." Chapters include: The Nov. 20, 1952 Contact: The Memes are Implants; George Hunt Williamson and the Baileys; William Pelley and the American Fascists; The Messages from "ET"; Adamski's Techno-logical Descriptions and Another ET Message: The Danger of Weaponized Gravity; A Doozie of an Anachronistic Revelation; Adamski's Retro-Looking Saucers, and the Nazi Saucer Myth; The Strange Case of Dr. Hermann Oberth: Dr. Oberth's 1968 Statements on UFOs and Extraterrestrials; more.
262 Pages. 6x9 Paperback. Illustrated. $19.95. Code: SSPY

PIRATES & THE LOST TEMPLAR FLEET
The Secret Naval War Between the Templars & the Vatican
by David Hatcher Childress
Childress takes us into the fascinating world of maverick sea captains who were Knights Templar (and later Scottish Rite Free Masons) who battled the ships that sailed for the Pope. The lost Templar fleet was originally based at La Rochelle in southern France, but fled to the deep fiords of Scotland upon the dissolution of the Order by King Phillip. This banned fleet of ships was later commanded by the St. Clair family of Rosslyn Chapel (birthplace of Free Masonry). St. Clair and his Templars made a voyage to Canada in the year 1298 AD, nearly 100 years before Columbus! Later, this fleet of ships and new ones to come, flew the Skull and Crossbones, the symbol of the Knights Templar.
320 PAGES. 6x9 PAPERBACK. ILLUSTRATED. BIBLIOGRAPHY. $16.95. CODE: PLTF

SECRETS OF THE MYSTERIOUS VALLEY
by Christopher O'Brien
No other region in North America features the variety and intensity of unusual phenomena found in the world's largest alpine valley, the San Luis Valley of Colorado and New Mexico. Since 1989, Christopher O'Brien has documented thousands of high-strange accounts that report UFOs, ghosts, crypto-creatures, cattle mutilations, skinwalkers and sorcerers, along with portal areas, secret under-ground bases and covert military activity. This mysterious region at the top of North America has a higher incidence of UFO reports than any other area of the continent and is the publicized birthplace of the "cattle mutilation" mystery. Hundreds of animals have been found strangely slain during waves of anomalous aerial craft sightings. Is the government directly involved? Are there underground bases here? Does the military fly exotic aerial craft in this valley that are radar-invisible below 18,000 feet? These and many other questions are addressed in this all-new, work by one of America's top paranormal investigators. Take a fantastic journey through one of the world's most enigmatic locales!
460 pages. 6x9 Paperback. Illustrated. Bibliography. $19.95. Code: SOMV

THE LOST WORLD OF CHAM
The Trans-Pacific Voyages of the Champa
By David Hatcher Childress
The mysterious Cham, or Champa, peoples of Southeast Asia formed a megalith-building, seagoing empire that extended into Indonesia, Tonga, and beyond—a transoceanic power that reached Mexico and South America. The Champa maintained many ports in what is today Vietnam, Cambodia, and Indonesia (particularly on the islands of Sulawesi, Sumatra and Java), and their ships plied the Indian Ocean and the Pacific, bringing Chinese, African and Indian traders to far off lands, including Olmec ports on the Pacific Coast of Central America. Statues of the Champa show men and women distinctly African in appearance and the Champa royalty were known to consist of nearly every racial group. They had iron tools and built megalithic cities of finely-cut basalt and granite, such as the city of My Son in Vietnam, identical to that at Tiwanaku. Topics include: Cham and Khem: Egyptian Influence on Cham; The Search for Metals; The Basalt City of Nan Madol; Elephants and Buddhists in North America; The Olmecs; The Cham in Colombia; The Cham and Lake Titicaca; Easter Island and the Cham; the Magical Technology of the Cham; tons more. 24-page color section.
328 Pages. 6x9 Paperback. Illustrated. Bibliography. $22.00 Code: LPWC

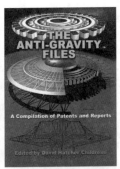

THE ANTI-GRAVITY FILES
A Compilation of Patents and Reports
Edited by David Hatcher Childress

In the tradition of *The Anti-Gravity Handbook* and *the Time-Travel Handbook* comes this compilation of material on anti-gravity, free energy, flying saucers and Tesla technology. With plenty of technical drawings and explanations, this book reveals suppressed technology that will change the world in ways we can only dream of. Chapters include: A Brief History of Anti-Gravity Patents; The Motionless Electromagnet Generator Patent; Mercury Anti-Gravity Gyros; The Tesla Pyramid Engine; Anti-Gravity Propulsion Dynamics; The Machines in Flight; More Anti-Gravity Patents; Death Rays Anyone?; The Unified Field Theory of Gravity; and tons more. The book that finally blows the lid on suppressed technology, zero-point energy and anti-gravity! Heavily illustrated. 4-page color section.
216 pages. 8x10 Paperback. Illustrated. References. $22.00. Code: AGF

PROJECT MK-ULTRA AND MIND CONTROL TECHNOLOGY
A Compilation of Patents and Reports
By Axel Balthazar

People from around the world claim to be victims of mind control technology. Medical professionals are quick to marginalize these targeted individuals and diagnose them with mental illness. Unfortunately, most people are oblivious to the historical precedent and patented technology that exists on the subject. This book is a compilation of the government's documentation on MK-Ultra, the CIA's mind control experimentation on unwitting human subjects, as well as over 150 patents pertaining to artificial telepathy (voice-to-skull technology), behavior modification through radio frequencies, directed energy weapons, electronic monitoring, implantable nanotechnology, brain wave manipulation, nervous system manipulation, neuroweapons, psychological warfare, subliminal messaging, and more.
384 pages. 7x10 Paperback. Illustrated. References. $19.95. Code: PMK

HIDDEN AGENDA
NASA and the Secret Space Program
By Mike Bara

Bara looks into the Army Ballistic Missile Agency's (ABMA) study to determine the feasibility of constructing a scientific/military base on the Moon. On June 8, 1959, a group at the ABMA produced for the US Department of the Army a report entitled Project Horizon, a "Study for the Establishment of a Lunar Military Outpost." The permanent outpost was predicted to cost $6 billion and was to become operational in December 1966 with twelve soldiers stationed at the Moon base. Did this happen? Did NASA and the Pentagon expect to find evidence of alien bases on the Moon? Did the Apollo 12 astronauts deliberately damage the TV cameras in order to hide their explorations of one of these bases? Does hacker Gary Mackinnon's discovery of defense department documents identifying "non-terrestrial officers" serving in space mean that the US has secret space platforms designed to fight a war with an alien race? Includes an 8-page color section.
346 Pages. 6x9 Paperback. Illustrated. Bibliography. $19.95. Code: HDAG

HAARP: The Ultimate Weapon of the Conspiracy
By Jerry Smith

The HAARP project in Alaska is one of the most controversial projects ever undertaken by the U.S. Government. Jerry Smith gives us the history of the HAARP project and explains how works, in technically correct yet easy to understand language. At best, HAARP is science out-of-control; at worst, HAARP could be the most dangerous device ever created, a futuristic technology that is everything from super-beam weapon to world-wide mind control device. Topics include Over-the-Horizon Radar and HAARP, Mind Control, ELF and HAARP, The Telsa Connection, The Russian Woodpecker, GWEN & HAARP, Earth Penetrating Tomography, Weather Modification, Secret Science of the Conspiracy, more. Includes the complete 1987 Eastlund patent for his pulsed super-weapon that he claims was stolen by the HAARP Project.
256 pages. 6x9 Paperback. Illustrated. Bibliography. $14.95. Code: HARP

TECHNOLOGY OF THE GODS
The Incredible Sciences of the Ancients
by David Hatcher Childress

Popular *Lost Cities* author David Hatcher Childress takes us into the amazing world of ancient technology, from computers in antiquity to the "flying machines of the gods." Childress looks at the technology that was allegedly used in Atlantis and the theory that the Great Pyramid of Egypt was originally a gigantic power station. He examines tales of ancient flight and the technology that it involved; how the ancients used electricity; megalithic building techniques; the use of crystal lenses and the fire from the gods; evidence of various high tech weapons in the past, including atomic weapons; ancient metallurgy and heavy machinery; the role of modern inventors such as Nikola Tesla in bringing ancient technology back into modern use; impossible artifacts; and more.
356 PAGES. 6x9 PAPERBACK. ILLUSTRATED. BIBLIOGRAPHY. $16.95. CODE: TGOD

ORDER FORM

10% Discount When You Order 3 or More Items!

One Adventure Place
P.O. Box 74
Kempton, Illinois 60946
United States of America
Tel.: 815-253-6390 • Fax: 815-253-6300
Email: auphq@frontiernet.net
http://www.adventuresunlimitedpress.com

ORDERING INSTRUCTIONS

✓ Remit by USD$ Check, Money Order or Credit Card
✓ Visa, Master Card, Discover & AmEx Accepted
✓ Paypal Payments Can Be Made To:
    info@wexclub.com
✓ Prices May Change Without Notice
✓ 10% Discount for 3 or More Items

SHIPPING CHARGES

United States

✓ Postal Book Rate { $4.50 First Item / 50¢ Each Additional Item
✓ POSTAL BOOK RATE Cannot Be Tracked!
    Not responsible for non-delivery.
✓ Priority Mail { $6.00 First Item / $2.00 Each Additional Item
✓ UPS { $7.00 First Item / $1.50 Each Additional Item
    NOTE: UPS Delivery Available to Mainland USA Only

Canada

✓ Postal Air Mail { $15.00 First Item / $2.50 Each Additional Item
✓ Personal Checks or Bank Drafts MUST BE
    US$ and Drawn on a US Bank
✓ Canadian Postal Money Orders OK
✓ Payment MUST BE US$

All Other Countries

✓ Sorry, No Surface Delivery!
✓ Postal Air Mail { $19.00 First Item / $6.00 Each Additional Item
✓ Checks and Money Orders MUST BE US$
    and Drawn on a US Bank or branch.
✓ Paypal Payments Can Be Made in US$ To:
    info@wexclub.com

SPECIAL NOTES

✓ RETAILERS: Standard Discounts Available
✓ BACKORDERS: We Backorder all Out-of-
    Stock Items Unless Otherwise Requested
✓ PRO FORMA INVOICES: Available on Request
✓ DVD Return Policy: Replace defective DVDs only

ORDER ONLINE AT: www.adventuresunlimitedpress.com

10% Discount When You Order 3 or More Items!

Please check: ✓

☐ This is my first order   ☐ I have ordered before

Name				
Address				
City				
State/Province			Postal Code	
Country				
Phone: Day		Evening		
Fax		Email		

Item Code	Item Description	Qty	Total

Please check: ✓

☐	Postal-Surface	Subtotal ▶
		Less Discount-10% for 3 or more items ▶
☐	Postal-Air Mail (Priority in USA)	Balance ▶
		Illinois Residents 6.25% Sales Tax ▶
		Previous Credit ▶
☐	UPS (Mainland USA only)	Shipping ▶
		Total (check/MO in USD$ only) ▶

☐ Visa/MasterCard/Discover/American Express

Card Number:

Expiration Date: Security Code:

✓ SEND A CATALOG TO A FRIEND: